Real estate and urban development

1981 Third edition

Real estate and

urban development

Halbert C. Smith, D.B.A., S.R.E.A.
Professor of Real Estate and Urban Analysis
University of Florida

Carl J. Tschappat, Ph.D., S.R.E.A., A.I.P.
President
Land Development Analysts, Inc.

Ronald L. Racster, Ph.D.
Professor of Real Estate and Urban Analysis
The Ohio State University

RICHARD D. IRWIN, INC. Homewood, Illinois 60430
Irwin-Dorsey Limited Georgetown, Ontario L7G 4B3

ISBN 0-256-02445-6
Library of Congress Catalog Card No. 80-84484
Printed in the United States of America

1 2 3 4 5 6 7 8 9 0 MP 8 7 6 5 4 3 2 1

To Ruth, Barbara, and Janie

Preface

Since publication of the revised edition of *Real Estate and Urban Development*, the academic field of real estate has continued to change and expand. Courses and programs of real estate education are now offered at many of the leading universities in the United States and Canada. The growth in the number of students majoring in real estate in a number of collegiate business schools has exceeded the growth rate of other, better-established disciplines. Furthermore, real estate instruction has expanded dramatically in industry-sponsored and community college programs.

Research in the field of real estate and urban analysis has also continued to increase. Several universities have established centers for research in real estate and chairs for prominent faculty members in the field. The major academic-professional organization serving the field, the American Real Estate and Urban Economics Association, has continued to grow and prosper. Graduate programs have continued to expand in recognition of the growing sophistication required for real estate analysis. The supply of Ph.D.s in the field has also increased significantly, yet the demand for college and university teachers and researchers has not been satisfied.

Whether the academic interest both of students and of faculty will continue to expand or will moderate can only be known with the passage of time. Further expansion, however, will require the discipline to be interesting and relevant to important problems of individuals and society. To this end, we believe that beginning courses in real estate and urban analysis should rely upon basic disciplines such as economics, accounting, psychology, and sociology, and that the teaching-learning process should seek to enable students to solve problems and resolve issues relating to the interrelationships among land resources and other productive factors. Further, we believe strongly that a beginning course in real estate should be as rigorous as beginning courses in such fields as accounting, economics, and finance. The course should go beyond definitions and current practice; its focus should be real estate principles and analysis, not real estate brokerage. A general approach recognizing the relationships among investment decision making, urban development, and social problems, determined by the framework of legal, social, and economic systems, should be the goal for real estate education.

We were pleased by the acceptance of the first and revised editions of *Real Estate and Urban Development*. They were used in real estate courses in a number of leading universities. Our goal was to provide an integrative, theory-based learning aid for basic education in the field of real estate. This edition, we hope, retains the basic attributes of the prior editions, while providing new and updated materials, greater organizational cohesiveness, and improved clarity of style and content.

The third edition retains the same basic organization structure. It is divided into four parts: Framework for Analysis, Investment Opportunity and Constraint, Real Estate Functions, and Real Estate Administration in the Public Sector. New chapters have been added on Continuing Investment Decisions, Risk and Return Analysis, and Real Estate Financing. Some of the older materials have been deleted, while significant revisions have been made to most other chapters.

Like the earlier editions, this edition focuses upon real estate investment decision making and upon the execution of such decisions within the urban environment. The book further attempts to provide insight into the role of the investment decision-making process both in contributing to and in alleviating the social problems of cities. In so doing, it includes much of the material that is traditionally taught in real estate principles courses. To comply with the new approach, however, it inevitably omits some traditional material and reorganizes or de-emphasizes other such material.

Our primary goal for the book is that it serve the needs of students beginning their study of real estate in colleges and universities, either at the advanced undergraduate or graduate level. The book may also be useful in the growing number of courses and programs required both for the licensing of a new breed of professional real estate business people and for entrance to and maintenance of standing in professional organizations.

Halbert C. Smith
Carl J. Tschappat
Ronald L. Racster

Contents

munity income. Price structure. Determinants of supply: *Anticipations of demand. Utilization of existing real estate resources. Availability and prices of land and utilities. Availability and price of financing. Availability and prices of materials and labor. Taxes.* Conceptualizing the local housing market: *Filtering.* Market and feasibility analyses: *Market analysis. Feasibility analysis.*

ance and guaranty. Subsidized housing programs. Special aid for low-income housing and urban renewal. Taxation. Community development. Urban renewal: *Rehabilitation and conservation. Direct block grants.* Impact of federal housing programs: *Policy for the provision of adequate housing. Income redistribution effects.*

part one

Framework for analysis

chapter 1

Real estate administration

All people use real estate. "All Americans 'know' real estate. . . . At least most of us think we do."[1] Usage of the physical commodity brings a feeling of familiarity, but this is not sufficient for acquiring an understanding of the complex economic, social, and legal processes affecting land usage. This book attempts to provide an integrated study of these factors and their influence on our urban real estate resources. The principal viewpoint for this study is the individual decision maker who considers real estate to be an investment. The emphasis of the book is on economic principles which are manifest in decisions regarding the use of real estate, including the size and type of structure to be constructed, the legal rights to be obtained in a transaction, and many other kinds of decisions, such as whether to buy, sell, or improve a parcel of real estate or let it deteriorate. The rationale upon which such decisions are based, the process by which the decisions are made, and the considerations that enter into the decision-making process for real estate are all parts of the subject matter of this book.

Economic importance of real estate

Perhaps the first step in gaining an understanding of real estate is to obtain a feel for its relative importance and magnitude in the national

[1] Henry E. Hoagland, *Real Estate Principles* (New York: McGraw-Hill, 1955), p. 1.

3

economy. To grasp the importance of land resources, we may note that privately owned urban real estate constitutes approximately $3,200 billion (more than 50 percent) of the national wealth.[2] New construction annually contributes about 10 percent to the gross national product. The construction industry is the largest single industry classified and employs approximately 4.2 million people directly and millions more in related activities. Credit for real estate, which enables people to buy and build homes, offices, schools, apartments, churches, stores, and factories, is one of the largest components of debt in the country and expanded from 26.4 percent of all debt in 1960 to approximately 30.4 percent in 1978. In actual amounts, mortgage debt increased from $260 billion to more than $1,155 billion during this period. The purchase of a home is often a family's single largest investment, and about 65 percent of the occupied housing units in the United States are owned by the occupants.[3]

Nature of real estate

Real estate is a physical good, including the land and improvements affixed to the land. *Real property* is a legal concept which gives the individual the right to use and control the real estate. In everyday affairs, the terms *real estate* and *real property* are often used interchangeably.

In addition to the earth's surface the concept of real property includes the airspace above the earth's surface and the earth beneath the surface, extending theoretically to the center of the earth. Since this planet is a spheroid, the resulting shape of a square or rectangular parcel of surface land is an inverted pyramid, with the apex at the earth's center. Theoretically, the pyramid is not closed at the base because no limit is known in space. However, the public domain typically is declared to exist at a certain height above the surface of the earth, or above the highest building in the city.

Not all physical items within the inverted pyramid are considered to be real estate. The law makes a major distinction between real property and personal property. Usually real property consists of ownership rights in land, buildings permanently attached to the land, growing crops, trees, and other vegetation gaining its sustenance from the earth, minerals below the earth's surface, and the airspace. Problems and disagreements often come about with respect to whether given items, such as carpet, drapes, television antennas, and so on, are

---

[2] U.S. Bureau of the Census, *Statistical Abstract of the United States: 1979,* 100th ed. (Washington, D.C.: U.S. Government Printing Office, 1979), p. 472.

[3] Ibid., p. 782.

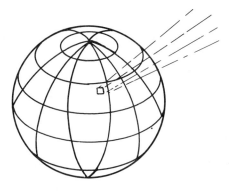

part of the real estate when it is being sold. However, if an item is considered a permanent part of a building, it is called a fixture and is legally considered to be real estate. (See Chapter 10.)

Finally, we may point out that there are many interests in real estate other than complete ownership. Life estates, reversions, remainders, and leaseholds are examples of real property interests that may have value and are governed by real property law.

REAL ESTATE ADMINISTRATION

Administration is the process of making a decision as to the proper course of action and the carrying out of a decision once it has been made. Administration of our real estate resources involves the functions of producing, marketing, appraising, counseling, managing, and consulting. Individuals, firms, and government agencies perform these functions in the administrative process. Rational behavior is implied in this process, and the administrative approach in this text is often based upon applied economic analysis and the rational behavior upon which it is based.

This viewpoint does not deny the value of using research results produced by the application of behavioral tools; indeed, we have incorporated such knowledge in various sections of the book, particularly in the chapter on real estate marketing (Chapter 14). Rather, a behaviorist framework constitutes another way of viewing the *same* problem or process, and it attempts to provide better data for the functional process. To state our position another way, psychological and social factors may determine the nature of the inputs to the various steps in the administrative process, but these steps or functions are still present.

Figure 1–1 outlines the characteristics of real estate administration in both the private and public sectors. A continuing theme in this book

FIGURE 1–1
Real estate administration

	Private sector	Public sector
Decision makers	Individuals, households Firms	Voter Legislature Executive branch Judiciary Bureaucracy
Objectives	Maximize wealth and utility	Maximize social welfare
Decision process	Determine objectives Develop hypotheses Collect and analyze data Specify alternatives Formulate conclusions Make a decision	Determine the portion of the nation's resources to be controlled by the public sector Allocate resources among perceived needs Analyze alternative programs to meet each need
Execution	Plan the operation Organize the factors of production (land, labor, capital, and management) Direct the operation Control the operation	Develop most efficient organization for implementation of programs Plan the program Organize the factors of production (at times through the operation of private sector firms) Direct the operation Control the operation
Type of decisions	Buy, sell, exchange Own, rent Borrow, lend Subdivide, build Maintain, repair Renovate, rehabilitate, remodel, preserve Abandon, reuse, demolish	Impose constraints by law or regulation (zoning, police power, environmental protection, lending regulations) Transfer income (housing subsidies, tax shelters, revenue sharing) Provide and manage real estate resources directly (public land and buildings, parks, streets, etc.)

is that the administration processes in the two sectors are interdependent. In a very fundamental way, the actors, or decision makers, in the private sector, through the political process, are also the ultimate decision makers in the public sector. The interrelationship, however, is much more complex in operation. For instance, the firm in the private sector is often an integral part of the execution of a public program, as when a private developer constructs subsidized housing for lower income households. Of course, all administration of real estate in the private sector is constrained by laws and regulations formulated in the public sector, such as zoning, building codes, and lending regulations. Programs, laws, and regulations from the public sector can induce particular types of real estate to be developed, can channel funds to housing versus other types of investments, and can cause certain neighborhoods to be rehabilitated. Such programs influence behavior and the administration process in the private sector. In turn, the administration process in the public sector is influenced by private sector decisions. Streets are improved and parking provided in response to real estate development that reflects the location decisions of firms and households. The decision to forgo maintenance and repair eventually can produce blighted areas which initiate public sector response. Laws and regulations are formulated to eliminate unfair practices in housing and lending perceived to have existed in the private sector.

Functional activities for administration

Often, in the administration process, many of the real estate functions are carried out by specialists or specialized firms, whose activities cause them to be considered part of the real estate business. As with all businesses in a private enterprise economy, a real estate business will exist only so long as it performs a useful service for which members of society are willing to pay an amount sufficient to enable the business to earn a long-run profit. The various types of real estate businesses are discussed under the activities they are organized to accomplish.

Producing. The production of physical real estate resources involves the construction of buildings, the modification of existing buildings, the application to land of nonbuilding improvements (such as blacktopping for a parking lot or landscaping for a public park), and the development of raw land so that additional capital improvements may be applied. These activities are usually performed by firms that specialize in development and construction—remodeling, demolishing, landscaping, and paving. Construction firms usually specialize by type of structures erected; for example, some firms build only single-family residences, while others specialize in erecting the steel framework for skyscrapers.

Marketing. Marketing activities are performed by real estate brokerage firms, speculative construction and development firms, individuals, government agencies, and businesses that wish to sell real estate without engaging a broker. Most real estate marketing activity is carried on by subdivision development and construction firms and by brokerage firms. Development and construction firms often build entire subdivisions and market each house on a speculative basis (that is, no buyer has agreed to purchase the house before construction).

Brokerage firms enter into a contract, usually with the owner of real estate, agreeing to attempt to find a buyer for the property. If the firm is successful, it will earn a commission percentage on the property's sale price. The Realtors National Marketing Institute (an affiliate of the National Association of Realtors) is the principal professional organization in this field.

Financing.   The financing of real estate is performed primarily by private financial institutions. Commercial banks, mutual savings banks, savings and loan associations, and life insurance companies provide approximately 75 percent of the dollar value of all mortgage financing. The remaining portion is furnished by trust funds, pension funds, endowment funds, government agencies, individuals, and nonfinancial businesses. When obtaining financing, the borrower (mortgagor) usually signs a note evidencing the debt to the lender (mortgagee) and also executes a mortgage. The mortgage pledges the property for possible sale in case the mortgagor defaults on the debt to the mortgagee. The decision-making phase of financing concerns whether or not a loan will be made, while the management (or execution) phase involves the actual lending and supervision processes (see Figure 1–1).

Appraising.   Real estate appraisal has as its objective the estimation of value of specific parcels of real estate. The activity is performed primarily by professional appraisers and real estate brokers. Brokers are usually knowledgeable about markets and the factors which create value, but they frequently cut short most of the appraisal function in order to arrive quickly at a *listing price.* Professional appraising involves rigorous analysis of various types of market data. Normally brokers have not been adequately trained in appraisal methodology, nor do they usually maintain the files of market information required to perform the appraisal function. The appraiser is a specialized consultant and in recent years has gained much prominence in the shaping of real estate decisions. Three professional organizations—the Society of Real Estate Appraisers, the American Institute of Real Estate Appraisers, and the American Society of Appraisers—have been instrumental in upgrading the standards and educational requirements for those wishing to enter the appraisal field in the United States. In Canada, the Appraisal Institute of Canada, as well as the Society of Real Estate Appraisers, has performed this function.

Consulting and counseling.   Various types of consultants are often required in matters concerning real estate. With the complexity of real property law, the lawyer is often required. Architects may be employed to design functional and aesthetically desirable buildings. Engineers may be required to design and oversee the construction of factories, bridges, roads, and other land improvements. Economists and business analysts may be needed to search out and analyze locations and to provide analysis, suggestions, and a continual review of administrative procedures.

Counseling is usually regarded as a more narrow term than consulting in the real estate field. The American Society of Real Estate Counselors (an affiliate of the National Association of Realtors) has popularized the term in regard to the type of service offered by its members, although the counseling function is not limited to those who are members of the organization. Counseling entails the rendering of investment advice to a client. An estimate of the value of a parcel of real estate may be one of the major considerations in the decision process of investors, but it is not the only important factor. The investors' financing requirements, their income tax situation, their portfolio of other investments, and their personal preferences should be considered by the counselor-consultant in advising clients about investment decisions.

Managing. The function of managing a property is often performed by a hired property management firm. For smaller investment properties the owner sometimes performs the management function. Whether a hired manager or the owner does it, however, management involves expense in terms of the manager's fees or the owner's time. Hired managers have become increasingly important since World War II because of the great mobility of the population which has led to increasing absentee ownership of real estate. It is not uncommon for the owner of a small parcel of investment real estate in the North to vacation in Florida during the winter months, leaving property in the hands of a professional manager. The Institute of Real Estate Management (also an affiliate of the National Association of Realtors), which awards the CPM (Certified Property Manager) designation to highly trained and qualified property managers, is the main professional organization in this field.

The investment process

It cannot be emphasized too strongly that the analysis and decisions concerning real estate are similar to the analysis and decisions concerning other factors of production and other investments which represent combinations of resources. Because real estate is often studied independently from other factors of production, the similarities between the various investments are obscured. Obviously, real estate, with its fixity of location and high unit value, can be differentiated from other resources, and the law affecting real property is in many ways different from that affecting personal property. However, of primary importance is not the differences, but rather an understanding of the total investment process and how the *process is applied to real estate.*

The theory of investment is relevant to the decision-making process involving the administration of real estate in the private sector. The theory may be defined as the identification of factors causing people and firms to make decisions about income-producing assets and the description and measurement of the relationships among those factors. Investment theory boils down the fundamental proposition that investors give up or pay a certain amount of valuable asset (often money) for the right to receive income or other valuable benefits in return. Algebraically, this proposition may be expressed in the following way:

$$P = (f)B$$

where P equals price or value, (f) is the functional relationship, and B equals the benefits to be derived, perhaps over a period of years. An understanding of investment theory allows one to analyze and predict how decisions will be made and thus how parcels of real estate will be developed. Analyzing patterns of decisions allows one to understand and predict city growth and development.

CONSTRAINTS UPON REAL ESTATE DECISIONS

Although real estate decisions are made within the framework of private enterprise, four major types of constraints limit an investor's scope of decision-making authority. These limitations represent the government's residual, but inherent, powers to legislate and regulate on behalf of the general welfare and to claim unowned property. While real estate is subject to many indirect influences (such as economic and social trends), all direct limitations from the public sector in the form of laws and regulations emanate from one or more of the following four categories: police power, right of taxation, right of eminent domain, and doctrine of escheat.

Police power

The police power represents the right of governmental units to limit the rights that individual property owners have in their property. The justification of the police power is for the protection of the general welfare of all people in the regulation of public health, morals, and safety. McQuillan has noted that this power concerns "the inherent right of people through organized government to protect their health, life, limb, individual liberty of action, property, and to provide for public order, peace, safety, and welfare."[4] Examples of uses of the

---

[4] Eugene McQuillan, *The Law of Municipal Corporations*, 3d ed. (Chicago: Calaghan, 1949), vol. 6, p. 464.

police power with respect to real estate are in the areas of zoning, building codes, open housing laws, and the licensing of real estate brokers.

Zoning. Zoning involves the division of a city or other area into districts for various types of land uses. The zones or districts are usually delineated within a pattern established by a city plan. Within a zone such aspects as the height of buildings, the proportion of land covered by the building, and the uses to which the building may be put are regulated. In zoning residential areas, density may also be controlled by requiring a specified number of square feet of area or a given number of lineal feet of frontage per structure. Most zoning laws will not allow the invasion into one zone of a use from another zone. Thus, industrial uses are not allowed to enter a residential district.

Although zoning necessarily places limitations upon the rights of individual property owners, most experts as well as the general population seem to feel that zoning accomplishes worthwhile objectives such as raising land values, reducing traffic problems and nuisances, and improving the allocation of public utilities and recreational facilities. In order for zoning to be successful, however, the right amount of land must be set aside for each type of use. If an oversupply of land is zoned for commercial use while insufficient land is zoned for industrial use, the prices of the latter will be bid up relatively out of proportion to the former. Thus, zoning authorities must be cognizant of the economic needs of the city both now and in the future. Furthermore, the zoning ordinance must not be a straitjacket of inflexibility. Exceptions are usually needed to allow the overall plan to be realistically workable; nevertheless, indiscriminate and unnecessary deviation should not be allowed. As with most restrictions, therefore, zoning must combine inflexibility with a tempering degree of flexibility so that legitimate exceptions to the rule may be made.[5]

Building codes. Building codes regulate the quality and strength of materials for the purposes of controlling safety, fire prevention, and sanitation. The thickness and height of walls, spacing of beams and girders, and allowable stresses are usually governed, as are the plumbing, vents, ventilation, height and size of rooms, and strength of materials that go into the building.

Building codes are established by local government agencies, usually the municipal governments. As with zoning ordinances, we should note that the regulations should attempt to temper rigidity with a degree of flexibility. In this case the flexibility refers to the ability to obtain changes in building codes as new materials and construction processes replace older methods and materials. In too many cases in the past, building codes have not measured up to this requirement. A

---

[5] Appendix B describes some typical zoning requirements and procedures.

result has been in some cases a lack of progress. A good example in St. Louis, Missouri, which for many years enforced very restrictive, archaic building codes. In 1961 a change in the building code allowing utilization of newer materials resulted in a downtown building boom which continued for several years after the change.[6]

Although building codes by their nature must deal with some details, the amount of detail should be limited to an absolute minimum, while the emphasis is placed upon the objectives to be accomplished. The modern approach is to state standards in terms of *capacity to perform* rather than in terms of the *amounts* and *kinds* of materials going into the structure. Such criteria would encourage the introduction of improved building methods and materials.

A major problem with building codes has been that they differ among communities within the same metropolitan area. This situation forces construction firms to know several different code requirements, unnecessarily complicating their work. In many cities it also has resulted in special interest groups having a great deal of influence over the code. Dealers of presently approved products and craft unions understandably fight code changes which could weaken their market positions. Such groups can form strong lobbies against major improvements, such as the acceptance of prefabricated units or more efficient new products. Recommendations for the improvement of building codes have included the placement of code formulation and enforcement at the state government level. The codes would be uniform for an entire state and would be less subject to pressures from local, special interest groups.[7]

Licensing of brokers.   Licensing is required in practically every state before one may perform the functions of a real estate broker or sales representative. Although this limitation is not directly concerned with an individual parcel of real estate, it does have considerable influence upon the total market activity for real estate resources. The license laws are designed to set a minimum standard of competence and honesty for real estate brokers. As is the case with respect to the licensing of physicians, attorneys, dentists, and other professionals whose activities are deemed to be in the public welfare, the licensing of real estate brokers has as its objective the protection of the public in an area where special, technical knowledge is required. It should be noted that the license laws presently do not contain standards that would elevate the real estate brokerage business to that of a profession.

---

[6] Robert L. Bartley, "Business Helps St. Louis Fight Decay," *The Wall Street Journal*, May 26, 1966, p. 14.

[7] Carl J. Tschappat, "The Modernization of Building Codes" (Unpublished paper, September 1965).

However, many states require varying amounts of basic education in real estate either prior or subsequent to licensing. While some licensed brokers and sales personnel pursue more advanced education, advancement of the field is limited by the vast numbers of licensees who achieve only the required, minimum levels of education and training.

Open housing laws.   Statutes and court decisions outlaw discrimination in real estate transactions on the basis of race, religion, sex, or national origin. Although the federal fair housing law, some state fair housing laws, and the U.S. Supreme Court decision outlawing discrimination occurred in the late 1960s, a number of laws had been enacted in the early and mid-1960s by a few cities and states to forbid housing discrimination. These early efforts were sporadic, and some suffered setbacks. For example, a state fair housing law enacted by the legislature in California was overturned by referendum. However, a 1966 decision of the California Supreme Court declared the referendum to be unconstitutional. Also in 1966, a federal fair housing law was introduced in Congress as part of civil rights legislation. And in 1963 an order barring discrimination in transactions involving government-underwritten loans was issued by President Kennedy.

On April 11, 1968, Title VIII of the Civil Rights Act of 1968 was signed into law by President Johnson. This law bans discrimination in the sale, rental, and leasing of housing *except* in the rental of apartments up to four units in size if the owner occupies one of the units, by religious organizations or private clubs, and by homeowners not using the services of an agent. These exemptions were negated by a decision of the U.S. Supreme Court in 1968 that the federal Civil Rights Act of 1866 outlawed *all* racial discrimination in housing. Additionally, some states also passed laws closing all avenues of discrimination in housing. For example, the Ohio fair housing law (House Bill 432) which took effect on November 12, 1969, outlaws discrimination in the sale, rental, or leasing of housing on the basis of race, color, religion, national origin, or ancestry.[8]

Taxation

Although the right of taxation has been said to be the right to stifle or kill worthwhile projects, the lack of the right of taxation would be even more disastrous. Collective action through governments is a necessity for the operation of modern societies. Therefore, governments (other than the federal government) have the right to impose taxes upon the property within their jurisdictions. Much of the burden of providing needed services and facilities by local governments is incurred by the

---

[8] See Appendix A for the provisions of these major antidiscrimination housing laws.

tax on real property. As with other liens, when tax payments are not made, the property may be sold to satisfy the debt.[9]

Although the federal government is prohibited from taxing property directly, the earnings produced by property are taxable in the form of federal income taxes. The federal income tax has an important bearing upon the decision-making process and will be considered in those investment calculations.[10] Suffice it to note here that the income tax is in reality merely an *indirect* tax upon property of all types, real and personal.

Eminent domain

The right of eminent domain is the right of governments and other designated agencies to take private property for public use. When relinquishing private property for public use, the owners must be compensated for the value of the property taken. Although they have the right to be paid, title holders do not have the option of refusing to give up their property. The right of eminent domain is one which can force owners to sell for just compensation even if owners do not wish to sell.

Often the governmental agencies cannot agree with the owner of the property as to what just compensation for the property is. When agreement cannot be reached, the governmental agency will condemn the property, and the court will determine the amount of just compensation. The right of eminent domain is vested in the federal government, the various state governments, municipal governments, and other public corporations such as public utilities whose function is regarded as essential to the public welfare.

Doctrine of escheat

The doctrine of escheat, although much less onerous than other limitations, nevertheless restricts the absolute control of property by private individuals. This doctrine is of common-law origin and states, in effect, that when there are no longer any identifiable owners of a particular parcel of real estate, ownership or title to the real estate will vest in the state. This doctrine has greater influence upon private personal property such as bank accounts, savings and loan accounts, and so on, which many times go unclaimed by owners. With respect to real estate this type of occurrence is much less frequent, but nevertheless it does occur.

---

[9] Real estate taxation is discussed in Chapter 12.

[10] This is discussed more fully in Chapter 13.

SUMMARY

If this brief overview of the real estate field seems to describe a large, multifaceted, complex sphere of activities, the impression is correct. In the administration of our real estate resources, decisions are made and actions are taken in a number of different types of business firms. Appraisal firms, consulting firms, land development firms, and financial institutions all play important roles in the field of real estate.

Many decisions involving real estate are also made by public or government agencies. Local governments pass zoning ordinances, and building and housing codes. They also levy real estate taxes. State governments build highways and decide who can and cannot be in the real estate business. The federal government owns and leases much real estate and occasionally buys and sells property. More importantly, however, several government agencies, such as the Department of Housing and Urban Development, the Federal Home Loan Bank Board, the Federal Reserve System, the Federal National Mortgage Association, the Federal Housing Administration, the Government National Mortgage Association, the Federal Home Loan Mortgage Corporation, and the Environmental Protection Agency, regulate many aspects of real estate activity and help channel funds into the mortgage market.

The results of all these decisions and influences within a framework of legal constraints produce patterns of types of institutions, funds flows, and land uses which can be studied in the area of macroadministration. Basic mechanisms contributing to these patterns are commonalities in laws, economic behavior, psychological makeup, and social mores. The legal framework results from the four types of public limitations on property rights—police power, taxation, eminent domain, and the doctrine of escheat. The decision-making or investment process is the means by which these commonalities are translated into patterns of behavior. This process, the legal framework, functions performed, and the influences of public decision makers are the general topics for consideration in this book.

QUESTIONS FOR REVIEW

1. Why is the term *administration* important to an understanding of real estate?
2. How would you distinguish between administration and decision making?
3. What control do you have of activities that may occur in the airspace above your land?
4. Can you identify real estate firms in your community engaged in each of the functional activities of producing, marketing, financing, appraising, counseling, managing, and consulting?

5. Why is investment theory important in understanding real estate?

6. Would you pay more or less than $2,000 for the right to receive $1,000 per year for the next two years? Would you pay more or less than $10,000 for the right to receive $1,000 per year for the next ten years? Why?

7. What are the reasons for limiting private property rights of real estate owners? Do you believe additional limitations will be placed on ownership rights? If so, what types of additional limitations do you foresee?

8. The real estate tax is often cited as being an unfair and regressive tax. Can you think of reasons that it could be regarded in this way?

REFERENCES

Calkins, Robert D. "The Decision-Making Process in Administration." *Business Horizons* 2, no. 3 (Fall 1959): 19–25.

Hoagland, Henry E. *Real Estate Principles.* New York: McGraw-Hill, 1955, chap. 1.

Kinnard, William N., Jr. "Reducing Uncertainty in Real Estate Decisions." Beyer-Nelson Distinguished Lecture at Ohio State University, 1968. Published in *Real Estate Appraiser* 34, no. 7 (November–December 1968): 10–16.

Ratcliff, Richard U. *Real Estate Analysis.* New York: McGraw-Hill, 1961, chap. 1.

Simon, Herbert A. *The New Science of Management Decision.* New York: Harper & Row, 1960.

Weimer, Arthur M. "Real Estate Decisions Are Different." *Harvard Business Review* 44, no. 6 (November–December 1966): 105–12.

Weimer, Arthur M.; Hoyt, Homer; and Bloom, George F. *Real Estate.* 7th ed. New York: John Wiley and Sons, 1978, chaps. 1 and 2.

chapter 2

The investment approach

Premises

The investment approach to decision making in real estate is based upon the premise that many alternatives are available to the investor. Individual investors have a choice of purchasing stocks, bonds, real estate, a private business, or many other items. If the decision is made to purchase stock, they have an endless variety of companies and industries from which to choose equity investments. If the investors decide to purchase bonds, an almost infinite variety of legal provisions and features are available from many firms in different industries. Similarly, real estate investments are as varied as all the individual properties and legal provisions compounded. Investors have almost an infinite variety of investment alternatives from which to choose.

A second premise is that market imperfections may cause the price of an investment property to be higher or lower than the property's value. If perfect competition reigned, the market price would by definition equal value, and the price the purchaser paid would be justified. Markets, however, are not perfectly competitive. For example, real estate prices may fluctuate during the year if the market is more active in some seasons than others. Sellers may harbor an inflated opinion as to their property's worth. Or owners may be under pressure to sell because they need their capital quickly or because they are moving out of town. If investors pay too high a price, their return on investment

(ROI) will be lower than necessary. But if investors pay a price lower than the property's market value, their ROI will be higher than market returns on properties of comparable risk. Smart investors should continually be watching for "good buys"—properties whose prices are less than their long-term values. Successful investment strategy usually requires the ability to exploit market imperfections.

A third premise—and a corollary of the first two—is that the investors (or their advisers) must collect, assimilate, analyze, and draw conclusions from a large quantity of market data. To make choices among the almost infinite variety of investments and to identify good buys or bad buys, information must be available concerning the types of available properties, income and expense characteristics of the properties, rates of return being obtained in the market by other investors, and rates of return obtainable from other types of competing investments. Investors who do not rely upon analyses of market data to guide their investment decisions are really not investors; they are gamblers.

Objectives

With the great diversity of people, motives, and criteria applied by investors, one might expect chaos to reign without public planning and dictated decisions. Such is not the case. Even with the diversity of criteria and weights applied to these criteria, investors, as well as business enterprises, have certain ultimate objectives in common. These have been termed the profit, service, and social objectives.[1]

Although there may be disagreement as to the relative importance of the three objectives, most people in the real estate market, as in other markets, attempt to fulfill these objectives in a variety of ways. We do not contend that one thinks explicitly about the objectives; rather, these objectives are in the nature of economic and social norms, the fulfillment of which determines in the eyes of contemporaries whether one has been successful or not.

Profit objective. Economic science is based upon the premise that people attempt to maximize their welfare by acquiring an optimal mix of valuable commodities and services. The extent to which one purchases any one commodity or service depends upon the benefit—financial or psychological—to be obtained from the item relative to the price that must be paid for it. Income is one of the primary benefits to be obtained from owning a productive commodity such as real estate. Income is desirable because with it one can purchase other commod-

---

[1] See John F. Mee, "Management Philosophy for Professional Executives," *Business Horizons,* Bureau of Business Research, School of Business, Indiana University (December 1956): 5–11.

ities and services for ultimate consumption; the rental income to many landlords buys their groceries.

Another major type of benefit to be obtained from owning real estate is the psychological benefit (or amenities) buyers expect when they purchase residential real estate for self-occupancy. As in the case of the purchasers of income-producing properties, home purchasers are investors in the sense that they attempt to buy the type of house at the lowest price which will give them the greatest psychological "profit" or satisfaction.

At times, business real estate is purchased for the prestige and status that may be attached to an impressive building. Business firms often construct buildings that are much more elaborate than would be necessary to carry on the firm's functions adequately and efficiently. The Seagram Building on Park Avenue in New York City, for example, is constructed of bronze, which is artistically more striking, but it is also much more expensive than functionally comparable steel. In such cases it is doubtful whether the increased prestige will result in income that is sufficient to justify the increased cost of the building in a purely financial sense. Thus, profit must be measured in both financial and psychological terms.

Service objective. The service objective can be described from two points of view—both relative to the profit objective. First, service may be regarded as the ultimate objective. In this view each economic unit—a person or business—should strive to provide a service. If a needed service is provided at a reasonable price, the business or investor will indeed make a profit.

The second viewpoint regards profit as the ultimate objective. If business firms or investors obtain a profit in the long run, a service has been provided.

Since debating which of the two viewpoints is correct is a little like arguing which came first, the chicken or the egg, it may be well to regard profit and service as equally important. Certainly the two go hand in hand, and the accomplishment of both is necessary for the continued existence of an economic unit.

Social objective. If the profit and service objectives are regarded as having equal importance, they must share the glory with yet another motivating force. The social objective recognizes an investor's or a business's responsibility to society. This responsibility stems from the fact that no business executive or investor is truly "self-made." As Samuelson points out:

> If ever a person becomes arrogantly proud of *his* economic productivity and *his* level of real earnings, let him pause and reflect. If he were transported with all his skills and energies intact to a primitive desert

island, how much would his money earnings buy? Indeed, without capital machinery, without rich resources, without other labor, and above all without the technological knowledge which each generation inherits from society's past, how much could he produce? It is only too clear that all of us reap the benefits of an economic world we never made.[2]

How does the investor-business executive pursue the social objective? By engaging in an economically and socially useful activity which is both legal and ethical. The danger of engaging in illegal activities is evident. The danger of engaging in unethical activities is not so clear. Consider the case of a landlord who creates or maintains an unsafe, unhealthful slum tenement. In most cases, refusal to improve undesirable conditions has been defended by landlords on the ground that the additional rent cannot be sufficiently charged to justify the added expenditure of maintaining or improving property. In some cases this contention is valid. Particularly where government-imposed barriers exist—such as the long-standing rent control in New York City or confiscatory levels of the property tax—proper maintenance of existing units, as well as the construction of new units, is inhibited. Public policy should effect a more viable economic framework that will justify maintenance expenditures. However, in other cases slumlords have condoned unacceptable living conditions in their rental units when the income produced by the units would have justified greater maintenance expenditures. Such practices may be extremely profitable in the short run, and for individuals the short run may be a sufficiently long period of time to enable them to acquire desired wealth. Over a longer period of time, however, such activities will be limited or precluded by society.

In attempting to accomplish the three objectives, investors often arrive at similar conclusions about how best to go about the task. For example, in striving to maximize the benefits of home ownership within their capacities, many people have similar ideas of what type, size, and location of a house best fulfills their wants. Thus, we find districts and neighborhoods having homes with similar characteristics. Further, the residents of those homes are likely to have similar income levels, educational attainment, and social status in the community.

Investment criteria

The real estate decision maker needs to consider certain criteria in judging alternative investments. In effect the following questions are asked: "What is a good investment for my particular purpose? What

---

[2] Paul A. Samuelson, *Economics*, 6th ed. (New York: McGraw-Hill, 1964), p. 435.

purchase price should be paid?" The following criteria provide the standards by which to answer these questions.

Return on investment. Return on investment, or yield, is a percentage relationship between the price investors must pay and the stream of income dollars they obtain from the investment. For example, if $1,000 was paid for a piece of land from which investors expected to receive net $100 per year for as long as they held the land, their return on investment would be 10 percent.

In the case of land, investors assume it does not wear out or lose value during the life of the investment; therefore, the investors could recover their capital at any time simply by selling the land, which should bring about $1,000. The ROI calculation becomes more complicated for investments such as buildings which wear out and lose value during the life of the investment. In addition to receiving a return *on* their invested capital, the investors must plan for the return *of* their capital from the income stream. For example, if investors pay $10,000 for a building and the building loses value (depreciates) over the next 20 years, the investors must obtain, in addition to their 10 percent on the outstanding balance of the investment, 5 percent of $10,000 ($500) so that at the end of the 20th year they will have recovered the $10,000 invested capital.[3]

Business risk. Two types of risk enter into a determination of whether an expected return for a specific investment is sufficiently high—business risk and financial risk. Business risk concerns the probability that the income-producing ability of the investment (or business) will not be as great as expected. Although a return on the investment has been estimated, there is some probability that this expectation will not be realized. Any cause of such a loss that has its source in the investment itself would constitute a part of the business risk. For example, if an apartment building cannot be rented at the rates anticipated by an investor, the property may have to be sold to pay the investor's obligations. Manifestation of business risk will have resulted in loss of the investment.

Business risk stems from two sources—internal operating difficulties (or inefficiencies) and external factors. The ROI calculation may assume that revenues and expenses will be kept at a particular level. Perhaps, however, poor management does not achieve a high tenant occupancy or does not take advantage of discounts in purchasing supplies. Because of such internal operating inefficiencies the return will be lower than expected.

Externally the demand for a particular product or the services provided by real estate may diminish. New apartment buildings may be

---

[3] Note: Compare this with the purchase of a corporate bond.

erected, causing the relative attractiveness of older buildings to decline; or general economic conditions may force business tenants to get by with less office space, thus affecting the ability of management to lease space designed for this purpose.

The uncertainties associated with investment ventures of this kind can be compared to relatively riskless investments such as government bonds. With the latter type of investment there is virtually no business risk. The investor can be confident of receiving interest as scheduled and return of principal at the bonds' maturity. Obviously, the increased risk associated with real estate investments causes the investor to demand a greater return expectation before investing. The greater the business risk, the higher must be the expected return over and above the available rate on relatively riskless government bonds.

Financial risk.   Most real estate investors use borrowed funds in the purchase of real estate. Although business risk is present even when no borrowed funds are used, financial risk is strictly dependent upon the amount of and legal provisions concerning borrowed funds. If the income produced by an investment falls below the payment which was specified in the debt agreement, the owner will have to either sell the property to satisfy the debt or make the payments from other resources. For most investments, of course, the property's income-producing ability is expected to cover all expenses, including debt service.

In deciding upon an acceptable rate of return, investors should consider financial risk. They should not accept a return that barely compensates them for the burden of losing the property if debt payments cannot be made. On the other hand, if investors have adequate personal resources to cover any such deficiency, the financial risk is lower.

Cost of capital.   An investor's cost of capital determines whether the expected return on investment is sufficiently high. Investors should not purchase any investment which does not provide a return equal to the price they must pay for borrowed funds and the return they could obtain on competing investments. In calculating their cost of capital, investors should weight the cost from each source by the percentage of funds obtained from that source. For example, if a $100,000 investment property were financed by 60 percent debt funds and 40 percent equity (the investor's own funds), the cost rates of each would be weighted accordingly. Suppose the debt funds cost 8 percent interest on a mortgage and other equity investments with a comparable risk yield 12 percent. If the proportion of debt and equity funds employed by investors are expected to remain constant, the cost of capital calculation would be as follows:

Mortgage debt (0.60 × 8%) 4.8%
Equity (0.40 × 12%) 4.8%
Weighted average cost of capital 9.6%

The investment should not be purchased unless its expected return is
at least 9.6 percent.

Stability of income.   The stability of income can be of importance
in an investment situation. Particularly with respect to the financial
expenses, the income pattern can be crucial. If the income should fall
below the debt service requirement for any period, the owner would
have to use other resources to make the payment, allow the property to
be sold, or make special arrangements with the lender. Over a longer
period the income might be adequate to provide the desired return; in
the short run it could mean loss of property.

This graph depicts a dangerous situation for investors. During two
months of the year the income is less than the debt service requirement. The difference of $250 per month will have to be paid out of
investors' personal funds, or they must be prepared to lose the property.

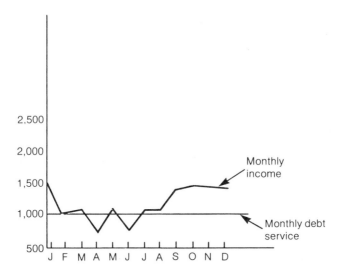

Liquidity.   While the aforementioned criteria may be favorable,
investors might not find the investment desirable. They may realize
that at any time they might have to sell the investment to meet a
specific need. Real estate is sometimes vulnerable to a lack of liquidity, which is defined as the ability to sell the property quickly for at
least as much as the amount invested. Therefore, in most such invest-

ments there should be a high probability that neither the equity funds nor the borrowed funds will be needed on short notice.

Investments providing high liquidity typically yield a lower return than less liquid investments. In other words, investors must be willing to pay for liquidity, and if they need a high degree of liquidity, they would probably resort to lower-yielding, high-grade corporate or government bonds.

The degree of liquidity for real estate is often a function of the type of property under consideration. Special-purpose properties of relatively high value are less liquid than general-use properties. Houses of medium-price range (say $60,000 to $70,000) are more liquid than very large or small houses. Usually, the wider the market for any investment, the greater is the chance for recovering the capital invested.

Applicability of the investment approach

In this book we include our entire study of the administration of real estate within the framework of the investment approach. We feel that this approach is superior to others because it facilitates the important aspect of decision making. Decision making was shown in Chapter 1 to be the key element in the administration of real estate resources, and it is through the investment approach that decision making is understood.

Non-income-producing properties. The investment approach might be regarded as inappropriate for the analysis of properties that do not produce dollar income, such as single-family residences, public parks, school buildings, and libraries. The benefits from properties of this type may not accrue in the form of monetary income and may be indirect or even unmeasurable. Coons and Glaze have shown that in buying a home most people are concerned with consumption motives, such as the services the home will provide and the prestige and status to be obtained, rather than financial advantage.[4] A "good address," an impressive architectural design for a home, the beauty of a park, or attractiveness of a school are intangible benefits. Decisions are made whether to develop or purchase these types of properties. Upon what basis are these decisions made? What type of analysis goes into these decisions? We submit that the investment approach, which recognizes that the outlay must be justified by the expected returns—whether these returns be monetary or psychic—provides the best approach for understanding the ubiquitous decision-making requirement.

---

[4] Alvin E. Coons and Bert T. Glaze, *Housing Market Analysis and the Increase in House Ownership* (Columbus: Bureau of Business Research, Ohio State University, 1964).

The expected future stream of psychic benefits (amenities) can be considered analogous to financial benefits in a dollar-income-producing investment. For dollar-income-producing investments a percentage relationship (or ROI) is calculated between these benefits and the price that must be paid. For psychic-income-producing investments we cannot make such a calculation because the benefits themselves are not directly measurable in dollar terms. This does not negate the theory or analytical approach, however. Rather, it means that we must compare prices of alternative properties, as these prices are related to the benefits and to the other criteria discussed in this chapter.

The home purchaser should recognize that the business risk associated with a home purchase concerns the probability that the production of amenities by the home will not be as great as anticipated. Will the location continue to provide the expected benefits? What is the probability the neighborhood will decline more rapidly than anticipated?

As with income properties, financial risk associated with amenity-producing properties concerns the probability that the mortgage payment cannot be met. To assess this probability purchasers must weigh their expected future incomes against personal expenses, housing expenses, and the periodic mortgage payments. Two rough rules of thumb are that purchasers having no abnormal personal expenses can pay up to 2½ times their annual gross incomes for a home, and that they can afford to pay up to 25 percent of their monthly income in housing expense.

Homebuyers should also consider the liquidity of their investments. Can they sell the home in a reasonable time if they should so desire? What is the probability they will need to sell within two, three, five, or ten years?

Lastly, stability of benefits should be considered. Will the home provide satisfactory benefits in winter as well as summer? Is it sufficiently well decorated that a family will enjoy the benefits of homeownership as soon as they move in, or will they have to wait some period of time until the home can be redecorated?

The investment approach to home ownership thus involves a weighing of costs against returns. The principal returns are the psychic benefits or amenities produced by the property and the right not to pay rent. Costs include the interest that must be paid for borrowed money and the alternative monetary or psychic benefits that could be obtained from an alternative investment. These burdens comprise the home investor's cost of capital.

Social problems. One last question about the applicability of the investment approach concerns its role in social analysis: How does the macroapproach to real estate problems fit within this microlevel framework? What justification would we have for including in this book a discussion of urban decay and redevelopment, mass transit, city planning, low-income housing, and so forth? Market imperfections and inadequate regulation and enforcement may contribute to the continuance of socially unhealthful consequences such as slums and racial ghettos. Understanding of the investment process may reveal ways the decision-making process can be altered to effect more desirable social results.

Additionally, however, knowledge of the investment approach can help identify those areas where social action must be taken to remedy patterns that cannot be changed efficiently through the private decision-making process. One such area is neighborhood rehabilitation. The housing market is generally considered an inadequate device to renew and rehabilitate slum areas of our cities. Several owners of slum properties cannot fix up their properties while the rest of the area remains deteriorated; rents cannot be increased to justify the expenditure. Furthermore, no one developer is large enough to accumulate all the properties in a slum area so as to be able to rehabilitate the entire area. Clearly the market is inadequate, and governmental assistance is needed. The investment in such a rehabilitation project must be justified from a social standpoint rather than from the standpoint of a private investor's potential return.

SUMMARY

The investment approach can be regarded as a philosophy of making decisions and solving problems. It entails identifying and measuring the benefits to be derived from a course of action and the costs that must be incurred to achieve that action. The costs are weighed against the benefits for alternative courses of action in order to decide which way to proceed.

Real estate analysis is particularly appropriate for the investment approach because benefits in the form of income or amenities are usually present and, at least for income-producing properties, are measurable. Similarly, the costs of purchase and maintenance can usually be identified and estimated. Relationships between costs and benefits for several properties or projects can then be calculated and evaluated.

Several motivating and constraining forces serve to channel real estate investment decisions into observable patterns. Common objectives of profit, service, and so ial function stimulate investors to seek the same rewards. Common expectations about future growth and development tend to cause investors to evaluate similarly the various ways of achieving their objectives.

Investment criteria relevant to real estate are return on investment, the amount of cash generated after the payment of expenses, the liquidity of the property, and the business risk and financial risk associated with the property. The cost of obtaining funds for investment is determined by a weighted average cost of equity and debt funds and is a major determinant of the rate of return on investment that is demanded by investors.

QUESTIONS FOR REVIEW

1. What is the role of the profit, service, and social objectives in producing patterns of land use?
2. Why are the service and social objectives given equal weight with the profit objective?
3. What is meant by *liquidity?* Look up in a book on finance a definition of *marketability.* How do the two terms differ? Which is more important in real estate analysis? Why?
4. What are some of the considerations that should be taken into account when deciding what an appropriate ROI should be?
5. What would you say are the costs and the benefits of obtaining a college education? Can the question of whether to pursue a college education be regarded as an investment decision? Why or why not? Would everyone come to the same conclusion regarding the relationship between costs and benefits associated with four years spent at a college or university? Why or why not?
6. How would you measure business risk? In what way is business risk reflected in ROI?
7. Why are investment criteria in addition to ROI important? Can you think of a situation in which the expected ROI might be acceptable but another criterion would cause a proposed investment to be unfavorable?
8. Visualize a side-section profile through the center of a large city. How does the height of buildings illustrate the principle of proportionality? How is the principle of proportionality related to the economic principle of increasing and decreasing returns?

REFERENCES

Harvey, Robert O., and Clark, W. A. V.   "The Nature and Economics of Urban Sprawl." *Land Economics* 41, no. 1 (February 1965): 1–9.
Hoyt, Homer.   "The Growth of Cities from 1800 to 1960 and Forecasts to Year 2000." *Land Economics* 39, no. 2 (May 1963).
Lynch, Kevin.   "The Pattern of the Metropolis." In *Metropolis: Values in Conflict,* edited by C. E. Elias, Jr., James Gillies, and Svend Riemer. Belmont, Calif.: Wadsworth, 1964.
Ratcliff, Richard U.   *Real Estate Analysis.* New York: McGraw-Hill, 1961, pp. 306–31.

Ricks, R. Bruce. "New Town Development and the Theory of Location." *Land Economics* 46, no. 1 (February 1970): 5–11.

Sauvain, Harry C. *Investment Management.* 3d ed. Englewood Cliffs, N.J.: Prentice-Hall, 1967, pp. 3–20.

Seldin, Maury, and Swesnik, Richard H. *Real Estate Investment Strategy.* 2d ed. New York: Wiley-Interscience, 1979, chaps. 1–3.

Wendt, Paul F., and Cerf, Alan R. *Real Estate Investment and Taxation.* 2d ed. New York: McGraw-Hill, 1979, pp. 1–9.

chapter 3

Value: The central idea

Decision making in real estate centers on the investment calculation. Potential investors wish to pay a price which is sufficiently low to allow them to obtain a future return on their investments. Sellers of real estate wish to obtain a price high enough to allow them to have obtained a return on their investment in the past. Each transaction affecting ownership or use of real estate involves such basic investment calculations, whether the real estate is an owner-occupied single-family residence, an investment property, a lease arrangement, or a share in a syndicate or some other form of joint ownership. The investment calculation may involve income and expenses in dollars or, in the case of the owner-occupied home, it must be conceptualized in terms of amenities–housing services provided by the unit and net satisfaction. Further, investors compare the risk and return available from a real estate investment with the risk and return of alternative investments, resulting in a decision process which considers a portfolio of investments.

Investment calculations recur during the period of ownership of real estate. Owners must repeatedly determine whether or not to spend for maintenance and repair. Less frequently, decisions must be made about rehabilitation, modernization, expansion, property conversion to another use, or demolition of the existing improvements and reuse of the site. Even the decision to abandon the real estate involves an investment calculation.

The investment process consists of two phases. Phase 1 is the esti-mation of market value or the most probable selling price of the prop-erty. Phase 2 is the investment calculation. The concepts of market value and investment value and the procedures by which the value of real estate is measured are discussed in this chapter and in Chapter 4. A discussion of the investment calculation is reserved for Chapter 5. In Chapters 6 and 7, the investment calculation is broadened by further consideration of risk and returns and by analysis of continuing invest-ment decisions.

VALUE AS A MARKET CONCEPT

The concept of value is a market concept. It is the result of interact-ing forces of supply and demand. It rests upon the presence of willing buyers and sellers freely bidding in competition with one another. The modern concept of value was synthesized by Alfred Marshall, whose famous book *Principles of Economics* became the world's leading economics textbook.[1] In this book Marshall introduced the famous scissors analogy of supply and demand operating in the market. As each blade of a pair of scissors is necessary for the unit to function, so are supply and demand necessary for the economic unit—a market—to function. The interaction of both of these forces is important in the determination of price.

Value in a perfectly competitive market

Value is a phenomenon of a competitive market. If real estate mar-kets were perfectly competitive, supply and demand would *determine* value, which would be identical with price. The criteria of a perfect market are:

1. Homogeneity of products.
2. A product divisible into small economic units.
3. A transportable product enabling supply to flow to areas of high demand.
4. Many buyers and sellers.
5. No buyer or seller large enough to influence the market.
6. No external influence.
7. Complete knowledge as to possible uses.
8. Agreement as to expectations.

If the requirements of this model were met, there would be no need for value estimates to be made. In analyzing any market, however, it soon becomes clear that the requirements are impossible to attain. For

---

[1] Alfred Marshall, *Principles of Economics*, 8th ed. (London: Macmillan, 1920).

example, the wheat market is often cited as a market closely approaching the idea of a perfect market; yet, even in this market the product is not homogeneous (there are different grades of wheat). Additionally, the market is influenced by governmental activities and has within it buyers and sellers who do not have complete knowledge and are not in agreement as to the future. If the characteristics of the real estate market are compared with the requirements in this same way, the extreme imperfections become apparent. Because real estate markets are far from perfect, real estate analysts look at many indications of market activity, including transaction prices, in an effort to *estimate* value.

Real estate market characteristics

Real estate markets are imperfect in part because real estate is different from other economic goods. The differences between real estate and other economic goods concern its physical immobility, its length of economic life, and its economic size. Real estate markets may also have relatively few buyers or sellers at any given time.

Physical immobility. The physical immobility of real estate, although an obvious characteristic, leads to several important economic considerations discussed in this section.[2]

Because of the physical immobility of real estate, the market for each parcel is largely determined by those who demand and supply properties in a localized area. Although the demand side of the market may contain buyers from outside the local area, in many instances prospective purchasers of real estate come from the local area. The supply side is, of course, local. To the extent, however, that a parcel in one locality may substitute for one in another locality, the supply side becomes broader in scope. The fact remains, however, that each parcel of real estate is imperfectly substitutable for other parcels.

The physical immobility of real estate has an important implication for the valuation of real estate. Since the parcel of real property cannot be moved from its location, its value is subject to the effects of economic, social, or political developments emanating from the national, regional, community, and neighborhood levels. With respect to movable economic goods, such as a refrigerator or rug, purely local economic forces have much less effect on their values. Why? Simply because they can be moved to escape such influences.

Social, political, and·economic developments at all levels require subjective assessment and often are tenuous in their relationship to

---

[2] These economic considerations in turn provide the reasoning and justification for the valuation procedures discussed in Chapter 4.

value. Nevertheless, value estimates should be based upon some assumptions about future conditions in the society, although quantification of their effects is difficult. The appraiser or investment analyst considers these influences by beginning with the broadest influence and working down to more and more localized influences, that is, from national to regional to city to district or neighborhood factors. Favorable trends tend to increase estimates of the gross income to be derived from a property or to increase one's confidence in a predicted level of income. Trends supporting demand have the effect of reducing vacancy expectations, reducing the risk factor in capitalization rates, or lowering one's expectation of future depreciation or obsolescence. Unfavorable trends would have opposite effects.

Examples of some of the large-scale social trends that might be considered in evaluating the worth of a property are those toward the formation of smaller families, delayed marriages, urban living, and long-term apartment tenancy. These trends may be accentuated or mitigated within any one region or community, although social conditions in local communities are usually reflective of national trends.

Political trends are even more difficult to assess. The emphasis upon housing programs by Congress; the status of zoning laws, housing and building codes, open occupancy laws, and programs; and school integration efforts are but some of the current political conditions that may affect property values.

Although it is fairly obvious that national economic conditions can influence a property's value (during the recession of 1973–74, many parcels of real estate declined in value), the more localized types of influences may be more obscure. Examples: the decline in coal mining in southern Illinois from 1945 to 1960 caused the entire region to suffer economically and produced a commensurate loss in real estate values. During the 1950s and early 1960s, for a variety of reasons, several cities, such as Evansville, Indiana, and Pittsburgh, experienced economic declines which were accompanied by sluggishness and value decreases in real estate markets.[3] Probably every reader can think of several examples of district and neighborhood developments that have adversely affected real estate values in an area.

Economic trends generally are more amenable to quantifiable analysis. Such considerations would include an analysis of income levels, availability of financing and interest rates, outlook for monetary policy, levels of savings, prices of housing relative to other economic goods, expected investment in housing and other kinds of real estate, and

---

[3] In the case of Evansville, the decline was caused by several large industries leaving the town following labor difficulties and mergers. The Pittsburgh decline was largely attributed to increasing automation in steel plants.

various demographic data, such as numbers of population and mobility trends.

Short-term analysis of the national economy is particularly helpful in determining an appropriate capitalization rate. As we shall see in the income approach to value, capitalization rates are simply interest rates added to capital recovery rates. Since capitalization rates are used to convert a real estate parcel's earning expectancy to value, a property's value would tend to be inversely correlated with interest rates in the economy.

At the local level economic trends become more directly translated into market analyses for a particular type of property being considered. In assessing economic trends affecting housing, social and demographic factors are combined with income projections to estimate housing requirements and their predicted effects on rents, vacancy rates, and transaction prices. Similar types of analyses are important in the valuation and investment analyses of offices, commercial property (including shopping centers), and industrial property.[4]

In addition to an analysis of social, economic, and political factors at the national, regional, and local levels, a thorough examination and analysis of the physical and legal characteristics of the property must be made. The physical immobility of real estate means that every parcel is different from every other parcel. If similar in every other respect, it differs in its location relative to other parcels; it is either closer to or farther from the corner than the adjacent parcel. Similarly the legal rights and obligations may vary between two otherwise similar parcels. One seller may be contemplating the sale of an estate for life, another the sale of a leasehold, and still another the sale of a fee simple estate. The appraiser or investor must be aware of the exact physical items to be included in a purchase and of the legal rights and obligations accompanying the physical items.

Long length of economic life.   Another major atypical characteristic of real estate is its relatively long economic life. Land, or more specifically location, lasts forever, and buildings usually are built to last from 25 to several hundred years. In contrast are other economic goods which last much shorter periods of time. For example, automobiles may last five to ten years, clothing two to five years, and groceries one day to a month. What is the implication of this characteristic for the economics of real estate? It is that the purchase of real property represents a long-term commitment. The purchaser's viewpoint should be long range, and he or she should be convinced of the ability of the property to provide the services desired over its entire economic life.

---

[4] Market analysis is discussed more fully in Chapter 9, and an outline of market analyses conducted by the Federal Housing Administration is contained in Appendix D.

The purchase of real estate thus requires a thorough analysis aimed at predicting the type, amount, and quantity of future benefits to be obtained from the property. It also requires a prediction of the *expected* expenses to be incurred by the property, for the resultant of the two—net operating income (NOI)—is the generating engine of value.

Economic size.   Another major atypical characteristic of most parcels of real estate is their relatively large economic size. To purchase a parcel of real estate one usually must pay a price of anywhere from several thousand dollars on up. It is not unusual for a family to spend $60,000 to $150,000 for its home or for purchasers of investment properties to pay $500,000 or more. Contrast this with the price of groceries, clothes, or even automobiles. Thus, the single largest purchase of most families throughout their lives is a home.

The relative size of most real estate transactions has two implications from an economics standpoint for real estate investors. The first of these is that the purchase of real estate must be viewed as an important, long-term commitment, and the second is that financing considerations are important determinants of the investment feasibility. Although one can trade in real estate—as one trades in stock, bonds, or other investments—traders in real estate, even to a greater extent than traders in other types of investments, should be convinced of the long-term soundness of their purchases. A real estate investment may be less liquid and less marketable than other types of investments. Even traders in real estate may have to hold property one or perhaps even five years to expect to profit from their purchases. Investors, as contrasted with traders or speculators, are concerned with the income-producing potential of the property. Thus, in purchasing property for trading, the basic question is simply whether the price for which the property can be purchased is less than the price warranted by a long-term investment analysis.

The second implication of the large economic size of real estate transactions is that the investor must consider the present state of financing conditions and the impact of the specific financing arrangement on each transaction. A complex structure of financing institutions has evolved for the purpose of financing real estate transactions. Savings and loan associations, commercial banks, mutual savings banks, real estate investment trusts, and life insurance companies are all important institutions in this area. The cost of borrowing funds and the terms demanded by these institutions are obviously important considerations to the real estate investor.

Because of the large amount of money that must usually be borrowed for a family to purchase its home, long-term amortized loan arrangements have been developed. It is not unusual for a family to agree to repay a large loan over a period of 25 years in monthly installments which include both interest and repayment of the principal amount of the loan. Real estate investors, whether they are home purchasers or commercial property purchasers, should attempt to obtain the most favorable terms and interest rate possible from a reliable institution. But more important, they must analyze the effect this will have upon their total income position. Will the income from the real estate or the amenities derived from home ownership be sufficient to more than offset the financing expense? What income will be left over after paying the financing expense? How does this amount compare with the income to be obtained from other investments?

The individual terms and interest rates that investors can obtain from various institutions vary from time to time in relation to the fiscal and monetary policies of the U.S. government. Investors should be aware of the basic determinants of interest rates and financing terms and should understand the relationship between fiscal and monetary policies and loan arrangements for real estate investment. One study of the cyclical effect of these policies showed a close relation between restrictive monetary and fiscal policies of the government and significantly decreased levels of real estate construction and investment.[5] In such times marginal buyers are excluded from the market because of the high cost and their inability to obtain financing.

Few buyers and sellers. Real estate markets may have relatively large numbers of potential buyers and sellers, but not all of these buyers and sellers are active in the market at any one time. A community may have 1,000 single-family residences similar enough to be in the same submarket. Only 50 residences may be offered for sale, and fewer than 50 families may be shopping the market for a home. The going price for this type of housing will be determined by the forces of supply and demand, and the prices will indicate the value of all properties of this type in the submarket. Markets for shopping centers, warehouses, and office buildings may be even thinner, that is, have fewer buyers or sellers. The real estate analyst often must estimate the market value of properties competing in thin markets. In these instances, the transaction price negotiated in the open market may vary from estimated market value within a wider range than when the appraiser is working with a property that competes in an active market where buyers and sellers of similar properties are numerous.

Money and the value concept. An addendum to our explanation of the value concept is now necessary to clarify the role of money in economic (value) decisions. The role of money is often misunderstood because of its own characteristic ability to change in value. Although

---

[5] Halbert C. Smith and Carl J. Tschappat, "Monetary Policy and Real Estate Values," *Appraisal Journal* 34, no. 1 (January 1966): 18–26.

money serves as both a medium of exchange and a standard of value, the standard itself can change from year to year, day to day, or hour to hour. Some currencies, in fact, have experienced such rapid devaluation (for example, the German mark following World War I) that the change was noticeable almost minute by minute.

Since the values of economic goods are cited and compared in money terms, the value of an economic good may not have changed, even though the number of dollars measuring its value is different from one time to another. Thus, in order to compare dollar measurements of value over a time period during which the value of the dollar has changed, it is necessary to adjust the dollar measurements to conform to each other. This is done by the familar method of inflating or deflating one of the dollar measurements to the level represented at the time of the other dollar measurement.

Value is a real concept. As expressed by Adam Smith, it is "the power of a good to command other goods or labor services in exchange."

An illustration of this definition of value and the clouding role of money is provided by two appraisals that were performed on the same downtown commercial building four years apart. The first appraisal estimated the building's value at approximately $200,000, while the second appraisal estimated the value at $220,000. As measured by the consumer and wholesale price indexes, there had been about a 10 percent decline in the value of the dollar during that four-year-period. Thus, it is clear that the real (constant dollar) value of the building was about the same four years after the first appraisal, even though the dollar measurement increased by $20,000. Stated differently, the real estate would command about the same goods in exchange as it did four years previously.

MARKET VALUE

Real estate appraisers have definitions of value which provide workable, measurable concepts in an imperfect market and which are recognized by the courts. One such definition of *market value* formulated by the Society of Real Estate Appraisers and the American Institute of Real Estate Appraisers is the following:

> The highest price in terms of money which a property will bring in a competitive and open market under all conditions requisite to a fair sale, the buyer and seller, each acting prudently, knowledgeably and assuming the price is not affected by undue stimulus.
>
> Implicit in this definition is the consummation of a sale as of a specified date and the passing of title from seller to buyer under conditions whereby:

1. Buyer and seller are typically motivated.
2. Both parties are well informed or well advised, and each acts in what he or she considers his or her own best interest.
3. A reasonable time is allowed for exposure in the open market.
4. Payment is made in cash or its equivalent.
5. Financing, if any, is on terms generally available in the community at the specified date and typical for the property type in its locale.
6. The price represents a normal consideration for the property sold unaffected by special financing amounts and/or terms, services, fees, costs, or credits incurred in the transaction.[6]

Although the definition is somewhat similar to the definition of value under perfect competition, some of the perfect competition requirements are missing and some are less stringent. The real world thus dictates a compromise between the theoretically pure concept of a market and the necessity to make decisions and settle disputes.

Market value is but one kind of value of concern to the real estate analyst. Other values that sometimes must be estimated are included in the following list:

Assessed value: A dollar amount assigned to taxable property by an assessor for the purpose of taxation; frequently a statutorily determined percentage of market value.

Condemnation value: Value sought in condemnation proceedings is market value. In the instance of a partial taking, adjustments to the value of the part taken may be made for damages and/or special benefits to the remainder property.

Excess value: Value over and above market value which is ascribable to a lease that guarantees contract rental income in excess of market rental at the time of the appraisal.

Fair market value; fair cash value: Market value.

Forced "value"; liquidation "value": The price paid in a forced sale or purchase when time is not sufficient to permit negotiations resulting in market value being paid; should be called forced price or liquidation price, rather than value.

Going concern value: The value of the business enterprise and the real estate it occupies; includes goodwill.

Insurable value: Value of the destructible portions of a property.

Intangible value: A value not imputable to any part of the physical property, such as the excess value attributable to a favorable lease, or the value attributable to goodwill.

Investment value: Value to a particular investor based upon individual investment requirements, as distinguished from the concept of market value, which is impersonal and detached.

---

[6] Byrl N. Boyce, *Real Estate Appraisal Terminology* (Cambridge, Mass.: Ballinger, 1975), p. 137; this publication is jointly sponsored by the American Institute of Real Estate Appraisers and the Society of Real Estate Appraisers.

Leasehold value: The value of a leasehold interest; the right to the use, enjoyment, and profit existing by virtue of the rights granted under a lease instrument.

Mortgage value: Value for mortgage lending purposes.

Stabilized value: A value estimate which excludes from consideration an abnormal relation of supply and demand . . . a long-term value; or which excludes from consideration any transitory condition which may cause excessive cost of construction . . . and which may cause an excessive sale price.[7]

Many of these value concepts are basically market value, as previously defined, to which certain adjustments have been made to reflect the purpose or use to which the value estimate will be put. Assessed value, condemnation value, insurable value, leasehold value, and mortgage value are examples.

INVESTMENT VALUE

Investment value is the basis of phase 2 of the two-phase investment process in real estate. Investment value can be defined for the buyer and for the seller. In both instances, investment value is the "value in use," that is, what the property is worth to that particular individual. A buyer's investment value is the *maximum* that he or she would be willing to pay for a particular property. The seller's investment value is the *minimum* he or she would be willing to accept. Both the buyer and seller have their respective investment values determined by the same factors. The individual's assessment of risk and future productivity of the property is reflected in the investment value, in addition to the financing arrangements, tax situation, and other personal investment requirements. Investment value also depends upon how well matched the real estate is to the individual's needs and preferences.

Example

Fifty potential buyers may be shopping the local market for a small apartment property of eight units. Each of these buyers could have a different investment value for the various properties offered for sale. For seller X's property, buyer A may be willing to pay $160,000; buyer B, $145,000; buyer C, $165,000; and so on. Buyer C may foresee productivity that A and B do not; C may be misinformed. Buyer C may be willing to accept a lower return on investment than A or B, perhaps because of a lower opportunity cost; C may have more favorable financing or may be more creative in the

---

[7] Ibid.

financial arrangements; C could be in a higher tax bracket; the property may be more suited to C's needs. All of these factors, and the list is not intended to be inclusive, could cause C to have a higher investment value for this property than A or B. The seller of the property, X, has an investment value of $150,000 for the property. If this price cannot be obtained for the property, it will not be sold.

In a competitive, although imperfect, real estate market, competition among buyers interested in similar properties and among sellers offering these properties results in transaction prices. These transaction prices array themselves in a distribution. The real estate analyst observes this distribution of prices and uses it as factual evidence in the estimation of market value for a property of that type. The more active the market (the larger the number of buyers and sellers), the more similar the properties and the buyers and sellers, and the more knowledgeable the buyers and sellers about the uses to which the property can be put, the narrower will be the range within which transaction prices are negotiated and the more reliable will be the estimate of market value as an indication of probable transaction price.

Each transaction price in this market will be equal to or below the investment value of the buyer involved and equal to or above the investment value of the seller of that property. In a competitive market, properties are sold without buyers or sellers having to pay or accept their investment value. Competition among sellers of similar properties, who are aware of alternatives available to potential buyers, prevents a seller from differentiating among buyers—from singling out a buyer and extracting the maximum investment value. On the other side of the market, competition among buyers prevents a buyer from forcing a particular seller to accept the minimum reservation price for the property. Competition among sellers sets the ceiling on transaction prices in the market; competition among buyers sets the floor under price. Between this floor and ceiling, individual transaction prices are negotiated for properties of this type.

Example

In the above example, a transaction could only occur between seller X and buyer A or C. Buyer B had an investment value below that of seller X. Suppose that buyer A paid $159,000 for the property. If the seller had been more aware of the demand for the property and had been a better negotiator or had been willing to engage in a longer bargaining process, a transaction might have been consummated with buyer C, who would be willing and able to outbid A. Buyer A is a satisfied purchaser in an imperfect market. A is pleased to have obtained the property for $1,000 less than the maximum investment value, for this means A will attain a greater ROI than A was willing to accept if A had paid $160,000 investment value. The return which A will earn on the $159,000 investment has been market-determined, that is, determined by the competition of buyers and sellers for properties of this type. Seller X is satisfied because the price of $150,000 would have been accepted, if competition had forced X to the minimum reservation price. The seller has received a windfall profit—a profit greater than that which would have induced X to supply the property. Other owners of similar properties who are not now part of the active supply can be viewed as having investment values greater than the going price for properties of that type.

In summary, market value is an estimate of most probable selling price in a competitive market. Market value is estimated from observed transaction prices of similar properties. These transaction prices are negotiated in an imperfect market between buyers and sellers, each having his or her own investment value for the property. Awareness of alternatives and the need to compete cause these transaction prices to exhibit some central tendency. Investment value and market value thus are linked through the competitive market process that determines transaction prices.

MARKET VALUE, PRICE, AND COST

The preceding discussion of the determination of transaction prices and the use of these prices as indications of market value clearly demonstrate that the price paid for real estate can vary from its estimated market value. Price is the dollar amount actually paid; market value is the estimate of what should have been paid given the conditions described by the definition of market value.

Cost is a historical fact; market value is dependent upon future productivity, either income or amenities. A building may have cost $100,000 to produce ready for occupancy and use. The improvements may be on a site which "cost" the investor $30,000 (the price paid for the site). The price paid for the site, which is viewed by the investor as part of the total investment in the property, can differ from its market value. The cost to create the improvements also may have been more or less than their market value. A favorable lease, creative financing, a change in the character of the neighborhood, or a strong demand for that type of property can result in value for the improvements in excess of their cost. Conversely, a building which cost $100,000 to create may have a market value upon completion of only $90,000. This circumstance could occur when the site is improved with the wrong type of improvement or when the site is over- or underimproved. An overimprovement results when too much has been invested in improvements on a given site; an underimprovement results from too little investment in improvements.

The discrepancy between the costs of production of real estate improvements, including a normal profit as part of cost, and the value of these improvements can result from actions of misinformed individuals and from the necessity that value estimates be made at a point in time. The real estate analyst is always providing value estimates in market time periods in which supply, demand, and price may not be in long-run equilibrium. Market disequilibrium in the form of a rising demand not yet met by the supply can result in market value greater than cost. The cost to create improvements does not necessarily set the upper limit on improvement value. In the long run, of course, competition and supply adjustments would result in no unit's being supplied unless price (value) covered the costs of production. Market disequilibrium in the form of excess supply can result in market values lower than cost. The real estate analyst provides value estimates at all points on the cycle of real estate starts and values, both at the peak of a cycle and in the trough; in times of inflation and in times of recession. The value estimates are made using current market data and reflect existing supply and demand conditions. Only if "stabilized value" is estimated are the existing market data adjusted to reflect long-run "normal" conditions.[8]

THE CONCEPT OF HIGHEST AND BEST USE

Highest and best use is a profit maximization concept which provides an explanation for the type and intensity of improvements initially developed and now in place on urban sites. The developer-investor is assumed to be a rational, knowledgeable individual who strives to maximize profitability, that is, to achieve the greatest dollar ROI. Sites are assumed to sell in a competitive market under conditions inherent in the definition of market value (buyers and sellers are knowledgeable about possible uses to which the site can be put, no coercion, normal offering time, and so on). In such circumstances, sites would sell at a price (value) reflecting their productivity under the improvements constituting their highest and best use. A knowledgeable seller would accept no less than this price; a knowledgeable buyer would pay no more. The concept of highest and best use attempts to show how development decisions are made in the private sector only. Decision making in the public sector may result in the site's being developed for a public purpose such as a park or school. In this instance, social benefits and costs become the determinants of land use.

The real estate analyst always values the site under its highest and best use. To make this concept workable in "real world" situations, the

_____
[8] Defined on p. 38.

analyst visualizes highest and best use in two separate circumstances. One situation involves a vacant site; the second is a site with existing improvements.

Vacant site

Highest and best use of a vacant site is that use of the site which will provide the greatest income to the site after deducting the capital and labor expenses of the improvements. The highest and best use is the most profitable use of the vacant site. The program of use to which the land is put must be long term in nature. If the site is vacant, all of the logical, feasible alternative uses can be analyzed to decide which use would provide the greatest income residual to the site. This analysis involves estimating total NOI under each proposed use and subtracting from it the portion of income allocable to the improvement. The improvement's required income is calculated by multiplying the capitalization rate by the improvement cost.

The highest and best use decision may be simplified by constraining conditions. For example, in an area zoned for single-family residential structures, the analysis is limited to considering alternative homes. Commercial, industrial, or multifamily uses need not be considered; they are illegal. Although it is often easy to eliminate many potential uses, a decision about what is the highest and best use may require a considerable amount of comparative analysis of several properties. For single-family residential properties, the highest and best use decision usually requires analysis of such factors as location, style, design, quality of construction, relation to lot, and size. All such factors must be considered in terms of the surrounding properties. Do the style, size, design, and so on, blend in with neighboring uses? Too great a deviation in these factors would signify an over- or underimprovement.

For income properties the decision as to whether a particular improvement is the highest and best use requires comparative analysis of income streams and economic lives. Where there is a wide variety of possible income-producing uses, the return provided to the land by each use must be calculated and compared with other possible returns. The following example should clarify how this determination is made.

Suppose that you have the opportunity to buy a vacant corner lot on a well-traveled commercial "strip" street. The location is zoned for commercial usage, but it is adjacent to residential areas.

In the preliminary analysis it is noted that the most apparent needs are for a supermarket or a dry cleaner. A demand-analysis survey is favorable for both types of stores, and the following cost and expected rental figures are indicated for two sizes of supermarkets and a dry-cleaning store and processing unit.

> Supermarket: $40/square foot
>> 10,000 square-foot supermarket: $400,000 cost
>>> Expected revenue: 1 percent of gross sales of $4,000,000, or $40,000
>> 8,000-square foot supermarket: $320,000 cost
>>> Expected revenue: 1 percent of gross sales of $3,600,000, or $36,000
> Dry cleaner: $40/square foot
>> 7,000 square feet: $280,000 cost
>>> Expected revenue: flat $2,400/month, or $28,800/year

All leases would provide net income to the owner. The market-determined rate of ROI on the alternative capital improvements must be obtained. For simplicity, let us assume that each of the three alternative improvements would yield an 8 percent return in the market. Combining the 8 percent ROI with a 2 percent straight-line recapture rate (each improvement has a 50-year economic life expectancy) gives a 10 percent capitalization rate for investment in the alternative improvements. For the 10,000-square-foot supermarket, a $40,000 income would be required to support the $400,000 investment in improvements. The 8,000-square-foot supermarket would require a $32,000 income; the dry-cleaning establishment, $28,000. Subtracting the "building income" from the expected NOI of each property leaves $–0–, $4,000, and $800 residual income to the site. The conclusion is that the 8,000-square-foot supermarket is the highest and best use. In a competitive market of knowledgeable buyers and sellers, this site would be expected to sell for $50,000 ($4,000 ÷ 0.08), its value under the highest and best use.

If the $50,000 market value were paid for the site and the 8,000-square-foot supermarket were constructed, the investor would receive 8 percent on investment in the site and improvement and recapture a $320,000 improvement cost out of the stream of future NOI over the economic life of the improvement. Construction of either the 10,000-square-foot supermarket or the 7,000-square-foot dry cleaner would result in the investor's making less than 8 percent on investment or, viewed in another way, the value of the improvements in either instance would be less than the cost of creating them.

Assuming the site to be purchased at $50,000 (its value under highest and best use), $4,000 would be required to provide an 8 percent return on site value. The 10,000-square-foot supermarket would have $36,000 income remaining to support the investment of $40,000 in improvements. The $36,000 of income capitalized at 10 percent provides a value of $360,000 for improvements costing $400,000 to create. The dry cleaner improvement costing $280,000 would be valued at

$248,000. The 10,000-square-foot supermarket is an overimprove-
ment; the dry cleaner is an underimprovement. *When the proper type
and intensity of land use have been achieved (the highest and best
use), the value of improvements equals the cost of creating them.*

Improved sites

Existing improvements may be the highest and best use of the site,
if they continue to produce income or amenities and thus have value
in their own right. In fact, existing improvements remain the highest
and best use until it becomes economically feasible to reuse the site
for a more profitable purpose. At this time, the existing improvements
are said to contribute nothing to the value of the site. The value of the
site under the new program of use is great enough to permit purchase
of the property (existing improvements and site), demolition of the
existing structure, and preparation of the site for reuse. Until this point
in time is reached, the existing improvements remain the highest and
best use, and the site is valued under that type of use.

Suppose that the site in the preceding illustration is improved with
an older single-family residence, rather than being vacant. The market
value of the house and lot is $60,000 and is estimated by comparison
with similar residences that have sold recently. In this instance, the
analyst would conclude that the existing single-family residence is the
highest and best use of the site. The value of this site would be
$10,000, which is the value of a single-family residential lot in this
location; the structure is appraised at $50,000. The site in this instance
is valued under a single-family residential use, not a commercial use.

As time passes, the house may suffer further loss of value because of
physical wear and deterioration of its location for residential purposes. At the same time, the value of a vacant site under the highest
and best commercial use may rise. At some future date, the site will
have "ripened" for reuse. Site value under the new commercial highest and best use might reach $58,000; the market value of the site and
the deteriorating single-family residence has fallen to $56,000, with
$2,000 required to demolish the existing improvements and to prepare
the site for reuse. At this point, the highest and best use becomes the
commercial structure, and the site would be valued as though vacant
and put to commercial use. The existing single-family residence
would add nothing to the value of the site. Until this point in time, the
residential improvements remain the highest and best use of the site.
In either instance, whether valued under an existing residence or
under a commercial use, the site's value is determined by its highest
and best use.

SUMMARY

Investment decisions are based upon an appraisal of a property's value. Although investment analysis requires consideration of other factors in addition to value (such as financing requirements and income taxes), the primary criterion is value. The process of estimating value can thus be regarded as a major portion of investment analysis.

Value is a market phenomenon which is the resultant of the interaction of supply and demand. In turn, supply and demand are the market effects of the relative scarcity and utility associated with an economic good. Under perfect competition value would equal the price paid for the good. There would be no necessity to measure value independently; it would be automatically measured by the price of each transaction. However, since markets (particularly the real estate market) are less than perfectly competitive, value must be estimated independently by competent appraisers or analysts.

Real estate appraisers have a definition of market value that accommodates some market imperfections. Other "values" are defined according to the purpose or use to which the value estimate will be put. Investment value is one of these other value concepts. Investment value and market value are shown to be linked through the negotiations that produce transaction prices in imperfect real estate markets.

Market value, price, and cost can differ at any point in time. Market value can be regarded as the consensus of knowledgeable buyers and sellers about the price that should be paid for the real estate; price is the number of dollars actually paid in an imperfect market. The cost of creating the improvements may be greater or less than their market value at the date of the market value estimate. Special considerations affecting the particular property under appraisal, such as a favorable lease, could result in a value for the improvements greater than their cost. Shifting market demand and supply conditions, which may not be in long-run equilibrium at the date of an appraisal, can produce a value that varies from the cost of creating the improvement.

The concept of highest and best use provides an explanation of why land in the private sector is developed with a particular type and intensity of land use. A site is developed to its highest and best use when improvements are constructed that maximize profitability (overall return on investment) and, at the same time, produce the highest land value. A vacant site would sell under conditions of perfect competition at a price (value) determined by its highest and best use. A knowledgeable seller would not accept less; a knowledgeable buyer would be willing to pay the price, knowing that a use exists that will produce sufficient income to provide the required return on investment. Although real estate markets are less than perfect, the analyst estimates the value of the vacant site under its highest and best use. When the site under appraisal is improved with an existing building, the analyst concludes that the present improvement is the highest and best use unless a new improvement would generate sufficient site value to enable the present improvements to be demolished. As long as the present improvement remains the highest and best use, the site is valued under that type of land use.

QUESTIONS FOR REVIEW

1. What role does money play in the identification and measurement of value? How does money both help and hinder the measurement of value?
2. Discuss the contention that "value is the basic criterion of all decision making."
3. What are the characteristics of real estate and real estate markets that result in a definition of real property value different from value under perfect competition?
4. How does *market value* differ from a *normal* or *stabilized* value?
5. How does *investment value* differ from *market value?*
6. What are the two concepts of highest and best use?
7. Why would the cost to create improvements differ from the market value of the improvements when either an overimprovement or an underimprovement has been constructed?

PROBLEMS

1. A large home on the crest of a hill commanding a beautiful view of the river below was offered for sale at $250,000. The home had been built 15 years earlier by a wealthy business tycoon near the small town of his birth in southern Missouri. Although no one in the town could afford such an expensive property, all of the town's epople agreed the home was probably worth at least $250,000. A local businessman offered $100,000, but the offer was rejected. Finally, the property was sold for $150,000 to a Chicago family as a summer vacation home.
    a. Did an effective market exist for the property?
    b. In your opinion, what was the value of the property?
    c. Does sale price necessarily equal value?
    d. Would you have paid $150,000 for the property?
    e. Would you have sold for $150,000?
2. Assume that you own a parcel of land for which you paid $10,000 three years ago. The annual real estate tax amounts to $175. You now need your money and want to sell. If inflation has been averaging 5 percent per year, would you accept $11,576 ($10,000 plus 5 percent compounded annually)? Why or why not? What additional costs might you want to cover in your asking price?

REFERENCES

American Institute of Real Estate Appraisers. *The Appraisal of Real Estate.* 7th ed. Chicago, 1978.

Boyce, Byrl N. *Real Estate Appraisal Terminology.* Cambridge, Mass.: Ballinger Publishing Co., 1975.

Featherston, J. B. "Historic Influences on the Development of the Theory of Value," *Appraisal Journal* 43, no. 2 (April 1975): 165–82.

Smith, Halbert C. *Real Estate Appraisal.* Columbus, Ohio: Grid, 1976.

Smith, Halbert C., and Maurais, Mark R. "Highest and Best Use in the Appraisal Profession," *Real Estate Appraiser and Analyst* 46, no. 2 (March-April 1980): 27–37.

Society of Real Estate Appraisers. *An Introduction to Appraising Real Property.* Chicago, 1975.

Turvey, Ralph. *The Economics of Real Property.* London: George Allen and Unwin, 1957.

Wendt, Paul F. *Real Estate Appraisal: Review and Outlook.* Athens: University of Georgia Press, 1974.

chapter 4

The measurement of value

The problem of value measurement arises because of the existence of market imperfections. Price may or may not equal value in any less-than-perfect market; therefore, an independent measurement is required to arrive at a value figure. And even after a value figure is obtained by an independent process, it is not certain the figure is the price that will occur in an active, viable market. Thus, the best that one can do is to estimate the value of an economic good.

Obviously, since real estate is an economic good, these general statements are applicable—even more so than for most economic goods—to the estimation of real property values. Real estate markets are fraught with hazardous variances from the concept of an ideal market; therefore, the estimate of value of a parcel of real estate requires a wider range of possible error than do value estimates for other economic goods. The price obtained for a special-purpose, income-producing property valued at $300,000 might vary by as much as 25 percent in either direction from the appraised value. In contrast, the price of a bushel of wheat is probably so close to its value that there would be little discernible difference between value and price. These differences among markets in the efficiency and accuracy of the price-setting process largely result from the economic nature of the products themselves.

In Chapter 3, the features of real estate that lead to its economic uniqueness were discussed, and the economic implication of each characteristic was related to its influence on value. The following methods and procedures of value measurement should incorporate the effects of economic characteristics into estimates of income, capitalization rates, costs, and market prices.

There are three classical approaches, or frameworks of analysis, by which the value of a parcel of real estate is estimated. These are the income approach, the direct sales comparison approach, and the cost approach. Occasionally appraisal literature contains reports of newly developed approaches to real estate valuation; however, upon close examination it can be seen that many so-called new approaches have their roots in one or more of the three classical approaches.

Although we discuss each of the three approaches separately from the others, each approach is closely related to the other two. Since all roads lead to the final objective—the concept of value—the three approaches can be regarded as being different ways of looking at the same problem. The analyst needs to understand clearly the relationships among the three approaches and to be able to discern which approach is appropriate in a given situation.

VALUE ESTIMATION BY INCOME CAPITALIZATION

Nature of the income approach

The income approach focuses attention upon the value to investors of an expected future stream of net income to be derived from a parcel of real estate.[1] The right to receive the income in future years is the right associated with property ownership. This legal right has value, and it is this value which the income approach measures. In carrying out the income approach, several variables must be considered, all of which constitute inputs to the basic value formula that:

$$V = I \div R$$

where

V = Value
I = Income
R = Relationship between value and income

In estimating value, we attempt to predict total income (I) and to estimate the appropriate, current (R) or capitalization rate. Income is net operating income (NOI). The capitalization rate is a composite of

---

[1] A thorough treatment of the income capitalization approach to estimating market value is contained in William N. Kinnard, Jr., *Income Property Valuation* (Lexington, Mass.: D. C. Heath, 1971), and Halbert C. Smith, *Real Estate Appraisal* (Columbus, Ohio: Grid, 1976), chaps. 5 and 6.

the discount rate and the recapture rate. The latter rate is a function of the remaining economic life of the depreciating portion of the asset and the pattern of capital recapture.

The capitalization process

The process of capitalization involves conversion of a forecasted stream of future income into its present value. This conversion process is termed capitalization and is based upon the principles of discounting.[2] The present value of any economic good is an amount less than the sum total of all the future income payments to be derived from that economic good. There are basically two reasons for this. The first is that if investors already had all the payments to be derived in the future from the property, they could put these in a perfectly safe governmental or institutional investment and receive a return. Investors presumably would be incurring no risk of not obtaining their money at the end of the time. The second reason is that on top of the pure payment for the use of money, the investors must be compensated for added risk—the risk that they will not obtain their capital back. The percentage amounts for each of these two reasons, the pure interest rate and the risk rate, are the two components that make up the rate of return on investment (ROI). The ROI and the straight-line or sinking fund recapture rate make up the capitalization rate. The sinking fund recapture rate for estimating the value of an annuity is the amount necessary to be obtained each period, compounding at the discount rate, to accumulate to one dollar.[3] The ROI is also often termed the discount rate.

$$ROI + ROC = R$$

where

ROI = Return on total investment
ROC = Rate of recapture of capital
R = Capitalization rate

Valuation inputs

The income capitalization process requires that decisions be made regarding a property's expected net operating income, its remaining economic life, the expected pattern of the income stream, and the

---

[2] The mathematics of discounting and the use of the compound interest tables are explained in Appendix F. The reader who requires further explanation of the derivation and use of these tables should carefully read this appendix.

[3] Column 3 in Appendix G is a table of sinking fund factors, which are used as rates of recapture under this premise.

appropriate capitalization rate. When the decisions have been made, the valuation process is reduced to arithmetic calculation.

Net operating income.   In attempting to predict future net income, the most useful type of information is the historical experience of the property itself. In the case of a commercial, industrial, or apartment property, the first step is to analyze past years' income figures. How far back should one go? There is no definite answer, but preferably the record for at least five years should be examined. In analyzing past revenues, the following two questions should be answered:

1. *Is each source of revenue appropriate and reasonable?*

Sometimes certain revenues should be discounted or eliminated. For example, some income statements show revenue from tenants for janitorial service. The offsetting expense will, of course, reduce or eliminate this item. But in some cases, even when the revenue is currently larger than the commensurate expense, it is unreasonable to project this situation into the future.

Whether each amount of revenue is reasonable can be ascertained only in relation to comparable sources. If an apartment rental is either too low or too high it should be adjusted to the proper or reasonable rent. This is termed the *market rent* and is distinguished from *contract rent* which is the amount actually paid. Market rent is what should be paid and, therefore, the amount that can be expected in the future.

2. *What is the trend of revenues for the time being analyzed?*

If the trend is either upward or downward, there may be some reason for the trend that the analyst has not discerned. Before proceeding, it should be decided whether the trend is expected to continue or to change. This, of course, is the reason for analyzing a period of several years. Whether the past is an accurate predictor of the future can never be known for certain at the prediction stage of any analysis, but this makes it all the more important for analysts to utilize available data, their analytic powers, and their judgment derived from experience.

In analyzing past expenses, four questions should be considered:

1. *Is each item of expense appropriate and reasonable?*

The same comments that were made with respect to revenues are appropriate here. Additionally, however, we should mention that the problem of discerning and eliminating inappropriate expense figures from an owner's statement is usually greater than for revenues. Most owners' income statements include expense items that are not appropriate to the property's value. Typical of such items are financing expense and income tax expense. These expenses are not allocable to the real estate. They do not necessarily have to be incurred by the real estate for it to produce income. Some owners would not need to bear such expenses, but all owners would have to expect janitorial or fuel expense. The former are thus personal or business expenses of the owner and should be eliminated from a statement of property expenses.

2. *What is the trend for each expense?*

As with the analysis for the trend of revenues, the trend of each expense should be noted and analyzed if necessary. If the trend of an expense is either upward or downward (and most expenses will be upward), there may be some reason for predicting higher or lower expenses in the future. On the other hand, analysts may uncover an upward trend of some expenses that effective and efficient management could correct. If so, analysts would then adjust the predicted expense downward under the assumption that effective and efficient management will be available for the property. The point to be emphasized with respect to analysis of the expense trend is that the trend should not be extrapolated blindly into the future. Often trends can be changed with proper management, and these possibilities will be detected by analysts when they look at the causes for basic factors underlying the trends.

3. *Should any expenses not included in the owner's statement be included?*

Often an owner's statement has been compiled for tax purposes or for other accounting reasons and not for the purpose of estimating the property's value. In these cases only the actual expenses incurred should be included. However, since the objective is to predict all the *future* expenses necessary for the property to have value—regardless of who owns the property—certain expenses should be added. Two good examples of such expenses typically are vacancy and collection losses and management expense.

Vacancy losses and often collection losses involve little or no out-of-pocket expense. Yet, in predicting the future net income for a parcel of real estate, analysts would be remiss in not recognizing the high probability that reductions from total possible gross income will result because of these reasons. Keep in mind that the objective is to predict future net income, and that particularly as buildings become older, their owners should expect to experience some periods between lessees when their property will not be drawing income and some tenants who for various reasons will not pay their rent. Thus analysts should include this expense as one expected for the future.

Particularly with respect to a small, owner-managed investment property the expense of managing the property is often not included in an owner's statement of income and expenses. The owner in such a case manages the property, and management does not represent an out-of-pocket expense. Management is thus not entered as a specific and identified expense. The function of property management, however, will have to be performed in the future for the property to obtain income for the owner. This reasoning provides the justification for including management as an expense that will be incurred by a property in the future—whether accomplished by the owner or by a hired manager. In cases where the owner has hired a manager and this expense is identified in the operating statement, and provided the expense is reasonable both with respect to amount and trend, this figure could be entered as the analyst's best estimate of the future expense. In cases where the owner has not hired a manager and no management expense is indicated in the statement, the analyst should impute a future management expense to the property. The owner's time is worth money, since he or she could be earning money during the time spent managing the property. The amount imputed usually varies between 2 and 10 percent of effective gross income, which is the difference between total possible gross income and vacancy and collection losses.

4. *Are large replacement item expenses amortized over the expected life of the replacements?*

Some large components of a building such as its heating system, air-conditioning system, water heater, or roof can be expected to wear out faster than the building itself. A roof, for example, may have to be replaced every 15 years, while the building can be expected to last perhaps 50 to 100 years. Over its total life, then, the building will undoubtedly have several roofs. Many times, analysts will find that the owners have not amortized these large expenditures over their expected lives. Rather, as the large expense is incurred for replacing a roof or heating system, this expense will be included as a deduction from that year's income. This is not the proper procedure, however, for forecasting stabilized income. It must be recognized that the roof wears out each hour each day and each year, rather than all at once. It is fallacious to assign the entire expense of a new roof to one earning period only. Therefore, in predicting future expenses to the real estate, analysts typically allocate an amount to each period for major repairs and replacements of components of the building that last a shorter time than the building itself. These items are not included in depreciation assignable to the basic building.

In predicting future revenues and expenses for a parcel of real property through the procedure of analyzing past operating statements of the owner, the analyst obtains a new statement of expected revenues and expenses which is called a reconstructed operating statement.[4]

---

[4] Examples of the owner's operating statement and of the appraiser's reconstructed operating statement are shown in Figures 4–2 and 4–3.

Remaining economic life.   Another variable to be considered is the length of economic life of the building. All material things wear out over some period of time, and buildings are no exception. Buildings wear out, meaning that expenses will increase over the life of the building, while revenues at some point will begin to decline and will decline more and more as time goes along. Eventually, the property will no longer generate a competitive rate of return on market value and the building adds nothing to the value of the property. The property's value at this time is site value only.

Certain income capitalization procedures (land residual, building residual, and property residual techniques) require that the remaining economic life of the improvements be estimated, because this is the period during which an owner can expect to obtain a competitive return from an investment. Typically the economic life for buildings runs from 25 to 75 years, although exceptions can be found at both ends of the range. The actual measurement of this variable can only come from knowledge of construction techniques and judgment associated with long experience in dealing with buildings and estimating their economic lives. Other income capitalization techniques, such as the Ellwood technique, use an assumed investment holding period and project net operating income over, say, ten years rather than over the entire economic life of the improvements. The building and land are often assumed to have value at the end of the holding period. The value of this property reversion is dependent upon the market value of the site and the productivity of the building over its remaining economic life.

Pattern of income.   Another input in the income approach is the pattern of the income to be received over the remaining economic life of the building (or over an assumed investment holding period). While any pattern can be discounted to present value, an income stream's pattern will usually be forecast as one of the following two basic forms.

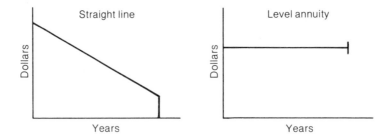

The straight-line pattern assumes that the net income will decrease by the same percentage every year to the end of the building's economic life, while the level annuity assumes the net income will remain constant. The decision as to which pattern will be most realistic for a property being appraised must be based upon the analyst's assumption about the most probable experience of net income.

Both the straight-line and level annuity methods of capitalization assume that the capital investment in the building will be recovered over the remaining economic life of the improvement. The annual rate of recapture is a sinking fund concept which assumes that the capital recaptured each period is reinvested in another property or investment yielding the same rate of return as the property being appraised. The straight-line capitalization process is but one special case of the more general discounting process based upon this assumption.[5]

The straight-line declining income stream would be an appropriate assumption if the net income were expected to decline at approximately the same average annual percentage rate. The average annual percentage rate of decline can be computed with the formula:

$$\frac{R \times d}{R + d}$$

where R is the capitalization rate and d is the rate of recapture expressed as the reciprocal of the remaining economic life of the improvement. Thus, if the remaining economic life of a building were estimated to be 40 years, d would be $1/40$, or 2.5 percent. The capitalization rate, R, is the sum of the rate of recapture and the rate of discount. If the return on investment were 8 percent, R would be 10.5 percent. The annual rate of decline in income would be:

$$\frac{R \times d}{R + d} = \frac{0.105 \times 0.025}{0.105 + 0.025} = \frac{0.002625}{0.13} = 0.0202, \text{ or } 2.02\%$$

The present value of this declining income stream could be found by discounting each year's income by the present value of $1 factor at 8 percent (from Appendix G). Figure 4–1 demonstrates this process.

Graphically, the income stream in Figure 4–1 produces a straight line falling at the annual rate of 2.02 percent, or approximately $243 each year, as shown below.

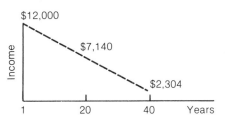

⁵ Only recently has the annual recapture under straight-line capitalization been assumed to be reinvested at the speculative rate of discount. Formerly, the most common assumption was that the annual recapture was not invested. See Appendix F.

FIGURE 4–1
Present value of a straight-line declining income stream

Year	Income	8 percent factor present value of $1	Present value
1	$12,000 ×	0.9259	$ 11,111
2	11,757 ×	0.8573	10,079
3	11,514 ×	0.7938	9,157
4	11,271 ×	0.7350	8,284
5	11,029 ×	0.6806	7,506
40	2,524 ×	0.0460	116
			$114,286

A shortcut method to obtain the answer depicted in Figure 4–1 is to develop a "straight-line capitalization rate" by adding the rate of discount (0.08) and the reciprocal of the building's remaining economic life ($1/40$ years = 0.025) to obtain a rate of 10.5 percent. This rate can be divided into the $12,000 income to obtain the present value of an income stream forecast to decline at an average annual rate of 2.02 percent, that is,

$$\frac{\$12,000 \text{ net income}}{0.105} = \$114,286$$

In level annuity capitalization, a sinking fund factor is added to the ROI rate to obtain the total capitalization rate. If the same income used in the above example of straight-line capitalization were capitalized by the level annuity method of capitalization, the capitalization rate would be 0.08 plus 0.00386 (annual sinking fund factor at 0.08, 40 years), or 0.08386. Note that the capitalization rate is lower than in the shortcut straight-line method and produces a higher value of about $143,096 ($12,000 ÷ 0.08386). The higher value results because the income stream is level, rather than declining.

When deciding whether to use straight-line or level annuity capitalization, it is apparent that the net income pattern produced by the property should be the basis for the decision.

One additional point about the pattern of the net income stream is that although the actual amount of net income that will be received in any particular year may vary considerably from the amount forecasted under either the straight-line or level annuity pattern, the deviations on either side are likely to cancel out—leaving the basic pattern. In other words, the estimate may turn out to be too low in some years but will turn out to be too high in other years. These theoretical income streams are thus estimates of the pattern and not of the actual amounts to be received in any particular year. Alternatively, the annual income may be estimated in each year as the analyst foresees it, with the irregular amounts discounted to present value using the present value of $1 factors at the appropriate rate of discount.

Estimation of capitalization rates.   We now return to a determination of the capitalization rate to be used in discounting the future income stream. The two components of the discount rate are (1) the pure cost for the use of money and (2) the additional business risk involved in a real estate investment. The addition of the discount rate and the recapture rate provides the capitalization rate. The reciprocal of the capitalization rate is a factor obtainable from a table.[6] Discount rate determination, then, involves the question of what rate investors demand and can obtain for a given level of risk in a particular real estate investment.

At any point in time the pure interest for long-term investments is determined by the yield on long-term government bonds. If this latter rate is, say, 6 percent, a real estate investor would demand an additional return to compensate for the added risk. Rather than trying to determine the rate to be added to the pure rate of interest, however, the analyst or investor can usually more easily look at the overall rate of discount for similar real estate investments. If similar parcels were purchased for yields of 10 percent, the analyst would impute a 10 percent discount rate to the property in question. Similarly, if the going rate for the comparable parcels were 12 percent, this would be the return imputed to the parcel and used in the analysis. The idea is simple; only the implementation is difficult.[7] In Chapter 6, the potential of the capital asset pricing model (CAPM) in the development of a capitalization rate is explored.

Site or property reversion.   The only remaining variable to be determined in estimating the value of a property by the property residual technique is the value of the site. With an income capitalization method using an investment holding period assumption (Ellwood), the value of the property (site and improvements) at the end of the holding period must be estimated.

The site reversion value is necessary in the property residual technique, since the investor would be entitled to the continued use of the land after the building is worn out and no longer has value. For analysts to estimate the value of the total property, therefore, they must estimate the value of the reversionary right to use the land after the building is gone.

---

[6] Column 5 of the compound interest table in Appendix G contains these factors.

[7] Other methods for determining capitalization rates are given in books on real estate appraising cited at the end of this chapter; in specialized valuation problems these methods may be appropriate and useful.

Since no analyst has a crystal ball and can say what the value of the site will be, say, 25 or 50 years into the future, most real estate analysts, unless they have better information, assume that the value of the site at the end of the life of the building will be the same as the value of the site today. The problem, therefore, becomes one of estimating the value of the site today and discounting that value for the remaining economic life of the building. The valuation procedures for the site are (a) by direct sales comparison with comparable vacant parcels of land and (b) by hypothetical highest and best use computation.[8] The direct sales comparison approach is discussed later in this chapter.

Site value can be estimated by capitalizing the difference between (a) the total net operating income available to the real estate if it were improved with the most profitable long-term use and (b) the part of the income stream attributable to the building. The portion of the income stream remaining after building income is subtracted from total income is attributed to the site, and this income stream is capitalized to provide a present value for the land. In capitalizing an income stream to land, however, it must be recognized that this income stream theoretically can continue forever. That is, the legal right cannot be terminated so long as the owner lives up to the basic requirements of society. The income stream to a parcel of land, therefore, is capitalized to perpetuity. This process involves dividing the site's annual income by the discount rate (ROI) used in capitalizing the building's income.

In income capitalization methods that project NOI over an investment holding period, rather than over the economic life of the improvements, a judgment must be made about the dollar amount of property reversion at the end of the typical or average holding period. This property reversion includes both site value and improvement value, assuming that the improvements will have remaining economic life after the holding period. These techniques avoid assigning an absolute dollar amount to this property reversion. Instead, the analyst assumes that the present market value of the property will increase by some percentage (appreciate), decrease by some percentage (depreciate), or remain level. Factors causing an expected increase include inflation or long-run demand forces pressing against a limited supply. A percentage decrease in the property reversion could result from physical deterioration, functional obsolescence, and locational obsolescence (the site becomes less well suited for the existing improvements). Often appraisers do not attempt to forecast either increases or decreases in property value over a holding period that may be as long as ten years. Instead, the assumption is made that the prop-

---

[8] The second procedure of estimating the value of a site was discussed in Chapter 3 as the highest and best use decision.

erty will sell for today's market value at the end of the investment holding period.

Examples of the income approach

Estimating the value of the ABC office property (described in the next section) illustrates many aspects of various income capitalization approaches. The reader is cautioned to remember that a real estate analyst would typically use only one of the following approaches in obtaining an indication of market value for a client.

Estimation of net operating income. The first step in a valuation problem is to estimate the future net operating income in the format of a reconstructed operating statement.

Assume that you are asked to estimate the value of the ABC property, a ten-year-old office building on a major artery near downtown. Other commercial and office buildings of fairly high quality occupy the area, and this usage is expected to continue. The building contains 9,000 gross square feet and 7,650 net rentable square feet, which is renting at $8.60 per square foot.

The owner's operating statement is shown in Figure 4–2. The real estate analyst critically examines the owner's statement as well as

FIGURE 4–2
ABC office property owner's operating statement

Gross rents collected (1981)		$63,250
Expenses:		
Power.....................................	$ 5,900	
Real estate tax.........................	2,675	
Garbage removal	500	
Supplies	1,000	
Mortgage payments	25,000	
Insurance	2,520	
Decorating	6,500	
Repairs	500	
Depreciation.........................	7,500	
Cleaning	2,500	54,595
Net income before taxes		$ 8,655

current and foreseeable market conditions for properties of this type. The present rent of $8.60 per net rentable square foot is confirmed as reasonable at this time. The experience of similar buildings over time indicates that vacancy and collection losses typically are 5 percent of potential gross income. Expenses that do not vary significantly with occupancy are classified as fixed; expenses which vary with occupancy are shown as variable. The reserve for replacement account, which is a noncash depreciation reserve, is a separate category.

All expenses are placed on an annual basis, requiring proration of a three-year insurance premium and determination of the average annual cost of decorating and repairs. Expenses inappropriate for an appraisal, such as the mortgage payment and depreciation, are omitted. The reader is referred back to the discussion of net operating income for the factors to be considered in estimating NOI. The analyst's reconstructed operating statement is shown in Figure 4–3.

FIGURE 4–3
ABC office property reconstructed operating statement

Potential gross income		$65,790
Vacancy and collection losses		3,290
Effective gross income		$62,500
Expenses:		
Fixed		
Real estate taxes	$2,675	
Insurance	840	
Variable		
Maintenance*	4,585	
Cleaning	2,500	
Utilities	5,900	
Supplies	1,000	
Management	2,500	
Reserve for replacement	3,000	23,000
Net operating income		$39,500

* Includes decorating, repairs, and trash removal.

Property residual technique.   Estimating the market value of this commercial property using the property residual technique requires an estimate of (*a*) the remaining economic life, (*b*) the value of the site reversion, and (*c*) the market-determined overall rate of return on investment (discount rate). The analyst knows that the building is ten years old and that it has been well maintained. The property is in an attractive, well-located commercial district that serves a prosperous and stable residential area. In the judgment of the analyst, the building has 30 years of remaining economic life.

The site measures 100 by 200 feet. Recent sales of comparable vacant sites indicate a market value for the subject property's site of $3 per square foot, or $60,000.[9] Today's market value is assumed to be the

---

[9] Alternatively, site value might be estimated by hypothesizing the highest and best use of the site, as though vacant, and capitalizing the income residual to the land.

The highest and best use of the site, if vacant, would be a new, more modern office building costing $400,000 and having a 50-year economic life. The building would have

value of the site at the end of the 30-year remaining economic life of the building. Investors in properties of this type are requiring a 10 percent return on their investment. A higher rate of discount (return on investment) would produce a lower value, while a lower rate would result in a higher value. When market value is to be estimated, the rate of return should be justified from market experience.

The property residual technique produces a present value of $375,800 for the property (see Figure 4–4). The level annuity premise

FIGURE 4–4
Valuation of ABC office property: Property residual technique

Value of NOI for 30 years:	
$39,500 × 9.427 (PV annuity of $1,	
10%, 40 years)	$372,366
Value of site reversion:	
$60,000 (by market comparison) ×	
0.0573 (PV of $1, 10%, 30 years)	3,438
Value of property	$375,804, say $375,800

was used in capitalizing future income into present value. The site's value at the end of the building's economic life is assumed to be equal to its current market value. The discounted value of the site reversion was added to the present worth of the NOI to obtain total property value. Final value estimates are rounded to avoid spurious accuracy.

Building residual technique. Estimating the market value of the ABC office property using the building residual technique requires that the analyst estimate the remaining economic life of the building

the same number of units, but all rents could be increased by $50 per month. Operating expenses would increase by $1,500 per year. Investors in the market are able to obtain a 10 percent rate of return on an investment in this type of real estate, as demonstrated below. The indicated value for the site under its highest and best use is $59,570.

Site value under highest and best use

Potential gross income	$74,500
Vacancy and collection losses	3,700
Effective gross income	$70,800
Less: Expenses	24,500
Net operating income	
(highest and best use)	$46,300
Value of site:	
Net operating income	$46,300
Less: Building income:	
$400,000 ÷ 9.915	
(PV of annuity of $1, 10%,	
50 years)	40,343
Site income	$ 5,957
Site value ($5,957 ÷ 0.10)	$59,570

(30 years) and the value of the site ($60,000). The market-determined rate of return on properties of this type also must be ascertained (say 10 percent).

The building residual technique produces a present value of $375,800 for the property (see Figure 4–5). The income necessary to

FIGURE 4–5

Valuation of ABC office property: Building residual technique

NOI	$ 39,500
Income required to support site value:	
Site value ($60,000 × 0.10 site capitalization rate)	6,000
Income residual to building	$ 33,500
Value of building:	
$33,500 × 9.427 (PV of annuity of $1, 10%, 30 years)..............................	$315,804
Value of site:	
$60,000 (by market comparison)	60,000
Property value	$375,804, say $375,800

give the investor a 10 percent return on the market value of the site was subtracted from NOI to find the income residual to the building. The building's income is capitalized into present value using the level annuity factor at 10 percent.[10]

[10] The examples in Figures 4–4, 4–5, and 4–6 demonstrate that identical answers are obtained when the same data are used to work each of the three residual techniques. (Discrepancies are the result of rounding.) The property residual technique typically is worked using the level annuity tables. The building and site residual techniques, however, are sometimes worked using straight-line capitalization. If the preceding problem is worked by the building residual technique using straight-line capitalization of income, the answer would be $317,100. The discrepancy between answers obtained by the property residual and building residual techniques is caused by the different assumptions in the two capitalization methods. The level annuity premise assumes an equal annual income to the property; straight-line capitalization assumes an income stream which decreases annually in a straight-line pattern.

Valuation of ABC office property: Building residual technique using straight-line capitalization

NOI	$ 39,500
Income required to support site value: Site value ($60,000 × 0.10 land capitalization rate)	6,000
Income residual to building................	$ 33,500
Value of building: $33,500 ÷ 0.1303 (0.10 percent return on investment plus 0.0303 percent recapture of investment assuming 30-year remaining economic life)	$257,099
Value of site	60,000
Property value	$317,099, or $317,100

Site residual technique. When working with the site residual technique, the analyst assumes that the cost to create the building equals its market value. The site residual technique would *not be* used to appraise the ABC office property, which is improved with a ten-year-old structure. The assumption that the cost to create this building is equal to its market value would not be realistic, since the structure suffers from varying amounts of deterioration and obsolescence. The site residual technique is used only when new or almost new improvements exist—improvements which have yet to suffer loss of value because of deterioration or obsolescence and which could be the highest and best use of the site if it were vacant.

The example in Figure 4–6 demonstrates that the site residual technique provides the same value estimate as the building and prop-

FIGURE 4–6
Valuation of the ABC office property: Site residual technique

NOI	$ 39,500
Income required to support building value (cost to create): Building cost (value) assumed to be $315,804 ÷ 9.427 (PV of annuity of $1, 10%, 30 years)	33,500
Income residual to the site	$ 6,000
Value of site: $6,000 ÷ 0.10 land capitalization rate	$ 60,000
Value (cost) of building	315,804
Property value	$375,804, say $375,800

erty residual techniques, when building cost (value) is assumed to be $315,804. The income necessary to provide the investor a market-determined 10 percent return on investment, and to return the initial investment of $315,801 over the economic life of the building, is deducted from NOI to give the income residual to the site. The income residual to the site is then capitalized as a perpetuity at 10 percent to obtain site value. Site value is added to building cost (assumed to equal building value) to give property value.

Direct capitalization with an overall rate. Direct capitalization can be accomplished simply by dividing the property's NOI by an overall capitalization rate. An overall capitalization rate can be derived from market evidence by dividing the NOIs of comparable properties by their verified sale prices. Each comparable sale provides an indication of the appropriate overall capitalization rate (reciprocal of the net income multiplier). Analysts use a number of comparable sales to provide evidence in support of their selection of this market-determined rate. These comparable properties must have sold recently under conditions that permitted their market values to be realized, that is, arm's-length negotiation among knowledgeable buyers and sellers, no coercion, and a normal offering time.

Direct capitalization is demonstrated in Figure 4–7, where the overall capitalization rate of 0.1050 is divided into the $39,500 NOI of

FIGURE 4–7
Valuation of the ABC office building: Direct capitalization

Selection of overall capitalization rate:
   $41,000 NOI ÷ $381,400 sale price of comparable A: 0.1075 indicated overall rate
   $37,000 NOI ÷ $355,800 sale price of comparable B: 0.1040 indicated overall rate
   $40,500 NOI ÷ $395,120 sale price of comparable C: 0.1025 indicated overall rate
Selected overall capitalization rate: 0.1050
   This rate was selected by the analyst because comparable B most closely resembles the ABC commercial property, and 0.1050 approximates the mean OAR from all three comparables.
Value of ABC office property:
   $39,500 NOI ÷ 0.1050 overall capitalization rate: $376,190, say $376,200

the ABC commercial property to obtain a value estimate of $376,200. Only three comparables are used in Figure 4–7 to derive the overall capitalization rate; additional sales would be desirable when available.

Mortgage-equity and Ellwood techniques. Mortgage-equity appraisal methods, of which the Ellwood technique is an example, divide the NOI into that part required to pay the installments on the mortgage debt (typically, these payments are for principal and interest on a level payment, fully amortized mortgage) and into the cash flow to the equity position. In contrast to the income capitalization techniques described above, mortgage-equity appraisal explicitly incorporates financing into the appraisal methodology. A complete explanation of the derivation of the Ellwood overall capitalization rate is beyond the intent of this basic text.[11] The example in Figure 4–8 computes Ellwood's overall capitalization rate (R), and defines the components of the formula. The Ellwood overall capitalization rate is divided into NOI to obtain property value.

The assumptions incorporated into the Ellwood overall capitalization rate are summarized below.

---

[11] The interested reader is referred to L. W. Ellwood, *Ellwood Tables for Real Estate Appraising and Financing,* 4th ed. (Cambridge, Mass.: Ballinger, 1977). The Ellwood technique of mortgage-equity appraisal is, of course, named for its originator.

FIGURE 4–8
Valuation of the ABC office property: Ellwood (mortgage-equity) technique

Ellwood overall capitalization rate (R):

$$R = Y - MC + (\text{Depreciation} \times 1/S_n) \text{ or}$$
$$- (\text{Appreciation} \times 1/S_n)$$

where

Y = Equity yield rate (0.12)
M = Loan to value ratio (0.75)
C = Mortgage coefficient (0.019853)*

Depreciation
or Appreciation = Percent depreciation or appreciation assumed in the value of the property over the investment holding period. In this calculation no depreciation or appreciation in the property's reversion value is forecast.

$1/S_n$ = Annual sinking fund factor (Column 3 in Appendix G) at the equity yield rate for the assumed investment holding period. This term is not needed unless depreciation or appreciation has been assumed.

Substituting:

$$R = 0.12 - 0.75(0.019853)$$
$$R = 0.1051$$

Value of ABC office building:

$$\$39,500 \div 0.1051 = \$375,832, \text{ say } \underline{\$375,800} .$$

* C was obtained from precomputed coefficients in *Ellwood Tables for Real Estate Appraising and Financing,* given the equity yield rate (0.12), income projection period (10 years), and mortgage terms (10%, 30 years, 75% loan to value). The value of C can be computed by formula for any combination of these variables.

1. A level NOI is projected over a typical or average investment holding period. Investors usually do not hold a property over the entire economic life of the improvements; 7 to 12 years is a more common holding period. Ellwood's tables are calculated for holding periods of 5, 10, 15, 20, and 25 years.

2. The NOI is divided between the income necessary to service the mortgage and the income flowing to the ownership position. The analyst builds into the Ellwood capitalization rate the typical financing terms available for the property at the time of appraisement. It is assumed that potential purchasers of the property would shop the market for the most favorable financing terms and that market value will reflect those terms.

3. The property is assumed to be sold at the end of the investment holding period. The outstanding balance of the mortgage debt is retired at that time, and the remainder of the reversion price is available to the equity position.

4. Provision is made for anticipated appreciation or depreciation in the market value of the property over the investment holding period. In contrast to the property residual technique, in which the projection of NOI over the economic life of the improvements results in a reversion of site value only, the assumption of an investment holding period produces a reversionary value that contains both site and improvement value.

5. The market value of the equity investment is the discounted value of the stream of income to the equity over the investment holding period, plus the discounted cash reversion to the equity when the property is sold. The appropriate rate of discount is the market rate necessary to attract equity funds to this type of investment.[12]

6. The present value of the equity can be added to the initial amount of the mortgage to give the property value. In effect, the initial amount of the mortgage represents the present value of the level debt service plus the present value of the mortgage reversion at the end of the holding period discounted at the mortgage rate of interest. Ellwood's method splits NOI into cash flow and a cash reversion to the equity and a flow of debt service and reversion to the lender, each of which is discounted at its respective rate to obtain present value.

Figure 4–9 demonstrates what is assumed to occur over the investment holding period after valuation of the property using the Ellwood technique. For illustrative purposes, it is assumed in this example that the property is purchased for $375,832, the precise value estimated using the Ellwood formula.

Purchasing the property for $375,832 and financing its acquisition with a $281,874 mortgage (75 percent of value) requires an equity of $93,958. The example demonstrates that the equity value will be attained, given all the assumptions which the analyst has built into the appraisal. The value of the equity is shown to be the present value of the cash throw-off to the equity over the ten-year holding period, plus the present value of the cash reversion to the equity at the end of the ten-year holding period. (The assumed sale price of the property, with no depreciation or appreciation, is $375,832; subtracting the outstanding unpaid balance of the mortgage, or $256,372, gives a reversion to the equity of $119,460.) The cash throw-off and cash reversion to the equity are discounted at the equity yield rate of 12 percent.

---

[12] This equity rate is an after-financing, before-tax internal rate of return on equity value.

Although circuitous reasoning seems inherent in this conceptualization of Ellwood's mortgage-equity technique, his formulation of an overall capitalization rate avoids assuming that the absolute dollar value of the mortgage is known at the time of appraisal (only the loan to value ratio, the interest rate, and the maturity need to be specified), or that the absolute dollar sale price for the property reversion must be specified (only the percentage of expected appreciation or depreciation in property value over the holding period needs to be predicted).

FIGURE 4–9
Assumptions in the Ellwood technique

Purchase price of the property		
(market value)	$375,832	
Mortgage loan at 75 percent of value	281,874	
Equity required for purchase	$ 93,958	
Annual cash throw-off to equity over		
ten-year holding period	$ 39,500	NOI
	−29,681	Annual mortgage payment
	$ 9,819	Cash throw-off
Cash reversion to the equity at end		
of the holding period	$375,832	Assumed sale price
	−256,372	Outstanding balance
		of mortgage
	$119,460	Cash reversion
Present value of cash throw-off and cash		
reversion discounted at 12 percent:		
$9,819 × 5.6502 (PV of annuity of 1,		
12%, 10 years, Appendix G) = ...	$ 55,479	
$119,460 × 0.3220 (PV of 1, 12%,		
10 years, Appendix G) = ...	38,466	
Indicated equity value ....:......	$ 93,945*	
Mortgage at time of purchase	281,874	
Property value	$375,819*	

* Discrepancy from $93,958 and $375,832 due to rounding.

The sum of the present value of the equity plus the amount of the mortgage equals the estimated market value of the property, or approximately $375,832.

Several techniques, but only one estimated market value

Proper application by the analyst of each of the several income capitalization techniques appropriate for the ABC commercial property would, in theory, produce identical estimates of market value. Market value is determined by demand and supply conditions and not by the methodology chosen by the appraiser to measure it. In practice, of course, we would be surprised if the answers obtained by use of two or more methods were identical. The realities of the imperfect markets that provide the valuation inputs, such as discount rates, sale prices, and loan terms, will result in discrepancies among market value estimates.

If each of these techniques is capable of providing the "correct" estimate of market value, why do we need more than one? Analysts and academicians vary in their support of the methods. Kahn, Case, and Schimmel, for instance, have contended that "the property residual technique is sufficiently elastic to meet any given appraisal problem. It is the preferred technique."[13] The basic appraisal textbook published by the American Institute of Real Estate Appraisers is less conclusive in recommending a particular income capitalization technique.

> In order, these are the considerations leading to the selection of a suitable method and technique, applicable in any appraisal situation:
>
> 1. The data available.
> 2. The rate of return that is appropriate to attract investment capital.
> 3. The capitalization method that conforms to the character and prospective behavior of income and the assumptions concerning recapture.
> 4. The residual technique that is most applicable to the circumstances of the property being appraised.[14]

In applying these income capitalization techniques in the "real world," the real estate analyst is continually faced with imprecision and uncertainties in the data. The lack of perfect information results in advocacy of the more complex techniques. For instance, an overall capitalization rate obtained directly from the market evidence by dividing the NOIs of comparable properties by their sale prices can produce a relatively wide dispersion of indicated overall rates. On the other hand, explicitly incorporating value-creating factors, such as financing, the investment holding period, and potential appreciation or depreciation in property value over the holding period, raises these components in the valuation process to the level of consciousness. Here the appraiser can determine the value of the variables, rather than permitting them to remain buried in a relatively imprecise overall capitalization rate derived from the sale of comparable properties.

Real estate investment properties are increasingly being financed with mortgage instruments that permit adjustment of the mortgage interest rate over time as market conditions warrant. The rise to a higher level of mortgage interest rates in the late 1970s resulted in lenders being less willing to commit to a long-term mortgage at a fixed interest rate. Today, the rollover mortgage, in which the interest rate and/or the rate of amortization is renegotiated periodically, and the variable rate mortgage, with the rate of interest tied to an index, are becoming common. Mortgage-equity appraisal methodologies will need to be adapted to the potential for variation in mortgage interest rates, debt service, and reversion value. If the mortgage interest rate

---

[13] Sanders A. Kahn, Frederick E. Case, and Alfred Schimmel, *Real Estate Appraisal and Investment* (New York: Ronald Press, 1963), p. 153.

[14] American Institute of Real Estate Appraisers, *The Appraisal of Real Estate*, 7th ed. (Chicago, 1978), p. 429.

changes, with no change in the mortgage amortization rate, the annual debt service and cash flow to the equity can vary. If the mortgage amortization rate is permitted to change to offset the effect of a change in the mortgage interest rate, the debt service and cash flow to the equity remain the same over the investment holding period, but the cash reversion will be altered at the end of the holding period, since a different proportion of the original mortgage will have been paid off. These realities pose interesting methodological problems for the analyst who continues to use mortgage-equity techniques. Although beyond the scope of this text, the Ellwood formula can be adapted for a rising net operating income over the holding period, for junior financing, and for equity participation by the lender. A reformulation of the mortgage-equity concept is needed for today's financing. Pending this innovation, analysts may increasingly use methodologies which do not explicitly consider financing, such as direct capitalization with an overall rate.

If increasing the variables that require conscious analysis and judgment on the part of the analyst improves the value estimate, why stop with the explicit introduction of financing into valuation methodology? Why not include income taxes as well and capitalize an aftertax cash flow and aftertax cash reversion to the equity? This approach is developed in the next chapter as a technique for determining investment value. Investment value, it may be recalled, is defined as a personal value that depends upon the particular financing that an individual investor can secure, the individual's required return on investment, and the individual's needs and investment goals. These investment goals cause an investor to select a particular tax depreciation schedule which, given his or her income tax bracket, will determine the amount of tax that must be paid, or the tax savings that will be obtained, as well as the magnitude of any aftertax cash reversion to the equity. The concept of investment value differs from the concept of market value in that the latter represents a consensus among knowledgeable buyers and sellers concerning the price for which the property should sell under defined conditions. Market-derived data are used in the various appraisal methods that estimate market value. Even the financing arrangement in the mortgage-equity technique is assumed to be typical for a given type of property—even when the financing is defined as the best obtainable. Rational and knowledgeable buyers are expected to shop to obtain these terms, and nothing less would be acceptable. On the other hand, income tax considerations vary among buyers and sellers to the extent that generalization about "typical" tax factors for the type of property under appraisal becomes tenuous.

VALUE ESTIMATION BY DIRECT SALES COMPARISON

The idea of the direct sales comparison approach is straightforward: by comparing prices for similar properties, the analyst can judge the price (and thus the value) of the property under consideration. The properties for which these prices are compared must be similar; it would be fallacious to compare prices of dissimilar properties. But how similar to each other must the properties be? Although a quantitative answer is not possible, the general rule is that the properties must be sufficiently similar so that all the differences among the properties can be identified and dollar values assigned to these differences. For example, a comparison between two houses which have as their only difference the lack of a basement in one of them would be quite feasible. A value difference could easily be assigned to the basement and the resulting market price imputed as one evidence of value.

In making comparisons, it should be recognized that the determinants of supply and demand are operating to produce market prices, and that the analyst is looking at the end results of the market process. The actions of the market produce a price which can be viewed as a discounted value of the benefits that are expected from the property in the future. Thus, if buyers discount a property's expected benefits to a certain price they will tend to discount similar benefits available from other properties to similar prices.

This basic assumption of the direct sales comparison approach clearly shows its relation to the income approach. In the income approach the future net operating income to a property must, of course, be estimated, while this step is not necessary in the direct sales comparison approach. The benefits or income to a property are expected when the analyst employs the direct sales comparison approach, just as in the income approach. The fact that they are not estimated does not mean that a buyer will agree to forgo these benefits.

By the same reasoning, the income approach must contain a measurement from the market to determine the value that should be placed upon the expected income. This measurement comes through the capitalization rate. In effect, there is a market of capitalization rates just as there is a market of prices. In the direct sales comparison approach, analysts go to the market to determine prices; in the income approach, analysts go to the market to determine capitalization rates. They compare the capitalization rates for properties having similar risk and make adjustments to the rate for any differences that are perceived.

The adjustments that must be made reflect differences among physical characteristics (such as number of rooms and baths, lot size, physical condition, and architectural desirability), location, and market conditions. Dollar or percentage adjustments are assigned to each differential in the comparables, based upon how much more or less the property would be expected to bring in the market with or without the feature. For example, lack of a second bath in a property being appraised results in a subtraction from the price of a comparable property having a second bath. Similarly, better architecture or design of the subject property over that of a comparable property results in an addition to the price of a comparable property having inferior characteristics. Location of a single-family residential subject property in a less desirable neighborhood, or its exposure to a high-volume traffic artery, can result in a subtraction from the verified sale price of the comparable.

If the time of sale of a comparison property is over four to six months in the past, an adjustment often must be made to reflect changed market conditions. The adjustment takes account of any change in the value of the dollar and the real estate market that may have occurred. With the value of the dollar decreasing and many real estate markets experiencing price increases, an adjustment of 6 to 10 percent per year will often be required. This adjustment was made to the comparable properties in Figure 4–10.

Additional adjustments to the comparable's sale price for terms and conditions of sale are sometimes attempted. An adjustment for terms of

FIGURE 4–10
Grid analysis, direct sales comparison of a single-family residence

	A	B	C	D	Subject
Price	$71,900	$52,600	$61,800	$61,500	?
Market conditions	This year	Three years ago +18% +$9,468	Two years ago + 12% +$7,416	One year ago + 6% +$3,690	Now
Location	Equal	Equal	Poorer +$1,000	Equal	—
Architecture	Better −$1,200	Poorer +$1,200	Equal	Equal	—
Rooms	6½ −$1,500	6	7½ −$3,400	6	6
Baths	1½	1 +$2,400	1½	1 +$2,400	1½
Condition of property	Better −$1,800	Poorer +$1,500	Equal	Equal	—
Indicated value	$67,400	$67,168	$66,816	$67,590	

sale might reflect the amount, timing, type of repayment, and other obligations assumed by the buyer. The most stringent terms would be all cash at the time of sale. In a real estate transaction the seller may take a mortgage from the buyer as part payment, sell on installment contract, require no payment for a period of time, or lend the buyer funds at an attractive interest rate. The analyst may compensate for such terms by adjusting all transactions to a figure the analyst believes would be appropriate for a normal or typical transaction.

Adjustments for conditions of sale concern the relationship between buyer and seller. Was each acting under undue pressure? Did each have knowledge of market conditions? Was the property on the market for a reasonable time? Was the transaction at arm's length, that is, was there a personal relationship between buyer and seller? *Although adjustments for terms and conditions of sale may be attempted, it is believed to be better practice not to use these properties as comparables.*

Direct sales comparison: Single-family residence

In carrying out the direct sales comparison approach, a useful technique is to construct a grid, showing on one axis each comparison property and on the other axis each item for which the properties are different. Such a grid is shown in Figure 4–10. Values are assigned to each difference and either added to or subtracted from the known price of the comparable to derive a price for the property under appraisal. The adjustments can be shown in absolute dollars or as percentages.

Direct sales comparison, ABC office property

Figure 4–11 shows the direct sales comparison method applied to our previously analyzed ABC office property. In our example, the ABC property is compared with two comparable office buildings. A larger number of comparables would be preferred in the practical application of this method of value estimation. The reader also is cautioned that the format and methods used in the direct sales comparison of income properties vary with the type of property and its characteristics.

The ABC property and the two comparables differ in the size of the buildings, the availability of on-site parking, net rentable area, and effective age/overall condition. They are similar in location; each property is on the same high-volume traffic artery in a suburban commercial district of offices, restaurants, and commercial establishments. The sites are very similar; all three measure 100 feet × 200 feet and are level at street grade. The three properties rent for $8.60 per square foot of net rentable area.

FIGURE 4–11
Direct sales comparison, ABC office property

	Comparable A	Comparable B	ABC building
Price	$425,000	$350,000	
Gross income	$71,000	$63,960	
Price per square foot of building (includes land)	$44.74 (9,500-sq.-ft. building)	$40.00 (8,750-sq.-ft. building)	(9,000-sq.-ft. building)
Market conditions	Current	One year ago +5.0% +$2.00	
Location	Equal	Equal	
Parking	10,700 sq. ft.	8,800 sq. ft. +0.32% +$0.13	10,800 sq. ft.
Efficiency ratio	0.87 −2.0% −$0.89	0.85	0.85
Effective age and condition	Eight years Very good −4.3% −$1.92	Ten years Average	Ten years Average
Indicated value per square foot	$41.93	$41.70	$41.80*
GIM	5.98	5.47	5.70*

* Indicated from market evidence.

   The comparability of sites and site value permits the use of a unit of comparison obtained by dividing the sale price of the comparable by the gross square feet of building area. Thus, comparable A sold for $44.74 per gross square foot of building area ($425,000 ÷ 9,500 square feet); comparable B sold for $40.00 ($350,000 ÷ 8,750 square feet).

   Adjustments are then made to the sale price per square foot of building area. Rising values in this market necessitate an upward adjustment of 5 percent to comparable B, or $2 per square foot. Comparable B also has 2,000 square feet less parking, requiring an upward adjustment which, in this case, reflects the cost of paving the additional area.

   Comparable A has a higher ratio of rentable area to gross building area. The reduction in value in this instance is the present value of the additional gross rent produced by the higher efficiency ratio.

   The age/condition adjustment shows that comparable A is in better overall condition and is judged by the appraiser to have an effective age of eight years. The ABC office building is in average condition and has been given an effective age of ten years. In this instance, effective age and actual age are the same. The appraiser could assign an effective age different from the building's actual age. Effective age is defined as "the age of a similar structure of equivalent utility, condition, and remaining life expectancy as distinct from chronological age."[15] Maintenance and remodeling can result in an effective age less than the chronological age. The better condition of comparable A requires a downward adjustment in its price per square foot of building area.

Figure 4–11 also shows gross income multipliers of 5.98 for comparable A and 5.47 for comparable B (sale price divided by gross income). The GIM is another unit of comparison in the direct sales comparison technique.

After adjustments, the analyst must carefully select the appropriate value of the unit of comparison from the values indicated by the comparables. In selecting the appropriate value for a unit of comparison, the appraiser asks such questions as: "Which comparable was most similar and required the least adjustment?" "Am I satisfied with the accuracy of the data used to obtain my adjustments?" "Do I know all that I should about the conditions of sale of each comparable?" In selecting the market value estimate from indications of value using alternative units of comparison, the appraiser again uses judgment and may ask the question, "Is the unit of comparison accepted in the market by investors?" Selecting $41.80 and 5.70 is not a simple mathematical averaging of value indications, but once again requires the informed judgment of the appraiser.

In estimating the market value of the ABC office building using the direct sales comparison approach, the appraiser uses a GIM of 5.70 and an indicated value of $41.80 per gross square foot of building. The following conclusion is reached:

$65,970 total gross income × 5.70 GIM = $375,003 value

9,000 gross square feet of building × $41.80 value per square foot = $376,200 value

Indicated market value of ABC office property: $375,500

In conclusion, the direct sales comparison approach is appropriate for value estimation when there are active, viable markets in which sales prices can be obtained and in which properties are truly comparable. Usually such markets exist for single-family residential properties and for some general-purpose commercial and industrial properties. For more specialized types of properties, direct comparison of sales is impossible or implausible, and the appraiser must rely upon the income or cost approach.

---

[15] Boyce, *Real Estate Appraisal Terminology,* p. 74.

VALUE ESTIMATION BY COST ANALYSIS

The cost approach to value estimation attempts to measure value by adding all the costs necessary to reproduce a building, subtracting therefrom any losses in value, and adding to this figure the site value. Because of its reliance on historical cost figures, the approach can be used when both market and income data are unavailable or unreliable. The main assumption upon which the cost approach is based, however, constitutes a theoretical weakness, and the task of measuring reductions in value on older buildings becomes its Achilles' heel in practicality.

Relation of cost to value

The principal assumption of the approach is that the cost of creating an economic good equals its value. However, since value of improvements is determined by the forces of supply and demand in the market, the equality of cost and value only rarely exists. Investors pay only scant attention to the historical cost of the good. Differences between value and reproduction cost can be identified and measured, but only with uncertainty.

As discussed in our previous analysis of highest and best use,[16] a vacant site is improved with its highest and best use when a building or other improvement provides the owner of the land with the highest percentage return. In this situation the cost of the improvement equals its value, and no further adjustments are required to estimate value. If too much capital is sunk into the building, the percentage return to the land is lowered, and this condition is termed an overimprovement. If too little capital is invested in the improvement, which also would lower the land's return, an underimprovement results.

To repeat, the value of the building equals its cost when the improvement is the highest and best use of a vacant site. It is important that this relationship be understood—specifically, why value equals cost at the highest and best use. The answer most simply is that when the improvement is the highest and best use, the cost incurred is justified. Intelligent, well-informed investors will gladly incur this cost so as to obtain the highest possible return.

Therefore, the cost approach is quite properly used whenever the analyst believes a new, or almost new, improvement to be the highest and best use of a vacant site. In this instance, no accrued depreciation need be deducted from the building's reproduction cost new to estimate its value. The value of the land is determined either by direct

---

[16] See Chapter 3.

sales comparison or by assuming a hypothetical highest and best use of the site and capitalizing the site's residual income (as demonstrated in the income capitalization section of this chapter). Older buildings and some new buildings suffer loss of value from various deficiencies. For these improvements, reproduction cost new less accrued depreciation provides a measure of value. Site value obtained independently and added to the value of the improvements equals property value through the cost approach.

Reproduction cost

Estimation of reproduction costs can be accomplished in several different ways. These are (*a*) the quantity survey method, (*b*) the unit-in-place cost method, and (*c*) the comparison method.

The quantity survey method of estimating costs refers to the costing of each item and service going into the building. All the nails, lumber, bricks, concrete, plaster, and services of laborers, plasterers, carpenters, electricians, and others would be added up. The total cost of all such items and services would be the final reproduction cost. The quantity survey method is a lengthy and onerous procedure that would be used by a contractor or architect to determine a bid price for a new building. For value estimation the additional accuracy is not usually great enough to warrant its use over more concise methods.

The unit-in-place cost method is a shortcut of the quantity survey method. It usually involves the use of a cost service—a manual that is updated periodically and shows cost figures for various components of a structure. Examples of cost services appropriate for a variety of types of buildings are the Marshall-Swift *Valuation Quarterly* and the Boeckh *Building Valuation Manual;* Means' *Construction Costs* specializes in large buildings.

Basically, the method involves estimating the cost of a unit of a major structural component or assembly and multiplying the cost of the unit by the number of units. For example, the cost of a square yard of roof would be multiplied by the number of square yards; the cost of a square foot of brick wall would be multiplied by the number of square feet; and the cost of a lineal foot of foundation would be multiplied by the number of lineal feet. The cost services provide such unit costs. They are kept current and are adjusted for regional cost differences.

The third method, the comparison method, requires the appraiser to keep personally up to date on construction costs and to keep current a set of "benchmark" buildings whose costs are known. A surprisingly small number—usually 10 to 15—of benchmarks will provide the bases for estimating the costs of a fairly large number of types of buildings. The appraiser does this by applying the square foot or cubic foot cost of a benchmark structure to the structure under appraisal and making adjustments for differences between the structures. For example, if a subject house had a downstairs bath while the benchmark did not, an adjustment would have to be made.

Cost estimating is a crucial part of the cost approach; however, this discussion can do no more than acquaint the reader with the fundamental ideas of cost estimating. The important point to remember is that costs are prices and prices occur in markets; therefore, it is imperative for the cost estimator to keep up to date on the current market prices of materials, labor, and services. The use of published cost services can help the process, but they should be used with caution. Costs vary from locality to locality, and costs that are not current or that have not been determined for a specific city are likely to be inaccruate.

Accrued depreciation—penalties

Deductions from the reproduction cost new of a building in order to estimate the value of an existing structure are of three types and are perhaps most appropriately termed penalties.[17] These are penalties for physical deterioration, functional obsolescence, and locational obsolescence. The analyst measures each penalty and deducts the penalties from the reproduction cost.

Physical deterioration. The first penalty, physical deterioration, reflects the fact that all material things wear out. Every physical thing is on the road to the junkyard, and buildings are no exception. Therefore, in valuing a building over two or three years old, one must deduct accrued depreciation for both the building's structure and for its replaceable parts.

First, analysts make a schedule of replacement items such as water heaters, roofs, and bathroom fixtures that are worn out. They would obtain cost figures for these items. Second, they make a schedule of items and conditions that are partially worn out (depreciated). Such things as the furnace, water heater, roof, and paint job again would constitute candidates for this schedule. Again, these would be costed out (new), but the amount of remaining useful life would be deducted from the penalty. This is usually done by prorating the cost over the total expected life of the item. For example, a three-year-old paint job that should last five years and cost $1,000 would have an indicated penalty of $600. Next, analysts would recognize the physical deterioration in the building itself (sometimes termed the bone structure). This penalty would be measured by multiplying the ratio of the building's effective age to its total economic life by the portion of reproduction

---

[17] Robert O. Harvey, "Observations on the Cost Approach," *Appraisal Journal* 21, no. 4 (October 1953): 514–18.

cost representing the "bone structure" of the building less physical deterioration already charged (such as the $600 penalty for painting).

Functional obsolescence.   Functional obsolescence is the loss of a building's relative ability to perform its function. The development of new materials and processes and the acceptance of different styles and designs cause older buildings to become less desirable. The second penalty in the cost approach recognizes those differences between modern buildings and the existing building.

Possible sources of functional obsolescence are lack of air conditioning and elevators, out-of-date kitchens, old designs, rooms too small, ceilings too high, and so on. In some instances such a deficiency can be corrected, and the value increase will be equal to or greater than the cost incurred. In other instances the cost incurred to remedy a functional obsolescence deficiency will be greater than the value produced by incurring the cost. The former is termed a *curable* penalty, while the latter is known as an *incurable* penalty. Obviously, these terms do not apply to the physical ability to make the change; any building can be completely changed. Rather, the terms *curable* and *incurable* refer to the financial justification for making a change.

The distinction between curable and incurable penalties is an important one for deciding how to measure functional penalties. The procedure is simple for curable penalties; the cost of correcting the deficiency is used, since this cost equals the value loss of the deficiency. For incurable penalties, however, the matter is a bit more complex. Since the cost of correcting the deficiency is greater than the value, some other method must be employed to estimate the value. Either the lost income can be capitalized, or direct sales comparisons can be made with properties that are similar but do not have the deficiency.

Measurement of the value loss by the income approach rests on the fact that many deficiencies will cause various types of expenses to be larger. For example, ceilings that are too high require larger fuel and maintenance expense; unattractive architecture and design result in vacancy losses; out-of-date kitchens result in lower sales prices; and inconvenient arrangements produce a need to hire additional, part-time help. These negative income (or loss) streams can be estimated and capitalized, and the resultant penalties subtracted from the reproduction cost of the building.

The direct sales comparison approach can also be utilized to estimate incurable penalties. Ideally this would be accomplished by comparing the transaction prices of properties that are similar in every respect except the deficiency. If, for example, houses similar to a house having an incurable kitchen deficiency sell for $8,000 more than other like houses having out-of-date kitchens, the penalty would be $8,000 (while the cost of putting in a new kitchen might be $12,000).

   Locational obsolescence. The third penalty, locational obsolescence, is defined as a loss in value of the building because the site is no
longer as desirable as it was for the purpose served by the building. It
represents, in other words, a relationship between the land and the
building that is less ideal than it once was. It does not, however,
connote a value loss for the land. In fact the land has in many such
cases increased in value due to its increased desirability for commercial or industrial uses. Keep in mind that the building suffers the
penalties; the land value is estimated separately.
   How, then, is the locational obsolescence penalty measured? Answer: *By deducting the present value of the income stream lost because of the lack of adaptation to its site or by the increased value of
similar buildings on sites more suitable.* When a dollar rent can be
imputed to the property, a loss of rent due to the deterioration of the
site for that purpose can be capitalized and taken as the penalty. However, when a special-purpose property that does not generate dollar
income is under valuation, the penalty for locational deterioration can
be taken by shortening the remaining economic life of the improvement (as in the following example). The theory is that the deteriorated
relation between land and building will cause the building to be
profitable for a shorter time. (Physically, the building would be torn
down sooner than would otherwise occur.) The percentage relationship of the present value of the income stream lost to the value of the
income stream without the penalty can then be applied to the replacement cost less the first two penalties.[18] An example should clarify
this complex description, as well as the entire cost approach.

---

   [18] Several other methods for estimating accrued depreciation are available to the
analyst. For instance, the market value of the improvements (obtained by some other
method, such as the building residual technique of income capitalization or by direct
sales comparison) might be subtracted from the cost new of the improvements, with the
difference representing accrued depreciation (cost new, $100,000, less market value of
improvements, $60,000, gives total accrued depreciation of $40,000). Or, straight-line
depreciation may be used, with the rate of depreciation depending upon the economic
life of new improvements of that type ($1/50$ years economic life = 2.0 percent). The rate of
depreciation times the chronological age of the improvements provides an estimate of
the percentage loss in value due to accrued depreciation from physical deterioration and
functional obsolescence, but not loss of value due to locational obsolescence (0.02×20
years chronological age = 40 percent loss of value $\times$ $100,000 cost new = $40,000 depreciation from physical and functional causes; locational obsolescence would be measured separately). In the observed condition method, the analyst may break the total cost
new of the building into the cost of its component parts (footings, walls, roof, heating
system, and so on) and by observation (judgment) assign a total depreciation rate to each
component (roof is 20 percent depreciated; heating system is 30 percent depreciated;
and so on). The cost new of each component part times the percent depreciated, when
aggregated, provides an estimate of accrued depreciation from physical deterioration.
Loss of value resulting from functional obsolescence and locational deterioration must
be derived separately. These alternative methods for taking accrued depreciation in the
cost approach are illustrative only; other methods are available. See AIREA, *Appraisal
of Real Estate,* 7th ed., pp. 236–62.

Cost approach examples

Assume that we wish to estimate the value of a ten-year-old school building (see Figure 4–12). Although in good physical condition, the building is located in an area that has become ripe for industrial de-

FIGURE 4–12
Valuation of school property: Cost approach

Cost new for building		$462,000
Less accrued depreciation (penalties)		
1. Physical deterioration:		
Curable		
Repainting	$ 4,000	
Roof leaks	2,000	
Incurable		
Structural decay 1 percent per		
year—10 percent × cost new less		
physical curable already charged	45,600	51,600
2. Functional obsolescence:		
Curable		
Poorly fitting windows	$ 6,000	
Needs acoustical tile in classrooms	5,000	
Incurable		
Inefficient heating system requires		
an extra part-time janitor—		
$3,000/year at 6 percent for 15		
years—life of heating system	29,136	40,136
3. Locational obsolescence:		
Life of new school at appropriate site		
100 years: 6 percent PV factor	16.62	
Life of new school at present site		
40 years: 6 percent PV factor	15.05	
	1.57	

$$\frac{1.57}{16.62} = 9.4\%$$

Reproduction cost	$462,000	
Less: Total physical and functional		
obsolescence penalties	91,736	
9.4% × $370,264	$370,264	$ 34,804
Value of building		$335,460
Value of site (by market comparison)		80,000
Value of school property		$415,460, say $415,500

velopment. The school board has decided to determine whether the value of the building and land justifies abandonment of the school in favor of construction of a new building in a more desirable location.

By use of the Marshall-Swift *Valuation Quarterly* we have classified the building as "Class B" in "good" condition. Class B construction has reinforced concrete frame in which the columns and frames can be either formed or precast concrete. "Good" quality refers to the second from best, out of four quality classes. Such a building is designed for good appearance, comfort, and convenience. The cost cited of $38.50 per square foot totals $462,000 for the 12,000 square feet.

The penalties for accrued depreciation are subtracted from the cost new of the building. The penalty for physical deterioration contains both curable and incurable elements. The painting and roof repair can be accomplished readily and relatively inexpensively. The structural decay cannot be remedied without complete reconstruction of the building. Such a task would not add as much value to the building as it would cost. With the total economic life of the building, if new, estimated at 100 years, approximately 10 percent deterioration is estimated to have occurred.

The functional penalty is also divided between curable and incurable components. The windows and acoustical problems can be remedied by spending $11,000, and such cost would be justified. The heating system requires supervision that a newer system would not require; nevertheless, the cost of installation would be greater than the value lost by the present system.

The locational penalty is estimated by the percentage of the present value of the economic life lost to the total economic life of the building at an ideal location. This percentage is applied to the building in its existing condition—that is, after deducting the first two penalties from reproduction cost.

To the building value of $335,460 would be added the site value. If the site value were $80,000, the total property value would be $415,000 (rounded). The school board should not sell the property unless it could obtain at least that amount and construct a new school of comparable quality on a different site for a total cost (including land) not to exceed the price obtained for the old school. If the land value has appreciated sufficiently, this proposal could be feasible.

Cost approach for the ABC office property

Figure 4–13 shows an application of the cost approach to the ABC office property in our previous examples. The market value of the site has been obtained independently by direct sales comparison. Similar sites suitable for commercial use have sold for an indicated value of $3 per square foot. The ABC site contains 20,000 square feet and has a market value of $60,000. The cost new of the ABC building has been calculated at $46.14 per square foot, or $415,260.

The ABC office building is in average physical condition and suffers from no significant functional or locational obsolescence. Rather than employ the breakdown method of classifying the causes of depreciation by type, as in the previous example, the appraiser uses an eco-

FIGURE 4–13
Cost approach: ABC office property

Market value of site	20,000	square feet
	×$3.00	per square foot
	$60,000	site value
Cost new building	9,000	square feet
	×$46.14	cost per square foot
	$415,260	building cost new

Building depreciation

$$\frac{10 \text{ years effective age}}{40 \text{ years economic life}} = 25.0 \text{ percent depreciation}$$

$415,260 × 0.25 = $103,815
total depreciation

Parking lot cost new	$6,000	(no accrued depreciation)
Value of ABC office property	$415,260	building cost new
	+6,000	parking area cost new
	$421,260	improvements cost new
	−103,815	depreciation
	$317,445	improvements depreciated cost
	+60,000	site value
	$377,445	say $377,400 indicated market value

nomic age-life relationship to estimate total accrued depreciation. The ABC building, if new, would have a 40-year total economic life. The building is ten years old at the time of the appraisal, and is in average condition. An effective age of ten years is considered to be appropriate. The appraiser, in making this judgment, has observed that similar structures in the same overall condition as the ABC building are also about ten years old. The parking area, if new, would have a total physical life expectancy of 15 years. No depreciation is taken on the $6,000 cost new of the parking area because of recent resurfacing.

Dividing the effective age of the ABC building by its total economic life (effective age plus remaining economic life) indicates that the structure has suffered a 25.0 percent loss of value from cost new due to physical deterioration and functional obsolescence, if any. Depreciation in the amount of $103,815 is deducted from the $415,260 cost new to produce a value for the ABC building of $311,445. Building and parking area value ($6,000) plus site value gives an indicated market value from the cost approach of $377,400.

Reconciliation of value indications

The analyst engages in reconciliation throughout the value estimation process. Whenever observed data vary and a choice must be made concerning the most probable outcome of uncertain events, the analyst must logically select the most appropriate data and the most likely outcome. For example, informed sources may differ about the prospects for the local economy. Local business conditions influence real estate markets and the rent and vacancy levels that will be experienced by the subject property. Conflicting factors may be affecting the neighborhood in which the property is located. A transition in land use may be in process, which would shorten the remaining economic life of the building, while, at the same time, the area may be the focal point of a government-sponsored improvement program. Elsewhere in the appraisal problem, market data from comparable properties may show a range of rents, vacancy experiences, return on investment, and other necessary inputs. When the direct sales comparison method has been worked, the analyst must reconcile the indicated value of each of the comparable properties into a single value estimate from this approach. Finally, having used each of the three appraisal methods (direct sales comparison, income, and cost new less depreciation) for which data are available and which are appropriate for the subject property, the analyst has a range of value indications to reconcile into a final estimate of market value.

At every step of the appraisal process, the reconciliation process requires informed judgment and expert opinion. The reconciliation process is not a simple averaging of divergent data.

Application of the three approaches to the ABC office property has resulted in three indications of value (Figure 4–14). All three ap-

FIGURE 4–14
Reconciliation and value estimation, ABC office property

Value indication from direct sales comparison	$375,500
Value indication from income capitalization	375,800
Value indication from cost new less depreciation	377,400
Final value estimate	375,800

proaches are considered valid for the appraisal of this property. However, the analyst considers the income approach to be the most appropriate valuation method for an investment property. Also, the data used in the income approach have been verified and are believed to be accurate and supportable from market evidence. The analyst's final conclusion of market value for the ABC office building is $375,800. The analyst then states that this value estimate is supported by the value indications from the cost and direct sales comparison approaches.

SUMMARY

This chapter describes the methods and techniques of value estimation. Emphasis is placed upon the valuation function because all decisions regarding real estate involve a consideration of value (price) or rate of return. Rates of return are a function of prices paid and received, and transaction prices in a market determine values. The central concept and beginning point for understanding investment analysis is that of market-determined prices—or value. The estimate of value is an important criterion in the investment decision-making process. Presumably, investors would not want to pay more than the market value for a property, even though their financing arrangements and income tax situation would permit them to pay a higher price.

The valuation process requires a consideration of all factors believed to influence income expectancy and capitalization rates. These factors are complex and play an exceedingly important role in the valuation of real estate because of its physical nature. Immobility, long life, and large size make real estate particularly vulnerable to economic, social, and political-legal developments. Trends in each of these areas must be considered at the national, regional, community, and neighborhood levels. Since real estate investment decisions require a long-term, future-oriented viewpoint and great reliance is placed upon financing, a real estate investor's success or failure is in large measure dependent upon perceptive analysis and prediction of such value-determining trends.

The steps required in each of the three approaches to value are shown in Figure 4–15. Theoretically, if each approach were equally applicable to a valuation problem and if equally complete and reliable data were available, all three approaches would produce the same estimate of market value. Depending upon the nature of the property and the market in which it would be bought and sold, one approach is usually more appropriate than the other two. Before embarking on the appraisal procedures, the legal rights being valued must be identified.

FIGURE 4–15

QUESTIONS FOR REVIEW

1. Why does the cost approach produce an estimate of market value? In other words, what market data are used in the cost approach?

2. Why does the income approach produce an estimate of market value? What market data are used in the income approach?

3. How does level annuity capitalization differ from straight-line capitalization? Which is more realistic?

4. What is meant by *functional obsolescence?* Could a new building contain functional obsolescence? Why?

5. How is business risk reflected in a capitalization rate? Would a higher level of business risk result in a higher or lower value for a property, other factors remaining unchanged?

6. How does an analyst know whether expenses are reasonable or unreasonable?

7. What main difficulty would you foresee in attempting to estimate the value of a 30-year-old property via the cost approach?

PROBLEMS

1. Calculate the value of an income stream of $12,000 for the first year, with a discount rate of 8 percent and capital recapture required over 25 years under straight-line capitalization. What would be the value under level annuity? Can you explain the reason for the difference?

2. Estimate the value of the following property:

". . . the building is a frame five-apartment structure which was constructed in 1960, with additions in 1972 and 1977. The structure is in excellent physical condition, but the neighborhood is in rapid transition from residential to light-industrial usage. Four of the apartments rent for $200 a month each, with the owner paying all of the expenses. The owner, who functions as both janitor and manager, lives in one of the apartments. If vacant, his apartment would rent for $175 a month. The demand for apartments has been strong in the community and should continue at high levels."

Other interesting data:

Expenses:

Fuel, water, power, and telephone	$ 800
Building supplies	200
Mortgage payments	1,500
Decorating and painting	400
Repairs and maintenance	600
Reserve for wasting parts	400
Insurance	500
Real estate tax	1,200
Land value (by market comparison)	10,000
Estimated economic life of building	40 years
Rate of return derived from market	10%

a. Convert the given information into a reconstructed operating statement.
b. Identify the assumptions involved in your calculations.
c. What is your final value estimate?

3. You have been asked to appraise a vacant site on the north side of town. The neighborhood is zoned C-2 (allowing small commercial uses), but it is predominantly residential in character. The residences are mostly around 40 years old; doubles and some small apartment buildings (up to eight units) are also in the neighborhood. The site is a double residential lot, 120 feet wide by 160 feet deep. After surveying the neighborhood and other comparable neighborhoods, you find the following sales that you believe can be used for comparison purposes. Assume a current date of January 1982.

	1	2	3	4
Size	60 × 160	60 × 160	60 × 160	120 × 160
Terrain	Equal	Equal	Equal	10% better
Market conditions	1/81	11/81	9/81	1/82
Location...................:	10% better	Equal	Equal	15% worse
Condition of sale*	Arm's length	Forced purchase*	Arm's length	Seller required to sell*
Surroundings	5% better	Equal	5% worse	Equal
Price	$26,000	$28,000	$24,000	$50,000

* Forced conditions of sale are believed to result in prices 5 percent higher or lower than would have otherwise occurred.

The market has been rising about 6 percent per year; however, you believe no market adjustment is necessary for less than three months. Make any indicated adjustments, and estimate the value of the site.

4. You are appraising the city hall of a town with a population of about 100,000. The building measures 100 feet by 100 feet and is one story in height (10 feet). It was constructed in 1965, and the city is now considering selling it and erecting a new city hall in another location. You are unable to find any sales of buildings you feel would be sufficiently comparable to justify use of the direct sales comparison approach. The remaining economic life of the building is estimated at 25 years. The date on which you are making the appraisal is December 1981.

The highest and best use of the land, were it vacant, would be a 16-unit apartment building which would gross $57,600 per year and would net before depreciation about $35,000 per year. Such a building would have an expected economic life of 50 years. From comparable sales you feel that investors today must be able to foresee an 8 percent return on such an investment. You obtain cost estimates that indicate the 16-unit building could be constructed for $20,000 per unit.

The present building was built in 1965 at a cost of $189,500, and several contractors have told you the building could be replaced today for approximately $3.25 per cubic foot. Although the building has been well maintained, some wear and tear has occurred, and you believe physical deterioration of about 1.5 percent per year should be counted. Also, because of the inefficient room arrangement, not all of the city employees have been housed in the city hall, and five rooms in other locations have been rented to house some employees. The rental on these rooms has run $1,000 per year, and (according to the employees) about $300 per year has been consumed in gasoline in going back and forth so that the outlying employees could use the candy and coke machines at city hall. The building needs decorating at a cost of $1,800.

You believe that the new, more centrally located city hall will have an expected economic life of about 60 years, while the same building at the subject site would serve for only 30 years.

a. Estimate the value of the property.
b. How do you account for the difference between your value and the original cost? Do you believe the property will increase in value in the future?
c. How do you account for the difference between the cost of a highest and best use structure and the value of the existing property?
d. Would you recommend demolishing the existing structure in order to erect the 16-unit apartment building?
e. Should the cost of demolishment be deducted from the value of the land? Why or why not?

REFERENCES

American Institute of Real Estate Appraisers. *The Appraisal of Real Estate.* 7th ed. Chicago, 1978.

Ellwood, L. W. *Ellwood Tables for Real Estate Appraising and Financing.* 4th ed. Cambridge, Mass.: Ballinger, 1977.

Goulet, Peter G. *Real Estate A Value Approach.* Encino, Cal.: Glencoe, 1979.

Kinnard, William N. *Income Property Valuation.* Lexington, Mass.: D. C. Heath, 1971.

Kinnard, William N., and Boyce, Byrl N. *An Introduction to Appraising Real Property.* Chicago: Society of Real Estate Appraisers, 1975.

Shenkel, William M. *Modern Real Estate Appraisal.* New York: McGraw-Hill, 1978.

Smith, Halbert C. *Real Estate Appraisal.* Columbus, Ohio: Grid, 1976.

Smith, Halbert C., and Racster, Ronald L. "Should the Traditional Appraisal Process Be Restructured?" *Real Estate Appraiser* 36, no. 7 (November–December 1979): 6–11.

chapter 5

The investment calculation

The two preceding chapters deal with the concept of market value and its measurement. We emphasized that value is an opinion; transaction price is a fact. Professional appraisers are often called upon to estimate the market value of parcels of real estate because the market value figure is the basis for economic transactions. A buyer does not usually wish to pay more, nor the seller to take less, than the market value of the property.

Nevertheless, for many purposes the market value estimate is not the whole story. It is only phase 1 of the calculation for decisions having an investment motive, that is, a conscious consideration of the expected returns in relation to the capital required. Since most decisions that determine the role of real estate resources in shaping the future of cities are made with the investment motive, it is our contention that the professional approach to the study of real estate and the making of intelligent decisions must employ the investment calculation as its base. Investment calculations are made whenever a property transaction is contemplated; when a maintenance or repair decision is made; when a structure is modernized, renovated, converted, abandoned, or demolished; and when a site is developed with a new set of improvements. Richard Ratcliff, a strong proponent of the investment approach, has stated: "Most of the critical real estate decisions which confront families, professional real estate operators, bankers, and businesses are, broadly speaking, investment decisions which call for predictions of productivity of value."[1]

The investment calculation begins where the value calculation ends. We can regard the valuation calculation as phase 1 and the investment calculation as phase 2. Actually both phases may be viewed as the investment process, with phase 2 taking into account the personal and business considerations peculiar to the investor. Phase 1 will already have taken into account the general or average investment conditions in the market. To the extent that a particular investor's situation is different, the price that investor is willing to pay will differ from market value. However, the fact that investors may be willing to pay a price higher than market value does not necessarily mean that they will do so. They may pay a higher price if the seller is an astute negotiator and the investor is eager to buy and uncertain of the bids from other purchasers. The less competitive the market, the greater is the likelihood that a transaction price will vary from market value. As we have seen in previous chapters, estimation of market value becomes more difficult in these circumstances. The range of observed transaction prices may be quite broad, and the market consensus is difficult to ascertain.

INVESTMENT VALUE AND INVESTMENT PROFITABILITY

Investment value was defined as the maximum the buyer would be willing to pay and the minimum the seller would be willing to accept.[2] Investment value in this manner can be expressed as an absolute dollar amount. Often, however, buyers find it more useful to analyze the profitability of an investment, assuming that they purchase the property for a given price. This type of investment calculation permits buyers to compare alternative investments in terms of relative profitability and risk. These alternative investments may be real estate or other investments generating a calculable yield, such as securities, orange groves, cattle, or business ventures.

In the following sections, we first develop a calculation of investment value in terms of a dollar amount and then examine various measures of return on investment and other profitability criteria.

INVESTMENT VALUE CALCULATION

Income flows

The basic figure with which phase 2 begins is net operating income as determined in the valuation phase. This figure, you will recall from

---

[1] Richard U. Ratcliff, *Real Estate Analysis* (New York: McGraw-Hill, 1961), p. 4.
[2] See Chapter 3.

Chapter 4, is the resultant of the analyst's estimate of future gross income less future expenses attributable to the real estate. For income-producing real estate, this figure is a measure of its productivity. The sources and analysis of real estate productivity are examined in Chapter 8. Our purpose in this chapter is to complete the framework of analysis so that the role of productivity in the investment approach may be clearly understood.

In investment analysis of income properties, the net operating income used in the appraisal process is adjusted by adding back the replacement reserve. Net operating income was defined in Chapter 4 as total gross income less vacancy and collection losses and less operating expenses. Included as an operating expense was a "reserve for replacement." This reserve for replacement resulted from the need to replace short-lived components of the building before the remaining economic life of the building had ended. In effect, the replacement reserve is a depreciation account and, as such, is a noncash expenditure which does not reduce the cash flow experienced by an investor. Investors typically consider the entire available cash flow in their decision process. Consequently, the replacement reserve has been added back to the net operating income in the examples presented in this chapter.

Although NOI after adjustment for the replacement reserve is the one best estimate of the future income to a parcel of real estate and would be the same under competent management no matter who the owner, no such agreement may be reached with respect to the price each potential owner would pay. Personal considerations, such as the financing required for a potential investor to purchase the property, the expected effect of the purchase on the investor's income tax position, and other unmeasurable influences, such as the disposition of the investor's spouse, may enter into the bid price and the acceptable return. It is the function of phase 2 of the investment calculation to take into account the measurable personal and business influences (such as financing and income taxes) on the price investors are willing to pay, or to determine their possible returns given the price they must pay to acquire the property.

The injection of financing and income tax into the investment calculation produces several measures of income or flow in addition to net income. These measures in turn can be related to appropriate investment amounts in order to measure profitability. These items are defined as follows:

1. *Cash throw-off and cash flow*
   Net income (NOI + reserve for replacements)
      Less: Annual mortgage payment (debt service)

Cash throw-off (before-tax cash flow)
Less: Annual income tax liability
Cash flow (aftertax cash flow)

2. *Taxable income and tax liability*
Net income
Less: Depreciation for tax computation
Less: Annual interest on mortgage debt
Annual taxable income (or loss) from the investment times investor's tax rate
Annual income tax liability

3. *Tax shelter*
Tax shelter is usually defined as a net loss for income tax purposes. That is, if net income minus tax depreciation and mortgage interest is negative, the negative income is a loss for calculating income tax liability. The loss can be deducted from other income before computing the tax. Thus, if a tax loss of $1,000 occurs and the investor's tax bracket is 50 percent, approximately $500 less in tax would be paid on other income than would be paid without the tax loss. This deduction from other taxable income is the tax shelter.

Of course, no investor wants a real loss. The tax loss occurs because investors can deduct interest and higher levels of depreciation and possibly expenses other than those they actually incur. Thus, a tax loss may be claimed even though positive net income is being produced by the property at more realistic depreciation charges and even though the property may actually be increasing in value.

In a broader sense, tax shelter occurs whenever an expense deducted for income tax is larger than the actual expense. Although such an expense may not be great enough to produce a tax loss, the investor's tax liability is lower than it would be otherwise.

Investment value from appraisal methodologies

The income capitalization methods for estimation of market value would each produce an investment value if the requirements of an investor were substituted for market-determined variables. Instead of a market-determined rate of discount, the rate of return required by an investor can be substituted. Instead of a typical or average investment holding period, the anticipated holding period of the investor would be used. The particular financing arrangements would replace the most typical arrangements for the property. The absolute dollar investment value is computed using the property's adjusted NOI (before financing and before tax) if the property residual, building residual, land residual, or Ellwood technique is used. If the Ellwood methodology or other mortgage-equity techniques are employed, investment value is determined by capitalizing cash throw-off. None of the appraisal methodologies gives explicit consideration to income taxes and the potential influence of tax factors on investment value.

Investment value from aftertax cash flow

An absolute dollar investment value can be obtained by discounting the projected aftertax cash flow and aftertax cash reversion to the equity position at the investor's required rate of return on the equity investment. An investor must determine the financing arrangements, the most probable investment holding period, the tax depreciation schedule, the desired equity rate of return, and any anticipated appreciation or depreciation in the market value of the property over the holding period.

In Figure 5–1, investment value is computed for an investor who is considering the purchase of the ABC office property having a market value (phase 1) of $375,800. This property has an adjusted net income of $42,500. The investor, after shopping for the best financing terms available, discovers that a mortgage for $281,850 at 10 percent for 30 years can be obtained. The annual debt service on this mortgage will be $29,681. The investor is in the 50 percent income tax bracket (50 percent of taxable income will be paid in taxes). Commercial property which has been previously owned, such as the ABC property, must be depreciated for income tax purposes using straight-line depreciation. Allocation of the assumed $375,800 market value between building value and site value indicates that the depreciable basis is $315,800 (improvements value). The investment holding period is five years. The property is assumed to be sold for $375,800 at the end of the holding period (no appreciation or depreciation in market value is projected). A 9 percent aftertax return on the equity investment in this property is required by the investor.

The property's investment value for this prospective purchaser is the sum of (a) the present value of the equity position and (b) the amount of the mortgage. The present value of the equity is the sum of (a) the aftertax cash flow to the equity for five years discounted at 9 percent and (b) the aftertax cash reversion at the end of the holding period discounted at 9 percent. In Figure 5–1, the value of the equity position is shown to be $102,167, and the total investment value is $384,017. Thus, the maximum amount that the investor can pay, given all the assumptions, and earn a 9 percent aftertax return on equity is about $384,000.

If an investor could purchase the property for less than $384,000, the return on equity would increase. Purchasing the property for its

FIGURE 5–1
Calculation for determining investment value

			Year		
	1	2	3	4	5
Net income (NOI + replacement reserve).............	$42,500	$42,500	$42,500	$42,500	$42,500
Less: Interest	28,114	27,950	27,769	27,569	27,569
Less: Depreciation (straightline, 30 years)	10,522	10,522	10,522	10,522	10,522
Taxable income	$ 3,863	$ 4,028	$ 4,209	$ 4,409	$ 4,630
Net income	$42,500	$42,500	$42,500	$42,500	$42,500
Less: Mortgage payment	29,681	29,681	29,681	29,681	29,681
Less: Taxes (50%)	1,932	2,014	2,104	2,205	2,315
Aftertax cash flow	$10,887	$10,805	$10,715	$10,615	$10,504

Sale price $375,800
Less: Outstanding mortgage balance 272,192
Equity $103,608
Less: Capital gain tax 10,522*
Aftertax cash reversion .... $ 93,086

* Calculated as follows:

Original basis $375,800
Less: Accumulated depreciation 52,612
Adjusted basis $323,188
Sale price $375,800
Less: Adjusted basis 323,188
Capital gain .... $ 52,612
Capital gain tax rate .... ×0.20
Capital gain tax .... $ 10,522

Solution:

Payment		PV of $1 at 9 percent		
$10,887	×	0.9174	=	$ 9,958
10,805	×	0.8417	=	9,094
10,715	×	0.7722	=	8,274
10,615	×	0.7084	=	7,519
10,504	×	0.6499	=	6,826
93,086	×	0.6499	=	60,496

Value of equity $102,167
Plus: Mortgage 281,850
Investment value $384,017

market value of $375,800 produces an aftertax return on equity of about 11.27 percent. If the amount of the mortgage can be increased or more favorable terms can be obtained, the return on equity would increase. The student will note later in this chapter that the 9 percent used in Figure 5-1 as the investor's required aftertax return on equity is also the "internal rate of return" on equity, if the price of $384,000 is paid for the property. If the property is purchased at its market value of $375,800, the aftertax internal rate of return on equity is 11.27 percent, as shown in Figure 5-3.

Determinants of the required return on equity

In the problem example of Figure 5-1 a discount rate of 9 percent is used with no explanation as to why. This rate is the aftertax return required by a specific investor. The magnitude of the rate reflects the characteristics of the investment and the investor. Some real estate investments generate more cash throw-off than others, which may offer greater tax shelter. An individual investor, perhaps a widow, may require cash income; tax shelters have little value to her. Physicians, on the other hand, can often afford to hold for appreciation in market value and are interested in investments that generate tax shelters rather than cash income. Real estate investments also vary in the amount of personal attention required, which must either be hired from professionals or be done by the investor. Investors with a high opportunity cost for their time might require a larger return on their equity than investors who are able to handle profitably the chores of managing the property.

Real estate investments vary in the level of business risk associated with the property. Business risk reflects the stability of income, the potential loss of future income and capital value, and the marketability of the investment (ability to cash out of the investment at market value without an unreasonable delay). Much of this text is concerned with the determinants of business risk. The physical characteristics of the property, its location, the character of the neighborhood and community, and real estate and financial market conditions are all determinants of business risk. Investors vary in the amount of risk they are willing or able to tolerate. The widow may require stability of income and value and can be expected to worry if the vacancy rate is greater than 5 percent. Another investor may be better able to tolerate fluctuating income and value, particularly if potential exists for long-run appreciation in market value.

The 9 percent return on equity used in the preceding example is a discount rate composed of two parts—the pure rate for the use of riskless capital and an additional premium required to compensate the investor for business risk. Further, the investor must consider financial risk.

Financial risk concerns the level and stability of income in relation to financing requirements. Mortgage payments are a contractual obligation upon the mortgagor, and any lack of income to meet that obligation could cause the investment project to fail. Obviously, then, the investor should be able to foresee an income stream that provides a considerable margin of safety above operating expenses, reserves, taxes, and financing charges. Since most real estate investors utilize credit and thus incur fixed charges when purchasing real estate, the capitalization rate would usually contain a "normal" level of financial risk. But when an individual investor's financial risk level becomes greater than some minimum level acceptable to the market, an additional percentage must be added in determining the necessary return rate. For example, if the analyst believes the aftertax market discount rate is 14 percent, but a particular investor would have to incur a greater than average financial obligation to purchase the property, the desired rate of return should be increased proportionately to reflect the additional risk.

An investor's particularly strong financial situation and the ability to meet financial obligations out of personal funds can also be considered in determining the return rate. Since the discount rate includes a normal rate for financial risk, a lower-than-normal financial risk for a particular investor could serve to reduce the desired return below the market discount rate. The investor would then be in a position to bid a somewhat higher price for the property than could the "average" investor who would have to incur a normal level of financing.

Net present value

The net present value method for analyzing the feasibility of an investment involves discounting both the aftertax cash flow to the equity position over the holding period and the aftertax cash reversion at the investor's required rate of return. If the present value of the aftertax income to be received by the investor is equal to or greater than the initial equity investment, the purchase is feasible.

The net present value for the ABC office property at the end of a five-year holding period is shown in Figure 5–2. The new present value is a positive $8,217, indicating that the true internal rate of return that will be earned is greater than the investor's required 9 percent rate of return.

Figure 5–2 also computes a "profitability index" for the ABC office property. The profitability index is the present value of the aftertax cash flows divided by the initial equity investment. An index of 1.0 or

FIGURE 5–2
Net present value and profitability index,
ABC office property

Net present value:

Aftertax cash flow		PV of $1 at 9 percent		
$10,887	×	0.9174	=	$ 9,958
10,805	×	0.8417	=	9,094
10,715	×	0.7722	=	8,274
10,615	×	0.7084	=	7,519
10,504	×	0.6499	=	6,826
93,085	×	0.6499	=	60,496

Value of equity $102,167
  Less: Initial equity 93,950

Net present value.................. $ 8,217

Profitability index:

$$\frac{\text{Value of equity at 9\%}}{\text{Initial equity}} = \frac{\$102,167}{\$93,950} = 1.087$$

greater indicates that the investment will yield the required 9 percent return. In comparing alternative investments of the same risk, the property having the greatest net present value or the highest profitability index would be chosen.

INVESTMENT CRITERIA

In addition to calculating an absolute dollar investment value or net present value, an investor may find it desirable to determine the attractiveness of the investment by analyzing a number of ratios and by assuming a seller's required minimum price. These ratios can be grouped into three categories—multipliers, financial ratios, and profitability ratios. The ratios are calculated using the data from our ABC office property for which an investment value was calculated previously. The calculations assume the following facts:

Purchase price (at market value)	$375,800
Mortgage	281,850
Equity	$ 93,950
Gross income	65,790
Less: Vacancy and collection loss	3,290
Less: Operating expenses (less replacement reserve)	20,000
Net income	$ 42,500
Mortgage payment	29,681
Cash throw-off..................................	$ 12,819

Multipliers

Two kinds of multipliers can be used. The net income multiplier is not often used since its reciprocal, the capitalization rate, is commonly employed in real estate analysis. The gross income multiplier is used more frequently; however, it must be used with great care. To compare gross income multipliers, the properties should be traded in the same market and should be equivalent in expense patterns, risk, location, physical attributes, time, and terms of sale.

$$\begin{matrix} \text{Gross income} \\ \text{multiplier (GIM)} \end{matrix} = \frac{\text{Value or price}}{\text{Gross income}} = \frac{\$375{,}800}{\$65{,}790} = 5.71$$

$$\text{Net income multiplier} = \frac{\text{Value or price}}{\text{Net income}} = \frac{\$375{,}800}{\$42{,}500} = 8.84$$

The multipliers can be used to obtain a quick estimate as to whether a property is priced reasonably in relation to its gross or net income. The gross income multiplier is usually regarded as less relevant for larger, more complex properties, as their expense levels may vary greatly. However, one recent study showed that the use of the GIM produces value estimates almost as accurate as those produced by more sophisticated techniques.[3] If expense patterns among a class of properties vary significantly, however, use of the GIM as other than a rough guide to value is hazardous.

The multipliers are within the realm of reasonable expectation for an apartment property. While multipliers vary greatly, the range for annual gross income multipliers is normally between 4 and 10. Net income multipliers for apartment properties usually range between 5 and 12. Appropriate multipliers for a specific property would be estimated from actual transactions of comparable properties in the same market area.

Financial ratios

These ratios deal with the income-producing capacity of the property to meet operating and financial obligations.

$$\text{Operating ratio} = \frac{\text{Operating expenses}}{\text{Gross income}} = \frac{\$20{,}000}{\$65{,}790} = 30.4\%$$

$$\begin{matrix} \text{Break-even} \\ \text{cash throw-off} \end{matrix} = \frac{\begin{matrix}\text{Operating expenses} \\ + \text{ Mortgage payment}\end{matrix}}{\text{Gross income}} = \frac{\$49{,}681}{\$65{,}790} = 77.51\%$$

---

[3] Richard U. Ratcliff, "Don't Underrate the Gross Income Multiplier," *Appraisal Journal* 39, no. 2 (April 1971): 264–71.

$$\text{Loan to value ratio} = \frac{\text{Loan}}{\text{Price or value}} = \frac{\$281,850}{\$375,800} = 75.0\%$$

$$\text{Debt service coverage} = \frac{\text{Net income}}{\text{Mortgage payment}} = \frac{\$42,500}{\$29,681} = 1.43$$

The investment analysis should compute the operating and break-even cash throw-off ratios for all properties that will require the investor to incur operating expenses and financing charges. A relatively efficient property will exhibit a low operating ratio. Operating ratios are affected significantly by lease terms which require tenants to pay all or a portion of utilities or the property tax. Similarly, the break-even cash throw-off ratio provides an indication of the magnitude of all cash charges relative to gross income. The margin of safety between cash inflows and cash outflows is the difference between 100 percent and the break-even cash throw-off ratio. For the ABC property both ratios are reasonable. Operating ratios typically range from 25 to 50 percent, while the break-even cash throw-off ratio typically varies between 60 and 80 percent.

The loan to value ratio and the debt service coverage ratio are measures of the financial risk associated with the investment and should be computed for every investment using borrowed funds. The loan to value ratio on a newly financed property normally runs from 60 to 90 percent, while the debt service coverage ratio should normally be at least 1.3.[4] Legal requirements are usually imposed on the maximum loan to value ratios that institutional lenders can incur; the debt service coverage ratio provides an indication of safety from legal default in the event revenues fall and the mortgage payment is in jeopardy.

Profitability ratios

The ultimate determination of an investment's desirability is its capacity to produce income in relation to the capital required to obtain that income. Measures of relationship between income and capital for investment properties result in the following ratios:

$$\text{Payback period} = \frac{\text{Equity capital}}{\text{Cash throw-off}} = \frac{\$93,950}{\$12,819} = 7.3 \text{ years} \qquad (1)$$

$$\begin{array}{l}\text{Equity dividend rate} \\ \text{(before-tax return} \\ \text{on equity)} \end{array} = \frac{\text{Cash throw-off}}{\text{Equity}} = \frac{\$12,819}{\$93,950} = 13.64\% \qquad (2)$$

---

[4] When borrowers obtain loans of 100 percent of value or price paid, they are said to have "mortgaged out." A loan in excess of 100 percent produces a "windfall."

$$\text{Overall rate} = \frac{\text{Net income}}{\text{Total investment}} = \frac{\$42,500}{\$375,800} = 11.31\% \qquad (3)$$

Aftertax dividend rate
$$\begin{matrix}\text{(aftertax return} \\ \text{on equity)}\end{matrix} = \frac{\text{Aftertax cash flow}}{\text{Equity}} = \frac{\$10,887}{\$93,950} = 11.59\% \quad (4)$$

Calculation of tax and aftertax cash flow:

Net income		$42,500
Less: Mortgage interest (monthly payments)	$28,114	
Less: Tax depreciation (0.033 straight-line rate,		
30 years × $315,800 improvements)	10,522	38,636
Taxable income		$ 3,864
Net income		$42,500
Less: Debt service	$29,681	
Less: Tax (50% marginal tax rate × $3,864)	1,932	31,613
Aftertax cash flow		$10,887

Gross yield on equity
$$= \frac{\text{Aftertax cash flow} + \text{Mortgage principal repayment}}{\text{Equity}} \qquad (5)$$
$$= \frac{\$10,887 + \$1,567}{\$93,950} = \frac{\$12,454}{\$93,950} = 13.25\%$$

Average aftertax return on equity

$$= \frac{\begin{matrix}\text{Sum of aftertax} \\ \text{cash flows over} \\ \text{investment} \\ \text{holding period}\end{matrix} + \begin{matrix}\text{Aftertax cash} \\ \text{reversion at end} \\ \text{of holding period}\end{matrix} - \begin{matrix}\text{Equity} \\ \text{invest-} \\ \text{ment}\end{matrix}}{\text{Number of years in holding period}} \qquad (6)$$
$$\div \text{ Equity investment}$$

Example

Sum of aftertax cash flows:*

Year 1	$ 10,887
Year 2	10,805
Year 3	10,715
Year 4	10,615
Year 5	10,504
Total	$ 53,526
Aftertax cash reversion (year 5) . . .	93,085
Total aftertax income to equity . . .	$146,611
Less: Equity investment	93,950
Return on equity investment	$ 52,661

$$\frac{\$52,661}{3 \text{ years}} \div \$93,950 \text{ equity} = \frac{\$10,532}{\$93,950} = 11.21\%$$

* Figure 5–1.

While most investors do not usually calculate all six of the above ratios in evaluating an investment, they are useful indexes of a project's profitability for a given year. We recommend that when the necessary data are available, at least five of the six ratios be calculated—and preferably for each of several years. The payback period is less important, since it is the reciprocal measure of the equity dividend rate. It also has the theoretical weakness, of course, of not discounting future years' earnings.

The equity dividend rate shows investors what percentage of their equity investment will be returned to them in cash before income taxes for one year. The amount of mortgage repayment is deducted in arriving at cash throw-off. Thus, if mortgage principal repayment approximates actual depreciation the ratio is a good approximation of the true before-tax yield, on equity. The aftertax equity dividend rate provides a comparable yield on an aftertax basis, while the gross yield adds back the mortgage principal repayment. The latter ratio would be a more accurate aftertax yield *if* the property were believed not to be depreciating in value.

The overall capitalization rate measures the profitability of the entire property. It is produced by both the equity and debt portions of the investment and thus falls between the mortgage interest rate and the equity dividend rate. This ratio (computed using net operating income) is often used by appraisers in estimating the market value of an entire property—not just the equity portion.

The average aftertax return on equity provides a single measure of profitability that recognizes aftertax cash flow over an assumed investment holding period, as well as the aftertax cash reversion at the end of the holding period.[5] The average rate of return, of course, does not utilize the time value of money. Two properties, each of which generates the same total aftertax income over an investment holding period, could have an identical average return on equity even though the income from one property is concentrated early in the holding period, while the investor has to wait until the other property is sold to obtain the bulk of its total income. This absence of discounting future years' earnings can be partially overcome by using the payback period in conjunction with the average return on equity. The payback period reveals the pattern of the future income stream; the average rate of return measures the magnitude of future income relative to the investment required to produce it.

---

[5] A variety of average return calculations are possible. The average return on equity can be computed by using before-tax cash throw-off over the holding period; by using before-tax cash throw-off plus equity buildup resulting from paydown of the mortgage over the holding period; and by using only aftertax cash flow.

It should be recognized that each of these ratios has been calculated for one year only. The changing mortgage balance, depreciation, and income tax would cause some of the ratios to change each year. It is often advisable to calculate the ratios for each of several years, as demonstrated in Figure 5–4 and in Appendix C.

Internal rate of return. The internal rate of return is defined as the interest rate which discounts a stream of future earnings equal to the cost of the investment outlay. To compute an internal rate of return, the following data must be known or projected: equity investment outlay, aftertax cash flow, holding period, and selling price of the property at the end of the holding period. The calculations in Figure 5–3 produce an internal rate of return for the ABC office property over a holding period of five years. It is assumed that the property can be sold for the price paid, or $375,800.

The internal rate of return differs from previous measures of profitability in that it discounts the stream of earnings to be obtained over several future years. The internal rate of return is the most defensible of all profitability ratios. Unfortunately, it has not received widespread use among real estate investors. We recommend the internal rate of return measure of profitability whenever adequate data are available and the necessary predictions about the holding period and selling price can be made realistically.

VARYING THE ASSUMPTIONS

Estimates of gross income and operating expenses are presumably based upon market experiences of comparable properties (as well as the subject property), but market conditions cause variations over the holding period. The assumptions involved in calculating mortgage payments and income taxes also may be variable. These *investment expenses* are usually dependent upon the investor's financial position and capacity, not just the project or property being considered for purchase. Furthermore, given a certain financial capacity, loan terms and depreciation expenses may be variable within limits. For example, investors may have the option of obtaining a 70 percent, 25-year, 10 percent face rate loan or a 75 percent, 20-year, 11 percent face rate loan. They may be able to calculate depreciation for tax purposes over 25, 30, or 40 years or to use accelerated methods.

Role of computers

Differences among the variable assumptions will cause the value of the investor's equity position to change. Or, given a certain price or

FIGURE 5–3
Internal rate of return

	Year				
	1	2	3	4	5
Net income (NOI + replacement reserve)	$42,500	$42,500	$42,500	$42,500	$42,500
Less: Interest	28,114	27,950	27,769	27,569	27,569
Less: Depreciation (straight-line, 30 years)	10,522	10,522	10,522	10,522	10,522
Taxable income	$ 3,863	$ 4,028	$ 4,209	$ 4,409	$ 4,630
Net income	$42,500	$42,500	$42,500	$42,500	$42,500
Less: Mortgage payment	29,681	29,681	29,681	29,681	29,681
Less: Taxes (50%)	1,932	2,014	2,104	2,205	2,315
Aftertax cash flow	$10,887	$10,805	$10,715	$10,615	$10,504

Sale price	$375,800
Less: Outstanding mortgage balance	272,192
Equity	$103,608
Less: Capital gain tax	10,522*
Aftertax cash reversion	$ 93,086

* Calculated as follows:

Original basis	$375,800
Less: Accumulated depreciation	52,612
Adjusted basis	$323,188
Sale price	$375,800
Less: Adjusted basis	323,188
Capital gain	$ 52,612
Capital gain tax rate	×0.20
Capital gain tax	$ 10,522

Solution:

$$\$93,950 \text{ equity} = \frac{\$10,887}{(1+r)^1} + \frac{\$10,805}{(1+r)^2} + \frac{\$10,715}{(1+r)^3} + \frac{\$10,615}{(1+r)^4}$$
$$+ \frac{\$10,504}{(1+r)^5} + \frac{\$93,085}{(1+r)^5}$$

12%	11%		ATCF		12%	11%	
$ 9,720	$ 9,808	=	$10,887	×	0.8928	0.9009	(PV of 1, 1 year)
8,613	9,475	=	10,805	×	0.7972	0.8116	(PV of 1, 2 years)
7,627	7,835	=	10,715	×	0.7118	0.7312	(PV of 1, 3 years)
6,746	6,972	=	10,615	×	0.6355	0.6587	(PV of 1, 4 years)
5,960	6,233	=	10,504	×	0.5674	0.5934	(PV of 1, 5 years)
53,255	55,664	=	93,805	×	0.5674	0.5934	(PV of 1, 5 years)
$91,891	$96,007	≈	almost 11.3%				

r = Aftertax internal rate of return.
  = Approximately 11.3% (11.27%).

cost to obtain a property, the rate of return on the investor's equity will change with differing loan terms or tax requirements. When considering a proposed investment, investors (or their advisers) should usually calculate several equity values or rates of return, using different assumptions about items such as loan terms and taxes. It is normally desirable to project the calculations over several years, so that the expected rate of return can be seen separately each year.

Although investment values and rates of return can be determined by hand calculation, the computations are greatly facilitated by the use of electronic computers, especially when a variety of inputs are considered for each of several years. Among the inputs that might be varied, in addition to loan terms and income taxes, are gross income, expected vacancy rate, type of depreciation expense (straight-line, declining balance, and so on), and individual expense items such as real estate taxes or maintenance expense. The estimated remaining economic life or expected holding period and the expected selling price of the property at the end of the holding period (reversion value) can also be varied. Investors or investment counselors can then see return rates (or investment values, given capitalization rates) within a range of most favorable to least favorable expected experiences.

A large firm may have its own computer and investment analysis programs. Medium- and smaller-sized firms can more efficiently either (*a*) utilize their own programs on a time-sharing computer service or (*b*) subscribe to a computerized investment analysis service. Perhaps the most widely used of the latter type of arrangement is provided by Realtron Corporation. Realtron offers an investment analysis service to subscribers who pay a monthly fee. The subscriber telephones the input data to a central computer and recieves the output back within a few minutes. Some investment analysis computer programs, such as those developed by the Educational Foundation for Computer Applications in Real Estate (EDUCARE), a number of universities, and some business firms, are more complex and provide greater sophistication in their output analyses. They require more input data and compute a greater variety of ratios and return rates, while allowing more variables in the input data.

A computer-assisted investment analysis called REALVAL is shown in Figure 5–4 for our ABC office property.[6] Figure 5–5 provides the input forms and definitions for the program. Much of the output shown in Figure 5–4 has already been explained in this chapter. The reinvestment rate of return and the marginal rate of return have not been

---

[6] Jeffrey Fisher, *Computer-Assisted Investment Analysis and Valuation of Income Property*, Research Report no. 6, (Columbus: Center for Real Estate Education and Research, Ohio State University, 1979).

FIGURE 5-4

REALVAL pro forma operating period cash flows

	YEAR	1	2	3	4	5
POTENTIAL GROSS INCOME		65790	65790	65790	65790	65790
VACANCY AND COLLECTION		-3290	-3290	-3290	-3290	-3290
EFFECTIVE GROSS INCOME		62501	62501	62501	62501	62501
EXPENSES		-20000	-20000	-20000	-20000	-20000
NET OPER. INCOME		42500	42500	42500	42500	42500
DEBT SERVICE		-29681	-29681	-29681	-29681	-29681
LAND LEASE		0	0	0	0	0
PARTICIPATIONS		0	0	0	0	0
B.T. CASH FLOW		12819	12819	12819	12819	12819
NET OPER. INCOME		42500	42500	42500	42500	42500
LAND LEASE		0	0	0	0	0
PARTICIPATIONS		0	0	0	0	0
INTEREST		-28114	-27950	-27769	-27569	-27348
DEPRECIATION		-10522	-10522	-10522	-10522	-10522
AMORTIZED EXP.		0	0	0	0	0
TAXABLE INCOME		3863	4028	4209	4409	4630
FEDERAL INCOME TAX		-1932	-2014	-2104	-2205	-2315
B.T. CASH FLOW		12819	12819	12819	12819	12819
FEDERAL INCOME TAX		-1932	-2014	-2104	-2205	-2315
AFTER TAX CASH FLOW		10887	10805	10715	10615	10504
NPV AFTER TAX		1738	3442	5102	6708	8253
PROFITABILITY INDEX		1.017	1.035	1.053	1.070	1.086
MORTGAGE BALANCE		280283	278552	276639	274527	272192
DEBT COVERAGE RATIO		1.43	1.43	1.43	1.43	1.43
LOAN/ORIG. VALUE		0.75	0.74	0.74	0.73	0.72
LOAN/CURR. VALUE		0.75	0.74	0.74	0.73	0.72
LENDERS YIELD		10.00	10.00	10.00	10.00	10.00
BREAKEVEN RATIO		0.76	0.76	0.76	0.76	0.76
B.T.C.F./EQUITY		13.64	13.64	13.64	13.64	13.64
A.T.C.F./EQUITY		11.59	11.50	11.40	11.30	11.18
ESTIMATED SELLING PRICE		375800	375800	375800	375800	375800
B.T. IRR ON EQUITY		15.32	15.28	15.24	15.20	15.17
A.T. IRR ON EQUITY		11.02	11.09	11.16	11.22	11.27
REINV. RATE OF RETURN		9.20	9.39	9.58	9.75	9.92
MARG. RATE OF RETURN		0.0	11.17	11.31	11.44	11.56

PURCHASE PRICE IS $375800.0

REVERSION AT END OF 5 YEAR HOLDING PERIOD

SELLING PRICE		375800.
SELLING COSTS		0.
MORTGAGE BALANCE		272192.
BEFORE CASH FLOW		103608.
SELLING PRICE		375800.
SELLING COSTS		0.
COST BASIS	375800.	
ACCUM. DEPREC.	52612.	
AMORTIZED EXP.	0.	
ADJ. BASIS		323188.
TOTAL GAIN		52612.
ACCUM. DEPREC.	52612.	
ST. LINE	52612.	
RECAP. CREDIT	0.	
ORDINARY INCOME		0.
CAPITAL GAIN		52612.
ORD. INCOME	0.	
TAX RATE	0.5000	
ORDINARY INCOME TAX		0.
CAPITAL GAIN	52612.	
TAX RATE	0.2000	
CAPITAL GAIN TAX		10522.
AFTER TAX CASH FLOW		93085.

FIGURE 5–5
REALVAL data input

Project identification (60 alphanumeric characters):	ABC Office Property
20 Purchase price	$375,800
21 Land/value (decimal)	0.16
22 Initial rent before vacancy	$ 65,790
23 Operating expense ratio	0.32*
24 Initial vacancy (decimal)	
25 Rent-up rate per quarter	
26 Normal vacancy (decimal)	0.05
Financing information	
30 First mortgage ($ or decimal)	0.75
31 Interest rate	0.10
32 Loan term	0.30
33 Points (decimal)	—
34 Years interest only	—
35 Second mortgage ($ or decimal)	
36 Interest rate	
37 Loan term	
38 Points (decimal)	
39 Years interest only	
Investment horizon	
40 Holding period	5.
41 Printout for (maximum 60) years	10.
Tax information	
42 Initial ordinary income tax rate	0.50
43 Revised tax rate	
44 Starting in year	
45 Capital gains tax rate	0.20
Discount and reinvestment rates	
46 Required equity yield	0.09
47 Reinvestment rate	0.09
Growth rates	
50 Initial income growth rate	
51 Revised income growth rate	
52 Starting in year	
53 Revised income growth rate	
54 Starting in year	

* Percent of potential gross income (rent).

FIGURE 5–5 (continued)

55 Initial property value growth rate ⎯⎯⎯⎯

56 Revised property value growth rate ⎯⎯⎯⎯

57 Starting in year ⎯⎯⎯⎯

58 Revised property value growth rate ⎯⎯⎯⎯

59 Starting in year ⎯⎯⎯⎯

60 Selling commissions (decimal) ⎯⎯⎯⎯

Tax depreciation

Depreciation basis ($ or decimal of total)		Depreciable life		Rate	
61	1.00	62	30.	63	1.
64		65		66	
67		68		69	
70		71		72	
73		74		75	

Show rate as decimal of straight-line, i.e., 1.0 for straight-line, 1.5 for 150% declining balance, and 2.0 for double-declining balance. A 3.0 indicates sum-of-the-years' digits.

Additional financing alternatives

90 Price of land for sale-leaseback to lender ⎯⎯⎯⎯

91 Land lease payments ($ or decimal of land price) ⎯⎯⎯⎯

92 Growth rate for lease payments ⎯⎯⎯⎯

93 Participation type: (1) Effective gross income ⎯⎯⎯⎯

  (2) Net operating income ⎯⎯⎯⎯

  (3) Cash flow before tax and participation ⎯⎯⎯⎯

94 Initial participation (decimal) ⎯⎯⎯⎯

95 Incremental participation (decimal) ⎯⎯⎯⎯

96 Starting at (base $) ⎯⎯⎯⎯

97 Incremental participation ⎯⎯⎯⎯

98 Starting at (base $) ⎯⎯⎯⎯

99 Mortgage prepayment penalty (% of mortgage balance) ⎯⎯⎯⎯

REALVAL input requirements: Existing property

Purchase price (20)

The purchase price must be specified for an investment analysis but can be left blank for an appraisal. In the case of an appraisal, the model searches for the price or value which provides the investor a specified equity yield.

Land/value (21)

This input is necessary for any aftertax analysis since it determines the depreciable basis of the property.

Initial rent before vacancy (22)

FIGURE 5–5 (*continued*)

This variable is the potential gross income. If the analyst chooses to ignore the rental growth rate options (variables 50–54), this will normally be an average or stabilized rent for the holding period.

Operating expense ratio (23)

This input will be total operating expenses as a percentage of effective gross income.

Initial vacancy (24)

If the user desires to have a higher than normal vacancy when the project is first purchased or construction completed, the initial vacancy would be specified in variable 24. If left blank, initial vacancy will be the same as the normal vacancy specified in variable 26.

Rent-up rate per quarter (25)

This variable will determine how soon normal vacancy is reached. That is, normal vacancy will be reached after a number of quarters equal to the difference between variables 24 and 26 divided by variable 25.

Normal vacancy (26)

This input will be the vacancy after the rent-up period described above.

First mortgage (30)

The amount of the first mortgage (if any) can be specified either in dollars or as a percentage of the purchase price. In an appraisal, the analyst would typically specify a typical loan/value so that financing is a function of the value estimate.

Interest rate (31)

The annual interest rate should be specified. The model assumes monthly payments, however.

Loan term (32)

The variable should be the loan term in years, including any interest-only year.

Points (33)

Points are specified as a percentage of the mortgage. The investor will receive net financing equal to the mortgage amount (variable 30) less the points. Payments, however, are based on the mortgage amount (variable 30).

Years interest only (34)

This input will be the number of years that only interest is paid. Amortization doesn't start until after the interest-only period. The mortgage balance will, of course, not decrease during this period.

Second mortgage (35–39)

The second mortgage is entered in the same manner as the first mortgage.

Holding period (40)

This variable is used in two different ways. First, the details of all reversion calculations are printed for this year, including selling commission and tax information. Second, for an appraisal, the model searches for the value estimate which results in the specified rate of return for this holding period. The specified holding period can be the economic life of the property.

FIGURE 5–5 (continued)

Printout years (41)

The model computes certain return measures assuming a hypothetical sale in each year up to that specified in variable 41. In other words, all reversionary calculations printed out for the holding period (variable 40) are actually made for every year. This is useful in determining the optimal holding period. Thus, all annual calculations and returns are calculated for all years up to and including that specified in variable 41. Variable 41 should never be specified to be less than the holding period specified in variable 40. If so, the model will assume variable 41 equal to variable 40.

Initial tax rate (42)

For aftertax investment analysis or valuation, the initial ordinary income tax rate is specified. It will normally be the investor's marginal tax rate.

Revised tax rate (43)

The tax rate can be changed after a specified number of years by putting the new rate in variable 43 and the year of change in variable 44.

Capital gains tax rate (45)

For aftertax investment analysis or valuation, the tax rate applicable to capital gains is specified here.

Required equity yield (46)

This variable is used in two different ways. First, it is used in finding the investor's net present value (NPV). Second, for an appraisal, the model searches for the value that gives this equity yield for the specified holding period. If no financing was entered, this will be a return for the entire property; if financing is presumed, it is the return on equity. If tax rates are entered, it is an aftertax return.

Reinvestment rate (47)

One of the returns computed by the model explicitly assumes the investor reinvests his annual cash flows. This is the rate at which his reinvested cash flows are assumed to compound.

Income growth rates (50–54)

These variables allow the analyst to explicitly specify the income pattern by allowing for three different growth rates (positive or negative).

Property value growth rates (55–59)

Three different patterns for property value growth and/or decline can be assumed.

Selling commissions (60)

These are brokerage and other costs of making the sale and are assumed to be tax deductible. They are specified as a percentage of the sale price.

Tax depreciation inputs (61–75)

Up to five different components can be depreciated at once, or one rate can be applied to the entire depreciable basis. The depreciable basis can be specified either in dollars or as a percentage of the total depreciable basis. When dollars are specified, the total should equal the purchase price less the land value.

When the input is a decimal, the component will be a percentage of the depreciable basis (purchase price less land cost as specified by land/value in variable 21). For example, a "1" in component one will automatically cause the entire depreciable basis to be depreciated by the rate and years specified in variables 62 and 63.

The depreciable life will normally be the minimum allowed for tax purposes.

FIGURE 5–5 (concluded)

The "rate" is expressed as a multiple of straight-line. That is, a "1" indicates straight-line depreciation. A "2" indicates double-declining balance; "1.5" indicates 150 percent declining balance; and so on. A "3" is a special input that indicates sum-of-the-years'-digits depreciation.

Price of land for sale-leaseback (90)

If the land is to be sold, and leased back simultaneously with the purchase of the property, the price of the land is specified here. The purchase price of the property (20) must include the land. The selling price will be adjusted for the sale-leaseback. It is assumed that the lender purchases the land, and his yield is affected accordingly.

Land lease payments (91)

The payments for a sale-leaseback can be specified either in dollars or as a percentage of the price specified in variable 90.

Growth rate for lease payments (92)

If the payments specified in variable 91 are to escalate each year, the rate is specified here.

Participation type (93)

The lender may receive a participation based on a percentage of effective gross income, net operating income, or cash flow before tax and before participation.

Initial participation (94)

This is the percentage of EGI or NOI for the initial participation.

Revised participations (95–98)

The percentage participation can be changed twice as specified in these variables.

Mortgage prepayment penalty (99)

Specification of a prepayment penalty effectively results in a cash flow greater than the mortgage balance going to the lender at reversion. The investor, of course, receives less cash flow. This input item can also be used to give the lender a "participation" in reversion cash flows.

discussed previously. The reinvestment rate of return is an aftertax internal rate of return that assumes the annual recapture of investment is reinvested at some rate other than the equity yield rate, in this instance, at 9 percent. The marginal rate of return is the return earned by holding the property one additional year. The marginal rate of return decreases when loss of tax shelter dominates increases in before-tax cash flows and any increase in property value. The marginal rate of return may be a determinant of the investment holding period, with the investor considering the sale of the property at the time the marginal rate of return falls below the required rate of return on equity.

Figure 5–6 provides the results for selected performance measures given different assumptions regarding financing, rents, operating ex-

FIGURE 5-6
Sensitivity analysis, ABC office property

	Fifth-year performance					
	Equity dividend (BTCF/equity)*	ATCF/equity*	Aftertax IRR†	NPV‡	Profitability index‡	Debt coverage ratio
Base case: No change in rent or reversion value; 75% L/V, 10%, 30-year mortgage	13.64%	11.18%	11.27%	$ 8,253	1.086	1.43
1. Rent and operating expenses increase 5% per year	23.39	16.05	13.36	16,178	1.171	1.74
2. 75%, 10%, 30-year mortgage plus two points additional interest§	12.87	10.64	9.95	3,592	1.035	1.43
3. 80%, 10%, 30-year mortgage	14.42	12.56	12.83	11,154	1.147	1.34
4. 85%, 10%, 30-year mortgage	15.72	14.85	15.42	14,056	1.247	1.26
5. 75%, 11%, 30-year mortgage	10.95	10.03	9.80	2,896	1.030	1.32
6. 75%, 12%, 30-year mortgage	8.21	8.83	8.31	-2,495	0.973	1.22
7. 75%, 10%, 25-year mortgage	12.52	9.75	11.16	8,023	1.083	1.38
8. 75%, 10%, 30-year mortgage and a 10% L/V, 12%, 10-year second mortgage	11.26	9,93	14.34	12,412	1.215	1.18

* One year's before-tax or aftertax cash flow divided by equity.
† Aftertax cash flow and aftertax cash reversion over holding period.
‡ Uses 9 percent as investor's required rate of return.
§ Lender's yield increases to 10.52 percent.

penses, and reversion value. The computer allows the analyst to perform such sensitivity analysis by varying only one variable or by altering a number of variables simultaneously. Further, simulation can be accomplished with REALVAL and other computer-assisted investment programs by permitting variables to change simultaneously over a prescribed range. This is accomplished by assigning probabilities to expected values of the variable. Thus, probabilities may be assigned to a range of future rents which varies from a potential decrease of 2 percent per year to an increase of 5 percent annually. REALVAL requires only that the analyst assess the lowest value believed plausible, (a 2 percent decrease), the most probable value (stable), and the highest plausible value (a 5 percent increase). Using Monte Carlo simulation, the computer then arrays a frequency distribution of aftertax rates of return of property value.

A case example projecting various rates of return under different sets of assumptions is presented in Appendix C, Queens Gate Apartments.[7] An investor's rates of return under three sets of assumptions are projected for the first year. The most logical and defensible of the three investment structures is then calculated for each of ten years—a normal holding period for such an investment.

MOTIVATION OF INVESTORS

A survey of apartment investors by the U.S. Department of Housing and Urban Development shows that cash flow is the most important criterion considered by all types of investors.[8] Individuals ranked tax shelter as the second most important motive, while real estate groups and investment trusts ranked this consideration third in importance.

Other important reasons for investing were financial leverage, capital appreciation, and low risk. Location, demand for housing, the housing supply, and mortgage financing opportunities influenced active investors, while passive investors rated location and builder reputation high among nonfinancial criteria for investment.

With respect to earnings, over two thirds of the active investors spoke in terms of the average annual rate of return. Thirteen percent used total dollar return, and 11 percent used payback period. Only 4 percent used the discounted rate of return, which gives less weight to earnings in future years and more weight to early earnings. This result

---

[7] Although some of the concepts used in the case are not covered until Chapters 13 and 17, Appendix C should be studied in conjunction with this chapter as well as Chapters 13 and 17.

[8] Arnold H. Diamond, "Tax Considerations Affecting Multi-Family Housing Investments" (paper presented at the Annual Meeting of American Real Estate and Urban Economics Association, New Orleans, Louisiana, December 28, 1971).

is surprising in view of the emphasis given to present value concepts in real estate and financial investment courses.

About one third of the apartment investors believed that apartments yielded more tax shelter than other real estate investments; 25 percent thought apartments yield a higher return; and 20 percent believed apartments provided a better hedge against inflation than other real estate investments.

A previous study by Ricks showed that equity investors and other participants in the real estate investment process regard the rate of return on equity investment as the most important measure of profitability and the rate of return on cost as the second most important measure.[9] The after-financing, before-tax return on equity was listed as the most important decision guide. Second and third in importance were the before-financing, before-tax return and the after-financing, aftertax return.

Among the factors considered in making a decision to commit funds to a real estate investment, Ricks found that investors and other participants regarded market value appreciation, safety of investment funds, and a high rate of return on equity as first, second, and third in importance. Loan terms were generally more important than characteristics of the property in decisions to commit funds.

SUMMARY

The valuation process, as described in Chapter 4, may be regarded as phase 1 of the investment calculation. Phase 2, discussed in this chapter, extends phase 1 to include personal or business expenses which would be incurred with an investment, but which are omitted in the valuation process. Income taxes and financing charges are the two most important investment-related expenses which are often not directly associated with real estate for valuation purposes.

Phase 2 may also involve a different discount rate from the rate which is appropriate in estimating market value. The market rate includes risk levels applicable to the average or typical buyer; any individual investor's risk situation or return requirements may justify a higher or lower discount rate. Financial risk, to the extent that it is greater or less than the normal market level, is also reflected in the investor's discount rate.

Assumptions about financing terms, depreciation expense, and in-

---

[9] R. Bruce Ricks, *Real Estate Investment Process, Investment Performance, and Federal Tax Policy*, Report of the Real Estate Investment Project for the U.S. Treasury Department (Los Angeles: University of California Press, 1969).

come taxes can be varied; investment value and rates of return can be calculated under several different combinations of assumptions. The calculations can be carried out for several years to show trends. Electronic computers greatly aid the calculation process and are a necessity if several investments are to be analyzed.

Other investment criteria, in addition to investment value, include multipliers, financial ratios, and profitability ratios. Given a selling price, a limited holding period, and an aftertax cash flow, an internal rate of return can be computed for an equity investment.

Finally, we have noted some attitudes that investors claim to hold with respect to investment criteria. Cash flow and tax shelter are the two most important factors. Rate of return on equity is the most important profitability measure, while little attention seems to be paid to discounting processes that weigh future earnings less heavily than immediate earnings.

QUESTIONS FOR REVIEW

1. Why might an investor be willing to pay more for a property than its market value?
2. Why might an investor not be willing to pay as much as market value for a property?
3. Why might an investor not be willing to purchase a property at any price?
4. What is *financial risk?* How is it accounted for in investment analysis?
5. What is *business risk?* How is it accounted for in investment analysis?
6. How do you explain the results of investor surveys which show that little reliance is placed upon discounted cash flows in evaluating investments?
7. Do you believe that the Queens Gate Apartments case contained in Appendix C describes a realistic investment situation? Why or why not? What types of investment calculations are presented in the case?
8. What is a *tax shelter?* Would you purchase a parcel of real estate to obtain a tax shelter? Why or why not?
9. Distinguish between depreciation for tax purposes and capital recovery for valuation or investment analysis purposes.
10. What is *profitability?* Upon which profitability ratios would you place primary reliance in evaluating an investment?
11. What is an *internal rate of return?*
12. What is *investment value?* How does it differ from market value?
13. Why is the face value of the mortgage loan added to the value of the equity benefits in arriving at investment value?
14. What is net present value? How is net present value similar to investment value? How is it related to the profitability index?

PROBLEMS

1. An investment is expected to produce $10,000 per year to perpetuity. If a 12 percent annual rate of return is required, how much is the investment worth?

2. If the life of the investment in problem 1 were expected to be 20 years, how much would the investment be worth?

3. A purchaser paid $80,000 for an investment property. How much annual income must the property produce to yield an 11 percent rate of return?

4. A couple purchase a home and obtain a $60,000 mortgage loan at 12 percent for 25 years to finance the deal. How much would their total mortgage payments be, including both principal and interest (annual debt service), if payments are made annually? If payments are made monthly?

5. In problem 4, how much of the first year's payment would be interest? How much interest would be paid in the second and third years? Approximately how much total interest would be paid over the 25 years? What would be the *average* amount of annual interest paid?

6. Look in a Federal Tax Rate Schedule, and determine the tax liability of a married taxpayer having a $20,000 taxable income, filing a joint return, and having one dependent. What amount of tax would the same individual pay in the succeeding year if the income were increased to $25,000? How much is the difference in tax on the two amounts (or the incremental tax)?

7. A property produces $10,000 annual NOI. The owner charges $2,000 per year depreciation and pays $5,000 in interest on an outstanding loan. The total annual debt service on the loan is $7,500. The owner is in the 34 percent tax bracket.
   a. How much is the cash throw-off?
   b. How much income tax must the owner pay on the income generated by the property?
   c. How much is the owner's aftertax cash flow?
   d. If the owner has $20,000 equity funds invested in the property, what is the equity dividend rate?

8. An individual has been willed a remainder estate in a parcel of land which allows her to obtain possession at the termination of a lease ten years from now. If the land is forecast to be worth $25,000 at that time, how much could the estate be sold for today to an investor demanding a 10 percent rate of return?

9. A property is expected to generate NOI of $10,000. Debt service will amount to $6,000 per year. If the investor contributes $25,000 in equity, how long is the payback period?

10. Calculate the internal rate of return for an investment property which is expected to yield $30,000 per year NOI and which can be purchased for $225,000. The investor plans to sell the property after five years for $250,000. The investor will pay all cash, use straight-line depreciation, and is in the 40 percent tax bracket.

11. Calculate an investment value for projection 1 in the Queens Gate Apartments case (see Appendix C).

REFERENCES

Beaton, William R., and Robertson, Terry. *Real Estate Investment*. 2d ed. Englewood Cliffs, N.J.: Prentice-Hall, 1977.

Kelting, Herman. *Real Estate Investments*. Columbus: Grid, 1980.

Kinnard, William N. *Income Property Valuation*. Lexington, Mass.: D. C. Heath, 1971.

Seldin, Maury, and Swesnik, Richard H. *Real Estate Investment Strategy*. 2d ed. New York: Wiley-Interscience, 1979.

Smith, Halbert C. "Investment Analysis in Appraising." *Real Estate Appraiser* 32, no. 9 (September 1967): 19–25.

Wendt, Paul F., and Cerf, Alan R. *Real Estate Investment Analysis and Taxation*. 2d ed. New York: McGraw-Hill, 1979.

Wiley, Robert J. *Real Estate Investment*. New York: John Wiley and Sons, 1976.

chapter 6

Risk and return analysis

The typical goal of investors is to maximize their wealth position by making intelligent decisions based on risk-return analysis. Investors contribute a certain amount of assets to a business venture from which they expect to receive a return on their investment in addition to the eventual return of the investment. By committing the use of their assets to another party, the investors are taking the chance of losing some or all of their assets, or losing the opportunity to invest in another venture with more amenable expectations. In order to attract investor funds, the investment project must offer some sort of anticipated compensation in proportion to the amount of risk investors will be undertaking; the greater the risk, the greater the compensation must be. Otherwise, investors would always invest in low-risk projects only. The compensation for risk among different investment alternatives, which otherwise offer equal returns, changes investors' expected returns from each venture. The value of a project is dependent upon the anticipated returns. Therefore, it becomes extremely important to quantify and measure risk when valuing an investment project.

There are many different types of investments from which an investor may choose. The most common of these include stocks, bonds, and real estate. Each type of investment can be further classified by degree of risk and investment characteristics. Bonds, for example, are assigned a quality rating by a rating agency (usually Moody's Investors Service or Standard & Poor's Corporation). Vital statistics concerning stocks and bonds are published daily in many local newspapers as well as in financial publications. This information, along with advice from stockbrokers, enables investors to analyze effectively the quality of a particular stock in relation to other investments. Because investments of different types with similar risk and return characteristics are competitive, real estate can be a viable alternative investment to stocks and bonds. Unfortunately, there is a lack of information on real estate investments comparable to the information available for stocks and bonds. There is no major publication containing rates of return and selling prices for actual real estate transactions. Therefore, it is necessary that expected returns and risk be individually analyzed for each potential real estate investment project and compared to similar measurements in other capital markets. This procedure provides a common basis for comparative decision making.

The chapter examines the methods most commonly used to measure risk, and the more recent developments of risk analysis involving the capital asset pricing model of finance. This material contains a discussion of how measures of risk are included in the valuation of real estate.

Types of risk

The risk involved in any investment project stems from a variety of sources. However, a given type of risk does not necessarily apply to all types of investments. Some types of risk may be alleviated or eliminated. In order to know what must be done to mitigate losses, it is necessary to identify which categories of risk apply to each individual investment project.

Market risk. This type of risk is the result of downward market trends causing a loss in the market value. It is also known as systematic or nondiversifiable risk.

Business risk. Business risk refers to the uncertain projections of future operating income, and the potential for loss due to actual income that is lower than expected.

Financial risk. This is the risk of holding interest-bearing debt. The more heavily a firm is debt-financed, the more sensitive it is to financial risk.

Total corporate risk. Business risk plus financial risk comprise total corporate risk.

Interest rate risk. This risk applies directly only to those investing in bonds. It refers to a bond price change in reaction to interest rate changes on bonds.

Marketability risk. This is the risk that an asset cannot be sold quickly for an amount equal to or above its market value.

Liquidity risk. This is the risk that an asset cannot be sold quickly for an amount equal to or above the amount invested.

Default risk. This is the risk that principal and/or interest payments will not be made on time. It is the basis on which bond ratings are made.

Purchasing power risk. The value of certain assets may decline due to inflation and the decreasing purchasing power of the dollar. Fixed-income securities are very sensitive to purchasing power risk, while real estate, whose returns generally rise with inflation, is at least somewhat protected.

Political risk. This risk is the result of the unpredictable actions of any governmental unit on the federal, state, or local level. The most common types of regulations affecting land use include zoning ordinances, building codes, the various federal and state environmental acts, and the tax laws.

Real property values are affected by each of these types of risk. Real estate is extremely sensitive to financial risk because most real estate investments are highly leveraged (debt-financed). If operating income does not meet expectations, debt service payments may not be made on time. This leads to default risk on the part of the lender. Real estate is generally thought to be immune from purchasing power risk, but this theory does not always hold true. Each individual project reacts to the forces of inflation in a different manner.

Some risks, such as liquidity risk, default risk, and political risk, bear fairly obvious relationships to real estate. Arguments now being advanced assert that real property returns, and thus market values, are influenced by returns on alternative investments such as stocks and bonds. Therefore, the types of risks which influence the returns on these investments must also influence the returns on real estate. The precise relationships between real estate and investments in other capital markets are the topic of much current research.

Despite being subject to numerous types of risk, real estate projects can be advantageous as investments if risk and potential return analysis shows the projects to be feasible. Real estate ownership can be highly profitable. In addition, direct control over operating procedures and management is more easily exerted in most real estate investments than in the stock or bond market. This provides a more flexible tool with which an investor may work.

Risk evaluation of real estate projects has traditionally been imprecise and difficult to quantify. Due to the unique problems and characteristics of real estate ownership and the collection of real estate data, risk calculations are rather subjective. This problem occurs when individuals must assign probability distributions to the occurrence of certain events. The next section describes how probabilities can be used to express the relative riskiness of competing investments.

RISK EVALUATION

Probability distributions

A probability distribution defines the likelihood of a certain event's occurrence. A probability distribution includes designations for all possible events in one category. For example, economists may state that there is a 20 percent chance the economy will boom, a 60 percent chance it will remain normal, and a 20 percent chance it will slide into recession. Notice that the sum of the probabilities in a distribution must be 100 percent.

Outcomes may be linked to the occurrence of a certain event. Investors may expect different investment returns, depending on the state of the economy. Under a boom situation, they may predict a return of $5,000, while under normal conditions they will predict a return of $2,000, and during a recessionary period they will anticipate a loss of $1,000. This distribution is easily described in chart form.

State of economy	Probability	Outcome
Boom	.20	$5,000
Normal	.60	2,000
Recession	.20	(1,000)

However, future economic conditions may actually be much better, in between, or more severe than the three state possibilities indicate. Therefore, consideration of a myriad or unlimited number of possibilities is a more realistic approach. This situation is represented by a continuous probability distribution, which is usually presented in a graph (see Figure 6–1). The area under a probability curve represents

FIGURE 6–1
Continuous probability distribution

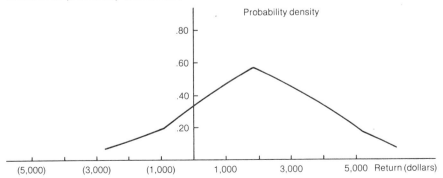

the probability of occurrence. Therefore, the probability that investors will earn exactly $2,000 is quite slim, while the probability that they will earn between $1,000 and $3,000 is considerably greater.

If an investor is considering more than one investment, data from probability distributions provide useful information for comparisons. Graphs of distributions may show that the outcomes tend to group in a central area. While the outcomes of two different investments may group around the same values, the dispersion around the central area may be quite dissimilar. Notice in Figure 6–2 that the returns for both

FIGURE 6–2
Graph of a risky project versus a less risky project

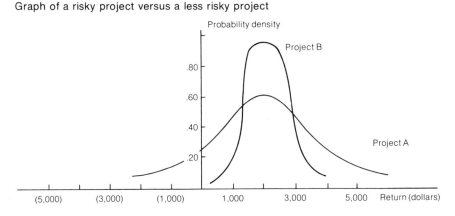

investment projects center on $2,000 but that the project A returns are more widely dispersed. The narrower the range of distributions around a central value, the less the chances are that the actual value will be outside this range. Project B is therefore less risky and should be chosen over project A. However, if Project A returns centered on $5,000 while project B returns centered on $2,000, the investor would have to choose between a riskier project with a good probability of earning a greater amount and a less risky project earning a lesser amount. This decision is based on investor preferences. If project B is chosen, the investor is said to be risk averse. But before a choice can be made, the investor must generate numerical data which can be used to assess the riskiness of all investment projects in comparison to each other. The characteristics of both central tendency and dispersion can be measured for normal distributions.[1]

---

[1] A normal distribution, sometimes referred to as a bell-shaped curve, is a unimodal curve symmetrical about the mean, and contains an infinite range of possibilities. The area beneath any normal curve equals 100 percent. See any good statistics book for a more complete description of the characteristics and properties of the normal curve.

Measurement of central tendency and dispersion

Risk in income-producing investments is essentially the margin of error present in the estimation of a project's net present value. Variance, a statistical term, is a measure of the volatility of the occurrence of each identified possible return or situation outcome. To demonstrate, consider the example of an investor considering the purchase of a 40-unit student apartment complex which currently yields rents of $280 per month for a two-bedroom apartment. The local university is examining the possibilities of increasing enrollment limitations. However, the size of the increase is still subject to much debate. The campus department of housing believes there is an 80 percent chance that the increase will be moderate, a 15 percent chance that the increase will be large, and a 5 percent chance that the increase will be extremely small. If the increase is moderate or large, area apartment complex owners can raise rents due to increased demand for student apartments. A moderate enrollment increase will result in rental rates of $310 per month, while a large increase will result in rates of $330 per month. In other words, three different states and outcomes could occur.

	State	Outcome	Probability of occurrence
I.	Small increase	$280/month	.05
II.	Moderate increase	$310/month	.80
III.	Large increase	$330/month	.15

The investor is considering alternative projects and wants to know which project will produce higher returns with the least amount of risk. An analysis of the apartment project follows.

A reconstructed operating statement for the project demonstrates the differences in net operating incomes (NOIs) for each of the possible outcomes.

	State I	State II	State III
Potential gross income (rent × 12 × 40)	$134,000	$148,800	$158,400
Less vacancy and collection losses (5%)	6,720	7,440	7,920
Effective gross income	$127,680	$141,360	$150,480
Less operating expenses	60,000	60,000	60,000
NOI	$ 67,680	$ 81,360	$ 90,480

A weighted average of these NOIs using the probabilities of occurrence as weights is defined as the *expected value* of the NOI. Expected value is a measurement of central tendency; it identifies the average value that would be reached if the experiment were repeated over and over. While this specific act may not be repeated, the expected value provides at least some indication of the risk involved.

$$E\,(\text{NOI}) = \sum_{i=1}^{N} (\text{NOI})_i)P_i$$

$$
\begin{aligned}
E\,(\text{NOI}) &= P_1(\text{NOI}_i) + P_2(\text{NOI}_2) + P_3(\text{NOI}_3) \\
&= (.05)(\$67,680) + (.80)(\$81,360) + (.15)(\$90,480) \\
&= \$82,044
\end{aligned}
$$

To measure the dispersion about the expected value, or mean of the distribution, the variance is calculated.

$$\sigma^2 = \sum_{i=1}^{N} (K_i - K)^2 P_i$$

where

σ^2 = Variance
K_i = Outcome for each state
K = Expected value
P_i = Probability of outcome occurring

However, another measure, the standard deviation, is more typically used as a measure of dispersion, or risk. The standard deviation is simply the square root of the variance and is written as σ (sigma). Calculation of the variance and the standard deviation is shown below.

State	K_i	$-$	K	$= (K_i - K)$	$(K_i - K)^2$	$\times\ P_i$	$=\ (K_i - K)^2 P_i$
I	$67,680		$82,044	$(14,364)	$206,324,496	.05	$10,316,225
II	81,360		82,044	(684)	467,856	.80	374,285
III	90,480		82,044	8,436	71,166,096	.15	10,674,914
							$21,365,424

$\sigma^2 = \$21,365,424$

$\sigma = \sqrt{\sigma^2} = \sqrt{\$21,365,424} = \$4,622$

One standard deviation is the distance of $4,622 in either direction from the expected value. Two standard deviations are double that distance, and three standard deviations are triple that distance. Therefore, assuming a normal distribution, the standard deviation $4,622 means that the actual NOI will be within $4,622 of the expected NOI 68.26 percent of the time. This ranges from a NOI of $77,422 to $86,666. The actual outcome will lie within two standard deviations of the expected value 96.46 percent of the time and within three standard deviations 99.74 percent of the time (see Figure 6–3). The smaller the standard deviation, the smaller the range of outcomes becomes, and thus the more likely it is that the actual outcome will fall close to the expected value.

Perhaps the investor is more interested in the rate of return. The same procedure described above may be applied to this measure. Assuming the investor expects to provide 100 percent equity, or

FIGURE 6–3
The normal curve

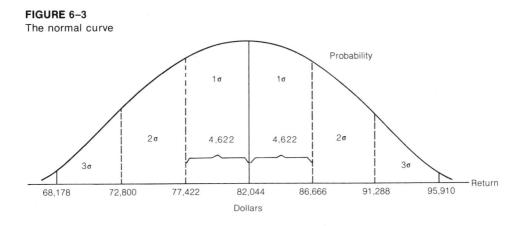

$650,000, then a rough rate of return, the equity dividend rate (EDR), can be estimated.

$$\text{Equity dividend rate} = \frac{\text{Cash throw-off}}{\text{Equity}}$$

Note that cash throw-off is the same as NOI when financing is not considered.

EDR		Probability
$\dfrac{\$67,680}{\$650,000} = 0.104$		.05
$\dfrac{\$81,360}{\$650,000} = 0.125$		.80
$\dfrac{\$90,480}{\$650,000} = 0.138$		.15

$E\,(\text{EDR}) = (.05)(0.104) + (.80)(0.125) + (.15)(0.138) = 0.126 = 12.6\%$

The risk is now found by calculating the standard deviation as before:

$$\sigma = \left[\sum_{i=1}^{N} P_i(K_i - K)^2 \right]^{1/2}$$

$$= [(.05)(0.104 - 0.126)^2 + (.80)(0.125 - 0.126)^2 \\ + (.15)(0.138 - 0.126)^2]^{1/2}$$

$$= \sqrt{0.00005}$$
$$= 0.00683$$

In this case, the equity dividend rate will lie between 11.92 percent and 13.28 percent approximately 68 percent of the time. Of course, the expected value and the standard deviation have little meaning unless they are compared to similar computations on alternative investments. Assuming the investor's alternative investment also has an expected EDR of 12.6 percent, but has a standard deviation of 2 percent, the investor will choose the apartment complex over the alternative.

Sensitivity analysis and computer simulation

An outgrowth of the mean-variance risk analysis method is sensitivity analysis. This method recognizes that each term of the NOI equation is subject to variation. NOI is calculated repeatedly by substituting several different values of one variable in the equation. The value of each variable can be plotted against NOI on a graph. The result is a line whose slope represents the sensitivity of the NOI to the variable. The steeper the slope, the more sensitive is the variable. If two projects are being compared, the project with steeper sensitivity lines would be the riskier. The process can be repeated for each term in the equation. Usually the analysis is carried out further to include cash throw-off or aftertax cash flow.

It is easy to see how such a process could become tedious and time consuming. With computers, however, this analysis can be completed with relative ease. Using a Monte Carlo computer simulation technique carries the process a step further. This attempts to imitate or simulate project results for each probable combination of inputs. Each variable term can be expressed as a probability distribution. This information enables the computer to recalculate NOI many times, using randomly picked values. These values picked by the computer are available for use only as often as specified by the probability distribution for that variable. The resulting NOIs also appear in the form of a probability distribution. This range of values is more informative than just a point estimate. From the distribution, an expected value for NOI and a standard deviation representing risk can be calculated. It must be noted that this risk represents total project risk. In the next section total risk is divided into two categories.

A shortcut method of simulation is *scenario analysis*. This process involves specifying an optimistic, a pessimistic, and a most likely outcome. The three scenarios for two or more projects are compared, and the project most appealing to the investor is accepted. This is a rather subjective method, as there is no specific quantification of risk.

Another variation of computer simulation is to link NOI values (or cash throw-off or aftertax cash flow) to the investor's utility preference curve. This implies that the derived expected utility is more important than the actual returns.

Although computer simulation provides a single, concrete estimate of risk, this number means nothing unless it is compared to a similar computation for an alternative project. In addition, the final figure is based on probability distributions which can only be subjectively determined. These limitations reduce the usefulness of the risk-level figure. If, however, risk levels affect the value of an investment, a measure must be developed which accounts for the amount and direction of change in the value related to risk. The remainder of this chapter discusses the development of such a measure, which finally results in a risk-adjusted capitalization rate.

The portfolio concept of risk

Most of today's sophisticated investors adhere to the portfolio concept of investment. This theory asserts that an investment should be accepted or rejected on the basis of its effect on other assets held by the investor. Major investors do not invest in one asset only, but rather in many assets. This collection of investments is called a portfolio. Portfolios usually consist of diverse investments stemming from different financial markets and submarkets. A portfolio may include eight different types of stock, or a few stocks and a few bonds, or several pieces of real property, or gold, or combinations of all of these.

Portfolios are usually well diversified in an attempt to decrease risk and raise returns. The literature of finance categorizes risk as either *systematic* or *unsystematic*. Unsystematic risk, also called diversifiable risk, can be eliminated from the portfolio by holding securities and other investments with returns that are less than perfectly correlated. Perfectly positively correlated returns always move exactly together when market conditions change; perfectly negatively correlated returns always move exactly opposite. If one asset in the portfolio reacts negatively to a market downturn, losses may be offset through another asset held which reacts positively. However, some assets react in different degrees to a change in market conditions. The objective is to develop an efficient portfolio by eliminating risk (loss potential). This is achieved through the inclusion of assets with varying return correlations in the portfolio. The degree of correlation and the effect this correlation will have on a portfolio can be estimated in order to help the investor choose the optimal collection of assets.

All risk cannot be eliminated from a portfolio. To the extent that asset returns are correlated, portfolio risk exists. This risk is termed systematic risk, or sometimes market risk, and is the relevant risk with which investors need to be concerned when valuing projects. This type of risk stems from market conditions which affect all firms, such as inflation, recession, and high interest rates.

Financial theory values securities through the capital asset pricing model (CAPM). This model requires a measurement of systematic risk. CAPM and the measurement of systematic risk are described in the following sections. Later, applications to real estate projects are discussed.

The capital asset pricing model

The capital asset pricing model states that the required return on an investment to keep the market in equilibrium is composed of a compensation for time, measured by the riskless rate of return, and a risk premium. The general equation takes the form:

$$K = R_f + b(K_m - R_f) \tag{1}$$

where

K = Required rate of return on an individual security
R_f = Risk-free rate of return
b = Beta coefficient
K_m = Required rate of return on an average stock or portfolio consisting of all stocks in the market
$(K_m - R_f)$ = Market risk premium
$b(K_m - R_f)$ = Risk premium on the specific stock being evaluated

R_f and K_m are difficult to measure exactly, but a proxy from historical data is generally used. For example, R_f may be expressed as the long-term U.S. Treasury bond rate and K_m may be the return on New York Stock Exchange stocks. Beta, however, is more difficult to estimate.

Beta coefficients

The key variable in the CAPM equation is the beta coefficient. This measures the sensitivity of a given stock's return to the overall market rate of return. Beta weights the market risk premium by the specific stock's relative riskiness. In other words, beta represents the systematic risk of a stock. A stock whose risk moves exactly with the market is assigned a beta value of one. A beta coefficient of 0.5 indicates a stock with half the systematic risk of the average stock, while a beta coefficient of 2 indicates a stock with twice the risk. Betas for many stocks are listed in several major financial publications (for example, *Value Line*) and are also published by such institutions as Merrill Lynch, the Wharton School, and Wells Fargo Bank. Betas for other investments must be calculated by the investor.

Beta is determined statistically by regressing the historical returns of the specific stock to the historical returns of the general capital market. Linear regression is a method of determining the relationship between a dependent variable and an independent variable. In the

CAPM model, the dependent variable is the expected return on the specific investment (K_j), and the independent variable is the market portfolio's return (K_m). Beta is the coefficient of the independent variable. Intuitively, beta is represented as follows.

Historical returns on the stock in question are plotted on a graph against historical market returns. Usually, Standard & Poor's 500-stock index is used as a proxy for the historical returns of the total market. When all points are plotted, a line is statistically fitted through the points.[2] This line will have the general equation:

$$K_j = \alpha_j + b_j K_m + e_j \qquad (2)$$

where

K_j = Expected return on the jth stock
α = Return on the jth stock when $K_m = 0$
b = Slope of the regression line
K_m = Market portfolio's return
e_j = Random error term

From the drawn line, α and b can be estimated. α is the point where the line cuts the vertical axis, while b is the slope of the line $(\Delta Y/\Delta X)$. These numbers may be substituted in the equation along with K_m, the current market return. The result is an estimation of beta which can be used in equation 1.[3]

The Security Market Line

The relationship between risk, as measured by the beta coefficient, and security rates of return is represented by the Security Market Line (SML). The SML is a curve that represents the CAPM equation. As an example, assume the risk-free rate, R_f, is 8 percent, the market rate of

---

[2] This can be done through least squares analysis, which is explained in most statistics books.

[3] Beta can also be calculated as the stock's covariance with the market divided by the market variance:

$$b_1 = \frac{\text{COV}(K_i, K_m)}{\sigma_m{}^2} = \frac{\sigma_i \sigma_m \rho_{i,m}}{\sigma_m{}^2} = \frac{\sigma_i \rho_{i,m}}{\sigma_m}$$

where

K_i = Stock's returns
K_m = Market's returns
σ_i = Standard deviation of the stock
σ_m = Standard deviation of the market
$\rho_{i,m}$ = Correlation coefficient between the stock and the market returns

For a more complete explanation, see Eugene F. Brigham, *Financial Management Theory and Practice* (Dryden Press: Hinsdale, Ill., 1979), appendix 5A.

return, K_m, is 12 percent, and the beta of a certain stock is 1.5. Therefore,

$$K = R_f + b(K_m - R_f)$$
$$= 8\% + 1.5(12\% - 8\%)$$
$$= 8\% + 1.5(4\%)$$
$$= 14\%$$

Where beta is 1.0 percent:

$$K = 8\% + 1.0(12\% - 8\%)$$
$$= 12\%$$

Figure 6–4 shows the graph of this relationship.

FIGURE 6–4
Graph of the Security Market Line

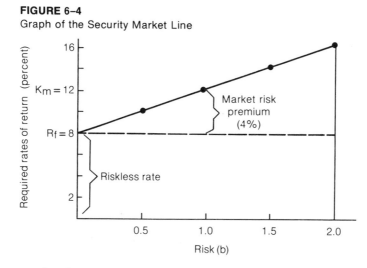

This line represents the market at equilibrium and reflects a stock's required rate of return at every level of risk in the market. The Y-intercept of this line indicates the return for a risk-free asset. An equity yield rate can be derived from the SML if the risk level, beta, of the project is known. For example, if the beta of a specific project is 0.5, then the graph shows the equity yield rate to be 10 percent. This rate can also be found by substituting 0.5 for b in the CAPM equation. The resulting equity yield rate can then be used to find a capitalization rate. If the Ellwood formula is used, 10 percent is substituted for Y in the equation. Because the market is rarely in equilibrium, most individual stocks will be illustrated by a point lying off the SML. A point above the SML represents a stock earning a higher return than expected. The price of a high-return stock will tend to be bid up until its return falls to that of equilibrium, and the price of a low-return stock will tend to drop until its return is raised to equilibrium. The slope of the SML reflects the risk preferences of investors. A steep slope indicates aversion to risk, while a horizontal slope represents no risk aversion. Of course, the SML is altered when the risk-free rate of return or the market rate of return is changed.

Application of CAPM to real estate

The CAPM approach has the potential to be extremely useful in the valuation of income-producing properties. In developing a capitalization rate, the appraiser must first estimate the equity yield rate. The traditional method of estimating equity yields has been through the calculation of the internal rate of return (IRR). The rate of return K expressed by the CAPM equation, however, is equivalent to the equity yield rate. The determination of this rate through CAPM would yield several advantages over the IRR method. The IRR requires that the appraiser specify cash throw-off, purchase price, and reversion value. CAPM is especially useful when there is not enough information available from comparable properties to make these calculations. In this case, beta is estimated by using historical data for the subject property, or possibly by using an adjusted version of the beta for stocks of a publicly traded real estate corporation investing in properties similar to the subject property. Traditionally, risk has been subjectively determined. The CAPM approach allows the analyst to quantify risk explicitly through the calculation of the beta coefficient.

But perhaps the most important contribution of CAPM is its ability to reflect the relationship of capital market conditions on risk and equity yield rates. Intuitively, this relationship seems logical. Real estate investments, after all, must compete in the capital market for funds. Since investors may consider all potential investments, the expenditure which would be required to purchase an equally desirable alternative determines the value of an investment. In addition, real estate investors are usually assumed to be knowledgeable and rational. Therefore, in an attempt to mitigate risk and improve their financial positions, real estate investors will tend to hold diversified portfolios. These portfolios may include stocks, bonds, and other investments. Investors are interested in the performance of a real estate investment only to the extent that it affects their total portfolio risk and returns. The investment must be analyzed with a method reflecting this concern, and that method is CAPM. Finally, the real estate market and the securities market are being linked closer together as corporations invest more of their assets in real estate and as more instruments, such as REITs and GNMA mortgage-backed securities, are utilized.

The current literature of the real estate and appraisal community is beginning to acknowledge the potential benefits of the application of CAPM to the development of capitalization rates. The results of early empirical tests show that relationships between real estate market returns and capital market returns do indeed exist. The exact type and degree of correlation has not yet been determined; various tests have yielded somewhat different results. Generally, however, it seems that the strongest correlation exists between real estate yields and yields on utility bonds or BBB-rated bonds. This is logical, as bonds represent an investment similar to a mortgage,[4] and as utilities have a large percentage of their assets invested in land and buildings.

Although arguments advocating the use of CAPM-determined equity yield rates are strong, actual application of CAPM to real estate is impractical at this point in time. The major problems concern the development of a beta coefficient for individual real estate investment projects. For example, many real estate projects are development projects and have no record of past returns. Suggestions to overcome this drawback include using betas of similar existing projects or using adjusted betas of publicly traded corporations which invest in similar properties. Both these methods, however, are imprecise and not fully developed.

Another problem exists when the regression technique of beta estimation is used. This method regresses project returns against market returns. Because of the difficulty involved in obtaining actual market return figures, a surrogate index representing the stock market is used (for example, Standard & Poor's 500). The index, however, does not include other types of investment returns. This is unfortunate because all investors are assumed to be rational and knowledgeable, and thus hold *diversified* portfolios consisting of many types of assets. It has been rather convincingly argued that a new index must be developed to account for other types of investments, including real property and human capital.[5] Although the use of such an index is theoretically more correct, the measurement of real property returns and human capital is extremely difficult.

SUMMARY

This chapter examines a few of the methods currently used to measure the risk involved in a real estate project. The more traditional

---

[4] Both bonds and mortgages represent loans with periodic repayments of principal and interest.

[5] Human capital is defined as "the value of the earnings stream resulting from individuals' particular talents and abilities (doctor, lawyer, brick mason, *etc.*)." This helps to differentiate the investment needs of various types of investors. See Mike Miles and Michael Rice, "Toward a More Complete Investigation of the Correlation of Real Estate Investment Yield to the Rate Evidenced in the Money and Capital Markets: The Individual Investor's Perspective," *Real Estate Appraiser and Analyst*, 44, no. 6 (November–December 1978), pp. 8–19.

method involves a mean-variance analysis in which potential profitability is expressed as an expected value and risk is expressed as the standard deviation of a probability distribution. A short review of computer risk analysis is also provided. This method, however, is simply a more sophisticated application of the mean-variance model. The figures resulting from these methods are useful only as standards for comparison.

A more pragmatic, concrete measure is then developed through the capital asset pricing model, a method which explicitly quantifies risk. This risk measurement is incorporated in an equity yield rate, which in turn is included in a capitalization rate. As a result, the capitalization rate will reflect not only risk but also the effects of the capital and money markets on real estate values. The inclusion of these two characteristics—risk quantification and capital and money market conditions—in determining capitalization rates should result in more accurate final value estimates. Some of the subjectivity of valuation is thereby eliminated, and thus the values arrived at should be more defensible.

Unfortunately, the use of the CAPM method as it exists today is impractical. Many problems exist with its application not only in the real estate market but also in the stock market, for which it was originally developed. Current research in real estate is focusing on adjustment of the CAPM formula to correct its deficiencies. This requires research into the relationships between the capital and money markets and real estate yields. But even though the adaptation of the CAPM to real estate is in its infancy, the concepts employed in the model add meaningful insight into real estate yields and returns.

QUESTIONS FOR REVIEW

1. Review the different types of risk. How do each of these affect real estate investment projects? Can any of these types of risk be eliminated?
2. How does risk affect value?
3. What do the terms *variance, expected value,* and *standard deviation* mean? How do these measures relate to risk and return?
4. What are some of the problems associated with computer simulation?
5. What is a portfolio? Why are portfolios diversified? Include a discussion of systematic risk versus unsystematic risk.
6. What is the relationship expressed by the CAPM equation? Do you think that this relationship holds true for real estate investments? Why or why not?
7. Discuss the calculation of beta. If necessary, do some additional reading on beta estimation. What are some of the problems associated with the calculation of beta and with the application of beta to real estate?

8. How does CAPM fit into the overall framework of real estate valuation? What are the advantages of using an equity yield rate determined by the CAPM equation?

9. What are the links between real estate values and rates of return in the capital and money markets?

REFERENCES

Brigham, Eugene F. *Financial Management Theory and Practice*. Hinsdale, Ill.: Dryden Press, 1979, chap. 5 and pp. 412–20.

Chou, Ya-lun. *Statistical Analysis*. 2d ed. New York: Holt, Rinehart & Winston, 1975.

Goulet, Peter G. *Real Estate A Value Approach*. Encino, Calif.: Glencoe, 1979, chap. 9.

Pellatt, Peter G. K. "The Analysis of Real Estate Investments under Uncertainty." *Journal of Finance*, 27, no. 2 (May 1972): 459–71.

Pyhrr, Stephen A. "Real Estate Risk Goes Scientific." *Real Estate Review*, 3, no. 3 (Fall 1973): 62–67.

Ratcliff, Richard U., and Schwab, Bernhard. "Contemporary Decision Theory and Real Estate Investment." *Appraisal Journal*, 38, no. 2 (April 1970): 165–87.

Real Estate Appraiser and Analyst. Chicago: Society of Real Estate Appraisers, 44, no. 6 (November–December 1978). Entire issue devoted to articles on the correlation of real estate yields with yields in the money and capital markets.

chapter 7

Continuing investment decisions

Real estate administration and the investment decisions which administration involves are continuing processes that extend beyond the initial purchase or the decision to supply the real estate. Throughout the investment holding period, an owner makes decisions which affect the value of the equity position. For purpose of discussion, we have classified these continuing decisions into (1) decisions which affect capital structure and ownership and (2) decisions which alter both the capital structure and the physical property. Both categories of decisions affect in some manner the value of the investor's equity in the property. This chapter is primarily concerned with the economics of the continuing decisions which also affect the physical property.

Decisions affecting only the capital structure. Decisions which only influence the capital structure of the investment include rent adjustments, refinancing, alteration of tax depreciation schedules within allowable limits, syndication, conversion to condominiums, sale of the property outright, sale and leaseback, exchanging for a property of like kind, or even abandonment. These decisions have the potential of altering the rate of return earned on the equity, and thus the value of the equity position. Partial "cashing out" of the equity can be accomplished by refinancing or syndication, which, again, will alter the value of the equity remaining with the investor. Or, the equity position can be terminated entirely by a sale or exchange of the property.

Decisions affecting the physical property. Recurring decisions that result in alteration of the physical property include decisions to maintain and repair the building, decisions to improve or alter the building, and, at times, the decision to demolish an existing building, with or without reuse of the site.

Continuing investment decisions are often interdependent and may occur simultaneously or sequentially, with each successive decision reflecting prior actions. The property may be simultaneously improved, refinanced, and syndicated, with the original owner remaining as a general partner with only partial claim to cash flow, tax shelters, and capital gains. Or, a property may be rehabilitated after years of decisions not to spend on maintenance and repair, later to be refinanced and, still later, exchanged for a property of like kind, with the owner reinvesting the equity while postponing some or all of the capital gain tax.

CAUSES OF CONTINUING INVESTMENT DECISIONS

In Chapter 3, we indicated that the characteristics of real estate as an economic good, such as its fixity of location, durability, and large economic size, result in real estate markets being less than perfectly competitive. In Chapter 6, we recognized that real estate investments and their markets, although imperfect, are competitive with alternative investments. Rational investors in real estate realize and act upon the opportunity to increase their rate of return and the value of their equity positions. At the same time, investors are conscious of the profitability of investments in the stock market, gold, and other alternatives to real estate. If markets become unbalanced, or out of equilibrium, so that investors can obtain a higher risk-adjusted rate of return on, say, gold than on real estate, funds will flow into gold, driving its price up and its yield down. At the same time, the scarcity of funds available to real estate will have the opposite effect until risk-adjusted yields are in balance. At this point, the nominal return on the two types of investments could be different if they are in different risk classes. In the same manner, if it is more profitable to own slum housing than luxury apartments, funds will flow into slum properties until the risk-adjusted returns on investment are in balance in these two real estate markets. Again, the nominal rate of return on slum housing would be greater than the return on less risky apartment developments. It is this nominal rate of return that is used by the real estate analyst in the appraisal process to estimate market value, discussed in Chapter 4.

If markets were completely efficient, all investment properties would earn the same risk-adjusted rate of return. Although real estate markets have characteristics that render them less than completely efficient, the fact that investors are continually altering and fine-tuning their investments in real estate is evidence of both competition and of some degree of efficiency in the markets and the mechanism through which rates of return on alternative real estate investments are brought into proper relationship.

Exogenous determinants

The constant changes in the basic determinants of the need for real estate and the supply of real estate can alter the relative prices and yields on real estate investments. Thus, the in-migration of households into a community can reduce the level of vacancies in the local housing stock and result in an increase in rents, which, in the short run, increases the rate of return earned by fortunate investors in rental housing. If the higher yields persist, funds will be attracted, triggering a supply response. Additional new housing will be supplied in markets where rents are high enough to make new construction economically feasible. The supply of housing also can be increased by enlarging existing buildings or by converting nonresidential real estate into rental units. Further, the supply of real estate can be increased by improving the quality of the existing stock of units. An expenditure of funds to cure physical deterioration and functional obsolescence can be a result of relatively higher yields on rental housing.

Conversely, the loss of population and households, perhaps due to the closing of a local industry, causes disinvestment in housing. Rents, prices, and the rate of return on rental housing decline (or fail to keep pace with alternative investments), and property owners disinvest by forgoing maintenance and repair. This disinvestment continues until the standing stock provides only the quantity and quality of housing services which, given the net income generated, produces the equilibrium risk-adjusted rate of return on investment. At this point, the community may have a physically deteriorated housing stock and a high proportion of abandoned units. New construction and improvements to existing units will have been negligible.

The characteristics of real estate as an economic good, which render real estate markets imperfect, result in a slower adjustment to changes in demand or supply factors than in some other markets, but competition in real estate markets does result in alterations in the physical stock of real estate over time in response to changing needs and supply conditions.

Exogenous, or external, determinants of continuing investment decisions are discussed throughout this text. For instance, changing money and capital markets can produce mortgage interest rates which make refinancing feasible. The federal government creates opportunities to improve real estate by providing special tax depreciation methods to encourage renovation of central city properties, rehabilitation of housing for lower income families, and preservation of historic structures. State and local governments may provide incentive for renovation by forgiving part or all of the real property tax. Or, industrial bonds may be authorized by the community, and the lower cost of capital may make a renovation project feasible.

Endogenous determinants

Continuing investment decisions also result from factors which are internal, or endogenous, to the investment and investor. If the property has been held by an investor for a long period of time, the original mortgage may have been retired or paid down to the point where refinancing is feasible; tax shelters may have evaporated, and action may be taken to renew them. The physical aging process alone can influence the decision to spend for maintenance and repair if the property is held for an extended period of time. Larger and larger expenditures for maintenance and repair will be required to keep the property competitive in the market, until it is no longer feasible to prevent the onslaught of physical deterioration. Investment decisions also are influenced by the changes in the investment needs of the owner over time as the family progresses through its life cycle. An investment which fulfilled the needs of a successful young executive may no longer be suitable in the retirement years. The need for cash flow in retirement may result in forgoing maintenance and repair to the property. Even though prolonged undermaintenance can result in higher vacancies, lower rents, and a lower property value, an elderly investor may not be concerned with these eventualities.

THE REPAIR AND MAINTENANCE DECISION

The decision to spend on maintenance and repairs is the most frequent investment decision during the holding period. Annually, or more often, the owner may decide to fix a leaking roof, to repair a broken window, to paint, to strip and refinish the floor, and to perform other routine tasks. Or, the owner may choose not to spend for maintenance and repairs, or elect to spend less than would be required to maintain the building in its present condition. A deteriorated building is the end result of successive decisions over a long period of time to make few or no repairs and to forgo adequate maintenance.

Maintenance and repair expenditures are made to prevent a loss of property value or net income. Ideally, maintenance and repairs would be performed over the investment holding period to the point where the present value of the outlays for maintenance and repair (above a minimum necessary to keep the building habitable) equals the present value of the loss of net income and reversion value averted over the holding period. Another way of stating this decision rule is that expenditures for maintenance and repairs will be made at a level which maximizes the internal rate of return on the equity over the holding period or which maximizes the net present value of the investment. In an efficient market, this "maximum" return on investment over the long run would be the equilibrium return.

A simplified example of the maintenance and repair decision may be helpful. The investor thinks: "If I spend $1,000 a year on the average for ten years on maintenance and repair, my cash flow will be reduced annually by this amount. However, if I do not spend $1,000 each year on the average, I will not over time be able to keep my rents at market level, my vacancy losses will increase, and when I sell the property in ten years, its value will be lower. In fact, I expect to lose about $800 a year in net income and will realize a loss of $7,500 in a lower property value at the time of sale." If 10 percent is the appropriate rate of discount, the investor concludes that the present value of the $1,000 annual maintenance and repair outlays, or $6,144 ($1,000 × 6.144567, Appendix G, column 5, 10 percent, ten years), is less than the present value of the loss averted, or $7,806 ($800 × 6.144567, plus $7,500 × 0.385543, Appendix G, column 4, 10 percent, ten years). The maintenance and repair outlays represent a cost to the investor; the losses of net income and reversion value averted are the investor's gain.

In this instance, the property is kept in a state of "normal" maintenance and repair over the investor's holding period. There would be a limit, however, to the amount which would be spent on maintenance and repair over the holding period. This limit would be reached when the present value of the outlays for maintenance and repair equals the present value of the loss averted.

While the above example conceptualizes the maintenance and repair decision, it is obvious that market imperfections and other characteristics of real estate as an investment prevent such precision in the maintenance and repair decision. Investors cannot forecast the loss of net income or reversion value over the entire investment holding period; the length of the investment holding period is itself an uncertain variable. The time horizon involved in the maintenance and repair decision is, as a practical matter, the foreseeable short run. An investor can recognize how the property compares with other properties in the market and can judge the level of maintenance and repair necessary to keep the property competitive in the short run.

The simple example above also overlooks the fact that, as the building ages, larger expenditures on maintenance and repair are required to prevent a given loss in net income and reversion value. The onset of

physical deterioration cannot be indefinitely postponed by maintenance and repair, and both functional and locational obsolescence can
render additional maintenance and repair expenditures infeasible.
Decisions made early in the investment holding period to keep the
property in good repair may not be made later when no amount of
expenditure on maintenance and repair would overcome the debilitat-
ing effects of a neighborhood in transition to another land use or of a
functionally obsolete heating system. However, an investor can recognize when market conditions have changed to the extent that maintenance and repair can no longer prevent loss of net income. Again, the
time horizon for the maintenance and repair decision under such circumstances is the short run.

A structure that has reached the end of its economic life will be
"milked," with little expenditure on maintenance and repair. Some
buildings reach their end abruptly, such as a structure taken for a
public park. In most instances, however, a building has suffered prolonged undermaintenance before it is removed from the standing
stock. This structure obtains the lowest rents in the market and is
occupied by tenants with the least ability to pay. Forgoing maintenance and repair on the building will not result in a higher vacancy
loss or lower rents. The net income over the remaining economic life
of the building or its reversion value will not be significantly affected
by lack of maintenance and repair.

A landlord who is in a strong market position, where less housing
services (in the form of reduced quality) can be offered for the same
dollar of rental income, and who will not lose tenants if the property is
undermaintained, can reduce maintenance and repair without affecting rental income or the value of the property. This landlord faces a
relatively inelastic demand, where the quantity of housing services
demanded is not particularly responsive to price. Does this situation
exist in the inner city, where minority groups may be hindered in their
access to the entire housing market? Do landlords of ghetto housing
have a quasi-monopoly position? Are inner-city properties undermaintained because they are occupied by minorities, or are they undermaintained simply because they are occupied by low-income households? This issue continues to be debated. Our concept of the housing
market as reasonably competitive suggests that undermaintenance occurs because people are poor. Consequently, blight and deteriorated
housing, which are the symptoms of undermaintenance, exist primarily because of poverty, not because of prejudice.

THE DECISION TO IMPROVE OR ALTER THE STRUCTURE

During the investment holding period, the decision to improve the
structure is less frequent than the decision to maintain and repair it. In

contrast to maintenance and repair expenditures, which are operating expenses, the improvement (alteration) decision involves a capital expenditure that increases the value of the structure. This increase in value can result from a larger net income or an increased flow of amenities, from extending the building's remaining economic life, or from changing the discount rate used to capitalize net operating income into value. For income tax purposes, a capital improvement increases the depreciable basis of the property and can change the annual depreciation expense and the eventual capital gain at termination of ownership.

An improvement to the structure can involve rehabilitation, historic preservation, remodeling, modernization, conversion, or adaptive reuse. *Rehabilitation* has been defined as "restoration of a property to satisfactory condition without changing the plan, form, or style of a structure."[1] Rehabilitation removes the effects of prolonged under-maintenance. It only removes physical deterioration and might involve painting, replacement of a roof, replastering, or replacement of rotten or termite-infested portions of the building. Rehabilitation which only cures deferred maintenance, such as patching a roof or painting, is not a capital expenditure. More substantive rehabilitation, as when the roof is replaced, is a capital improvement. *Historic preservation* is rehabilitation which retains the character of the structure intact, or which returns the building to its original form, complete with any functional obsolescence that it may suffer.

Remodeling "changes the plan, form, or style of a structure to correct functional or economic deficiencies."[2] Remodeling may rearrange partitions to alter a floor plan, or it may replace obsolete electrical, plumbing, and heating systems. Remodeling may result in a *conversion* of the property from a use no longer suitable for the site to a use which is competitive in the market. An *adaptive reuse* is a conversion where the remodeling produces a creative reuse of the structure that is different from its original purpose. Remodeling and substantive rehabilitation, from an economic point of view, represent positive actions which add value to the property. Maintenance and repair, on the other hand, are preventive measures and are undertaken to prevent a loss of value.

An improvement should be undertaken only if the value added to the property at least equals the cost of the improvement. For example, a $50,000 rehabilitation project for the ABC office property analyzed in previous chapters would be feasible if the cost were at least matched by value added to the property. The uncertainties in a less than perfect

---

[1] Byrl N. Boyce, *Real Estate Appraisal Terminology* (Cambridge, Mass.: Ballinger, 1975), p. 174.

[2] Ibid., p. 175.

market result in the need for a margin of safety for the investor who undertakes a capital improvement in an ever-changing market. The margin of safety is the excess of value added over the cost of the improvement.

An exception to the rule that the value added should at least equal the cost of improving the property exists in the situation where a structure has been cited for code violations and where the alternative may be to improve or to have the building condemned. The improvements will be made in this instance if the cost does not exceed the remaining value of the structure. The value of this dilapidated property may increase very little following the renovation, the cost of which greatly exceeds the value added. However, failure to spend $10,000 to improve the building to code may result in the condemnation and loss of tenants and future income; that is, the remaining value of the building will fall to zero. If the structure, even in its dilapidated condition, has a value of $20,000 based upon remaining productivity, then the investor will expend $10,000 on improvements rather than suffer the $20,000 loss.

Capital improvements have the potential of affecting rents, vacancy and collection losses, operating expenses, financing expenses, tax depreciation expense, and the before- and after-tax reversion value of the property at the end of the investment holding period. Many improvement decisions will affect rents, in some cases because the building after alteration will have more net rentable area or because the quality of the services which the building provides will have been increased. Vacancy and collection losses also may be reduced if the improved property is more competitive. The operating expense ratio can change as the increased property value is realized in tax assessments and insurance premiums. Other expenses, such as utilities, can increase, perhaps because the building is now larger, or decrease, perhaps due to the greater energy efficiency of the improvement. Factors such as property tax abatements or energy-efficient improvements can cause operating expenses not to change proportionately with gross income.

The capital improvement must be financed with additional debt, new equity, or both. In all likelihood, the after-financing return on equity will be different following the improvement, perhaps because the new debt has different terms or because the debt to equity ratio has been changed. A changed interest expense following the improvement also can alter the aftertax return on equity. Finally, the basis for tax depreciation and the annual tax depreciation expense will be changed. The effect of the capital improvement on tax depreciation will be determined by the type of property and its use. Historic preservation, older commercial real estate, and apartment property to be used as subsidized housing have been given tax incentives in the form of rapid write-offs for rehabilitation expenditures. The feasibility of an improvement will reflect the interaction of all these variables in the determination of property value after the improvement.

Valuation analysis

Figure 7–1 provides a "before and after" valuation analysis of the feasibility of rehabilitation of the ABC office property discussed in

FIGURE 7–1
Valuation analysis of the rehabilitation of the ABC office property:
Before and after improvements

	Before	After
Rent per square foot	$8.60	$9.70
Net rentable square feet	7,650 s.f.	7,650 s.f.
Vacancy and collection losses	5%	3%
Operating ratio	35%	32%
Net operating income	$39,500	$48,232
Financing	75%, 10%,	80%, 11%,
	30-yr.	30-yr.
Ellwood overall capitalization rate	0.1051	0.1119
Market value	$\left(\dfrac{\$39,500}{0.1051}\right),$	$\left(\dfrac{\$48,232}{0.1119}\right),$
	or $375,800	or $431,000
Building value	$315,800	$371,000
Site value (from market)	$60,000	$60,000

Gain in value ("after" less "before")	$55,200
Cost of improvements	50,000
Excess over cost	$ 5,200 (or 10.4%)

previous chapters. Net operating income is expected to increase from $39,500 before rehabilitation to $47,936 after rehabilitation; this increase is the net result of higher rents, lower vacancy losses, and a lower operating ratio. The financing terms will change following rehabilitation. The owners will be able to obtain a higher loan to value ratio (80 percent) but will have to pay a higher interest rate (11 percent). Using the Ellwood mortgage-equity valuation technique, the after-rehabilitation financing produces an overall capitalization rate of 11.19 percent, compared with a 10.51 percent rate before the property was improved.[3]

---

[3] The Ellwood formula is $R = Y - MC$ plus depreciation $\times (1/S_n)$ or minus appreciation $\times (1/S_n)$. Substituting: $Y = 0.12$, $M = 0.80$, and $C = 0.010132$ for an 11 percent, 30-year mortgage and a 10-year holding period. Thus the overall rate, or R, is: $R = 0.12$ $0.80(0.010132) = 0.1119$.

The market value of the ABC property is expected to be $431,000 after rehabilitation, a gain of $55,200 in value. The gain in property value of $55,200 is compared with the cost of the improvements, which includes material, labor, the contractor's profit, architect's fees, any interim interest expense on money borrowed to accomplish the rehabilitation, and an allowance for contingencies. Further, if the improvements prevented renting part or all of the structure, the loss of rental income should be included as a cost. The estimated total cost of the improvements to the ABC property including a contingency reserve but no loss of rental income or interim expense, is $50,000.

The value added ($55,200) exceeds the estimated cost of improvements ($50,000) by $5,200, which is about 10.4 percent of the cost of improvements. The uncertainties surrounding estimated rents, vacancy level, operating expenses, and the expected costs of the improvements result in a need for this margin of safety of value added over cost. The investor contemplating this rehabilitation project would undertake it only if sufficient confidence existed in the factors influencing the after value and the improvement cost.

Aftertax analysis

An investor contemplating an improvement to an existing building should explicitly consider tax factors in analyzing the feasibility of the proposed expenditure. The "before" and "after" internal rate of return, net present value, and profitability index should be estimated, as well as the new debt service coverage and the break-even ratio. Although all rehabilitation and modernization projects should have an explicit aftertax analysis, such an analysis is particularly needed when a large part of the "after" property value is contributed by tax factors.[4] This situation can exist because of the special tax treatment of rehabilitated historic structures, housing for lower income families, and older commercial and industrial buildings.

---

[4] A valuation methodology which used net operating income with or without explicit consideration of financing would capture the effects of taxes on property value in the rate of discount used to capitalize net operating income (building, land, and property residual techniques) or in the equity yield rate (Ellwood mortgage-equity technique) or in the equity dividend rate. Precise derivation of discount rates from market evidence would theoretically permit tax factors to be implicitly incorporated into the valuation process, since similar properties would be selling in the market for higher prices relative to their net operating incomes or to their cash throw-offs to the equity due to these tax factors, and thus would be realizing lower yields (rates of discount). These lower returns on investment or on equity, when used in the "after" valuation of the improved property, would cause the value added by income tax consideration to be reflected (capitalized) in the final property value estimate, which would be higher. As a practical matter, however, market evidence for discount rates is difficult to obtain and to verify with such precision.

The investor should realize an aftertax internal rate of return, net present value, and profitability index of *at least* the same magnitude as before the improvement. Higher "after" values for the investment criteria are needed for the same reasons as those given for the need to have the value added to the property exceed the cost of the improvement. The uncertainties in estimating after-improvement cash flows require a safety margin.[5]

Figure 7–2 shows the investment effects of the $50,000 improvement to the ABC office property. The changes in gross income, vacancy and collection losses, and operating ratios, shown in Figure 7–1, are incorporated into the "after" investment analysis. The operating ratio, however, changes from 30.41 percent before rehabilitation to 27.9 percent after, rather than from the 35 percent to 32 percent in Figure 7–1, because of the absence of the $3,000 replacement reserve in the operating expenses used for aftertax investment analysis. The financing changes are the same as in Figure 7–1.

The $50,000 cost of rehabilitation is separated into $40,000 in capital improvements, which are depreciated at the straight-line rate over the remaining 30-year useful life of the building, and $10,000 of tangible personal property used in trade or business.[6] Qualified tangible personal property used in trade or business provides both first-year bonus depreciation and an investment credit against taxes owed. To receive the first-year bonus depreciation, the tangible personal property must have a useful life of six or more years and is limited to

---

[5] In a completely efficient market where risk-adjusted rates of return are equalized among investments, the risk-adjusted aftertax internal rate of return following improvement of the structure should be identical to the "before" return. Unless the property has been shifted to a different risk class, the nominal rate of return would be the same after rehabilitation as before rehabilitation. In this situation, the entire increase in aftertax cash flow would be capitalized into property value. Again, this increase in property value should equal the expenditure for rehabilitation for the improvement to the structure to be feasible.

The ABC office property in Figure 7–1 was appraised before and after improvement using a 12 percent equity yield rate. In an efficient market, this rate would have fallen and the property value would have risen to more than $431,000 until the aftertax return on equity was the same as it had been before improvement.

In a completely efficient market, the equilibrium rates of return are the result of the actions of investors operating at the margin where prices and yields are determined in this market. Other investors in this market, however, experience different rates of return since they can differ from the marginal investor with respect to, say, their income tax brackets or other characteristics. Another way of stating this observation is that different investors in a certain type of property can have different investment values, as explained in Chapter 5.

[6] The capital improvements can be depreciated using allowable rapid write-off methods at the election of the taxpayer. Substantial rehabilitation or modernization may result in the Internal Revenue Service extending the remaining useful life of the structure. However, the ABC office building retained its 30-year remaining useful life following rehabilitation.

FIGURE 7–2
Investment analysis of the ABC office property rehabilitation

---

Before

Property value $375,800
Financing .... 75% L/V, 10%, 30 years
Holding period .... 10 years
Rent before vacancy .... $65,790 ($8.60 per s.f. × 7,650 s.f.)
Operating expenses $20,000
Vacancy ratio .... 5 percent
Depreciable basis $315,800
Useful life .... 30 years
Depreciation method .... Straight-line
Estimated selling price in ten years $375,800

Pro forma operating period cash flows

	Year		
	1	5	10
Potential gross income	$ 65,790	$ 65,790	$ 65,790
Vacancy and collection	−3,290	−3,290	−3,290
Effective gross income	62,501	62,501	62,501
Expenses	−20,000	−20,000	−20,000
Net operating income	42,500	42,500	42,500
Debt service	−29,681	−29,681	−29,681
Cash throw-off........................	12,819	12,819	12,819
Net operating income	$ 52,500	$ 42,500	$ 42,500
Interest	−28,114	−27,348	−25,841
Depreciation	−10,522	−10,522	−10,522
Taxable income	3,863	4,630	6,137
Federal income tax	−1,932	−2,315	−3,068
Cash throw-off........................	$ 12,819	$ 12,819	$ 12,819
Federal income tax	−1,932	−2,315	−3,068
Aftertax cash flow	10,887	10,504	9,751
NPV after tax..........................	$ 1,738	$ 8,253	$ 14,897
Profitability index	1.017	1.086	1.157
Mortgage balance	$280,283	$272,192	$256,303
Debt coverage ratio	1.43	1.43	1.43
Loan/original value	0.75	0.72	0.68
Loan/current value	0.75	0.72	0.68
Lender's yield	10.00	10.00	10.00
Break-even ratio......................	0.76	0.76	0.76
BTCF/equity	13.64	13.64	13.64
ATCF/equity	11.59	11.18	10.38
Estimated selling price	$375,800	$375,800	$375,800
BT IRR on equity	15.32	15.17	14.99
AT IRR on equity	11.02	11.27	11.46

FIGURE 7–2 (continued)

Reversion at end of ten-year holding period

Selling price		$431,000
Selling costs		0
Mortgage balance		318,107
Before-tax cash flow		112,893

Selling price		$431,000
Selling costs		0
Cost basis	$431,000	
Accumulated depreciation	128,600	
Amortized expense	0	
Adjusted basis		302,400
Total gain		$128,600

Accumulated depreciation	$128,600	
Straight line	128,600	
Recapture credit	0	
Ordinary income		0

Capital gain	$128,600

Ordinary income	0	
Tax rate	0.50	
Ordinary income tax		0

Capital gain	$128,600	
Tax rate	0.20	
Capital gain tax		$ 25,720

Aftertax cash flow	$ 87,173

After

Property value	$431,000
Financing	80% L/V, 11%, 30 years
Holding period	10 years
Rent before vacancy	$74,205 ($9.70 per s.f. × 7,650 s.f.)
Operating expenses	$20,730
Vacancy ratio	2 percent
Depreciable basis	$365,800, with $10,000 basis eligible for bonus depreciation and investment credit
Useful life	30 years for $355,800 basis; 7 years for $10,000 basis
Depreciation method	Straight-line
Estimated selling price in ten years	$431,000

Pro forma operating period cash flows

	Year		
	1	*5*	*10*
Potential gross income	$ 74,205	$ 74,205	$ 74,205
Vacancy and collection	−2,226	−2,226	−2,226
Effective gross income	71,979	71,979	71,979
Expenses	−20,730	−20,730	−20,730
Net operating income	51,249	51,249	51,249

FIGURE 7-2 (continued)

Debt service	-39,404	-39,404	-39,404
Cash throw-off	11,845	11,845	11,845
Net operating income	$ 51,249	$ 51,249	$ 51,249
Interest	-37,851	-36,998	-35,244
Depreciation	-15,003*	-13,003‡	-11,860§
Taxable income	-1,605	1,248	4,145
Federal income tax	803	-624	-2,073
Cash throw-off	$ 11,845	$ 11,845	$ 11,845
Federal income tax	1,803†	-624	-2,073
Aftertax cash flow	13,648	11,221	9,773
NPV after tax	—	—	$ 23,474
Profitability index	—	—	1.269
Mortgage balance	$343,247	$335,018	$318,107
Debt coverage ratio	1.30	1.30	1.30
Loan/original value	0.80	0.78	0.74
Loan/current value	0.80	0.78	0.74
Lender's yield	11.00	11.00	11.00
Break-even ratio	0.81	0.81	0.81
AT IRR on equity	—	—	13.35

Reversion at end of ten-year holding period

Selling price		$375,800
Selling costs		0
Mortgage balance		256,303
Before-tax cash flow		119,497
Selling price		$375,800
Selling costs		0
Cost basis	$375,800	
Accumulated depreciation	105,224	
Amortized expense	0	
Adjusted basis		270,576
Total gain		$105,224
Accumulated depreciation	$105,224	
Straight-line	105,224	
Recaptured credit	0	
Ordinary income		0
Capital gain		$105,224
Ordinary income	0	
Tax rate	0.50	
Ordinary income tax		0
Capital gain	$105,224	
Tax rate	0.20	
Capital gain tax		$ 21,045
Aftertax cash flow		$ 98,453

* Composed of:

$11,860 Annual depreciation on $355,800 basis ($375,800 property value less $60,000 site value, plus $40,000 capital improvement, using 30-year remaining useful life).

2,000 First-year bonus depreciation ($10,000 tangible personal property ×0.20).

FIGURE 7–2 (concluded)

1,143   Annual depreciation of tangible personal property ($10,000 less $2,000 bonus deprecia-
            tion = $8,000 basis ÷ seven years useful life).

$15,003   Total first-year depreciation

   † Composed of:

$ 803   Total savings from $1,650 tax loss × 0.50 marginal tax rate of investor
   1,000   Investment credit ($10,000 tangible personal property × 0.10 rate)

$ 1,803   Total tax savings (shown as a positive number because it increased cash throw-off)

   ‡ Composed of:

$11,860   Annual depreciation on $355,800 basis
   1,143   Annual depreciation (over seven years) of tangible personal property

$13,003

   § Annual depreciation in years 8–10 is $11,860.

$10,000 of new or used property purchased on any one year ($20,000 on a joint return).[7] The $10,000 tangible personal property in the ABC office building rehabilitation has a useful life of seven years and results in bonus depreciation of $2,000 (0.20 × $10,000 cost) in the first year and $1,142 depreciation expense each year over the seven-year useful life ($10,000 cost less $2,000 bonus depreciation = $8,000 basis ÷ 7-year useful life = $1,142 annual straight-line depreciation expense). Tangible personal property can be depreciated under allowable rapid write-off methods at the taxpayer's election.

In addition, the investor is entitled to an investment credit against taxes owed of 10 percent in the first year. The investment credit applies to new or used depreciable personal property in certain qualified types of property, such as the ABC office building. To be eligible, the tangible personal property must have a useful life of three or more years, and it must have a seven-year useful life to receive the full 10 percent credit.[8] The $10,000 of tangible personal property in the ABC

---

[7] Tangible personal property is not land or buildings and generally is not items that are part of the structure by manner of attachment. Office equipment, carpeting, movable partitions, individual window air-conditioning units, and so on, are examples of tangible personal property.

[8] The tax credit available varies with the useful life of the tangible personal property: three–five-year life—one third of 10 percent credit; five–seven-year life—two thirds of 10 percent credit; seven-year life or longer—full 10 percent credit.

The investment credit is limited to the investor's tax liability. If the tax liability exceeds $25,000, the tax credit cannot exceed $25,000 plus 70 percent of the tax liability over $25,000 (80 percent in 1981; 90 percent in 1982). Unused credit carries back for three years and forward for seven years. The credit does not affect the depreciable basis of the property. Apartment properties do not qualify; hotels and motels, office buildings, and commercial buildings do qualify. Sale of the tangible personal property before its useful life has ended results in recapture of all or part of the investment credit taken.

office building rehabilitation generates a $1,000 credit against taxes in the first year.

The effects of the first-year bonus depreciation and investment credit are shown in the "after" analysis of the ABC office property in Figure 7–2. Rehabilitation increases the first-year depreciation expense to $15,003, which, together with $37,851 in mortgage interest, is sufficient to shelter completely net income from taxes.

The $803 tax saving generated in the first year by the tax shelter provided by depreciation and interest is further increased by the $1,000 investment credit received, producing a total tax saving of $1,803. Aftertax cash flow in the first year increases from $11,845 to $13,648. By the fifth year of the investment holding period, the investor is paying tax of $624 on a taxable income of $1,248. The $10,000 in tangible property has been fully depreciated by the end of the seventh year, and in the tenth year taxable income has increased to $4,145 and taxes paid have increased to $2,073.

The net result of the expected changes in rents, vacancy losses, operating expense ratios, and depreciation expense resulting from the additional $50,000 investment in the ABC office property rehabilitation increases the aftertax internal rate of return from 11.46 percent before rehabilitation to 13.35 percent after rehabilitation. Net present value over the ten-year holding period increases from $14,897 before to $23,474 after, and the profitability index increases from 1.157 before rehabilitation to 1.267 after the capital improvement. This investment analysis of the proposed rehabilitation project, when combined with the before and after valuation analysis, would indicate that it is economically feasible to undertake the improvement. Because of the uncertainties of forecasting future rents, vacancy levels, and so on, the investor would be well advised to continue the investment analysis with a sensitivity analysis that would demonstrate the effects of different rents, vacancy levels, operating ratios, or tax depreciation schedules on the profitability of the proposed rehabilitation project. This further analysis of the risk-return relationship would expose the vulnerability of the rehabilitation project to "downside" risks and would assist in demonstrating the potential for improved profitability.

Tax incentives for rehabilitation and preservation

In addition to the first-year bonus depreciation and investment credit for qualified tangible personal property used in the rehabilitation of the ABC office property, certain types of real estate enjoy tax benefits intended to promote the continued use of existing structures. Tax benefits are available for renovation of commercial and industrial buildings (not apartments) which have been in use for 20 or more years; for the preservation of historic structures; and for rehabilitation of apartments as housing for lower income families. Each of these tax benefits and their allowable options can be analyzed as shown in Figure 7–2 to find the effects on the profitability of the investment. However, the analysis would also incorporate recapture of excess depreciation at the time of sale, which can occur with each of the above tax shelters and which moderates the benefits received. The minimum and maximum tax provisions of the current tax law may also reduce the beneficial impact of accelerated depreciation of amortization of rehabilitation expenditures on the profitability of the investment.[9] These factors are mentioned to illustrate the complexities of an aftertax analysis of the alternatives available to the investor engaging in the rehabilitation or preservation of qualified investment properties. Expert advice should be sought to assist in the analysis.

Older commercial and industrial structures. Rehabilitation of commercial and industrial buildings (not apartments) which have been in use for 20 or more years can generate a 10 percent investment credit against taxes owed. The credit does not reduce the depreciable basis. To qualify, at least 75 percent of the existing external walls must be retained, although the walls may be reinforced or siding may be installed.

The rehabilitation expenditure must be for components with useful lives of at least seven years for the full 10 percent credit to be obtained (five to six years' useful life receives 6.67 percent credit; less than five years, no credit). No credit is given for expenditures which enlarge the property, for acquisition costs, for expenditures on parking lots, or for expenditures which qualify for investment credit under another provision (such as the tangible personal property in the ABC office rehabilitation). Qualified expenditures could be for interior and exterior rehabilitation, heating and cooling systems, plumbing, electrical systems, and so forth.

Historic preservation. The Tax Reform Act of 1976 permits certified rehabilitation expenditures on "certified" historic structures to be amortized at the straight-line rate over five years (20 percent per year).[10] Or, the investor may elect to be treated as the original user of the property and use the allowable rapid write-off depreciation

---

[9] Gailen L. Hite and Anthony B. Sanders, "Excess Depreciation and the Maximum Tax," Ohio State University, 1980. C. F. Sirmans, "The Minimum Tax, Recapture, and Choice of Depreciation Methods," University of Georgia, 1980. Papers delivered at American Real Estate and Urban Economics Association annual meeting, Denver, Colorado, September 5, 1980.

[10] A certified historic building is either on the National Register, in a Registered Historic District and certified by the secretary of the interior to be of historic significance to the district, or in a historic district designated by state or local statute and approved by the secretary of the interior.

method for the rehabilitation expenditures. The allowable methods for the original user of residential real estate are double-declining balance, sum-of-the-years' digits, and straight-line. Nonresidential buildings can be depreciated by the original user at 150 percent of straight-line and straight-line. Component depreciation of the capital improvements at allowable rapid write-off rates or at the straight-line rate is also available. (The reader is referred to Chapter 13 for an explanation of these depreciation methods.) The rehabilitation expenditures must be made during a two-year period and must exceed $5,000 or the undepreciated basis of the building at the beginning of the period, whichever is the greater. Unless extended, this tax benefit lapses July 1, 1981.

Whether the investor chooses to amortize certified rehabilitation expenditures over five years or to depreciate the expenditures as an original user, the acquisition cost of the building or, if already owned, its remaining basis at the time of rehabilitation will continue to be depreciated as "used" property over its remaining useful life. Again, rehabilitation may result in a longer useful life being assigned to the structure. Investors in certified commercial (nonresidential) historic structures have the option, in lieu of the five-year amortization of rehabilitation expenditures, of taking the 10 percent investment credit on these expenditures, which was discussed above. The investor is not allowed both the five-year amortization and the investment credit. Both alternatives should be analyzed to determine which will maximize the return on investment.

Low-income housing. Apartment properties which are rehabilitated as housing for lower income families can have capital improvements amortized over five years, if the items have a useful life of at least five years. The rehabilitation expenditures must total at least $3,000 over a two-year period and cannot exceed $20,000 per apartment unit. The acquisition cost of a used apartment building would be depreciated under allowable methods (straight-line or 125 percent of straight-line) over its useful life. The amortization of the rehabilitation expenditures would result in substantial additional depreciation. This rapid amortization of capital improvements to low-income housing projects applies until 1982, unless extended by Congress.

The federal housing programs for low-income households are discussed in Chapter 20. Apartment units constructed new or rehabilitated in one of these programs, such as Section 8, obtain much of their market value from the tax shelters which they generate from the use of allowable rapid write-off depreciation methods, or if rehabilitated, from the five-year amortization of rehabilitation expenditures. The market value of these projects is also enhanced by the favorable capital gain treatment which they receive at time of sale, which moderates the recapture of the capital gain.

Property tax incentives. Renovation and preservation may receive additional incentive by abatement of the real property tax. Structures eligible for abatement are typically in areas of the city designated as blighted (impacted) or historic, or the proposed project has been declared to be in the public interest. State and local statutes and practices differ in the manner in which the property tax abatement is given. In most instances, property taxes continue to be levied as assessed prior to the improvement, but the value added by renovation is not taxed. The tax abatement can be granted for periods of time up to 40 years, and the investor may be required to make payments to the municipality in lieu of the property tax forgiven. Alleviation of part of the property tax burden can, by itself, be a significant incentive for reuse and preservation, and when combined with the special depreciation rules and investment credits for qualified projects, real property tax abatement can be the marginal inducement to reuse of existing structures.

DEMOLITION AND REUSE

Casual inspection of any urban area will reveal demolitions of existing buildings. Sometimes the site is to be left vacant, or perhaps to be put to an interim "taxpayer" use, such as a parking lot; at other times, another building is immediately constructed on the site. Demolition may occur only after the existing building has accumulated substantial physical deterioration and functional and locational obsolescence. In some instances, the building may have been abandoned at the time of demolition and may have been removed only after the court found it to be a hazard to the public health and safety. However, the removal of relatively new buildings for a replacement use can sometimes also be observed. Such demolitions may be the result of a "taking" for a public purpose, or they may reflect profit-motivated decisions in the private sector.

The speed of reuse will depend upon the factors which affect the demand for the type of land use appropriate at the given location and upon the competition of alternative sites. At the time of reuse, the value of the site is determined by the new building, which is judged to be the highest and best use of the site. As discussed in Chapter 3, if an existing improvement already occupied the site, it no longer represented the highest and best use of the site and no longer contributed to property value.

Reuse of an urban site occurs when the site value under the new structure is sufficient to permit acquisition of the site and existing building at market value and to pay the costs of demolition and preparation of the site for the new structure. The reuse will yield a competitive return on investment and would have a positive net present value and a profitability index of 1.00 or greater. Reuse can involve assemblage of sites in order to increase the intensity of use. The value of the assembled sites when used as a single site for the new, more intense land use is typically greater than the sum of the values of the sites if used separately. This marginal increase in market value is known as plottage value.

Our ABC office property can be used to demonstrate the reuse decision and the concept of plottage. Let us suppose that the ABC office building was constructed by combining two adjacent lots. One lot was vacant; the second was improved with a small, older office building. The market value of the vacant site was $20,000; the value of the existing office building and lot was $32,000 ($20,000 site value; $12,000 building value). Demolition and site preparation for reuse were expected to total $5,000. The investor in the proposed reuse, our ABC office building, purchased both properties at market value ($52,000 total price) and, after paying the $5,000 demolition and site preparation costs, had $57,000 invested in a site suitable for the proposed ABC office building. Site value under the proposed reuse was estimated at $60,000, making the project feasible.[11] In this reuse, $20,000 of plottage value was created ($60,000 value of the combined sites under the new use, less $40,000, the sum of the values of the two sites used separately). The $20,000 site value of each lot used separately was the value under their respective highest and best use as a location for a smaller new office building. The aftertax investment analysis of the ABC office property in Chapter 5 further supports the feasibility of the reuse. A competitive aftertax internal rate of return was expected, and the investment was anticipated to generate a positive net present value.

SUMMARY

Real estate administration is a process involving continuing investment decisions. After the purchase or initial supply decision, the investor is faced with numerous decisions over the investment holding period. This chapter analyzes three of these decisions which have the

---

[11] The reader is referred to Chapter 4 for discussion of the estimation of site value for the ABC office property. Site value can be estimated by using the site, building, or property residual techniques, by mortgage-equity appraisal methods such as Ellwood, or by direct capitalization with an overall rate. The supposition is that building value equals the cost to create the structure when the site is improved to its highest and best use. Given this contention, site value under an assumed highest and best use (the proposed ABC office building in this instance) can be estimated by substracting the cost to create the building, or $315,800, from the total estimated value for the property ($375,800) found by using one of the above valuation techniques. The site residual technique, of course, estimates site value directly. The reader is referred to Chapter 4 for discussion of these valuation methodologies.

potential of altering both the capital structure of the investment and the physical property.

The decision to spend on ordinary maintenance and repair is made to avert a future loss of income and property value. Conceptually, expenditures are made for maintenance and repair to the point where the present value of the expenditures over the investment holding period equals the present value of the averted loss of income and property value. As a practical matter, the decision to spend for maintenance and repair is made within the time horizon of the foreseeable future. The investor decides whether spending for maintenance and repair will keep the property competitive in the short run.

The decision to rehabilitate, remodel, convert, or engage in the historic preservation of an existing building involves an expenditure of funds that adds value to the property. The value added must at least equal the cost of the improvements, including labor, materials, contractor's overhead and profit, architectural fees, interest on construction financing, contingency reserves, and any rent loss during the rehabilitation period. The analysis of value added should be supplemented by a before and after investment analysis which examines changes in the aftertax internal rate of return, net present value, profitability index, debt service coverage, and break-even ratio. These indicators of investment performance should perform at least as well after rehabilitation as before. The uncertainties in forecasting the variables which contribute to changes in property value and investment profitability following rehabilitation or modernization result in the need for a margin of safety in the after analysis, which would be demonstrated by improved profitability measures or an excess of value added over cost.

Tax incentives have been provided by the government to encourage reuse of existing buildings, including first-year bonus depreciation and investment credit against taxes owed for tangible personal property purchased in the renovation of structures put to qualified uses. Historic preservation is promoted by the provision for a five-year amortization of rehabilitation expenditures or treatment of the investor as a "first user" of the property, who can elect to use allowable accelerated depreciation. Or, the investor in a historic preservation project may elect to take a 10 percent investment credit on the rehabilitation expenditures. Investors in rehabilitated housing for lower-income families are benefited by five-year amortization of capital improvements; renewal of older commercial and industrial structures is encouraged by a 10 percent investment credit for rehabilitation expenditures. In addition to these various income tax incentives, in many communities abatement of the real property tax has given impetus to the rehabilitation and preservation of selected properties.

Demolition of an existing structure and the reuse of an urban site occur when the existing building is no longer the highest and best use of the site and contributes nothing to the value of the property, which has become site value only. Reuse occurs when the site value under the new use is sufficient to permit purchase of the existing structure and site at market value and to pay for the costs of demolition and site preparation for the new use. The proposed reuse will yield a competitive rate of return on investment and will produce a positive net present value.

In addition to decisions which affect both the capital structure of the investment and the physical property, the investor must periodically make decisions which have the potential of altering the value of the equity and the investor's ownership position. These decisions include rent adjustments, refinancing, altering tax depreciation schedules, conversion to condominiums, sale of the property, sale and leaseback, an exchange for a property of like kind, and abandonment. In making these investment decisions, the real estate investor must continually fine-tune the investment to maximize the value of the equity position. In this process, the investor is sensitive to the returns available on competitive investments and to the portfolio considerations discussed in Chapter 6.

QUESTIONS FOR REVIEW

1. How can altering the rent schedule of an apartment building affect the capital structure (debt/equity relationship) of the investment?

2. Ms. X purchased a property with an equity investment of $100,000 and a $800,000 mortgage. She has held the property for five years, and the mortgage now has a balance of $750,000. The market value of her property is $950,000. What is her present equity investment, and why?

3. When performing an explicit aftertax investment analysis of a proposed rehabilitation project, why might expected market value after rehabilitation be used to compute return on investment, rather than "before" market value plus the estimated cost of rehabilitation?

4. What should be included as costs to be matched by value added after rehabilitation?

5. Distinguish among rehabilitation, remodeling, and historic preservation.

6. In what ways are the maintenance and repair decision and the rehabilitation decision similar? How do they differ?

7. What factors can change in the appraisal to estimate property value after rehabilitation to produce a higher "after" value?

8. What might result in a different rate of discount or a different equity yield rate in the "after" valuation?

9. Distinguish among a nominal rate of return, a real rate of return, and a risk-adjusted rate of return.

10. The demand for office space has intensified in the community. How may the standing stock of office structures be changed to meet this increase in demand?

11. Does the contention "You get what you pay for" have any relevance to the housing condition of American households?

REFERENCES

American Institute of Real Estate Appraisers. *The Appraisal of Real Estate.* 7th ed. Chicago, 1978, pp. 497–505.

Higgins, J. Warren. *A Federal Guide for Real Estate Decisions.* Real Estate Report no. 31. Storrs: Center for Real Estate and Urban Economic Studies, University of Connecticut, 1980.

Martin, Thomas J., et al. *Adaptive Use.* Washington, D.C.: Urban Land Institute, 1978.

Morton, W. Brown, and Hume, Gary L. *The Secretary of the Interior's Standards for Historic Preservation Projects.* Washington, D.C.: U.S. Department of the Interior, 1979.

part two

Investment opportunity

and constraint

chapter 8

Productivity analysis

The measurement of market value and the calculation of rates of return lead to the question of what factors are responsible for producing market value and investment value. Modern value theory emphasizes the role of productivity in relation to scarcity as the essential cause of real estate's ability to produce income. In this chapter, we are concerned with identifying and understanding the elements of real estate productivity. This understanding is essential if the investor is to attain insight into all the important factors that may affect a property's income-producing ability.

NATURE OF PRODUCTIVITY

The concept of productivity involves the relationship between the value of inputs and the value of outputs. A productive enterprise is one in which the value of the outputs is greater than the input values. Usually this phenomenon is accomplished by a rearranging of the inputs into a final product or service that has greater value than the sum total of the inputs. For example, various materials (such as steel, glass, and rubber), machines, labor, and managerial talent go into the production of automobiles. The materials are purchased, the machines are depreciated, and workers' wages and managers' salaries are paid. Yet the automobile company may end up with a surplus above the payment of all costs. This surplus is a profit, and over the long run it represents the productivity of the firm.

ELEMENTS OF PRODUCTIVITY

Real estate can have value because it too enters into the productive process. It is combined with other factors of production to yield services and other goods, the sum total of which have a greater value than that of the factors added together. In the automobile example, real estate should also be listed as one of the input factors. The land provides a location for assembling the automobiles, and a building provides shelter for the employees and a base for the machines used in the production process.

The use to which a property is put is dependent upon the relationship between two relevant prices for any property—the maximum price that a buyer will pay for the property and the minimum price for which the owner will sell the property. As explained by Bish and Nourse, a buyer's ceiling price can be conceptualized as the present worth of the property's expected future cash flow, less any costs of construction, demolition, and redevelopment:[1]

$$V_b = \sum_{i=1}^{n} \left[\frac{R_i - O_i}{(1 + r)^i} - \frac{C_i}{(1 + r)^i} \right]$$

where

V_b = Buyer's ceiling price
n = Remaining economic life of property or planned investment period
R_i = Receipts, including rents and other periodic income and net cash receipts upon resale
O_i = Property operating expenses
C_i = Cost of construction or demolition and redevelopment
r = Buyer's cost of capital—the rate of return on alternative, equally risky alternatives

If a building desired by the buyer were already on the site, construction cost (C_i) would be zero. If, however, the building on the site were old and inappropriate for the buyer, the cost of demolishing the old building and constructing an appropriate building would be included in C_i.

The seller's minimum price (V_s) is determined by the same formula, except that C_i includes the cost of an alternative property that

---

[1] Robert L. Bish and Hugh O. Nourse, *Urban Economics and Policy Analysis* (New York: McGraw-Hill, 1975), pp. 80–81.

will satisfy the seller's needs equally well. This cost is included by owners because they will either continue to require the same type of property or they will convert the value of the property to another type of asset, such as cash. In other words, owners seek to avoid diminishing the value of their asset when selling a property.

When the seller's minimum price is equal to or lower than the buyer's maximum price ($V_s \lessgtr V_b$), a transaction occurs. If a seller's minimum price remains higher than all buyers' maximum prices for the property, no transaction for that property occurs. Thus, at any point in time, the real estate market can be conceptualized as a set of properties for which each owner has a floor price and potential buyers have ceiling prices. Market activity, in the form of transactions, occurs when one of the potential buyers' ceiling prices becomes at least equal to a seller's floor price, or when an owner's floor price becomes equal to the ceiling price of one or more buyers.

A buyer's ceiling price and a seller's floor price are established by each market participant's evaluation of the future ability of the property to experience the input variables: What receipts and expenses will be associated with the property? What amount of construction costs must be incurred to make the property useful? And what is the appropriate rate of return for the investment?

The assessment by each market participant of these variables is ultimately dependent upon the property's productivity—that is, the extent to which it will be able to generate net income, cash flow, appreciation, or other economic advantages. In the case of residential property, the productivity of property in terms of its ability to provide amenities is also considered.

While a great many factors determine a property's productivity, these factors can be grouped into three categories: *locational characteristics, physical characteristics,* and *legal characteristics.* The first two, locational and physical characteristics, may be regarded as *inherent* to the property; that is, they are not determined by a set of man-made *rules* or formulas. The last category, legal characteristics, may be regarded as less inherent to the property itself and more determined by external, third-party organizations and agencies—the U.S. Congress, state legislatures, federal and state courts, local governing bodies, and administrative agencies.

The basic legal structure surrounding real estate is presented in Chapters 10 and 11. The federal income tax and the real estate tax are also important productivity factors within the legal category that are discussed in separate chapters. In this chapter, we discuss the two categories of inherent productivity factors—locational characteristics and physical characteristics.

Location is an important element in the productivity of real estate because of the transportation and communication necessary between parcels of real estate. In the manufacture of automobiles the factory's access to raw materials, labor inputs, and consumer markets partially determines whether the manufacturer makes a profit. Similarly, the ability of a parcel of real estate to fulfill certain physical requirements is a determinant of its income-producing ability. If the automobile factory had been built on marshy land, or if the building were too small, the company's profit position would be impaired. Thus real estate, can be productive in two general ways: first, in a parcel's convenience or location relative to other parcels of real estate; and second, in a parcel's physical capacity to provide desirable materials or services.

LOCATIONAL CHARACTERISTICS

Locational characteristics involve the costs of transferring people, information, goods, and services from one site to other sites. Locational characteristics are concerned with a property's geographic relationship to other parcels of real estate. As Ratcliff puts it:

> The essence of location derives from one of the elemental physical facts of life, the reality of space. We cannot conceive of existence without space; if there were no such thing, all objects and all life would have to be at one spot. If this happened to be the case, real estate would have no such quality as location; all real estate would be in the same place, equally convenient to every other piece of real estate and to every human activity and establishment. But under the physical laws of the universe, each bit of matter—each atom, molecule, stone, dog, house, and man—takes up space at or near the surface of the earth. As a result, no two objects can be at the same place at the same time. Necessarily, then, all people, animals, and objects are distributed in a spatial pattern.[2]

From this explanation we can realize that location involves transfer and that transfer costs arise because the user of a parcel of real estate is not in immediate proximity to users of other parcels of real estate. The conveyance of people, information, goods, and services is hindered by the geographic barrier or friction of space. An analysis of transfer costs and advantages is thus concerned with the cost of overcoming this friction associated with a parcel of real estate relative to such costs associated with competing parcels.

Most probable use

The use to which real estate is put is an important determinant of its transfer costs. For example, the transfer costs of a single-family resi-

---

[2] Richard U. Ratcliff, *Real Estate Analysis* (New York: McGraw-Hill, 1961), p. 62.

dence will differ greatly from those of a retail store. Therefore, an analyst must attempt to identify the most likely future use of a parcel of real estate. In some cases the future use is already determined. The zoning ordinance, for example, may limit the parcel to single-family residential or light industrial usage. Also, many parcels of real estate include a costly improvement component. A building that is several times as valuable as the land will ordinarily not be torn down even if some other improvement would be a better use of the land; the costs of demolition and erection of a new structure usually outweigh the benefits to be gained. The analyst has little choice but to assume that the existing land use will be continued into the foreseeable future.

In cases where land-use determination has considerable leeway— for example, vacant, unzoned land or land improved with structures having relatively low value and not subject to stringent zoning regulations—the analyst cannot necessarily assume that the current use will continue. Instead, it must be decided what use will provide the greatest return on investment after both processing and transfer costs have been deducted. Conceptually, this is done by holding constant the income and processing costs of several potential uses to see how the transfer costs vary among them. When one finds several uses having low transfer costs, the total income expected, less anticipated expenses or processing costs, is examined. The combination yielding the lowest transfer costs and the highest income after processing costs is the financially justified use to which the land should be put.

Analysis procedure

Transfer costs can be regarded as linkages with other parcels of real estate. The term *linkage* implies that there is a need or desire for communication or for conveyance of goods, services, or persons between the subject parcel and other parcels of real estate. To the extent that one parcel of real estate is more favorably located with respect to the linkages for the use to which it is likely to be put than are other parcels having similar use expectations, the subject parcel enjoys transfer advantages. An identification of expected linkages, judgment as to their relative importance to each other, and comparison between the expected linkages of the subject parcel and the linkages of other parcels having the same use potential are the steps necessary to carry out an analysis of transfer advantages.

Identification of expected linkages. Linkages arise because of the need for persons, goods, services or information to come to the subject parcel or to go from the subject parcel to other locations. When the people, goods, services, or information come to the subject parcel they are termed inputs; when they go from the property they can be regarded as outputs. Thus, a manufacturing plant receives people (managers and laborers), goods (raw materials), capital (buildings and machines), and information as inputs. It processes all of these factors and puts out manufactured products.

A residential property typically has inputs of capital (the structure and other improvements), people (the occupants), goods (groceries, clothes, furniture, and so on), and information; its outputs are people who have been sheltered, clothed, maintained, and pleasantly comforted. The output of residential services, as well as the produce of the manufacturing plant, must be transferred to (have linkages with) schools, stores, place of work, churches, and so forth. In a like way, commercial establishments, public service facilities, and other land uses have inputs and outputs. Both types of transfer needs must be analyzed.

The significance of the input-output distinction lies in the determination of the most desirable location and physical situation for a particular function. If we think of input markets on one side and output markets on the other, we may graph the relative desirability of potential sites in terms of their total transfer costs, as shown in Figure 8–1.

FIGURE 8–1
Input, output, and total transfer costs

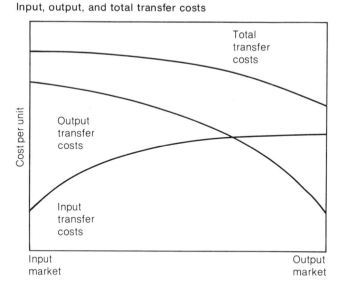

There is an optimal location, assuming equal physical facilities, between the two markets. This optimal location is usually much closer to one market or the other, depending on whether the product is weight-gaining or weight-losing. A weight-gaining product is one such as beer or soft drinks which by the addition of material (water) gains weight in its processing. Obviously the transportation of water is very expensive relative to the value of the product; therefore, the choice between locating a brewery at the source of raw materials and locating it at the consumption market should be made in favor of the latter.

Some products, iron for example, lose weight in processing. When relatively valuable material must be separated from other, heavy waste material, as in the case of separating iron ore from the earth, the location dictated is near the source of raw materials. Sometimes such a decision is determined by the presence of a vital input, such as cheap labor, in one location but not in others. This factor, however, is a physical factor involving processing costs and does not properly fall under the category of transfer costs.

When identifying linkages which are believed to be important in the expected future use of a particular location, the analyst can often usefully employ a mapping technique such as that shown in Figure 8–2 for a residential property. The advantages of visualizing expected

FIGURE 8–2
Linkages with single-family residence

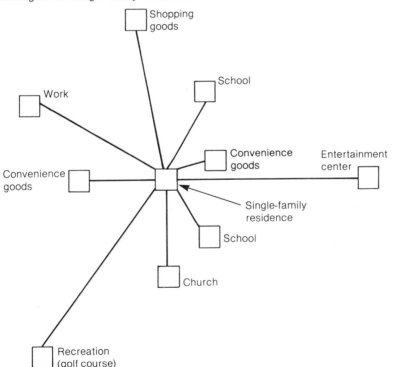

Note: The linkage lines are effective distances; that is, they account for difficulty as well as distance between the site and the linked establishments.

linkages are twofold: the analyst is less likely to omit important linkages, and in viewing the total linkage situation, the relative importance
of the linkages can be assessed. Only the important linkages need be
shown. Minor linkage requirements will tend to even out in terms of
relative advantage among prospective sites.

Judging relative importance of expected linkages.   The importance of the various linkages must often be judged for the average or
typical user of the real estate. For example, in deciding whether to
invest in an apartment project, the investor must consider the places to
which the typical occupant will desire to commute. If adequate
facilities are not available for some necessary linkages, such as shopping centers and schools, the project should be rejected, or means
should be found to provide these services in nearby locations. Similarly, in analyzing linkages for a speculative housing development, the
analyst must consider what linkages will be found desirable by most
people in the market the developer hopes to serve.

The prospective buyer-occupants can also analyze the linkages
with respect to their own specific requirements. Unless definite plans
can be made to stay permanently, however, the linkages other possible
purchasers would find desirable should also be considered.

Comparison of transfer costs.   The advantages of transfer provided
by competing sites should be analyzed for the obvious reason that
another site may have lower total transfer costs for the desired linkages. If the other important variables (incomes or benefits, processing
costs, and price) are equally favorable, a decision to reject the subject
site in favor of the competing site is required by financial sanity. The
real estate specialist (broker, sales representative, investor, appraiser,
or consultant) who works in a fairly small market area usually knows
the relative advantages of all or most sites for fulfilling various
functional requirements. Although the analysis may not be written or specified in the above manner, it is performed nonetheless.
The person less familiar with the site and its surroundings would
do well to perform the steps prescribed here in a definite, detailed
manner.

PHYSICAL CHARACTERISTICS

The physical characteristics of a property include physical aspects
of both the land and improvements. With regard to the land, the physical characteristics include the chemical and physical makeup of the
site (for example, ore mining), the availability of water, the suitability
of the soil and climate for agriculture, the natural flora and fauna (for
trapping, fishing, hunting, forestry, or grazing), the amenities of the
site (climate, view, and terrain), and those features of the site which

determine construction and maintenance cost (primarily terrain, soil structure, and climate).[3] Additionally, the site may have been leveled and graded, had storm and sanitary sewers installed, had drives and walks paved, and been landscaped.

Even when no detectable improvements have been made to the site itself, public improvements (off-site improvements or improvements in common) serve to make the land more valuable. Streets, the lighting system, public sewers, parks, and sidewalks are all important value-determining characteristics. All such improvements, as well as on-site improvements, represent applications of labor, capital, and managerial talent to the parcel of land. They become wedded in an inseparable marriage in which the contribution of one factor cannot be separated from that of the others. In almost every instance of urban land analysis, it must be recognized that much more is involved than simply the original and indestructible qualities of the land. In this sense, real estate is, as Ratcliff has emphasized, a manufactured product.[4]

Physical characteristics of improvements refer to their size, shape, quality, condition, architectural style, and subsidiary systems (such as heating, air-conditioning, electrical, and plumbing systems). In addition to major improvements, such as a principal building, secondary or support improvements (such as garages, barns and other agricultural outbuildings, cooling towers, and so forth) must be evaluated in terms of their physical characteristics.

All such characteristics and modifications of urban land may be thought of as imparting processing advantages. They determine the efficiency and capacity with which real estate can perform services and provide benefits. They determine how well a parcel of real estate provides the amenities of home ownership, how much corn another parcel can produce, how well an office building performs its function, how many cattle can be supported on a range, how many automobiles can be produced in a factory, and how many lobsters can be caught in a particular oceanic area. The real estate analyst must examine and consider each characteristic or feature of a given parcel that would have a bearing on its future processing advantage. Poor construction, inadequate utilities, inappropriate style, and insufficient lighting would be examples of unfavorable factors that would influence the processing advantage of a parcel of real estate relative to other, competing parcels. Such characteristics obviously would tend to reduce future net income or services in relation to other properties and thus to reduce its value.

---

[3] Edgar M. Hoover, *The Location of Economic Activity* (New York: McGraw-Hill, 1963), p. 91.

[4] Ratcliff, *Real Estate Analysis*, pp. 1, 43, 54–55.

Analysis of physical characteristics—the site

The physical characteristics of a parcel of real estate determine the property's processing costs. Characteristics of the site are usually analyzed separately from those of major on-site improvements. The major improvement will often dictate the type of analysis performed for the site, although this distinction would be unrealistic for some types of improvements. For example, an intensive analysis of the agricultural fertility of a parcel of real estate that is already improved with an appropriate, costly commercial structure would be inappropriate. Beginning with the site, then, analysis of the processing characteristics includes the following possible categories of factors: (a) geological characteristics, (b) agricultural fertility, (c) surface characteristics, and (d) facilitating improvements.

Geological characteristics. Subsurface characteristics of the soil are important in determining the support which can be provided to buildings, drainage and seepage, and the possibility of mineral extraction. The degree to which the last would be profitable can be analyzed only by competent specialists.

Subsurface soil characteristics may also impose strict limitations to the type of improvement that can be erected on the surface. Marshy, swampy areas or areas subject to volcanic activity require more costly construction techniques to support buildings, although in most cases suitable structures can be built if costly, specialized techniques are used. The Imperial Hotel in Tokyo, designed by Frank Lloyd Wright, is a foremost example of how potential damage from earthquakes can be overcome. It was erected in the years 1916–22, using a revolutionary, floating cantilever construction to provide the required flexibility to absorb shocks. A tremendous earthquake shortly after the construction left the structure standing unaffected, while almost every other building in Tokyo was destroyed.

In Chicago, where land is marshy, huge piers must be sunk to bedrock to support tall buildings. The costs of this additional construction requirement limited the height of Chicago's skyscrapers to fewer than 45 stories until the mid-1960s, when newer construction techniques allowed the 100-story John Hancock Center and the 60-story First National Bank Building to be constructed. Since then the Sears Tower, which is the world's tallest office building, has been constructed. Sometimes the culprit is quicksand. An adequate number of borings to test for the presence of quicksand and other geological characteristics should always be made before construction contracts are signed.

Where rock is close to the surface of the land, additional costs for excavation are encountered. Basements are much costlier, and subsurface sewage, electrical, and telephone placements are more difficult and costly. Also, impervious soils and subsurface rock may affect the drainage and seepage of the land. The area may be subject to flooding, precluding the proper drainage of storm and sanitary sewage. The elevation of the surface in relation to surrounding land can also be a determinant of drainage.

Agricultural fertility. This factor should obviously be considered when a prospective real estate investment will involve agronomic endeavors. Appropriate agricultural experts should be employed to perform such analysis. A resort to do-it-yourself analysis, opinion by the owner or neighbors, or other nonscientific approaches will usually yield unreliable results.

Surface characteristics. The terrain, size, shape, vegetation, and exposure are characteristics of the surface of a parcel of real estate which may possibly influence value. Hilly terrain and woods require costly modifications for commercial, industrial, or low-cost residential uses. Long, narrow lots are not suitable in today's market for single-family residences. Extreme irregularity in the shape of a residential lot is undesirable, while pleasant views and attractive neighborhood structures are important advantages. Additionally, the freedom from obnoxious odors and noises is a virtual necessity for middle- and upper-class residential neighborhoods. Having adequate foot traffic and exposure to appropriate clientele is necessary for commercial uses.

Sometimes a lot is of insufficient size to accommodate a desired use, and two or more parcels are combined to produce the desired size. When the combined parcels have a greater value than the sum of the values of the individual parcels before being combined, the difference is called *plottage value.*

Facilitating improvements. These represent capital expenditures on *and* off the site for such improvements as utilities, paving, subsidiary buildings (for example, a garage), and landscaping. The analyst should identify all such improvements and consider their adequacy or the cost of installing adequate facilities. For well-established uses the amount of analysis may be relatively small; facilitating improvements would have been needed and installed already. New uses, however, may require significant attention to such items. For example, before Anheuser Busch located a new brewery near Columbus, Ohio, a great deal of analysis was required to determine whether the water supply would be adequate to meet the great needs of a large brewery.

Analysis of physical characteristics—the major improvement

Analysis of the major improvement must be tailored to the specific type of structure. Often experts are required to judge the quality and condition of the construction of large, steel-frame buildings or of special-purpose structures, such as a grain elevator or a refinery. For any building the following items should be examined relative to their physical characteristics: (*a*) construction, (*b*) functional capability, and (*c*) subsidiary systems.

Construction.   Quality and condition of the structural components are the criteria to be considered in evaluating construction. Studs, rafters, joists, subflooring, foundations, footings, and the roof are examples of such components. Quality of the physical components should be judged relative to their original character and workmanship, while condition should indicate how much physical deterioration has occurred. A ten-year-old bathtub that was of high quality when installed and is in good condition may contribute more to a home than a new tub of lesser quality. If the ten-year-old tub is functionally less desirable than a new tub, that penalty should be reflected under the following category.

Functional capability.   The degree to which the size, shape, arrangement, lighting, and general appropriateness of the building and its component rooms are adequate determines functional capability. Such considerations can be of overriding importance to the financial success of a real estate venture. For example, a large, high-rise, luxury apartment building in a midwestern city experienced financial difficulty because of the small size of the rooms and apartments. Persons seeking that type of housing were unwilling to accept the small quarters even at reduced rents. The investors lost their shirts, and the Federal Housing Administration, which insured the mortgage, was forced to take over the building.

Subsidiary systems.   Heating, air-conditioning, electrical, plumbing, and elevator systems contribute to the overall productivity of the property. These systems should be examined with respect to their *future* capacity and efficiency. Usually the analyst must estimate the age of these components, their condition, and their capacity to continue to perform their intended functions. These systems will normally have to be replaced one or more times over the life of a building.

Use of checklists

To lessen the likelihood of omitting small but important details, the analyst should develop a checklist for use in analyzing a major improvement. In single-family residential buildings, for example, one should begin in the basement, examining such items as the floor, walls, foundation, plumbing, furnace, water heater, laundry facilities, subflooring, windows, and stairs. Upper floors should be examined in respect to room size, layout, shape, and decorating; condition of walls, floors, and ceilings, electrical outlets, and heating ducts; and condition and adequacy of fixtures such as the kitchen sink, disposal, and bath appliances. The attic should be examined with respect to rafters, sheathing, insulation, ventilation, and general condition. Obviously, an analysis of larger commercial, industrial, and apartment buildings would be more complex.

Lastly, the exterior of a building should be examined. The siding, foundation, chimneys, porches, and windows should be noted for quality and condition. Aspects of the site, such as landscaping and paving, will have been considered under site-processing advantages or costs, discussed above.

PRODUCTIVITY AND LAND-USE PATTERNS

The ability of a particular parcel of real estate to enter the productive process can differ according to its favorable or unfavorable locational or physical characteristics relative to those of other parcels. Differences in future productivity expectations—whether due to physical or transfer factors—usually result in different values among properties. Even with significant differences in physical and locational characteristics among properties, however, similarities among properties result in land-use patterns that are both discernible and predictable. Similarities in the transfer advantages of a number of sites cause supply competition to take place, thus refuting the idea that land income is more of a monopolistic rent than is the income to other factors of production.[5] Certainly elements of monopoly may be motivating factors in producing land income, but no more so than for the return to labor or capital. When any commodity or service is in short supply, the owners thereof have some monopolistic control over it. A general theory of factor income would impute no difference between land and other production factors with respect to whether the income was caused by monopoly.

Patterns of development

Decision makers, whether they be private investors, government agencies, or business firms, apply different weights to the various loca-

[5] See Edward Chamberlin, *Monopolistic Competition* (Cambridge, Mass.: Harvard University Press, 1939), appendix D, "Urban Rent as a Monopoly Income," pp. 214–17, for the viewpoint that income to real estate represents a monopoly return. This viewpoint derives from the contention that each parcel of land is unique in its locational characteristics and therefore cannot be considered as in direct competition with other parcels of real estate in supplying specific locational needs. According to Chamberlin, the locational characteristics of urban land are different from those of agricultural land. Urban land carries its market with it, and the rent paid represents the value of the monopoly privilege of providing retail services *at that particular place.*

tional and physical characteristics upon which they base their decisions. For example, some homebuyers demand five bedrooms, while others want three bedrooms; some buyers prefer a brick house, while others want frame or stone. Even when the same criteria are used, different weights are assigned to them by the various buyers in the market. For example, while the availability of water is important to all industrial firms in choosing a location, it is of relatively greater importance to a brewery than to most other types of firms.

We have pointed out, however, that even with the great diversity of investors, there are common objectives and investment criteria operating within the private enterprise framework. In pursuing common objectives, investors rank the various productivity characteristics and produce patterns of similar decisions. Groups of similar decisions, in turn, result in discernible patterns of land use and types of structures. We now consider these patterns and the tendencies toward proportionality that result from the actions of a myriad of individual real estate decision makers.

Land-use patterns

If the types of land use are categorized and a map is made showing the categories, it would show for all cities definite areas devoted predominantly to a particular use. Figures 8–3 and 8–4 show two views

FIGURE 8–3
Land-use map of Columbus, Ohio

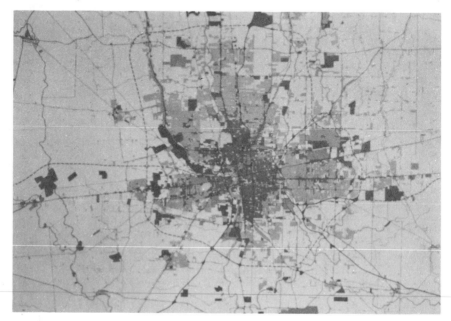

FIGURE 8–4
Close-up view of land-use map of Columbus, Ohio

(one, a close-up view) of a land-use map of Columbus, Ohio. The uses shown on the map are categorized into various degrees of residential density and other land uses, such as industrial, commercial and office, and public and quasi-public facilities. One can notice that commercial usage predominates at the center of the city, while high-density residential areas surround the core.

Relatively independent residential areas develop outward from the older residential, commercial, and light manufacturing areas. These may be communities within the major city, or they may be suburban communities having separate governments. They are satellites to the major city, however, in that many of their residents work in the major city. In short, there is usually economic integration of the major city and outlying suburban communities, but there is also segregation of economic classes, races, and social structure. The satellite communities, whether within the major city or politically separate, are served by stores selling primarily convenience goods, but with some stores having shopping goods. From an everyday living standpoint the satellite communities are independent; from the point of view of the breadwinner's source of income, the location of major shopping purchases, and the location of entertainment and cultural activities, the satellite communities are part of the major city.

Industrial areas are scattered somewhat sporadically around the city, although heavy manufacturing is usually located on the periphery of the densely occupied area or along railroad tracks or riverfronts.

Theories of urban growth

In looking at land-use patterns that have developed in the expansion of urban areas, one may begin to wonder what forces brought about the quiltwork of uses that at the same time seems to have both chaos and order. The identification and description of these forces would be an important step in the prediction of the future growth patterns of cities. Growth theory would also help to decide what is an optimal distribution or quantity of various land-use types and at least provide some clues about how to cope with the social problems of poverty, crime, and juvenile delinquency which occur in overpopulated areas. If some of the expansionary forces that breed these problems could be controlled and regulated, both privately and through action of city governments, perhaps the problems could be attacked more intelligently.

Several theories of urban growth have been advanced by economists and sociologists. These so-called theories have described urban areas as developing in concentric circles,[6] in sectors,[7] around multiple nuclei,[8] or along lines of transportation. While these so-called theories may hold some value for descriptive purposes, they lack predictive capabilities, and thus fail to qualify as legitimate theories. For example, the theories do not explain or predict how wide the concentric circles should be, where new sectors or nuclei will begin or how large they will be, or where new or expanded lines of transportation will be established. Such theories are incapable of predicting spontaneous events or of anticipating reactions of market participants to investment opportunities and constraints.

Because of the inadequacies of descriptive theories to forecast development trends and patterns, a real estate analyst can more profitably rely upon knowledge of the investment decision-making process as applied to land resources in order to formulate forecasts of future land use. We must recognize that many real estate decisions are unpredict-

---

[6] Ernest W. Burgess, "The Growth of the City," in *The City,* edited by Robert E. Park, Ernest W. Burgess, and Roderick D. McKenzie (Chicago: University of Chicago Press, 1925), pp. 47–62.

[7] Arthur M. Weimer, Homer Hoyt, and George F. Bloom, *Real Estate,* 7th ed. (New York: Ronald Press, 1978), p. 212.

[8] Chauncey D. Harris and Edward L. Ullman, "The Nature of Cities," in *Building the Future City, Annals of the American Academy of Political and Social Sciences,* no. 242 (November 1945), pp. 7–17.

able. A rundown warehouse may seem a candidate for demolition to most observers; yet some entrepreneur may recognize an opportunity to rehabilitate the building to a profitable theme restaurant. A parcel of land may seem to be useful only for agricultural purposes; yet a developer may recognize an opportunity to develop the land into a high-value residential area. Nevertheless, some generalizations have been observed and tested in urban real estate markets.

Market equilibrium

Land is bought and sold in markets, as are other economic goods and services. Since land is a market good, its prices tend toward an equilibrium in which no owner of a particular type or quality of land has an economic advantage over other owners. Thus, all users of a particular type and quality of land tend to pay prices for land that will equalize their position with that of other users and with their own potential use of other competing parcels.

Since there are almost always numerous parcels of land that are physically suitable for a particular use—such as construction of an automobile assembly plant, a brewery, or a residential subdivision—location becomes the crucial variable in the tendency toward equilibrium. That is, access to input and output markets will determine whether production at a particular site will allow a firm to be competitive with other firms. As noted earlier in this chapter, firms (and households) analyze their competitive position in terms of linkages and transfer costs between various potentially usable parcels and their input and output markets. The tendency toward equilibrium of land prices and economic rents often results in discernible patterns of land use and development. Thus, compatible types of commercial uses tend to locate in proximity to each other, as do compatible types of residential and industrial uses.

Location analysts must recognize that the tendency toward equilibrium assumes that bidders for a given parcel need the same type and quality of land. However, this assumption is unrealistic in that there are always differences among demanders (firms and households) that will cause each bidder to perceive the costs and advantages of a particular site slightly differently. Therefore, as transportation costs increase with distance from a market, there will be differences among demanders in the costs they will experience. As shown in Figure 8–5, as distance from a market increases, the price that each demander can pay changes in such a way as to form a separate price-distance curve. Thus, for parcels of land located closer to the market than point S, firm 1 (F_1) will be able to outbid firm 2 (F_2); for market differences greater than S, F_2 will be able to outbid F_1. Since firms within an industry, or

FIGURE 8–5
Price-distance relationships

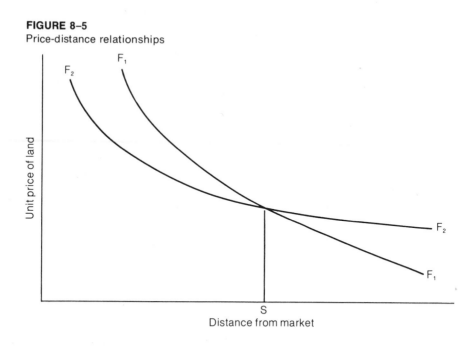

Distance from market

firms performing the same economic function, experience costs that are relatively similar as compared with the costs of firms in other industries, patterns of similar land uses tend to develop in urban areas. As noted previously in this chapter, economists and sociologists have described these patterns in terms of concentric circles, sectors, and nuclei.

Population density gradient

Since transportation costs tend to increase with distance from common destinations within an urban area, population density tends to decrease as distance from central activities increases. Since the central business district (CBD) of many cities contains the greatest concentration of common activities, a number of studies of population density relative to the CBD have been conducted. These studies have confirmed the hypothesis that population per unit of land decreases with an increase in distance from the CBD. This decrease is known as the population density gradient. However, over the history of the United States, the population density gradient appears to have become less pronounced. This phenomenon can be seen in Figure 8–6, which shows two population density gradients, representing population-distance relationships at two different times for one city. Over time,

FIGURE 8–6
Population density gradients

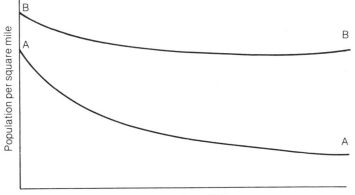

many U.S. cities have experienced shifts in population density gradients resembling the shift from AA to BB in Figure 8–6.

What are the causes of these shifts? We could cite several potential reasons, all of which undoubtedly play a role in the shifting relationship between population and distance from the CBD. The absolute increases in population have required the use of larger amounts of land, and there has been a tendency toward a trade-off between density and proximity. At the same time, the trends toward urbanization and economic specialization have lessened dependence on the CBD. Outlying employment and shopping centers have enabled larger numbers of people to reside at greater distance from the CBD. Racial and ethnic discrimination constrained growing numbers of minority population to central areas, but the social and economic problems generated by these nonmarket considerations produced an even greater population flight to outlying areas. Finally, increasing household incomes, coupled with low transportation costs, enabled increasing numbers of people to live farther from central activities in order to enjoy the benefits of more space and recreation. With the rapidly escalating energy costs experienced in recent years, it is reasonable to expect a shift toward higher population density gradients.

Household decisions

The preceding analysis provides a framework of the considerations that determine land values in an urban area. The framework applies equally well to business firms and households. If households, like business firms, can construct an equally appropriate improvement on a variety of sites, they will tend to bid up prices for residential sites that will minimize transportation costs while maintaining the desired set of physical characteristics (including such factors as terrain, elevation, neighborhood, vegetation, size, and shape).

For many households (and small businesses as well), however, the analysis must be reversed between locational and physical characteristics. Many parcels of residential and commercial land have existing structures which are appropriate substitutes for constructing new structures on vacant parcels. Furthermore, transportation costs do not vary significantly among parcels within one portion of an urban area. Thus, a household seeking a home in an urban area can hold constant the locational variable by confining the search to one part of town (such as the northwest or southeast quadrant) and considering only homes in this area having the desired physical characteristics (for example, five bedrooms, three baths, and a two-car garage). All sites within this area will be equally satisfactory from a locational standpoint; the decision variable is the desired set of physical characteristics.

Whether a household or a business firm regards (explicitly or implicitly) locational or physical characteristics as the decision variable, however, the model of market equilibrium still applies. Demanders attempt to maximize their economic position, given their needs and desires—for business firms, access to input and output markets; for households, access to employment, recreation, shopping, and a desirable set of existing physical characteristics. Demanders will bid prices which reflect their perception of the property's ability to meet their needs and desires within the constraint of their ability to pay. Generally, the highest bidder will be successful in obtaining and occupying the property.

Locational considerations in intraurban decisions

While the model of market equilibrium serves as the basis for explaining the development of land-use patterns, it provides only limited guidance in locational decisions regarding specific parcels of real estate. Thus, we now consider some principles and rules of thumb regarding locational aspects of specific site uses. Our analysis thus far has been largely deductive; that is, we have applied generalizations and theory to explain actual occurrences in the form of patterns and trends. Site-specific principles have been developed largely by inductive reasoning; that is, analysts have observed sites that have been successful for certain uses and unsuccessful for other uses and demanders' behavior that appears to account for success or the lack thereof.

These observations formulated as principles and rules of thumb are presented as guides to successful locational analysis for specific site uses.

Access is related to use.   Some types of uses require better or greater access than others. In general, establishments selling convenience goods and services require the highest degree of access. Convenience goods and services are relatively inexpensive items that are sold by a number of highly competitive establishments. Examples of such establishments are drugstores, variety stores, beverage carryouts, fast-food restaurants, service stations, dry-cleaning stores, barbershops, and beauty shops. Such uses require a high volume of passing traffic (automobile or foot traffic, or both), easy access to the establishment, and ample parking.

Often convenience establishments are located in shopping centers or are otherwise in close proximity with larger establishments which generate traffic. Convenience establishments are not major traffic generators, but rather rely upon customers generated by other establishments. The latter type of establishments are those which customers intend to visit when they begin a shopping journey and are known as *generative* establishments. Convenience establishments which rely on passersby are known as *suscipient* establishments.

Location is less crucial to establishments selling shopping goods—items for which customers will compare price and quality at several stores. Shopping goods are generally big-ticket items such as furniture, automobiles, musical instruments, jewelry, and clothing. Buyers of shopping goods are usually willing to travel farther and overcome more obstacles in order to patronize a shopping goods establishment. For example, it is not unusual for customers to travel 50 or 100 miles to purchase furniture or to travel 25 or 50 miles to enjoy the culinary delights of a particular restaurant.

The important point for real estate investors and analysts is that convenience establishments which do not generate customers must be located on sites that have easy access to passersby and customers generated by other establishments. A small shopping center comprised entirely of convenience goods establishments will probably be doomed to financial difficulties and potential failure unless it has easy access to a high volume of traffic. A single convenience store has similar requirements. Service stations must be located in the flow of traffic, with easy entry and exit.

Access is dependent upon transportation system design.   Access to establishments from transportation systems and routes is highly dependent upon the nature of the system. It is obvious, for example, that convenience stores located close to an interstate highway will not obtain customers from highway travelers unless the stores are also in close proximity to an exit from and entry to the highway. Similarly, travelers on mass transit modes such as airplanes or trains will not be able to patronize stores that are not located at points of origination or destination. Thus, hotels, motels, apartments, and shopping centers must be located at breakpoints of major transportation systems. Access to and from the systems must be easy, fast, and safe.

Less obvious aspects of access concern location relative to highway intersections and traffic flows. Many highway and street intersections exhibit uneven traffic flows. For example, in a four-way intersection the predominant traffic flow may be north to south. In such an intersection the best location, particularly for a convenience establishment, would be in the northwest quadrant. Southerly traffic would slow or

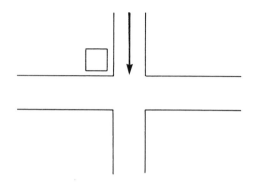

stop at the intersection and thus be more likely to stop at the establishment than if the establishment were located in other quadrants. If the establishment were located in the southwest quadrant, automobile traffic would tend not to stop because it would be accelerating after the intersection. The northeast and southeast quadrants would probably pose even greater obstacles to safe and easy access by southbound travelers.

Medians, one-way traffic patterns, and absence of on-street parking tend to lessen access. Some medians are crossable; some are not. Noncrossable medians limit access to the traffic proceeding in only one direction. Even crossable medians reduce access from traffic flow on the far side of the median. In such situations establishment entrepreneurs should locate on the side of predominant traffic flow.

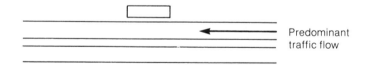

Predominant
traffic flow

Access is dependent upon timing of traffic flows.   Particularly in urban areas, the volume of traffic often varies with the time of day. Workers traveling to employment centers will cause traffic flows to be heavy in one direction in the mornings and heavy in the opposite direction in the evenings. Similarly, major recreational centers, such as a football or baseball stadium or a concert hall, will cause heavy traffic flows in one direction before events and in the opposite direction after events.

Typically travelers will not stop on their way to work or to recreational or other events. Unless they have allotted a specific amount of time for a stop, they would be tardy in reaching their destination. Therefore, an establishment can be located along a heavily traveled highway and obtain few customers, if most of the traffic has a specific destination other than home. If, however, most of the traffic is homeward bound, and time schedules are less pressing, travelers will stop to patronize convenience establishments.

As an example of the importance of the timing of traffic flows in relation to access, consider a small shopping plaza containing a moderate-price restaurant, a beverage carryout store, a pizza parlor, and a barbershop. The plaza is quite attractive, having been constructed only three years ago. It is located on a four-lane highway that has a crossable median and heads to the center of a large midwestern city. Although traffic counts along the highway were high, a real estate consultant counseled against the project. The accompanying sketch

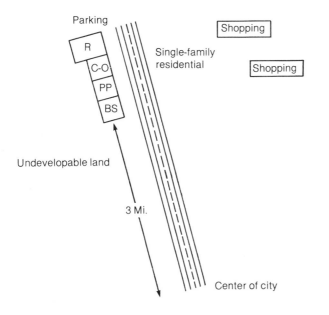

shows the relationships between the plaza and surrounding land uses. The real estate consultant advised the owner-developer to build an office building rather than the shopping plaza. The consultant's reasons for recommending against the shopping plaza were that the heavy traffic flows going toward the center of the city in the mornings would generate few customers. The evening traffic flows would also generate few customers because, although the median was crossable, a left-turn crossing would be hazardous, particularly with no deceleration lane and the threat of rear-end collision.

Residents of the area across the highway might be expected to patronize the plaza; however, the highway is a formidable barrier, and given alternative sources, residents prefer to purchase convenience goods without having to overcome such an obstacle. Certainly parents would not send their children across a hazardous four-lane highway to obtain nonessential items. The restaurant was the only traffic-generating establishment in the plaza, and the other establishments were not complementary to a restaurant. For example, dinner customers of the restaurant would usually not want to buy a pizza or get a haircut.

The experience of the plaza confirmed the consultant's advice. Although the volume of the restaurant was sufficient for it to remain in business, the other three establishments went out of business within a year after opening. The turnover of tenants has continued to be high, and the developer sold out for less than the investment cost. The plaza is an example of a real estate development whose locational factors were not favorable. The physical characteristics were acceptable— even good, since the improvements were new. However, poor timing of traffic flows, lack of access for the surrounding residents, and incompatibility between the one traffic-generating establishment and the other establishments were major negative locational factors.

Desirability of location depends upon compatibility of surrounding uses. In retailing businesses, location in terms of other compatible or incompatible businesses within the same trading center will affect the level of business volume. A drugstore located near a supermarket, bakery, or hardware store in a large shopping center would probably attract 10 to 20 percent more customers than it would if the surrounding businesses were gardening or household repair shops; its location near auto repair services or eating drive-ins would have a negative effect. Mortuaries tend to have a negative effect on many types of retail businesses.[9] Trade and professional organizations and unions

---

[9] Richard Lawrence Nelson, *The Selection of Retail Locations* (New York: McGraw-Hill, 1958), pp. 70–77, lists tables predicting the degree of compatibility, or interchange between various types of stores, in rural trading centers, neighborhood convenience centers, large shopping centers, and the central business district.

frequently locate near state capitals or in Washington, D.C., to conduct lobbying activities with state legislators, congressmen, and senators. They may also require ready access to state and federal agencies, such as a state banking regulatory authority (by a state bankers' association) or the U.S. Department of Labor (by a national labor union). Fire departments locate along major arteries close to the center of the area to be served.

Access can be created or destroyed. Changes in transportation systems and routes can greatly affect the desirability of a location. New travel routes will create desirable new locations and cause old ones to wither away. For example, many new locations for retail and service establishments were created at interchanges of interstate highways, while many locations along older major highways deteriorated rapidly after the construction of interstate highways.

In one case a developer acquired land and built a shopping center close to the intersection of an interstate and secondary highway. At the time there was no entrance to or exit from the interstate. However, the developer was able to persuade the state highway department and the federal highway administration that a cloverleaf was needed (partially on the basis of the existence of the shopping center). The cloverleaf greatly increased the center's business, which justified expansion of the center.

Similarly, the redesign of transportation systems within an urban area can enhance or downgrade a location. The closing, narrowing, or widening of streets can have a drastic impact upon locational desirability, as can the conversion of two-way streets to one-way. The removal of parking spaces along streets in downtown areas is often cited as a contributing factor to deterioration of the downtown retailing function.

SUMMARY

The productivity of real estate consists of two elements—physical characteristics and location (transfer characteristics). The physical characteristics of a property determine how well the property can be used for its intended purpose. The transfer characteristics determine how conveniently a property is situated in relation to other properties. The criterion for deciding whether some aspect (such as building design, convenience to a bus stop, or view) is a physical characteristic or a locational factor is whether the transfer of people, goods, or messages is involved. If transfer is involved, the factor under consideration is locational; if not, it is a physical characteristic.

The distinction between transfer and physical characteristics facilitates analysis of the productivity of a parcel of real estate. Although the physical characteristics of a property might be quite attractive, its location could be detrimental to the property's intended use. Conversely, a well-located property might be much less valuable than other equally well-located properties because of an unattractive, poorly constructed, or dysfunctional building. The analysis procedure for physical characteristics requires identification and evaluation of each principal physical aspect of a property. In analyzing transfer characteristics, all important linkages must be identified and their time-distances compared with those of competing properties.

The market process applied to land-use decisions tends to produce patterns of land uses. While some descriptive "theories" of urban growth have attempted to explain the phenomena of land-use patterns, these theories provide little predictability of future growth and use patterns. Thus, more meaningful analyses for real estate decision makers usually involve recognition of ceiling and floor prices, the tendency toward market equilibrium, and knowledge of population density gradients in urban areas.

Finally, we noted some principles and rules of thumb that are often useful in analyzing the locational aspects of specific sites. In considering proposed uses for sites, an analyst must evaluate the accessibility of the site in relation to a particular use. In this evaluation, an analyst must consider the timing of traffic flows, the transportation system design, and the compatibility of surrounding uses. The probability of changes in transportation systems and routes that can favorably or adversely affect access should always be assessed.

QUESTIONS FOR REVIEW

1. What is a buyer's ceiling price? How does the seller's minimum price differ from this?
2. What is meant by location?
3. In what ways is real estate considered to be productive?
4. What is meant by linkage? What are transfer costs? Why are these concepts important in finding desirable locations?
5. Why is the term *physical characteristics* more appropriate than the term *processing costs* for improved real estate?
6. Is the view from an apartment overlooking San Francisco Bay a physical or a locational characteristic? What about an attractive neighborhood in relation to a single-family residence? Why?
7. Can you think of examples in a city or cities of the growth patterns suggested by each of the theories of urban growth?
8. How could a real estate developer use each of the theories of urban growth to identify desirable areas for residential development?
9. Why does the population density gradient decrease as distance from the CBD increases?

10. What factors relating to access are important in retail trade? Is access important to an office building? If so, are the important factors different from those of retail establishments? How?

11. Why is the financial center of the United States concentrated around Wall Street at the southern tip of Manhattan?

12. Why did Pittsburgh and Gary develop into steel-producing centers?

REFERENCES

Barlowe, Raleigh. *Land Resource Economics*. 3d ed. Englewood Cliffs, N.J.: Prentice-Hall, 1978, chap. 9.

Bish, Robert L., and Nourse, Hugh O. *Urban Economics and Policy Analysis*. New York: McGraw-Hill, 1975, chaps. 3 and 4.

Haggett, Peter. *Locational Analysis in Human Geography*. New York: St. Martin's Press, 1966.

Hoover, Edgar M. *The Location of Economic Activity*. New York: McGraw-Hill, 1963.

Lawrence, Richard L. *The Selection of Retail Locations*. New York: McGraw-Hill, 1958.

Nourse, Hugh O. *Regional Economics*. New York: McGraw-Hill, 1968, chap. 4.

Ratcliff, Richard U. *Real Estate Analysis*. New York: McGraw-Hill, 1961, pp. 62–80.

Smith, Wallace F. *Urban Development: The Process and the Problems*. Berkeley: University of California Press, 1975, chaps. 3 and 6.

chapter 9

Community and market analysis

The extent to which any parcel of real estate is productive and thus has value is determined by the market within which it is bought and sold. Any decision about a property's most productive use or its most likely use—whether to buy, sell, improve, let deteriorate; what type of building to construct; how many stories a building should have; what the internal features of a building should be—and the timing of all these decisions can only be determined within a market framework. This chapter thus deals with the nature of real estate markets, the many types of forces influencing decision makers within a market, and the methods of analysis for estimating and predicting market decisions and trends.

A market may be conceptualized as including all the people, both potential buyers and potential sellers, and all the influences which tend to determine the price for which a property will be transacted. Beckman and Davidson define the term *market* as

> a sphere within which price-making forces operate and in which exchanges of title tend to be accompanied by the actual movement of the goods affected. . . . On a more general plane, the market is the mechanism by which the valuable resources of our society are allocated among the various alternative ends that compete for their use.[1]

---

[1] Theodore N. Beckman and William R. Davidson, *Marketing*, 8th ed. (New York: Ronald Press, 1967), pp. 3–6.

In analyzing a market, one must at least conceptually consider the types and characteristics of the people on both the buying and selling sides of the market and all of the activities, actions, and opinions occurring within society that may play a role in influencing the decisions of potential buyers and sellers. Obviously, there are so many potential influences on the motivations of human beings that all considerations can never be completely identified and measured. The reactions of people in the market to some new government policy or to a decision on land-use control by a city council can never be known with certainty. The influence on a community of a major industry's plans to expand can never be predicted with complete accuracy. Nor can the actions of a foreign government or an institution, such as a bank, be translated into some precise effect upon the value of an individual parcel of real estate. Nevertheless, the analyst's job is to attempt to discern which influences are important and what approximate effect such influences may have upon real estate productivity, decisions, and value.

Also, it must be pointed out that although important influences may be correctly identified, the quantification of these influences may be extremely difficult and their translation into value changes extremely hazardous and qualitative. Social trends occurring in our society are among the most important considerations that will influence long-run real estate values. The trend toward industrialization and urbanization, for example, has been one of the most important conditioners of life in our society. Industrial growth indicates new development of industrial real estate resources, which in turn leads to increased needs for commercial and residential resources. The effects of the trend toward industrialization, however, can be shown only in the most general terms, such as a general determination of which areas will grow, which areas will grow faster than others, and what types of growth to expect.

Social or behavioral trends may be of interest and value by themselves; however, real estate analysts attempt to relate them to the market with which they are dealing. A behavioral approach to the analysis of real estate would place primary reliance upon social and psychological variables. Only incidentally would social trends and psychological analysis result in economic measures of productivity. Since the purpose of this book, however, concerns the investment decision-making process, the social and psychological variables discussed in this chapter are placed within an economic framework. They are regarded as constituting some of the determinants of market prices. One of the most fertile areas for further research in real estate is the relation of behavioral (social and psychological) variables to real estate values and trends.

The first section of the chapter examines some economic models of market behavior. The purpose of this section is to allow the reader to understand the alternative models that are available and to build a case for one model, that of monopolistic competition, as being the most relevant for the economic good of real estate. Identification of a relevant market model allows the analyst to gain insight into the types of influences that may prevail in a market and what effects these influences may have upon potential buyers and sellers. Next, the chapter deals with the important types of influences on market behavior. These are divided into forces influencing demand and those influencing supply. A systematic identification and analysis of these forces is necessary in any market analysis. Then, the local housing market is conceptualized as interrelated submarkets. The filtering process is examined within the context of the conceptual model. Finally, the chapter deals with market analysis and feasibility analysis. The steps in each of these types of analysis are presented, and a step-by-step procedure for completing a market study is outlined.

MARKET FUNCTIONS

All markets perform the basic task of allocating resources among various uses in the economy. This allocation process involves the accomplishment of several functions by a market. Weimer, Hoyt, and Bloom identify three such functions: (*a*) apportioning existing quarters among those who need them, (*b*) contracting or expanding the space available in order to meet changed conditions, and (*c*) determining land use.[2] Ratcliff adds a fourth market function—price establishment,[3] which could be included in Weimer, Hoyt, and Bloom's first function. The market conditions associated with the first function can be illustrated with a graph of short-run supply-demand relationships as shown in Figure 9–1.[4]

In the short run the supply of housing space is shown to be price inelastic. Over a period of one to six months, or even a year, rents and prices may advance because of an increased demand. Such an increase may have been caused by a new employment source locating in the city or by an expansion in an existing source. Although the demand may increase, as shown in Figure 9–1, from D_1 to D_2, the supply of housing available cannot increase proportionately. The market thus serves to allocate the available space among those who need it. Such a

---

[2] Arthur M. Weimer, Homer Hoyt, and George F. Bloom, *Real Estate*, 7th ed. (New York: Ronald Press, 1978), p. 175.

[3] Richard U. Ratcliff, *Real Estate Analysis* (New York: McGraw-Hill, 1961), p. 229.

[4] Weimer, Hoyt, and Bloom, *Real Estate*, p. 177.

FIGURE 9–1
Short-run supply-demand relationships

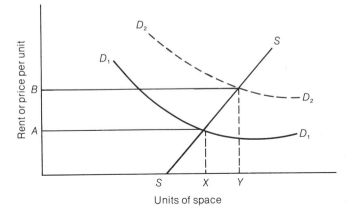

Units of space

lag in housing construction usually lasts six months to a year, partly because in many cases the construction process will take at least six months or longer. Additionally, however, it should be recognized that potential investors in new housing to be made available for sale or rental must be convinced that the increased demand will be a long-term rather than a temporary phenomenon.

Sometimes builder-investors produce additional housing units in anticipation of future increases in demand. Sometimes builder-investors continue to add new units after demand has slackened. For example, in a speech to the Biennial Congress of the International Fraternity of Lambda Alpha and the Land Economic Foundation on October 7, 1971, James Downs, chairman of the board of Real Estate Research Corporation, stated that "the effective demand is not there to absorb units at today's construction costs. . . . residential vacancy in the effective market is going up very rapidly and is going to continue to go up very rapidly until we cut the amount of building which we're doing next year."[5] Most desirably, however, increases in supply will occur when builder-investors correctly forecast additional demand for the immediate future. Ideally, the builder wants to be Johnny-on-the-spot with available housing when new long-term demand appears. This is the *raison d'être* for market analysis by suppliers of housing units.

The production of new units of housing space involves longer run adjustments in the quantity and quality of space—function 2 of the real estate market. This function operates during a time period long

---

[5] *Appraisal Briefs* (Chicago: Society of Real Estate Appraisers, October 1971).

enough to allow new units to be created (usually six months or longer). Conceptually, the time period is not so long as to allow a shift in the usage to which the land can most profitably be put.

The third market function—land-use determination—operates over a sufficiently long time period for all factors to vary. Buildings can be torn down, and new ones constructed in their place. Although the market forces of competition must operate within the constraints of the zoning law, the market determines over a long period of time what land use is the most profitable. Presumably the most profitable land use (highest and best use) will provide the greatest service to the community, since people will pay more for that use than for alternative uses.

MARKET MODELS

As we discussed in Chapter 3, the concept of a perfect market contains several assumptions about participant behavior and the character of the goods exchanged. The perfect market has homogeneity of products; the product is divisible into small units and is transportable; there are many buyers and sellers, with no single buyer or seller able to influence price; entry into the market is not hindered; and buyers and sellers have complete knowledge about possible uses for the product and are in agreement about expectations.

The wheat market might be visualized as an example of the most nearly competitive market. Each kernel of wheat is nearly like every other kernel (at least within a grade); most sellers must accept the going market price when they sell their wheat; and many buyers and sellers actively bid in a well-organized market. Even here, however, the imperfections are evident. The product is not homogeneous; there are several grades of wheat. Some buyers and sellers are large enough to affect the market price by withholding from or bringing to the market their wheat or bids. Entry to the market is not free or easy; considerable capital is required. And knowledge about the potential worth of the wheat is subject to disagreement. In fact, an active futures market for grain has developed. In this market, buyers bid to purchase grain which will be delivered at a future date. If the price goes up in the meantime, they will profit; if the price goes down, they will lose. On the other side, sellers are betting that the price of wheat will go down and thus agree to sell wheat they will obtain later at the present price, which they believe to be high.

In contrast with the wheat market, the real estate market is one of the least perfect markets we could identify. The product (a parcel of real estate) is highly differentiated. Large owners or buyers can sometimes affect the market price. Entry to the market usually requires a

sizable amount of capital, and knowledge about the potential productivity and value of real estate is subject to a lack of information as well
as disagreement. Because of these market imperfections, some economists have stressed the monopolistic characteristics of urban real estate. According to this view, each parcel of real estate is a monopoly for
its particular group of characteristics; no other parcel will substitute
equally well. Greater profits will accrue to some parcels than to others
because the elements of productivity (transfer and physical characteristics) are superior in some parcels and inferior in others. Thus, a
well-located office building will produce more income than an equally
attractive poorly located one. A dime store located on a "100 percent"
site will do better than one located a block away. And a residential
property having desirable architectural and design qualities will tend
to sell for a higher price than another property that is equally well
located but has less desirable physical characteristics.

If each parcel of real estate were a true monopoly, we know from
economic theory that the monopolist-owner would be assured of a
profit—at least in the long run. In pure monopoly, where there is only
one producer or seller, the level of output that will maximize total
profit can be chosen, given market demand conditions. Although the
monopolist may lose money or do no better than break even in the
short run, the fact that the level of output may be chosen is assumed to
insure in the long run that the monopolist will operate at a level that
will provide a profit.

It should be evident that the case for urban real estate's falling
under the classification of pure monopoly is no stronger than the case
for its falling under the model of pure competition. To refute the long-
standing emphasis on the monopolistic aspects of urban land, Ratcliff
has emphasized the "economic mobility" of urban land.[6] In this view,
perfect substitutability is not required for effective competition.
Woolworth or Kresge *can* accept a 98 percent location, particularly
when it is obtainable at a disproportionately lower price than a 100
percent location. Thus, the fact that many parcels of urban land are to
some extent in competition with one another for a given usage would
seem to refute the idea of monopolistic control of urban land. As
pointed out in Chapter 8, Chamberlin includes this product within the
vast majority of commodities whose markets contain aspects of both
competition and monopoly.[7] Since the real estate market is far from
being a perfect market, we could conclude, by definition, that it con-

---

[6] Richard U. Ratcliff, *Urban Land Economics* (New York: McGraw-Hill, 1949), chap.
12.

[7] Edward Chamberlin, *Monopolistic Competition* (Cambridge, Mass.: Harvard University Press, 1939), appendix D.

tains elements of monopoly. Whether these are greater or less than the monopoly elements in other markets makes little difference. But the concept of monopolistic competition does seem appropriate in describing the operation of real estate markets.

In monopolistic competition, the firm decides at what level of output to operate in the same way as does the monopolist. However, monopolistic competition differs from pure monopoly because there is no true market demand for the product. Every firm or entity differentiates its product or service by producing a different brand or type of the economic good. Nevertheless, each brand or type is related to the other brands and types of the same commodity. That is, each is a close substitute (not a perfect substitute) for the others. For example, Gleem toothpaste is a close substitute for Crest or Colgate. Thus, the level of output each firm can sell depends upon the prices and types of close substitutes, as well as its own price. Similarly, the prices of urban sites depend upon the prices and types of close substitutes.

There is another important difference between pure monopoly and monopolistic competition. The firm in monopolistic competition does not have a monopoly over the ability to satisfy the market, as does the pure monopolist. In pure monopoly, firm equilibrium is the same situation as market equilibrium. In monopolistic competition, however, the presence of profits will lead new firms to come into the market with closely substitutable products. Assuming that market demand remains unchanged, profit levels in the industry shrink as new firms continue to enter the industry. Thus, in long-run equilibrium, the profit levels of monopolistically competitive firms shrink toward zero.

Implications of theory

The real estate market's lack of qualification for being a perfect market implies justification for the role of intermediaries in the market. The existence of relatively few buyers and sellers at any one time for a given type of real estate, the incomplete knowledge and lack of agreement about future market conditions, the potential for any one buyer or seller to influence the market, and the lack of mobility into and out of the market necessitate the facilitating function of the real estate broker.

Nevertheless, the competitive aspects of real estate imply that investors must realize that, with a few possible exceptions, there are always substitutable parcels of real estate for any other parcel. If there is an active, viable market, an owner cannot expect to extract an unreasonable price from informed, intelligent potential buyers. At the same time, potential buyers can take comfort from the knowledge that there are normally a number of parcels of real estate that will serve a given need equally well. Some may be better than others, however, and a buyer must expect to pay a premium for those parcels having the greatest productivity potential. The point is that true monopoly profits are almost never attainable in real estate. Large profits will attract competitors, who will tend to drive prices and profits down.

On the other hand, it should be recognized that each parcel of real estate holds some—be it ever so small—degree of monopoly advantage. One parcel of residential real estate is located nearer the corner than other similar parcels. One house has a more desirable floor plan than another house in a comparable location. One commercial property is located at the center of pedestrian traffic patterns, while another is not. One industrial property has more complete docking and storage facilities than other comparably located properties. Prices reflecting these monopolistic advantages can be expected to be paid—but only in proportion to the degree of advantage perceived by the market. True monopoly prices reflecting total market demand will not be attainable.

DETERMINANTS OF DEMAND

The various types of influences on market behavior and prices can for convenience and for purposes of analysis be divided between the demand and supply sides of the market. The determinants of demand are all of those forces or influences that tend to cause real estate to be needed or desired plus the conditions making it possible for people to purchase and own property. Influences tending to cause real estate to be produced or supplied are all of those forces and conditions which motivate the suppliers of real properties to create and construct new real estate resources. Thus, this section of the chapter deals with the demand side of the market, and the next section deals with the supply side.

Although we make the distinction between demand and supply determinants, in reality it may be very difficult to separate the two. The fact that the population is growing is usually considered to be a demand factor, although realistically the growing population is a major determinant of supply as well. Similarly, the availability and relative prices of materials and labor are usually regarded as supply factors. They also influence demand, however, because of the competition of real estate with other economic goods. If the prices of real estate rise relative to other goods, demand will tend to be decreased, while if the prices of real estate decrease relative to other goods, the demand for real estate will tend to increase. We recognize the difficulties of arbitrarily assigning the various forces to the demand or the supply side of the market; however, it must be recognized that this classification is for convenience and analysis, and others are welcome to change the classification to fit their own needs.

Need for housing and other types of real estate

The productivity and the value of real estate are derived from its ability to be used beneficially by human beings. Many types of real estate are needed or desired to satisfy and fulfill the human condition. A broad classification of types of properties consists of residential, commercial, and industrial properties. The value of all these types of properties is dependent upon the presence of people to utilize them effectively. Thus, housing is needed to provide shelter and a measure of privacy for individuals and groups. Commercial properties are needed and desired because they provide the means by which other economic goods are made available to people. Industrial real estate is needed and desired because it provides shelter and a base for the production of other economic goods. The demand for commercial and industrial real estate is a derived demand and is dependent upon the need for the goods and services produced or sold by firms requiring such real estate.

In considering the demand for residential real estate, the need for shelter must be regarded as basic. Protection from the elements, however, is only one of the functions which most housing in the United States provides today. Housing is much more than shelter; it involves emotional needs and desires as well. Most housing today is a luxury good which attempts to fulfill the psychological and sociological, as well as physical, needs of people. Housing, as distinguished from shelter, includes architecturally pleasing designs, divided interior space, attractive wall and floor coverings, indoor plumbing, attractive kitchen and bathrooms, air-conditioning systems, space that may go unused for substantial periods of time, and many appliances and gadgets that make living more comfortable and more socially fulfilling.

People make a market, and therefore the first determinant of demand must be people, or population. Population is important not only in terms of sheer size, but also in terms of characteristics (or subgroupings) of the total population, such as age groupings, educational levels, race, and occupation. Migratory patterns, indicating where people are moving to and where they came from, are a further dimension of population trends that determine the need or demand for real estate.

Marketing analysis begins with identifying broad characteristics and movements, including studying and analyzing national trends in population growth, movements of people to and from different regions, and identifying the characteristics of the people moving, as well as hypothesizing reasons for such movements. Regional population changes can then be more accurately predicted, and the impact of population mobility translated to the community and neighborhood levels. The prime source of demographic information is the U.S. Bureau of the Census.

Data from the "100 percent coverage" portion of the 1970 census and intermittent census news releases reveal some of the current trends which are potentially useful to real estate market analysts. These trends include the following:

1. Internal migration of the population:
   a. From rural to urban areas.
   b. From central cities to suburbs.
   c. Into white and nonwhite concentrations in large central cities.
   d. From central geographic divisions of the nation to the coasts.
   e. From North to South in the case of blacks and the poor.
   f. Among the states, resulting in changes in their size rankings.
2. Differing decade rates of growth among racial groups, including:
   a. Reduced fertility and total growth rate of white populations.
   b. Greater fertility and total growth rate of black populations.
   c. Extremely high total growth rates of other nonwhite populations.
3. Older population.
4. Smaller family size and reduced importance of male family heads.[8]
5. Increase in number of nonfamily households.

Shifts in population among states and regions may have dramatic effects for real estate marketers operating in those states experiencing significant shifts. Figure 9–2 shows the shifts among the states between 1970 and 1975. As a general pattern, the South, Southwest, and West have been gaining population by net in-migration, while the Northeast and North Central states have been experiencing population outflows. Between 1970 and 1979, the greatest population increases occurred in California, Texas, and Florida, while only New York, Pennsylvania, Rhode Island, and the District of Columbia lost population. There are exceptions to the general trend—particularly New Hampshire, Washington, and Louisiana.

Within the state and regional patterns, however, population changes of cities can accentuate or mitigate the general trend. As can be seen in Figure 9–3, the largest, older cities have been losing popu-

---

[8] James C. Yocum, "Population Changes in Two Decades," *Bulletin of Business Research* (Ohio State University) 46, no. 9 (September 1971): 1.

FIGURE 9–2

U.S. migration trends, 1970–1975

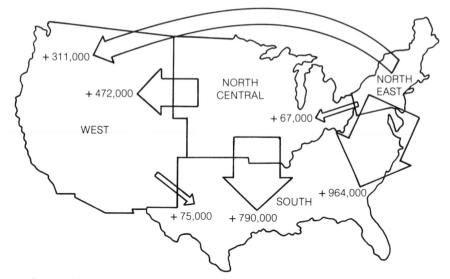

Source: Brian J. L. Berry and Donald C. Dahmann, *Population Redistribution in the United States in the 1970's,* Washington, D.C.: National Research Council, National Academy of Sciences, 1977.

FIGURE 9–3

Growth and decline among U.S. cities, 1970–1976

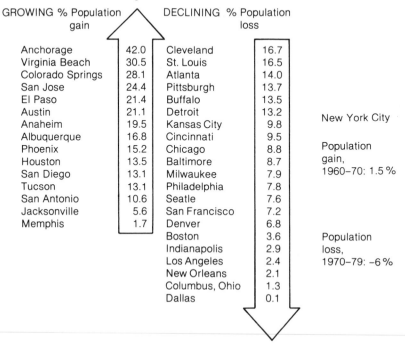

GROWING % Population gain		DECLINING % Population loss		
Anchorage	42.0	Cleveland	16.7	
Virginia Beach	30.5	St. Louis	16.5	
Colorado Springs	28.1	Atlanta	14.0	
San Jose	24.4	Pittsburgh	13.7	
El Paso	21.4	Buffalo	13.5	
Austin	21.1	Detroit	13.2	New York City
Anaheim	19.5	Kansas City	9.8	
Albuquerque	16.8	Cincinnati	9.5	
Phoenix	15.2	Chicago	8.8	Population
Houston	13.5	Baltimore	8.7	gain,
San Diego	13.1	Milwaukee	7.9	1960–70: 1.5%
Tucson	13.1	Philadelphia	7.8	
San Antonio	10.6	Seattle	7.6	
Jacksonville	5.6	San Francisco	7.2	
Memphis	1.7	Denver	6.8	
		Boston	3.6	Population
		Indianapolis	2.9	loss,
		Los Angeles	2.4	1970–79: –6%
		New Orleans	2.1	
		Columbus, Ohio	1.3	
		Dallas	0.1	

Source: U.S. Department of Commerce *News,* November 19, 1978.

lation while the smaller, younger large cities have been gaining. Certainly the demand for most types of real estate will remain stronger in those regions, states, and urban areas which are experiencing population growth than in those which are experiencing declines. The types of real estate needs will also probably differ between growth and nongrowth areas.

As can be seen in Tables 9–1 and 9–2, the total percentage of nonwhites increased substantially during the 20-year period 1950–70, a reflection of the higher than average rate of increase in the birthrate for the nonwhite population as compared with the white population. Blacks and other minorities migrated from the South to the more industrialized states of the North. (There is evidence that this trend has not held during more recent years.)

The age composition of the United States during the 20 years shifted to a lower average age; however, the median age in 1979 increased to 30 years from the median age of less than 28 years in 1970. This increase is a result of the baby boom babies reaching middle age and lower birthrates. The age composition of the U.S. population will be low relative to that of former years for several years into the future; however, the long-term prospect is for an increasing average age of the population. The rate of population growth is already decreasing, and the number of children below the age of five has dropped dramatically—an 11.2 percent decrease since 1970. As the rate of population increase slows, the average age of the population will increase. As the relatively large numbers of younger people in the 10–20 age category become older, they will tend to cause the average age to increase also (see Figure 9–4).

The effects of these trends can already be noted in the real estate market, particularly in the larger cities. The increased percentages of apartments being constructed in almost every large city attest to the growing numbers of young people entering the housing market at this time. Nonfamily households have increased by two thirds since 1970. These trends reflect a rising divorce rate, a falling birthrate, and the propensity of younger people to wait longer to get married and of married couples to wait longer to have children and to have fewer children. The advent of apartments for singles only or for young married couples without children is simply a manifestation of these population changes. In fast-growing regions of the country, such as Florida, the Southwest, and the West, complete new communities are being developed with increased emphasis on apartments and condominiums which provide smaller sized units with more complete services and facilities for the occupants.

Tables 9–3, 9–4 and Figure 9–5 show how migration, births, and deaths affect population changes for the United States as a whole and for regions within the United States.

TABLE 9–1

Resident population of United States and geographic divisions, 1979, 1970, and 1960*

Area	(Number of states)	Number, 1979‡	Number, 1970	Percent increase		Percent of U.S. total			Percent urban		Percent nonwhite	
				1979 from 1970	1970 from 1960	1979	1970	1960	1970	1960	1970	1960
East North Central	(5)	41,287,000	40,252,678	2.5	11.1	18.8	19.8	20.2	74.8	73.0	10.2	8.2
Middle Atlantic	(3)	36,711,000	37,152,813	(1.4)	8.7	16.7	18.3	19.0	81.7	81.4	11.5	8.5
South Atlantic†	(9)	34,976,000	30,671,337	14.0	18.1	15.9	15.1	14.5	63.7	57.2	21.5	22.8
Pacific	(5)	30,469,000	26,525,774	14.8	25.1	13.8	13.1	11.8	86.0	81.1	11.1	8.9
West South Central	(4)	22,470,000	19,322,458	16.3	14.0	10.2	9.5	9.5	72.6	67.7	16.3	16.9
West North Central	(7)	17,118,000	16,324,389	4.8	6.0	7.8	8.0	8.6	63.7	58.8	5.1	4.2
East South Central	(4)	14,105,000	12,804,552	10.1	6.3	6.4	6.7	6.7	54.6	48.4	20.5	22.5
New England	(6)	12,291,000	11,847,186	3.7	12.7	5.6	5.8	5.9	76.4	76.4	3.8	2.5
Mountain	(8)	10,673,000	8,283,585	28.7	20.8	4.8	4.1	3.8	73.1	67.1	5.8	5.0
U.S. total	(51)	220,099,000	203,184,772	8.3	13.3	100.0	100.0	100.0	73.5	69.9	12.6	11.4

* Total U.S. population, 1970, including U.S. citizens stationed abroad (U.S. armed forces and federal employees, and their dependents), 204, 765, 770.
† Includes the District of Columbia.
‡ Estimates.

Source: James C. Yocum, "Population Changes in Two Decades," *Bulletin of Business Research* (Ohio State University) 46, no. 9 (September 1971); and U.S. Department of Commerce *News*, March 5, 1980.

TABLE 9-2

Distribution of the population, by region for selected years, 1790 to 1975

Area and race	1790	1870	1910	1940	1960	1970	1975
Black							
United States (millions)	1	5	10	13	19	23	24
Percent, total	100	100	100	100	100	100	100
South	91	91	89	77	60	53	52
North	9	9	10	22	34	39	39
Northeast	9	4	5	11	16	19	18
North Central	—	6	6	11	18	20	20
West	—	—	1	1	6	8	9
White							
United States (millions)	3	34	82	118	159	178	183
Percent, total	100	100	100	100	100	100	100
South	40	23	25	27	27	28	30
North	60	74	67	62	56	54	52
Northeast	60	36	31	29	26	25	24
North Central	—	38	36	33	30	29	28
West	—	3	8	11	16	18	18
Blacks as a percentage of the total population							
United States	19	13	11	10	11	11	11
South	35	36	30	24	21	19	19
North	3	2	2	4	7	8	9
Northeast	3	1	2	4	7	9	9
North Central	—	2	2	4	7	8	8
West	—	1	1	1	4	5	6

— Represents zero.
Source: U.S. Department of Commerce, Bureau of the Census, *Current Population Reports,* special studies series P–23, no. 80, table 5.

TABLE 9-3

Components of population change for the United States for selected years: January 1, 1970, to January 1, 1979 (000)

Calendar year	Population at beginning of period	Total increase*	Natural increase	Births	Deaths	Net civilian immigration
1979	219,530	n.a.	n.a.	n.a.	n.a.	n.a.
1978	217,785	1,745	1,403	3,328	1,925	343
1974	211,207	1,541	1,225	3,160	1,935	316
1970	203,849	2,227	1,812	3,739	1,927	428

n.a.: Not available.
* Includes estimates of overseas admissions into and discharges from the armed forces and for 1970 includes error of closure between censuses.
Source: Data consistent with Bureau of the Census, *Current Population Reports,* series P–25, no. 793. Estimates of births and deaths (with an allowance for deaths to armed forces overseas) are from the National Center for Health Statistics. Estimates of net civilian immigration are based partly on data from the Immigration and Naturalization Service.

TABLE 9-4

Components of population change—states: 1960–1970 and 1970–1977 (000)

State	April 1, 1960 to April 1, 1970					April 1, 1970 to July 1, 1977				
	Net change		Births	Deaths	Net total migration†	Net change		Births	Deaths	Net total migration†
	Number	Per cent*				Number	Per cent*			
United States	23,912	13.3	39,033	18,192	3,070	13,027	6.4	23,870	13,982	3,140
New England	1,338	12.7	2,169	1,147	316	394	3.3	1,180	822	37
Maine	24	2.5	203	109	-69	91	9.2	117	78	52
New Hampshire	131	21.5	133	71	69	111	15.0	87	54	78
Vermont	55	14.1	85	45	15	39	8.7	52	32	18
Massachusetts	541	10.5	1,040	574	74	93	1.6	545	402	-51
Rhode Island	90	10.5	171	93	13	-15	-1.6	91	67	-39
Connecticut	497	19.6	537	255	214	76	2.5	288	190	-22
Middle Atlantic	3,034	8.9	6,725	3,749	59	-175	-.5	3,739	2,682	-1,232
New York	1,458	8.7	3,361	1,852	-51	-318	-1.7	1,850	1,295	-873
New Jersey	1,101	18.2	1,259	645	488	158	2.2	721	487	-76
Pennsylvania	475	4.2	2,105	1,252	-378	-16	-.1	1,168	901	-283
East North Central	4,028	11.1	7,832	3,652	-153	791	2.0	4,689	2,701	-1,197
Ohio	946	9.7	2,047	975	-126	44	.4	1,225	718	-464
Indiana	531	11.4	1,023	475	-16	135	2.6	630	349	-146
Illinois	1,033	10.2	2,153	1,077	-43	132	1.2	1,295	781	-382
Michigan	1,052	13.4	1,754	729	27	248	2.8	1,052	557	-247
Wisconsin	466	11.8	856	395	4	233	5.3	487	296	42
West North Central	930	6.0	3,133	1,604	-599	557	3.4	1,835	1,178	-100
Minnesota	391	11.5	744	327	-25	169	4.4	423	244	-11
Iowa	68	2.4	541	291	-183	54	1.9	306	209	-43
Missouri	358	8.3	857	502	2	123	2.6	523	367	-33
North Dakota	-15	-2.3	135	55	-94	36	5.8	75	41	1
South Dakota	-14	-2.1	146	65	-94	23	3.4	82	49	-11
Nebraska	72	5.1	291	146	-73	76	5.1	175	108	10
Kansas	70	3.2	419	218	-130	77	3.4	250	160	-13
South Atlantic	4,700	18.1	5,965	2,598	1,332	3,627	11.8	3,719	2,192	2,100
Delaware	102	22.8	109	45	38	34	6.1	64	35	5
Maryland	822	26.5	740	303	385	215	5.5	411	237	42

	(1)	(2)	(3)	(4)	(5)	(6)	(7)	(8)	(9)	(10)
District of Columbia	−7	−1.0	182	89	−100	−67	−8.8	83	57	−92
Virginia	682	17.2	909	369	141	483	10.4	541	291	233
West Virginia	−116	−6.2	339	190	−265	115	6.6	210	144	49
North Carolina	526	11.5	1,032	412	−94	441	8.7	633	334	142
South Carolina	208	8.7	573	216	−149	285	11.0	359	172	98
Georgia	646	16.4	975	379	51	460	10.0	623	307	144
Florida	1,838	37.1	1,107	596	1,326	1,661	24.5	797	614	1,478
East South Central	754	6.3	2,665	1,213	−698	1,029	8.0	1,658	940	311
Kentucky	181	6.0	647	313	−153	238	7.4	408	242	72
Tennessee	357	10.0	755	353	−45	373	9.5	478	282	178
Alabama	177	5.4	729	319	−233	245	7.1	444	248	49
Mississippi	39	1.8	534	228	−267	172	7.8	329	169	13
West South Central	2,371	14.0	4,012	1,599	−42	2,380	12.3	2,655	1,314	1,040
Arkansas	137	7.7	401	193	−71	221	11.5	249	156	128
Louisiana	386	11.9	832	316	−130	277	7.6	504	247	19
Oklahoma	231	9.9	461	244	13	251	9.8	314	195	133
Texas	1,617	16.9	2,318	847	146	1,632	14.6	1,587	716	760
Mountain	1,429	20.8	1,724	602	307	1,741	21.0	1,265	509	985
Montana	20	2.9	144	66	−58	67	9.6	88	49	27
Idaho	46	6.9	146	58	−42	144	20.3	112	47	79
Wyoming	2	.7	70	28	−39	74	22.2	48	22	49
Colorado	453	25.8	401	163	215	409	18.5	290	130	249
New Mexico	65	6.8	263	68	−130	173	17.0	157	58	74
Arizona	470	36.1	365	122	228	520	29.3	282	119	358
Utah	169	18.9	245	65	−11	209	19.7	221	54	42
Nevada	203	71.3	91	31	144	145	29.6	67	31	108
Pacific	5,328	25.1	4,808	2,028	2,547	2,683	10.1	3,129	1,642	1,196
Washington	556	19.5	591	284	249	245	7.2	378	218	85
Oregon	323	18.2	346	182	159	285	13.6	241	147	191
California	4,236	27.0	3,634	1,511	2,113	1,925	9.6	2,342	1,235	817
Alaska	76	33.6	73	13	16	105	34.6	53	11	62
Hawaii	137	21.7	164	37	11	125	16.2	115	31	40

Note: Total resident population. Minus sign denotes decrease or net out-migration.

* 1960 to 1970 based on 1960 population; 1970 to 1977 based on 1970 population.

† Comprises both net immigration from abroad and net interdivisional or interstate migration according to the area shown. Includes movements of persons in the armed forces.

Source: U.S. Bureau of the Census, *Current Population Reports*, series P–25, no. 460, and forthcoming report; and unpublished data.

FIGURE 9–4
Population by age and sex, 1978

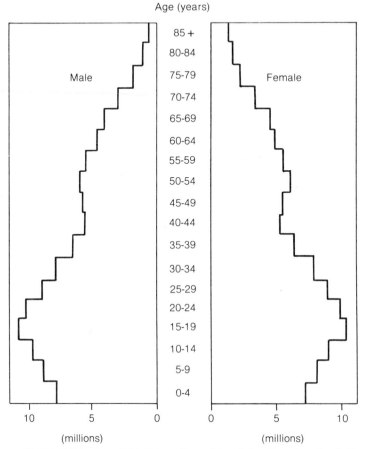

Age (years)

Source: U.S. Bureau of the Census, *Current Population Reports,* series P–25, no. 800, tables 6 and 24.

Societal trends

Many changes occur in society which result in changing living patterns, changes in class structure, changes in work conditions and lifestyles, and changes in the way that people use their time. Most of these changes are a result of the increasing capabilities of technology. In the area of transportation and communication, improved technology has resulted in the beginnings of mass transit systems in some cities that formerly did not have them, new road systems allowing people to live farther from their work, and better communications among all parts of the country. As new transportation systems are developed or

FIGURE 9-5
Annual levels of net growth, births, deaths, and net immigration,
1930–1978

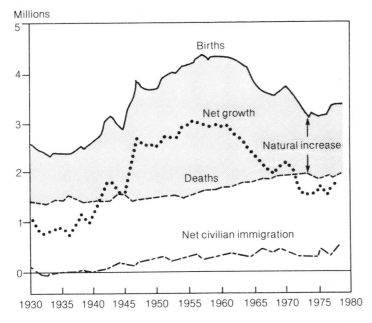

Source: U.S. Bureau of the Census, *Current Population Reports*, series P–20,
no. 336, table 1.

additions to old systems are made, real estate values in the areas affected are changed, often dramatically. As many people have made the move to suburbia, their entire lifestyle has changed, or at least it has been different from what it would have been had they lived in an apartment close to the center of a city. This trend, while much maligned, would seem to offer advantages in the minds of many people, or they would not have made the decisions to live in the outlying areas. It is not surprising that many people desire to have green space, trees, and desirable surroundings for their children when they can afford it. Without the ability to transfer themselves to and from important destinations, such as work, schools, and cultural centers, few people would have had the opportunity for these types of advantages.

Improved technology has also resulted in the greater use of machines and correspondingly increasing levels of efficiency. The requirement of fewer man-hours to produce the same amount of output as previously has led to more and more people obtaining greater amounts of time free from work. Greater emphasis upon leisure living and informality has created entire new markets for outdoor recreational equipment. Color televisions, picnic tables, and charcoal grills are but a few of the products demanded to satisfy this type of living pattern. Similarly, new houses are expected to contain patios, sliding glass doors, attractive yards and recreational areas, and often a pleasant view with green areas for recreation and relaxation. Bowling alleys, golf courses, and other recreational facilities have proliferated.

The new technology has made available for many homemakers such gadgets as self-cleaning ovens, dishwashers, built-in vacuum systems, automatic ice makers, electronic ranges, and many others. In short, changes in technology have shifted the society from an agricultural one to an industrialized one. An industrialized society has produced an urban society, where even rural residents have adopted and pursued the goals of their urban counterparts.

Values and attitudes

The values and attitudes adopted by a society change over time, and these changes, as well as the values and attitudes themselves, can have an important bearing upon the types of commodities, goods, and housing that people demand. Some values are associated with the entire society, while some are characteristic of subgroups or subcultures within the society. Religious groups, racial groups, members of social classes, and ethnic groups are some of these subcultures that may form values which vary somewhat from the values of the overall society.

From the standpoint of society as a whole, some of the more important values and attitudes that seem to prevail are that leisure time is important in obtaining the benefits of the good life. People's homes, and possibly their offices, are important measures of their social status. Informality in daily life and a willingness to make changes are more characteristic of families today than was the case before World War II. These attitudes and values are interrelated, of course, since the importance of leisure time is reflected in the type of home that one purchases. Greater informality is reflected in smaller living rooms, larger family rooms, and patios. Also, as people are willing to make changes—to move from one section of the country to another, to change houses within the same city, and to change sources of employment—these trends are reflected in the emphasis placed upon new housing and new office buildings of every type. Only the new structures can adequately reflect the new tastes and preferences.

One of the most important types of subgroups that is important in determining demand is social class. Lloyd Warner's work in identifying social classes in U.S. cities showed that four characteristics are important in explaining class differences.[9] These variables are income, occupation, house type, and area of residence; they produce a class structure as follows:

1. Upper class (0.9 percent of the population).
    a. Upper upper—old-line, wealthy families.
    b. Lower upper—socially prominent, newly rich families.
2. Upper-middle class (7.2 percent of the population).
    Professionals and highly-successful business executives.
3. Lower-middle class (28.4 percent of the population).
    Teachers, technicians, most sales representatives, white-collar workers.
4. Upper-lower class (44.0 percent of the population).
    Skilled workers, production workers, service workers, local politicians, and labor leaders.
5. Lower-lower class (19.5 percent of the population).
    Unskilled laborers, racial immigrants, and people in unrespectable occupations.

Social class, like any other subgrouping, holds significance for the real estate market analyst because people within one group have different needs and desires than people in the other groups. Studies have shown that people in different social classes respond differently to advertising media, have differing levels of interest in products and brands, and want to be treated differently by sales personnel. Given the same number of dollars to spend, they will spend the money differently.

The implications for real estate market analysts and real estate marketers are that as the size and composition of social classes in the society and within a community change, the types of housing and other real estate demanded will change.

Values attributed to different social classes are translated into different housing needs. Upper-middle-class families, for example, place high value on privacy, whereas upper-lower-class families value friendliness and openness to the community. In the first instance, high fences around yards are acceptable, while in a lower-class community such physical barriers will be rejected and, if erected, would be interpreted as an act of snobbishness. Dobriner illustrates in *Class in Suburbia* how hostilities arose in a new community as a result of value clashes (and, in particular, as a result of how values were translated into everyday living patterns) between two differing social classes

---

[9] W. Lloyd Warner, *Social Class in America* (New York: Harper, 1960).

moving into the same neighborhood.[10] Friction between the two classes ultimately led members of one of the classes to move from the community.

While suburbia typically has been portrayed as an upper-middle-class phenomenon, in actuality the metropolis is a network of suburbs of the various class groups, with the exception of the lower-lower class. Suburbs exist which are identical economically, in terms of property values and the income levels of the residents, but which differ in class structure and mode of living. In the Dobriner study cited above, the intermixture of two classes residing in the same community was temporary. The community, a new development, was the first Levittown constructed at the end of World War II, a time when demand for housing was exceptionally great. The houses appealed to two diverse groups: young middle-class families who traditionally were homeowners and found that Levittown was what they could afford at that stage of their life cycle, and working-class families who had accumulated enough savings during the war years to escape the crowded city and achieve for the first time the all-American dream of home ownership. While studies indicate that class differences do exist, assessing their effects upon real estate development is difficult, offering a potentially fertile area for investigation.

National income

Along with people, who are the ultimate source of demand for real estate, must be income. Income turns potential demand into effective demand. If the people are there and they have the income to purchase real estate, properties will be sold and purchased in the market. As with population, at least three levels of income must be considered and analyzed. Income trends at the national, regional, and local levels ultimately determine the effective demand for an individual parcel of real estate. To analyze income trends at the national level, one may refer to three types of accounting systems. Each of these systems is designed to provide a different type of information and is useful for different purposes. It is likely that the greatest weight in analyzing market demand will be placed upon the first system to be discussed—the gross national product/national income accounts—since the other two systems do not deal directly with income. Nevertheless, the other two systems can be useful for specialized types of analyses; the flow of funds system is particularly useful in analyzing financial transac-

---

[10] William M. Dobriner, *Class in Suburbia* (Englewood Cliffs, N.J.: Prentice-Hall, 1963).

tions.[11] Similarly, the input-output accounts can be useful to an industrial real estate broker in analyzing industry trends.

Gross national product/national income accounting system. The gross national product/national income accounts provide a broad picture of national production and income. Predictions about the economic health of the country are made in terms of the gross national product (GNP). Trends in the components of GNP and national income can be analyzed to detect changing patterns of production and income. While it is not consistent with the purpose of this book to describe in detail the GNP and income accounts, several trends illustrating the use of this accounting system can be cited. Within the GNP accounts, the services category of personal consumption expenditures has been the fastest growing component. This trend is in part a result of the growing affluence of a large part of the population, combined with the relatively maturity of the economy in being able to produce and provide physical goods. Investment in residential structures has been growing comparatively slowly, as have other categories of private investment. State and local government purchases of goods and services have been growing rapidly. While national defense and other federal government expenditures have held fairly level in recent years, state and local government expenditures have increased dramatically.

Flow of funds. The flow of funds accounting system describes how funds or assets have been used in the economy and the sources from which they came. This system is particularly useful in analyzing financial changes in the economy.[12] Some interesting trends that could be discerned from the flow of funds accounts, however, can be cited. The first of these is that the greatest percentage of funds in the economy was used by real estate mortgages during the decade of the 1960s. During the latter five years of the decade, however, this percentage dropped significantly. Corporate bonds and stocks increased in the percentage of funds used. Nevertheless, real estate mortgages continue to be the single most important use of funds, although the decline in importance is one that needs to be watched and analyzed by real estate market analysts. On the supply side, commercial banks have furnished the greatest proportion of funds. Savings and loan associations, while for several years the fastest growing suppliers of funds, leveled out in the percentage of funds they supplied and then resumed their increase during the mid-1970s.

Input-output analysis. Input-output analysis involves the use of a

---

[11] See Chapter 16.

[12] These financial changes in the economy are analyzed more fully in Chapter 16.

matrix which quantifies the use of goods and services among major sectors or industries in the economy. Figure 9–6 is an example of an input-output matrix using a seven-industry classification. The rows indicate the monetary amounts of products from each industry in the re-

FIGURE 9–6
Hypothetical input-output matrix ($ millions)

Industry producing	Industry purchasing							
	Agri-cul-ture	Manu-factur-ing	Power	Trans-porta-tion	Educa-tional ser-vices	Con-struc-tion	House-holds	Total gross output
Agriculture	21.0	25.0	0.5	1.0	1.5	5.0	13.0	67.0
Manufactur-ing	5.0	60.0	0.3	1.1	5.0	6.0	7.0	84.4
Power	1.0	2.0	1.3	0.6	0.5	5.0	1.5	11.9
Transporta-tion	2.6	4.0	0.2	1.1	0.5	0.1	6.0	14.5
Educational services	—	—	—	—	24.4	—	25.0	49.4
Construc-tion	0.3	5.0	0.5	1.2	0.5	—	0.1	7.6
Households	30.5	50.0	7.0	13.0	15.0	12.0	2.0	129.5
Total inputs	60.4	146.0	9.8	18.0	47.4	28.1	54.6	364.3

gion that are sold to a particular industry, while the columns show how much (in dollars) each industry bought from other producers. For example, the table shows that the agriculture industry sold $25 million worth of products to the manufacturing sector, and the construction industry bought $5 million of agricultural products. The breakdown of industrial classifications may be as broad or as refined as is necessary for the analysis, or as the obtainable data permit.

Input-output analysis can also be used to project future uses of goods and services. In this function, future household consumption determines total production and purchases. After future household consumption has been estimated, the other sectors are increased in the same proportion as the original matrix indicates. The mechanics of this method involve dividing the figures in each column by the column total to determine the percentage of each dollar consumed by an activity. A new matrix is produced using these *constant production coeffi-*

cients. These coefficients are assumed to be constant over time. (This assumption, of course, may be totally invalid!) Next, each coefficient in a specific column is multiplied by the amount shown in the corresponding row of the household column. For example, if household consumption of agricultural items is expected to increase to $20 million (row 1, column 7), then all coefficients under the first column are multiplied by 20 to obtain the amounts of input from each sector necessary to produce the required amounts of agricultural products. These inputs are called the "first round of input requirements" because additional second-round inputs will be needed to produce the original inputs, and then more inputs will be needed to produce the second-round inputs, and so on. Eventually, the additions become minimal and the process of determining required inputs may be stopped. The sum of all inputs from all rounds yields the production levels necessary for each sector to satisfy household demand.

Input-output analysis is useful to show transactions between industries and the relative importance of different activities to one another. However, input-output tables are not available in series at the present time. There is an increasing interest in this type of analysis, and when federal agencies are able to accumulate the types of data needed on a continuing basis, input-output tables may become available on a regular basis. The model does make several assumptions which may be unrealistic, so the user should be cautious in applying strict interpretations of the results.

Regional income

Real estate productivity and values also depend upon the level of income within a region. The regional income and economic prospects may differ significantly from national trends. Low per capita incomes in the Appalachian region, the demise of coal mining as a major industry in southern Illinois and the consequent depression of economic activity in that area, and the great growth and prosperity in southern California during the 1960s are but a few examples of regional trends that have varied substantially from the national experience. Real estate values in depressed regions have suffered commensurately with the decline in economic activity, while values in areas experiencing greater than average growth and prosperity have increased faster than the national average.

Although it is important for the real estate market analyst to keep abreast of regional economic trends, measures of these trends are less readily attainable than measures for trends at either the national or local levels. Two reasons for this lack of data can be cited. First, there is no standard delineation of regions. A region may vary in size from a group of states to a section of a city. A regional breakdown for one analyst or for one government agency would not be functionally useful for another analyst or another agency. Thus, there has not been agreement on how to divide up the country for the collection of regional data.

The second reason is that the boundaries of U.S. regions are much less meaningful than the national boundaries as determinants of economic activity. It is much easier to identify the production of goods and services within the United States and to keep track of products and services flowing into and out of the country than it is to keep track of these same flows among regions. The federal government has shown much more interest in data collection for the entire country than for regions of the country. In recent years, however, many groups have become concerned about regional analysis, and government agencies, as well as academic and professional groups, have devoted more attention to the understanding and collection of regional data.

Input-output analysis.   Input-output analysis would seem to hold some of its greatest potential as a tool for analyzing regions. While no regional input-output analysis is done on a series basis, the idea has been advocated, and indeed input-output analysis has been performed for a state. Hopefully, this tool may become operative and useful for states, and the state data could then be combined into regional groupings.

Other measures.   Without a regular system of measuring regional income and production, a market analyst must keep track of other indicators of economic activity. Personal income and buying income are estimated for states. Personal income measures can be found in *Business Week* magazine, while *Sales Management* magazine publishes estimates of buying income for states and other geographic areas in its annual "buying power" issue. The bureaus of business research of many state universities are also valuable sources of data on regional economic trends and prospects. State departments of development and chambers of commerce are other potential sources of statewide information.

Community income

Community income analysis is similar to regional analysis. Depending on the strength of the relationships between the region and the community and on the boundaries of each area, the incomes may be related. In some cases community income may be synonymous with regional income. Nevertheless, there are several methods of measuring income which are particularly useful for analyzing communities with established boundaries.

Economic base theory.   One tool or method for analyzing community income and economic prospects is economic base analysis. In its original concept, economic base analysis was designed as a tool to predict future population for a community. This prediction was accomplished by identifying all sources of employment in a community and dividing the number of employees between two categories—basic and service (or primary and secondary). Basic employment is recognized as the type for which products and services are exported beyond the community's borders. In other words, these are activities which bring income into a community. Service employment redistributes the income within the community. Examples of the first category are the automobile industry in Detroit, from which the community derives much of its income by the shipment of automobiles out of the city, and a large university within a city which brings income from students who come from beyond the city's borders. Examples of the second category are barbershops, beauty shops, real estate and insurance offices, and other types of service businesses that do not draw customers primarily from outside the community. Total employment (E_t) therefore consists of base or export employment (E_x) and service or local employment (E_l).

$$E_t = E_x + E_l \tag{1}$$

Figure 9–7 shows the various components of total community income.

Economic base analysis assumes the growth of a community is based on community employment levels and on the outside markets for which the community serves as a center of base activities. The more a community exports, the larger it grows. Service employment is ancillary to base employment and can be expressed as a fraction of total employment.

$$E_l = kE_t \qquad 0 < k < 1 \tag{2}$$

Substituting into equation 1:

$$E_t = E_x + kE_t$$

$$E_t = E_x \left(\frac{1}{1-k} \right) \tag{3}$$

From this equation, a ratio, known as the employment multiplier, is obtained between the number of basic employees and the number of service employees.

$$\frac{\Delta E_t}{\Delta E_x} = \frac{1}{1-k} \tag{4}$$

The basic sources of employment are surveyed in an attempt to determine whether increases in this type of employment will be taking place in the future. Increases in service employment are then predicted in relation to the ratio between service and basic employment

FIGURE 9–7
How the community earns its living

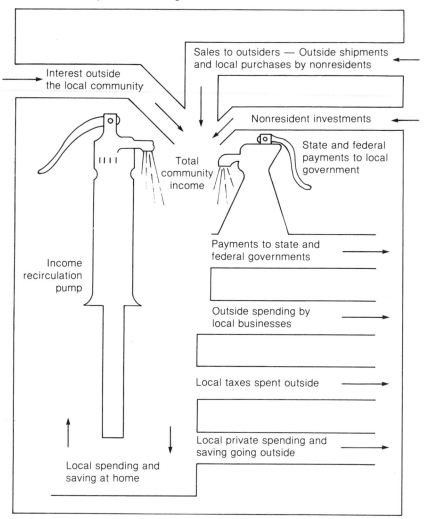

Source: Bank of America, Area Development Service, San Francisco.

existing previously in the community. The total increase in population, ΔP_t, deriving from the increase in basic employment can be projected on the basis of the ratio of the total population to the total employment existing in the community.

$$\Delta P_t = \left(\frac{P_t}{E_t}\right)\ (\Delta E_t) \tag{5}$$

As an example, assume research has revealed the following information:

Local population 100,000
Local employment 48,000
Local basic employment 20,000
Local employment increase in five years .... +3,000

The employment multiplier is calculated to be 2.4 ($E_t/E_r = 48/20$).
The increase in total employment is 7,200 [$\Delta E_t = (\Delta E_r)(1/1 - k) = 3,000 \times 2.4$]. Total employment in five years is the sum of the original
figure for total employment and the increase in employment, or
55,200. For every person added to the labor force, population increases
by 2.08 persons ($P_t/E_t = 100,000/48,000$). The population increase is
found as the total employment increase adjusted by the population
multiplier ($\Delta P_t = \Delta E_t \times 2.08 = 14,976$). The total population in five
years is then estimated as 114,976 ($P_{t1} = P_t + \Delta P_t = 100,000 + 14,976$).

When gathering information pertinent to the economic base analysis, the analyst must examine all influences which could modify the
results. For example, the importance of income sources should be analyzed along with the potential for new income source development.
Centers which may provide pertinent information for use in economic
base analysis include the Bureau of the Census, state employment
firms, chambers of commerce, tax authorities, specific firms and employment centers in the area, and research bureaus of local universities.

However, the process of surveying basic employment sources to
determine planned increases in employment has proved to be an unreliable predicting method for determining future basic employment.
Therefore, in carrying out economic base analysis, several techniques
are usually employed to project employment in various industry
classifications. In a mammoth study of the Columbus, Ohio, economic
base performed during the 1960s, the Ohio State University Bureau of
Business Research utilized three projection techniques. First, county
share of U.S. total value added per employee was determined for each
industry classification, and ratios were projected into the future on the
basis of total U.S. industry forecasts. Second, manufacturers were surveyed to determine future employment expectations according to the
amount of sales expected within and outside the community. Third,
input-output tables were constructed to show the interrelationships
among the various industries in metropolitan Columbus. Projected
sales of each industry were computed from the coefficients developed
in the input-output matrix, and then were converted to projected employment. This large study of the Columbus economic base projected
employment at various intervals 20 years into the future, to 1985. A
summary of the study is contained in Appendix E.

Despite the relative simplicity of the economic base analysis, it is not without serious limitations. The employment multiplier tends to be unstable in the short run for the same city. The multiplier also varies from city to city. This instability weakens the model as a reliable forecasting tool. In addition, the model assumes the supply of facilities supporting growth (such as transportation networks) is completely elastic; this assumption is obviously unrealistic. Many times, it is impossible to predict the appearance of latent income source activities. This occurred in Orlando, Florida, when Disney World was in the planning stages—the whole operation was kept very secret for a long time. Time dimensions also pose problems. For example, how long does it take before the multiplier becomes fully effective? In the long run, the differences between basic and service activities may diminish until it is difficult to separate the two. Perhaps the most important critique is best stated by Nourse:

> Theoretically, economic development does not necessarily occur because exports expand. Only to the extent that resource increases, technological changes, or productivity increases are associated with export increases would exports provide the mechanism for development. In fact, the comparative advantage for export production may depend on service sector efficiency, so that the causal relation may be the reverse of that hypothesized.[13]

The model as it stands, if taken to the extreme, implies that because world population is growing, the world must be exporting off the globe!

Location coefficient and location quotient. The location coefficient and the location quotient measure the percentage of an activity in a local area to that of the nation as a whole. The coefficient is the ratio of national employment in industry A to total national employment subtracted from the ratio of local employment in industry A to total local employment.

$$LC = \frac{L_a}{L_t} - \frac{N_a}{N_t} \qquad (6)$$

If the coefficient is positive, then the community is producing more product than it needs and must therefore be exporting it. Alternatively, a negative number implies imports, and thus industry A would be a nonbasic activity.

The location quotient (LQ) is similar, but it is represented by the ratio of local percentage employment to national percentage employment.

---

[13] Hugh O. Nourse, "Equivalence of Central Place and Economic Base Theories of Urban Growth," *Journal of Urban Economics* 5 (1978): 546.

$$LQ = \frac{L_a}{L_t} \div \frac{N_a}{N_t} \qquad (7)$$

A ratio greater than 1 suggests that some of the basic employment in the city is in industry A. The larger the quotient, the more important the industry is as an exporter. A ratio of 1 represents a city which neither imports nor exports products produced by industry A.

Central place theory.   Central place theory was originally developed by geographers to explain the distribution of city sizes. The theory assumes a flat landscape; uniform distribution of resources, including population, farms, and transportation routes; no external economies; and homogeneous households. Boundaries for various markets are set by the total cost of the product or service to the consumer. The total cost consists of the price plus transportation costs. Because transportation costs usually increase with distance, the point where the additional burden of transportation costs becomes too burdensome for the consumer sets the market boundary. In Figure 9–8 the maximum

FIGURE 9–8
Distance from market center to boundary

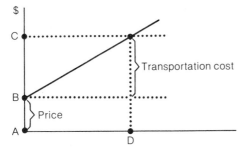

price consumers are willing to pay is $C; therefore, the market boundary is set at a distance D from the center. If extended in all directions, the boundary becomes a circle.

Beyond the boundary, another marketplace serves as the center to provide products and services to rural residents. A pattern of circles, each tangent to the next, appears on the plain. However, some areas on the plain are still left unserved, as shown by the shaded areas of Figure 9–9. Other producers will take advantage of these gaps and move in to fill in the unserved area. Excess profits by the original suppliers will force competition to develop between suppliers, and market area boundaries will soon expand and contract until an equilibrium is reached. The final equilibrium boundaries result in a pattern of hexagonals, as shown in Figure 9–10. The boundary represents the dis-

FIGURE 9–9
Circular market boundaries

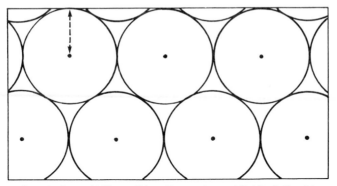

Source: James Heilbrun, *Urban Economics and Public Policy* (New York: St. Martin's Press, 1974), p. 78.

tance from the center where the delivered price is the same for each producer. Notice that all areas on the plain are served by a supplier.

When market area boundaries for all products and services, each of which serves an area of different size, are laid on top of one another, a fishnet pattern emerges. Certain market areas will tend to have greater concentrations of suppliers. These areas become cities or towns, and a hierarchy of central places is formed. For example, a farm market having the smallest market area and the least number of activities is a central place of the first order. A town containing activities with larger market areas in addition to the smaller farm markets is a central place of a higher order. The highest order central place comprises the largest

FIGURE 9–10
Hexagonal market boundaries

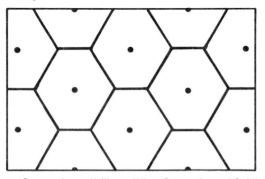

Source: James Heilbrun, *Urban Economics and Public Policy* (New York: St. Martin's Press, 1974), p. 78.

of the cities that contain all activities, including activities with a market so large that only one supplier exists for the entire plain. The market area for each order necessary for a firm's survival is known as the *threshold size*.

Mathematically, the population of these central places may be found as a proportion of the entire population of the market area. The population of the town with the smallest threshold size of the first order is represented as:

$$C_1 = k(C_1 + r) \qquad 0 < k < 1 \tag{8}$$

where:

C_1 = Population of town
r = Rural hinterland population
$C_1 + r$ = Entire population being served
k = Fraction of population required to serve the market

Solving for C_1, the equation becomes:

$$C_1 = \left(\frac{1}{1-k}\right) kr \tag{9}$$

To find the population of a larger town with many markets, the equation may be modified to:

$$C_1 = \sum_{i=1}^{n} k_i(C_i + S_i) \tag{10}$$

where:

C_n = Population of any place of order n
k = Fraction of population required to serve the market
S_i = Population of $n - 1$ satellite areas of the central place
i = Market order

Again, solving for C_n yields:

$$C_n = \sum_{i=1}^{n} \left[\left(\frac{1}{1 - \sum_{j=1}^{n} k_j} \right) k_i S_i \right] \tag{11}$$

Equivalence of the economic base theory and the central place theory. Economic base theory and central place theory can both be used to estimate population growth. The models—developed at the same time, one by economists and one by geographers—seem at first glance to be totally unrelated. Economic base analysis has been much discredited, but central place theory is usually considered to explain city size, not growth, and thus would be totally different in nature.

Nourse,[14] however, contends that the two theories are in fact equivalent and that neither is really a theory of growth.

Economic base theory estimates population growth according to the number of workers employed in basic activities. Notice that $k_i S_i$ in the central place theory equation is equivalent to basic employment. Total employment may be expressed as:

$$E_t = LC_n \tag{12}$$

where:

E_t = Total employment
L = Labor participation rate
C_n = Population of the central place

Alternatively,

$$C_n = \frac{E_t}{L} \tag{13}$$

Therefore, substituting $E_x(1/1 - k)$ into equation 13 for E_t yields:[15]

$$C_n = \frac{\left(\dfrac{1}{1-k}\right) E_x}{L} = \left(\frac{1}{1-k}\right)\left(\frac{E_x}{L}\right) \tag{14}$$

The multiplier $1/1 - k$ is the same in both theories. The expression E_x/L of economic base theory is the basic employment figure; this can also be expressed as kr, as previously discussed. The two theories are therefore equivalent, and all criticisms of one theory can be applied to the other. This is not to say, however, that an analysis using economic base theory or central place theory might not provide useful information. The analyst must be wary of all limiting factors and assumptions when using economic base theory or central place theory in analyzing market areas.

Other measures. Buying income is estimated by *Sales Management* for metropolitan areas. The magazine also estimates the number of people in various income categories. The analyst can use these data both in comparing a community with similar communities and in developing trends for the community under analysis. Chambers of commerce also usually maintain data on incomes and numbers of households in a community, as well as information on the number and types of industries, the number and types of commercial establishments, current and expected development in the community, and other economic measures.

---

[14] Ibid., pp. 543–49.

[15] The expression $E_x(1/1 - k)$ is from economic base theory.

The Federal Housing Administration periodically performs market analyses for metropolitan areas. These studies can be extremely useful in analyzing a real estate market. Trade and professional organizations within a community, such as a home builders' association or an apartment owners and managers association, may also maintain useful data and perform market studies.

Price structure

The prices of real estate in a community also help determine the demand for real estate. The price structure refers to the relationships among the prices of properties within the community and to the relationship between the prices of real estate and the prices of other economic goods. If real estate prices rise relative to the prices of other goods, people who would otherwise be in the market may refrain from buying until real estate prices seem to be more reasonable. By the same token, if people expect the prices of real estate to increase in the future relative to the prices of other goods, they may decide to purchase now rather than later.

In addition to total price, other elements of price must be considered. The down payments required on real estate may become more liberal or more rigorous. As money conditions tighten in the overall economy, for example, lenders often require larger down payments than during periods of relatively easy money. Also, institutional regulations are sometimes adjusted to allow smaller down payments. When this occurs, the demand for real estate is likely to be affected.

The monthly housing expense can be regarded as part of the price mechanism for residential real estate. Families must budget their housing expense, and the extent to which monthly housing expense is expected to increase can affect the willingness of families to purchase homes.

DETERMINANTS OF SUPPLY

Anticipations of demand

Perhaps the single most important determinant of the supply of new real estate resources is the expectation that suppliers have of demand. If developers and builders are optimistic about future demand, they will tend to bring forth newly created resources. If, however, they are relatively pessimistic about the coming year's demand, they will tend to hold back the level of development and construction activity. These anticipations result from forecasts of national economic activity, regional changes, and community income and economic activity.

Utilization of existing real estate resources

If the existing stock of real estate resources is not being utilized at close to its capacity, the suppliers of new real estate resources will be hesitant to bring new properties onto the market. The degree of utilization of existing resources is usually measured by the vacancy rate in residential property, the vacancy rate in office buildings, the number of square feet utilized per employee in office buildings and other commercial buildings, the sales per square foot for commercial property, and the number of employees per square foot or the income generated per square foot for industrial property. If these ratios indicate an unusually high level of unused or underused space, developers and builders will tend not to supply new properties. For residential property, the normal or average vacancy rate may run around 5 percent; this rate may go as low as 2 percent, and it may go considerably higher than 5 percent. When the rate is much above 5 percent, however, suppliers tend to reduce the amount of new development and construction.

Availability and prices of land and utilities

Suitable land must be available for development; furthermore, land must be available at reasonable prices, or development will be impeded. Land by itself, however, is not sufficient. Sewage facilities, storm drains, water mains, and power sources must be available. Some of the stickiest problems of real estate development today revolve around the obtaining of proper and adequate facilities of all types. Many communities have resisted the further provision of utilities without the payment of higher fees by developers. At the same time, communities have become cognizant of the ecological damage that can be done by septic tanks, the use of private water systems, and the unregulated development of new projects. Suppliers of new real estate resources today must work carefully with city planning commissions, zoning boards, city councils, other administrative bodies of local governments, and private groups of interested citizens.

Availability and price of financing

The importance of financing in real estate markets is indicated by its position as a determinant of both demand and supply. On the supply side of the market, financing for land development and construction are at least of equal importance with the availability and relative prices of financing for long-term mortgage commitments. Most developers and contractors operate with relatively small amounts of their own capital. If development and construction financing are not available, or are available only at relatively high prices, new development and construction will be unresponsive to any needs that exist.

Availability and prices of materials and labor

In normal times, materials and labor are available to real estate developers and contractors. During times of war, however, materials may be in short supply because they are diverted to a war effort. Very little building of nonstrategic resources took place in this country during World War II and the Korean War. The Vietnam War saw little constriction of the supply of materials because this war was less of a drain on our national economic resources. Undoubtedly, however, the Vietnam War helped to inflate the prices of building materials above what they would have been otherwise.

The prices of labor, or wages, in the construction industry have been one of the country's severe unresolved economic problems. As discussed in the chapter on real estate production,[16] the structure for bargaining between the construction industry and the labor unions is not ideal. Unions have not received the assurances of security that their members want and need. As a substitute for security, unions have demanded wage rate increases consistently above the national average. Thus, the prices for labor in the construction industry have been inordinately high, helping to push the prices of housing and other types of real estate beyond the reach of many people. Only wholesale reform in the relationships between unions and industry and in the provision of adequate security for construction workers will resolve this problem and serve to make real estate more realistically priced relative to other economic goods.

Taxes

The real estate tax and the federal income tax play an important role in influencing both the demand and the supply of real estate resources. The real estate tax serves as the principal means of financing for local communities, and faced with increasing demands, these communities have continually increased the levels of real estate taxation. In recent years there has been a revolt against the payment of higher and higher real estate taxes. Furthermore, the real estate tax has served to discourage improvements in existing properties and desirable changes in land uses.

The federal income tax has an influence on both the form and the financing of capital investment. Rules governing the deductions of

---

[16] See Chapter 15.

various expenses applicable to real estate may produce favorable or unfavorable conditions for real estate investment. Deductions for interest on a mortgage loan, for depreciation of the improvements in a real estate investment, and for other legitimate expenses may make some properties relatively desirable and others less desirable. Changes in the income tax laws[17] have changed the relative attractiveness of various types of real estate projects. No properties other than new apartments today receive the benefits of the most rapid form of depreciation allowed for computing income tax—200 percent declining balance. Before the Tax Reform Act of 1969, however, other properties received this advantage.

CONCEPTUALIZING THE LOCAL HOUSING MARKET

The basic determinants of demand and supply come into play in the process of allocating households among available housing units in the local housing market.[18] Households are diverse in their incomes, number of persons, stage in the family cycle, location of their places of employment, tastes, and preferences. Somehow, these heterogeneous households obtain shelter in a wide variety of housing units that differ in size, type (single-family detached, row house, apartment), physical condition, architectural features, and locational attributes. In this allocation process, each household apportions its income between expenditures for housing and expenditures for all other goods and services and, simultaneously, decides how much of the housing budget will be spent on quality and how much on quantity. The quantity attribute of housing is the size of the housing unit that will be occupied; the quality attribute is multidimensional and accounts for all other characteristics of the standing stock, including locational attributes. The quantity and quality dimensions of housing combine in a myriad of physical forms, resulting in the diversity of the standing stock of housing units. Each household locates in the housing unit that maximizes the total satisfaction of that household, given the price and amount of housing services provided by that unit and the prices of other goods and services.

This household joins other households as demanders of housing units in a local housing submarket. A housing submarket results from a group of households which, influenced by their incomes, needs, tastes

---

[17] See the discussion in Chapter 13.

[18] Antecedents of this conceptualization of a local housing market include the following: Wallace F. Smith, "An Outline Theory of the Housing Market with Special Reference to Low-Income Housing and Urban Renewal," Ph.D. dissertation, Seattle, University of Washington, 1958; Chester Rapkin, Louis Winnick, and David M. Blank, *Housing Market Analysis* (Washington, D.C.: Housing and Home Finance Agency, 1953); and William G. Grigsby, *Housing Markets and Public Policy* (Philadelphia: University of Pennsylvania Press, 1963).

and other factors, consider the housing units in the submarket to be closer substitutes, one for another, than they are for other units in the market. From the supply aspect, housing units in a submarket are similar in prices, in physical characteristics, and in locational attributes, although units in a submarket can be widely dispersed in the community or grouped in more than one geographic area. For instance, households may consider single-family homes in the $50,000 price range to be satisfactory substitutes for each other, although the neighborhoods containing such homes are on opposite ends of the community. Such housing units may, on balance, produce linkages providing the same amounts of satisfaction to households in the submarket.[19]

Housing submarkets are generally more homogeneous with respect to supply characteristics than with respect to the characteristics of demanders in the submarket. Households demanding units in a submarket will display differences in income and other factors affecting their housing choices. It is the combined effect of these factors that allocates the households to units in the submarket, even though one household has an annual income of $30,000, and another, $20,000, and one household is an elderly couple, and another, a young family of five persons.

Figure 9–11 depicts a local housing market composed of interrelated submarkets. Each submarket has its demand and supply functions, price, and vacancy rate. Submarket A consists of dilapidated one-

FIGURE 9–11
Interrelated housing submarkets

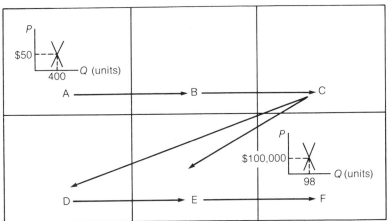

Key: Submarket A is 500 units of dilapidated one-bedroom apartments in the inner city, and submarket F is 100 units of luxurious single-family residences in preferred locations. Submarkets B, C, D, and E are intermediately linked with A and F.

---

[19] See Chapter 8 for discussion of these locational attributes.

bedroom, walk-up apartments in the inner city, renting for $100 per month. Households in these units have a median income of $8,000 a year; a large proportion of the units are occupied by minority families with school-age children. The supply of housing units in submarket A is fixed in the market time period (highly inelastic supply), and the demand for such units determines price, the number of available units occupied, and the vacancy rate. In submarket A, 400 of the 500 available units are occupied at $100 per month rent; the vacancy rate is 20 percent.

In a time period too short to adjust supply, vacancy rates can vary substantially among submarkets. The vacancy rate in submarket A may be 20 percent, while in submarket F only 2 percent of the available units are vacant. Submarket F contains high-priced, single-family homes that perhaps are currently in great demand because of a recent in-migration of high-income households into the community. The housing units in submarket F are selling for around $200,000, which is a premium price in the market at this point in time. Suppliers of such units are earning an above-average profit, as price exceeds long-run production costs.

The arrows in Figure 9–11 indicate linkages among submarkets. Linkages are an expression of the degree to which households in a submarket consider the housing units in a linked submarket to be acceptable (preferred) substitutes. Households in submarket E would prefer living in F, but were outbid by households occupying units in F. If the price of units in F falls sufficiently in the future, households in E will move from E to F. A linkage, then, expresses the cross-elasticity of demand in one submarket given a change in price in the linked submarket. The strength of a linkage (responsiveness of demand to a change in price in the linked submarket) depends upon the degree of substitutability of units in the two submarkets. A submarket can be linked to more than one other submarket (for example, submarket C is linked to both D and E); all submarkets are either directly or indirectly linked to one another. In reality, the local housing market is composed of many more submarkets and linkages than are depicted in Figure 9–11. Discrimination preventing the free movement of minority households, the lack of knowledge about available alternatives, simple inertia, and other factors contributing to market imperfection weaken linkages and lessen adjustments of demand to changing supply conditions in the various submarkets.

Premium rents and prices and abnormally low vacancy rates could not be maintained in the long run in a competitive market. In long-run equilibrium, each household would be occupying the housing unit that maximizes the household's total satisfaction; no household would have an incentive to move (given the prices of housing and of other goods and services, and all other supply and demand factors operating to affect housing choice). Supply adjustments would have produced "normal" vacancy rates in each submarket and an array of rents and prices equal to the costs of producing the volume of housing services comprising the various housing units (production costs include a normal profit to the supplier). A uniform risk-adjusted rate of return on capital investment would tend to be earned by suppliers across submarkets. The nominal return earned on investment would vary among submarkets in long-run equilibrium. Submarket A may have a 20 percent aftertax return on investment, and submarket C a 12 percent aftertax return. However, when these returns are adjusted for the relative risk of investing in properties in the two submarkets, a uniform return on investment of, say, 10 percent is obtained. This risk-adjusted rate is earned by suppliers of housing services in all submarkets.

Suppliers in long-run equilibrium would have no incentive to increase investment by modernization, rehabilitation, or conversion, nor would they desire to disinvest by forgoing repairs and maintenance. Capital improvements to the housing unit would increase the quantity of services provided by the unit. The costs associated with a capital improvement must be compensated by added value. Value is increased by generating a larger net operating income due to higher rents, by a reduction in vacancy losses, or by a lower operating ratio, or by all three combined. The capital improvement could also extend the economic life of the improvement, or it might shift the property to a different submarket in which risk and the required return on investment are less; either result would increase the value of the property. Capital improvements made to shift the property to another submarket may be a response to persistent abnormal profits in the other submarket.

Disinvestment can occur in response to persistent high-vacancy losses; in response to rents and net operating income continuing below the costs of producing the level of services provided by the unit; or by permitting the housing unit to fall into another, lower valued submarket that is experiencing continued above-normal profits. In long-run equilibrium, these abnormal profits would disappear, and supply and demand in the several submarkets would be in equilibrium.

Filtering

The literature of housing economics contains several concepts of filtering.[20] Some authors have used the term synonymously with the

---

[20] The interested reader will find a discussion of several of these concepts in Grigsby, *Housing Markets and Public Policy*, pp. 84–130. Also see William B. Brueggeman, "An Analysis of the Filtering Process with Special Reference to Housing Subsidies," in *National Housing Policy Study Papers* (Washington, D.C.: U.S. Dept. of Housing and Urban Development), November 5, 1973.

turnover of housing resulting from movement of households among units. Grigsby defines filtering as occurring "only when value declines more rapidly than quality so that families can obtain either higher quality and more space at the same price or the same quality and space at a lower price than formerly."[21] Ratcliff conceptualizes filtering by assuming demand factors constant and introducing additional housing units (new construction) into the market. The process referred to as filtering down "—is described most simply as the changing of occupancy as the housing that is occupied by one income group becomes available to the next lower income group as a result of decline in market price, that is, in sales price or rent value."[22]

Cast in our housing submarket framework, an increase in housing units supplied in submarket E will depress price (given demand) and permit lower income families to move from linked submarkets into submarket E. The vacancies created in linked submarkets (such as D and C) exert a downward influence on rents or prices in those submarkets, permitting still lower income families to improve their housing condition at the same or less expense. Ultimately, through the linkages among submarkets, units are vacated in submarket A, which contains the lowest quality, least desirable housing in the community. No demand exists for units in submarket A, and they are abandoned.

Filtering as described above is a slow, uncertain process. The multiplicity of linkages among submarkets can diffuse the impact on prices or rents. The filtering process can be impeded or halted by discrimination, lack of knowledge about available housing alternatives, undoubling (an existing household forms two separate households, leaving no vacancy behind), and in-migration of households which absorb vacancies.

Has filtering improved the housing condition of American households over time? Our answer would be, "No, it has not." This reply is not dependent upon market imperfections that slow or stop the filtering process. Rather, it is based upon the contention that the housing market is reasonably competitive. Suppliers of housing seize opportunities to achieve abnormal profits; households consume housing in a manner that maximizes their net satisfaction. The "benefits" view of filtering, where households by moving are able to improve their housing condition at the same or less expense, will not be sustained in the long run.[23] Households obtain only the quality and quantity of housing for which they are willing and able to pay. Any supply-induced reduction in price or rent in the market will result in disinvestment by

---

[21] Grigsby, *Housing Markets and Public Policy*, p. 97.

[22] Ratcliff, *Urban Land Economics*, pp. 321–22.

[23] Brueggeman, "Analysis of the Filtering Process."

suppliers until the equilibrium return on investment is again attained and until price again covers the cost of production of the housing services provided.

Our nation over time has indeed become better housed. This overall improvement in housing condition has resulted from numerous factors affecting housing demand and supply. Among these factors are the rising standard of living enjoyed by American households, technological innovations in construction and materials, tax advantages provided homeowners and investors in housing, and various institutional arrangements that reduce the cost and increase the availability of mortgage financing. Such basic determinants of supply and demand increase the total expenditure for housing, make it possible to buy more housing per dollar spent, or increase the supply of housing made available at a given price. Collectively, these factors contribute to the overall improvement in the housing condition of American households. The movements of households among units and housing submarkets are observable adjustments in a market continually affected by changing supply and demand conditions.

MARKET AND FEASIBILITY ANALYSES

Market and feasibility analyses are the end results of the consideration of all the factors that have been discussed in this chapter.[24] These studies attempt to relate all the determinants of supply and demand to the problem of anticipating future real estate needs in a community. As such, they represent the practical application of the theory of market behavior. Whether market studies and feasibility analyses are reliable and useful is thus a function of two considerations—validity of the theory and ability to attach accurate measures to the elements and relationships of the theory.

To be reliable, market and feasibility analyses must be painstaking and thorough. Past trends and relationships may not hold for the future. The analyst may have to dig beneath the surface to find qualitative indicators of future quantitative changes. Household size may not remain steady but may decline because of a declining birthrate, greater financial independence of older and younger persons (leading to undoubling), older marriage ages, and an increasing divorce rate. To predict such a change, the market analyst must understand social

---

[24] Although we discuss only market studies and feasibility studies, other types of economic studies are sometimes useful. For a discussion of a number of different types of studies, including highest and best use studies, land-use studies, land utilization studies, marketability studies, reuse appraisals, and cost-benefit studies, see Anthony Downs, "Characteristics of Various Economic Studies," *Appraisal Journal*, July 1966, pp. 329–38.

trends and changes in values and attitudes, as well as economic conditions and trends.

Market analysis

A market analysis is a study designed to determine the types and quantities of additional real estate resources which can be absorbed by the market over a reasonable period of time. Typically, market studies are limited to an analysis of a particular type of real estate, such as housing, industrial, or commercial real estate. The predominant type of study concerns housing.

Individual businesses, industry trade groups, and governmental agencies at local, state, and federal levels have interest in market studies. Businesses with markets of national scope, such as lumber and hardware suppliers, appliance manufacturers, and home furnishers, base their budgeting procedures on the estimated aggregate demand for new real estate for the coming year. Home builders' associations usually engage in market research to help their members plan the types, styles, and price ranges of new homes to produce during the coming year. And governmental agencies need to understand the economic and social needs of their constituencies in order to formulate policies that will encourage the proper amounts and types of housing and other real estate to be produced. In short, market analysis is a planning or budgeting tool. As one well-known analyst has said, "Market analysis is a study of the reasons why prices are being paid. It has far more to do with the future than with either the present or the past."[25]

Most cities and urban areas are concerned with housing market analyses in order to measure and identify housing needs in the community. The Federal Housing Administration (FHA) of the U.S. Department of Housing and Urban Development has also developed comprehensive techniques and instructions for the undertaking of market analyses in local communities across the country.[26] The FHA uses these studies in determining which projects that it has been requested to underwrite can be absorbed by the market. Most market analyses are concerned with the following broad subject areas:[27]

1. *Delineation of the market area*—the area within which dwelling units are competitive with one another.

---

[25] W. A. Bowes, "What Is Market Analysis?" *Real Estate Appraiser,* July–August 1968, p. 11.

[26] Federal Housing Administration, U.S. Department of Housing and Urban Development, *FHA Techniques of Housing Market Analysis* (Washington, D.C.: U.S. Government Printing Office, 1970).

[27] Ibid., p. 5. (Note: A detailed outline for FHA housing market analyses is shown in Appendix D, this volume.)

2. *The area's economy*—principal economic activities, basic resources, economic trends.
3. *Demand factors*—employment, incomes, population, households,
   family size.
4. *Supply factors*—residential construction activity, housing inventory, conversions, demolitions.
5. *Current market conditions*—vacancies, unsold inventory, marketability of sales and rental units, prices, rents, building costs,
   mortgage defaults and foreclosures, disposition of acquired properties.
6. *Quantitative and qualitative demand*—prospective number of
   dwelling units that can be absorbed economically at various price
   and rent levels under conditions existing on the "as of" date.

Most housing analyses estimate demand, or new housing construction, with an equation similar to the following one:

$$D_y = (H_y + V_{ny}) - (H_b + V_{nb}) - (V_s + C) + R_{b-y} \qquad (15)$$

where:

D_y = Number of new units needed in year y
H_y = Number of households forecasted for year y
V_{ny} = Normal vacancies in year y
H_b = Number of households in base year b
V_{nb} = Normal vacancies in base year b
V_s = Surplus vacant units
C = Construction in base period
R_{b-y} = Demolitions during the period

The results of the use of this equation for the city of Gainesville,
Florida, are shown in Table 9–5. The estimated number of housing
units needed between 1980–85, as projected in 1976, is 859–1,270
owner-occupied units and 962–1,402 rental units. Table 9–6 shows the
effective demand for sales units broken down into price categories,
while Tables 9–7 and 9–8 do the same for multifamily housing units.
Table 9–9 is a summary of the projections made for the study period.
By keeping track of any changes in the conditions upon which these
forecasts were made and the numbers and types of units supplied
during the projection period, the FHA, local builders, lending institutions, and local government agencies can determine whether housing
demand is being fulfilled, whether shortages continue to exist, or
whether overbuilding is occurring. If actual construction differs from
the projected numbers, then interested organizations would want
to determine the reasons which explain the situation and to identify
more precisely any submarkets that have been experiencing overbuilding.

TABLE 9–5

Estimated housing requirements: Gainesville urban area, 1985

	Total	Owner	Renter
Household growth	8,541–12,653	4,185–6,200*	4,356–6,453*
Demolitions†	250	25‡	225‡
A. Required growth and replacement	8,791–12,903	4,210–6,225	4,581–6,678
B. Vacancies required for additional units§	313–459	84–125	229–334
A + B: Estimated required units	9,104–13,362	4,294–6,350	4,810–7,012
Annual demand	1,821–2,672	859–1,270	962–1,402

   * Additional home ownership expected by 1980–85, causing tenure shift (owner-renter ratio of 49:51).
   † Demolitions averaging 50 per year.
   ‡ Owner-renter ratio of 1:9.
   § Vacancy rate: 2 percent owner, 5 percent renter.
   Source: City of Gainesville, Florida, Department of Community Development, *Housing Market Analysis, 1975–1985,* part 1: *Housing Element Gainesville Comprehensive Development Plan,* June 1976, p. 58.

TABLE 9–6

Effective demand for multifamily housing: Gainesville urban area, 1985
(low estimate—793 units)*

Price categories	Percent of purchasers	Cumulative	Percent above mini- mum price*	Absolute distri- bution annual demand	
				Low	High
Under $25,000	3%	3%			
$25,000–29,999	5	8			
$30,000–34,999	6	14	6%	40	56
$35,000–39,999	9	23	10	66	93
$40,000–44,999	9	32	10	66	93
$45,000–49,999	9	41	10	66	93
$50,000–54,999	8	49	9	59	84
$55,000–59,999	9	58	10	66	93
$60,000–64,999	8	66	9	59	84
$65,000–69,999	8	74	9	59	84
$70,000–74,999	7	81	7	46	65
$75,000–79,999	5	86	5	33	47
$80,000–84,999	4	90	4	27	37
$85,000–89,999	2	92	11	73	102
$90,000–94,999	2	94	—	—	—
$95,000 or more	6	100	—	—	—
	100%		100%	600	931

   * Minimum new sale price: $30,000 (lowest price at which housing industry can now provide new housing in the urban area).
   Source: City of Gainesville, Florida, Department of Community Development, *Housing Market Analysis, 1975–1985,* part 1: *Housing Element Gainesville Comprehensive Development Plan,* June 1976, p. 62.

TABLE 9–7
Annual qualitative demand for multifamily housing:
Gainesville urban area, 1985 (low estimate—793 units)*

Gross rent	0 BR	1 BR	2 BR	3 BR
$150	40			
160	24			
170	14			
180	9			
190	5	347		
200	3	226		
210	2	147		
220	1	95	358	
230		62	269	
240		40	202	
250		26	151	48
260		17	113	41
270		11	85	35
280		7	64	29
290		5	48	25
300			36	21
310			27	18
320			20	15
330			15	13
340			11	11
350+			9	9
	(40)	(347)	(358)	(48)

* Assumes a 793-unit annual demand 1975–85 and a unit size distribution of 5 percent for 0 BR, 43.8 percent for 1 BR, 45.2 percent for 2 BR, and 6 percent for 3 BR. (Distribution based upon table B–3, *Metropolitan Housing Characteristics, Gainesville, Florida*, HC (2)–79, U.S. Bureau of the Census, 1970.) Minimum gross rent based upon two-bedroom walk-up apartment renting at $220; other sizes are a proportion of this minimum.

Source: City of Gainesville, Florida, Department of Community Development, *Housing Market Analysis, 1975–1985: part 1: Housing Element Gainesville Comprehensive Development Plan*, June 1976, p. 67.

Feasibility analysis

While closely related to market analysis, feasibility analysis differs in that it deals with the acceptability and desirability of a particular real estate project. Market analysis may establish the need for more apartments of a particular type and price class in a community; whether a specific apartment project is sufficiently desirable to be absorbed by the market is another question. This question can be answered only by an intensive examination of the property's ability to

TABLE 9–8
Annual qualitative demand for multifamily housing:
Gainesville urban area, 1985 (high estimate—1,095
units)*

Gross rent	0 BR	1 BR	2 BR	3 BR
$150	55			
160	33			
170	20			
180	12			
190	7	480		
200	4	312		
210	3	203		
220	2	132	495	
230	1	86	371	
240		56	279	
250		36	209	65
260		24	156	55
270		15	117	47
280		10	88	40
290		7	66	34
300			50	29
310			37	25
320			28	21
330			21	18
340			16	15
350+			12	13
	(55)	(480)	(495)	(65)

* Assumes a 1,095-unit annual demand 1975–85 and a unit
size distribution of 5 percent for 0 BR, 43.8 percent for 1 BR,
45.2 percent for 2 BR, and 6 percent for 3 BR.
Source: City of Gainesville, Florida, Department of Community Development, *Housing Market Analysis, 1975–1985*, part 1: *Gainesville Comprehensive Development Plan*, June 1976, p. 68.

meet various requirements and its relative desirability to prospective consumers.

A feasibility study involves one of three basic types of problems:[28]

1. A site or building in search of a user.
2. A user in search of a site or certain improvements.
3. An investor looking for an opportunity.

A specific hypothesis is usually advanced as to how each type of problem may be solved. A site may be analyzed to determine whether an

[28] James A. Graaskamp, *A Guide to Feasibility Analysis* (Chicago: Society of Real Estate Appraisers, 1970), p. 11.

TABLE 9–9
Gainesville urban area: Summary of projections

	1975–80	*1980–85*
1. Population growth during the projection period	15,841–19,876	19,000–30,028
2. Estimated number of new household formations during projection period	4,982–6,408	8,541–12,653
3. Estimated total number of housing units required during projection period	5,425–6,903	9,104–13,362
Annually	1,085–1,380	1,821–2,672

	Annually (1975–85)*
	1,453–2,026
4. Total annual effective demand for new sales units†	660–931
$30,000–40,000	106–149
40,000–50,000	132–186
50,000–60,000	125–177
60,000–70,000	118–168
70,000–80,000	79–112
80,000+	100–139
5. Total annual effective demand for rental units	793–1,095
$150–179	31–43
180–209	207–286
210–239	265–366
240–269	159–221
270–299	74–100
300+	57–79

* Annual demand for ten-year period 1976–85. Figures are an average of the low projections for 1980 and 1985 and the high projections for the same periods.

† The new sales-rental ratio of the total is 45:55 (average over ten years). In 1975, the city had an owner-renter ratio of 49:51. It is assumed that tenure shift will lean toward rentals, particularly in the 1975–80 period, based upon the growing gap between the high cost of new housing and a decline in real income. Home ownership may represent a higher percentage from 1980 to 1985.

Source: City of Gainesville, Florida, Department of Community Development, *Housing Market Analysis, 1975–1985*, part 1: *Housing Element Gainesville Comprehensive Development Plan*, June 1976, p. 53.

apartment project would be a desirable type of use; an oil company may analyze an available site to determine whether a service station would be a profitable investment for the company; or analysts may study the desirability of a shopping center investment for clients wishing to liquidate their stock holdings in favor of a real estate venture. In short, a feasibility study attempts to forecast whether a particular course of action regarding a parcel of real estate fulfills the objectives of an owner-investor and meets externally or internally imposed conditions or requirements.

One of the most common objectives of an investor in a real estate project is that the project must produce a specified or desired rate of return. If the specified rate is the market rate of return, the capitalized value of the project will be its market value. And, as G. I. M. Young points out, if this value equals or exceeds cost, the project is *prima facie* justified.[29] However, *prima facie* justification of feasibility is not the end of a feasibility study. Other conditions and objectives may have to be met, and income may be further maximized.

The requirements which must be met by a real estate use are economic, political, legal, physical, and ethical in nature. A proposed use must be consistent with market needs, may depend on convincing community officials to provide water or sewer service, and must be within the realm of permissible uses and conform to space, site planning, and design standards imposed by zoning and planning commissions. Furthermore, the site must be capable of supporting the proposed improvements, and the proposed use must meet the ethical requirements of environmental concerns, the requirements of prospective tenants and employees, and the self-imposed standards of conduct of the investors themselves in providing resources that will usually be used for many years. Failure on any one of the counts is sufficient to render a proposed project "unfeasible."

The following examples illustrate how each of these types of conditions or requirements may affect a project's feasibility:

1. A proposed 60-story office building in Cincinnati was rejected before design work was begun because a market study showed that the projected demand for high-quality office space was amply supplied for the next five years.

2. An apartment project on the outskirts of Orlando, Florida, was stymied because sewer facilities were not available to the project and the city commission had ruled that septic tanks were unacceptable.

3. A low-rent housing project to be constructed in a section of $40,000–50,000 homes in a medium-sized Southern city was unacceptable because the number of square feet of living space in each unit was less than required by the zoning ordinance.

4. Before the 1960s the height of Chicago's skyscrapers was limited to about 50 stories because the subsoil conditions would not support taller buildings. Newer technology developed after World War II allowed caissons to be sunk to bedrock economically so that taller buildings could be supported. Today several buildings, including the John Hancock Center, First National Bank Building, Standard Oil Building, Lakepoint Tower Apartments, Marina Towers, and Sears Tower all exceed 60 stories.

5. An oil refinery which was thought to be of great economic benefit to Maine was disapproved by the state because of the potential for ecological damage from oil spills and leaks.

---

[29] G. I. M. Young, "Feasibility Studies," *Appraisal Journal*, July 1970, p. 379.

6.   A high-rise public housing building for families in Columbus, Ohio, was converted to other uses because of the social and physical problems that tenants experienced by being grouped into small areas with only one elevator for access to the entire building.

In addition to meeting certain conditions and requirements, for a project to be feasible it must meet other objectives, in addition to a desired rate of return. A project that does not produce tax shelter for high-income investors would not be feasible from their standpoint. Cash flow may be important to one investor, while maximizing return on total investment may be important to another investor. Generally, the investor's objective for an overall rate of return on the total investment can be incorporated into an appraisal of the property. As one well-known real estate analyst puts it, "An apartment project is economically feasible when its projected future net income affords an investor an appropriate rate of earnings on capital and provides for its recapture."[30]

The necessity of identifying the objectives of the potential owner-investor suggests that criteria need to be established to judge whether the objectives will be attained. Minimum requirements should be established for tax shelter, cash flow, return on equity, or return on total investment. Sometimes, however, an objective may be less definable and the criteria less specific. One firm was willing to spend up to $1 million for a relatively small office building if the building would enhance the firm's image. It is difficult enough to define image, let alone to measure its enhancement. Nevertheless, criteria were established calling for an "air of quality" about the building, its access to view by many passing motorists, aesthetically enriching landscaping, hidden parking, and proximity to a body or stream of water. In this instance cash flow, tax shelter, and return on investment were relatively unimportant.

Sometimes it may be desirable to develop a mathematical model to measure the returns produced by alternative uses or by differing intensities of development. Singer has developed such a model for identifying that intensity which provides the maximum rate of return on overall investment.[31] The model is built around the relationships between profit, value, and costs; rentable building area, gross building area, and building efficiency; and development costs, developer's profit, and investment profit.

In any type of feasibility study, analysts should understand that

---

[30] James F. Gibbons, "Apartment Feasibility Studies," *Appraisal Journal*, July 1968, p. 326. Gibbons further develops the point that a carefully prepared appraisal constitutes a feasibility study—a viewpoint that would be contested by some others.

[31] Bruce Singer, "Determining Optimum Developmental Intensity," *Appraisal Journal*, July 1970, pp. 406–17.

their clients have a problem which they need help in solving. A feasibility analysis that does not identify the client's objectives or establish meaningful decision criteria will produce meaningless results. A study that has not analyzed in depth the relevant variables for measuring the criteria may produce erroneous results. And a study that is undertaken with a prior positive conclusion helps either the client nor the analyst's reputation for objectivity. Unfortunately, many feasibility studies that the authors have seen could be accused of one or all of these defects.

If the situation warrants, one of the most valuable types of advice an analyst can give a client is *not* to undertake a project—or at least how to modify a project to render it feasible. Any positive bias should be toward helping the client, not toward a proposed project. In turn, the client should grant analysts complete freedom of objectivity. Without this freedom, the investor will probably be misled and analysts will find that their professional integrity has been undermined.

SUMMARY

The analysis of real estate markets is facilitated by a concept or model of the way in which these markets function. An examination of the models of pure competition and pure monopoly shows that neither is applicable to real estate markets. Rather, the model of monopolistic competition, we contend, best explains how the forces of price determination operate.

Market activity can be analyzed and forecast through the determinants of demand and supply. Market analyses can be carried out that are national, regional, community, or district in scope. Markets can also be divided into submarkets on the basis of various characteristics, such as price class of property, income class of buyers, ethnic and racial composition, legal tenure of occupants (owners versus renters), and geographic location. Although a direct relationship between national economic and social trends and the value of an individual parcel of real estate is often difficult to demonstrate, careful evaluation of these factors can often provide clues about broad patterns of demand that may be developing.

Market and feasibility studies are the most common types of useful economic studies requiring market analysis. While market studies attempt to analyze and predict the future demand for various types of real estate and to relate the demand to existing supply, feasibility studies attempt to determine whether a particular use will fulfill the objectives of a potential investor. Additionally, a project must meet externally and internally imposed physical, legal, political, ethical, and financial conditions or requirements. One of the requirements normally is that a project be absorbable by the market.

QUESTIONS FOR REVIEW

1. What is a *market*? How many potential buyers and sellers must there be before a market can exist?
2. What is the role of social class in real estate markets? Can you think of some examples of the way social class affects housing patterns?
3. Are real estate markets efficient? Why or why not? How do you measure and judge efficiency?
4. Consider the population mobility trends cited in the chapter. What implications for real estate values do these trends have? What changes in the mobility trends do you anticipate in the coming ten years?
5. How has the change from a rural to an urban society affected real estate markets and values? What do you see as the future trend of urbanization?
6. What is the relationship between a market analysis and a feasibility study? What is the viewpoint of each?
7. What is the "benefits" view of filtering? Describe the filtering process in a housing market comprising interrelated submarkets.
8. Has filtering improved the housing condition of families in the United States? Why or why not?
9. What is meant by a hierarchy of central places? What factors determine this hierarchy?
10. What criticisms are associated with the economic base model? the central place theory?
11. What type of problems would you expect to encounter in utilizing input-output analysis? How is input-output analysis useful as a market analysis tool?
12. Do you agree with the argument that economic base theory and central place theory are equivalent? Why or why not?

PROBLEMS

1. Assume city X has a current population of 250,000. Total employment is 175,000, and basic employment is 100,000. If 1,500 new jobs in basic activities are expected to be created over the next four years, then what would be the expected total population of city X at the end of this period?
2. Find the location quotients and coefficients for each of the following industries, and interpret the results.

	Employment	
	City Z	Nation (millions)
Manufacturing	20,000	20
Government	12,000	10
Retail sales	18,000	30
Construction	30,000	40
	80,000	100

REFERENCES

Dobriner, William M.   *Class in Suburbia*. Englewood Cliffs, N.J.: Prentice-Hall, 1963.

Federal Housing Administration, U.S. Department of Housing and Urban Development.   *FHA Techniques of Housing Market Analysis*. Washington, D.C.: U.S. Government Printing Office, 1970.

Goulet, Peter G.   *Real Estate A Value Approach*. Encino, Calif.: Glencoe Publishing, 1979, chap. 10.

Graaskamp, James A.   *A Guide to Feasibility Analysis*. Chicago: Society of Real Estate Appraisers, 1970.

Heilbrun, James.   *Urban Economics and Public Policy*. New York: St. Martin's Press, 1974.

Isard, Walter.   *Methods of Regional Analysis: An Introduction to Regional Science*. Cambridge, Mass.: MIT Press, 1960.

Leven, C.; Little, J.; Nourse, H.; and Read, R.   *Neighborhood Change*. New York: Praeger, 1976.

McCarthy, E. Jerome.   *Basic Marketing*. 4th ed. Homewood, Ill.: Richard D. Irwin, 1971, pp. 89–164.

Stegman, Michael.   *Housing Investments in the Inner City*. Cambridge, Mass.: MIT Press, 1972.

Weimer, Arthur M.; Hoyt, Homer; and Bloom, George F.   *Real Estate*. 7th ed. New York: John Wiley and Sons, 1978, chap. 6.

chapter 10

Property ownership rights

In most instances, real estate investors are in the fortunate position of being able to choose consciously the precise legal form of ownership they are to employ. Investors have the prerogative to make decisions about leasing or owning outright and can elect to own individually or jointly with others. Investors are able to specify the fixtures which are to be acquired with land and are in a position to adjudge the impact that various easements, private deed restrictions, and zoning ordinances will have on the use of the land. Ownership can involve establishing a corporation or entering a partnership, syndicate, or investment trust which owns property. Such forms offer tax benefits and limited liability which could be critical to the fulfillment of the investor's objectives, although the magnitude and quality of property ownership rights are not affected by the interjection of the separate holding entity.

For the investor to make sound decisions concerning ownership, an awareness of the types of situations which might arise is necessary when potential investment properties are considered. The investor cannot acquire a greater ownership right than that of the existing owner, so complete information about those rights must be obtained before the venture is undertaken. This requires a familiarity with the types of ownership rights which exist and with the means available for transferring them.

Several ownership rights, such as fee tail and qualified fee estates, rarely appear and are generally in disfavor with courts of law and with investors in general. However, the individual investor must analyze the minimum ownership rights required to make use of a given property before condemning a particular right. A determinable fee estate or a lease from period to period may be adequate. In any event, the investor should be cognizant of all possible types of rights when deciding whether or not to enter a specific transaction.

The investor's option to join with others in an investment situation also requires careful attention to ownership form. Ownership with others can be effected in a manner that permits the various owners to freely deed or will their individual rights to others, or ownership can be established with a right of survivorship under which the surviving owners acquire the share of any owner who dies. The first form, *tenancy in common,* is by far the more frequently used. It grants investors more freedom of action, and it permits them to use the property ownership to provide for their heirs in the event of their death. The second form, *joint tenancy,* leads to continuity of the ownership venture by preventing the heirs of a deceased owner from interfering with the plans of the surviving owners. Here again, the specific plans of the individual investors dictate the ownership form to be used.

The development of a proper group ownership form is one of the most important decisions that must be made in any real estate investment. The corporation and the trust permit the loss liability of investors to be limited to their cash or property investment in the project. The partnership, tenancy in common, and joint tenancy forms fail to limit liability, but they permit individual investors to obtain personal income tax deductions. The limited partnership form allows liability limitation for one category of partners while retaining the full tax deduction status for all partners. The strategy implications of selecting a group ownership form are considered in this chapter.

A different type of multiple-ownership situation arises through special legislation providing for married couples. Some states recognize a special form known as *tenancy by the entireties* wherein the right of survivorship exists between the married partners. Upon the death of one partner, title to all properties held in tenancy by the entireties automatically passes to the other, a situation which is true even if one of the partners sells his or her share to a third party (without the signature of the other partner). State laws vary considerably in this area; tenancy by the entireties and other ownership forms such as community property and condominium require state enabling laws. For investors this means two things: (1) they must be familiar with the possible forms of ownership in each state where they consider investments; and (2) they must decide which forms they prefer when an option is available.

REAL ESTATE VERSUS REAL PROPERTY

An awareness of the distinction between the terms *real estate* and *real property* is essential to an understanding of property ownership rights. As mentioned in Chapter 1, *real estate can usually be defined as land and anything permanently attached to land.* A parcel of real estate is tangible; it is described in terms of size, shape, and location, and it extends from a point at the center of the earth outward to the outermost layer of the earth's atmosphere. Minerals, oil, and water contained in the land and air rights above the land are included. Anyone standing upon the parcel or on an adjoining parcel can physically view it. *Real property, on the other hand, is an embodiment of intangible ownership rights.* These ownership rights are available to individuals in a free enterprise economy such as that of the United States, and they are retained by sovereign government in directed economies such as that of the USSR. They are described in terms of extent of ownership, considering factors of possession, control, enjoyment, and disposition.

Given a society in which private property prevails, ownership rights can range from virtually absolute to highly limited. An individual is entitled to own a parcel of real estate "outright," with complete rights to possession, control, enjoyment, or disposition in whole or in part. The government which permits private ownership imposes only one restriction—to refrain from creating conditions which could be harmful to public health and/or welfare. Limited ownership usually occurs by contract, where one individual acquires part of the ownership rights of the outright owner. Examples are leasing agreements, public utility easements, and mineral rights purchases.

REAL ESTATE DESCRIPTIONS

Legal documents involved in real estate transactions should describe the property as precisely as possible. Such documents include sale contracts, deeds, mortgages, and long-term leases. Precise descriptions of real estate are also necessary in subdividing, building, and financing activities. Generally, there are five ways of describing real estate—one method of general, everyday usage and four that are more precise.

Street and number

A description by street and number is sufficiently precise for most nonlegal purposes, such as providing general locations and postal delivery. It is also legally acceptable in contracts for the sale of real estate and other legal documents, provided the street and number can be found. However, for taxation, conveyancing, and other purposes which require that the real estate be described precisely, one of the "legal" methods should be used. If one of these methods is used properly, no misunderstanding about the size of the parcel or the location of its boundaries should occur. Disagreements and lawsuits will be avoided.

Metes and bounds

A metes and bounds description utilizes instructions as to direction and distance (metes) between the boundaries, or corners (bounds), of a parcel of land. The description begins at a point on the site's boundary and proceeds around the outer limits of the property until the point of beginning is reached and the entire parcel has been circumscribed. An example of a metes and bounds description is as follows:

> Beginning at a point in the east line of Goddard Avenue 50 feet north of the north line of 22d Street 200 feet to the center of Hogtown Creek; thence northwesterly along the center line of Hogtown Creek 175 feet; thence west on a line parallel to the north line of 22d Street, 182 feet to the east line of Goddard Avenue; thence south along the east line of Goddard Avenue, 180.5 feet to the place of beginning.

Metes and bounds descriptions are used in those parts of the country where the government has not surveyed the land. Figure 10–1 shows the extent of the government survey system. It can be seen that New England, the Middle Atlantic states, and Texas are the principal areas not surveyed and thus are the areas in which one is most likely to find metes and bounds descriptions. Nevertheless, such descriptions can be used in any part of the country and are often used in combination with the rectangular survey system when a tract has not been platted.

Monuments

Description by monuments is similar to metes and bounds; however, the measurements along the boundaries are not given. The corners of the property are indicated by permanent monuments, such as trees, rocks, streams, or street intersections, concrete markers, or steel stakes. One corner of the property is described by its monument, and the directions are then prescribed to the succeeding circumferential monuments, until the point of beginning is reached.

A difficulty in describing real estate by monuments is that the monuments may not be so permanent as was originally believed. Trees can die, rocks can be moved, stream and street intersections can change, and man-made monuments can deteriorate or be lost. Thus, the use of this method is not recommended.

FIGURE 10–1
Principal meridians of the federal system of rectangular surveys

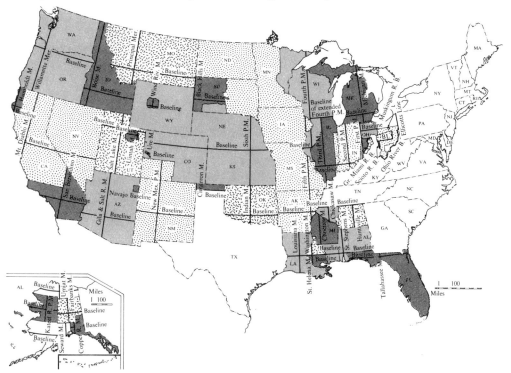

Note: The shading shows the area governed by each principal meridian and its base line.
Source: U.S. Department of the Interior, Bureau of Land Management.

Government or rectangular survey

As shown in Figure 10–1, much of the country has been surveyed by the federal government. The survey consists of a system of grid lines running north and south, and east and west, on a map of the earth's surface. The origin for an area of description is the intersection of a principal meridian (running north and south) and a base line (running east and west). Secondary meridians and parallels are established at 24-mile intervals. The area contained within such a 24-mile square is termed a *check*, and each check is subdivided into 16 six-mile squares called *townships.*

A township is the largest subdivision identified in land descriptions. It is identified by the number of tiers (rows) of townships north or south of the base line and the number of ranges (columns) of townships east or west of the principal meridian. Thus, in Figure 10–2, the subdivided townships would be described as Township 2 North,

FIGURE 10–2

Rectangular survey system

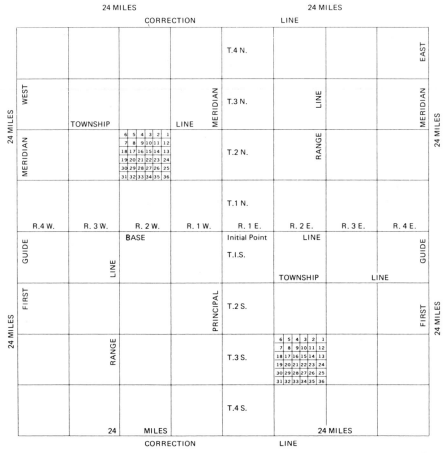

Source: William Atterberry, Karl Pearson, and Michael Litka, *Real Estate Law* (Columbus, Ohio: Grid 1974), p. 62.

Range 2 West and Township 3 South, Range 2 East of the specified principal meridian and base line.

Since a township consists of a six-mile-square area, it obviously contains 36 square miles. This area is further divided into 36 one-mile-square units, called *sections*. The sections are numbered beginning with the northeastern corner, as shown in Figure 10–2. A section contains 640 acres and is identified by its number within the specified township.

A section can be further subdivided into halves, quarters, subhalves, and subquarters. Each quarter of a section contains 160 acres, each half of a quarter section contains 80 acres, and each quarter of a quarter section contains 40 acres. Additional subdivisions can be made, if necessary. The description of the crosshatched area in Figure 10–3 would be the NW ¼ of the SE ¼ of the SW ¼ of Section 17 of Township 2 North, Range 2 West.

FIGURE 10–3
A divided section

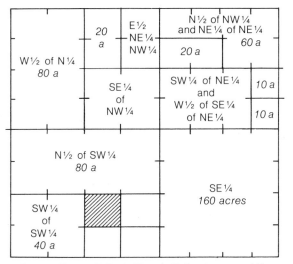

Source: Richard F. Fleck, Thomas P. Henderson, and Ross H. Johnson, *Real Estate Principles and Practices* (Columbus, Ohio: Charles E. Merrill, 1976), p. 24.

Recorded plat

Usually when areas of 40 acres or less are developed or subdivided (and often when this is done with larger areas), a map, or *plat*, must be filed with the county clerk or recorder. Each street or block must be named or numbered, and each lot assigned a number. Sometimes only a subdivision name and lot numbers are required. Upon acceptance and recording of the plat by the appropriate county official, the lot and block numbers of the named subdivision constitute an exact legal description. The exact size, dimensions, and boundary locations may be obtained by referring to the recorded plat. For example, a lot in a plat recorded under the name "STR Acres" might be identified as

> Lot No. 7, Block 16 of STR Acres,
> as recorded on page 31 of Book 27
> in the Tippecanoe County Recorder's Office.

Of course, the recorded plat would often be contained in an area originally surveyed by the government. The recorded plat would therefore refer to the section and township identified by government survey.

PERSONAL PROPERTY AND FIXTURES

Our definition of real estate in terms of land and its permanent attachments is very vague insofar as the word *permanent* is involved. Items not permanently attached to land are considered to be personal property, personalty, or movables. They are not real estate, and they can be removed from the real estate at any time by the holder of the personal property rights.

A *fixture* is an item that was once personal property but later attached to real estate in a permanent manner. Fixtures go to the buyer in a sale of real property, and they cannot be removed from the real estate without the permission of the real estate owner. The law of fixtures is one of the most complex areas in the study of real estate law, with every case having unique considerations. In general, the courts apply four tests to determine whether or not an article is permanently attached to real estate.[1]

Intention of the parties. The most important test is whether or not the article was intended to be permanently attached at the time of attachment. This is a commonsense approach which attempts to determine whether or not a reasonable person would consider an item to be a fixture.

Manner of attachment. In general, an item is permanently attached if its removal damages the real estate.

Character of the article and its adaptation to the real estate. Articles built especially for a particular building are normally considered fixtures.

Relation of the parties. Courts tend to favor certain parties in disputes, primarily on the ground that their adversaries should know better than to permit fixture disputes to arise. For example, buyers tend to be favored over sellers where sale agreements are indefinite, and tenants are normally favored over landlords in gaining permission to remove personal property they may have inadvertently attached to the landlord's property.

Residential property transactions create many problems of defining personal property and fixtures. Buyers sometimes assume that they are buying houses completely equipped with storm windows, carpets,

---

[1] Robert Kratovil and Raymond J. Werner, *Real Estate Law*, 7th ed. (Englewood Cliffs, N.J.: Prentice-Hall, 1979), chap. 3.

elaborate light fixtures, special plumbing attachments, and so on, which the sellers do not wish to sell. A deal is closed, and the buyers learn to their dismay that the items which were so instrumental in their decision to buy are gone when they prepare to take possession. Thus, investors must question all fixtures and personal property items to determine whether or not they are part of the sale agreement. When they are in doubt as to the permanence of any item, they should state in the offer to buy that they plan to acquire it. Sellers then have an opportunity to reject the offer, but no confusion or misunderstanding is likely to arise. The two parties agree as to the items included in the price, and the sale is either consummated or canceled.

REAL PROPERTY OWNERSHIP RIGHTS

The interest that an individual holds in real estate is referred to as an estate. Estates are of two types: estates in possession and estates not in possession. Estates in possession are by far the more common, being divided into freehold estates and estates of less than freehold. Freeholds represent substantial ownership rights and are treated as real property by the law; estates of less than freehold, that is, leaseholds, are considered personal property. Estates not in possession represent future interests in property which convert to estates in possession upon the occurrence of a specified event. The relationship between types of estates is presented in Figure 10–4.

Freehold estates of inheritance

The most complete forms of ownership are those which can be enjoyed by the owners during their lifetimes and then passed on to designated heirs or lineal descendants. Fee simple absolute and fee tail estates endure throughout the lifetimes of the owners. The owners can change the form of the estate by grant or by will, such as the establishment of a life estate for their daughter with the property to go to specified heirs upon her death, but the estate remains fee simple or fee tail in the absence of such actions. Qualified fee estates endure either indefinitely or until a specified event occurs—this event not normally being the death of the estate holder.

Fee simple estates.   The fee simple owner is entitled to freedom of action with regard to the property as long as the actions are lawful and do not conflict with public interest. It may be improved in any manner, leased to anyone, given away, sold; trees may be removed or planted; and soil and minerals may be removed or added. Fee simple ownership can be restricted by law through zoning, where only specified uses of the land are permitted, or by voluntary deed restric-

FIGURE 10–4
Estates in land

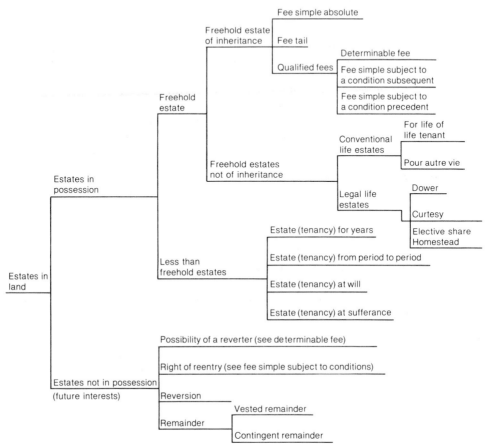

tions which specify permitted uses. Nuisances cannot be maintained, such as a deep hole which could endanger children; the public welfare is harmed by jeopardizing the health and safety of others.

Fee tail estates.   The concept of fee tail is a carry-over from feudal times, when the ownership of property was granted to individuals and their heirs. Early common law held that the property reverted back to the original grantor when the blood line of the grantee terminated, but modern (U.S.) statutory law either refuses to recognize a fee tail or limits it to lives in being at the time of the original grant. Fee tail estates are rarely encountered today, but investors must be aware of what they are and be certain that they can derive a fee simple ownership from the seller's fee tail.

Qualified fee estates. A qualified, determinable, or base fee estate is one which terminates upon the occurrence of a specified event. Words such as "as long as" or "during" are used in its creation. An example of a determinable fee estate is an individual's grant of property to a peace-promoting charity for as long as the United States remains a member of the United Nations. If the United States later withdraws from the United Nations, ownership reverts to the grantor or grantor's heirs. The grantor's right in the property between the time of grant and the time of U.S. withdrawal is called a *possibility of a reverter* rather than a *reversion,* since the United States might never withdraw from the United Nations. If an event had been stated which is reasonably certain to occur, such as granting the property until January 1, 2000, the grantor would possess an outright reversion. The charity's right to the property prior to U.S. withdrawal is a fee simple right, since ownership could continue forever. The charity can sell the property, but the buyer obtains only the determinable fee subject to the possibility of a reverter.

Two other forms of qualified fee estates, fee simple subject to a condition subsequent and fee simple subject to a condition precedent, work the same way as a determinable fee, except that a condition must be fulfilled by the grantee. In the U.S.–UN situation, ownership reverts to the grantor following an action taken by the U.S. government. The grantee has no control over this action, and the reversion occurs automatically at the time of U.S. withdrawal. The fee simple subject to a condition subsequent requires action (or lack of action) on the part of the grantee, such as a situation in which grantors grant their property to a school as long as it is used for school purposes. If the school sells the property or converts it to a nonschool use, the grant becomes void and the grantors or their heirs have the right to reenter the property and assume absolute ownership. However, in recent years courts have held that sale of land owned under qualified fee is permitted if the proceeds are put to a use which fulfills the conditions of the agreement with the grantors. This would occur if the school sold the land held under qualified fee and used the proceeds to buy a parcel of land better suited for school business.

The fee simple subject to a condition precedent is identical to the fee simple subject to a condition subsequent except for the timing of the condition. A condition must be met by a grantee prior to the title conveyance. To use the above example, a condition precedent would arise if the property owners were to grant their property to the school as of the date the school instituted a new program—for example, the teaching of real estate courses. As long as the school continued to teach real estate, it would retain ownership of the property. If it did not begin teaching real estate, title would not be conveyed; if it discontinued the real estate courses, ownership of the property would revert to the grantors. The condition precedent fits few practical situations. Most states have abolished estates on condition precedent.

The qualified fee estate has been in disfavor with courts for many years. It provides a vehicle for unusual situations which inevitably require court action before the rightful owner of a property can gain possession. An individual might grant property to a distant nephew so long as the nephew refrains from drinking alcoholic beverages, while another individual might devise a grant in which the grantee must follow a specified religious faith. The extent to which conditions of this type are upheld is impossible to measure, and the courts tend to interpret the law in such a manner that the fee simple character of the grantee's right outweighs the conditions imposed. An investor must be very careful whenever a deed contains peculiarities of this type. An attorney should be consulted to ascertain whether or not fee simple absolute could be achieved in the purchase.

Freehold estates not of inheritance

A life estate is an interest in real property granted to an individual for the duration of his, her, or someone else's lifetime. At the time of death of the designated person, the property reverts to the original owner or heirs.

Life estates are of two types: conventional and legal.[2] Conventional life estates are created by the grantor and grantee involved in the estate. In most cases life tenants receive the property right for the duration of their own lifetime. If they retain their right for the lifetime of another person, such as would be the case where a man grants his son the rights to a property for the lifetime of his (the grantor's) wife, the estate is known as a life estate *pour autre vie*.

A life estate can be sold or leased, but the buyers or lessees must realize that they might have to surrender the property on short notice after the death of the life estate holder. Thus, the economic value of a life estate is normally based on personal utilization or a composite of short-term leases.

Legal life estates are created by operation of law. They are of three types: dower and curtesy, elective share, and homestead.

Dower and curtesy.   Dower refers to the ownership rights of a wife in her husband's property during her lifetime. As long as the husband is alive, dower is said to be "inchoate," which means that the wife has only the possibility of a right rather than the right itself. Upon the

---

[2] William B. French and Harold F. Lusk, *Law of the Real Estate Business*, 4th ed. (Homewood, Ill.: Richard D. Irwin, 1979), p. 63.

husband's death, the dower right becomes "consummate." Under the laws of many states, the dower ripens into a life estate in one third of the real property owned by the husband during the marriage. All real property owned by the husband during the marriage is included, even though part or all might have been sold prior to his death.

Dower right, in those states which recognize it, is an important consideration for purchasers of real property. To obtain an unencumbered title, they must be certain that the seller's wife relinquishes her dower right to the subject property in writing. Otherwise, she is entitled to a life estate upon her husband's death, although the property is not a part of his estate.

As in any life estate, property acquired by a wife through her dower right is hers to use in any manner she pleases during her lifetime. Upon her death, the property passes on to a party named by the husband in his will, or to his natural heirs of succession, if he dies intestate (without a will). The party named by the husband or his heirs holds the *rights of remainder*. This right is normally vested (that is, absolute and definite; cannot be taken from them), but it is contingent in situations where a remainderman cannot be ascertained at the time of transfer. Some people still retain the practice in wills of naming "my oldest son" or "my firstborn child" where no such son or child has been born at the time the life estate is created. A remainder exists in either the vested or contingent situation, however, and the property eventually passes on to the remainderman. Even in those rare cases when a person dies with no heirs or assigns, the government is a contingent remainderman through the power of escheat.

Dower provides the wife a claim to real property superior to claims of the husband's debtors. Dower is terminated by divorce in nearly all states; however, a few states terminate dower only where the wife is at fault in the divorce proceedings.

Curtesy is a man's right in real property owned by his wife during their marriage. Very few states recognize curtesy today, and where it exists it is usually treated the same as dower. The laws of some states grant the husband dower rather than curtesy. Other states grant curtesy only where the wife is survived by a child of the marriage to the surviving husband. Regardless of the requirements imposed on curtesy, to be certain of obtaining an unencumbered title a buyer of real property should obtain a release of curtesy in the same manner as a release of dower is obtained.

Elective share.   Some states have replaced dower and curtesy with "elective share" provisions for surviving spouses. For example, the Florida probate code was amended effective January 1, 1976, to abolish dower and curtesy rights and to provide for an elective share for the surviving spouses. An elective share is defined as 30 percent of the decedent's personal property and Florida real estate, except homestead property and claims. A surviving spouse also has a statutory family allowance and rights in homestead property, regardless of whether he or she chooses an elective share.

In order for a surviving spouse to be eligible for an elective share, the deceased spouse must have owned property in Florida at the time of death and have been a resident of Florida at the time of death. The surviving spouse must file a formal election of share within four months of the first notice of administration.

In addition to an elective share, or any other benefits obtained upon the death of a spouse, the surviving spouse is entitled to "exempt property." Such property consists of households furniture, furnishings, and appliances in the decedent's residence, and automobiles up to a net value of $5,000. The surviving spouse is also entitled to the decedent's personal effects up to a net value of $1,000 unless they were legally bequeathed to someone else by a will.

A surviving spouse is not required to take the elective share. The provisions of the decedent's will may be more favorable. Or, if the decedent has died intestate, the intestate share may be more favorable than the elective share.

Homestead.   The laws of a few states permit a family to declare either a specified amount of land or a specified dollar value of property as a homestead.[3] A properly declared and recorded homestead is exempt from foreclosure by creditors to the extent of the legal maximum amount of area or dollar value. The family cannot be evicted from the land during the husband's lifetime, and his widow is protected after his death. The state laws which provide for homestead generally require that a family exist, that the homestead be used as the family's residence, and that the head of the family possess an ownership interest in the property.[4] Most of the states with homestead laws also require that the family file for homestead and have it recorded in the county records.

The right of homestead is actually a protection of other ownership rights rather than an independent estate in land. Homesteads are owned either in fee simple or fee tail, with the homestead right granting protection of ownership. The homesteader's widow receives substantial protection through this right; the husband cannot convey clear title during his lifetime without the wife's permission, and the wife's right to the homestead is prior to the claims of the husband's creditors upon his death.

---

[3] No choice is involved; each state determines how the homestead is to be established.

[4] French and Lusk, *Law of the Real Estate Business*, p. 73.

Less than freehold estates

Earlier in this chapter, we noted that an individual does not have to be the absolute owner of a parcel of real estate in order to derive valuable benefits. Many business firms have found that they can create extra profits by selling their business realty and obtaining long-term leases. Physical use of the property is not disturbed by this financing arrangement, but fee simple ownership is transferred into the hands of an absentee landlord. The former owners no longer have capital tied up in realty, and they can deduct all rents for tax purposes. The new owners acquire an investment which should yield a satisfactory return.

A leasehold can be defined very simply as the right to use the property of another. Complete utilization with no restrictions is rarely granted; the most common situation is one in which the use to which the land can be put by the lessee and the manner in which the use is carried out are regulated by a contract between the lessor and the lessee. Leases generally can be calssified by duration of lease. Four types of estates can be created by varying the length of time for which the property is leased:

Estate for years—beginning and ending point of lease specified. Leases of this type are usually measured in periods extending over several years, but they can be for any specified period—even less than a year. The key distinguishing factor is that the exact duration of the lease must be specified.

Tenancy from year to year. As with the estate for years, the period of measurement can be something other than a year. A tenancy from year to year (actually period to period) is automatically renewed every period until one of the parties gives sufficient notice of termination.

Tenancy at will. In most states, a tenancy at will exists without a definite agreement among the parties. It can be terminated at any time (without notice) by either party. A tenancy at will frequently arises where the tenant holds over without objection by the landlord after the expiration of the lease.

Tenancy at sufferance. This final form of tenancy arises when a tenant continues to use property after the agreement with the landlord has completely expired. It is a wrongful tenancy, and it cannot exist if the owner exercises the right of reposession. Tenancy at sufferance also arises where a person moves onto a property owned by someone else without the owner's knowledge or consent.

The differences in the four types of leasehold described here are significant to both lessors and lessees. Lessees must beware of the last two forms if a fairly permanent lease is contemplated. Where termination without notice is possible, unscrupulous landlords can let a tenant build up a successful business and then cancel the lease in order to take over the business. Lessees of homes can find themselves evicted if they fail to comply with unreasonable rent demands. From the lessor's standpoint, some degree of certainty of income is required for sound planning. The "midnight movers" who leave under the cover of darkness on the day the rent is due create significant management problems for the landlord. For either party, a temporary arrangement may be desired for a test period. However, the benefits of a lease of known duration outweigh the disadvantages, and a test arrangement should be replaced in a reasonable time if trouble is to be avoided.

Incorporeal property rights

The owners of an estate in land can, if they wish, grant the privilege of using their land to others without surrendering any of their property ownership rights. Such privileges do limit freedom of use, however, and they normally must be included in the definition of ownership. They are of three types: (*a*) easement, (*b*) license, and (*c*) profit.

Easements.   An easement is a nonpossessory interest one person holds in the real estate of another. It is not considered to be an estate in land, although it cannot be revoked by the landowner. The most common form of easement is the *commercial easement in gross,* such as a right-of-way for a pipeline, electric line, telephone line, or railroad. An easement in gross also exists as an individual's personal right. The commercial form can be assigned, conveyed, or inherited, but the individual form is granted to a single individual for his or her lifetime only. Few courts recognize the individual, noncommercial easement in gross today, since the easement appurtenant and the license are defined broadly enough to include nearly every situation which may arise.

The easement appurtenant is a grant made by the owners of one parcel of property, the *servient tenement,* to permit their land to be used in some manner by the owners of an adjoining parcel, the *dominant tenement.* The most common easement appurtenant is a right-of-way granted to a neighbor for ingress and egress. Once granted, the benefits attach to the dominant tenement and the obligation to permit use attaches to the servient tenement. Both dominant and servient tenements exist in an easement appurtenant, while only the servient land is involved in an easement in gross.

Most easements are formed through express grants in writing, although they can arise by will, by implication, or by prescription. Easements established by grant are normally part of a conveyance by deed, although they can be created by written contract. Implied easements arise where landowners sell a portion of their parcel which is completely surrounded by other land that they own. The buyers can safely imply that they are entitled to establish a right-of-way across the sellers' land, although the sellers are entitled to select a reasonable location for the right-of-way. An easement by prescription arises where a person's land is used by another on an adverse, visible, open, notorious, and continuous basis under claim of right by the user for an uninterrupted period of time as prescribed by law. The owner of the property in question can stop the running of the prescribed period by interrupting use of the easement for a short time, thereby making the prescribed easement exceptionally difficult to obtain. Permission may also be granted for the use at one point in time, thereby eliminating the essential requirement of adverse use. Easements by prescription arise almost exclusively in the case of vehicular rights-of-way, although courts tend to include nonadverse party driveways under this procedure.

License.   A license is a privilege granted to a single individual permitting him or her to go upon the servient land. Permission to hunt or fish is one example; another is the sale of admission tickets for theatrical or sporting performances. Licenses can be made orally, and they are revocable by the owner of the servient land.

Profit.   A profit, or *profit a prendre*, is the right to remove soil or minerals from the servient tenement. Profits are personal rights which can be assigned, conveyed, or inherited, although they can be established in favor of a single dominant tenement.

OWNERSHIP BY MORE THAN ONE PERSON

Many parcels of real estate are owned by more than one individual. The total parcel is usually owned in fee simple, so the problems of multiple owners arise in determining how to divide interests among the various owners. The following types of multiple ownership are prevalent in the United States.

Tenancy in common.   Ownership in the form of tenancy in common works like a common stock corporation. A single parcel of real property, undivided in the sense that each owner exercises the rights of ownership of the entire parcel rather than a staked-off portion, is operated by the owners exactly as though it were a business firm. The individual owners have a say in making decisions about the parcel and can sell their interest, give it away, or grant it to their heirs as they wish.

Joint tenancy.   A tenancy in common is created automatically whenever two or more people acquire concurrent ownership of a parcel of real estate. Joint tenancy, on the other hand, requires a formal written instrument evidencing the desire to create an ownership situation different from that of tenancy in common. In a joint tenancy, all owners have equal ownership rights. The ownership rights of individual owners pass upon their deaths to the other owners—again being split equally among them.

A joint tenancy between two or more persons is enforced by the courts only where four "unities" exist. These unities, or common bonds, are:

1. *Unity of interest.* The ownership rights of each of the parties must be equal and endure for the same length of time.
2. *Unity of time.* The interests of each of the parties must be acquired at the same time.
3. *Unity of title.* All joint tenants must receive their interest through a single conveyance of title.
4. *Unity of possession.* All joint tenants must have equal rights of possession, although these rights do not have to be exercised by any of the parties.

The unique characteristic of joint tenancy is that it can exist for either the entire parcel or part of the parcel. For example, a group of five men pool their money to buy an investment property. Each man supplies 20 percent of the money for an undivided 20 percent ownership right. A tenancy in common is formed among the five men. Three of the men wish to form a joint tenancy as to their 60 percent combined interest, so they prepare a binding legal agreement to that effect. They have their wives sign the agreement in order to avoid any claim of dower right, and they make use of the property with their two partners by tenancy in common. If one of the three men dies, his two joint tenant partners each receives 10 percent additional ownership— the property now being owned 30 percent by each of the two joint tenants and 20 percent by each of the two tenants in common.

If one of the three joint tenants does not die, but grants his 20 percent interest to an outside party, the joint tenancy is upset as far as his share is concerned. His 20 percent falls back into the tenancy in common status. However, the other two joint tenants can continue the joint tenancy on the 40 percent.

Joint tenancies have created many problems over the years and are currently in disfavor with the courts. An ironclad agreement must exist for the joint tenancy to be recognized over the rights of the surviving spouse of a joint tenant.

Tenancy by the entireties. Tenancy by the entireties is a special form of joint tenancy in some states which can be employed only by husband and wife. Any real property acquired by them during their marriage can be established as a tenancy by the entireties, thereby guaranteeing each partner a right of survivorship to the other's share. The right of survivorship continues even when one of the partners conveys his or her share to a third party. Like joint tenancies, tenancy by the entireties is held in disfavor by many states, and they require a binding written agreement for the tenancy to be enforced.

Community property. The concept of community property is of Spanish origin, and it is prevalent in several Western states. It holds that husband and wife each own 50 percent of all real property purchased after their marriage. The only property excluded is that which is purchased with funds which are clearly owned by only one of the married partners. Both owners must sign transfer papers on community property.

Condominium. Many state laws have been passed in recent years to permit the development of condominium apartment units. Each owner holds a fee simple interest in an apartment and a tenancy in common in halls, elevators, lawns, and so on. The separate ownership forms have been discussed previously, but the condominium combination is unique.[5]

Corporation, trust, and partnership. A parcel of real estate can be owned by a single legal entity that is in itself an aggregation of individual owners. The legal framework that unites the owners also defines the manner in which ownership interests are divided. The use of corporations, trusts, and partnerships is considered here in terms of property ownership strategy.

PROPERTY OWNERSHIP STRATEGY

The goals of investors and the risks associated with individual properties determine the proper form of ownership structure in each investment situation. In general, high-risk projects are more properly structured as corporations or trusts. These two forms are also excellent choices for situations in which large numbers of investors are called upon to provide equity capital.

Partnership and tenancy in common structures are well suited for tax shelter investments and other investments that involve small numbers of investors. The limited partnership is particularly popular as a vehicle for syndicators to use in assembling equity money from small numbers of investors who seek limited liability and freedom from management decisions.

The major consideration in selecting an ownership form is the objectives of investor groups. Small-scale investors frequently fear the partnership form in which the ownership shares have no active market and cannot be sold easily. Larger investors at times find the corporation and trust forms useful for projects that are to be subdivided and

---

[5] Condominiums are discussed further in Chapter 16.

sold at ordinary income rates or for projects that are to be operated to yield tax-sheltered cash income. The same investors might prefer the partnership form for projects yielding tax deductions via depreciation or yielding capital gains through sale.

The variables in the ownership decision are: (*a*) avoidance of double taxation when using a corporation, (*b*) avoidance of personal liability for investors, (*c*) marketability of shares, and (*d*) acquisition of maximum income tax deduction benefits. These variables are reflected in the four basic ownership forms as follows.

Corporation.   The corporate form is designed for easy transfer of small portions of ownership, and it offers total limitation of liability for investors. However, it creates a taxable entity that pays tax in addition to that which must be paid by investors individually. Also, the corporate form fails to permit investors to deduct net taxable losses from their personal income tax returns.

The corporate form is of maximum value to investors who place a much higher priority upon easy transferability of ownership and liability limitation than on income tax minimization. However, careful tax planning can lead to a need for one or more corporations in achieving desired salaries, pension plans, medical plans, deductibility of automobiles and other expenditures, and so on. These issues go beyond basic real estate planning and are not considered in this text.

Tax-free real estate investment trust.   The tax-free real estate investment trust (REIT) became popular in the 1960s and early 1970s as a vehicle for achieving a single tax on income plus the desired liability limitation. However, tax losses cannot be passed through to investors. To retain its tax-free status, the trust must pay 90 percent of its income to investors, and it must follow numerous rules regarding the percentage of investments that must be in real estate and the length of time that investments must be held. Virtually all income must be passive in nature rather than the result of direct project operation by a trust's management. Substantial losses caused REITs to lose popularity during the mid-1970s, but they returned to greater favor more recently.

Partnership.   The partnership form avoids double taxation and allows tax losses to be deducted by individual investors. Liability is unlimited for all investors in the general partnership, but it can be limited in the limited partnership for partners who are not involved in project management. Broadly based markets for partnership shares rarely exist, but shares are easily transferred and purchasers can usually be found for shares in a quality offering.

Most states have securities registration laws that affect partnership interests (as well as trusts and tenancies in common). When out-of-state investors are involved, the Securities and Exchange Commission (SEC) requires registration of partnerships. These laws frequently have exemptions for entities that stay intrastate and maintain small ownership groups. Registration is time consuming and expensive, and the form of ownership and size of share are often kept small to achieve exemption from registration laws.

Tenancy in common.   The tenancy in common shares most of the features of the partnership. Liability is more difficult to limit, but an agreement among tenants in common can be devised in which one owner assumes all of the liability incurred by the owners. If the other owners pay off a partnership debt to an outside party, they can secure reimbursement from the managing (liable) owner.

Summary regarding strategy.   The proper ownership form for a group of individuals or for a combination of individuals, trusts, partnerships, and corporations is a function of investor objectives and project characteristics. Tax implications, transferability of shares, and liability limitations must be considered. Compromise solutions can lead to an optimal ownership structure. These compromises must be minor in nature; investors with widely divergent objectives usually should not invest together. Individuals structuring a real estate ownership arrangement should learn everything possible about the objectives of their investors and carefully place each investor in a project that best meets his or her objectives.

Sophisticated real estate syndicators frequently attempt to construct large files of investors in which investors having a common interest are brought together. This has been an exceptionally effective approach for Realty Research Corporation in Atlanta, Georgia.

Large-scale developers tend to employ a joint-venture arrangement with one or more financial institutions that can be used repeatedly on different projects. Cousins Properties, Inc., of Atlanta, Georgia, has followed this pattern in several major developments with Fidelity Mutual Life Insurance Company. U.S. Steel Realty Company has joint-ventured projects with Connecticut Mutual Life Insurance Company, and John Hancock Life Insurance Company has devised a successful joint-venture format that it has used in conjunction with many developers throughout the nation. The limited partnership tends to be the most popular form for these joint ventures, but any of the other forms could meet investor objectives.

SUMMARY

Real estate is land and everything permanently attached to the land. Four "legal" methods of describing real estate are available for use in any situation or document where the exact boundaries and dimensions of a parcel of land may be required. These are (*a*) metes and bounds. (*b*) monuments, (*c*) government or rectangular survey, and (*d*) recorded plat. The last method, recorded plat, is usually available for residential subdivisions. The first three are normally applied to larger tracts. In most sections of the country that have been surveyed by the government, the government or rectangular survey system is the preferred method for describing land. Metes and bounds or monuments are used predominantly in areas not so surveyed, although they can also be used in surveyed areas. Description by street address is satisfactory for everyday usage—situations in which disputes are not likely to arise.

Real property is a legal concept that refers to the right to own, use, or occupy real estate. Fixtures are items of personal property which have become real property, often because of permanent attachment to the real estate. Property rights can take several forms, called *estates* in real property, such as the fee simple, fee tail, determinable fee, fee subject to condition subsequent or precedent, life estate, estate for years or from period to period, reversion, remainder, dower, and community property. The market value and investment value of real property are dependent upon the legal interest under valuation, which should always be carefully defined by the analyst.

The ownership form selected for a real estate investment situation determines the relationship among investors, between investors and lenders, and between investors and their officers or partners. Many forms of legal protection for all of the parties involved can be created in corporate charters, trust agreements, partnership agreements, or agreements among tenants in common.

When real estate is owned by only one person, fee simple ownership is the most desirable form. It provides the maximum ownership rights. However, some property titles are encumbered with conditional titles, life estates, and other limitations which prevent the investor from gaining the maximum bundle of ownership rights.

At times, an investor might prefer to lease, rather than own outright, a parcel of property. Leases can be established for any period of time and on several renewal bases, and most state laws are quite articulate about what constitutes an enforceable clause or an act of renewing a lease.

Given many alternative ownership forms and structures, investors must plan workable strategies for their projects that optimize their protection from liability, their income tax deduction status, and their protection against lenders, officers, and other investors. The corporate and trust forms offer excellent liability protection, but they limit opportunities for investors to obtain income tax deductions. A tenancy in common form offers excellent deductibility from income tax liability, but unlimited liability for debts of all types. The limited partnership form provides liability limitation, tax deductions, and protections among limited partners, but it requires that the limited partners refrain from making managerial decisions, thereby causing them to lose ownership control. Thus, investors must devise the optimal structure for each project based upon their goals and a project's risks.

QUESTIONS FOR REVIEW

1. What is *real estate?* How does this term differ from *real property?*
2. How does one determine whether an asset is a fixture or an item of realty?
3. Distinguish between estates in possession and estates not in possession.
4. Distinguish between freehold estates of inheritance and freehold estates not of inheritance.
5. What are the three types of incorporeal rights to real property?
6. What are the four unities of a joint tenancy?
7. Indicate the ownership form that appears to be most practical for a joint venture. Defend your choice.
8. Why must legal descriptions, rather than street and number, often be used to describe real estate?
9. What are the four methods of legal description?
10. How many sections are in a township? How many acres are in a section? How many square feet are in an acre?
11. What is the principal difficulty in describing real estate by monuments?
12. When describing a parcel of real estate by rectangular survey, why must the principal meridian and base line be cited?
13. Make a rough sketch of Section 3 of Township 1 North, Range 2 East of the Tallahassee Principal Meridian and Base Line and indicate the S ½ of the NW ¼ of the NE ¼.

REFERENCES

Atterberry, William; Pearson, Karl G.; and Litka, Michael P. *Real Estate Law.* Columbus, Ohio: Grid, 1974.

Creteau, Paul G. *Principles of Real Estate Law.* Portland, Me.: Castle, 1977.

Curtis, Clayton C. *Real Estate for the New Practitioner.* 6th ed. Gainesville, Fla.: B. J. Publishing, 1980, chap. 2.

French, William B., and Lusk, Harold F. *Law of the Real Estate Business.* 4th ed. Homewood, Ill.: Richard D. Irwin, 1979.

Kratovil, Robert, and Werner, Raymond J. *Real Estate Law.* 7th ed. Englewood Cliffs, N.J.: Prentice-Hall, 1979.

Unger, Maurice A., and Karvel, George R. *Real Estate Principles and Practices.* 6th ed. Cincinnati: South-Western, 1979, chap. 3.

chapter 11

Conveying ownership rights

Ownership of real property can be transferred (or conveyed) in several different ways. These methods reflect the status of the owners of real estate who are conveying title (called grantors) or the parties to whom title is being conveyed (called grantees).

METHODS OF CONVEYING TITLE

Public grant

A public grant is the conveyance of title to land by the federal government to a private party. It is accomplished by means of a special type of deed called a *patent*. Since most of the land in the United States was originally owned by the government, the first transactions involving the land were public grants. Many abstracts of title pertaining to small, individual parcels contain a reference to the patent which originally conveyed title to the land (usually part of a much larger tract) from the government to a private party.

Private grant

The usual type of property transfer involves a voluntary conveyance during the grantor's lifetime and is known as a private grant.

Whether the transfer is a sale or a gift, it is accomplished by means of a deed.

A deed is a written instrument that conveys title to real estate. Whether property rights are sold outright, given away, or sold at a public auction to satisfy a lien, every exchange requires a properly prepared and properly recorded deed in order for a legally recognized exchange to occur. There are several types of deeds, including these: (*a*) general warranty deed, (*b*) quitclaim deed, (*c*) deed of bargain and sale, (*d*) special warranty deed, and (*e*) officer's deed.

General warranty deed.   The most desirable type of deed from the buyer's viewpoint is the general warranty deed. In such a deed, the seller normally makes the following three guarantees or convenants:

1. The seller possesses a legally recognizable title to the property conveyed. This is known as the *covenant of seisin.*
2. There are no encumbrances against the title other than those stated therein. This is the *covenant against encumbrances.*
3. The seller will protect the grantee against persons claiming to have superior title to the conveyed property. This is the *covenant for quiet enjoyment.*

The buyer must keep in mind that the seller's guarantees are worthless when the seller is financially irresponsible, but they do provide grounds for legal action when the buyer finds that a good title did not pass, when unknown encumbrances arise, or when claims are made against the property. Aside from this margin of protection, the guarantees in a warranty deed give the buyer a feeling of security in the transaction.

Quitclaim deed.   A quitclaim deed passes the seller's ownership rights to the buyer without guarantees. Buyers are, and should be, suspicious of such deeds. They are definitely meant to be advantageous to sellers. However, they are used frequently in situations where partial ownership rights are involved. A woman who possesses dower rights in a parcel of real estate sold by her husband might be willing to sign a quitclaim deed after the sale in order that the buyer can pass unencumbered title to other parties. Heirs of former owners of property who might wish to bring claims against the property due to slight legal technicalities in title transfer will often sign a quitclaim deed for a price. Many nuisance situations of this type arise, and the quitclaim deed is an effective means of handling them.

Bargain and sale deed.   A third type of deed, the deed of bargain and sale, is worded in such a manner that the land itself is said to be conveyed rather than the ownership interest therein. A fine line of distinction exists between the deed of bargain and sale and the other two forms, but there are times when a seller wishes to convey ownership without warranties but also without using the quitclaim deed, which a buyer might not accept. Corporations frequently use the deed of bargain and sale to effect such an arrangement.

Special warranty deed.   The special warranty deed is one in which grantors convenent only against claims arising from the time during which they owned the property. It is typically used when the title has an old encumbrance that cannot be cured but is not expected to create a difficulty for subsequent purchasers.

Officer's deed.   Officer's deeds are used in conjunction with mortgage foreclosure sales and to convey tax titles. They record transfers from a public official to an auction purchaser, with the ownership rights of the foreclosed being cut off after a stated redemption period. No warranties are made.

Deed requirements.   Regardless of which type of deed is employed, the following requirements must be met:

1. There must be a grantor, and a grantor's legal name must appear in the body of the deed. The grantor must be of full age and sound mind and must be acting without duress.
2. There must be a grantee. The deed must state to whom the property is to be conveyed.
3. Words of conveyance from the grantor to the grantee must be included.
4. A description of the conveyed property that is adequate to permit identification is needed.
5. There must be a statement of consideration—that is, something to be paid in exchange for the real estate. The amount paid for the property may not need to be stated, the usual consideration being "one dollar plus other valuable consideration." Some states, for example, Nebraska, require the exact amount to be stipulated.
6. The grantor must sign the deed, and in some states must affix a seal. The grantee is not required to sign or seal, although it is usually customary to do so.
7. The deed must be delivered to the grantee. Further, delivery must be accomplished in such a manner that the grantor and grantee have a meeting of minds that the transaction has been consummated. Improper delivery, such as when the grantee picks up the deed from the grantor's secretary without the grantor's knowledge, does not result in a valid transaction.

The above list represents the absolute minimum requirements for a valid deed. Some states also require that the deed be dated, witnessed, and acknowledged, and the parties involved may agree that it should contain warranties of title and statements of encumbrances. The investor should note that the law offers only partial protection in deed transactions; the investor must make an individual effort to bring out the warranties and the statement of debts or liens.

State revenue stamps. A final requirement to have a deed recorded is that it must contain an adequate number of state (or county) revenue stamps, where required. A federal tax was formerly imposed on all deeds conveying real estate, except in the case of gifts or other transactions where there was no monetary consideration. Federal revenue stamps are not required on deeds recorded after December 31, 1967, but a number of state governments require state revenue stamps. Florida, for example, requires documentary stamps on deeds at the rate of 40 cents per $100 valuation or any part thereof.

A few essentials on deeds can save the investor many legal problems.

1. The investor should always sign his or her full legal name (middle initial is satisfactory). The other party to the contract should do the same.
2. Words, phrases, or clauses that are uncertain, unneeded, or ambiguous should not be used. Many phrases which sound very legal and impressive do not further the purpose of the deed and can raise legal questions.
3. A deed form that is recognized by the state in which the real estate is located must be used. Ownership rests in the state containing the property, rather than the owner's state of residence (where different), and variations in state laws can affect the validity of the deed.

While the property conveyed in a private grant often consists of the fee simple ownership rights, lesser estates (such as life estates) and incorporeal rights (such as easements) are also conveyed by means of a deed in a private grant.

Devise

When an owner of real estate dies, leaving a will indicating who is to obtain title to the property, title to the property is conveyed by devise. The deceased person is termed the devisor, while the party who obtains title in this manner is termed the devisee. (With respect to personal property, the parties are called, respectively, the legator and the legatee.) A will is the legal instrument by which title is conveyed in this situation.

Descent

When an owner of real estate dies without leaving a will (intestate), title to the real estate is conveyed according to the provisions of the state's probate law. The portion of the law specifying the parties to whom title is conveyed in various situations is often called the statute of descent and distribution. For example, the Florida statute specifies the following order of succession for the real and personal property of a person who dies intestate in situations where there is and is not a surviving spouse.

1. The surviving spouse receives:
   a. If there is no surviving lineal descendant of the decedent, the entire intestate estate.
   b. If there are surviving lineal descendants of the decedent, *all* of whom are lineal descendants of the surviving spouse also, the first $20,000 of the intestate estate, plus one half of the balance of the intestate estate. Property allocated hereunder to the surviving spouse to satisfy the $20,000 shall be valued at the fair market value on the date of the decedent's death.
2. The part of the intestate estate not passing to the surviving spouse, or the entire intestate estate if there is no surviving spouse, descends as follows:
   a. To the lineal descendants of the decedent.
   b. If there is no lineal descendant, to the decedent's father and mother equally, or to the survivor of them.
   c. If there are none of the foregoing, to the decedent's brothers and sisters and the descendants of the deceased brothers and sisters.
   d. If there are none of the foregoing, one half of the estate shall go to the decedent's paternal kindred and the other half to the decedent's maternal kindred, in the following order:
      (1) To the grandfather and grandmother equally, or to the survivor of them.
      (2) If there is no grandfather or grandmother, to uncles and aunts and descendants of deceased uncles and aunts of the decedent.
      (3) If there are no paternal kindred or if there are no maternal kindred, the estate shall go to such of the kindred as shall survive in the order aforesaid.
      (4) If there are no kindred of either part, the whole of such property shall go to the kindred of the last deceased spouse of the decedent as if the deceased spouse had survived the decedent and then died intestate entitled to the estate.

Foreclosure

The holder of a valid lien on real property is entitled to request that the property be sold at public sale when the fee simple owner defaults in satisfying the claim which caused the lien to arise. The fee simple owner's rights of ownership are cut off at the time of sale by a court-appointed official, and the buyer at the sale receives a fee simple title. The court does not guarantee the quality of this title; the buyer takes it subject to any defects that existed when it was in the hands of the former owner.

Adverse possession

Individuals can take away the title of another person if they use that person's property on an actual, continuous, hostile, visible, and exclusive basis for a period of time prescribed by law. This change of title is based upon the concept that land should be used rather than left idle. In other words, anyone who owns property for the prescribed period—usually 7 to 21 years—and fails to use the property or assert a claim of ownership against the adverse possessor should lose the property if the adverse possessor did make profitable use of the land.

Prescription

When an individual uses the land of another for a period of time stated by law, such as using a roadway across a neighbor's land, the user obtains a right of easement in the neighbor's land. This use must have most of the attributes of adverse possession, except that it need not be exclusive.

Title from nature (riparian rights)

As discussed above, recorded deeds contain a legal description of the owner's parcel of property. Many descriptions are expressed in terms of monuments or natural boundaries, and these can change. Where a body of water washes land into the described area, title is obtained through accretion. Where boundary water recedes and leaves dry land, reliction adds to the title holder's land. The only case in which such changes do not convey title is when a boundary river or stream changes course (avulsion). The dry bed is still the boundary.

CONVEYANCING FUNCTIONS

The laws pertaining to real estate conveyancing require that formal procedures be followed in all types of transactions. Offers, contracts, closings, title transfers, rentals, and many other activities are framed in legal terms, with precisely worded documents evidencing them. Many of these documents appear to be cumbersome, but less precise terminology leads to ambiguity, and failure to insert the many clauses can easily cause disagreement among the parties at a later date.

Nearly all real property transactions are governed by state statutes of frauds, laws requiring that all transactions other than short-term leases must be in writing. Oral clauses or oral agreements pertaining to the transaction document are not enforceable until they have been set down in writing and incorporated properly into the document. This is a reasonable statute; many disagreements are avoided where oral testimony is not permitted, and people tend to plan more carefully when all provisions are stated in writing.

Investors who enter into written agreements concerning real property should have all pertinent documents examined by an attorney to be certain that agreement is reached on all essential points and to provide a measure of protection against undesirable provisions. However, the attorney cannot do the entire job. The investor is the person who will be bound by the agreement and who is in a position to know exactly what his or her objectives are and what clauses can meet them best. For example, a land contract containing a forfeiture clause (which states that failure to make a payment causes the land to revert to the seller) might be advantageous for a speculator who would like to withdraw from the investment if it proved unprofitable. The same clause would be disadvantageous for a low-income couple who are buying their home under land contract to avoid making a large down payment. Speculators know that the decision to forfeit or not forfeit is their own; the person who cannot afford the down payment is at the mercy of the seller if illness or other problems cause one or more payments to be missed.

The frequent investor in real estate must learn to analyze documents thoroughly in a short period of time. The investor must be able to determine whether or not all pertinent items are included, and investment objectives must be analyzed to determine which clauses should or should not be inserted. Other clauses are subject to negotiation, and investors must know enough about them to determine that an agreement is equitable, given their particular objectives.

The first step in preparing a document for a real estate transaction is to determine whether or not it is proper for the purpose. Warranty deeds, deeds of bargain and sale, and quitclaim deeds all transfer ownership rights, but only the warranty deed employs wording that calls for the seller to guarantee the quality of the ownership right which is transferred. A quitclaim deed conveys only the seller's interest, no matter how encumbered. The use of these and other documents varies among the states, and thus it is important for investors to become familiar with practices within their realm of operation.

Many of the documents involved in real property transactions are preprinted in standard form. Offers to purchase, deeds, closing statements, mortgages, liens, leases, trading agreements, trust agreements, escrow agreements, and brokers' listing contracts are examples of documents that are typically prepared en masse by trade groups and individual firms. Local boards of Realtors usually prescribe a certain set of forms for their members, but each board can prescribe a different form, and not all members of a particular board adhere to the entire package of prescribed forms. Also, many brokers do not have access to Realtor-approved forms. Lenders normally develop their own forms, as do escrow agents, trustees, and landlords.

Many functions must be performed in even the least complicated conveyancing transaction. The most frequently encountered activities are considered here, presented in chronological order from the initial purchase offer to the transaction close.

Listing property

People who wish to sell a real estate holding frequently list the property with a real estate broker. A listing contract is an agreement between a real estate broker and individuals who plan to sell property, stipulating the price to be asked for the property, the amount (usually a percentage of the selling price) the broker is to receive for finding a buyer, and the duration of the agreement. There are three basic types of listing contracts: (*a*) open listing, (*b*) exclusive listing, and (*c*) exclusive right-of-sale listing. A fourth type, net listing, is mentioned frequently in the literature but is frowned upon in practice, and a fifth, multiple listing, is a subtype of the exclusive right-of-sale contract.

Open listing.   The open listing contract permits the seller to grant a similar contract to all brokers who will accept it. No broker has an exclusive right to sell, and the first broker to produce an acceptable offer for the property is entitled to the commission. No other brokers are entitled to any portion of the commission. If the owner sells the property without the help of a broker, no commission is paid.

Open listings require a minimum commitment by the seller, but they rarely occur, because few brokers will accept them. In most cases, the broker must cultivate potential buyers for days or even weeks to convince them to buy. Sellers may believe that open listings "keep brokers honest," but the rationale for brokers not accepting such a contract is strong.

Exclusive agency listing.   In an exclusive listing, the seller hires only one broker, but retains the right to sell the property through his or her own efforts without paying a commission. Even if another broker sells the property, the broker holding the exclusive listing is entitled to a commission. This type of contract is more common than open listing, but brokers are somewhat reluctant to accept a contract when they must compete with the seller.

Exclusive right-of-sale listing.   The contract type which grants the major legal advantage to the broker is the exclusive right of sale. Regardless of who sells the property—the owner included—the broker with an exclusive right-of-sale listing is entitled to receive the commission (see Figure 11–1). Obviously, brokers prefer the exclusive right-of-sale listing arrangement, and sellers are frequently satisfied to accept it, particularly after they have failed to sell their properties through their own efforts. Under this contract type, the broker can proceed in obtaining contracts without fear of being too late to make the sale.

Net listing.   The net listing contract is one in which the seller specifies a price desired from the sale and the broker keeps everything in excess of that amount. Obviously, this type of contract would encourage brokers to attempt to establish low net prices for sellers, and this would give the brokerage profession a bad name.

Multiple listing.   One arrangement that has been very satisfactory for sellers, buyers, and brokers is the multiple listing, in which the seller grants an exclusive right-of-sale listing to a broker who agrees to put the property in a pool operated by an organized group of brokers. All of the brokers work to sell the property, and all or part of the commission is shared by the participating members of the group. The seller finds the multiple listing advantageous because the prospective buyers being serviced by several brokers become potential buyers for the property. Brokers find that a rapid turnover of properties brings in more business and promotes greater profit and greater efficiency than are possible through individual operation. However, the multiple listing concept does have two problems which keep it from being used more widely: (1) some brokers tend to rely upon their coparticipants to bring in most or all of the listings; and (2) some brokers withhold choice listings for their individual sale. The latter problem can be quite serious; "vest-pocket listings" can dissolve a multiple listing arrangement very quickly. The first problem can also cause serious difficulties with the multiple listing service and, particularly in small organizations, may ultimately cause its downfall.

Establishing a reasonable duration for listing contracts is an important problem faced by brokers. Many legal actions have been brought by brokers who introduced a buyer to a seller only to find that the two of them conspired to wait until the listing contract terminated so that they could transact a sale without paying a commission. Today the courts generally hold that a broker is entitled to a commission when the following situations occur.[1]

---

[1] Robert Kratovil and Raymond J. Werner, *Real Estate Law*, 7th ed. (Englewood Cliffs, N.J.: Prentice-Hall, 1979), pp. 81–82.

FIGURE 11–1
Listing agreement

GAINESVILLE BOARD OF REALTORS
EXCLUSIVE RIGHT OF SALE
RESIDENTIAL LISTING AGREEMENT

1. Dated _____. In consideration of the agreements of the REALTOR and Owner as set forth herein concerning the described property.

ML#		Street or Road		City	B/B		Price		Sec	L.O
Legal				Tax #				Zoning		
				Taxes				HE 19		
				Lot Size						
				Abst Loc						
Foyer	Const		Mortgagee			%		Balance		P + I
LR	Yr Blt	1								
DR	Roof	2								
FR	Attic Ins	3								
# BR	Fireplace	Loan #						Escrow		
# Bath	Walls	VA	FHA	CONV		C/D		Total		
Other	Flrs	Remarks								
	Heat									
Main	Air									
Gar/CP	HW Type									
Util	Elect									
Porch	Water	Owner					Ph			
	Sewer/Septic	Address								
Equip		Listed		19		Com		L	S	
		Slsmn				Hm Ph				
Termite Con		How Show				Vac		LB		

_____ as REALTOR and
_____ as Owner, agree to the following:
Owner warrants to the REALTOR that the above representations of the property furnished to the REALTOR by the Owner are true and correct, and that there are no misstatements in any of said representations which would have any material effect on the property value. Owner agrees to indemnify and save REALTOR harmless of and from any and all loss, damage, suits and claims, including reasonable attorneys' fees and costs of defense incurred by REALTOR on account of any representations made by REALTOR in reliance on the Owner's representations herein. The Owner agrees to furnish the REALTOR with keys to the property, will allow the REALTOR to place an appropriate sign and lock-box and allow the REALTOR to use the Owner's name when necessary or desirable in marketing the property, and will make the property available for the REALTOR to show during reasonable hours to prospective purchasers.

The Owner hereby gives to the REALTOR for a period of six _____ months from the date hereof, the exclusive right and authority to find a purchaser for the above described property, upon the following terms or at any other price and terms acceptable to Owner.

Price: _____ Terms: FHA ☐ VA ☐ CTM ☐ CONV. ☐
Other Terms: _____
All taxes for the current year, rentals, monthly mortgage insurance premiums, hazard insurance premiums and interest on existing mortgages (if any) shall be pro-rated as of the date of closing.
Personal property to be included in the purchase price: All fixed equipment, including drapery hardware, plants and shubbery now installed on said property. Additional personal property _____

2. The Owner agrees, at his expense, to provide for: (a) preparation of and delivery to the Purchaser of a good and sufficient warranty deed (unless otherwise required) conveying an Insurable title free and clear of all liens except encumbrances of record assumed by the Purchaser as part of purchase price: (b) binder for fee title insurance policy or abstract; (c) documentary and state surtax stamps for the deed; (d) Seller's attorney fee; (e) recording fee for satisfaction of existing mortgage, if mortgage is paid off; (f) Mortgage discount; (g) evidence from a licensed pest control firm that property is visibly free from infestation or damage by termites or other wood destroying organisms) (h) and to furnish ownership statement as required by the Real Estate Settlement Procedures Act.

3. The Owner agrees that the REALTOR has the exclusive right, at the REALTOR's discretion to: Arrange for financing and order and obtain all items necessary to consummate a closing on subject property, such as, but not limited to, pest control, title insurance, survey, etc.

4. (a) For finding a purchaser ready, willing and able to purchase the above property, Owner agrees to pay REALTOR a commission of _____% of the total purchase price on the terms herein mentioned, or at any price and upon terms acceptable to Owner, whether the Purchaser be secured by REALTOR or Owner, or by any other person, or, if the property is afterwards sold within four months from the termination of this agreement, or extensions thereof, to any person to whom the said property has been shown by the REALTOR or his representatives or by a co-operating Broker. However, no commission shall be due the REALTOR if after this listing is terminated, the property is relisted with another REALTOR.
(b) In any exchange of this property, permission is given REALTOR to represent and receive commissions from both parties.
(c) In the event the property is rented or leased the Owner will pay the Listing REALTOR's rental or leasing fee.

5. In consideration of this exclusive right of sale the REALTOR agrees to: (a) process the property through the Multiple Listing Service. (b) advertise the property as REALTOR deems advisable. (c) furnish information requested by any REALTOR or real estate broker and (d) the REALTOR agrees to devote the resources of his/her firm in an effort to market said property.

6. In consideration of the above, the Owner agrees to immediately refer to REALTOR all inquiries relative to purchase of his property.

7. Owner authorizes REALTOR or cooperating broker to accept, receipt for and hold all money paid or deposited as a binder on his property and if such deposit is forfeited by the prospective purchaser, after deducting any funds expended for Buyer or Seller's processing costs, the Owner shall retain as liquidated damages one half of the remainder of the binder deposit. The remaining one half of net deposit shall be paid to the Agent as compensation not to exceed the total amount of his commission.

8. Owner and REALTOR acknowledge that this agreement does not guarantee a sale and that there are no other agreements, promises or understandings either expressed or implied between them other than specifically set forth herein and that there can be no alterations or changes to this contract except in writing and signed by each of them. They also agree that this agreement supersedes any prior agreement regarding this property. They each agree that this property is offered to any person without regard to race, color, creed, national origin or sex.

9. This is a legal and binding contract on all parties hereto, including their heirs, legal representatives, successors and assigns and if it is not fully understood Owner should seek competent legal advice.

10. In connection with any litigation arising out of the Agreement, the prevailing party shall be entitled to recover all costs incurred, including reasonable attorney's fees.

_____   _____
REALTOR   Owner

By: _____   _____
                                             Owner

Owner's Mailing Address: _____
                    White Copy to Realtor—Pink copy to Owner—Yellow copy to MLS

MLS 1979 Rev # 1   2M-480-41360

1. The deal falls through because owners change their minds and refuse to sign the deed to the purchaser or the contract to sell. The rule is the same when the land has increased in value and the owner rejects the broker's buyer for this reason. If the seller refuses to sign, giving as the reason the fact that the seller has changed his or her mind, the seller cannot thereafter shift ground and claim that the buyer's offer was not in compliance with the listing. (*Russell* v. *Ramm*, 200 Calif. 348, 254 Pac. 532.)

2. The deal falls through because the owner's wife refuses to sign the contract or deed. (*Pliler* v. *Thompson*, 84 Okla. 200, 202 Pac. 1010.)

3. The deal falls through because of defects in the owner's title. (*Triplett* v. *Feasal*, 105 Kans. 179, 182 Pac. 551.)

4. The deal falls through because of the owner's fraud. (*Hathaway* v. *Smith*, 187 111. App. 128.)

5. The deal falls through because the owner is unable to deliver possession within a reasonable time.

6. The deal falls through because the seller insists on terms and provisions not mentioned in the listing contract, as where the seller insists on the right to remain in possession after the deal has been closed. (*Brown* v. *Ogle*, 75 Ind. App. 90, 130 N.E. 147.)

7. After the contract of sale has been signed, the seller and the buyer get together and cancel the contract. (*Steward* v. *Brock*, 60 N.Mex. 216, 290 P. 2d 682.)

8. The deal falls through because the buyer cannot procure financing and the contract is not contingent on ability to procure financing.

Even when there is no reluctance on the part of the seller to pay the broker's commission, a question arises as to the point in time when the commission has been earned. In general, the broker has earned a commission when he or she introduces the seller to a buyer who is ready, willing, and able to buy the property according to the terms specified in the listing. *Ready* and *willing* mean that the buyer wishes to purchase immediately; *able* indicates that the buyer has financial means to acquire the property. A sale need not result from this union of seller and buyer in order for the commission to be earned; the seller must pay the commission even though he or she refuses to consummate the deal (unless the refusal is due to the buyer's being other than ready, willing, and able). If the seller and the potential buyer both sign a contract of sale but later cancel for any reason, the commission must be paid. This is true even if the buyer fails to fulfill the contract, the seller's remedy being to sue the buyer for damages because of breach of contract—the damages being primarily the commission.

To avoid the possibility of paying a commission without having sold the property, a seller may specify in the listing contract that the broker is entitled to a commission only if the property is sold to a buyer introduced by the broker.[2]

Making an offer

Upon finding a desirable property, investors normally prepare a formal, written offer to submit to the owner. This offer ripens into a contract for sale if it is accepted by the owner, and it permits the owner to make a counteroffer if a change in terms is desired. As a practical matter, investors usually learn of the property's availability through a broker who holds a listing contract with the seller. The investor thus has a statement of the owner's desired terms as a guide in preparing the offer.

Two points are worth noting about the offer to purchase: (1) The buyer should be specific as to exactly what he or she is offering to buy. The buyer should specify whether storm windows and screens, light fixtures, carpets, and so on, are to be included in the sale or excluded from it. Anything the buyer wishes to receive which might be considered personal property should be listed. (2) The seller might wish to state the terms of the listing contract in a manner general enough to permit the rejection of offers to buy because of certain specific items they contain, or the seller might wish to make the listing extremely specific and to hold that the listing must be agreed upon exactly by the buyer. Either way, the seller may accept any offer, even if the terms deviate widely from the listing.

Once an offer to buy is tendered to the seller, the potential buyer and the seller can negotiate as to the price and what the sale includes until they make a satisfactory arrangement or terminate negotiations. The offer to buy is merely an offer; many counteroffers and counter-counteroffers might be necessary to effect a sale.

The offer must state formally that an offer is being made, and it must indicate clearly each of the following items:

1. Name of offeror, offeree, and broker.
2. Detailed description of property and fixtures, including a listing of all items that are to be made part of the transaction.
3. Amount to be paid and terms of payment. The offer can be worded to make it contingent upon obtaining a specific financing arrangement.

---

[2] Under such a provision the buyer may be introduced indirectly by the broker, such as when a broker's newspaper advertisement leads to a sale; in that case the broker is still entitled to a commission. Such a provision cannot be specified in an exclusive right-to-sell listing, however, since the broker gets a commission regardless of who sells the property.

FIGURE 11-2
Contract for sale

CONTRACT FOR SALE AND PURCHASE   BAR/FAR Form No. 3

PARTIES: _____ , as "Seller",

of _____ (Phone _____),

and _____ , as "Buyer",

of _____ (Phone _____),

hereby agree that the Seller shall sell and Buyer shall buy the following property upon the following terms and conditions WHICH INCLUDE the Standards For Real Estate Transactions on the reverse hereof or attached hereto, hereinafter referred to as "Standard(s)".

I.   DESCRIPTION:
    (a)   Legal description of real estate located in _____ County, Florida:

    (b)   Street address, if any, of the property being conveyed is _____ .

    (c)   Personal property included:

II.   PURCHASE PRICE: . . . . $ _____
    PAYMENT:
    (a)   Deposit(s) to be held in escrow by _____
                             in the amount of . . . . . $ _____
    (b)   Subject to AND assumption of Mortgage in favor of _____
                        bearing interest at _____ % per annum and payable as to principal and
          interest $ _____ per month, having an approximate present principal balance of . . . . . . $ _____
    (c)   Purchase money mortgage and note bearing interest at _____ % on terms set forth herein below, in the
          principal amount of . . . . $ _____
    (d)   Other _____ . . . . $ _____
    (e)   Balance to close, (U.S. cash, certified or cashier's check) subject to adjustments and prorations . . . . $ _____
                                           TOTAL . . . . . $ _____

III.   FINANCING: If the purchase price or any part thereof is to be financed by a third party loan, this Contract for Sale and Purchase, hereinafter referred to as "Contract", is conditioned upon the Buyer obtaining a firm commitment for said loan within _____ days from date hereof, at an interest rate not to exceed _____ %; term of _____ years; and in the principal amount of $ _____ Buyer agrees to make application for, and to use reasonable diligence to obtain said loan. Should Buyer fail to obtain same, or to waive Buyer's rights hereunder within said time, either party may cancel Contract.

IV.   TITLE EVIDENCE: Within _____ days from date of Contract, Seller shall, at his expense, deliver to Buyer or his attorney, in accordance with Standard A, either (CHECK) ☐ (1) or ☐ (2): (1) abstract, or (2) title insurance commitment with fee owner's title policy premium to be paid by Seller at closing.

V.   TIME FOR ACCEPTANCE AND EFFECTIVE DATE: If this offer is not executed by both of the parties hereto on or before _____ , the aforesaid deposit(s) shall be, at the option of Buyer, returned to him and this offer shall thereafter be null and void. The date of Contract shall be the date when the last one of the Seller and Buyer has signed this offer.

VI.   CLOSING DATE: This transaction shall be closed and the deed and other closing papers delivered on the _____ day of _____ 19 _____ , unless extended by other provisions of Contract.

VII.   RESTRICTIONS, EASEMENTS, LIMITATIONS: The Buyer shall take title subject to: Zoning, restrictions, prohibitions and other requirements imposed by governmental authority; Restrictions and matters appearing on the plat or otherwise common to the subdivision; Public utility easements of record, (provided said easements are located contiguous throughout the property lines and are not more than 10 feet in width as to the rear or front lines and 7½ feet in width as to the side lines, unless otherwise specified herein); Taxes for year of closing and subsequent years, assumed mortgages and purchase money mortgages, if any; other _____ provided, however, that none of the foregoing shall prevent use of the property for the purpose of _____

VIII.   OCCUPANCY: Seller represents that there are no parties in occupancy other than Seller, but if property is intended to be rented or occupied beyond closing, the fact and terms thereof shall be stated herein, and the tenant(s) shall be disclosed pursuant to Standard G. Seller agrees to deliver occupancy of property at time of closing unless otherwise specified below. If occupancy is to be delivered prior to closing, Buyer assumes all risk of loss to property from date of occupancy, shall be responsible and liable for maintenance thereof from said date, and shall be deemed to have accepted the property, real, and personal, in its existing condition as of time of taking occupancy unless otherwise noted in writing.

IX.   ASSIGNABILITY: (CHECK ONE) Buyer ☐ may assign ☐ may not assign, Contract.

X.   TYPEWRITTEN OR HANDWRITTEN PROVISIONS: Typewritten or handwritten provisions inserted herein or attached hereto as Addenda shall control all printed provisions in conflict therewith.

XI.   SPECIAL CLAUSES:

- - - - - - - - - - - - - - -
THIS IS INTENDED TO BE A LEGALLY BINDING CONTRACT.
IF NOT FULLY UNDERSTOOD, SEEK THE ADVICE OF AN ATTORNEY PRIOR TO SIGNING.
THIS FORM HAS BEEN APPROVED BY THE FLORIDA ASSOCIATION OF REALTORS AND THE FLORIDA BAR
Copyright 1978 by The Florida Bar and the Florida Association of REALTORS
- - - - - - - - - - - - - - -

WITNESSES: (Two recommended)   Executed by Buyer on _____

_____   _____ (SEAL)
                                                       (Buyer)
_____   _____ (SEAL)
                                                       (Buyer)

WITNESSESS: (Two recommended; required if Homestead)   Executed by Seller on _____

_____   _____ (SEAL)
                                                       (Seller)
_____   _____ (SEAL)
                                                       (Seller)

Deposit(s) under II (a) received; if check, subject to clearance.

By: _____
        (Escrow Agent)

BROKERAGE FEE: Seller agrees to pay the registered real estate Broker named below, at time of closing, from the disbursements of the proceeds of sale; compensation in the amount of _____ % of gross purchase price for his services in effecting the sale by finding a Buyer, ready, willing and able to purchase pursuant to the foregoing Contract. In the event Buyer fails to perform and deposit(s) is retained, 50% thereof, but not exceeding the Broker's fee above computed, shall be paid to the Broker, as full consideration for Broker's services including costs expended by Broker, and the balance shall be paid to Seller. If the transaction shall not be closed because of refusal or failure of Seller to perform, the Seller shall pay said fee in full to Broker on demand.

_____ (SEAL)   _____ (SEAL)
      (Name of Broker)   (Seller)

                                                     _____ (SEAL)
REV.: 7/78   (Seller)

FIGURE 11–2 (*continued*)

STANDARDS FOR REAL ESTATE TRANSACTIONS

A. EVIDENCE OF TITLE: [1] An abstract of title prepared or brought current by a reputable and existing abstract firm (if not existing then certified as correct by an existing firm) purporting to be an accurate synopsis of the instruments affecting the title to subject real property recorded in the public records of the county wherein the land is situated, through date of Contract. An abstract shall commence with the earliest public records, or such later date as may be customary in the county wherein the land is situated. Seller shall convey a marketable title in accordance with Title Standards adopted from time to time by The Florida Bar, subject only to liens, encumbrances, exceptions or qualifications set forth in this Contract and those which shall be discharged by Seller at or before closing. Upon closing of this transaction such abstract shall become the property of Buyer, subject to the right of retention thereof by first mortgagee until fully paid; or [2] a title insurance commitment issued by a qualified title insuror agreeing to issue to Buyer, upon recording of the deed to Buyer, an Owner's policy of title insurance in the amount of the purchase price, insuring title of the Buyer to the real property, subject only to liens, encumbrances, exceptions or qualifications set forth in this Contract and those which shall be discharged by Seller at or before closing. Buyer shall have 30 days, if abstract, or 5 days, if title commitment, from date of receiving evidence of title to examine same. If title is found defective, Buyer shall, within 3 days thereafter, notify Seller in writing specifying defect(s). If said defect(s) render title unmarketable, Seller shall have 120 days from receipt of notice within which to remove said defect(s), and if Seller is unsuccessful in removing them within said time, Buyer shall have the option of either (1) accepting the title as it then is, or (2) demanding a refund of all monies paid hereunder which shall forthwith be returned to Buyer and thereupon Buyer and Seller shall be released as to one another, of all further obligations under the Contract; however, Seller agrees that he will, if title is found to be unmarketable, use diligent effort to correct the defect(s) in title within the time provided therefor, including the bringing of necessary suits.

B. EXISTING MORTGAGES. Seller shall furnish a statement from the mortgagee(s) setting forth principal balance, method of payment, interest rate and whether the mortgage(s) is in good standing. If a mortgage requires approval of the Buyer by the mortgagee in order to avoid default, or for assumption by the Buyer of said mortgage, and [1] the mortgagee does not approve the Buyer, the Buyer may rescind the Contract, or [2] requires an increase in the interest rate or charges a fee for any reason in excess of $100.00, the Buyer may rescind the Contract unless Seller elects to pay such increase or excess. Seller shall pay 50% of such fee up to $50.00. Buyer shall use reasonable diligence to obtain approval. The amount of any escrow deposits held by mortgagee shall be credited to Seller.

C. PURCHASE MONEY MORTGAGES: The purchase money note and mortgage, if any, shall provide for a 30 day grace period in the event of default if it is a first mortgage and a 15 day grace period if a second mortgage; shall provide for right of prepayment in whole or in part without penalty; shall not provide for acceleration in event of resale of the property, and shall be otherwise in form and content required by Seller's attorney; provided, however, Seller may only require clauses customarily found in mortgages and mortgage notes generally utilized by savings and loan institutions in the county wherein the property is located. Said mortgage shall require the owner of the property encumbered to keep all prior liens and encumbrances in good standing and forbid the owner of the property from accepting modifications of or future advances under prior mortgage(s). All personal property being conveyed will, at option of Seller, be subject to the lien of the mortgage and evidenced by recorded Financing Statements.

D. SURVEY: The Buyer, within time allowed for delivery of evidence of title and examination thereof, may have the property surveyed at his expense. If the survey, certified by a registered Florida surveyor, shows any encroachment on said property or that improvements intended to be located on the subject property in fact encroach on lands of others, or violate any of the Contract covenants, the same shall be treated as a title defect. Any survey prepared in connection with or as a consequence of this transaction may include a description of the property under the Florida Coordinate System as defined in Chapter 177, Florida Statutes.

E. TERMITES: The Buyer, within time allowed for delivery of evidence of title and examination thereof, or no later than 10 days prior to closing, whichever date occurs last, may have the improvements inspected at Buyer's expense by a Certified Pest Control Operator to determine whether there is any visible active termite infestation or visible existing damage from termite infestation in the improvements. If Buyer is informed of either or both of the foregoing, Buyer will have 4 days from date of written notice thereof or 2 days after selection of a contractor, whichever occurs first, within which to have all damages, whether visible or not, inspected and estimated by a licensed building or general contractor. Seller shall pay valid costs of treatment and repair of all damage up to 1½% of Purchase Price. Should such costs exceed that amount, Buyer shall have the option of cancelling Contract within 5 days after receipt of contractor's repair estimate by giving written notice to Seller, or Buyer may elect to proceed with the transaction, in which event Buyer shall receive a credit at closing of an amount equal to 1½% of said Purchase Price. "Termite" shall be deemed to include all wood destroying insects.

F. INGRESS AND EGRESS: Seller covenants and warrants that there is ingress and egress to the property.

G. LEASES: Seller shall, not less than 15 days prior to closing, furnish to Buyer copies of all written leases and estoppel letters from each tenant specifying the nature and duration of said tenant's occupancy, rental rates and advanced rent and security deposits paid by tenant. In the event Seller is unable to obtain such letters from each tenant, the same information shall be furnished by Seller to Buyer within said time period in the form of a Seller's affidavit, and Buyer may thereafter contact tenants to confirm such information. Seller shall deliver and assign all original leases to Buyer at closing.

H. LIENS: Seller shall, both as to the realty and personalty being sold hereunder, furnish to Buyer at time of closing an affidavit attesting to the absence unless otherwise provided for herein, of any financing statements, claims of lien or potential lienors known to Seller and further attesting that there have been no improvements to the property for 90 days immediately preceding date of closing. If the property has been improved within said time, Seller shall deliver releases or waivers of all mechanic's liens, executed by general contractors, subcontractors, suppliers, and materialmen, in addition to Seller's lien affidavit setting forth the names of all such general contractors, subcontractors, suppliers and materialmen and further reciting that in fact all bills for work to the subject property which could serve as a basis for a mechanic's lien have been paid or will be paid at closing.

I. PLACE OF CLOSING. Closing shall be held in county wherein property is located, at the office of attorney or other closing agent designated by Seller.

J. TIME: Time is of the essence of this Contract. Any reference herein to time periods of less than 6 days shall in the computation thereof exclude Saturdays, Sundays and legal holidays, and any time period provided for herein which shall end on a Saturday, Sunday or legal holiday shall extend to 5:00 p.m. of the next full business day.

K. DOCUMENTS FOR CLOSING: Seller shall furnish deed, mechanic's lien affidavit, assignments of leases, and any corrective instruments that may be required in connection with perfecting the title. Buyer shall furnish closing statement, mortgage, mortgage note, and financing statements.

L. EXPENSES: State surtax and documentary stamps which are required to be affixed to the instrument of conveyance, intangible tax on and recording of purchase money mortgage to Seller, and cost of recording any corrective instruments shall be paid by Seller. Documentary stamps to be affixed to the note or notes secured by the purchase money mortgage, cost of recording the deed and financing statements shall be paid by Buyer.

M. PRORATION OF TAXES (REAL AND PERSONAL): Taxes shall be prorated based on the current year's tax with due allowance made for maximum allowable discount and homestead or other exemptions if allowed for said year. If closing occurs at a date when the current year's millage is not fixed, and current year's assessment is available, taxes will be prorated based upon such assessment, and the prior year's millage. If current year's assessment is not available, then taxes will be prorated on the prior year's tax; provided, however, if there are completed improvements on the property by January 1st of year of closing, which improvements were not in existence on January 1st of the prior year, then taxes shall be prorated based upon the prior year's millage and at an equitable assessment to be agreed upon between the parties, failing which, request will be made to the County Property Appraiser for an informal assessment taking into consideration homestead exemption, if any. However, any tax proration based on an estimate may at request of either party to the transaction, be subsequently readjusted upon receipt of tax bill on condition that a statement to that effect is set forth in the closing statement.

N. SPECIAL ASSESSMENT LIENS: Certified, confirmed and ratified special assessment liens as of date of closing (and not as of date of Contract) are to be paid by Seller. Pending liens as of date of closing shall be assumed by Buyer, provided, however, that where the improvement has been substantially completed as of the date of Contract, such pending lien shall be considered as certified, confirmed or ratified and Seller shall, at closing, be charged an amount equal to the last estimate by the public body, of the assessment for the improvement.

O. PERSONAL PROPERTY INSPECTION, REPAIR: Seller warrants that all major appliances, heating, cooling, electrical, plumbing systems, and machinery are in working condition as of 6 days prior to closing. Buyer may, at his expense, have inspections made of said items by licensed persons dealing in the repair and maintenance thereof, and shall report in writing to Seller such items as found not in working condition prior to taking of possession thereof, or 6 days prior to closing, whichever is first. Unless Buyer reports failures within said period, he shall be deemed to have waived Seller's warranty as to failures not reported. Valid reported failures shall be corrected at Seller's cost with funds therefor escrowed at closing. Seller agrees to provide access for inspection upon reasonable notice.

P. RISK OF LOSS: If the improvements are damaged by fire or other casualty prior to closing, and costs of restoring same does not exceed 3% of the Assessed Valuation of the improvements so damaged, cost of restoration shall be an obligation of the Seller and closing shall proceed pursuant to the terms of Contract with cost therefor escrowed at closing. In the event the cost of repair or restoration exceeds 3% of the assessed valuation of the improvements so damaged, Buyer shall have the option of either taking the property as is, together with either the said 3% or any insurance proceeds payable by virtue of such loss or damage, or of canceling Contract and receiving return of deposit(s) made hereunder.

Q. MAINTENANCE: Notwithstanding provisions of Standard O, between Contract date and closing date, personal property referred to in Standard O and real property, including lawn, shrubbery and pool, if any, shall be maintained by Seller in conditions they existed as of Contract date, ordinary wear and tear excepted.

R. PROCEEDS OF SALE AND CLOSING PROCEDURE: The deed shall be recorded upon clearance of funds and evidence of title continued at Buyer's expense, to show title in Buyer, without any encumbrances or change which would render Seller's title unmarketable, from the date of the last evidence and the cash proceeds of sale shall be held in escrow by Seller's attorney or by such other escrow agent as may be mutually agreed upon for a period of not longer than 5 days from and after closing date. If Seller's title is rendered unmarketable, Buyer shall within said 5 day period, notify Seller in writing of the defect and Seller shall have 30 days from date of receipt of such notification to cure said defect. In the event Seller fails to timely cure said defect, all monies paid hereunder shall, upon written demand therefor and within 5 days thereafter, be returned to Buyer and, simultaneously with such repayment, Buyer shall vacate the premises and reconvey the property in question to the Seller by special warranty deed. In the event Buyer fails to make timely demand for refund, he shall take title as is, waiving all rights against Seller as to such intervening defect except as may be available to Buyer by virtue of warranties, if any, contained in deed. In the event a portion of the purchase price is to be derived from institutional financing or re-financing, the requirements of the lending institution as to place, time and procedures for closing, and for disbursement of mortgage proceeds, shall control, anything in this Contract to the contrary notwithstanding. Provided, however, that the Seller shall have the right to require from such lending institution at closing a commitment that it will not withhold disbursement of mortgage proceeds as a result of any title defect attributable to Buyer-mortgagor.

S. ESCROW: Any escrow agent receiving funds is authorized and agrees by acceptance thereof to promptly deposit and to hold same in escrow and to disburse same subject to clearance thereof in accordance with terms and conditions of Contract. Failure of clearance of funds shall not excuse performance by the Buyer. In the event of doubt as to his duties or liabilities under the provisions of this Contract, the escrow agent may in his sole discretion, continue to hold the monies which are the subject of this escrow until the parties mutually agree to the disbursement thereof, or until a judgment of a court of competent jurisdiction shall determine the rights of the parties thereto, or he may deposit all the monies then held pursuant to this Contract with the Clerk of the Circuit Court of the County having jurisdiction of the dispute, and upon notifying all parties concerned of such action, all liability on the part of the escrow agent shall fully terminate, except to the extent of accounting for any monies theretofore delivered out of escrow. If a licensed real estate broker, the escrowee will comply with provisions of Section 475.25 (1) (c), F.S., as amended. In the event of any suit between Buyer and Seller wherein the escrow agent is made a party by virtue of acting as such escrow agent hereunder, or in the event of any suit wherein escrow agent interpleads the subject matter of this escrow, the escrow agent shall be entitled to recover a reasonable attorney's fee and costs incurred, said fees and costs to be charged and assessed as court costs in favor of the prevailing party. All parties agree that the escrow agent shall not be liable to any party or person whomsoever for misdelivery to Buyer or Seller of monies subject to this escrow, unless such misdelivery shall be due to willful breach of this Contract or gross negligence on the part of the escrow agent.

T. ATTORNEY FEES AND COSTS: In connection with any litigation including appellate proceedings arising out of this Contract, the prevailing party shall be entitled to recover reasonable attorney's fees and costs.

U. DEFAULT: If Buyer fails to perform this Contract within the time specified, the deposit(s) paid by the Buyer aforesaid may be retained by or for the account of Seller as liquidated damages, consideration for the execution of this Contract and in full settlement of any claims; whereupon all parties shall be relieved of all obligations under the Contract; or Seller, at his option, may proceed at law or in equity to enforce his legal rights under this Contract. If, for any reason other than failure of Seller to render his title marketable after diligent effort, Seller fails, neglects or refuses to perform this Contract, the Buyer may seek specific performance or elect to receive the return of his deposit(s) without thereby waiving any action for damages resulting from Seller's breach.

V. CONTRACT NOT RECORDABLE, PERSONS BOUND AND NOTICE: Neither this Contract nor any notice thereof shall be recorded in any public records. This Contract shall bind and inure to the benefit of the parties hereto and their successors in interest. Whenever the context permits, singular shall include plural and one gender shall include all. Notice given by or to the attorney for either party shall be as effective as if given by or to said party.

W. PRORATIONS AND INSURANCE: Taxes, assessments, rent, interest, insurance and other expenses and revenue of said property shall be prorated as of date of closing. Buyer shall have the option of taking over any existing policies of insurance on the property, if assumable, in which event premiums shall be prorated. The cash at closing shall be increased or decreased as may be required by said prorations. All references in Contract to prorations as of date of closing will be deemed "date of occupancy" if occupancy occurs prior to closing, unless otherwise provided for herein.

X. CONVEYANCE: Seller shall convey title to the aforesaid real property by statutory warranty deed subject only to matters contained in Paragraph VII hereof. Personal property shall, at the request of Buyer, be conveyed by an absolute bill of sale with warranty of title, subject to such liens as may be otherwise provided for herein.

Y. OTHER AGREEMENTS: No prior or present agreements or representations shall be binding upon any of the parties hereto unless incorporated in this Contract. No modification or change in this Contract shall be valid or binding upon the parties unless in writing, executed by the parties to be bound thereby.

4. Type of deed to be received and specific ownership restrictions and encumbrances that will be permitted.
5. Manner in which expenses, taxes, rentals, and so on, are to be prorated between buyer and seller.
6. Options available to the offeror if the property is damaged or destroyed before the final closing and statements evidencing the insurable interests of the parties.
7. Duration of offer.
8. Time and place of closing and length of time permitted for title search and removal of objections to title.
9. Manner in which earnest money deposits are to be handled and provision for the broker's commission.
10. Statement of how the broker's commission is to be computed.
11. A complete agreement clause that excludes all facts and material items not considered in the writing. This clause requires that oral agreements be incorporated into the document.
12. Offeror's witnessed signature, owner's acceptance of the offer, and receipt for deposit.

A standard offer form approved by the Florida Bar Association and the Florida Association of Realtors is presented as Figure 11–2 to indicate the manner in which these factors are commonly considered. The offer to purchase is designed to meet the needs of the offeror. The standard clauses contained in Figure 11–2 avoid most of the problems that could arise in the event of damage to the property, failure to obtain clear title or proper financing at closing, failure to pay the broker's commission, and so forth. Other clauses can be inserted to meet any types of needs, such as those regarding an exchange of properties, a sale of previously owned properties, or the establishment of a corporation or syndicate to hold the real estate assets. The standard form is a logical and desirable instrument for most transactions, but specialized activities call for individualized provisions. The wording of these provisions must be precise, and an attorney should normally be consulted in preparing them.

Reaching agreement—contracts for sale

When a buyer and seller agree as to the exact terms of a real property transaction, a written contract is prepared that describes the property and all extras, states the price to be paid, and indicates the time at which title is to pass. A contract for sale does not have to be a formal document to be legally enforceable. It is frequently represented as an accepted offer to purchase. Kratovil provides an example of a contract

similar to the following that was enforced by one court, indicating that
the contract does not even have to state the specific details of transfer:[3]

New York

February 29, 1908

Received of John Smith $200 on said purchase of property 2293
Jones Avenue, New York, New York, at a price of $18,000.

T. Wilson

Obviously, this is not a good practice. The contract should clearly
identify the parties; the property to be transferred, including personal
property, if any; and the type of deed to be granted. It should specify
that a merchantable title is to pass, and it should contain the signatures
of both parties.

One of the most important functions of the contract for sale is to
stipulate the time when title is to be passed from the seller to the
buyer. If the time is not specified, the law holds that title must be
conveyed within a reasonable time after the signing of the sale contract. Adequate time is allowed to permit the buyer to ascertain the
seller's ownership rights and determine whether or not any encumbrances exist that could prevent a clear title from passing. Both parties
must work out their financial arrangements within this time.

Searching title

A deed conveys title, but it can convey a bad title as well as a good
one. The investor seeks a good title in every transaction, as evidenced
by one of the following: (*a*) abstract or certificate of title, (*b*) title
insurance policy, or (*c*) Torrens certificate.

Abstract and attorney's opinion. The most common evidence of
title in the United States is the *abstract* and *attorney's opinion*. An
abstract is a summary of all deeds, liens, land contracts, or any other
recorded instruments that may affect ownership. If lost or destroyed, it
can be replaced by a new abstract or a title insurance policy. Many
abstracts are lengthy when a property has changed hands frequently,
but fortunately the attorney who traces title can update the abstract
from the last transfer and review earlier documents effectively in a
short period of time. An opinion is then expressed as to the probability
that the buyer will encounter claims against the property. This opinion
is not legally binding against the attorney unless the research was
negligent. However, an expert researcher's opinion is usually quite
reliable, especially when the property has changed hands infre-

---

[3] Kratovil and Werner, *Real Estate Law*, p. 98.

quently and is purchased from a person who has owned it for a long period of time.

Title insurance. Investors will usually find that lending institutions require that they be provided with a title insurance policy which protects their interests against most possible claims. The mortgagee's policy does not protect the investors' equity in the property, but the owners can obtain a separate equity policy at a cost lower than that of the mortgagee's policy. The title insurance company searches the title through the abstract and the public records, granting a policy only when the probability is low that the company will have to pay a claim. If a policy is issued, a single premium is charged to the property buyer at the initiation of coverage. After that time, the insurance company handles any claims or lawsuits relating to title.

Torrens certificate. The Torrens certificate involves a formal land registration approach to title verification. A list of persons who could have an interest in the property can be developed from the abstract. This list is submitted to a county registrar of Torrens certificates with an application for a certificate. The application serves as a lawsuit against those named on the list, requiring them to contest any claims they might have to prevent issuance of the certificate. The registrar also publishes the application in local newpapers, advertising for claims against the property. If no claims arise, a certificate is issued declaring the applicant to be the owner of the land. Declared owners need have little worry about future claims after this procedure has been followed, but they must defend themselves if a claim should arise. Indemnity funds are provided by counties for paying claims, but these accumulated funds are often insufficient to provide complete indemnity.

The Torrens certificate is an inexpensive means of obtaining freedom from fear as to title claims, but it is a time-consuming and complicated procedure. Future transfers require both a deed passage and a certificate transfer, thereby adding further complications. For these reasons, and because (a) covered property cannot be removed from the system without court permission and (b) the system has not been tested for constitutional validity, Torrens certificates are not widely employed.

Closing the sale

The contract for sale is a binding legal contract that states the manner in which ownership rights are to be transferred. At the time of transfer, a statement is prepared indicating the manner in which expenses are to be prorated, the costs to be paid by the buyer, and the costs to be paid by the seller. All expenses are subject to negotiation, but the purchaser normally is required to pay (a) appraisal fees, survey

FIGURE 11–3
Closing statement

Month _____ Day _____ Year _____
Composite closing statement

Seller's statement		Item	Buyer's statement	
Debit	Credit		Debit	Credit
$ .00	$ .00	Total purchase price	$ .00	$ .00
_____	_____	Binder deposit	_____	_____
_____	_____	First mortgage—balance	_____	_____
_____	_____	Second mortgage	_____	_____
		Prorations and Prepayments:		
_____	_____	Rent	_____	_____
_____	_____	Interest—first mortgage	_____	_____
_____	_____	Interest—second mortgage	_____	_____
_____	_____	Prepayment—first mortgage	_____	_____
_____	_____	Prepayment—second mortgage	_____	_____
_____	_____	Insurance	_____	_____
_____	_____	Taxes—city	_____	_____
_____	_____	Taxes—county	_____	_____
		Expenses:		
_____	_____	Abstract/continuation	_____	_____
_____	_____	Attorney's fee	_____	_____
		Documentary stamps:		
_____	_____	Mortgage—note	_____	_____
_____	_____	State on deed	_____	_____
_____	_____		_____	_____
_____	_____	Intangible tax—mortgage	_____	_____
		Recording:		
_____	_____	Mortgage	_____	_____
_____	_____	Deed	_____	_____
_____	_____	Title insurance	_____	_____
_____	_____	Brokerage	_____	_____
_____	_____	Miscellaneous	_____	_____
_____	_____	Total—debits and credits	_____	_____
		Balance due: Balance due:		
_____	_____	to seller from buyer	_____	_____
		Grand totals		

Broker's statement

	Receipts	Disbursements
Binder deposit	$ .00	$ .00
Check from buyer at closing	_____	_____
Brokerage fee	_____	_____
Check to seller at closing	_____	_____
Seller's expense (less brokerage)	_____	_____
Buyer's expense	_____	_____
Grand totals	_____	_____

FIGURE 11–4
RESPA

A. U.S. DEPARTMENT OF HOUSING AND URBAN DEVELOPMENT DISCLOSURE/SETTLEMENT STATEMENT	B. TYPE OF LOAN

B. TYPE OF LOAN

1. ☐ FHA   2. ☐ FMH/   3. ☐ CONV. UNINS.

4. ☐ VA   5. ☐ CONV. INS.

6. FILE NUMBER	7. LOAN NUMBER

8. MORTG. INS. CASE NO.

C. NOTE: This form is furnished to give you information about your settlement costs.

☐ STATEMENT OF ACTUAL COSTS. Amounts paid to and by the settlement agent are shown. Items marked "(p.o.c.)" were paid outside the closing; they are shown here for informational purposes and are not included in totals.

D. NAME OF BORROWER	E. SELLER	F. LENDER

G. PROPERTY LOCATION	H. SETTLEMENT AGENT	I. DATES
		LOAN COMMITMENT
	PLACE OF SETTLEMENT	SETTLEMENT	DATE OF PRORATIONS IF DIFFERENT FROM SETTLEMENT

J. SUMMARY OF BORROWER'S TRANSACTION		K. SUMMARY OF SELLER'S TRANSACTION	
100. GROSS AMOUNT DUE FROM BORROWER:		**400. GROSS AMOUNT DUE TO SELLER:**	
		401. Contract sales price	
101. Contract sales price		402. Personal property	
102. Personal property		403.	
103. Settlement charges to borrower (from line 1400, Section L)		404.	
104.		Adjustments for items paid by seller in advance:	
105.		405. City/town taxes to	
Adjustments for items paid by seller in advance:		406. County taxes to	
		407. Assessments to	
106. City/town taxes to		408. to	
107. County taxes to		409. to	
108. Assessments to		410. to	
109. to		411. to	
110. to		**420. GROSS AMOUNT DUE TO SELLER**	
111. to			
112. to			
120. GROSS AMOUNT DUE FROM BORROWER:			
		500. REDUCTIONS IN AMOUNT DUE TO SELLER:	
200. AMOUNTS PAID BY OR IN BEHALF OF BORROWER:		501. Payoff of first mortgage loan	
		502. Payoff of second mortgage loan	
201. Deposit or earnest money		503. Settlement charges to seller (from line 1400, Section L)	
202. Principal amount of new loan(s)			
203. Existing loan(s) taken subject to		504. Existing loan(s) taken subject to	
204.		505.	
205.		506.	
Credits to borrower for items unpaid by seller:		507.	
		508.	
206. City/town taxes to		509.	
207. County taxes to			
208. Assessments to		Credits to borrower for items unpaid by seller:	
209. to			
210. to		510. City/town taxes to	
211. to		511. County taxes to	
212. to		512. Assessments to	
220. TOTAL AMOUNTS PAID BY OR IN BEHALF OF BORROWER		513. to	
300. CASH AT SETTLEMENT REQUIRED FROM OR PAYABLE TO BORROWER:		514. to	
		515. to	
301. Gross amount due from borrower (from line 120)		**520. TOTAL REDUCTIONS IN AMOUNT DUE TO SELLER:**	
		600. CASH TO SELLER FROM SETTLEMENT:	
302. Less amounts paid by or in behalf of borrower (from line 220)	( )	601. Gross amount due to seller (from line 420)	
		602. Less total reductions in amount due to seller (from line 520)	( )
303. CASH (☐ REQUIRED FROM) OR (☐ PAYAbLE TO) BORROWER:		**603. CASH TO SELLER FROM SETTLEMENT**	

HUD 1   REV. 1/76 AS & AS (1322)

FIGURE 11–4 (*continued*)

L. SETTLEMENT CHARGES	PAID FROM BORROWER'S FUNDS	PAID FROM SELLER'S FUNDS
700. SALES/BROKER'S COMMISSION based on price $ @ %		
701. Total commission paid by seller Division of commission as follows:		
702. $ to		
703. $ to		
704.		
800. ITEMS PAYABLE IN CONNECTION WITH LOAN.		
801. Loan Origination fee %		
802. Loan Discount %		
803. Appraisal Fee to		
804. Credit Report to		
805. Lender's inspection fee		
806. Mortgage Insurance application fee to		
807. Assumption/refinancing fee		
808.		
809.		
810.		
811.		
900. ITEMS REQUIRED BY LENDER TO BE PAID IN ADVANCE.		
901. Interest from to @ $ /day		
902. Mortgage insurance premium for mo. to		
903. Hazard insurance premium for yrs. to		
904. yrs. to		
905.		
1000. RESERVES DEPOSITED WITH LENDER FOR:		
1001. Hazard insurance mo. @ $ /mo.		
1002. Mortgage insurance mo. @ $ /mo.		
1003. City property taxes mo. @ $ /mo.		
1004. County property taxes mo. @ $ /mo.		
1005. Annual assessments mo. @ $ /mo.		
1006. mo. @ $ /mo.		
1007. mo. @ $ /mo.		
1008. mo. @ $ /mo.		
1100. TITLE CHARGES:		
1101. Settlement or closing fee to		
1102. Abstract or title search to		
1103. Title examination to		
1104. Title insurance binder to		
1105. Document preparation to		
1106. Notary fees to		
1107. Attorney's Fees to		
(includes above items No.:		
1108. Title insurance to		
(includes above items No.:		
1109. Lender's coverage $		
1110. Owner's coverage $		
1111.		
1112.		
1113.		
1200. GOVERNMENT RECORDING AND TRANSFER CHARGES		
1201. Recording fees: Deed $; Mortgage $ Releases $		
1202. City/county tax/stamps: Deed $; Mortgage $		
1203. State tax/stamps: Deed $; Mortage $		
1204.		
1300. ADDITIONAL SETTLEMENT CHARGES		
1301. Survey to		
1302. Pest inspection to		
1303.		
1304.		
1305.		
1400. TOTAL SETTLEMENT CHARGES (entered on lines 103 and 503, Sections J and K)		

The Undersigned Acknowledges Receipt of This Disclosure Settlement Statement and Agrees to the Correctness Thereof.

_____   _____
Buyer   Seller

fees, and photograph costs; (*b*) title search charges or title insurance premiums; (*c*) recording and transfer fees; (*d*) attorney's fees; and (*e*) costs incidental to obtaining a new mortgage, such as a credit report, mortgage origination fees, and special title insurance fees to protect the lender. The seller typically pays (*a*) broker's commission, (*b*) repair costs needed to improve the property to the condition specified in the contract for sale, (*c*) state revenue stamps, (*d*) attorney's fees, and (*e*) discounts charged by lenders on Federal Housing Administration (FHA) and Veterans Administration (VA) mortgages. The most important items to be prorated are property taxes, prepaid homeowner's insurance premiums, and prepaid tenant rent. Utility bills can be prorated when it is not convenient to obtain a special billing at the date of closing.

Closing costs vary widely among transactions, as would be indicated by the nature of the charges. A small single-family home in an established subdivision typically requires much less work in preparing an appraisal, a title search, a survey, or a cost proration than would a farm property or a high-rise apartment building. Nearly every service performed does have a minimum charge, however, making the minimum total cost several hundred dollars in most cases. Certain services such as the appraisal can be eliminated at times, but the title search and attorney's fee are almost inescapable. Thus, closing costs must be anticipated in nearly every real estate transaction.

The closing statement is the final accounting in a real property conveyance. All costs, services, and prorated expenses are listed in the closing statement so that all parties understand their responsibilities and the flow of funds that results from these responsibilities (see Figure 11–3 for an example of a closing document).

Closing documents similar to that shown in Figure 11–3 may remain in use to accomplish the final settlement. In addition to these forms, most lenders must complete a Uniform Settlement Statement (see Figure 11–4), to be given to the borrower when title to a one–four-family property is transferred.[4] This requirement was imposed by the Real Estate Settlement Procedures Act of 1974 (RESPA). RESPA resulted from the lack of uniformity in settlement procedures, from observed inadequate legal protection for the buyer in the settlement process, and from the belief that settlement costs were sometimes excessive.[5]

---

[4] Not all lenders must comply with the Real Estate Settlement Procedures Act. For instance, individuals are exempted from compliance if they are not lending on the security of a "federally assisted" mortgage. Most home mortgage loans, however, are subject to the act.

[5] Paul Barron, *Federal Regulation in Real Estate: The Real Estate Settlement Procedures Act* (Boston: Warren, Gorham and Lamont, 1975).

RESPA applies when title to one–four-family units is transferred. Exempted from the act are refinancings, construction loans, junior mortgages, transfers with the existing loan being assumed or taken subject to (unless the loan terms are modified or the lender imposes charges of more than $50), real estate purchased with intent to resell in the ordinary course of business, vacant lot sales (unless the loan will be used in part to finance construction of a dwelling), sales involving properties of 25 acres or more, and mobile home purchases (unless both the mobile home and the lot are purchased jointly).

A lender gives the homebuyer a booklet describing RESPA when the prospective buyer makes written application for a loan. At this time, the lender also provides a "good faith" estimate of the amount or range of the specific closing costs the borrower is likely to incur. Points or discounts associated with the loan, however, need not be estimated at this time. The Uniform Settlement Statement itself (see Figure 11–4) is to be made available to the borrower one business day prior to closing at the borrower's request. At this time all closing costs are specified, including points and discounts. The borrower is given a completed Uniform Settlement Statement within a reasonable period after closing, unless the borrower has waived this right.

Other functions

Purchasing an option. An *option* is an agreement between buyer and seller in which the seller agrees to hold an offer open for a specified time and the buyer agrees to pay a sum of money as consideration. No real property ownership rights pass at the time the option is granted. The buyer is merely purchasing the right to buy at a fixed price within a stated period. If the offer is accepted, a purchase contract results. The consideration paid for the option is kept by the seller regardless of the buyer's decision.

Employing an escrow agent. An escrow operation is one in which a person is asked to serve as a neutral third party to a business transaction. In the usual situation a banker or other lending institution official is employed to hold a seller's property deed and a buyer's purchase money until the property title has been cleared. The third party, referred to as an escrow agent, escrow company, or escrow holder, requires a detailed set of instructions regarding the provisions, such as when title is to pass, how delivery is to occur, and what actions are to be taken if impediments of title or other complications arise. Both parties to the business transaction can work together to terminate the escrow arrangement, but neither party can terminate it alone. Since the agreement is legally binding, it should be composed in such a manner that little or nothing is subject to interpretation by the escrow holder. The instructions should be complete and thorough, and provision should be made for means by which both parties can reach agreement upon any item of uncertainty.

Exchanging properties. Current tax laws concerning capital gains frequently make it desirable to trade one parcel of real estate for another rather than to effect separate sale and repurchase transactions. Most Realtors have a contract form for this that specifies the exact nature of each property and the manner in which the commission is to be paid. The exchange contract contains most of the aspects of the contract for sale discussed previously in this chapter.

The commission on an exchange is agreed to by all parties to the transaction. The amount is often determined by charging a flat percentage of the exchange value of each property (actually two commissions), although wide variations in practice are found. Most brokers who specialize in selling homes do not operate as intermediaries between two trading parties. In the residential real estate market very few cases arise in which a person wishing to trade a home would desire to trade the home for the exact home which another person wishes to trade. Therefore, the broker acts as a principal for both parties, buying their old homes and selling them new ones. The "pure" exchange arrangement in which the broker does not acquire title to either property is more commonly used in business and investment real estate.

SUMMARY

Basic conveyancing functions examined in this chapter include (a) listing property, (b) making offers, (c) searching titles, (d) closing transactions, and (e) transferring partial ownership rights. Legal documents are presented, and the important elements of each are discussed. The important point made in the chapter is that planning for investment return, income taxation, and liability protection can be the most productive use of time only when the investor achieves skill at conveyancing. He or she must learn to minimize time in activities that facilitate the basic task, and developing skills in conveyancing is the only way to avoid losing a great deal of time in working with deeds, mortgages, contracts, and other documents.

Attorneys can relieve the investor of much of the conveyancing burden, but only the investor can evaluate conveyancing documents in terms of varied objectives. A carefully drawn statement of objectives, coupled with sound ownership and tax planning, should help the investor develop a sound pattern of action to follow in conveyancing.

QUESTIONS FOR REVIEW

1. What is a statute of frauds?
2. Identify ten provisions normally covered in an offer for sale.
3. What costs are to be paid by the buyer and the seller in a normal closing statement?
4. What are the basic deed forms?
5. What is a listing contract? Identify the principal items covered in a typical exclusive right-of-sale listing.
6. How are titles searched? What evidence of a good title can one obtain?
7. What is a land contract?
8. What is an option on real estate?

REFERENCES

Crean, Michael J. *Principles of Real Estate Analysis*. New York: D. Van Nostrand, 1979, chaps. 3–9.

Curtis, Clayton C. *Real Estate for the New Practitioner*. 6th ed. Gainesville, Fla.: B. J. Publishing, 1980, chaps. 3, 4, and 5.

French, William B., and Lusk, Harold F. *Law of the Real Estate Business*. 4th ed. Homewood, Ill.: Richard D. Irwin, 1979.

Friedman, Milton R. *Contracts and Conveyances of Real Property*. New York: Practicing Law Institute, 1972.

Gray, Charles D., and Steinberg, Joseph L. *Real Estate Sales Contracts: From Preparation through Closing*. Englewood Cliffs, N.J.: Prentice-Hall, 1970.

Harvey, David C. B. *Harvey Law of Real Property Title and Closing*. 3 vols. New York: Clark Boardman, 1972.

Kratovil, Robert, and Werner, Raymond J. *Real Estate Law*. 7th ed. Englewood Cliffs, N.J.: Prentice-Hall, 1979.

chapter 12

Real estate taxation

Since real estate, unlike most economic goods and products, is physically immobile, it is particularly vulnerable to taxation. All that a government must do to levy and collect taxes is to identify the parcel of real estate and its owner. The property cannot be moved to another taxing district; and if the owner cannot or will not pay the tax, the property can be confiscated and sold to satisfy the government's claim.

The constitutional requirement that effectively prohibits a property tax to be levied by the federal government provides little solace to a property owner who must usually pay 2 to 4 percent of the property's value each year to local taxing authorities.[1] The property tax burden can be especially onerous to the moderate- or low-income family struggling to obtain the benefits of home ownership. And even for more affluent property owners, the tax liability may be a negative inducement to development of a site to its most efficient use, maintenance and rehabilitation of existing properties, or the conversion of older uses into new or combined uses.

Yet the property tax is probably the most pervasive of all taxes. In spite of heated criticism of both the theoretical basis for the tax and its practical effect and administration, the tax survives, just as important as ever to local governments and taxing districts—and perhaps more firmly entrenched than ever. Undoubtedly, its persistence stems from the several substantial advantages it carries over possible alternative taxes—its ability to raise large sums of revenue, its amenability to small incremental changes in tax rates, the immobility of the tax object, and its historic tie to local governments and local needs. Despite its many defects and possible inequities, the property tax seems likely to remain the most important revenue source for local governments and taxing districts during the foreseeable future.

---

[1] The U.S. Constitution (Section 9) states: "No capitation, or other direct, tax shall be laid, unless in proportion to the census or enumeration herein before directed to be taken." The 16th Amendment, ratified in 1913, specifically exempted taxes on incomes from this requirement.

Nature of the property tax

The property tax is calculated as a percentage (or millage rate) of a property's value, or some equally applied portion thereof. Therefore, it is called an *ad valorem* tax. For example, a property appraised for taxation at $50,000 (in a jurisdiction where the tax rate is applied to 100 percent of market value) and located in a taxing area in which the total tax rate is 2.5 percent, or 25 mills, would be taxed $1,250 for the year.

Obviously, the tax liability of the property can be increased either by raising its appraised value or by increasing the tax rate. And in jurisdictions where the rate is applied to some percentage of market value (say 50 percent), the tax liability can be increased by increasing the applicable percentage (to, say, 55 percent). It should be apparent that unless restrictions are placed on tax rates, percentages of market value that may be taxed, and appraisal procedures, a property's tax burden can be set at any required or desired level.

Many states have attempted to mitigate some of the inequities of the property tax by requiring professional appraisal procedures, limiting tax rates, requiring standardized value ratios for taxation, and exempting certain classes of owners from a portion of the tax. For example, Florida requires that all property be taxed at 100 percent of its market value and that tax rates be limited to 28 mills (10 mills per taxing authority of city and county and 8 mills per school district). Exempted from the rate limitation, however, is a rate for interest and capital retirement of bonds approved by voters in the jurisdiction. Florida also provides a $5,000 homestead exemption. After five years of residency, this exemption is increased to $25,000. There is no additional exemption for the elderly, but a disabled and immobile homeowner is entitled to a 100 percent exemption. Veterans who are disabled at least 10 percent receive a $500 exemption.

Thus, a homeowner who has lived in the state more than five years, qualifies for homestead, and lives in a community where the tax rates are ten mills for the county, eight mills for the city, and eight mills for the school district would have to pay $650 on property appraised at $50,000.

County	$0.010 \times \$25,000 =$	$250
City	$0.008 \times \$25,000 =$	200
School district	$0.008 \times \$25,000 =$	200
		$650

If the homeowner qualified for none of the exemptions, the total tax bill would be $1,300.

$$0.026 \times \$50,000 = \$1,300$$

Additional exemptions extend to certain corporate classes of property owners. Property owned by governments—federal, state, county, or city—is exempted. And property owned by nonprofit organizations, such as churches, schools, and public authorities, is usually exempted. Sometimes a public authority, such as a local housing authority or a port authority, will agree to make payments to the local community in lieu of property taxes.

Establishing the tax rate

The tax rate for a jurisdiction (such as a city, a county, or a school district) is calculated by dividing the budgeted expenditures less non-property tax income by the jurisdiction's total assessed valuation minus exemptions:

$$R = \frac{E - I}{V - X}$$

where:

R = Tax rate
E = Budgeted expenditures
I = Expected income from sources other than the property tax
V = Total assessed valuation
X = Value of exemptions

For example, if a community's budget calls for expenditures of $5 million, nonproperty tax income is expected to be $1 million, there is $450 million of assessed value in the community, and the value of all exemptions is estimated to be $50 million, the tax rate would be calculated as follows:

$$R = \frac{\$5,000,000 - \$1,000,000}{\$450,000,000 - \$50,000,000} = 0.01$$

Converted to mills (dollars per thousand), the tax rate would be ten mills.

Special assessments

A community may require that public improvements adjacent to private property be paid for by the private property owners. Taxes for this purpose are termed *special assessments* and are used to finance such improvements as streets, gutters, sewers, and sidewalks. The rationale for special assessments is that the improvements increase the property's value and therefore the property owner should pay at least part of their cost. Most cities share the cost of the improvements with the property owners, charging them only a percentage (say 75 percent) of the total cost or only for the materials used.

Most cities will not make specific improvements and assess property owners, unless owners of more than 50 percent of the street frontage request the improvements. The total cost assigned the property owners is usually allocated on a front foot basis and charged to each owner (on both sides of a street) according to the number of front feet owned.

Special assessments result in a lien on the property, equal in priority to regular property taxes. Unpaid assessments can result in foreclosure and sale of the property at public auction. Thus, a buyer should not purchase a property without knowing whether or not there are special assessments, and their dollar amount, if they exist.

ECONOMIC AND SOCIAL ISSUES

As mentioned earlier in the chapter, the property tax has been severely criticized for several reasons. Controversy continues to rage over the property tax. Occasionally modifications in the tax are made to lessen the impact of some criticism or to lessen the impact of the tax on a particular segment of the population. Recently in California the property tax was radically changed, but nowhere has it been repealed. Its important advantages seem to outweigh its disadvantages. For complete evaluation of the tax it is necessary to consider some of the criticisms and issues surrounding it.

The property tax is regressive.   When a tax falls more heavily on lower income than on higher income taxpayers, the tax is termed *regressive*. The property tax has been accused of this malady. The principal reasoning for this contention is that the value of housing does not increase proportionately to increases in income. People having incomes of $200,000 per year typically do not live in homes ten times as valuable as those occupied by people having incomes of $20,000 per year. The Keynesian consumption function applies to housing, as well as other consumer goods. Since the property tax is based upon property values (*ad valorem*), higher income taxpayers tend to pay less property tax *per dollar of income* than do lower income taxpayers. Thus, the tax is regressive.

Another, although secondary, reason for the contention that the property tax is regressive is that some studies have shown that owners of poor housing occupied by low-income tenants pay property taxes at a higher rate than do owners of higher value housing. For example, Peterson et al. found such a pattern in four major cities.[2] Presumably,

---

[2] George E. Peterson, Arthur P. Solomon, Hadi Madjid, and William C. Apgar, Jr., *Property Taxes, Housing, and the Cities* (Lexington, Mass.: Lexington Books, 1973).

however, such patterns result from poor appraisal practices and could be corrected.

Netzer, in his landmark study, agrees that the property tax *payments* are regressive. However, he realizes that there may also be disparities in the benefits or services derived from the tax. Perhaps lower income taxpayers require more police and fire protection, place more reliance on the court system, and utilize more heavily the public health, welfare, and school systems. Netzer's conclusion regarding this aspect is that the net result of the tax is *not* regressive, when the benefits are taken into account.[3] Thus, lower income taxpayers utilize the services provided by the property tax to a greater degree than the additional cost to them.

The property tax inhibits construction of new housing.   This criticism usually implies adoption of a single property tax on land only. Henry George denounced taxes on personal property, structures, and improvements to a site as inequitable and a deterrent to investment.[4] Certainly we would anticipate a much greater investment in all types of structures, including housing, if taxes were removed from them. A much greater burden would be shifted to landowners, and much earlier development of raw land would be encouraged. However, it is doubtful that a single tax on land could raise the revenue necessary to provide the existing level of municipal, county, and state services. Heilbrun has concluded: "These [disadvantages] are sufficiently important to make site value unacceptable as the sole basis of the contemporary real estate tax, but they do not rule out a compromise involving use of a relatively heavier land tax."[5] Also, econometric studies attempting to estimate land values separately from improvements have not been promising.[6] Netzer, however, has concluded that a combination of user charges, particularly for congestion and pollution, and land-value taxation would be the best system.[7]

The property tax inhibits maintenance and rehabilitation of existing housing.   Again, the argument is advanced that the absence of annual

---

[3] Dick Netzer, *Economics of the Property Tax* (Washington, D.C.: Brookings Institution, 1966), pp. 45–62.

[4] Henry George, *Progress and Poverty* (New York: Robert Schalkenbach Foundation, 1948), book 8, chap. 3.

[5] James Heilbrun, *Real Estate Taxes and Urban Housing* (New York: Columbia University Press, 1966), p. 169.

[6] See Eugene F. Brigham, "The Determinants of Residential Land Values," *Land Economics* 41 (November 1965): 325–34; and Paul B. Downing, "Estimating Residential Land Value by Multivariate Analysis," in *The Assessment of Land Value,* edited by Daniel M. Holland for the Committee on Taxation, Resources, and Economic Development (Madison: University of Wisconsin Press, 1970), pp. 101–23.

[7] Dick Netzer, "Is There Too Much Reliance on the Local Property Tax?" in *Property Tax Reform,* edited by George E. Peterson (Washington, D.C.: John C. Lincoln Institute and Urban Institute, 1973), p. 23.

property taxes would allow owners to maintain their properties in better condition. Such a contention, however, seems unlikely, since numerous properties today are maintained in superior condition. Most property owners probably could decrease their maintenance expenditures, if they so wished, but they realize such action would deplete their long-run income potential. Property tax forgiveness might have some beneficial impact on the maintenance of properties by lower income owners, but it is highly doubtful that all, if any, such tax savings would be channeled into property maintenance.

The effect of the property tax on rehabilitation is another matter, however. The property owner who considers the cost of rehabilitation may well regard the increased property tax (resulting from the property's increased value) to be sufficiently burdensome to forgo a modernization project. Undoubtedly, a substantial part of the "housing problem" could be alleviated if the cost impediment to rehabilitation could be eliminated.

Heilbrun suggests that "tax abatement" might be applied to the *additional* values created by new construction or rehabilitation.[8] Such an abatement would (compared with the present system) encourage new construction and rehabilitation that create greater values through the more efficient operation or better condition of properties. The original tax base would be maintained. And the revenue obtained from properties that were not allowed to deteriorate would offset the revenue lost by not taxing the increased values.

The property tax is not based on ability to pay. One of the prime criteria of an equitable tax is that it be related to the taxpayer's ability to pay. This criterion is often violated by the property tax, say its critics. Relatively high-income taxpayers may elect to live in modest homes, while other, lower income taxpayers may, because of large families or personal desires, stretch to afford larger, more valuable homes. The higher income taxpayers will undoubtedly hold their wealth in such assets as stocks, bonds, or savings accounts. Intangibles and other personal property are often taxed at lower rates than real estate. The property tax thus places a greater strain on the real estate owner than on the owners of other types of property.

It must be pointed out, of course, that the earnings of most assets are taxed by the federal government, and some assets are taxed by state and municipal governments as well. Homeowners gain the advantage of not having to pay income tax on rent saved. They also gain another substantial benefit from the mortgage interest deduction.

The property tax is inherently subject to poor administration. This criticism, while admitting that administrative improvements may be possible, contends that there will always be difficulties in administer-

---

[8] Heilbrun, *Real Estate Taxes and Urban Housing,* p. 171.

ing the property tax. The large number of assessing jurisdictions and the popular election of assessors seem to guarantee that many assessors will be less than totally competent to handle the task of property appraisal. While important progress in upgrading assessors' qualifications has been made in many counties, many assessing officials (particularly in small counties) have little or no education or background in property appraisal. Inefficiencies, inequities, and errors are bound to occur in these cases.

Additionally, because of the political nature of assessors' offices, assessors are usually subject to great pressure for favorable appraisals. Most assessors have wisely insulated themselves from individual requests, but assessors undoubtedly hesitate to raise the assessments of large groups of voters or politically influential property holders beyond an acceptable level. It should be noted that assessment decisions can be appealed to a board of review and to the courts.

Assessors have attempted to improve their own competence through their organization, the International Association of Assessing Officials (IAAO), and by attendance at courses sponsored by the major appraisal organizations. Also, some state governments have established statewide agencies to audit the appraisal practices and valuations of county assessing officials, to insure that minimum standards are met.

The property tax varies widely among geographic areas. Even if the property tax is applied uniformly within a county, it may be applied differently in the next county. And its variation among states may be even greater. Since each county employs a different appraisal staff, tax appraisals for similar properties are almost certain to vary among counties. And different states operate under differing legal requirements with regard to the assessment function. In order to create greater uniformity among counties, some states, as noted above, have established agencies to audit the assessments and appraisal practices of the counties. Their objective is usually to ascertain that laws mandating assessments at a specified percentage of market value (say 100 percent) are being carried out and that appraisal procedures are being uniformly applied. Undoubtedly such agencies contribute to a more equitable assessment of property taxes within a state.

Some critics, notably Benson, have suggested that the property tax be administered regionally.[9] Regional administration would reduce the number of assessors and facilitate uniformity in assessment prac-

---

[9] George C. S. Benson, Sumner Benson, Harold McClelland, and Procter Thompson, *The American Property Tax: Its History, Administration, and Economic Impact* (Claremont, Calif.: Claremont Men's College, Institute for Studies in Federalism and the Lincoln School of Public Finance, 1965).

tices. For the foreseeable future, however, local administration of the property tax appears to be firmly entrenched.

Proposition 13

Although property taxes are an important source of local revenue, taxpayers are beginning to protest high levels of taxation. The first major property tax cutback occurred in June 1978, when the voters of the state of California passed Proposition 13. This law cuts property tax assessments from 3.2 percent of market value to 1 percent of market value, a 68 percent decrease. The annual loss of revenue is about $7 billion.

Ironically, this tax cut has been increasing taxpayers' federal and state income taxes. A large federal deduction is lost due to the lowered property tax. California's income tax is tied to the federal income tax, so it also is increased. The actual amount of tax relief is about $6.4 billion.

There are many arguments for and against Proposition 13, including those discussed in this chapter. California, however, was operating under a state revenue surplus at the time of the tax cut. Therefore, the long-term effects of Próposition 13 still remain to be seen.

SUMMARY

Counties, cities, and taxing districts usually obtain most of their revenues from the property tax. The tax is levied within the geographic jurisdiction of the governmental unit. The amount of tax levied is determined by the unit's budgeted expenditures, less all nonproperty tax income. To obtain a tax percentage, this amount is then divided by the assessed value of all taxable property in the jurisdiction less the value of all exemptions. The millage rate can then be obtained by converting the tax percentage to dollars per $1,000 of value.

The property tax has received much criticism. The principal arguments against it are: (*a*) the tax is regressive; (*b*) it inhibits new construction; (*c*) it inhibits the maintenance and rehabilitation of existing housing; (*d*) it is not based on ability to pay; (*e*) it is inherently subject to poor administration; and (*f*) there are wide geographic variations in the tax. Even with such criticism, however, the property tax seems well entrenched.

The property tax's three big advantages are its ability to raise large amounts of revenue, its long history of usage in the United States, and its preference to other types of taxes that also produce problems and inequities. The advantages are so great that they counterbalance all of the criticisms and defects. Undoubtedly the property tax will continue to be the largest source of revenue for local governments. Owners of real property should not expect to be relieved of this burden in the foreseeable future.

QUESTIONS FOR REVIEW

1. How is a community's property *tax base* established?
2. How is a community's *tax rate* established?
3. Identify other important sources of a community's revenue.
4. What is a *mill?* How is the millage tax rate derived?
5. What is the role of the community's budget in determining its property tax rate?
6. Why is the property tax often considered regressive?
7. What effect does the property tax probably have on the maintenance and rehabilitation of housing?
8. Why is the property tax often considered to be poorly administered?
9. If the property tax were abolished, how could local governments raise needed revenues? Evaluate each method in comparison with the property tax.
10. A city's budget for the coming year calls for expenditures of $30 million. Non-property-tax income of $8 million is expected, and the city contains $1.4 billion of taxable property value. What tax rate is called for (*a*) in percentage terms? (*b*) In mills?
11. Calculate the amount of property tax you would be required to pay in the following situation. Your state allows a homestead exemption of $5,000; it also provides a $5,000 exemption for homeowners over 65 from school taxes only.
    a. You, a homeowner, are 68 years old.
    b. Your home in the city is assessed at $60,000.
    c. You qualify for homestead exemption.
    d. Millage tax rates are: city—ten mills; county—eight mills; and school district—six mills.
12. A street is to be paved and gutters installed in front of your property. The city assesses property owners 75 percent of the cost of such improvements, which are estimated to be $40 per running foot. Your property has 100 feet of frontage on one side of the street to be improved. How much will be your special assessment?

REFERENCES

Benson, George C. S.; Benson, Sumner; McClelland, Harold; and Thompson, Procter. *The American Property Tax: Its History, Administration, and Economic Impact.* Claremont, Calif.: Claremont Men's College, Institute for Studies in Federalism and the Lincoln School of Public Finance, 1965.

Curtis, Clayton C.   *Real Estate for the New Practitioner.* 6th ed. Gainesville, Fla.: B. J. Publishing, 1980, chap. 8.

Heilbrun, James.   *Real Estate Taxes and Urban Housing.* New York: Columbia University Press, 1966.

Holland, Daniel M., ed.   *The Assessment of Land Value.* Madison: University of Wisconsin Press, 1970.

Lindholm, Richard W., ed.   *Property Taxation and the Finance of Education.* Madison: University of Wisconsin Press, 1974.

Netzer, Dick.   *Economics of the Property Tax.* Washington, D.C.: Brookings Institution, 1966.

Peterson, George E., ed.   *Property Tax Reform.* Washington, D.C.: John C. Lincoln Institute and Urban Institute, 1973.

chapter 13

Federal income taxation

The profitability of real estate investment decisions often depends upon the amount and timing of the federal income tax. As demonstrated in Chapter 5, the federal income tax, as well as the annual debt service, is deducted from NOI in deriving cash flow from a property or project. The greater the amount of tax that must be paid, the lower will be an investor's cash flow. And even if the same total amount of taxes were paid over a property's useful life, lower taxes in earlier years would make the project more profitable than either a level annual tax liability or higher taxes followed by lower taxes.

Two important types of considerations have guided Congress in the formulation of tax policies and laws. The first consideration is equity. Since the federal income tax is levied on the general populace, relatively equal and fair treatment of all taxpayers is a desirable, if perhaps unattainable, goal. In this regard, economists and other tax experts generally agree that the taxpayer's burden should reflect the ability to pay. Thus, a taxpayer who earns $10,000 per year should pay less in taxes than one who earns $50,000 per year. Furthermore, Congress has decided that equity and fairness require the $50,000-per-year taxpayer to pay a higher *percentage* of income in taxes than is paid by a lower income taxpayer. This concept of equity is the basis for our graduated income tax system.

The second major consideration concerns the social and economic needs of the country. The tax burden can be imposed in such a way as to favor certain taxpayers over others. Taxpayers who make favored types of investments, or those who hold assets for long-term gains (rather than short-term speculative profits), have been awarded relatively favorable tax treatment. For example, the tax factors affecting real estate in part reflect the felt need to provide adequate housing and sufficient amounts of other real estate resources, such as factories, warehouses, shopping centers, and office buildings. The employment generated directly and indirectly by construction activity has been a continuing concern.

Income tax advantages promote the social goal of home ownership. When the federal government instituted supply-oriented housing programs, investors were given tax advantages in addition to subsidy dollars to induce the desired investment in housing for the disadvantaged. As the emphasis in federal housing programs switched from the provision of new low- and moderate-income housing to the use of the existing housing stock, renovation was encouraged by permitting rehabilitation expenditures to be amortized over a five-year period.

These are general statements regarding governmental objectives. The individual taxpayer has somewhat different objectives, seeking to maximize aftertax cash income by taking advantage of favorable tax provisions to the fullest extent possible.

Taxpayer objectives

Most persons who have investable funds are earning taxable income from their business or profession, investments in stocks, taxable bonds, interest-bearing certificates/accounts, or nonsheltered real estate. As a given person's annual taxable income increases, he or she finds that the investment objective must change to maximize profits. As an example, note that in the accompanying 1979 Federal Tax Rate Schedule for a married couple filing jointly, each dollar of taxable income above $60,000 is taxed at a 54 percent rate. For the person earning exactly that amount, investment in a 12 percent certificate of deposit would produce a 6 percent aftertax benefit. The same person could purchase a 7.5 percent tax-exempt bond, such as those issued by various instrumentalities of a state government, and increase the yield by 25 percent on an aftertax basis (7.5/6 = 125 percent of 6 percent yield).

This investor would also find desirable a real estate investment in which depreciation and interest exactly offset the net operating income. Such an investment is said to provide tax-sheltered income.

Some highly depreciable investments have a positive cash flow after operations and debt service, yet the depreciation is so great that

1979 Tax Rate Schedules

If you cannot use one of the Tax Tables, figure your tax on the amount on Schedule TC, Part I, line 3, by using the appropriate Tax Rate Schedule on this page. Enter the tax on Schedule TC, Part I, line 4.

Note: *Your new zero bracket amount has been built into these Tax Rate Schedules.*

SCHEDULE X—Single Taxpayers

Use this schedule if you checked Filing Status Box 1 on Form 1040—

Not over $2,300 .... —0—

Over—	But not over—	Enter on Schedule TC, Part I, line 4:	of the amount over—
$2,300	$3,400	14%	$2,300
$3,400	$4,400	$154+16%	$3,400
$4,400	$6,500	$314+18%	$4,400
$6,500	$8,500	$692+19%	$6,500
$8,500	$10,800	$1,072+21%	$8,500
$10,800	$12,900	$1,555+24%	$10,800
$12,900	$15,000	$2,059+26%	$12,900
$15,000	$18,200	$2,605+30%	$15,000
$18,200	$23,500	$3,565+34%	$18,200
$23,500	$28,800	$5,367+39%	$23,500
$28,800	$34,100	$7,434+44%	$28,800
$34,100	$41,500	$9,766+49%	$34,100
$41,500	$55,300	$13,392+55%	$41,500
$55,300	$81,800	$20,982+63%	$55,300
$81,800	$108,300	$37,677+68%	$81,800
$108,300	....	$55,697+70%	$108,300

SCHEDULE Y—Married Taxpayers and Qualifying Widows and Widowers

Married Filing Joint Returns and Qualifying Widows and Widowers

Use this schedule if you checked Filing Status Box 2 or 5 on Form 1040—

Not over $3,400 .... —0—

Over—	But not over—	Enter on Schedule TC, Part I, line 4:	of the amount over—
$3,400	$5,500	14%	$3,400
$5,500	$7,600	$294+16%	$5,500
$7,600	$11,900	$630+18%	$7,600
$11,900	$16,000	$1,404+21%	$11,900
$16,000	$20,200	$2,265+24%	$16,000
$20,200	$24,600	$3,273+28%	$20,200
$24,600	$29,900	$4,505+32%	$24,600
$29,900	$35,200	$6,201+37%	$29,900
$35,200	$45,800	$8,162+43%	$35,200
$45,800	$60,000	$12,720+49%	$45,800
$60,000	$85,600	$19,678+54%	$60,000
$85,600	$109,400	$33,502+59%	$85,600
$109,400	$162,400	$47,544+64%	$109,400
$162,400	$215,400	$81,464+68%	$162,400
$215,400	....	$117,504+70%	$215,400

Married Filing Separate Returns

Use this schedule if you checked Filing Status Box 3 on Form 1040—

Not over $1,700 .... —0—

Over—	But not over—	Enter on Schedule TC, Part I, line 4:	of the amount over—
$1,700	$2,750	14%	$1,700
$2,750	$3,800	$147.00+16%	$2,750
$3,800	$5,950	$315.00+18%	$3,800
$5,950	$8,000	$702.00+21%	$5,950
$8,000	$10,100	$1,132.50+24%	$8,000
$10,100	$12,300	$1,636.50+28%	$10,100
$12,300	$14,950	$2,252.50+32%	$12,300
$14,950	$17,600	$3,100.50+37%	$14,950
$17,600	$22,900	$4,081.00+43%	$17,600
$22,900	$30,000	$6,360.00+49%	$22,900
$30,000	$42,800	$9,839.00+54%	$30,000
$42,800	$54,700	$16,751.00+59%	$42,800
$54,700	$81,200	$23,772.00+64%	$54,700
$81,200	$107,700	$40,732.00+68%	$81,200
$107,700	....	$58,752.00+70%	$107,700

SCHEDULE Z—Heads of Household (including certain married persons who live apart (and abandoned spouses)—see page 7 of the Instructions)

Use this schedule if you checked Filing Status Box 4 on Form 1040—

Not over $2,300 .... —0—

Over—	But not over—	Enter on Schedule TC, Part I, line 4:	of the amount over—
$2,300	$4,400	14%	$2,300
$4,400	$6,500	$294+16%	$4,400
$6,500	$8,700	$630+18%	$6,500
$8,700	$11,800	$1,026+22%	$8,700
$11,800	$15,000	$1,708+24%	$11,800
$15,000	$18,200	$2,476+26%	$15,000
$18,200	$23,500	$3,308+31%	$18,200
$23,500	$28,800	$4,951+36%	$23,500
$28,800	$34,100	$6,859+42%	$28,800
$34,100	$44,700	$9,085+46%	$34,100
$44,700	$60,600	$13,961+54%	$44,700
$60,600	$81,800	$22,547+59%	$60,600
$81,800	$108,300	$35,055+63%	$81,800
$108,300	$161,300	$51,750+68%	$108,300
$161,300	....	$87,790+70%	$161,300

Source: Internal Revenue Service.

the investment shows a negative taxable income. The Internal Revenue Service typically treats the income from a rented parcel of real estate as a business income, and, when it is negative, it can offset income received from other sources. The investment is then said to "throw off" tax shelter.

The value of tax shelter is a function of tax bracket. For example, a person who can absorb a negative investment income into other earned income at the 70 percent marginal tax bracket would logically pay more for the negative income investment than would a person who can absorb it at 40 percent. For example, a $1,000 loss taken at 70 percent is worth $700 after tax, while the same loss taken at 40 percent is worth only $400.

Federal income tax laws cover a myriad of situations in great detail. There is discussion in Congress every year about the tax loopholes, and articles appear in newspapers and magazines about how little tax some of the wealthiest people pay. The fact is that one must have substantial resources to take advantage of all the tax laws and regulations which can lead to a zero income tax. Long-term capital gains must be offset by long-term capital losses, and the overall investment portfolio must be selected carefully to generate negative taxable income equal to taxable earnings from all noninvestment sources. Timing of transactions is critical, and a ready pool of prospective investments must be kept available.

The investor of more moderate means frequently finds some shelter of ordinary income when his or her marginal tax bracket exceeds 50 percent. Investment counselors of various kinds are utilized, ranging from attorneys and certified public accountants to neighbors and friends.

One of the most interesting aspects of this phenomenon is that investment brokers are designing tax shelters to meet the specific needs of very specialized investor groups. They are establishing precedents in tax courts, taking advantage of important tax court rulings, and "creating" tax shelters which meet the requirements of the Internal Revenue Service. Obviously not all counselors are completely informed, and even the best ones lose a case at times, but they have saved investors millions in tax dollars. An investor reading this section should note that tax counseling help can be obtained from the references listed at the end of this chapter.

Consider the following concepts:

Concept	*Authors' comments*
1. Investors in all tax brackets enjoy income that is sheltered from tax.	An aftertax dollar of income is worth more than a before-tax dollar of income.
2. Investors whose next dollar of income will be taxed above 50 percent desire tax-sheltered income, and they can gain greatest aftertax benefits from investments whose negative income offsets other taxable income.	The true benefit of tax shelter throw-off begins at the 50 percent tax bracket, although persons of all brackets can use a loss throw-off to their benefit. Note that below the 50 percent tax bracket, $1 of ordinary taxable income is worth more than 50 cents, while $1 of loss is worth less than 50 cents.
3. An investor can absorb tax losses only to the extent that other taxable income is earned to be offset.	A tax shelter throw-off divided among several investors allows each to absorb his or her share of a loss at a higher bracket than would be in effect if one investor took the whole loss at a succession of lower and lower brackets.
4. Tax shelter can be created for the benefit of counselors and investors by careful planning:	

Concept	*Authors' comments*

a. Build or purchase improvements on leased land. Deduct land rent as well as depreciation on improvements.

The counselor might own the land and collect taxable rental income. Note: Landownership can be severed from existing property to establish a land lease.

b. Place tax shelter investors in a limited partnership, and charge them (deductible) fees for a wide variety of services. Take present and future cash flow as fees.

The counselor develops, leases, manages, finances, brokers, and so on, with fees for all services. This makes sense up to the level of cash flow. Fees are deductible to investors, taxable to the counselor.

c. Take rapid depreciation.

(1) Use rapid depreciation methods—double-declining balance, 1.5 or 1.25 declining balance, and sum-of-the-years' digits.

Involves recapture as ordinary income if sold too soon. May result in additional annual tax by triggering the minimum tax.

(2) Make a component breakdown. Depreciate each element of the property separately over the shortest life accepted by IRS.

Keep good records. Cost of components must be justified by invoices or, at times, by an independent appraisal.

(3) Consider renovation of housing or historic structures which qualify for five-year straight-line deduction of renovation cost plus tax credits.

There are limits on amount, and the property must qualify with IRS.

5. Seek seller financing on extended-interest-only terms.

Principal is not deductible.

6. The counselor might mark up the property's price and take back a high-interest-rate junior mortgage.

If done properly, this increases the tax basis to investors and increases the depreciation potential. It might also reduce the possible capital gain.

7. The counselor might have an agreement to buy out the investors' equity shares for $1 after most of the depreciation has been taken.

This is to avoid capital gain tax upon disposition. An alternative is for the investors to default on their shares rather than sell for $1.

This list of concepts is designed to meet the needs of investors whose only desire is to acquire deductions that offset other taxable income. Logically such investors can consider only the aftertax net annual dividend on their capital investment, given that all of their income is to be received from their dealings with the Internal Revenue Service. If this yield is acceptable, the loss of cash flow and capital gain potential becomes irrelevant.

The variables in developing a strategy for decision making are as follows:

1. Counselor/developer/"deal maker."
    a. Land purchased at lower price than that at which it is transferred to investors.
    b. Developer fee. Usually 3–5 percent of total investment. Can be deferred to allow fee to be paid out of future cash flow from operations.
    c. Bonus for bringing project in under budget. Usually expressed as a percentage of unused funds in construction loan when permanent loan is closed.
    d. Fees for management of operations.
    e. Percentage of ownership received for services rendered.
    f. Percentage of refinancing and/or sales profits (not necessarily proportionate to percentage of project ownership).
2. Tax shelter investors.
    a. Minimize investment in nondepreciable land. Lease the land when possible. Note: Most tax shelter investors would pay a disproportionately high rental (relative to land value) if the lease payments were fully deductible.
    b. Seek little or no cash flow. Seek investments in which the developer takes fees and passes all deductions to investors.
    c. Seek investments on which the most rapid methods of depreciation can be taken. This criterion favors housing.
    d. Seek investments designed to minimize taxes on disposition. Plan disposition timing in advance of acquisition, considering both capital gain taxes and recapture of rapid depreciation.
    e. Predetermine a desired aftertax return on investment which can be measured annually.
3. Seller of property.
    a. Installment sale. Receive proceeds in stages to spread taxes over time.
    b. Deferred-payment sale. Tax deferral for sales not qualifying for installment sale. This involves taking back a purchase-money mortgage valued at less than its full amount.
    c. Tax-free exchange. Deferral of all income taxes on sale until substitute property is sold.
    d. Avoidance of tax related to tax preference items.

Structuring the investment[1]

Structuring involves combining the variables to meet simultaneously the objectives of developers, investors, and sellers. At the same time, the economic objectives of lenders must be met. An example of structuring involving apartments is as follows:

1. The developer purchases land for $200,000, acquires rezoning for 12 apartments per acre, and leases the land to the investment group for $40,000 per year, supporting a value of $400,000 at a capitalization rate of 10 percent. This land is subordinated (first-lien rights transferred) to the permanent first-mortgage lender.
2. The developer retains 2 percent of ownership, serving as a full-liability general partner, but contracts to receive one third of all proceeds from any future refinancing.
3. The developer contracts to retain one half of any savings for bringing the project in under budget; he agrees to cover personally all costs in excess of budget (including losses due to slow rent-up or lower-than-projected rents).
4. The developer contracts for a fee of $500 per unit, said fee to be paid out of the first five years' cash flow at a rate of $100 per unit per year.
5. The developer agrees to contract for management of the project at 6 percent of rents collected.
6. The project is to be depreciated at 200 percent double-declining balance. The developer offers to purchase the investors' shares at a capital loss to equity investors great enough to offset recapture of depreciation.

These are only a few of the ways a project might be structured.

Several concepts have been identified here without explanation. The important ones are described as follows.

Depreciation

Real estate on which depreciation can be taken must meet the following criteria:

1. Improvements (structures and other improvements on the site) and furnishings are depreciable. Neither land nor one's personal residence is depreciable.
2. The real estate must be held for the production of income or used in one's trade or business. Real estate considered to be one's stock-in-trade is not depreciable.

---

[1] A structured example is presented in Appendix C, Queens Gate Apartments.

3. The person or entity holding the property must be classified as an investor with respect to that property. Dealers in real estate cannot depreciate their stock-in-trade. Brokers, builders, and developers are dealers with respect to properties that they hold for sale to customers; these same individuals may be classified as investors with respect to properties they hold for the production of income. Investor versus dealer status remains a gray area in the tax laws and regulations. Investors may avoid dealer status if they remain passive by not improving their property for sale; if they refrain from continuous advertising of the property "for sale" and do not often sell property; or if they receive only a small portion of their total annual income from the sale of property.

Original tax basis and depreciable basis. The original tax basis is the cost of acquisition of the real estate, which is the price paid plus any acquisition expenses paid by the buyer or, in the case of improvements constructed by the investor, the cost of construction plus the acquisition cost of the site.[2] The tax basis is not affected by mortgage financing. The buyer giving a purchase-money mortgage to the seller or assuming (or taking subject to) an existing mortgage will not alter the original tax basis, which remains the cost of acquisition. Similarly, a mortgage placed upon the property after acquisition or after the construction of improvements does not affect the original tax basis. Thus, the real estate investor is able to depreciate both the equity investment in improvements and the portion of the improvements' value financed with borrowed money.

The original tax basis must be allocated between depreciable improvement value and land value which cannot be depreciated. In performing this allocation, evidence is presented to indicate the market value of land and improvements at the time of acquisition. Appraisals and the assessed valuations of land and improvements have been accepted as evidence of proper allocation. When the investor has constructed the improvements on an acquired site, the cost of construction becomes improvement value and the acquisition cost of the land is taken as land value.

The portion of the original tax basis allocated to improvements becomes the depreciable basis. The depreciable basis may be altered over the investment holding period by capital improvements to the property. Capital improvements add to the value of the real estate, extend its useful life, or adapt the property to a different use. Capital improvements are distinguished from expenditures for ordinary repair

---

[2] The tax bases for properties acquired by gift, will, exchange, foreclosure, or involuntary conversion are each defined by special provisions beyond the scope of this book.

and maintenance, which are expensed annually as made. The capital improvements may be a new roof, new wiring, remodeling, or modernization expenditures.

Salvage value must be considered in establishing the depreciable basis. Salvage value is the estimated market value of the improvements (or other depreciable assets such as furniture and furnishings) at the end of their useful life. The salvage value of improvements can be reduced by the cost of their removal, which typically exceeds the salvage value at the end of their useful life. Investors intending to hold the property over the useful life of the improvements therefore can use a zero net salvage value in establishing their depreciable basis.

The depreciation expense taken each year depends in part upon the useful life of the improvements. Guidelines to useful lives have been provided by the Internal Revenue Service for various broad categories of improvements and short-lived furnishings, equipment, and fixtures. Examples of these guidelines include the following:

	Years
Apartments	40
Hotels	40
Office buildings	45
Warehouses	60
Dwellings	45
Stores	50
Factories	45

The taxpayer, of course, usually prefers the shortest possible useful life when maximization of aftertax cash flow is an important consideration. Circumstances may enable the investor to justify a useful life shorter than that of the guideline. In Los Angeles an investor constructed a retail store on a site that was to be taken for a freeway within seven or eight years. He obtained a ten-year useful life for depreciation of the improvements, with the resulting tax losses creating substantial deductions from other income. The deductions made the property particularly desirable (and thus valuable) to investors having high incomes.

Allowable depreciation methods.   What methods of depreciation are allowable depends upon whether the improvement is residential or nonresidential and upon whether the investor takes a new property as a "first user" or purchases used real estate. Residential real estate is defined as having 80 percent of gross income from dwelling units. In accumulating the 80 percent, rent can be imputed for an owner-occupied unit. Taking a property as first user means that no other investor has taken depreciation on the property. Allowable depreciation methods are summarized below for new (first user) and used residential improvements and for nonresidential improvements.

New residential improvements (taken as first user)

1. Straight-line depreciation—taken at a constant rate of the original depreciable basis.

    ### Example

    Forty-year useful life = $1/40$, or 0.025, annual rate × $100,000 depreciable basis (cost of improvements; no salvage value is assumed) = $2,500 annual depreciation.

2. Double-declining balance—taken at no more than 200 percent of the straight-line rate and calculated on the outstanding balance of the depreciable basis. A rate less than 200 percent of the straight-line rate can be used. Salvage value is never considered with this method.

    ### Example

    Forty-year useful life = 0.025 straight-line rate × 2.0 = 0.05 double-declining-balance rate × $100,000 depreciable basis = $5,000 depreciation in the first year. Depreciation in the second year: 0.05 × $95,000 = $4,750; in the third year: 0.05 × $90,250 = $4,512; and so on.

3. Sum-of-the-years' digits—another rapid write-off depreciation method in which the annual rate of depreciation changes and is applied each year to the original depreciable basis. Salvage value is assumed to be zero.

    ### Example

    Forty-year useful life. The formula for determining the rate of depreciation in the first year is to sum the digits for each year of useful life and to divide 40 by this sum; in the second year, 39 is divided by the sum; and so on.

Year	1
	2
	3
	. . .
	40
Total	820

    A formula, $n(n + 1)/2$, can be used to obtain this total, where n = useful life. Depreciation in the first year is 40/820 × $100,000 = $4,878. Depreciation in the second year is 39/820 × $100,000 = $4,756; in the third year, 38/820 × $100,000 = $4,634; and so on.

4. Component depreciation—the component parts of the structure are depreciated separately over their respective useful lives. Rapid write-off methods may be used, provided the useful life of the component is longer than three years. Component depreciation is available for new improvements

(construction cost is the depreciable basis), and for used improvements (price paid must be allocated among components).

Example

Building cost—$100,000

Components	Depreciable basis	Life	Straight-line, first year	Double-declining, first year
Shell	$ 55,000	40	$1,375	$2,750
Roof	7,000	15	469	938
Electricity	6,000	20	300	600
Plumbing	7,000	20	350	700
Elevator	15,000	10	1,500	3,000
Air conditioner	10,000	10	1,000	2,000
Total	$100,000		$4,994	$9,988

Used residential improvements (not taken as first user)

1. Straight-line depreciation.
2. 125 percent declining balance—the depreciation rate is no greater than 125 percent of the straight-line rate. This method is allowed only if the useful life of the improvement is 20 or more years; otherwise, only straight-line depreciation is permitted. The allowable rate is taken times the outstanding balance.

Example

Forty-year useful life = 0.025 straight-line rate × 1.25 = 0.03125 × $100,000 depreciable basis = $3,125 depreciation in the first year; 0.03125 × $96,875 = $3,025 in the second year; 0.03125 × $93,850 = $2,933 in the third year; and so on.

New nonresidential improvements (taken as first user)

1. Straight-line depreciation.
2. 150 percent declining balance—the depreciation rate is no greater than 150 percent of the straight-line rate. Annual depreciation is calculated on the outstanding balance of the depreciable basis.

Example

Forty-year useful life = 0.025 straight-line rate × 1.50 = 0.0375 × $100,000 depreciable basis (no salvage value) = $3,750 depreciation in the first year; 0.0375 × $96,250 = $3,609 in the second year; 0.0375 × $92,641 = $3,474 in the third year; and so on.

3. Component depreciation—maximum depreciation rate allowable is 150 percent of the straight-line rate.

Used nonresidential improvements (not taken as first user)

Straight-line depreciation only.

Tangible personal property (furniture and furnishings)

Tangible personal property may be depreciated separately from the improvements, provided the item has a useful life of three or more years. Allowable methods are the following:

New
1. Straight-line depreciation.
2. Double-declining balance.
3. Sum-of-the-years' digits.

Used
1. Straight-line depreciation.
2. 150 percent straight-line.

Additional depreciation on tangible personal property (furniture and furnishings)

Additional "bonus" depreciation is allowed on furniture and furnishings in the first year, provided the useful life of the item is six years or longer. Up to 20 percent of the cost of new or used personal property is allowed, with taxpayers filing a joint return limited to a maximum of $20,000 of such depreciation. The depreciable basis of the tangible personal property is reduced by the "bonus" depreciation taken in the first year.

Qualified tangible personal property used in trade or business also provides an investment credit of 10 percent against taxes owed, if the tangible personal property has a useful life of seven or more years. The reader is referred to Chapter 7 for additional explanation and examples.

Rehabilitation expenditures for low-income housing, for older commercial structures, and for historic preservation

The tax treatment of rehabilitation expenditures for low-income housing, for commercial and industrial real estate in use for at least 20 years, and for historic preservation of qualified properties is discussed in Chapter 7.[3]

---

[3] The Section 8 housing program is discussed in Chapter 20.

Election of methods. An investor electing to use an allowable rapid write-off depreciation method is permitted to switch to straight-line depreciation during the investment holding period in order to depreciate fully the remaining balance of the depreciable basis. This election is in a year of the taxpayer's choosing and can be done only once in an investment holding period. The year in which the switch should be made to minimize the tax liability can be computed at the beginning of the holding period, given the depreciable basis, useful life, and depreciation method chosen. As the example below shows, allowable depreciation under the rapid write-off method will be less in year 22 than if the investor had switched to straight-line depreciation in year 21.

Example

Forty-year useful life; $100,000 depreciable basis. Double-declining-balance depreciation is used initially.

Year	Double-declining-balance depreciation	Straight-line rate	End-of-year balance
1	$ 5,000		$95,000
2	4,750		90,250
3	4,512		85,738
4	4,287		81,451
5	4,072		77,379
6	3,869		73,510
7	3,676		69,834
8	3,492		66,342
9	3,317		63,025
10	3,151		59,874
11	2,994		56,880
12	2,844		54,036
13	2,702		51,334
14	2,567		48,767
15	2,438		46,329
16	2,316		44,013
17	2,201		41,812
18	2,091		39,721
19	1,986		37,735
20	1,887		35,848
21*	1,792		34,056
22	1,702	$ 1,792	
23		1,792	
...		. . .	
40		1,792	
	$65,944†	$34,048†	$ 0

* The taxpayer would switch to straight-line depreciation in year 21. Depreciation of the remaining outstanding depreciable basis at the beginning of year 22 ($34,056) at the straight-line rate for the remaining years of useful life (19 years) provides greater depreciation than if he or she had remained with the double-declining-balance method. The more rapid the method of taking depreciation, the more quickly the switch will occur.

† Discrepancy of total depreciation taken from $100,000 caused by rounding.

Leasehold improvements. An investor who leases land and improves the site can depreciate the cost of the improvement over its useful life, if the useful life is less than the term of the lease.

Example

An investor leases a site for 49 years and constructs an office building with a 45-year useful life. The investor can depreciate the improvement cost over 45 years, using 150 percent declining-balance or straight-line depreciation.

If the term of the lease is shorter than the useful life of the improvements, the investor-lessee is permitted to amortize the cost of improvements over the term of the lease, using straight-line amortization. If the intention of the investor is to amortize improvement cost over the term of the lease, care must be taken that any renewal options are not construed by the Internal Revenue Service to be part of the lease term.

Rapid write-off depreciation and the return on investment. The use of an allowable method of rapid write-off depreciation permits a larger portion of the cash throw-off from investment real estate to be sheltered from taxation. If the total of depreciation expense, operating expenses, and interest expense exceeds the property's effective gross income, a negative taxable income (tax loss) is realized. The investor is permitted to use this "paper" loss as an offset against taxable income from other sources such as wages, salaries, and other investment income. The consequent reduction in the investor's total income tax bill represents a tax savings imputable to the property which produced the tax loss. The aftertax return on the equity investment in that property is increased because of the tax savings. Even if the total tax deductions do not exceed the property's realized gross income, a portion of the cash throw-off comes "tax free" to the investor as long as the depreciation expense exceeds the principal retirement portion of the annual debt service. This truism can be shown by comparing the deductions determining cash throw-off and taxable income.

Items 1 and 2 below are identities in the computation of cash flow and taxable income. To the extent that depreciation exceeds the principal retirement on the mortgage, taxable income will be less than cash throw-off and a portion of the cash throw-off comes tax free to the investor.

Cash throw-off	*Taxable income*
(1) Net operating income	(1) Net operating income
Less: Debt service	Less:
(2) Mortgage interest	(2) Mortgage interest
(3) Mortgage principal repayment	(3) Depreciation
Equals: Cash throw-off	Equals: Taxable income

Rapid write-off depreciation and the minimum tax.   Use of a rapid write-off method of depreciation will produce excess depreciation during the taxable year. Excess depreciation is the difference between depreciation expense taken using the rapid write-off method and what would have been taken if straight-line depreciation had been used. Excess depreciation is a tax preference item which can result in the investor being liable for an additional "minimum tax." Each taxable year the investor sums all tax preference items (there are ten categories of tax preference items, but excess depreciation is the only one of relevance for the real estate investor). The regular minimum tax is then computed by subtracting either (1) $10,000 or (2) one half of the regular income tax liability from the total of tax preferences. The net balance is taxed at a flat 15 percent rate.

Example

Investor X, using component depreciation and the double-declining-balance method, had $40,000 in depreciation expense in the taxable year. Had straight-line depreciation been used, depreciation would have been $20,000. The difference, or $20,000, is excess depreciation. This investor had a regular income tax liability of $16,000 for the year. The investor's minimum tax liability is:

Tax preferences	$20,000
Allowable deduction (which is greater than one half of $16,000)	−10,000
Subject to minimum tax	$10,000
Minimum tax rate	×.15
Minimum tax, which will be paid in addition to the tax on the $16,000 of taxable income	$1,500

The higher-income taxpayer is not necessarily always benefited by rapid write-off methods of depreciation, if the resulting tax preferences trigger the minimum tax. Many syndications of real estate today use the straight-line component depreciation method to avoid excess depreciation and the minimum tax while, at the same time, permitting greater depreciation expense than the composite method.

The reader also will recognize that the minimum tax complicates the internal rate of return and net present value calculations. The annual after-tax cash flow each year depends not only upon the real estate investment under consideration and the amount of cash throw-off and taxable income which it generates, but also upon the excess depreciation it produces and upon the investor's total tax preferences and other taxable income. Examples of after-tax rate-of-return calculations in Chapter 5 do not consider these complications.

Deduction of operating expenses and interest expense

Real estate investors are permitted to deduct from their taxable incomes all operating expenses associated with the property and the interest expense on money borrowed to finance the investment. Operating expenses are actual cash expenditures made to operate the property and to keep it in good repair; they are not capital expenditures.

Investment interest limitation. Noncorporate investors are permitted to deduct interest expense on investment real estate. Currently, however, these taxpayers are subject to an "investment interest limitation" on interest deductions in excess of investment income. The total interest deduction allowed is determined by the sum of these items:

1. The amount of $10,000 on a joint return.
2. Net investment income.

Interest expense in excess of that permitted as a deduction under the above formula can be carried forward under restrictive rules. Corporations are not affected by the investment interest limitation; there are no limitations on the amount of "business" interest expense that is deductible. Interestingly, rental real estate (apartments, shopping centers, office buildings, and so on) has been classified as business property by the Internal Revenue Service. The interest expense associated with such property is not subject to the investment interest limitation.

Real estate investors affected by the limitation are speculators in land, property owners who have a net lease arrangement where the tenant pays practically all of the operating expenses, and property owners who are guaranteed a rate of return on their investment. The investment interest limitation is designed to prevent the high-bracket noncorporate taxpayer from excessive use of interest expense to shelter other income from taxes, while holding the investment for appreciation in market value that will be given favorable capital gain treatment at the end of the investment holding period.

Points and discounts. Under certain conditions, points charged by the lender may be treated as additional interest expense by the taxpayer. The 1976 Tax Reform Act required points considered to be interest to be prorated and deducted over the term of the loan. However, points charged on a mortgage used to purchase or to improve a taxpayer's personal residence are deductible when paid, if it is the local custom to charge points when making such a loan.

Discounts are sometimes used by lenders to increase their effective interest yield on the mortgage. A discount is considered to be mortgage interest and is therefore deductible. However, accrual basis taxpayers must amortize the discount over the term of the loan; they deduct only the prorated amount as interest expense in any one taxable year. Cash basis taxpayers have an interest expense deduction annually when they pay their mortgage payment to the extent that a portion of the payment represents a pro rata portion of the discount.[4]

Construction period interest and real estate taxes. The 1976 Tax Reform Act required individuals and Subchapter S corporations to capitalize and amortize interest and property taxes paid during the construction period. The construction period begins when construction or reconstruction of the building begins, and it ends when the improvement is ready for use or for sale. Prior to the 1976 act, these expenditures could be deducted when paid or when capitalized and depreciated.

This provision becomes effective over time, depending upon the type of property. Nonresidential properties on which construction began in 1976 are subject to the provision. Residential properties have been affected since 1978, and low-income housing is to be covered in 1981. The amortization period will be progressively lengthened over time for each class of property until the permanent ten-year amortization period is reached in 1982 for nonresidential property, 1984 for residential property, and 1988 for low-income housing.

Capital gains

The taxable gain realized upon the disposition of real estate may be treated as a long-term capital gain if the following criteria are met:

1. The property is held for longer than 12 months. Properties sold within shorter periods of time result in a short-term capital gain, which is taxed as ordinary income.
2. The property is held as an investment, for the production of income, or is used in one's trade or business. Dealers in real estate cannot take a capital gain upon sale of their stock-in-trade.

Capital gains defined. A capital gain is defined as the net sale price less the adjusted basis. Net sale price is the sum of (*a*) cash received, (*b*) other consideration received (notes, market value of other property, and so on), and (*c*) any mortgages assumed or taken subject to by the buyer, less (*a*) the broker's commission and (*b*) other expenses of sale (legal fees, recording fees, but not the state or local transfer tax). The adjusted tax basis is the original tax basis (plus any capital additions) less depreciation taken during the holding period.

---

[4] Investors can report income and expenses on either a cash or accrual basis. The cash method recognizes income in the taxable year in which it is received; deductions are allowed in the year in which they are paid. The accrual method recognizes income and expenses in the year in which the right to receive the income or the liability for the expense occurs.

Example

Mr. and Mrs. A sold their apartment property for $50,000. They had invested $10,000 in capital improvements during the ten years they owned the property. Their original tax basis was $30,000, $23,000 of which was allocated to improvements and $7,000 to land. They have taken $7,250 depreciation (straight-line) during the holding period. Their capital gain is computed as follows:

Proceeds from sale (cash)		$50,000
Less: Broker's commission	$3,500	
Attorney's fee	200	3,700
Net sale price		$46,300
Original tax basis		$30,000
Plus: Capital additions		10,000
		$40,000
Less: Depreciation taken		7,250
Adjusted tax basis		$32,750
Net sale price		$46,300
Less: Adjusted basis		32,750
Capital gain		$13,550

Long-term capital loss.   Treatment of a long-term capital loss varies, depending upon whether the property qualifies as a Section 1231 property or as a capital asset. Section 1231 properties must be held for more than 12 months, and include real estate used in one's trade or business. Interestingly, many income-producing properties, such as apartment buildings, retail stores, and office buildings held by a noncorporate taxpayer, are also classified as Section 1231 properties. Although the owner may consider these properties to be "investments" held for capital appreciation and for the production of income, the Internal Revenue Service and the courts have permitted Section 1231 to apply.[5]

The advantage of Section 1231 is full deductibility of any long-term capital loss against other ordinary income. The taxpayer aggregates all long-term gains and losses from the disposition of Section 1231 properties during the year. If a net gain results, it is added to any other long-term capital gains and taxed accordingly. If a net loss results, the net loss is fully deductible against other ordinary income.[6] Whether or not the property qualifies under Section 1231 becomes important at

---

[5] Income-producing properties may not be eligible for Section 1231 treatment if the investor is protected against loss of income or is guaranteed a rate of return on investment. For instance, a property leased on a net basis, with the tenant paying all, or practically all, expenses, would not qualify.

[6] The tax treatment of long- and short-term capital gains and long- and short-term capital losses, realized in various combinations by noncorporate and corporate taxpayers in a given taxable year, are beyond the scope of this introduction to tax factors affecting real estate.

the time of disposition of the real estate. Depreciation methods applicable to the property during the holding period are not affected by this classification.

Since 1978 the noncorporate investor has been able to deduct up to $3,000 of a net long-term capital loss on a non–Section 1231 investment property in a joint return.[7] Any overage can be carried forward indefinitely. The long-term capital loss carried forward is first deducted from any capital gains and then from other income subject to the above limitation.

Recapture of excess depreciation.   The ability to depreciate certain types of real estate using rapid or modified rapid write-off methods produces excess depreciation, which is the difference between depreciation taken during the holding period and that which would have been taken using the straight-line depreciation method. Excess depreciation, of course, disappears if the real estate is held for its entire useful tax life. Investors in real estate enjoy a tax shelter if the depreciation taken exceeds the true economic depreciation of the property. The use of rapid write-off depreciation methods increases the probability that this circumstance will occur. Indeed, some properties appreciate in value over the holding period, rather than depreciating. The shelter afforded by rapid write-off depreciation would be even more beneficial if the investors could receive favorable treatment of their capital gains at the time of sale. This shelter, however, has been moderated by provisions which are designed to "recapture" all or part of the excess depreciation at the time of sale. The recaptured portion of the capital gain is taxed as ordinary income.

The provisions for recapture of excess depreciation tend to promote longer investment holding periods. Real estate operators who invest primarily for tax-sheltered income and who sell or exchange whenever their real estate begins to produce a taxable income are dealt with more severely than investors who buy and hold for the long term.

Residential and nonresidential real estate

1.   If residential or nonresidential real estate[8] is held less than one year, all the depreciation taken is recaptured and taxed as ordinary income to the ex-

---

[7] A net long-term capital loss can occur when long-term capital losses exceed long-term capital gains. If only one capital gain transaction occurs during the year, and it produces a loss, the loss is carried forward under the above rule.

[8] The holding periods for residential real estate financed under a federal housing program or state and local programs for low- or moderate-income families remain under less stringent 1969 regulations. The capital gain for such a property is recaptured to the extent of the depreciation taken if the property is not held 12 months. If the property is held for 12–100 months, all depreciation taken in excess of straight-line depreciation is recaptured to the extent of the capital gain. For each month past 100 months, a 1 percent reduction is permitted in the excess depreciation taken after December 31, 1975. A project held for 16 years 8 months (200 months) would have no portion of the capital gain recaptured as ordinary income.

tent of the capital gain. Any portion of the gain attributable to appreciation in market value will be taxed as a long-term capital gain.

Example

Mr. and Mrs. A's building on leased land had an original tax basis of $100,000 at the time of purchase, January 1, 1980. Mr. A sold his property on January 5, 1981, thereby qualifying for a long-term capital gain.

Net sale price (property had appreciated)	$110,000
Adjusted basis (original basis less	
approximate depreciation taken)	91,000
Total gain	$ 19,000
Portion recaptured and taxed as ordinary	
income (depreciation taken)	9,000
Portion taxed as a long-term capital	
gain (appreciation in market value)	$ 10,000

2. If real estate is held for longer than one year, the excess of the depreciation taken over what would have been taken using straight-line depreciation is recaptured and taxed as ordinary income. The balance of the total gain will be taxed as a capital gain. If these properties are not held for 12 months, any gain will be treated as short term and taxed as ordinary income.

Example

Mr. and Mrs. A's building on leased land had an original tax basis of $100,000 and was sold for $110,000 after a five-year holding period. Double-declining depreciation was taken over the five years.

Net sale price	$110,000
Adjusted basis ($100,000 less $18,550 depreciation)	81,450
Total gain	$ 28,550
Excess depreciation taxed as ordinary income	
($18,550 less $10,000 straight-line depreciation)	$ 8,550
Taxed as capital gain	20,000
Total gain	$ 28,550

The rules for recapture, all else equal, tend to reduce the aftertax return on equity investment and are a factor promoting longer invest-ment holding periods. Other factors in the investment decision, how-ever, are never constant. Rising rents contributing to appreciation in market value can result in an advantageous sale within one year or within 100 months. Even without appreciation in market value, recap-ture of a portion of the gain as ordinary income becomes less of a factor in the decision to sell as the investment holding period lengthens.

Capital gain tax bill. The investor since 1978 has been forgiven tax on 60 percent of the capital gain. Thus, only 40 percent of the capital gain is added to the investor's other ordinary taxable income, with payment of taxes at the appropriate ordinary income tax rate.

Example

Mr. and Mrs. A's building in the immediately preceding example would result in a total tax bill of:

Excess depreciation (taxed as ordinary income)	$ 8,550
Capital gain of $10,000 × 0.40	8,000
Total to be added to Mr. and Mrs. A's other ordinary income .	$16,550
Mr. and Mrs. A's marginal ordinary tax rate	×0.40
Tax attributable to the sale of this investment	$ 6,620*

* In addition, Mr. and Mrs. A may be liable for the minimum tax in the year of sale, since they had been using rapid write-off depreciation, or for the "alternative minimum tax" which can be triggered by a capital gain. The untaxed 60 percent of the gain is used in the computation of the alternative minimum tax, as well as "adjusted itemized deductions" (itemized deductions which exceed 60 percent of adjusted gross income after certain adjustments have been made to both total itemized deductions and adjusted gross income). The investor pays the larger of the regular minimum tax or the alternative minimum tax.

TAX DEFERRAL

Exchanges

Real estate held for investment purposes and meeting the "like kind" and "investment property" tests, can be exchanged for other real estate on a tax-free or partially tax-free basis. Only boot is taxed.

Boot. Boot is any asset or liability transferred as part of the realty exchange. The most typical forms of boot are cash, mortgages existing prior to the exchange, purchase-money mortgages created within the exchange, and debt instruments transferred in lieu of cash.

Neither party in a tax-free exchange is permitted to recognize a loss at the time of the exchange. The party receiving boot in any form will probably have a gain that is subject to taxation, but the party who gives up boot may only add the surrendered boot to the tax basis. The following rules apply to boot.

1. Cash received is subject to taxation; cash paid is added to the tax basis.
2. Mortgages exchanged as a part of the property exchange are netted against each other. The party who ends up with a smaller mortgage must report taxable boot on the difference between the mortgages. The party who accepts the larger mortgage adds the difference between the mortgages to the tax basis.

3. Notes made in lieu of cash are treated as mortgages. The party making the notes adds the amount of the notes to the basis.

For each party in a tax-free exchange, the adjusted basis after the exchange is calculated as follows.

To original basis of original property:

Add:
   Cash paid
   Notes issued
   Mortgage obligation accepted (assumed or taken subject to)
Deduct:
   Mortgage obligation passed to other party
   Cash received
   Notes accepted

This yields the new basis. If the exchange caused the party to achieve a taxable gain, any gain recognized (taxed) is added to the basis. This permits the avoidance of double taxation at the time the property is sold.

Apportionment of basis. In effecting the exchange, the relative values of land and depreciable improvements become very important. Both parties normally wish to achieve depreciable status on as much of their bases as possible, and increasing the building to land ratio is desirable in nearly any exchange of properties.

Assumption of a mortgage increases one's tax basis, as does paying cash. Also, tax paid on gain recognized at the time of exchange is added to the basis. Relative appraisals determine how these items are apportioned to buildings and land.

Depreciation recapture. Depreciation recapture must be considered at the time a tax-free exchange occurs. Unpermitted excess depreciation must be reported as ordinary income in the tax year that the exchange is consummated.

Example

Miss W purchased improved land on January 1, 1979, for $100,000—$80,000 building and $20,000 land. During 1979, 1980, and 1981, she deducted $10,321 at a 150 percent rate for a 33⅓-year life. Her adjusted basis on December 31, 1981, is $89,679, and she exchanges the property (without boot) for unimproved land valued at $93,800.

Straight-line depreciation during the three years was $7,200 at 3 percent per year. Miss W is entitled to no excess depreciation (100 percent recapture), so she must report ordinary income of $3,121 ($10,321 − $7,200).

In this example, the gain on property equals the recaptured depreciation. Had the gain been less than the recaptured amount, only the amount of the gain would have been recaptured. This rule recognizes that actual incurred depreciation is certain at the time of disposal and sets the gain limit. In other words, recapture cannot of itself create a loss in which the basis exceeds the value of the property held after the exchange.

The tax-free exchange creates a substantial amount of flexibility for the real estate investor. Any type of real property can be exchanged for any other type, without regard to whether raw land or improved property is involved. Thus, the investor who wants to acquire a particular parcel of property can find a substitute property that the owner of the desired property would accept in trade, purchase the substitute property, arrange for financing identical in amount to that of the desired property, and exchange the two parcels on a tax-free basis.

The original owner transfers the old tax basis to the new property, and incurs no tax detriment in the exchange. Normally the owner hopes to secure a greater value in the new property than was in the old.

The investor is able to secure the desired property, which usually is ready for immediate development. He or she may wish to use the exchange technique to upgrade the tax basis by assuming a larger debt in the exchange, or to transfer from a parcel of raw land to an income-producing property. Through careful planning, nearly any property acquisition or disposal can be worked out as a tax-free advantage.

Installment sale

The installment method of reporting permits the seller to defer taxable gain on each dollar of selling price until that dollar has been collected. If the total taxable gain is 25 percent of the contract price, then 25 cents per dollar collected is taxable in the year of collection. Any property eligible for long-term capital gain can retain its eligibility and be taxed accordingly.

The installment treatment helps the buyer to avoid bringing together dollars needed to purchase the property, and it permits the seller to pay tax only when the money is received. Income averaging is accomplished easily in this manner.

Qualifying for installment treatment.   The Installment Sales Act of 1980 eliminated the limitation that no more than 30 percent of the selling price could be received in the year of sale, and eliminated the previous requirement that at least two or more payments be received over two or more taxable years. However, at least one payment must be received beyond the year of sale. Election of the installment method is treated as automatic on installment sales of real estate.

The installment method is not available for sales of depreciable property between spouses; individuals and their or their spouses' 80 percent owned entities; individuals and their trusts or their spouses' trusts; or between 80 percent owned entities. The taxpayer in effect is required to use the accrual method of accounting for transactions of this nature. The rule is intended to serve as a deterrent to transactions that are arranged to permit the related purchaser to claim depreciation deductions based on a stepped-up basis while the seller is not yet required to include corresponding gain from the sale in income.

Imputed interest. For users of the installment sale method the Internal Revenue Code contains special provisions regarding interest-free payment plans. The installment sale permits capital gain treatment, and most sellers would prefer to receive all of the proceeds as principal rather than interest, with the Internal Revenue Service being required to impute 10 percent interest unless at least 9 percent is charged by the seller.

The benefits of an installment sale are obvious to a property seller. The buyers do not appear to achieve any personal benefits, yet they are usually able to accommodate the tax needs of the sellers while securing low-cost financing of the contract price. In practice, the sellers usually receive a lower than market interest rate on the unpaid balance.

The major problem that can arise in an installment sale transaction is that the buyers must arrange for property title releases to match their development schedule. If partial releases are established according to a fixed payment schedule, then the buyers might be unable to gain clear title when needed. Solving this problem usually leads to an installment sale that benefits both parties.

TAX FACTORS AFFECTING THE HOMEOWNER

Deduction of mortgage interest and the property tax. Homeowners who itemize their deductions in calculating their taxable income have their aftertax cost of home ownership reduced by being able to deduct (1) interest on indebtedness used to finance the purchase of the home and (2) any real property tax paid. Other housing expenses incurred by such homeowners are not deductible. The benefit to a taxpayer of deductibility of mortgage interest and the property tax is offset in part by the standard deduction permitted in lieu of itemizing deductions. Increases in the standard deduction reduce the net benefit obtainable from itemizing expenses. The tax savings generated by home ownership tend to permit a greater expenditure for housing and the purchase of a larger, better quality unit. Also, these tax advantages are influential in attracting families to home ownership, including the ownership of condominiums and cooperatives, and thus increase the number of dwelling units demanded for owner occupancy.

Capital gain on disposition.   A personal residence cannot be depreciated for tax purposes, but it can be sold for a capital gain. The capital gain is the difference between the adjusted sale price of the home and its tax basis. The adjusted sale price is the sale price received, less the broker's commission and other sale expenses (legal fees, prepayment penalties on the mortgage). The tax basis for a personal residence is its acquisition cost or the construction cost of the residence plus the acquisition cost of the lot. This original tax basis may be increased by capital improvements made during the holding period. A capital loss on the sale of a personal residence is not recognized.

Example

Mr. and Mrs. A bought a lot in 1976 for $5,000 and constructed a home costing $20,000. Their original tax basis was $25,000. In 1978 they added a family room costing $5,000, increasing their tax basis to $30,000. On March 1, 1981, Mr. and Mrs. A executed a contract for sale for $45,000 with Mr. and Mrs. B. Mr. and Mrs. A eventually paid a $3,150 commission to their broker and $100 to an attorney, netting $41,750 from the sale.

Mr. and Mrs. A's capital gain is:

Sale price		$45,000
Less: Commission	$ 3,150	
Legal fees	100	3,250
Adjusted sale price		$41,750
Less: Original tax basis	$25,000	
Capital addition	5,000	
Adjusted tax basis		30,000
Capital gain		$11,750

Deferment of the capital gain.   The taxpayer can defer payment of the tax on a capital gain realized from the sale of a personal residence if he or she reinvests the proceeds in another personal residence within 18 months prior to or 18 months after the sale. If the taxpayer is having a new home constructed, he or she has 18 months after the sale of the prior residence in which to provide evidence of reinvestment (securing a building permit will suffice) and 24 months in which to occupy the new home. However, only expenditures made on the new residence within the 36-month period (18 months before and 18 months after the sale of the former residence) are counted in the tax basis of the new residence. Whether an existing home is purchased or a new or rehabilitated property is obtained, the taxpayer will be liable for taxes on any part of the adjusted sale price realized from the former residence that is not reinvested in the new property. In effect, the taxpayer is taxed to the extent that he or she disinvests.

Example

Mr. and Mrs. A from the preceding example buy a new $35,000 home within the allotted time. Their adjusted sale price for their former residence was $41,750. They have a taxable capital gain of $6,750. The tax basis of their new home is:

Cost of home		$35,000
Less: Gain from sale of former residence	$11,750	
Gain taxed at time of sale	6,750	
Deferred gain		5,000
Tax basis of new residence		$30,000

These adjustments leave Mr. and Mrs. A in the same position after their reinvestment in a new residence as they were when they sold their former home. If Mr. and Mrs. A sell their new home for its purchase price of $35,000, they will have a $5,000 capital gain, given the $30,000 tax basis. Since they were taxed on $6,750 of gain at the time of sale of their former residence, they pay taxes on a total capital gain of $11,750, the same gain they would have realized upon the sale of their former residence without reinvestment. The provision for deferring part or all of the capital gain is tax postponement, not tax avoidance. The same circumstances exist when the taxpayer moves up to a more expensive home.

Example

Mr. and Mrs. A buy a new home for $60,000. Their tax basis for their new home is:

Cost of new home	$60,000
Less: Gain on sale of old home deferred	11,750
Adjusted tax basis of new residence	$48,250

In this instance, the $48,250 tax basis represents the $30,000 adjusted basis of their former home, plus a $18,250 additional investment in the more expensive home (cost of new home, $60,000, less adjusted sale price of former residence $41,750). Mr. and Mrs. A have postponed the entire $11,750 gain, which would be realized if they sold their new home for an adjusted sale price of $60,000.

Expenses incurred in "fixing up" the previous principal residence for sale are deductible in determining the adjusted sales price of the previous home, when the proceeds are reinvested in a new principal residence. The fixing-up expenses must be incurred within 90 days prior to sale, be paid within 30 days after sale of the previous home, are not otherwise allowable as deductions in computing taxable income, and cannot be taken into account in computing the amount realized from the sale of the previous home.

Avoidance of tax on the capital gain. A taxpayer 55 years of age or older is relieved of all or a portion of the taxable capital gain upon the sale or exchange of a personal residence (maximum $100,000). To qualify for this exemption, the following criteria must be met:

1. The residence must have been owned and used by the person at least three of five years prior to the sale.
2. Either spouse who is at least 55 years of age can elect to take the exemption for a couple holding joint ownership. A taxpayer can benefit from the exemption only once in his or her lifetime.

SUMMARY

The real estate investor and the homeowner remain beneficiaries of favorable treatment under the federal income tax statutes. Investors can depreciate certain improvements by using rapid write-off depreciation schedules, and they have the potential of sheltering part or all of the cash flow from taxation. Tax losses generated by an investment property can be used to reduce ordinary taxable income. Investment property can be sold for a capital gain, and the gain may be at least partially deferred by the exchange of life-kind properties or by the installment sale. In response to economic conditions and a perceived reordering of national priorities from housing to other needs, and in the desire to attain greater equity in the tax structure, Congress reduced real estate tax shelters in 1976. Although tax reform undoubtedly will again reduce the advantages enjoyed by the real estate investor, opportunities for tax planning to maximize aftertax income are expected to remain. The complexity of tax planning has only been suggested in this chapter; the assistance of a tax expert is important in this aspect of real estate.

Homeowners may take interest expense and the property tax in itemizing deductions to determine taxable income. A personal residence can be sold for a capital gain, and the gain may be deferred by reinvesting in another personal residence. The homeowner 55 years of age may avoid all or part of the gain upon the sale of his or her residence. Home ownership has been promoted by these tax advantages; it is unlikely that Congress will remove them.

QUESTIONS FOR REVIEW

1. Describe how tax factors affect investment value and market value.
2. What criteria must be met for real estate to be a depreciable asset and to be eligible for capital gains treatment upon sale?
3. How does allowable depreciation differ for new and used residential and nonresidential properties?
4. Why is part of the cash throw-off "tax free" as long as tax depreciation expense exceeds the principal repayment portion of the annual debt service?
5. What is meant by the term *depreciation recapture?*
6. What is the advantage of having a Section 1231 asset?
7. What is the intent of the surtax levied on tax preference items?
8. What are the potential advantages of an exchange of like-kind properties?
9. What are the tax advantages of home ownership?

REFERENCES

Anderson, Paul E. *Tax Factors in Real Estate Operations.* 5th ed. Englewood Cliffs, N.J.: Prentice-Hall, 1978.

Berman, Daniel S., and Schwartz, Sheldon. *Tax Saving Opportunities in Real Estate Deals.* Englewood Cliffs, N.J.: Prentice-Hall, 1971.

Case, Fred E. *Investing in Real Estate.* Englewood Cliffs, N.J.: Prentice-Hall, 1978.

Freeland, James A.; Lind, Stephen A.; and Stephens, Richard B. *Fundamentals of Federal Income Taxation: Cases and Materials.* 2d ed. Mineola, N.Y.: Foundation Press, 1977.

J. K. Lasser Tax Institute. *J. K. Lasser's Successful Tax Planning for Real Estate.* Rev. ed. Edited by Bernard Greisman. Garden City, N.Y.: Doubleday, 1979.

Kau, James B., and Sirmans, C. F. *Tax Planning for Real Estate Investors.* Englewood Cliffs, N.J.: Prentice-Hall, 1980.

Prentice-Hall Federal Tax Handbook, 1979. Englewood Cliffs, N.J.: Prentice-Hall, 1979.

Rice, Ralph S., and Solomon, Lewis D. *Federal Income Taxation: Problems and Materials.* 3d ed. St. Paul, Minn.: West, 1979.

Robinson, Gerald J. *Federal Income Taxation of Real Estate.* Boston: Warren, Gorham, and Lamont, 1979.

Sandison, Robert W.; Anderson, Robert L.; Faggan, Juan; Garber, Lawrence A.; Lipson, David E.; and Warwick, Gerald B. *Federal Taxes Affecting Real Estate.* 4th ed. New York: Matthew Bender, 1978. All authors are associated with Arthur Andersen and Co., CPA.

part three

Real estate functions

chapter 14

Real estate marketing

Marketing is one of the essential functions that must be performed by every business firm. A useful good or service may be produced and financed, but if it is not distributed to people or firms that will pay a fair price, the cycle of business activity has not been completed. One view (propounded mostly by marketing people) is that marketing is the most important business function of all. Marketing, this view holds, is the drive wheel of every economic enterprise. If a firm cannot identify and serve a particular demand in the economy, the other functions of producing and financing will be to no avail; the firm is doomed to failure. Of course, the same observation could be made with regard to producing and financing.

Consistent with the view of marketing as a broad, important business function is the following definition of marketing. "Marketing is the process by which the demand structure for economic goods and services is anticipated or enlarged and satisfied through the con- and services is anticipated or enlarged and satisfied through the conception, promotion, exchange, and physical distribution of such goods and services."[1]

---

[1] Marketing faculty of Ohio State University, *Statement of the Philosophy of Marketing* (Columbus: College of Commerce and Administration, Ohio State University, May 1964).

This definition implies or assumes several characteristics about markets and how to serve them. First, it suggests that demand cannot be created by a marketer. It can be magnified or pushed forward in time, but every demand function exists prior to a marketer's exploitation of it. Therefore, it is crucially important to a marketer to be able to "read" the demand structure. The marketer must collect relevant data and analyze them to determine what products and services can be marketed successfully.

The marketing mix

After identifying markets with specific needs that can be satisfied, enlarged, or pushed forward in time, the marketer must decide how best to accomplish the marketing job. The marketing mix in most cases is determined by the market and its needs.

Usually, the marketer will have several alternative products and services to offer. Deciding what these products and services are and in what proportions they are to be offered are the objectives of this step in developing a marketing strategy. Builders may offer homes of standard design in various styles and interior decoration. Or custom design and architecture may be offered in the higher priced homes. They may offer some combination—say 75 percent standard and 25 percent custom—depending upon their analysis of market needs. If real estate marketers find a low-medium income market in dire need of modern, safe, sanitary housing, they may find that the only way of attempting to serve this market economically would be through a government program, such as the Section 8 subsidized occupancy program.

The activities of marketing are extremely broad in nature. They include the formulation of ideas for new goods and services that will meet the expected demand. Ways in which the availability of these products can be made known to the public and methods by which the public can be convinced of their desirability are part of the marketing function. Finally, the marketer is concerned with the legal and physical arrangements for the transfer of title and possession to a purchaser.

The marketing of real estate is a major function of real estate brokerage firms, land developers, and builders. Brokerage firms specialize in bringing together buyers and sellers of all types of properties; land developers convert unused or agricultural land to residential or business uses, usually holding title to the land and selling parcels from their own account; and builders construct residences or business structures for sale to ultimate purchasers. Variations in the activities of these types of firms may occur. Builders may construct buildings which they do not own but for which they are paid a builder's fee. A brokerage firm may have a building constructed for speculative resale from its own account. And a land development company may also do construction work and have a brokerage division. Nevertheless, they all engage in the marketing of real properties.

Other types of real estate firms—management, appraisal, counseling, and financing companies—also have a marketing function to perform. They must market the services provided by their firms. They differ from brokerage, development, and construction firms, however, in that they do not create or maintain an inventory of real properties for sale. Our analysis of the marketing function is oriented primarily to firms maintaining an inventory of real properties, although marketing principles are applicable to other types of real estate firms as well. Brokerage firms are a focus of analysis because marketing is the principal business function of these firms; it is their reason for existence.

The term *marketing* carries a much broader connotation than does the term *brokerage*. Brokerage usually refers to the legal relationships—rights and obligations—among the parties to a real estate transaction.[2] While a knowledge of these relationships may be regarded as prerequisite to a viable marketing effort, they are not the whole story—or even most of it. Marketing, as we said before, deals with the entire process of enlarging and satisfying needs in society. It is the process by which resources are allocated in the economy.

The brokerage firm may specialize in the type, location, or price range of the homes it lists and attempts to sell. Or it may offer a variety of homes in each category. The decision as to the combination, however, should be made only after and in consideration of an analysis of market needs.

In addition to having a choice among types of properties to offer and sell, the brokerage firm has a choice among services to offer. It may offer only selling services for its own listings. Or it may participate in a multiple listing service and attempt to sell the listings of other firms as well. A brokerage firm may offer insurance along with its marketing service. It may also offer other real estate services, such as appraisal, management, or counseling. Its marketing service could include financial analyses for income properties, inspection and appraisal services for prospective purchasers, or a trade-in program for sellers wishing to purchase another property. Other possible services may come to mind. Whether they are provided or not should be a conscious decision of the firm's marketing strategy.

MARKETING STRATEGY

Since marketers cannot hope to fulfill all the needs of society, they must limit the market they hope to serve. They must decide which needs they will try to meet, which people have those needs, where

---

[2] These relationships are covered in depth in Chapter 11.

those people are, and when they are likely to experience the needs. Note that the decisions focus upon the needs and upon people having the needs—not upon a particular service or product.

Failure to focus upon needs has been termed marketing myopia.[3] Many examples could be cited of businesses that failed because of marketing myopia. Automobile companies such as Studebaker Corporation that did not provide the types of styling, design, engine performance, or other features the market desired have gone out of business. The major U.S. automobile companies suffered a loss of more than 25 percent of their domestic business in 1980 by failing to offer cars with the fuel efficiencies achieved by foreign producers. *Esquire* magazine lost its dominance of the would-be sophisticate male readership market to *Playboy* by not providing the desired mix of features, interviews, stories, and photographs. Railroad companies have experienced great difficulties because they did not realize they should be in the general transportation business.

In the world of real estate, many builders have failed because the properties they constructed did not have the desired features. Many apartment buildings have lost tenants to other properties because the owners or managers did not regard themselves as purveyors of housing services. They did not provide the features and services desired by the market. Brokerage firms have failed because they did not project the image of security, trustworthiness, or adequate service desired by homebuyers.

Our purpose is not to emphasize the negative—to dwell on how or why firms fail. We do want to point out that failures can occur because of a lack of proper attention to the marketing concept. Failures can occur for other reasons as well, of course. Improper management of the production, financing, organization, or personnel functions are just as likely to produce unfavorable results. Nevertheless, marketing myopia leads to a high proportion of failures and may be difficult to diagnose.

The best defense against marketing myopia is a marketing strategy. A strategy identifies long-range objectives and the general means for achieving those objectives. In marketing, the development of a strategy requires the identification and delineation of the market or submarket that exhibits needs or desires the firm believes it can serve and of the types, quantities, and prices of products or services that are required in order to serve that market.

Real estate is a field composed primarily of marketers whose strategy is to seek out buyers or renters for products within specialized categories. The most basic product differentiation is a delineation of

---

[3] Theodore Levitt, "Marketing Myopia," *Harvard Business Review* 38, no. 4 (July–August 1960): 45–56.

the type of land marketed by the firm. Few firms are capable of providing competent marketing services for the various types of land, including agricultural land, predeveloped suburban land (planned, zoned, and so on), developed building sites, and land which has been improved with buildings for commercial, industrial, residential, or other uses. Varied skills are needed, and firms which attempt to acquire all of these skills tend to expand beyond the top executives' ability to manage.

Each firm must identify its most efficient level of activity and devise a marketing strategy that is specialized to fit the talents of its members. As the firm's scale changes, its capabilities for extending its operations into new areas of specialization also change, and therefore its marketing strategy must be reevaluated frequently. Examples of possible strategies are as follows:

1. Devise reuse programs for existing structures which are inefficient at present. Locate new tenants, negotiate leases, and design the renovation effort to meet tenants' needs. Then sell the concept to a builder-renovator.

2. Serve as a catalyst which brings together a land developer and several home builders. Market developable land to the developer; market the lots to builders. Secure development, construction, and permanent financing. Market the builders' homes. This has been done by Bonner Realty Associates, Inc., in several of metropolitan Atlanta's most successful residential communities, developed by Cousins Properties, Inc.

3. Seek an exclusive relationship with a corporate home relocation service. Develop skills in the management, repair, and resale of the homes acquired by the relocation company.

4. Become a specialist in locating sites and purchasers for a retail franchise chain. Many brokerage firms have specialized exclusively in land sales to such firms as fast-food chains, oil companies, home improvement stores, and hotels/motels which seek multiple sites in a single community or a larger service area.

Most of these strategies are founded upon a thorough knowledge of a particular property type. A general categorization of property types follows.

Unimproved acreage sales

Most sales of unimproved acreage are made to purchasers who seek appreciation from future reuse demand. Potential reuse factors such as the following are typically highlighted by the marketer.

1. Proposed highways, proposed utility extensions, and redevelopment.

2. Residential and commercial growth in the direction of the subject property.
3. The subject property's superior forestation, topography, water amenities, and other amenities.
4. The subject property's price and terms relative to those of competitors.
5. A projection of the timing of expansion into the area with an identification of the subject property's best prospects.

The purchasers of unimproved acreage are typically speculators who seek land of many investment types. They depend heavily upon the reputation and performance record of a marketing specialist.

This specialty has been a popular one among marketers who have been highly aggressive and optimistic about development timing. Many states now require that formal prospectuses be prepared which provide facts, both positive and negative, about the subject property. Land syndications for investors have been both popular and profitable, but many syndicators have been overly optimistic and have generated projects at prices and on financing terms that require substantial appreciation for profit to occur. The market downturn of the mid 1970s caused many defaults and losses by investors, thereby leading to greater regulation of syndicators and a poor reputation for this marketing specialty.

Predeveloped land sales

The marketer of predeveloped land converts land from unimproved acreage to buildable sites without performing the physical site development. The steps usually taken to enhance the value of sites are to:

1. Prepare a land-use plan.
2. Secure rezoning of the site to higher density uses.
3. Secure agreements from the county or city to bring utilities to the site.
4. Secure agreements from the highway department to improve roads as needed.
5. Prepare engineering analyses:
   a. Two-foot-interval topographic analysis.
   b. Soils studies.
   c. Hydrological studies.
   d. Forestation analyses.
   e. Final land plan and staking out of lots/sites.
6. File plat.

The purchasers of predeveloped land are usually land developers. The predevelopment process minimizes the time required to commence physical development, and it renders the property ready for immediate consideration for a land development loan. The loan will normally fund the land at a "retail price," causing the services of the predeveloper to be recognized as value added.

Developed land sales

The land developer divides tracts into sites that are ready for immediate use by builders. The land price paid by the user includes all utilities, streets, curbs, gutters, sidewalks, streetlights, and other improvements desired by the builder-purchaser. If the developer is efficient, a sufficient profit is gained through the development process to pay the retail price for raw land and convert it to building sites that are worth more to builders than the developers' cost of preparation.

Improved land sales

The constructor of buildings for sale seeks a profit by creating user-ready structures primarily for non-real estate entities. Manufacturers, retailers, wholesalers, and others either purchase or rent existing buildings or commission new ones to be built. They are not in the business of constructing buildings. At times, the marketer creates an investment group to own a building created for rental and use by another party.

Resale property sales

Marketers of resale properties normally promote the virtues of owner occupancy or those of a seasoned, stable income. Resale properties are priced as a function of location, physical amenities, or capitalized income. The marketing specialist concentrates on reasons why the formerly owned property is superior to new space or alternative properties. Renovation planning is frequently a part of this process.

Leasing as a marketing specialty

The leasing agent's primary market is tenants who for one reason or another choose to rent rather than own. Such marketers sell freedom from making a down payment and the absence of a permanent user commitment to the property.

Marketing specialized services

The most sophisticated type of product to sell is the many service specialties in real estate. Research, management, and appraisal firms must develop strong reputations for performance and then support these reputations with each client. Direct solicitation is not permitted in those areas where professional associations are prominent, so performance and reputation are critical to success. The product specializations discussed here tend to occur in geographically separated market areas, as shown in Figure 14–1. The relationships between stages and location are simplified in an effort to separate strategy types showing the maximum extent of specialization that is typically found in the market. Obviously, many variations and combinations of product mix occur.

FIGURE 14–1
Real estate development stages

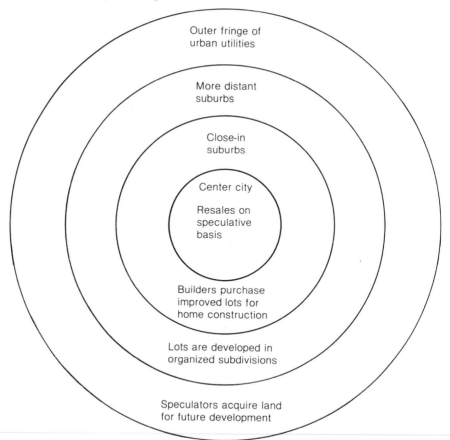

Land speculation is shown to exist primarily in the outer fringe of urban utilities. Large tracts of rural land are frequently purchased on long-range financial terms. Lot development occurs primarily in the more distant suburbs, and home builders are drawn from close-in suburbs to the slightly farther out areas as they seek lower land prices and more desirable lots. The center city rarely contains large tracts for new development, so resales and redevelopment represent the principal forms of activity.

Buyer market segmentation

Identifying and delineating the market to be served involves the process of market segmentation—carving out submarkets from larger, more general markets. This process recognizes that the needs and desires of consumers are not homogeneous. In the extreme, individuals would have their own private preferences for any type of want-satisfying product or service. Fortunately, however, preferences can usually be grouped into market segments, or submarkets. For example, some ethnic groups prefer to live in neighborhoods where their specialized foods are sold, church services are offered in their own language, and they can socialize with people sharing their interests. Gay people tend to seek out particular residential areas. Executives subject to frequent transfer seek expensive homes in new and prestigious neighborhoods where appreciation is expected to be at high levels.

Identification of potential submarkets should be undertaken in a systematic way. One of the best ways is to construct a marketing grid.[4] Ideally, such a grid contains characteristics of one dimension along one axis and characteristics of another dimension along another axis. For example, a construction firm seeking to identify potential markets for office buildings might construct the grid in Figure 14–2 showing desired features among several types of owners or occupants Marketers would emphasize those features which meet the specific needs of each user type interviewed.

Such a grid focuses upon the needs of potential customers, not upon specific ways of fulfilling those needs. For example, the need for variable space patterns in offices might be met with movable partitions, removable walls, or added units in modular construction. The need for a pleasant view might be met with an interior courtyard, a site with a natural view, or height. And climate conditioning would require a different mix of heating, cooling, and purification in New York, Miami, and Fairbanks.

---

[4] For a more thorough treatment of the development and construction of marketing grids, see E. Jerome McCarthy, *Basic Marketing: A Managerial Approach*, 6th ed. (Homewood, Ill.: Richard D. Irwin, 1978).

FIGURE 14–2
Market grid for new office needs

Savings and loans and banks	Real estate and in-surance officers	Attor-neys	Physi-cians	Account-ing firms	Finance com-panies	
	X	X		X	X	Variable space patterns
X			X			Special plumbing and fixtures
	X	X		X		View
	X			X	X	Informational service
X					X	Special security arrangements
X		X		X	X	Central location
	X	X	X	X	X	Climate conditioning
X	X	X	X		X	Customer parking
X		X		X		Prestige building
	X				X	Low rental rate
		X		X		Expansion potential

A grid identifying possible submarkets for a residential brokerage firm might appear as shown in Figure 14–3. A firm wishing to provide marketing services to purveyors and consumers of real estate services would find that it could serve the market for single-family residences, most of which are occupied by their owners, in all sections of the city except the center and northeast areas. Single-family units are available in all sections of the city except the center and northeast areas. Mul-tifamily units are available in all sections except the center, north, and northwest areas. High-income buyers and properties are located in the north, east, and northwest areas. And the low-income market is con-centrated in the south, east, center city, and west sections. Thus, brok-ers wishing to serve the high-income, single-family residence market could operate in the north, east, and northwest areas of the city. They might further wish to specialize by limiting their operations to one of those areas. Given, for example, a conscious decision to concentrate

FIGURE 14–3
Market grid for real property marketing services

Center city	North	South	East	West	NW	NE	SW	SE	
	X	X	X	X	X		X	X	Detached single-family residences (owner market)
		X	X	X		X	X	X	Multifamily units (rental market)
	X		X		X				High income
	X	X	X	X			X	X	Medium income
X		X	X	X					Low income
X	X		X					X	Condominium
X			X						Cooperative

the firm's efforts on marketing detached single-family homes in the north, east, and northwest areas of the city, the marketer must select a target segment of the buying public which can be defined at the outset of the marketing effort.

Homes in these areas are large and expensive, and purchasers tend to have the following characteristics:

1. *Age:* Head of household between 35 and 50.
2. *Income:* Household income above $60,000 per year.
3. *Employment:* Head of household holds professional position near perimeter highway or downtown.
4. *Family size:* Four persons.
5. *Locational requirements:* Must be near private schools and major shopping center.
6. *Qualitative factor:* Neighborhood must have significant "snob appeal."

If these characteristics are stated accurately, the firm can concentrate its time and advertising budget on locating such purchasers and meeting their home purchase needs.

A similar process is used when the firm specializes in the marketing of commercial property. Location is less important, but purchaser requirements can be cataloged and purchaser characteristics can be defined.

THE BUYING PROCESS

The goal of the marketing effort is to produce a consummated transaction with a satisfied purchaser and a satisfied seller. After developing a viable, consistent marketing strategy in both the market for properties and the market for marketing services, the marketing executive hopes the sales force will be able to convince individual members of the market that the services and properties offered by the firm are worthy of purchase. The analysis to this point helps to identify these individuals and their needs; it does not help in developing an approach to consummating a transaction. This step results from completion of the stages in the buying process.

Stages in the buying process

All buyers experience several phases during the time that they are considering a major purchase. Each phase may be short-lived or extended over weeks or even months. Nevertheless, the successful completion of each stage is prerequisite to a successful transaction.[5]

Need arousal.   The buying process begins when consumers experience a need. They realize for one reason or another that they may require a new home, office, or commercial facility. The need for a different home may be felt because of an impending family addition, a job transfer to another city, or the desire to upgrade or change location. Whatever the source, experiencing the need produces a state of tension in the potential buyer—a feeling that a problem requires resolution.

Information search.   Individuals, as a result of a felt need, become sensitive to advertising, bits of news, educational programs, experiences of others, and other cues in their environment which may bring them closer to satisfying the need. During the stage of prepurchase activity, the potential buyers' perception becomes tuned in to differences in size, style, design, location, price, and other characteristics; they learn and accumulate experience.

This is the stage during which the real estate marketer should provide information—not only about available properties, but about the entire purchase process. For most new buyers, and for many older buyers as well, the purchase of a home is a traumatic experience. The more they can learn about the process, the greater will be the possibility of overcoming their fears and consummating the sale.

Prepurchase activity can be used to create a sequence of changes in the buyer's state of mind that bring the buyer closer to the act of

---

[5] For a thorough analysis of buyer behavior, see Philip Kotler, *Marketing Management: Analysis, Planning, and Control*, 4th ed. (Englewood Cliffs, N.J.: Prentice-Hall, 1980), chap. 6.

purchase. Buyers proceed from a state of awareness of their needs and the necessity to satisfy them to knowledge about various alternative properties that could fulfill the needs. They then begin to like one or several properties and develop a preference for one property over the alternatives. The preference ripens into a conviction that one property can best satisfy their needs and relieve their state of tension. Conviction leads to purchase.

Purchase decision. The decision to purchase is made in relation to the amount of risk perceived by consumers. This depends on the degree of subjective certainty that they will do well by making the purchase. Consumers try to reduce this risk by gathering information and making comparative judgments as to the amount of risk involved among various alternatives. The purchase decision is in effect the manifestation of favorable prepurchase activity.

Use behavior. The buying process is not completed by the purchase decision. In some respects the consumers' "buying" has just begun. They must study and learn how to use the property just purchased; they must learn various aspects of its use, such as how the dishwasher works, when to pay taxes, and how to get the porch fixed. The marketer can be very helpful during this stage by anticipating the types of information buyers will want and by taking the initiative in providing that information. The property purchased should be viewed as part of the consumption system; it is the means by which the purchasers of the property attempt to meet their needs.

Postpurchase feelings. A buyer usually sees the purchase as both a reward and a punishment. It is a reward because it helps to satisfy a felt need. Buying the property is a lengthy process, and the new home is the end result of all the time, effort, and money expended. But it is also punishment because the purchaser continues to have doubts as to the wisdom of the purchase. Nearly all purchasers wonder whether they should have gone so far into debt, whether the house will be adequate for a growing family, whether the family should have gotten along a little longer in an apartment and gotten into better financial shape before purchasing a home. Opportunity costs—the passing up of alternative uses of their resources—become apparent during the postpurchase stage.

The anxiety experienced during this stage has been termed *cognitive dissonance*. The dissonant feelings that occur following a purchase can be allayed by an effective real estate broker and will produce a satisfied customer—and a potential client for the future. The broker should reassure buyers by visiting them, introducing them to the neighbors, pointing out the favorable aspects of the property, and perhaps giving them a housewarming gift. This should be regarded as one of the most effective ways of building a satisfied clientele—people who will recommend the broker to others and who will call the broker when they wish to sell.

Buying process roles

Different roles may be assumed by the various parties concerned with a real estate purchase. In a home-buying situation, one member of the family may dominate and be the principal decider. Yet, if one member dominates in that decision (say the wife), another member (the husband) may dominate in another decision—for example, the city where the family will live.[6] In the purchase of business real estate, the company president may be the final decider, but only after receiving advice from others in the firm. Other functions in the process may be undertaken by different persons. Kotler groups these activities into the roles of initiators, influencers, deciders, buyers, and users.[7]

Initiators are the people who first suggest or think of the idea of buying a particular product or service. For example, a housewife may first realize that her current home is too small and there suggests the family consider selling the house and buying a new or different one.

Influencers are those who provide information to, persuade, or stimulate a buyer during any stage of the buying process. Sales representatives, advertising media, and friends are examples of influencers. Some part of the real estate advertising budget should be aimed at those who will influence buyers. Children are often important influences or parents who are deciding whether to purchase a home or which home to purchase. Yet, how often do real estate sales representatives encourage children to speak up or express their opinions? Sometimes the sales representative encourages them to remain outdoors while the parents tour the property. The sales representative who does this may be passing up an opportunity to direct some marketing effort toward important influencers!

Deciders make the actual decision. It may be the wife who decides she likes one house better than another; it may be the husband's decision; or it may be a democratically formed family decision. The real estate marketer would do well to try to identify the decision maker(s) in every buying situation and to address a great deal of effort to that person or persons.

Those who make the actual purchase are termed the *buyers*. The buyer may be a different person than the decider, for example, a child

---

[6] James F. Engel, Hugh G. Wales, and Martin R. Warshaw, *Promotional Strategy*, 3d ed. (Homewood, Ill.: Richard D. Irwin, 1975), pp. 141–43.

[7] Kotler, *Marketing Management*, p. 134.

sent to the store to buy a carton of milk for her mother. For most real estate transactions both husband and wife are the buyers, since both usually sign the contract and/or deed. If, however, the buyers are different from the deciders, more attention should be directed to the deciders.

Those individuals who use or consume a product or service are the *users*. As with the buyer, the user may be someone different from the decider. The person who receives a gift or the employee who uses the facilities provided by an employer is a user but not a decider. The user, however, may be a strong influencer, and marketing effort directed to the user who is also an influencer may pay off handsomely. Apartment dwellers who complain to landlords about the noise level between apartments will induce the landlords to desire better soundproofing in their next apartment building investment. Workers who experience difficulty in performing tasks in a building with inadequate lighting will probably influence their employer to modify the lighting system. Supportive communication should be addressed to such users-influencers to make them aware of the availability of more adequate facilities.

Benefits of buying process analysis

Analysis of the stages in the buying process through which buyers progress and of the roles played by the various parties to a real estate purchase can be quite rewarding. Perceptive insight can tell the sales representative who the decider is, who the influencers are, and who the users are likely to be. The appropriate sales message can then be directed to each person.

By attempting to understand which stage of the buying process a prospective buyer is in, the sales representative will be better able to direct the appropriate type of information to the prospect. If the prospect is still in the prepurchase activity stage, the prospect will probably be offended if the sales representative attempts to close the sale; the buyer has not yet completed the information gathering and analysis necessary to make a decision.

Similarly, sales representatives may gain many new clients by understanding the significance of postpurchase feelings. By allaying fears and concerns after a purchase, a sales representative makes a satisfied convinced buyer who will use that sales representative the next time a need arises to buy or sell and who will recommend the sales representative and the firm to friends. It should be realized that a postpurchase gift by itself does not perform the function of allaying cognitive dissonance.

MARKETING PROPERTIES OR SERVICE?

The discussion relating to the development of a marketing strategy suggests that there is more involved in the marketing of real estate than simply lising properties for sale and making the listing available for public perusal. Indeed, with multiple listing services, all the brokerage firms in a community have essentially the same list of properties for sale as does one's favorite firm. Within a given market, every firm has the same function—to help expedite and consummate transactions of real properties. For fulfilling this function, a commission is paid.

Since a number of firms within a market attempt to achieve the same objective, the degree of success of any individual firm will be dependent largely upon how it goes about its pursuit of the objective, first, in terms of internal management of the firm, and second, in terms of ability to attract buyers and sellers. The first type of activity involves recruitment and training of personnel, cost accounting, control procedures, and so forth. A firm may be able to consummate a high volume of sales and yet receive a small return for its services because of unwise expenditures of time and money in the running of the business. The second type of activity, attracting buyers and sellers, is crucial to the survival (or maintenance) of the business and is the focus of this chapter. The nature of the competition suggests that the firm itself must be marketed. The firm must convince potential customers through deed and word that it provides a better service—or at least a different service—than do other firms serving the same market.

Thus, two markets are relevant to the real estate business—the market for the product and the market for the services of real estate intermediaries. Real estate markets and the marketing function presumably would exist even without broker-intermediaries. The broker-intermediary's role should be viewed as a facilitating, expediting, convenience-rendering function which causes the market to work *better* but which in itself does not "make the market."

Firms as monopolistic competitors

The economic analysis of the product in Chapter 9 developed the contention that the real estate market, in which the product is land and its improvements, best fits the model of monopolistic competition. Many parcels of real estate are sold and purchased each day, and each parcel is different from every other parcel. Each parcel is imperfectly substitutable for others, but each parcel usually is in competition with other parcels that are to some degree substitutable for it. Since there is effective competition among various parcels, the demand curve for one parcel may shift left as other substitutable parcels are brought onto the market. True monopoly prices will not be available in a well-functioning market, but purchasers will pay for perceived differential advantages of one property over another.

The model of monopolistic competition would seem also to fit many of the markets for the services of real estate firms. Particularly in the field of residential brokerage, this model realistically describes the market structure: many small firms in a community, each seeking to differentiate its service, vie for a share of the market. To a limited extent a firm may build up a loyal clientele; but as other firms enter the market, an individual firm's demand curve will shift to the left.

Firms as oligopolists

Some real estate markets, particularly those involving large, special purpose properties, are served by fewer, larger, more specialized firms. Commercial and industrial brokerage firms typically are more specialized, larger, and fewer in number than are residential brokerage firms. These markets and some residential markets, both for the product and for the services of the firms, may more appropriately be described by the model of differentiated oligopoly.

Differentiated oligopoly may be regarded as a special case of monopolistic competition. The difference is that there is even greater interdependence among the larger firms. This interdependence leads to the belief by a firm that if it lowers its price, other firms will follow suit. If, however, it raises its price, other firms will not. Whether in fact other firms behave according to these beliefs is irrelevant to the way in which a firm perceives its demand function. Its pricing policy and determination of level of operation will be decided on the basis of its assumptions about the actions other firms will take in response to its own pricing policy and level of operation.

Price-fixing

Many real estate firms formerly adhered to a schedule of suggested commission rates promulgated by a local trade or professional group—usually a board of Realtors. In the early 1970s the practice of requiring or even suggesting a standard structure of commission rates was attacked by the U.S. Department of Justice and by private individuals. Suits to require an end to such practices were filed under both the Sherman Anti-Trust Act and the Clayton Act against boards of Realtors and groups of brokers in a number of cities.

One important example of such actions was the suit against the

Atlanta Real Estate Board filed by the U.S. Department of Justice.[8] It was settled in early 1972 by agreement of the Atlanta Real Estate Board to accept a consent judgment which prohibited the fixing or recommending of commission rates or fees. It further required the board not to take any punitive action against anyone for failing or refusing to charge any particular commission or fee in connection with the sale, lease, or management of real estate.[9]

The recommended means of establishing commission rates is to negotiate a fee individually with each client. Most firms have their own fee schedules which serve as bases for their fee quotations. Competition among firms causes their fee rates to be similar, but recently discount brokers have evolved who typically offer limited services for reduced fees. Their concept is to educate the home seller in preparing his or her advertising, preparing the home for sale, and showing the home. Their fee is usually contingent upon the home sale, and it is frequently half or less than half the fee of the full-service firm. Some discount firms quote below-market flat fees for the sale of a home through their efforts, and even lower fees when the owner sells his own home.

In the late 1970s price-fixing charges were frequent in the area of computerized multiple listing services. Fees in some cases were divided among associated firms in such a manner that the listing agent, the listing firm, the selling agent, the selling firm, and the listing service participated according to a prearranged schedule. Most services today charge either a flat monthly fee to listing firms or a fee per listing, and the selling agent and firm pay no fee for the service. The requirements of the Justice Department and of state licensing commissions have been refined and clarified, and few legal problems are expected in the 1980s.

The legal status of nationally franchised brokerage firms, such as ERA, Gallery of Homes, Century 21, and Red Carpet, has also been clarified. Franchise holders agree to pay franchise fees which cover logos, advertising, and so on, and a schedule of referral fees is worked out on a firm-by-firm basis. A broker in Minneapolis might refer a client to a broker in Dallas, with all fee arrangements made through the franchise company in compliance with state reciprocity laws. The referring broker does not negotiate the commission with the client; this is done by the selling broker.

Price-fixing in real estate brokerage became an issue because the industry sought to prevent inexperienced or incompetent firms from

[8] *United States of America v. Atlanta Real Estate Board*, Civil Action No. 14744, February 17, 1971.

[9] "Atlanta Board Signs Agreement," *Realtor's Headlines* (Washington, D.C.: National Association of Real Estate Boards, January 10, 1972).

using low fees in lieu of quality services to obtain listings and sales. Recent emphasis upon the education of all license holders is helping to solve this problem.

During the late 1970s a number of the nation's largest retail and stock brokerage firms entered real estate brokerage. These businesses can afford to fund the start-up costs of new realty firms, and they can operate on a large-scale basis using the underlying firms' computers, offices, stores, and other overhead items. The trend appears to be for major growth of such realty firms, and future price-fixing and monopoly charges may arise if they become a high percentage of the market and are not careful to observe all governmental rules and requirements.

Discrimination

The Justice Department has been active in preventing real estate–related firms from discriminating against sellers or purchasers on the basis of race, color, sex, or national origin. Actions have been taken against (1) brokers who "steer" clients to neighborhoods known to contain large numbers of selected minorities; (2) lenders who reject the loan applications of unmarried couples, gay persons, or single women; and (3) lenders and appraisers who "redline" certain neighborhoods for rejection based upon structural or environmental criteria believed to be contrary to the interests of these neighborhoods. Violators have been fined and have been required to provide educational programs for their employees intended to prevent future violations.

Brokerage is a particularly delicate area with regard to discrimination. At what point is the broker who shows minority persons a home in a section known to have few minority homeowners observing the minority persons' civil rights, and at what point is the broker subjecting himself or herself to charges of "blockbusting"—to the claim that property values are being reduced because of the broker's efforts? The answer lies in strict adherence to laws and regulations, coupled with the display of consistent professionalism to all clients. Organizations such as the National Association of Realtors provide substantial literature and educational programs to keep the industry informed regarding operating methods that will avoid problems regarding discrimination.

DEVELOPING MONOPOLISTIC ADVANTAGE

A real estate marketing firm should attempt to carve out an area of operation that it can serve as well as or better than any other firm. Realization that the firm must market its own services and not just a list of properties also suggests the need for specialization and differentiation of its services. In other words, the firm needs to offer that combination of products and services that will be most useful to its target submarket.

The purpose of specializing and differentiating markets and services is, of course, to develop a monopoly advantage in one area of operation. A monopoly advantage will produce a profit above the minimum wage level as long as the firm is able to maintain its market position. As one real estate analyst has stated: "The ultimate objective of the firm within a free enterprise system is to create a monopoly to some extent either in fact or in the mind of the consumer."[10] Or as a marketing expert has put it: "The real dough is in what economists call monopoly profits. I don't mean in a restrictive sense. I mean being first, the guy who skims the cream."[11]

As demonstrated in the previous section, the firm engaged in real estate marketing competes in a market for services as well as in a market for real properties. Therefore, marketing strategy should be formulated with respect to the functions involved in the firm's entire operation. Through advertising, public relations, quality of personnel, management efficiency, and selling techniques (as well as segmenting markets), the firm can be different from or more efficient than other firms performing the same economic function. The job of top management, including marketing management, in a real estate firm is to perform the long-range planning necessary to identify target submarkets of properties and services, and to determine the appropriate mix of properties and services for these markets.

Advertising

This activity is one which every business executive must engage in to some extent. Good advertising practices and techniques can often mean the difference between a successful firm and one that is less than successful. In the advertising function, as we will maintain for the remaining four areas, the marketer of real estate products and services should keep in mind that the objective is to establish a monopolistic advantage. That is, the advertising program and the content and nature of the advertising should be formulated in such a way that prospective clients will tend to prefer the subject firm over other firms.

In carrying out the advertising function, the principal purposes of the advertising will be to gain attention for the firm and to present

---

[10] James A. Graaskamp, *A Guide to Feasibility Analysis* (Chicago: Society of Real Estate Appraisers, 1970), p. 35.

[11] Theodore Levitt, "Innovation and the Art of Thinking Small," *Sales Management*, October 1, 1965, p. 32.

specific properties which the firm has listed for sale to the public.
These two types of advertising are called firm advertising and specific
advertising. Another type of advertising, institutional advertising, has
as its purpose the popularizing of real estate in general. Such advertising is usually carried on by a trade or professional group. For example,
the National Association of Realtors® carries on a fairly extensive advertising campaign to promote real estate and the term *Realtor*. Similarly, local real estate boards often promote real estate activity and
encourage buyers and sellers to deal with members of the local board.

In seeking to establish a monopolistic advantage in this area of
activity, the broker-manager should consider how to use the various
advertising media. Most real estate firms rely heavily upon newspapers and signs for their advertising efforts. However, such media as
radio, television, posters, direct mail, streetcar and bus cards, calen-
dars, office displays, letterheads, pencils, and matchbooks might also
be used. Newspaper advertising is most appropriate for specific advertising, where the broker-manager wishes to present various properties
for sale. This type of advertising, however, also provides an important
opportunity for the broker to engage in name advertising. A unique
name or initials can be used for effective public identification. For
example, through successful advertising and promotion, the Harley E.
Rouda Company in Columbus, Ohio, has become known as HER. This
symbol has become identified with a fast-growing, progressive firm.
The initials appear in bold print on all the advertising media used by
this firm.

The choice of advertising media will also depend upon the market
segment that the firm wishes to exploit. For example, brokers dealing
in very expensive residential properties may want to advertise in *The
Wall Street Journal*, where executives with high incomes may be
likely to notice the advertisement. Firms catering to particular ethnic
groups may advertise in newspapers serving those groups. Some firms
in university cities seek to serve university-related personnel and may
advertise heavily in the campus newspaper. In all these kinds of advertising efforts, an effective analysis of the objectives and of the media to
accomplish those objectives will often mean the difference between a
favorable public image and a lack of public identification.

Public relations

Public relations can be defined as constituting all the activities in
which business executives and firms come in contact with the public.
Real estate marketers need to realize that a public image of the individual and the firm is built up in the public mind over a period of time.
All external activities of the firm, such as advertising, attendance at

public meetings, statements made on public issues, dealings with clients, functioning of the sales force, attractiveness and neatness of the office facilities, and manner of dress and personal appearance of the firm's personnel, blend together to create a public image of the firm. Business executives should consider all of these activities and whether they are helping to create the type of public image desired. Is the image desired, for example, that of a dynamic, progressive, fast-growing firm, or is the desired image one of stability—an old-line, conservative firm?

In attempting to establish a public image, the use of a theme, as well as a unique name or initials, may be helpful. Such a theme might emphasize the friendliness or courteousness of the firm's staff. Or it might emphasize the high volume of sales created by the firm. In a subtle way, a theme can quickly and efficiently help establish the public image desired.

Quality of personnel

The real estate broker-manager needs to consider the capacity and efficiency of the sales force. How well educated and trained are the sales associates who meet and deal with the public? This question needs to be considered in relation to the market being served. For example, an extremely high level of education may not be required to perform the sales function efficiently. Advanced degree training typically is not oriented to the persuasive techniques which lead to sales, and the years of advanced degree training frequently lead to an over-emphasis upon details rather than concentration upon issues associated with buyer motivation.

Too often sales personnel are chosen on the basis of the number of people they presumably know. Little thought or attention has traditionally been given to a prospective sales representative's education level, knowledge of art and music, level of success in other fields, or even aptitude for saleswork. With the growing sophistication of real estate investors, however, a background that includes a good education and the ability to converse intelligently on a variety of subjects is becoming more important than the number of people that a particular sales representative can call by their first names. It is often possible, we contend, to train and develop a good sales representative from a well-educated, personable individual; the reverse process is much more difficult.

The objective of personnel policies in a real estate marketing office should be to attract, train, and retain competent people who will take a *professional* approach to the sales function. This approach requires that sales personnel analyze prospective buyers, as well as the properties that they have listed for sale. It means that they should be aware of and should use the steps in the buying process as described earlier in this chapter. It means that they must be aware of investment principles and of what constitutes good and bad investment practice. It requires a desire to study continually to upgrade their competence in helping clients solve their real estate problems. This approach takes a longer run viewpoint than many sales representatives seem to have. It emphasizes the buildup of a clientele over a period of time, rather than maximizing the number of sales in any one month. If the sales representative develops an attitude of trying to help people solve real estate problems, he or she will indeed be successful over the long run.

Management efficiency

Few firms can be successfully and profitably operated for long without fairly good reporting and control. A sizable portion of the broker-manager's time should be spent in analyzing the performance of the firm as it relates to forecasted performance levels. Thus, budgeting and meaningful reports are essential.

Sales performance by the individual members of the sales staff should be analyzed regularly. Important items that should be correlated with sales performance include the time spent by each sales representative in the office, the time spent in transportation, the time spent in open houses, the time spent in analyzing potential customers, the geographic locations served by the sales representative, the length of time that the sales representative has been with the firm, and the educational level of the sales representative.

This type of analysis should be undertaken with a view to helping the sales force do a better, more professional job of marketing real estate. Reports and control devices should not be used with the objective of checking up or taking punitive action. A sales representative who has been employed by a firm for more than a probationary period should be considered a permanent part of the firm and should not be subject to dismissal except in very unusual circumstances. Thus, the objective of management efficiency should be positive rather than negative; management analysis should seek to develop ways in which greater service and more productivity can be attained, but should not be a tool for penalizing members of the sales force.

Selling techniques

The development of selling techniques can be overemphasized. A book answer to every possible objection, or a canned pitch to every prospect, will lead to an unthinking, unprofessional approach to real estate marketing. Rather, selling techniques should be related to the roles played by the various parties in a real estate transaction, as described above in this chapter. The sales representative needs to understand these roles and to analyze potential buyers in terms of whether they are actual buyers, influencers, users, or some combination of these. Furthermore, the sales representative needs to analyze potential buyers in terms of the stage in the buying process in which they happen to be. Some buyers will be going through the stage of prepurchase activity. It would be a mistake to ask such buyers to close a sale when they have not completed this stage of activity and are not yet ready to make a purchase decision. Furthermore, the professional sales representative needs to consider the long-run needs of the client relative to the properties available for sale and also relative to what the potential buyer says that his or her needs are. For example, a family may say that it needs a three-bedroom house. And such a house might be adequate for one or two years. If the sales representative has reason to believe that the family may have need for a larger house within a couple of years, he or she should point this out and attempt to have the family upgrade the size of house that it considers for purchase. Similarly, if the sales representative believes that a client needs a smaller or less expensive property than he or she is considering, the sales representative should encourage the prospective buyer to scale down his or her desires.

Books have been written about the ways in which sales personnel can overcome the objections of buyers. Such an approach has little to recommend it for two reasons. First, a buyer may have legitimate reasons why he or she does not consider a particular property appropriate. The design, the architecture, or the interior arrangement of the property might not be acceptable. To try to overcome such an objection when it is real and legitimate does not serve the buyer in a professional manner. Second, this approach assumes that a stock answer to an objection will be satisfactory to everyone. Obviously, no stock answer will satisfy all potential buyers, and a great injustice is done to the art of selling by trying to get by on stock answers. Again, if the philosophy of trying to help people solve real estate problems prevails, the sales representative will attempt to discuss the disadvantages as well as the advantages of a property with the potential buyer. By gaining the confidence of the buyer, the sales representative will ultimately be able to consummate a transaction with a happy, satisfied client. To high-pressure a buyer into a purchase which he or she will be regretful about afterward is to win a battle but lose the war.

The actual techniques of selling are as varied as the individual sales representatives. Sales representatives must develop a selling approach based upon their own personality, philosophy, and training. Nevertheless, we can identify the steps that a real estate sales representative should go through. They include these ten items:

1. Find and meet prospective buyers and sellers of properties.
2. Orient selling techniques to concerns of the individual buyer or seller.
3. Provide information and advice—help the seller list or the buyer buy.
4. Answer questions and objections.
5. Provide assurance about doubts.
6. Show several acceptable properties to buyers—help them compare.
7. Help indecisive buyers make up their minds.
8. Close the sale—ask the buyer to sign a contract.
9. Suggest steps the buyer should take before closing the transaction. Include the purchase of complementary items, such as insurance, that the buyer may purchase from the brokerage firm.
10. Assure the buyer's satisfaction: allay cognitive dissonance after the purchase.

These steps may seem obvious, but how many purchases can you recall in which the sales representative did not follow them? Unfortunately, the steps are all too often ignored or misapplied. Some sales personnel have never been exposed to them or have not been instructed in how to implement them. These responsibilities must also be borne by marketing management.

LEGAL FRAMEWORK OF REAL ESTATE MARKETING

Most real estate transactions are effected by intermediaries, licensed by the state, whose relationship to their principals is governed by the law of agency. The law of agency requires that an agent, such as a real estate broker, in effect stand in the shoes of his or her employing principal. Thus, a real estate agent must be careful to protect the interests of a client and do nothing that would compromise the probability of consummating a transaction. An agent must exercise the restraint of a "prudent man" in protecting the interests of the client. He or she cannot, for example, purchase the property from the client and then resell the property at a higher price, pocketing both the commission and the profit on the transaction.

A real estate agent's principal, to whom the agent owes legal fealty, is normally the owner of the property. The owner hires a real estate broker to attempt to sell the property. And it is the owner who agrees to pay a commission to the broker if the broker is successful in finding a buyer who is "ready, willing, and able" to buy the property on the terms specified by or acceptable to the seller. In most cases a transaction is not actually required to take place before the seller is liable for the commission.

The terms of sale that the seller is willing to accept and other aspects of the relationship between the seller and the agent are usually spelled out in a written listing contract. The listing is the legal document that gives the broker the right to attempt to sell the property. Upon agreement by a seller and a purchaser, each signs a contract verifying and legalizing the agreement. The contract must be in writing to be enforceable, and it should cover all the important concerns of both the buyer and seller.[12]

SUMMARY

Intelligent marketing is crucial to the success of every business firm. For those firms operating in a market characterized by effective competition, intelligent marketing requires the development of a marketing strategy. Identifying markets or submarkets having needs and devising the proper services or products to meet those needs are the components of strategy development.

Although the real estate market, including the market for properties and the market for the services of marketing firms, often fits the model of monopolistic competition, the marketing of larger, more specialized types of properties may better fit the model of differentiated oligopoly. The real estate market has changed dramatically since the mid-1970s, as small firms have grouped their marketing efforts through computerized multiple listing services and franchises, while corporate giants have entered the field. The Justice Department is watching the industry carefully to insure that a competitive market is maintained.

The job of marketing real estate can be analyzed in terms of buyer behavior and the roles that individuals play during the buying process. The stages of felt need, prepurchase activity, purchase decision, use behavior, and postpurchase feelings are sequential steps through which a purchaser of a major item progresses. It is helpful to a real estate marketer to know which stage a buyer is in and what roles are played in a group purchase. In addition to the final decision maker, there may be influencers, a buyer (as distinguished from the decision maker), and users.

A marketing strategy and analyses of buying stages and roles are useful, often indispensable, components of the marketing function. They do not guarantee success, however. Only their effective im-

---

[12] Listings and contracts, as well as other important documents and legal requirements, are discussed thoroughly in Chapter 11.

plementation by each member of the sales force can produce the desired results. To implement strategy and analysis, the real estate sales representative should carry through several basic steps, tailoring them to the individual customer. Selling techniques should be determined by the sales representative's own personality and the firm's policies and training procedures.

Real estate marketers operate within the legal framework of the law of agency and use several types of legal documents and procedures. They frequently owe legal fealty to one party in a transaction, but they must maintain professional objectivity in serving as intermediaries.

QUESTIONS FOR REVIEW

1. What is the difference between real estate *marketing* and *brokerage?*
2. What is a general definition or concept of strategy? Are other types of strategy relevant to real estate firms? If so, what are they?
3. What kinds of information would be required to identify appropriate submarkets for a new construction firm? For a new brokerage firm? For a new appraisal–investment analysis firm? For a new property management firm?
4. What would be some potential marketing mixes for a residential construction firm? A residential brokerage firm? An industrial brokerage firm?
5. How would a sales representative's approach differ between a buyer who is believed to be in the prepurchase activity stage and the same buyer in the felt need stage?
6. How would a sales representative's approach differ between a decider and a buyer (assuming they are different individuals)?
7. What do you believe should be the role of a "sales manager" in a real estate marketing firm?
8. What types of analyses might sales managers want to make, and what types of information would they need to make such analyses? What types of reports from the sales personnel would be required for these analyses?
9. Comment upon problems of the selling job that appear to be unique to the real estate sales representative.
10. Identify the actions of real estate firms that have led to recent charges of price-fixing and discrimination.

REFERENCES

Case, Fred E. *Real Estate Brokerage.* Englewood Cliffs, N.J.: Prentice-Hall, 1965.

Engel, James F.; Kollat, David T.; and Blackwell, Roger D. *Consumer Behavior.* 3d ed. New York: Holt, Rinehart & Winston, 1978.

Engel, James F.; Wales, Hugh G.; and Warshaw, Martin R. *Promotional Strategy.* 3d ed. Homewood, Ill.: Richard D. Irwin, 1975.

Hadar, Josef. *Elementary Theory of Microeconomic Behavior.* 2d ed. Reading, Mass.: Addison-Wesley, 1974, chaps. 5–10.

Kotler, Philip. *Marketing Management: Analysis, Planning, and Control.* 4th ed. Englewood Cliffs, N.J.: Prentice-Hall, 1980.

McCarthy, E. Jerome. *Basic Marketing: A Managerial Approach.* 6th ed. Homewood, Ill.: Richard D. Irwin, 1978.

chapter 15

Real estate production

Real estate investors can usually choose among properties that are already in existence or properties that can be created to their specifications. The principles and procedures governing any type of real estate investment, along with the legal and market framework, discussed previously, are now brought to bear upon the production of new properties.

Real estate production can be classified conveniently into two principal phases—land development and construction. Land development concerns all those steps taken to prepare raw land for building or improvement. Included in this phase are land procurement, land planning, land preparation, installation of utilities, and installation of streets and curbs. Construction of buildings can then follow. Included in the construction phase are planning the building, contracting for its construction, and managing the construction process. In most production operations both phases must be financed; typically each phase is financed separately.[1]

Economic significance

Real estate production is one of the most important segments of the national economy. New construction in the United States (including

---
[1] The financing function is discussed in Chapters 16 and 17.

land development) was 10.6 percent of gross national product (GNP) in 1965, 9.4 percent in 1970, 8.7 percent in 1975, and 9.5 percent in 1979. The year 1975 was a recession year for new construction, so no downward trend should be implied from these figures. In addition to new construction, maintenance and repair of existing structures serve to raise the value of total construction to about 15 percent of GNP. Investment in new residential and nonresidential structures is the principal component of gross private domestic investment in the GNP accounts. A measure of the importance of the construction industry is the fact that roughly 4 million people are employed in the production of real estate resources and that several million more are employed in related industries which manufacture products that become components of new properties.

Implications of theory

Elasticity of supply.   Chapter 9 is concerned with the interaction of demand and supply forces in the market. It was pointed out that in the short run the supply of real estate is inelastic relative to price increases. In other words, because of the length of time required to produce new real estate resources, an upward shift in the demand curve will result in relatively greater increases in rents and prices than in additional units of space supplied. As the time period of analysis lengthens, however, the supply curve becomes relatively more elastic.

The clear implication for those in the construction industry is that forecasting is of paramount importance to successful business operations. Because of cyclical fluctuations in demand conditions, it will often be too late to take full advantage of an increased demand situation after it has arrived. By the time builders get tooled up, organize their resources, and have construction well along, a period of six months to one year may have elapsed, and by then demand conditions may have slackened or another builder may have provided the needed units. Furthermore, by the time builders get their workers laid off and reduce their construction activities, cyclical variations are apt to produce another upturn, with builders being once again out of phase. Unfortunately, this description is not untypical of average builders today.

The difficulties and uncertainties with which the construction demand forecaster is faced must be realized. Unfortunately, the federal government's housing policies are more in the nature of short-run expedient tactics than of long-run strategies for significantly upgrading American housing. Shifts from tight money to loose money and back again are promulgated periodically by the Federal Reserve Board. Such shifts are sometimes reinforced and sometimes mitigated by ac-

tions of the Federal Home Loan Bank Board, the Federal Home Loan
Mortgage Corporation, the Federal National Mortgage Association, and
the Government National Mortgage Association. In addition, the fiscal
policies and actions of the Federal Housing Administration and the
Veterans Administration serve at times to run the forecasting art into
little more than a guessing game. Myrdal points out the need for longer
range planning in the United States.

> The main thing [needed] in long-range planning is all the separate
> pieces of the jigsaw should be integrated into a single comprehensive
> plan for the development of the economy as a whole. Such a plan,
> specifying not only the speed but also the main direction of economic
> growth, is vital for the framing of government policy. It is equally vital as
> a basis for planning in private business, which must otherwise operate
> with a complex of important parameters in the form of mere guesses,
> based on no real knowledge.[2]

Certainly, however, within the limits of forecasting ability, a six-month
to one-year forecast is crucial to construction firms.

Filtering. Filtering is the movement of people of one income
group into homes which have recently dropped in price and which
were previously occupied by those in the next higher income group.
The implication of the filtering phenomenon is that for the continual
improvement of housing standards, even in a static economy or community, new construction must occur to maintain a surplus of supply at
each family income level. To stand still in the production of housing,
even when economic conditions are static, means to regress. Urban
development and community progress require a continuing supply of
new housing above and beyond the level needed to house an increasing population. However, it is doubtful whether such a condition can
be sustained by the market.[3]

A critical problem in the past has been that old, in-town properties
often could not be economically upgraded. Lenders and appraisers
have found that older neighborhoods sometimes tend to reflect values
which are lower than those of newer and more modern neighborhoods.
The Department of Housing and Urban Development (HUD) has responded to this need through community development grants, and
some cities have experienced efforts by major lenders to revitalize
older neighborhoods. In April 1976 the U.S. Department of Justice
lawsuit filed against the American Institute of Real Estate Appraisers,
the Society of Real Estate Appraisers, the United States League of
Savings Associations, and the Mortgage Bankers Association for al-
leged discrimination against minority groups which typically purchase

---

[2] Gunnar Myrdal, *Challenge to Affluence* (New York: Pantheon Books, 1965), p. 84.
[3] See the discussion in Chapter 9.

homes in older, in-town neighborhoods. The suit requested that practices which downgraded values in such areas be stopped, and the defendants were asked to create new ways to appraise and underwrite older homes in older neighborhoods. Subsequently, the Department of Justice and the AIREA entered into a consent decree, and the suit against the other organizations was dropped.

The government-related secondary financing agencies (Federal National Mortgage Association and Federal Home Loan Mortgage Corporation) and the Veterans Administration responded positively to the government's efforts to stimulate greater amounts of mortgage lending in older and inner city areas. FNMA's urban commitment program provides for financing that includes both the acquisition and rehabilitation of property. Appraisers are instructed to evaluate homes "as renovated," reflecting values compared with those of other renovated homes. This has happened frequently in neighborhoods offering sound property shells; the values of homes in such neighborhoods have increased at approximately twice the average level. Neighborhoods in growing cities such as Atlanta, San Francisco, Dallas, and Houston approached an appreciation rate of 36 percent in 1979. Resales of renovated homes have provided comparables that have allowed VA, FHA, and FHLMC to approve loans at much higher levels than those of past years. Pressures to move back into the central city have resulted from higher gasoline prices, and the movement of middle-income families back to close-in locations has reduced the levels of crime and enhanced the qualities of inner-city life.

The new problem caused by central city renovation is that lower income families have been driven out of homes which had previously been lower in price and were available at rental levels which they could afford. Homes in Atlanta's Grant Park were purchased in 1978 and 1979 for less than $10,000 and resold for prices up to $40,000. The plight of the poor families whose leases were terminated has not been solved as of this writing, although FHA foreclosures have been made available at subsidized prices as low as $1 per home. The solution to this problem is a major challenge of the 1980s.

LAND DEVELOPMENT

Although land development is normally undertaken by private real estate developers and entrepreneurs, it is one of the most socially significant types of business activity. The individual or firm that converts raw agricultural land to urban use establishes land-use patterns and other physical arrangements that often prevail into the future for 100 years or longer. The productivity of the real estate after development will depend upon the extent to which the developer has made wise decisions and has established land-use patterns that will protect and enhance long-run values.

Much criticism has been leveled at land developers in recent years. Too often land developer–builders have failed in other businesses and have then moved on to try their hands at real estate production. Too often they have not been concerned with the long-run best interest of the community; instead, they have in many cases subdivided small acreages with inefficient layouts—small lots, narrow streets, insufficient services, unattractive designs—having little relation to previously established subdivisions, road systems, and utility services. Many times land developer–builders have had no education in real estate. They have been unknowledgeable about economic analysis, social trends, legal influences, and administrative concepts and tools. In more cases than not, real estate production has been performed by carpenters or other tradespeople who have attempted to go into business for themselves or to expand a limited operation. Clearly, with America's urban problems becoming increasingly crucial with each passing month and year, society cannot long tolerate the luxury of nonprofessional dominance in this field.

To bring some control and efficiency to land development, many communities have established various regulations and agencies which govern new real estate development. Developers are legally required to comply with some of these controls, and they should coordinate their developmental planning with other community plans and agencies whether or not there is a legal obligation. The plans and limitations that may be involved are briefly discussed in this section.

Zoning. Zoning is an exercise of the community's police power in regulating land usage, including the height, width, bulk, and density of buildings.[4] Zoning laws are well established in most communities, and compliance is mandatory, although not infrequently these laws have been subverted through political influence. Appointees to a planning commission are sometimes pressured to repay political debts or favors by voting favorably on a requested zoning change. Still, a change in the law or a "variance" is required to defeat the purpose of a zoning ordinance. Misinterpretations of the law or blatant favoritism will be overturned by the courts. In a few cases of noncompliance, developers and builders have been forced to tear down buildings and realign subdivisions. Obviously, the developer and builder should know and thoroughly understand the zoning laws applicable to their developments.

This issue works both ways. County and city zoning officials who have sought to win popular votes have been defeated in courts when

---

[4] See the discussion in Chapters 1 and 18.

their votes against developers have been judged capricious and arbitrary. *Hamby* v. *Barrett* (see Chapter 18) has achieved national stature in its finding that the commissioners of Cobb County, Georgia, discriminated against developers Beller and Gould (represented by the Hamby Estate) in defeating their zoning request. The Supreme Court of the state of Georgia laid down these tests that local officials must follow in determining the propriety of zoning requests:

1. The interests of the landowner and of society in general must be balanced, that is, the value lost to the landowner by failure to be zoned must be offset by value added to other property owners.
2. The proposed rezoning should not be adverse to the community's health (smoke, soot, dirt, garbage, etc.).
3. The proposed rezoning should not be adverse to the community's safety (traffic, combustibility, etc.).
4. The proposed rezoning should not be adverse to the community's morals (nightclub, X-rated movies, etc.).
5. The proposed rezoning should contribute to the community's general welfare (increased taxes, enhancement of surrounding values, etc.).

This case led to hundreds of developer-instigated lawsuits for equity between 1976 and 1980. It is the opinion of the authors that this issue has led, and will further lead, to greater professionalism in the zoning process. Local jurisdictions must now justify their denials on logical grounds, and landowners must defend their positions on similar grounds.

Master plan.   Many communities have developed a master plan, often on a metropolitan area or regional basis. The Franklin County Regional Planning Commission for example, has prepared a plan (known as the Blue Plan) for the entire Columbus, Ohio, metropolitan area. The plan concerns a number of municipalities, and it attempts to forecast and plan for future land development. The plan itself is not legally enforceable; however, most of the communities encompassed by the regional plan have developed their own city plans and zoning ordinances in conformity with it. Certainly professional real estate developers should coordinate their developments with a master plan so as to promote sound, long-run growth.

Building and housing codes.   These local codes regulate, respectively, construction standards and housing conditions and maintenance. Normally the latter would not be of concern to a developer except insofar as construction might influence future housing conditions. The builder obviously must be concerned with the building code and comply with it.

Transportation plans and facilities. Various governmental levels (city, county, and state) may have plans for street and highway development and for expansion of other public transportation facilities. Many cities, for example, have airport expansion plans which could drastically influence land development plans in the area. The large amount of freeway construction in recent years has cut through many existing and planned real estate developments. In many cases plans for extending city streets into newly developing areas will determine the basic street layout for a new subdivision.

Sewer extensions. As a community expands, both sanitary sewers and storm sewers should be extended to serve new areas. Developers must be aware of such plans. In some housing developments, subdivisions without storm sewers have been established, with disastrous results. In other situations, the sewage facilities were inadequate or the land was too low for adequate drainage.

Activities in land development

Land development encompasses all the steps taken from the inception of the decision to undertake a development project to the construction phase. In other words, it involves all the activities necessary to procure land and to prepare it for the construction of a building. Each of these activities is discussed in this section.

Land procurement. Although the necessity of this activity is obvious, the execution and problems associated with it can be quite complex. Furthermore, the considerations vary, depending upon whether the purpose of the land acquisition is to combine already improved parcels into a more intensive use or to develop agricultural land into single-family residential lots. Land should be procured for either purpose only after an adequate market analysis has been performed to determine the feasibility of the proposed undertaking.

In procuring previously developed land within an urbanized area, complex problems often arise from two sources: (1) the existence of improvements on the individual parcels and (2) the need to deal with the multiple owners of the required parcels. For example, in order to construct a new, larger building in a downtown area, the developer usually has to acquire a number of older, smaller parcels with structures of various ages and sizes. The owners may for various reasons have inflated opinions of the value of these parcels or may even refuse to sell the parcels at any price—particularly when they realize that it is imperative for the developer to obtain a given parcel to complete the land procurement plan. This problem has been especially significant in large-scale, private redevelopment efforts. Many urban projects have had to be developed as joint ventures with city governments. A combination of tax incentives and the power of eminent domain renders this type of arrangement practical and desirable.

The early 1970s were characterized by "land boom" which matched or exceeded that of the 1920s. The advent of real estate investment trusts, the attractiveness of real estate syndications, and the seemingly insatiable demand for lots, homes, commercial properties, and so on, attracted everyone from airline pilots to brain surgeons into land investment. Deals grew larger and larger, and "leverage," the nemesis of real estate, led a select, small number of people to become millionaires overnight. The bubble burst in 1973–74, and both institutions and individuals lost substantial sums. Caution became the watchword of the industry, and the need for sound market and financial feasibility analysis gained substantial prominence.

Zoning. The parcel must be zoned properly for the proposed use. If changes in zoning are needed, the developer must commence processing the rezoning request as quickly as possible. The rezoning procedure involves time delay that can be costly if land improvement and construction must be delayed.

Land preparation. Most tracts of land that are to be developed from agricultural to urban uses require the application of a considerable amount of labor and capital. Redevelopment projects in urbanized areas typically require much greater costs for land preparation. In either case the land must be cleared of unwanted debris, old buildings, and trees that hinder construction.

Subdividing. For residential developments, which typically involve the conversion of rural land to urban land, the site must be further developed after the land has been cleared. This phase is known as subdividing, and it usually involves the plotting of lots; the grading of the cleared site; and the installation of utilities, drainage facilities, and roads. Many substeps involving various kinds of costs are, of course, involved in this process. Surveying the preparation of blueprints for the subdivision, providing for water lines, and the installation of curbs, catch basins, and sewers are but a few of these substeps.

In addition to the above types of cash outlays, land developers must also consider the property taxes they will incur during the time they own the lots and also the equity cost that accrues because their capital is tied up. From an economic point of view, all of these costs plus the developer's profit must be considered the cost that society pays for obtaining the newly developed real estate.

Financing. Rarely can land developers pay cash for the land to be developed. Rather, they must finance the property by one of several methods. They might borrow from the seller (with a purchase-money mortgage serving as collateral), obtain an option from the owner to purchase the lots one at a time as they sell previously developed lots (with or without a house constructed on the lot), form a syndicate or a corporation to obtain equity capital from other individuals, or obtain a land development loan from a financial institution. In all such cases, the developers must usually convince the lenders (whether they be owners, investors, or financial institutions) of the feasibility of the project. Therefore, the developers need to have specific plans and budgets for the development and construction that is to take place on the land. A market survey or a number of sales reservations showing the demand expected for the completed units is usually necessary in convincing a seller or financial institution to advance the needed funds.

Significance to urban development

Our purpose is not to describe in detail the steps and processes involved in land development. Rather, we wish to identify and analyze some of the important considerations in the production of profitable and socially desirable real estate projects. Society has the responsibility of providing incentives to the developers who perform their function by creating the long-term utility that is to society's advantage; that is, developers who subdivide in accordance with future requirements and long-term values should be rewarded more than those who are in business to turn a quick dollar and get out. Developers, on the other hand, have the responsibility of understanding their social obligation as well as their means for realizing financial rewards. They should be educated in the area of long-run aesthetics and values. Too often they are not, and the zoning regulations are not intended or sufficient to preclude developments that may produce short-term profits but long-term slums.

Integrated development. The modern approach to land development is to assure proper relationships among the various land uses. Martin defines an integrated development as "one in which many kinds of land improvements are planned in relation to each other and constructed as a unit, as a whole."[5] Residential subdivisions which provide for shopping facilities, entertainment and recreational areas, public parks, and churches are integrated developments. A shopping center in which the various land uses are planned ahead of time and are related to one another is another example of an integrated development. Integrated developments are also related to land uses, utilities, and streets that now or in the future will border the development.

---

[5] Preston Martin, *Real Estate Principles and Practices* (New York: Macmillan, 1959), p. 96.

Integrated development contrasts with the so called add-on type, in which individual lots are developed and improved one at a time. Development of the latter type usually gives too much consideration to existing bordering uses which are probably obsolete. It also fails to provide for needed services and utilities. The ultimate result is unplanned, uncoordinated, nonhomogeneous land uses which do not retain their values as long as integrated developments.

Integrated development requires large-scale development and construction operations. The large firms that can engage in this type of development usually experience economies of scale that make integrated developments generally more profitable. Workers can be assigned to specialized functions, materials can be bought in large quantities, advertising is more rewarding, and managerial talent is applied equally to all phases of the job.

The integrated approach obviously facilitates planned, systematic urban development. Compliance with a master plan and the implementing provisions of the zoning regulations has become crucial in the effort to stem unplanned, topsy-turvy urban sprawl.

One note of caution is needed in analyzing integrated developments. All major lending institutions are fearful that common area facilities, such as parks, playgrounds, recreational amenities, parking garages, and so on, will become a burden on property owners after the developer has sold out and gone. Care must be taken to scale the common elements in such projects at levels which permit sound maintenance at reasonable costs.

Land planning and control.   Planning for the allocation and control of land uses within an integrated development requires an understanding of desirable and undesirable locational relationships. It is one thing to state that adequate shopping facilities should be provided in a residential development; it is quite another to decide the actual layout, and thus the relationships between the residential properties and the shopping area. In general, the shopping area should be convenient enough so that residents can travel there within five or ten minutes, but it must be located so as not to spoil the view or access of the residences. Consideration must be given to the relationships between the number, types, and sizes of the various stores and the number and the income characteristics of the people who are to be served.

The residential lots themselves must be developed so that the homes to be constructed will have adequate space and will be in pleasing relationships with neighboring properties and views, while being shielded from such nuisances as dumps, railroads, and highways. Street patterns should be planned to avoid monotony and high-speed traffic, yet should provide convenient access. The natural contours of the land and other natural advantages such as streams, trees, and views should be considered.

Once the subdivision has been planned and developed, steps should be taken to insure its continued existence as a planned, integrated development. The zoning laws may provide some control, but as discussed previously, these laws serve only to provide a broad framework within which many variations may occur. The developer of an integrated subdivision may well decide that more precise controls are needed. These usually take the form of deed restrictions.

Deed restrictions operate in addition to the zoning laws. The restrictions are placed on every parcel in the subdivision being developed, with provision for termination in 20 or 30 years unless the restrictions are extended by the property owners. Typically, the restrictions should place minimum limitations on the size or ground area of the structures, restrict the land uses and the types of structures, insist on adequate setback lines, and provide for architectural control through a committee of subdivision property owners. Formerly, restrictions limiting structures to those costing more than a given dollar amount were often placed in deeds, but such restrictions have become meaningless with the increasing price level over the years. Restrictions involving measures that are subject to change, such as prices and costs, and restrictions that run for indefinite periods should generally be avoided. Land uses change, and adequate flexibility (as well as the desired degree of control) should be provided.

Role of the developer-investor

Land developers are investors who commit their equity, equipment, labor force, and managerial talents to the conversion of land from one use to another. The developer's role is to conceptualize, plan, organize, and carry out the development of land resources. The developer's social responsibility must be regarded as of the highest importance when one considers the vast amount of wealth represented by the land and the fact that society must usually live with developers' accomplishments for many years. As such, then, the economic rationale for land development and redevelopment should be understood by developers so that they can carry out their function in the best interest of both society and themselves.

Most simply, land development or redevelopment is justified when the present value of the expected benefits is equal to or greater than the cost of obtaining those benefits. Developers should predict the future income levels and patterns that are obtainable under various uses. They should then estimate the costs necessary to develop the land for those purposes and compare the results. The costs for redevelopment projects should, of course, include the costs of demolishing existing uses and the forgoing of income from the existing uses. In either development or redevelopment projects, the developers' cost of capital should be the point below which they will not undertake the projects. The returns afforded by alternative uses above the cost of capital should be ranked, and the use showing the highest overall return should be chosen.

This suggests that the developer-investor must be intimately familiar with costs, income estimation procedures, and capitalization concepts. Income estimation requires knowledge of market analysis techniques, and this requires knowledge and understanding of data sources and research methodology. Certainly the development field should be no place for unsophisticated, nonanalytically oriented individuals. It should command the highest level of competence in business decision-making techniques.

The developer's role is also that of risk bearer. Developers' commitment of capital and labor subjects them to interest rate risk, and the projects in which they have their capital and labor committed are subject to business risk (failure of the undertaking) and market risk (the possibility that the project will decline in value). In most cases the financial risk associated with borrowed funds will also be incurred. Developers must know and understand these risks and be prepared to accept some, avoid some, and pass some along to insurers. As risk managers, developers must be aware of the alternative courses of action that are possible.

The land developer's role can be illustrated by the considerations involved in a decision made by one large land development firm. The firm, Winter and Company, purchases land for subsequent resale—either developed or undeveloped. All of the land purchased by the company is located in or around a large metropolitan area in the Southwest. The area has a well-defined economic base, the major categories of basic employment being heavy manufacturing, national defense, state government, and education. The area has a population of about 1 million persons, and it has been growing at a rate of about 10 percent per year. In short, the demand for well-located, high-quality raw acreage is expected to continue.

A tract of 55 acres of land has been offered for sale and is being considered for purchase by Winter and Company. The land is now zoned for agricultural and rural residential uses. Winter and Company believes that the land can be rezoned for urban residential usage (single family), at a density of 3.5 homes per acre (9,000–12,000-square-foot lots). The land is located about one-half mile outside a recently completed circumferential highway. The asking price for the land is $825,000 ($15,000 per acre). If the land is developed for single-family residences, Winter and Company estimates that the development costs will run approximately $5,000 per lot. It is believed that the lots can be sold within five years for an average price of $13,000. A bank line of credit will finance 75 percent of the land acquisition and development costs at 10 percent. Annual real estate taxes are expected to amount to 1 percent of the unsold land value. The company's marginal tax bracket is 50 percent, and its anticipated rate of return is calculated in Figure 15–1.

As can be seen in Figure 15–1, a discount rate of 16 percent comes close to equating the present value of the cash intake from the sale of lots with the present value of the cash outlays and expenses. The exact rate of return is somewhat more than 16.5 percent.

Several questions arise from this analysis. First, how reliable and accurate are the expected sales prices of the lots? Second, does the analysis include all the expenses that will actually be incurred? Third, are the financing assumptions valid and realistic? Obviously, any variation of substantial proportion will cause the yield to be different from that calculated. There is always some probability that the lot prices will be lower than expected or that sales cannot be made at the expected prices at the time anticipated. Are these risks adequately compensated by a 16 percent aftertax rate of return?

To state the problem differently, the land should not be purchased and developed unless the expected rate of return is above the firm's cost of capital. Its cost of capital is a weighted average of the cost of debt capital and equity. Since equity capital in land development will require a high rate of return to compensate for the risks, the weighted cost of capital will be relatively high—probably at least 15 percent. Winter and Company thus must consider its cost of capital in relation to the project's expected return. It should be confident that its predictions of sale prices, costs, and expenses are as complete and reliable as they can be. The company is then in a position to make a judgmental decision about whether to proceed with the project.

Role of the development lender

One of the major problems in forecasting by construction firms is that construction lenders have a tendency to overextend credit in times of "loose" money and to overrestrict credit when the availability of money is limited. Thus construction lenders accelerate rather than stabilize the cyclical swings of the market. Marginal loans made by lenders during expansion periods lead to substantial overbuilding, creating unsold or unrented inventory. When money is tight, the same lenders typically refuse to provide permanent loans on the products created through their loan efforts. This practice obviously places developers in financial jeopardy.

Good development lenders are moderately conservative, making only loans which can be supervised effectively. They stand behind the

FIGURE 15-1
Winter and Company calculation of investment project profitability

Year	1	2	3	4	5	Total
Sales revenue (38 lots/year)	$ 494,000	$494,000	$494,000	$494,000	$494,000	$2,470,000
Less costs:						
Real estate commissions (5 percent)	$ 24,700	$ 24,700	$ 24,700	$ 24,700	$ 24,700	$ 123,500
Title matters	5,000					5,000
Surveys	3,000					3,0000
Land acquisition cost	825,000					825,000
Land development cost ($5,000 per lot)	190,000	190,000	190,000	190,000	190,000	950,000
Real estate taxes	24,700	19,800	14,800	9,900	4,900	74,100
Total costs	$1,072,400	$234,500	$229,500	$224,600	$219,600	$1,980,600
Revenue minus costs	$ (578,400)	$259,500	$264,500	$269,400	$274,400	$ 489,400
Deduct:						
Loan interest at 10 percent*	$ 80,430	$ 57,840	$ 31,890	$ 5,440	$ –0–	$ 175,600
Income taxes at 50 percent	(329,415)	100,830	116,305	131,980	137,200	156,900
Net cash flow	$ (329,415)	$100,830	$116,305	$131,980	$137,200	$ 156,900
Present value of 1 factor at 16 percent	×0.8621	×0.7432	×0.6406	×0.5523	×0.4761	
Present value of cash flow	$ (283,989)	$ 74,937	$ 74,505	$ 72,893	$ 65,321	$ 3,667†

* Loan interest is based on the assumption that costs occur at the beginning of the year and revenues occur at the end of the year. The maximum loan is 75 percent of land acquisition and development cost. Thus, the loan balance at the end of year 1 is $1,072,400 times 75 percent equals $804,300. This loan is assumed to be reduced to $578,400 on January 1 of year 2, to $318,900 on January 1 of year 3, to $54,400 on January 1 of year 4, and to $0 on January 1 of year 5. All repayments are assumed to be made from project revenues.

† This figure represents value above a 16 percent (aftertax) rate of return. When discounted at a 17 percent rate, the ending balance is ($2,259), indicating that the project is capable of earning approximately 16.6 percent.

borrower and develop a financing plan that does not end until the unit is financed permanently. Savings and loan associations performed unusually well in this regard during the 1974–75 recession; real estate investment trusts performed poorly. The savings and loan industry performed equally well during the 1980 recession.

Role of the secondary financing market

Residential markets are by far the largest in dollar volume, number of loans, and amount of necessary supervision. The housing market is cyclical in the same direction as the general economy, but it tends to lag the economy by several months. In recent years the Federal National Mortgage Association (FNMA) and the Federal Home Loan Mortgage Corporation (FHLMC) have been geared to offer funding during periods of tight money. These secondary markets also supervise subsidized emergency assistance home loans issued by the Government National Mortgage Association (GNMA), another program to encourage market stability. During 1975 the GNMA program injected $10 billion into the economy for new single-family homes. In 1976 an initial injection of $3 billion was placed in multifamily homes, while approximately $5 billion went into loans for detached homes. A total of $10 billion of emergency assistance money was allocated for the year.

When money is tight, interest rates rise and yields increase on the home loans purchased by FNMA and FHLMC. However, FNMA sells forward standby commitments which permit knowledgeable developers to hedge against such increases. These commitments may be purchased at a price of 1 percent of the amount of the loans to be delivered. They are at a fixed yield rate, and they can be exercised or allowed to expire at the purchaser's option. If they are exercised, 0.5 percent is refunded. Commitments of this type tend to stabilize the market, but they have not been used extensively to date.

A secondary market vehicle that has been developed at the Chicago Board of Trade is the sale of forward commitments to buy FHA and VA home loans through the GNMA. The GNMA commits itself to purchase loans at fixed future dates and at fixed yields. Purchasers of the commitments bid on them in the same manner as they would on other types of commodities futures.

CONSTRUCTION

The building or construction process is carried on by an industry which, when considered in total, is our largest single industry. However, size alone—present and future—is not the only consideration that is expected to enhance the place of the construction industry in the national economy. Increases in the industry's efficiency and productivity may well occur at a faster rate than formerly and at faster rates than increases in the efficiency and productivity of other segments of the economy. Heretofore, the construction industry has been regarded as the least progressive of our major industries. Although productivity has increased, the gains have been lower than those of other fields. As Weimer, Hoyt, and Bloom point out:

> The industry continues to suffer from restrictive building codes, restrictive labor practices, and from its dependence on the development of regional supporting facilities by government to allow for new land development. Many builders, of course, continue to follow outmoded practices. Informal agreements sometimes result in price-fixing and the reduction of competition.[6]

To the extent that productivity gains in construction have not kept pace with those of other industries, the construction industry has contributed less growth to our total national wealth than have other segments of the economy. If productivity gains can be increased significantly, however, construction will contribute a greater share of increase to our national resources, Weimer, Hoyt, and Bloom also point out that the building industry may be having its industrial revolution, which suggests that the industry may shortly take off in productivity relative to its past performance and to other industries.[7]

Structure of the industry

Construction firms range in size all the way from very small companies to very large companies that engage in building operations in several countries. However, most of today's builders are relatively small operators. In home building, even the large builders such as Levitt and Sons, Inc., Ryan Homes, Inc., and U.S. Home are small in relation to the total market; each of the largest builders accounts for less than 0.5 percent of the industry's total production.

Also characteristic of the industry are the small outlays on research and development expended by construction firms and industry groups. Little research and development effort is undertaken by private firms, with the result that little new knowledge about construction materials and methodologies is obtained or distributed. Prefabrication techniques are considerably further advanced in European countries, and laborsaving techniques are employed more extensively. The conclusion is that profit squeezes will be felt increasingly by smaller firms

---

[6]Arthur M. Weimer, Homer Hoyt, and George F. Bloom, *Real Estate*, 7th ed. (Ronald Press: 1978), p. 327.

[7]Ibid., p. 330.

and that increases can be expected in the number of large-scale regional and national builders.

The construction process

Many steps and operations are involved in the construction of any major improvement to the land—whether the improvement be a home, apartment building, commercial structure, factory, or hydroelectric dam. Construction concerns the conversion of prepared but vacant land to a usable, productive parcel of real estate. It represents the creation of economic resources by the combining of various components into new time, form, and place relationships—both among themselves and with the land.

Functions

Planning. As with every complex task, the management functions of planning, organizing, and controlling must be performed in the construction process. In the planning function, provisions must be made for designing the structure, specifying the materials and components that will make up the structure, arranging for the purchase and timely availability of materials and components, arranging for the labor force required to assemble the materials and components, and providing for financing adequate to support these activities. Typically, an architect and a contractor are hired to perform all of these activities except the financing activity for the investor-builder.

The planning objective of the architect is to design a building that will serve most appropriately the functions or uses to which the building will be put. To do this the architect must thoroughly understand the requirements of the owner or user of the property.

> Design involves space planning, engineering design, and aesthetics. Space planning includes site planning—the disposition of the structure on the land—and interior planning—the distribution of the space within the building; engineering design relates to the structural features of the building, the floor and wall construction, roof framing, stairways, footings, and other features that determine the structural strength of the building. From an aesthetic standpoint, the architect endeavors to impart a pleasing appearance to the structure through the arrangement of masses and proportions and the selection of materials and architectural details.[8]

---

[8] Richard U. Ratcliff, *Urban Land Economics* (New York: McGraw-Hill, 1979), p. 177.

Under the planning function, the architect also specifies the quality, grade, brand name, or model number (hence the term *specifications* or *specs*) of the exact materials and component assemblies that are to go into the building. In writing the specifications, the architect must keep abreast of new materials, building techniques, and local building codes. Every subsurface and surface aspect of the structure must be designed and integrated into the plans. The architect must be able to visualize the finished product and to convert this visualization into a step-by-step plan for achieving it.

Organizing. Except for arranging for suitable financing, the activities involved in the organizing function are usually performed by the architect and/or the contractor. In addition to the architect who designs the structure and specifies its components, an architect may be engaged to supervise the building process. These architects control the activities of the builder to insure conformity with the plans and specifications. They check the construction process to see that the quality is acceptable.

Although architects are not ordinarily employed in the construction of single-family homes costing under $100,000, it seems likely that professional architectural services could be used profitably for the construction of many homes above the $100,000 level. The typical fee for full architectural service runs about 10 percent of the cost, and in higher priced homes the advantages of architectural design and supervision may more than make up for this fee. Studying the functional requirements of the family that is to occupy a dwelling and incorporating into the structure a design and features that will best meet these requirements is ordinarily not work for an amateur.

For their fee, architects attempt to provide an aesthetically pleasing environment and building, yet one which conforms to the pocketbook constraints of their employers. Since each family's makeup, age structure, personalities, and interests are different from those of every other family, it stands to reason that individual attention to the design of a home would be desirable for most families that can afford a relatively high-priced structure.

The purchase of a house that has been built for speculative resale (although constituting the largest source of new-home purchases) may not offer the best compromise between the desirable attributes of efficiency and beauty and the costs incurred. Indeed, the disadvantages may extend even further to inferior quality of work, materials, and components. To their credit, many of the larger, more experienced speculative builders now offer reliable warranties on ready-built houses. Furthermore, some recent court decisions have enforced the concept of vendor (builder-seller) warranty and in some cases have even extended the concept to financial institutions that have significant control over the building process. Nevertheless, the larger issue between architectural cost and advantage will not be resolved by the courts—only by the service provided.

Financing of the construction process is ordinarily organized by owners or contractors. The owners may be speculative builders who are erecting a large number of houses for resale or individuals who have contracted for the building of a home for their own occupancy. In the construction of multifamily residential buildings, commercial buildings, or industrial structures, the owners may be individual investors, partnership syndicates, corporations, or other types of organizations. In almost all cases, however, the individual or organization doing the actual construction must obtain the financing. Because of the large and unusual risks involved in this type of financing, a number of special safeguards and arrangements have evolved for construction financing.

The need for construction financing arises because the individuals who have contracted to have a building constructed will not pay for the work until it is completed, and builders cannot or do not want to pay the bills for labor and materials out of their own pockets before receiving payment from their employer. The builder's borrowing is done by means of a short-term (usually two to nine months), secured loan from a financial institution. The security for the loan is the land and a nonexistent building. Because of the risk that the building will not be built or will not be completed according to plans and specifications in the time period forecasted, the financial institution will typically not pay out the loan before construction has begun. Instead, the loan is usually paid out in stages after specified portions of the building have been completed—for example, after the foundation is in, after the roof is on, after the plumbing and electrical work have been completed, and when the building is finished. The financial institution will pay out portions of the loan, the total of which is smaller than the value of the security of the percentage of the job accomplished. For example, one third of the loan might be paid out after the roof is on, although the building might then be approximately 50 percent complete. Also, the lender will require the builder to show proof of payment of bills and to provide lien waivers from contractors and subcontractors.

Controlling. The controlling function for the construction process is performed by the owner, the architect, the contractor, and sometimes the financier. As discussed above, an architect representing the owner may control the construction process by supervising the builder. Owners could perform this function, of course, if they are qualified, but usually they are not capable of adequate supervision. Typically, for small, single-family home construction jobs, the owners employ contractors who are entrusted with the controlling function as well as the actual building process. The owners periodically check major aspects of the job, such as the general layout, the brand names of components, and the general construction quality. It would be quite easy in most cases, however, for a dishonest contractor to get by with inferior materials and poor work.

For large-scale development and construction projects, a team of engineers and inspectors representing the general contractor maintain constant supervision of the actual work. Spot checks by the owners, their architects, or the financial institution could cause nonpayment to the contractor. In large residential developments, the speculative builder's team of inspectors is charged with maintaining certain minimum standards of materials and an adequate quality of work. If a builder wishes to be able to sell houses on a continuing basis, the buying public must have a favorable image of the builder's capability and product. Also, in order to sell the houses, the builder may have to rely on government-underwritten financing for buyers and must therefore meet the standards required by the FHA and VA.

Role of the builder

Although various aspects of the functions of planning, organizing, and controlling are performed by parties other than the builders, the builders are the crucial element in the construction process. More of the construction process is performed by builders than by anyone else. The builders' role comprises a number of activities. Builders must estimate construction costs, submit bids on building jobs that will allow them an acceptable rate of return, assemble and organize materials and labor, arrange for construction financing, disburse payments to workers and subcontractors, supervise actual construction, and work with the owner.

The key to success for builders is their ability to estimate costs realistically and accurately. Reliable cost estimates and breakdowns will allow builders to submit acceptable bids, obtain materials and labor, cover their overhead, and make a profit. Figure 15–2 is a builder's house for which Figures 15–3 and 15–4 provide a detailed description and a cost breakdown. As shown in Figure 15–4, the costs are usually categorized according to the labor and materials going into the main structure, with heating, plumbing, and electrical systems considered separately from the main structure. If a builder's work force includes heating engineers, plumbers, and electricians, they would do this work. Often, however, smaller builders subcontract the heating, plumbing, and electrical work to specialized firms in these fields. The heating, plumbing, and electrical installations make up a significant proportion—18.38 percent—of the total cost of the house.

FIGURE 15–2
Builder's house plan

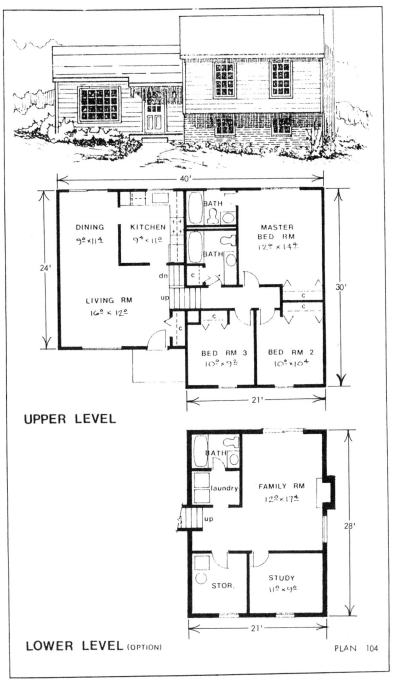

UPPER LEVEL

LOWER LEVEL (OPTION)

PLAN 104

FIGURE 15–3
Builder's house (detailed description)

Description:
  Three-bedroom, brick and stone, side split-level home.
  Seven rooms, 2½ baths.
  Built-ins in kitchen.
  Partial basement under living area.
  Brick fireplace in family room.
  Two-car garage.
Structure:
  Excavation and clay gravel: 11 courses, 8″ C.B., waterproofing; termite protection; metal windows.
  Chimney: C.B. with brick facing fireplace, flue size 12″×12″, gas vented into 8″ × 12″ flue; water heater vented.
  Fireplace (in family room): Firebrick lining; stone hearth; ceiling high mantle.
  Exterior walls: Sheathing Gyplap, ½″, 4′ × 8′, solid; face brick; frame backup, 2′ × 4′; door sills concrete; stone window sills; exterior painting lead and oil.
  Floor framing: #1 fir, 2″ × 8″–16″ O.C.; 1″ × 3″ bridging; joist anchors concrete slab basement floor.
  Fill under slab: 4″ gravel.
  Subflooring: ⅜″ plywood.
  Finish flooring: Nylon shag carpeting over 60-oz. foam pad.
  Partition framing: #1 fir, 2″ × 4″–16″ O.C.
  Ceiling framing: #1 fir, 2″ × 6″–16″ O.C.; bridging 1″ × 3″.
  Roof framing: #1 fir, 2″ × 6″ O.C.; collar beams 1 fir, 2″ × 4″–24″ O.C.
  Roofing: Asphalt shingle #210, size 12″ × 36″; tin flashing 26 ga.
  Gutters: Galvanized iron, 26 ga., 5″ o.g.
  Downspouts: Galvanized iron; 26 ga.; 3″ o.g.; number 4; connected to tile and to curb.
  Drywall: Walls and ceiling; ½″ thick; tape and sanded; joints cemented.
  Decorating: Kitchen and baths—3 coats I. & O. (1 flat, 2 enamel); living room, hall, and bedrooms—flat oil base paint, 2 coats; recreation room—paneled.
  Interior doors and trim: Doors—slab, flush; door trim—modern; finish—doors and trim. Stain shellac, varnish.
  Windows: Aluminum sliding—glass, single strength. Trim—molding W.P., painted 3 coats; screens—full aluminum; basement windows—Truscon or equal steel.
  Entrance and exterior detail: Main entrance door—3′ wide, 1¾″ thick; other entrance doors—W.P., head flashing 26 ga.; screen doors 1¼″ thick; railings and louvers, exterior millwork, redwood-plywood under overhang painted 3 coats.

FIGURE 15–3 (continued)

> *Cabinets and interior detail:* Westinghouse kitchen; base units, birch;
>   Formica counter top, stainless steel edging, 4″ backsplash; medi-
>   cine cabinet; all cabinets fruitwood stain—1 sealer, 1 filler, 1 finish
>   shellac.
> *Special floors and wainscot:* Kitchen and bath—Armstrong inlaid
>   linoleum, rubber base ⅝″ plywood underfloor; bath—ceramic tile
>   recess 4½″ high.
> *Plumbing:* 1 kitchen double-bowl sink, Westinghouse disposer and
>   dishwasher; 3 single-bowl sinks in bathrooms (tinted fixtures); 3
>   water closets (3 white fixtures); 2 bathtubs (tinted fixture); 2 show-
>   ers over tub (ceramic tile recess 4½′); 1 40-gallon glass-lined auto-
>   matic water heater.
> *Heating:* Gas forced air (100,000 Btu input—80,000 output capacity);
>   kitchen exhaust hood.
> *Electric wiring:* Circuit breaker—110–220 volts.
> *Hardware:* Chrome and brass.

Another category is indirect costs. These are costs for items that pertain to the entire property but are not functionally identifiable. The costs of utilities are lumped together in this category, together with such items as the building permit and the survey expense.

A much larger category is overhead and profit. Overhead includes the builder's office and general expenses. The breakdown in Figure 15–4 also identifies loan-related costs, surveys and soil tests, architect and engineering fees, and real estate taxes during the construction period. A normal builder's profit of about 15 percent of total costs is included in this example. A marketing cost of 5 percent provides for brokerage commissions, on-site personnel, and advertising.

Site improvements and the garage are shown as structural costs in Figure 15–4. These items are frequently shown separately when a builder offers such options as concrete drives and a one-car garage. When shown separately, they can be deleted or modified without affecting the basic house analysis.

The total costs of construction, site preparation, land, overhead, profit, and selling expenses comprise the anticipated sale price of the home. If they have been estimated accurately, an appraisal of the finished home will support this price and allow the purchaser to secure desirable financing while the builder earns the desired profit.

The possibility or, more accurately, the likelihood of being in error on the cost estimate, together with the vagaries inherent in the real estate market, should point up the hazards to small builders. A small

FIGURE 15–4
Builder's house (cost estimate)

Cost breakdown

Engineer's staking and materials ...	$ 100	Vanity tops	$ —
Excavation	560	Bath accessories.................	80
Concrete	3,250	Stairs	135
Termite treatment	72	Rails and dividers	45
Carpentry labor	2,450	Hardware.........................	—
Lumber and exterior trim; floor		Sliding glass doors	200
trusses and roof trusses	4,800	Glass and mirrors, carpet,	
Windows and front door	725	vinyl flooring	2,000
Plumbing.......................	3,400	Painting	2,000
Roofing material and labor	800	Ceramic tile	960
Metal gutters	—	Cleaning—unit final	100
HVAC	2,500	Mailboxes and number	—
Electric wiring and electric		Prefab chimney	700
fixtures.......................	1,250	Chimney surround	200
Insulation	450	Brick-stone	400
Sheetrock	2,400	Nails and carpentry	240
Trim wood interior	725	Garage	3,000
Metal bifold doors	250	Sitework (landscaping, seed,	
Metal closet shelves	85	asphalt)	2,500
Kitchen cabinet and vanity top	725	Contingency	1,000
Kitchen equipment	800	Total	$38,902

Cost analysis

	Dollar cost	Cost per square foot	Percentage of total cost
Construction	$38,902	$23.24	56.9%
Overhead and general conditions	2,500	1.49	3.6
Land (7,500 square feet)	9,000	5.38	13.2
Architect and engineering	300	0.18	0.4
Survey	200	0.12	0.3
Soil tests..	150	0.09	0.2
Taxes	200	0.12	0.3
Interest (six months)	2,400	1.43	3.5
Construction loan closing costs, legal fees,			
title insurance	2,000	1.19	2.9
Contingency.......................................	1,000	0.60	1.5
Total	$56,652	$33.84	82.8%
15% ± builder's profit.............................	8,500	5.08	12.4
Total before cost of sales	$65,152	$38.93	95.2%
Cost of sales (5%±)	3,258	1.95	4.8
Sale price (value)	$68,410	$40.88	100.0%

underestimation of costs can easily wipe out most of their profit. Or, if the demand for the type of property they have produced is not strong, they may not be able to sell it at the desired prices or at the times of completion. The supply of mortgage money may become tighter, an industry may leave town, the employment level may drop, or the market may just not react favorably to the new property. Relative to the profit, the structure may be too large, too small, unattractive, poorly designed, or low in quality. Thus, we find that many small builders go bankrupt or leave the business each year.

Administrative problems and considerations

Market analysis. Data available regarding demand are the same whether an existing or a new structure is being contemplated, but changes in supply require consideration of the possible adjustments in activity patterns that might result. A development of new retail shopping facilities might reroute traffic, causing great demand in the new shopping area and a deterioration of demand in the old area. Property values follow consumer demand, the problem being one of determining whether a new development can pull business from old ones. The investors in the older structures have a proven record, providing them with a sound base for holding their business.

A closely related problem is that of attempting to make a product that offers a competitive advantage over existing land uses in the vicinity. An apartment builder might find a strong demand for three-bedroom apartments, the meeting of which might draw families out of two-bedroom units located in the area. A residential subdivider might choose to specialize in $80,000–$90,000 homes for a given tract, even though the surrounding area is improved with homes of substantially less value. In all such cases it is much easier to determine the demand experience of existing uses than the demand for the proposed new use. Market research studies under these circumstances thus must be of two types: (a) analyses of the demand for the proposed use and (b) analyses of the demand for existing uses. The latter studies might indicate that a greater advantage could be gained by developing land in the same manner that surrounding properties have been developed than by developing land for new uses.

Once an initial program has been tested by market research, an exploratory development effort should be made. Unit sizes, price ranges, and development densities can be tested empirically before large-scale development is undertaken. Major home builders, such as Fox and Jacobs in Dallas, follow this approach and construct model homes to sell from rather than building an inventory of homes for immediate sale. They limit their financial risk to the investment in the models.

Financing. The cost of money changes frequently, and new construction is subject only to current costs. When current money costs are high, new structures are at a cost disadvantage as compared with existing structures. Rents and sale prices must be increased to accommodate high-interest rates on construction loans, and an increase in permanent loan interest rates can cause a permanent realignment in developmental economics. On a $100,000 loan for an apartment building, a 12 percent interest rate requires $2,000 more net income per year than does a 10 percent rate, an increase requiring higher rental charges in a new building than those received by older buildings. Of course, a low-interest-rate market has the opposite effect in terms of interest cost.

The complications of financing create administrative problems for developers. They must develop substantial written information regarding the project, the owners, and other projects developed by themselves. This information is submitted to a permanent lender who is asked to issue a letter of commitment for a future loan. If this is successful, the letter and the data package flow to a construction lender who is asked to issue the first funds. The construction loan, when approved, is disbursed in stages as the project is built. The construction loan is then repaid from the proceeds of the permanent loan.

Each lender in this process sets conditions that force the developer to get the project completed and rented or sold as quickly as possible. Most construction loans are issued for less than the full amount that the permanent lender has agreed to fund, so the developer must seek out a third lender for what is known as a "gap" loan. The interest rate on such financing is usually very high. As a further complication, most permanent loans require that the project achieve a predetermined level of rentals or sales before the permanent loan can be closed. This forces the developer to pay high interest rates on interim loans until occupancy reaches the required level.

Aside from the interest expense of money, the investor must consider the down payment required and the terms of repayment possible in the present market. Real estate investments normally involve loans that comprise a high percentage of appraised value.

Leverage, that is, the use of borrowed money to earn a sum greater than the cost of that money, provides a higher percentage return on investment than would be possible with 100 percent equity financing. High down payments and 10-year amortized repayments require a much higher net income than would be necessary with lower down payments and 20-year amortization. This increased net income would not be forthcoming where competing investments have competitive financing advantages.

Taxation. A common practice in recent years has been for developers to establish rapid depreciation techniques that minimize taxes in the first few years of operations. Reported profits are low or nonexistent, yet the cash flow from the investments are substantial. After about ten years the annual write-off is reduced, thereby increasing the annual income tax, but the investor has withdrawn much of the capital. It has been invested elsewhere in a manner that has earned more than it would have if a more gradual form of depreciation had been used.

The important point regarding the use of the depreciation concept is that investors look toward sources other than reported income to justify new improvements. A tax advantage today is more beneficial than an advantage gained after several years, and past exchanges of investment properties have indicated a tendency for different types of investors to operate in the short-run construction arena and the long-run operational arena. The investors who operate in the former arena look toward cash flow and capital gain through property sales for this return; those who operate in the latter arena look toward net income.

Zoning. New structures frequently do not fit the existing zoning plan. Zoning is nearly always a hindrance rather than a help to land developers. Existing structures operate under innumerable forms of former zoning regulations or variances. When a new use is contemplated that requires rezoning or the granting of a variance, the potential competitors are able to fight it through the city council or the zoning board. The competitors' position is more secure when new competition is thwarted.

Labor unions and productivity. Labor unions have frequently been attacked as a principal cause of the high costs and slow productivity advances in the construction industry. Certainly in an industry which requires large inputs of handwork, labor costs are bound to be high and the role of unions highly visible. In residential construction, for example, on-site labor costs typically run about 50 percent of the total costs. In the prefabrication of buildings the input of hand labor is still relatively high—both in the assembling of components at the site and in the manufacturing process. Undoubtedly labor practices have added to the rocketing costs of construction; in the overall picture, however, it is probable that too much of the blame for the industry's problems has been attributed to unions.

One way in which unions impede productivity in the construction industry is by attempting to dictate supply terms to the market by placing limitations on the number of new workers admitted to a trade; the effect, of course, is to maintain high wage rates. High initiation fees and trade examinations are sometimes used to control entrance to a trade. The degree to which unions are able to manipulate the labor supply varies from community to community.

Restrictive entrance requirements have had as one objective and effect the exclusion of racial minority groups from union membership. Such practices came under strong attack in the late 1960s with the push for civil, social, and economic rights. Today requirements by federal and state governments for more than token employment have resulted in the increasing employment of blacks and women in the building trades; many business firms building large structures specify that a certain percentage of the work force must belong to minority groups.

Another difficulty occurs because trade and craft unions are highly specialized, resulting in jurisdictional disputes and work stoppages where specific areas of work are unclear. Some unions demand jurisdiction in activities which do not involve specialized talent, such as demand of the painters' union that its members be given the right to clean paint spots.

Perhaps the greatest negative effect of the unions in limiting production comes from their efforts, often violent, to fight the use of laborsaving devices and new materials that threaten the need for skilled labor. As one example, the use of plastic pipe has been resisted stubbornly in many communities with arguments that the new type of pipe is inferior to cast iron or copper, which is untrue. Plumbers' unions have also argued that plastic pipe is a cheap substitute requiring no ability to install—arguments which are irrelevant to accomplishing the job. Some other examples have been forbidding the use of paint spray guns, limiting the size of paint brush used, and forbidding the use of premixed concrete.

It should be pointed out that underlying motivation for the restrictive practices of unions is the concern for job security. The nature of the construction industry and the construction process has resulted in quite unstable employment. Neither social legislation nor the approaches of employers have allowed unions to take a positive viewpoint toward laborsaving innovations.

> It seems likely, however, that labor unions have been criticized too harshly and assigned too much of the responsibility for the construction industry's slow productivity advances. The basic culprit must be identified as the structure of the industry itself, since a structure of larger firms would allow more effective dealings with unions. A situation in which small, weak, unsophisticated firms must deal with larger, more powerful unions is not the ideal model for collective bargaining.[9]

The impact of OSHA. The Occupational Safety and Health Act of 1973 established new construction safety standards which increased

---

[9] Halbert C. Smith, "Housing: Are We Paying More and Getting Less?" *Business Horizons*, Winter 1967, pp. 7–20.

substantially the cost of constructing new buildings. Workers are required to wear protective clothing and equipment; guardrails and barriers are to be constructed during the building period; and openings or holes are to be covered. Contractors must comply with these requirements, or financial penalties (fines) are imposed. The requirements have been controversial, and cost increases have been emphasized. After five years, however, the compliance enforcement agency has gained considerable experience, and the problems are becoming fewer. The law does produce improved safety conditions, and hopefully it will soon achieve a balance between costs and benefits.

SUMMARY

The production of new real estate resources is one of the country's most important economic functions, with new construction in the United States averaging about 10 percent of the GNP. The construction industry holds added significance for economic forecasters and related industries because of the difficulty of predicting future activity. Forecasting is difficult because supply lags demand, the industry is composed of primarily small, unsophisticated firms, and labor unions can interrupt work and increase costs after a project has been started.

Developers, builders, and lenders must coordinate their efforts to balance supply and demand relative to the final product of their efforts. The cost efficiencies of developing large land assemblages must be balanced against the potential cost of carrying improved land inventory for an extended period. The source of construction loans and permanent financing should be known before the improvement program begins.

Both land development and construction must operate in a framework of social controls such as zoning, building codes, community plans, and local regulations pertaining to streets, sewers, and utilities. Effective performance of the management functions of planning, organizing, and controlling are required in the construction field to minimize cost overruns, which are often disastrous to small builders. Important roles may be played in some or all of these functions by the owner, architect, contractor, and financier.

Professional real estate production administrators-investors need to estimate accurately all costs to be incurred in evaluating the desirability of a landholding and land development project or a construction project. They must then estimate the gross and net proceeds to be obtained, placing all proceeds and costs on a present value basis. A rate of return may then be calculated which can be compared with the firm's cost of capital.

QUESTIONS FOR REVIEW

1. How can zoning affect a land developer's rate of return?
2. Is the holding of land a useful economic function? Why? Can landholding be socially undesirable? How?
3. Do you believe that great increases in productivity are possible in the construction industry? Why or why not?
4. If you were to build a new home for your family, would you employ an architect? Why or why not?
5. Why does the structure of the construction industry contribute to an inefficient handling of labor disputes?

REFERENCES

Case, Fred E. *Investing in Real Estate.* Englewood Cliffs, N.J.: Prentice-Hall, 1978.

Crean, Michael J. *Principles of Real Estate Analysis.* New York: D. Van Nostrand, 1979, chaps. 10–14.

Cummings, J. *Complete Guide to Real Estate Financing.* Englewood Cliffs, N.J.: Prentice-Hall, 1978.

Hines, M. A. *Real Estate Finance.* Englewood Cliffs, N.J.: Prentice-Hall, 1978.

Hoagland, H. E.; Stone, L. D.; and Brueggeman, W. B. *Real Estate Finance.* 6th ed. Homewood, Ill.: Richard D. Irwin, 1977.

Martin, Preston. *Real Estate Principles and Practices.* New York: Macmillan, 1959.

Ratcliff, Richard U. *Real Estate Analysis.* New York: McGraw-Hill, 1961, pp. 269–305.

Roulac, Stephen E. *Modern Real Estate Investment.* San Francisco: Property Press, 1976.

Wendt, P. F., and Cerf, A. R. *Real Estate Investment and Taxation.* 2d ed. New York: McGraw-Hill, 1979.

chapter 16

Real estate financing 1:

Obtaining funds

Epic Homes Corporation, a relatively large local builder, began development of a 74-acre tract of land. Its objective was to create a well-planned subdivision of $80,000 to $100,000 homes at the edge of a medium-sized city. As preliminary work began at the site, an observer could not see and perhaps would not comprehend the importance of financing to this project. Neither James Randolph, the president of Epic, nor Epic Homes Corporation had invested any cash in the project. The land was purchased, development was begun, and homes would be constructed entirely with funds borrowed from others.

While most development projects require some financial input by the investor-entrepreneur, almost all real estate developments rely on a preponderant proportion of borrowed funds. The complex structure of institutions that lend money, the legal instruments and arrangements, the methods of evaluating risk, and many specialized conventions and techniques of the mortgage market form a system that is essential to real estate development. It is a system that must be studied one part at a time, and yet for effective understanding it should also be visualized *in toto*. The arrangements in any given real estate venture will constitute a unique combination; no two financing transactions are identical. However, the successful real estate entrepreneur understands thoroughly each component part of the system and is able to combine the parts in creative ways.

In the case of Epic Homes, the land was provided by the landowner in exchange for 25 percent of the profit to be derived from the project plus a 10 percent interest in the stock of Epic Homes Corporation. On the basis of the planned layout, engineering studies, and home designs, a local bank extended a loan for development and agreed to provide construction financing for up to one third of the homes. The bank also agreed to make long-term mortgage loans on prevailing terms for up to one third of the homes in the development to home purchasers who qualified under the bank's requirements. Other local lending institutions had expressed interest in financing both the construction and the long-term purchases of the remaining two thirds of the homes. Randolph was confident that with the successful completion and sale of one eighth to one fourth of the homes, public acceptance of the project would enable the remaining financing to be obtained.

The financing pattern for the Epic Homes project could have been quite different. Epic might have owned or purchased the land with its own capital—all or part of which might have been equity. Epic might have purchased the land partially with its own capital and partially with a loan from the landowner. The land development loan might have been obtained from the landowner at market interest rates, or the landowner might have been given a larger share of the profits to make the loan. Both the land development loan and the construction loan might have been obtained from a mortgage investment trust or a savings and loan association. Or one loan might have been obtained from one institution and the other loan from another institution. A permanent financing commitment might have been obtained for all of the new homes from a savings and loan association, a mutual savings bank, a mortgage banker, or a life insurance company. The terms—including interest rates, discounts and fees, maturities, privileges, and penalties—of the various loans could differ greatly among lenders. Thus, financing as an element in the real estate development process is subject to greater variation than almost any other factor.

In addition to making real estate development possible, financing often determines whether a project will be profitable. If the interest rate on a major loan is too high or a discount is too great, a project's profit may be eaten away. If a loan must be repaid before other funds are obtained, the entire project may be forfeited. If a lender exerts too much control over the project, unpopular designs and inefficient methods may be required or too much effort in paperwork may result. All of these considerations point up the great importance of financing to the production of new real estate resources and the significance for every real estate investor of understanding the role of financing.

FLOW OF FUNDS TO FINANCE REAL ESTATE

Funds may be defined as cash or any resource having value which is capable of being sold in order to buy some other asset. We may think of funds as being composed of deposits in banks and savings and loan associations, reserves built up in life insurance policies,[1] equity interests in investments such as stocks, bonds, or real estate, or other noninvestment assets such as homes, paintings, Oriental rugs, automobiles, or any item of value. The great bulk of funds used for real estate originates from two sources: (a) equity buildup in real estate and (b) cash savings of individuals and businesses in financial institutions.

Equity buildup in real estate is a continuous source of financing for the owner of real estate. Equity buildup occurs because (a) the real estate may increase in value and/or (b) the mortgage debt is paid down gradually, leaving more value to the owner or equity interest. Equity value results from legal ownership rights—the right to use the real estate in any legal manner, the right to sell it, and the right to convey title upon death. The cost of equity funds, however, may be high. This cost must be measured primarily by the opportunity of investing in other assets which might be higher yielding. Also, an equity interest in real estate may be relatively illiquid and unmarketable—and there may not be enough equity funds to finance the real estate. Because of the disadvantages of having to rely totally on equity funds, then, real estate users, as well as other capital users, use borrowed funds extensively.

Figure 16–1 shows that the principal sources of borrowed funds are the financial institutions, including banks, savings and loans, mutual savings banks, and life insurance companies. These are regarded as sources even though they depend on savings by individuals and companies. The institutions decide how the funds will be used and allocated among loan applicants. Of course, when individuals loan funds directly for real estate use, they are also regarded as sources. Real estate mortgages constitute the single largest use of funds in the U.S. economy, with government securities (federal, state, and local) being second. Although the importance of real estate credit in the employment of funds is great, the percentage of funds applied in this way declined from about 35 percent in the early 1960s to about 20 percent in 1980. This development reflected the increased demand for funds by large corporations and government agencies. Higher interest rates

---

[1] Savings or reserves build up in nonterm life insurance policies because a purchaser pays a higher premium than would be required for pure protection. Part of the premium of an ordinary life, limited pay life, or endowment policy thus accumulates as "cash value" and is available to the policyholder.

FIGURE 16–1
Model of flow of funds into real estate

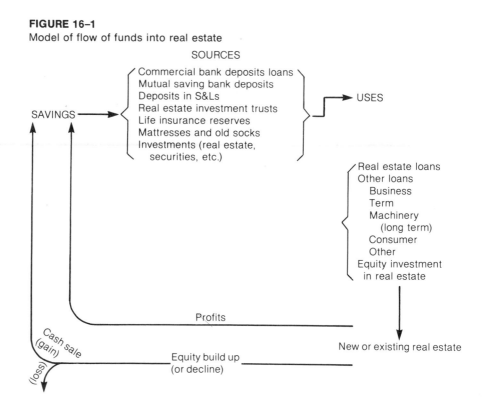

SOURCES

{ Commercial bank deposits loans
Mutual saving bank deposits
Deposits in S&Ls
Real estate investment trusts
Life insurance reserves
Mattresses and old socks
Investments (real estate,
  securities, etc.) }

SAVINGS

USES

{ Real estate loans
Other loans
  Business
  Term
  Machinery
    (long term)
  Consumer
  Other
Equity investment
  in real estate }

Profits

Cash sale (gain)

(loss)

Equity build up
(or decline)

New or existing real estate

prevailing during recent years have allowed securities other than mortgages to provide relatively more attractive yields.

Table 16–1 is a summary of the sources and uses of funds in the U.S. economy from 1970 to 1980. Commercial banks are the most important source of funds shown in Table 16–1, accounting for nearly 30 percent of the total. Individuals and others were the second largest source in 1979, but they have shown wide cycles of activity, ranging from second largest source to one of the largest user categories. Savings and loans have been a stable major source, accounting for over 10 percent of total funds in 1979.

In essence, then, the problem of the real estate investor is to be able to tap into the flow of funds at the best time and using the best sources to obtain the needed amount of funds at the least expense. Randolph and Epic Homes were able to tap the funds flow, although we cannot say without further information (nor can we ever be certain—except with hindsight) whether the best mix of equity and debt funds was used, whether the least expense was incurred, and whether the time was correct in relation to beginning the project. Perhaps a different

TABLE 16-1

Uses and sources of funds—summary: 1970–1980 (in $ billions)

Item	1970	1975	1976	1977	1978	1979 (estimated)	1980 (projected)
Uses, funds raised	92.3	200.5	263.5	337.5	388.5	385.8	361.7
Investment funds	66.4	119.5	145.9	192.8	216.8	232.8	224.8
Short-term funds	19.0	2.9	58.2	93.3	124.8	120.8	84.1
U.S. securities, privately held	6.9	78.1	59.4	51.5	46.8	32.2	52.8
Sources, gross funds supplied	103.9	205.8	278.7	365.1	437.6	435.7	404.6
Insurance company and pension funds	26.9	49.6	63.4	79.5	84.8	93.8	99.9
Insurance companies	13.0*	19.0	26.7	29.4	33.4	34.5	34.8
Private noninsured pension funds	7.8	14.1	12.5	16.5	16.0	22.0	34.8
State and local government retirement funds	6.1	10.5	11.7	14.4	16.2	18.8	23.3
Fire and casualty insurance companies	—	6.0	12.4	19.2	19.2	18.5	17.0
Thrift institutions	18.3	52.5	71.1	85.1	74.7	59.4	59.3
Savings and loan associations	12.5	36.6	51.9	64.9	57.2	50.4	47.9
Mutual savings banks	4.2	10.9	12.5	11.7	7.9	4.5	6.2
Credit unions	1.6	5.0	6.6	8.4	9.6	4.5	5.2
Investment companies	1.7	3.1	1.4	2.9	5.2	21.7	11.7
Other financial intermediaries	2.8	-1.6	7.2	17.6	19.7	23.8	14.2
Finance companies	0.7	2.0	8.3	16.2	17.7	21.7	12.4
Real estate investment trusts	2.1	-4.8	-3.8	-2.4	-1.0	-0.4	-0.2
Mortgage companies	—	1.2	2.7	3.8	3.0	2.5	2.0
Commercial banks	36.5	31.5	66.3	89.9	125.9	125.5	104.7
Business	2.5	13.4	16.0	11.6	11.1	18.3	13.4
Government	10.9	21.6	16.9	16.7	33.1	28.4	29.3
Foreign investors	11.0	10.4	17.9	42.1	40.1	-12.3	15.5
Residual: Individuals and others	-6.7	25.3	18.5	19.7	43.1	77.1	56.6
Less: Funds raised by financial intermediaries	11.6	5.3	15.2	27.5	49.1	49.9	42.9
Total net sources	92.3	200.5	263.5	337.6	388.5	385.8	361.7

* Includes fire and casualty insurance companies

Source: *Credit and Capital Markets* (New York: Bankers Trust Company, 1975 and 1980).

mix of types of funds, a different combination of sources, or different terms would have been more advantageous to Epic Homes. The problem of determining best mix, terms, and cost is a part of the return on investment calculus and is considered in depth in Chapter 17.

It is often the explicit or implicit strategy of a real estate investor to attempt to tap the funds flow on whatever terms fund suppliers will offer. Although not usually stated so bluntly, it is felt that no lender will grant a loan that is beyond the limit of reasonable risk. Furthermore, given a fairly high level of risk, which most real estate projects contain, the costs and terms among the various potential sources will not vary a great deal. Thus, for large, unique projects, the developer too often simply tries to obtain financing at whatever costs or terms are required. Instead of accepting the terms that are offered by one or two lenders, however, the developer should shop around thoroughly and be prepared, if possible, to wait until better terms can be obtained.

The inability to be selective or to have bargaining power in the borrowing process is a result of weakness in the equity position and should be avoided with three exceptions: (a) the investor has relatively little (in funds, reputation, or other commitments) to lose, while at the same time he or she has a great profit potential; (b) in spite of a slim profit potential and costly financing, there is little risk of default; and (c) the project is so large that a chunk of borrowed funds will be required even with a sizable chunk of equity.

Of course, risks and profit potentials are difficult to assess. In periods of growth and/or inflation, risks are underestimated and profit potentials overestimated. During recessions the opposite assessments are likely to prevail. The real estate investor needs to look beyond the immediate period to the long-run future.

In any event—whether to bargain for funds or merely to obtain a loan on any terms available—investor-borrowers should understand the concept of the flow of funds. Where to go to tap the flow and what to expect after they get there are items of information as important to real estate entrepreneurs as is the knowledge of construction techniques. Thus, we move on to a brief analysis of the principal sources and their characteristics and of the legal constraints in making real estate loans.

Savings and loan associations

A type of thrift institution which accumulates savings from individuals, savings and loan associations specialize in lending funds to purchasers of single-family homes. The lender obtains a personal note evidencing the debt and a first-mortgage lien on the property. Savings and loans may also loan a portion of their funds on other types of properties such as commercial and industrial properties, mobile homes, and apartment buildings, but the greatest bulk of their loans must be in one–four-family residences and government bonds. As shown in Tables 16–2 and 16–3, savings and loans hold twice as much of the outstanding mortgage debt as the next largest type of institutional lender and by far the largest percentage of mortgage debt to savings of these lenders.

TABLE 16–2
Mortgage debt outstanding on nonfarm residential property by type of holder, 1973–1979*

Year	Total	Mutual savings banks	Commercial banks	Savings and loans	Life insurance companies	Others†
1973	509,343	61,154	74,930	209,857	38,877	124,525
	(100.0)	(12.0)	(14.7)	(41.2)	(7.6)	(24.4)
1974	549,347	62,136	82,377	224,795	38,651	141,388
	(100.0)	(11.3)	(15.0)	(40.9)	(7.0)	(25.7)
1975	591,362	63,817	82,933	249,450	37,219	157,943
	(100.0)	(10.8)	(14.0)	(42.2)	(6.3)	(26.7)
1976	660,961	67,266	94,316	289,219	35,266	174,894
	(100.0)	(10.2)	(14.3)	(43.8)	(5.3)	(26.5)
1977	768,407	72,941	114,330	343,199	33,534	204,403
	(100.0)	(9.5)	(14.9)	(44.7)	(4.4)	(26.6)
1978	883,909	78,781	137,878	392,213	33,475	241,562
	(100.0)	(8.9)	(15.6)	(44.4)	(3.8)	(27.3)
1979 (2d quarter) ...	940,960	80,435	147,931	414,665	33,591	264,338
	(100.0)	(8.5)	(15.7)	(44.1)	(3.6)	(28.1)

* Amounts given in millions of dollars, with percentages given in parentheses.
† Government agencies, individuals, and other institutions (pension funds, mortgage bankers, and so on).
Source: Federal Home Loan Bank Board, *Federal Home Loan Bank Board Journal,* March 1980 (Washington, D.C.: U.S. Government Printing Office, 1980), tables S.5.5 and S.5.6, pp. 58–59.

TABLE 16–3
Mortgage loans as a percentage of savings by institution, selected years, 1960–1979 ($ billions)

Year	Mutual savings banks	Commercial banks	Savings and loans	Life insurance companies
1960	$73.9	n.a.	$ 96.8	$42.4
1965	84.5	$33.5	99.9	47.0
1970	80.3	31.0	102.7	44.3
1972	73.3	n.a.	99.7	39.9
1973	75.3	31.7	102.1	39.8
1974	75.4	30.3	102.6	39.8
1975	69.8	29.1	97.5	37.6
1976	66.0	29.9	96.2	34.9
1977	65.3	31.8	98.7	33.6
1978	66.2	33.7	100.4	33.0

n.a.—not available.
Source: U.S. Bureau of the Census, *Statistical Abstract of the United States, 1979* (Washington, D.C.: U.S. Government Printing Office, 1979), tables 864, 865, 867, and 900.

Savings and loan associations may be either state or federally chartered, and they may be either stock-owned companies or mutually owned by the savers. Federally chartered associations must belong to the Federal Home Loan Bank System and the Federal Savings and Loan Insurance Corporation (FSLIC). Many state-chartered associations also elect to belong. The FSLIC insures savings by investors and periodically examines loans made by the associations to determine whether there is any excess risk. The Federal Home Loan Bank Board establishes liquidity requirements, enforces rules and regulations, and maintains a source of funds at district Federal Home Loan banks which can be borrowed by member savings and loan associations.

Savings and loan associations can make a wide variety of types of loans. A summary of the current lending regulations of federal associations is provided below.

1. Home loans (one–four family).   At least 80 percent of a savings and loan association's loans must be invested in one–four family home loans. Federal associations currently may make fully amortized conventional loans up to 95 percent of the value of a one–four family residence for 40 years. Loans in excess of 90 percent of value must have the top 20 percent of the loan insured by a private loan insurer, or the savings and loan association must hold in reserve an amount equal to 1 percent of the unpaid balance until the unpaid balance is 90 percent or lower of the value of the property secured. There is no dollar limit on the size of loan that can be made. Federal associations can also make FHA and VA loans for amounts and terms specified by those agencies, and can make junior lien loans (second mortgages) for 15 years. The total mortgage indebtedness, however, may not exceed 95 percent of a property's value.

2. Multifamily property loans.   Savings and loans are permitted to make loans on multifamily properties (5 or more units) up to 90 percent of value for 30 years. Nonamortized loans may be made for 5 years up to 75 percent of a property's value.

3. Income property loans (commercial).   Fully amortized loans on nonresidential, income-producing properties are permitted up to 90 percent of value for 30 years.

4. Construction loans.   Savings and loan associations may make construction loans for maturities of 18 months on single-family residences (with a possible extension of 6 months) and 36 months on commercial properties (with a possible extension of 36 months). These loans may be combined with a permanent loan so that the total maturity on a single-family loan could be as long as 41 years 6 months. Amortization is not required on a construction loan.

5. Home improvement loans.   Two types of home improvement loans are made by savings and loans. FHA Title 1 loans may be made up to $15,000 in amount for 15-year maturities. Conventional home improvement loans may be made with a maximum maturity of 20 years and 32 days; there is no dollar limit on the size of such loans. They may be made either with or without mortgage security.

6. *Mobile home loans.* Savings and loan associations are permitted to make mobile home loans up to 90 percent of the costs (purchase price plus loan costs and insurance) for 20 years.

Recent legislation (the Financial Institutions Deregulation Act of 1980) and changes in rules have greatly expanded savings and loan associations' lending powers. They are now permitted to make consumer loans and second mortgages. Additionally, their first mortgage loans can include a renegotiable or variable interest rate provision. A reverse annuity mortgage (RAM), in which an owner can assign the equity in a property to the lender in exchange for monthly income, has been approved, but each association must submit for prior approval by regulatory authorities its plan for making such mortgages. Currently under consideration is a shared appreciation mortgage (SAM), in which a borrower agrees to share part of the gain upon resale of the property with the lender.

Most (but not all) savings and loans prefer to make conventional loans. Such loans have not been constrained by ceilings on interest rates or the extensive paperwork required by the FHA and VA. Savings and loans have obtained somewhat higher interest rates on their loans than have most other lenders, but they have given more liberal terms to borrowers.

Life insurance companies

Historically, one of the largest sources of funds for mortgages has been the approximately 1,500 life insurance companies. These companies obtain large amounts of investable funds from policyholders. Policy premiums must be held and invested during the time between policy origination and payout at the time of death. Insurance companies also invest funds in investment media other than mortgages, such as corporate stocks and bonds, government securities, and equity interests in real estate. These companies tend to invest more or less heavily in mortgages, depending upon the available yields. During recessions, for example, insurance companies usually reduce their mortgage lending drastically in favor of government and corporate bonds.

Large insurance companies have greater flexibility than other types of lenders in making loans over wide geographic areas. Most of the large insurance companies are qualified to do business in most or all states, and they utilize a network of mortgage bank correspondents to obtain and service loans.[2] Since the large insurance companies have vast amounts of funds to invest, they prefer to make large loans. The larger loans typically carry higher interest rates, and because there are fewer loans, less analysis and paperwork are involved. The correspondent typically continues to service such a loan for the insurance company, usually receiving a fee of about 0.3 percent of the outstanding balance.

For these reasons, loans on large commercial, industrial, and apartment properties are the dominant type made by insurance companies. When mortgage interest rates are favorable, life insurance companies also lend on entire groups (or packages) of single-family homes that are assembled by mortgage bankers. Because of their unfamiliarity with local real estate markets, the large national lenders usually demand that single-family home loans be underwritten by the FHA or the VA.

Commercial banks

Although primarily engaged in short-term business loans, commercial banks also participate extensively in the mortgage lending field. These institutions currently hold about 15 percent of the outstanding mortgages; their real estate loans average about 14 percent of their assets. While these percentages indicate that in absolute or relative terms banks are not nearly as important to the mortgage market as are savings and loans and insurance companies, their influence as a source of funds is keenly felt. The reasons for this influence are that (a) banks have attempted to expand their role in mortgage lending, (b) banks have fluctuated in the extent to which they have been active in the mortgage market, and (c) FHA and VA mortgages are not counted in the limits placed by law on the level of mortgages that banks may hold.

In recent years most progressive commercial banks have attempted to become the department stores of finance. Competitive pressures for savings by other institutions and the need for profitable investment outlets for funds have encouraged banks to offer a wide variety of financial services and to make other types of loans in addition to short-term commercial loans. Mortgage loans (as well as consumer loans, construction and development loans, and business term loans) are now made by most banks.

Mortgages have been attractive investment outlets for banks, particularly during periods of "easy money" and relatively low interest

---

[2] See Halbert C. Smith, *Interregional Mortgage Placement: Lenders' Policies, Practice, and Characteristics* (Storrs: Center for Real Estate and Urban Economic Studies, University of Connecticut, 1969) for a critical analysis of the operations of life insurance companies in this field.

rates. During these periods the yield on mortgages has been high relative to the yields on government and municipal bonds and business loans. While mortgage yields typically suffer in comparison with other yields during periods of "tight money," the large commercial banks that have entered the mortgage loan business have continued to grant mortgage loans during such periods. Nevertheless, the overall level of mortgage lending by commercial banks has decreased substantially during periods of monetary restraint.

Banks are limited in the volume of mortgage loans they may have. Current regulations limit their holdings of mortgage loans to no more than 70 percent of savings or 100 percent of equity capital, whichever is greater. Since FHA and VA loans are insured and guaranteed by the government, the risk of loss to a bank is very low on these loans, and they do not fall under the mortgage loan limitation.

Because of their background of conservative lending policies and more stringent regulations, banks typically grant less liberal loans than savings and loans. However, the interest rate charged has often been lower. Mortgage terms usually involve lower loan to value ratios and shorter maturities than those of savings and loans.

Banks strive to please their good customers. Consequently they will often grant a mortgage loan to a good customer when they would not make such a loan to a noncustomer. They typically prefer loans in the middle- to upper-value range in housing or larger loans on commercial and industrial property. Sometimes commercial banks grant a loan in order to service a good customer but then sell the loan to another financial institution, continuing to service the loan. This practice allows the bank to maintain a desirable liquidity position while maintaining the goodwill of customers.

Commercial banks are also good sources of construction and development loans. These loans are usually short term and are not counted in a bank's portfolio of mortgage loans. Often a bank makes a construction loan when another institution has agreed to make the long-term mortgage loan.

Many banks indirectly make mortgage lending possible by "warehousing" loans for mortgage bankers. Mortgage bankers often need short-term financing while they accumulate a package of loans to sell to a life insurance company. The mortgage company obtains the funds from a commercial bank, pledging mortgages held in the firm's inventory as security for the loan.

Because of these activities and the volatility of bank activity in the mortgage market, the influence of banks is quite important. Additionally, however, the absolute amount of mortgage lending by banks is significant. The role of banks in providing funds for construction and development is crucial for the creation of new real estate resources.

Mutual savings banks

From their depression-era image as perhaps the most staid and conservative type of lending institution, many mutual savings banks have become imaginative and aggressive leaders. Regarded as something of a cross between commercial banks and savings and loan associations, their relatively wide investment power has enabled mutual savings banks to grant mortgage loans on all types of real estate as well as to purchase stocks and bonds of private corporations and securities issued by all levels of government.

As shown by Table 16–2, mutual savings banks as of June 30, 1979, held over $80 billion in mortgage loans. This compares with about $148 billion and $415 billion in mortgage loans held by commercial banks and savings and loans, respectively, at the same date. Of the total assets held by mutual savings banks, mortgages are by far the most important. Their mortgage assets are almost five times as large as their next largest investment—corporate securities.

Compared with the volume held by the other major institutional lenders, the volume of mortgages held by mutual savings banks appears unimpressive. However, the concentration of these institutions in New York and the New England states emphasizes their importance as mortgage lenders in those states. The number of savings banks has decreased during the last decade. There were 486 in 1972 and only 464 in May 1980. In terms of savings held, New York is by far the largest state (see Table 16–4), while Massachusetts has the largest number of savings banks.

Real estate investment trusts

In 1960 the federal income tax law was amended to recognize the real estate investment trust (REIT) as a passive investment vehicle whose income passed on to beneficiaries is not taxed. Only the retained income of the REIT is subject to taxation. This provision gave investors in REITs the same tax advantage that investors in mutual funds have. Funds to purchase investment real estate are obtained from many investors (there must be at least 100 persons for the REIT to qualify for the tax advantage) in the same way that a corporation obtains capital by selling stock. The REIT sells shares, which are really certificates of beneficial interest in the trust. The shares are freely transferable and are limited in liability to the amount paid. A board of trustees runs the investment trust for the benefit of the shareowners.

REITs are a vehicle by which a relatively small investor can own a share of a much larger property. Actually, in most cases the shareowners in a REIT own shares of many properties. Thus, there is a great

TABLE 16–4
Amount of savings held in mutual savings
banks, by states, December 31, 1979

State	Savings ($millions)
New York	$ 75,895
City	53,790
Upstate	22,105
Massachusetts	20,466
Boston	4,841
Outside Boston	15,625
Connecticut	12,642
Pennsylvania	11,939
New Jersey	8,041
Washington	3,832
Maine	2,337
New Hampshire	2,301
Rhode Island	1,572
Maryland	1,513
Vermont	767
All other states*	2,597
Total	$143,903

* Includes Alaska, Delaware, Indiana, Minnesota, Oregon, and Wisconsin.
Source: National Association of Mutual Savings Banks, *Mutual Savings Banking: Annual Report of the President* (May 1980), p. 6.

amount of diversification through trust ownership of several properties. Shareowners are usually paid a regular dividend coming from the income produced by the real estate and from the depreciation expense charged on the books. If the property accumulates in value at a rate greater than the depreciation rate, the shareowners' equity capital may appreciate in value. An additional advantage to small investors is that they obtain the benefits of professional management, which they would not have if they saved their funds and invested them in a property on their own. Also, they may benefit from the use of leverage by the investment trust. That is, the trust may borrow funds from a financial institution to help finance properties that it purchases.

Two major types of trusts have evolved, one investing primarily in equity ownership positions and the other concentrating in mortgage loans. The equity trusts fared reasonably well during the stormy 1974–75 market period. The mortgage trusts tended to seek out high-risk loans through which they could invest substantial amounts of money in short periods of time. They frequently invested in combination land acquisition, development, and construction loans which relied upon uncertain permanent loan commitments. Many of these loans were made to purchasers whose financial strength and experience levels were marginal at best. The trusts were able to charge high rates of interest on borrowed funds, and they usually were able to secure a substantial percentage of profits in exchange for permitting the borrower to fund all costs plus a handsome draw for overhead. Investors found the mortgage trusts' earnings to be high, and the equity shares they purchased generated a sizable base for the issuance of bonds by the trusts. Within a few years the mortgage trusts were able to multiply their assets significantly, with their entire net worth being based upon the earnings generated from loans. The equity trusts were much more conservative, concentrating their property purchases in stable income-producing properties.

The excellent performance of the trusts in 1971–72 led to competition by commercial banks, and many formed their own trusts with remarkable results. The Chase Manhattan Realty Trust sold $100 million worth of shares on the first day of sales, and the Bank of America enjoyed a similar experience. At least half of the nation's 20 largest banks entered the market. Unfortunately, the number of good borrowers was limited, and nearly all of the mortgage trusts lowered their credit requirements to place their funds rapidly. Popular market areas such as Miami, Atlanta, and Houston became overbuilt with large-scale residential, commercial, and office developments, and borrowers began to default on interest and principal payments. The value of equity shares fell, and bonds began to mature before capital could be recovered from loans. The mortgage trusts incurred substantial losses.

Today some REITs are still attempting to recover from losses incurred in the 1970s. Other REITs have gone out of business or have changed their organizational status. Still, many REITs have recovered and are actively engaged in lending operations—usually more conservatively than before. REITs will undoubtedly continue as a viable source of funds for real estate. However, borrowers should expect to receive funds only for high-quality projects that can withstand temporary downturns in economic activity.

Mortgage bankers

Mortgage companies or bankers originate mortgage loans to individuals and firms, but they do not normally continue to hold the mortgage loans as assets. Rather, the mortgage banker usually sells the mortgage paper to a large lender, such as a savings and loan association, a life insurance company, or a mutual savings bank. As discussed in connection with life insurance companies, the mortgage banker typically continues to service the loan for its purchaser and is compensated for this service by the purchaser. Servicing is defined as taking all the steps necessary to make certain the loan provisions are carried out; the procedures include collecting the monthly payments from the borrowers and forwarding these to the investor-lenders, rendering accountings to investors and borrowers, and handling foreclosures. The servicing fee usually runs between about 0.25 percent and 0.5 percent of the outstanding balance of the loan.

Mortgage companies sometimes have continuing arrangements with large institutional lenders to obtain loans for them. A large lender will sometimes commit itself to purchase a specified amount of mortgage-secured loans from a mortgage company during a certain period. Or a lender may let a mortgage banker know what types of loans it would like to purchase. The mortgage banker is then invited to submit such loans to the lender, which determines whether or not it will purchase them. This procedure is usually followed for large loans. When a mortgage company has a continuing arrangement or commitment to sell loans to an institutional investor, the mortgage banker is known as a correspondent.

Miscellaneous sources of funds for real estate

Pension funds.   Pension funds are basically the accumulated savings which individuals set aside during their working lives for use in retirement. The assets of pension funds are estimated to total several billion dollars. Because of their magnitude, these assets would be an excellent source of funds for real estate activities, but as yet pension funds have been invested primarily in stocks and bonds. Only a small percentage of these assets has found its way into real estate financing. Recently, however, the Federal Home Loan Mortgage Corporation has been successful in attracting pension fund investments into mortgage finance through the creation and sale of mortgage participation certificates. These certificates represent security interests in pools of mortgages owned by FHLMC.

Mortgage brokers.   The chief function of mortgage brokers is to originate real estate loans for insurance campanies, commercial banks, and other investors. They act strictly as agents, never investing any of their own funds or servicing the loans originated. Frequently, mortgage brokers are real estate brokers who engage in this activity as a secondary business to accommodate clients with special financing needs.

Individuals.   In every community there are individuals with excess capital who are willing to invest in mortgage loans. Unlike financial institutions, these lenders are not regulated as to credit ratings, loan to value ratio, or maturity dates. This flexibility makes them valuable as an alternative form of financing for high-risk borrowers or projects.

In some cases, these lenders may be relatives or employers of the borrowers.

Summary of the flow of funds into real estate finance

In summary, Table 16–5 reflects the uses of credit funds supplied to real estate and the sources from which they came over a five-year period. The largest amounts of funds were placed in conventional home mortgages, and the bulk of these loans was supplied in order of decreasing importance by savings and loans, commercial banks, and mutual savings banks. Mortgage companies do not appear in the table because most of the mortgages they originate are sold to other institutional lenders.

INSTRUMENTS OF REAL ESTATE FINANCE

The principal instruments, or legal arrangements, used in financing real estate are the promissory note, the mortgage, and the deed of trust. Other instruments and arrangements are sometimes used. These include the condominium, the contract for deed, sale and leaseback, sale and contract-back, and the wraparound mortgage. In a review of these instruments, these questions should be kept in mind: (*a*) What is their essential nature? (*b*) What legal responsibilities do they create? (*c*) How are they used in real estate transactions?

If investors, as well as lenders, understand the implications of these questions, they should be able to structure creative financing arrangements for proposed investment opportunities. For example, one investor may find that an advantageous method of financing an investment is to create a split ownership situation by selling the land and leasing it back. Another investor with little or no capital may be able to obtain control of a property by purchasing on a land contract. A home builder may increase sales by obtaining prior agreement from a lender to finance major appliances in a package mortgage. Some investors may be able to decrease their tax liability by making installment purchases. And yet other investors may be able to finance properties by forming syndicates and selling limited partnership shares. Such arrangements and combinations require the creation of legal rights and obligations appropriate for each party to a transaction. These arrangements and combinations (as well as others) are created by the basic instruments of real estate finance, tailored to the individual situation and purpose.

Promissory note

A promissory note is a signed document acknowledging the existence of a debt and promising repayment. The chief function of the

TABLE 16–5

Mortgage activity of banks, insurance companies, and savings and loan associations, 1975–1979
($ millions, end of period)

Type of holder and type of property	1975	1976	1977	1978	1979
All holders	$801,537	$889,327	$1,023,505	$1,172,754	$1,334,373
One–four family	490,761	556,557	656,566	761,843	872,191
Multifamily	100,601	104,516	111,841	121,972	130,758
Commercial	159,298	171,223	189,274	212,746	289,093
Farm	50,877	57,031	65,824	76,193	92,331
Major financial institutions	581,193	647,650	745,011	848,095	940,268
Commercial banks	136,186	151,326	178,979	213,963	246,763
One–four family	77,018	86,234	105,115	126,966	146,077
Multifamily	5,915	8,082	9,215	10,912	12,585
Commercial	46,882	50,289	56,898	67,056	77,737
Farm	6,371	6,721	7,751	9,029	10,364
Mutual savings banks	77,249	81,639	88,104	95,157	98,924
One–four family	50,025	53,089	57,637	62,252	64,717
Multifamily	13,792	14,177	15,304	16,529	17,183
Commercial	13,373	14,313	15,110	16,319	16,965
Farm	59	60	53	57	59
Savings and loan associations	278,590	323,130	381,163	432,808	475,797
One–four family	223,903	260,895	310,686	356,114	394,436
Multifamily	25,547	28,436	32,513	36,053	37,588
Commercial	29,140	33,799	37,964	40,641	43,773
Life insurance companies	89,168	91,555	96,765	106,167	118,784
One–four family	17,590	16,088	14,727	14,436	16,193
Multifamily	19,629	19,178	18,807	19,000	19,274
Commercial	45,196	48,864	54,388	62,232	71,137
Farm	6,753	7,425	8,843	10,499	12,180
Federal and related agencies	66,891	66,753	70,006	81,853	97,293
Mortgage pools or trusts	34,138	49,801	70,289	88,633	119,278
Individuals and others	119,315	125,123	138,199	154,173	177,534

Notes:

1. Includes loans held by nondeposit trust companies but not bank trust departments.
2. Outstanding principal balances of mortgages backing securities insured or guaranteed by the agency indicated.
3. Other holders include mortgage companies, real estate investment trusts, state and local credit agencies, state and local retirement funds, noninsured pension funds, credit unions, and U.S. agencies for which amounts are small or separate data are not readily available.

Source: Board of Governors, Federal Reserve Board *Federal Reserve Bulletin*, Washington, D.C., current monthly data.

note is to make the borrower personally liable for payment of the debt. Once an individual has signed such a note, the terms of the repayment schedule must be made, regardless of the financial success of the property.

Mortgage

A mortgage is a pledge of security for the repayment of a debt. It is created by a formal written agreement in which the person who signs a promissory note pledges the property being financed as security (or collateral) for the debt. Therefore, the mortgage itself is a lien—not evidence of a debt. There are two parties to each mortgage, the mortgagor and the mortgagee. The mortgagor is the borrower, or the one pledging the property as security for the debt incurred. The mortgagee is the lender, or the one to whom the property is pledged.

Mortgage requirements.   Since a mortgage conveys an interest in real estate, it must be in writing. The actual wording of the document may conform to rather broad guidelines, but the document should contain essentially the same elements as the deed. The basic mortgage should meet the following requirements:

1. The mortgagor's legal name must appear. This implies that the mortgagor is of legal age for contracting.
2. The mortgagee's name must also appear.
3. The mortgage must contain words of conveyance or granting from the mortgagor to the mortgagee.
4. The mortgage must contain a description of the mortgaged property that is adequate to permit accurate identification.
5. The amount of consideration must be stated, or (as is more typical) reference must be made to the promissory note.
6. The mortgage must be signed by the mortgagor. Although it is not essential for mortgagees to sign documents, they usually do.

Mortgage theory.   Under old English law, a mortgage was an actual assignment of property to a lender. During the time that the mortgagor still owed the mortgagee part of the original loan, the lender could have the physical use of the land pledged and was entitled to any rents or revenues derived from it. Thus, in the earlier forms of mortgages, title to the land pledged as security for a loan was truly transferred to the lender.

Abuses on the part of lenders brought about more careful wording in the mortgage instruments. Slight delays in repaying the loan often resulted in legal default, with borrowers forfeiting any rights to recovery of title to their land. An outgrowth of the early experiences of both lenders and borrowers is the present-day distinction between the title theory and the lien theory of mortgages.

Fewer than 20 states subscribe to the title theory of mortgages. In title theory states, a mortgage is assumed to represent an actual conveyance of title to the mortgagee. This can be seen as very similar to the early mortgages in which the mortgagee owned legal title and could take possession of the property or collect revenues from it during the term of the loan. Two basic approaches to eliminating abuses in such mortgages have been developed, one or both of which all of the title theory states have adopted.

One approach is called intermediate title theory; it requires formal court action to rescind the borrower's legal rights in the property. Under intermediate title theory the mortgagee can assume possession of the property between the time of default and the sheriff's sale. While this system protects the lender against damage that may be committed by the mortgagor, who knows foreclosure is inevitable, it also protects the mortgagor from eviction without legal process. Another technique simply holds that a foreclosure proceeding must be held, as in lien theory states. This requirement makes borrower protection equal to that obtained under lien theory. The only difference is in the formal wording of the instrument.

Lien theory is a more modern and widely used approach to creating loan security. In lien theory states, the lender is considered to hold a lien, rather than title, against the property for security of the debt. A lien is the right to have property sold to satisfy a debt. In the event of default of the promissory note, foreclosure proceedings are initiated and the title is conveyed from the borrower to the lender. The mortgage remains with the property until the debt is paid, even if ownership of the property changes.

Deed of trust

As mentioned earlier, the typical mortgage involves only two parties, the lender and the borrower. However, in a deed of trust, also known as a trust deed, the borrower conveys the land, not to the lender, but to a third party. The third party holds the land in trust for the benefit of the holder of the note that represents the debt for which the property is pledged. The primary reason some states use this form is that the deed of trust can be foreclosed more easily and more quickly by a trustee's sale under a "power of sale" clause. In prescribed situations, court proceedings may be minimized or eliminated.

Mortgage loan clauses

Every mortgage loan contains several clauses which state the rights of the mortgagor and the mortgagee during the term of the agreement. These are as follows.

Renegotiable rate clause.   A renegotiable rate mortgage (RRM) is a series of short-term loans secured by a long-term mortgage. The short-term loans are automatically renewable at equal intervals of 3 to 5 years each. The mortgage term may not exceed 40 years. The monthly payments are made in equal installments. However, at the end of the life of each short-term loan, the interest rate may be changed to reflect the movement of the Federal Home Loan Bank Board's most recent monthly national average contract mortgage rate index of previously occupied single-family homes for all major lenders. This is the only term which may be altered. An interest rate modification results in a change of the monthly debt service payment. The new payment amount remains stable until the loan term has again expired.

To protect a borrower from excessive monthly payments, the Federal Home Loan Bank Board has issued regulations limiting the amount of fluctuation allowed in the interest rate. At renewal, the rate may not be increased more than one half of 1 percent per year of the loan term. (For a four-year loan this would be 0.5% × 4 = 2.0%.) The maximum change allowed over the life of the mortgage is 5 percent. Interest rate increases are optional, while decreases are mandatory. The mortgagor has the option of prepaying all or part of the mortgage balance at any time without penalty.

Acceleration clause.   Lenders usually insist that the instrument contain an acceleration clause which makes the entire debt due in the event of default. This clause makes it unnecessary for the lender to bring separate lawsuits against the same mortgagor for each late payment. The clause usually states that if any covenants are breached, including the obligation to pay when due the sums secured by the mortgage, the full amount is due immediately. This declaration of full payment due is at the option of the lender.

Prepayment clause.   Unless the mortgage loan instrument specifically states that the borrower is allowed to pay more than the scheduled amount, the borrower is not allowed to prepay. To prepay means to pay off the indebtedness before the original date. Prepayment, then, is a matter of contract and not an inherent right.

In typical prepayment clauses a statement is made as to whether (1) there is a penalty for prepayment, (2) an extra payment directly reduces the principal upon which interest is computed or eliminates the last payment, and (3) the number and size of extra payments in any one year are restricted. Some lenders try to discourage a fast turnover of funds, which is costly to them, by imposing prepayment penalties during the early years. These penalties are usually stated as a percentage of the unpaid balance, and the percentage charged is usually reduced in later years of the mortgage term.

Most savings and loan asociations have a prepayment clause in the note. Typically it states that the borrower has the right to prepay the principal amount outstanding in whole or in part and that the amount of the extra payment is applied against the principal amount outstanding. However, such clauses also usually state that extra payments do not extend or postpone the due date of subsequent monthly installments or change the amount of these installments.

Defeasance clause. This clause "defeats" the right of the lender to foreclose on the property so long as the borrower lives up to the terms of the agreement. Thus, as long as the borrower makes periodic payments according to schedule and fulfills all other requirements, the lender may not obtain the property or have it sold.

Exculpatory clause. An exculpatory clause relieves the borrower of personal liability to repay the loan. Thus, if the borrower defaults, the lender must look only to the property in foreclosure for recovery of the debt. In effect, the lender may not sue the borrower on the note or obtain a deficiency judgment if sale of the property at foreclosure does not provide sufficient funds to cover the loan's remaining balance. Obviously, borrowers prefer to negotiate loans with exculpatory clauses, but lenders are usually unwilling to allow them.

Subordination clause. When a lienholder consents to place his or her interest in lower priority than that of another lienholder, the lower priority is created by a subordination clause. A subordination clause is often used when the seller of vacant land takes back a purchase-money mortgage. Because many financial institutions require first priority on the lien, the seller agrees to lower his priority to a position inferior to a construction or permanent loan in order to make the sale. Sometimes landowners who lease their land will also subordinate their fee position to a construction or permanent loan obtained by the lessee.

Release clause. An acquisition and development loan obtained by a developer may be used to develop a number of building lots. Many such loan agreements contain clauses that allow the developer to have developed lots released as security for the loan as the lots are sold; a specified amount is then paid back to the lender. Usually the amount that must be paid to obtain a release is greater than the proportionate amount of the loan allocated to the lot. For example, if a developer borrows $100,000 to develop ten lots, the release amount might be $12,000 per lot—$2,000 more than the amount of loan per lot.

Cognovit clause. This clause is considered to be a confession of judgment. If borrowers allow it to be included, they in effect give up their right to "a day in court." The clause authorizes the lender's attorney to obtain a judgment lien against the debtor's real property. Without this clause, the lender must sue on the note and prove it to be in default.

Escalator clause. This clause allows the lender to increase the interest rate. Although an escalator clause in its most general sense could allow a lender to increase the rate for any reason, the increase is usually tied to an event or contingency—for example, if it is later discovered that the mortgagor-purchaser is an investor rather than an owner-occupant. Or the clause could provide that the interest rate is to escalate up to the legal maximum in the event of the borrower's default. Escalator clauses in which the interest rate change is at the lender's discretion are very unpopular with borrowers. The potential of escalator clauses for abuse and unfavorable public relations far outweighs any of their benefits.

Variable rate clause.   The variable rate mortgage (VRM) ties the interest rate to some specified index of market interest rates. As market rates fluctuate, either the periodic (usually monthly) payment *or* the loan's maturity would increase or decrease, depending on whether the rate went up or down.

Open-end clause.   Many institutions (particularly savings and loans) write loan agreements that allow a borrower to increase the amount of a loan after part of the loan balance has been paid. The loan can usually be increased to the original amount borrowed. While closing costs and loan fees are avoided by using an open-end provision, the lender usually reserves the right to adjust the interest rate if the current market rate is higher than the rate on the existing loan.

Redemption clause.   A borrower after default but prior to foreclosure has a right to pay whatever amounts are owed plus interest and to retain the property or his or her interest therein. This right is called the *equity of redemption,* and it is a matter of law, not negotiation. The right is stated in most mortgages, but it is present even if it is not stated.

The clauses discussed in this section are the principal variable provisions found in mortgages or notes. Other provisions that are sometimes used include equity participation and late payment clauses. Each lender usually has a standard form that outlines the rights of the lender and the borrower. All borrowers should carefully read such documents before signing, since the documents may contain clauses that are detrimental to their particular needs.

TYPES OF MORTGAGES

Mortgages may be classified according to several criteria—by whether or not they are underwritten by an agency of the U.S. government, by method of payment, by priority of lien, and by the purpose for which they were made. The classifications are not mutually exclusive; for example, a package mortgage could be either conventional or government underwritten. Similarly, a participation mortgage could be either fully or partially amortized. Thus, the classifications are simply different ways of looking at the same mortgage.

Government-underwritten versus conventional mortgages

Government-underwritten loans are insured or guaranteed by an agency of the U.S. government. The Federal Housing Administration insures loans made by private lenders to qualified buyers of properties that meet minimum standards. The Veterans Administration guarantees loans made by such lenders to veterans. No charge is made by the VA for a guarantee; however, the FHA charges a premium for loan insurance, as described below.

FHA-insured mortgage. The Federal Housing Administration was created under the National Housing Act of 1934. Under this act the FHA was granted the authority to insure mortgage loans made by private lenders. It is important to understand that the FHA issues an insurance policy, whose premiums are paid by the borrower, which guarantees that the lenders will receive their money even if the mortgagors fail to make their payments.

There are several types of FHA mortgage programs, including programs for low-income housing, nursing homes, cooperative apartments, and condominium apartments. The most common is the FHA program for single-family homes, which is authorized by Title II, Section 203, of the National Housing Act. Under this program the borrower pays an insurance premium equal to one half of 1 percent of the loan. The amount is included as part of the monthly payment. The lender sends this premium to the FHA, which in turn deposits it in the Mutual Mortgage Insurance Fund. If a borrower defaults on a loan, the FHA reimburses the lender from this fund. Reimbursement is made only after the mortgagor's interest has been foreclosed and the secretary of HUD has taken title to the property. The FHA must of course sell the property.

FHA-insured mortgages may be advantageous for some borrowers. Lenders will generally advance a higher percentage of the appraised value on an insured mortgage. There may be times when a potential homebuyer does not have a sufficient down payment to qualify for a conventional loan. In such cases an FHA-insured mortgage may be appropriate. The insurance premium, however, is an added expense for the borrower.

VA-guaranteed mortgage. The Servicemen's Readjustment Act of 1944 authorized the Veterans Administration to guarantee a stated percentage of real property loans made to qualified veterans by qualified lenders.

Although the Veterans Administration does not normally make mortgage loans, in areas where there are no lending institutions the VA will grant loans to veterans. Generally, the VA guarantees loans that are made by lending institutions to veterans. When a borrower defaults, the VA currently will pay up to $27,500 of any loss incurred by the lender. Because VA loans are available up to 100 percent of the selling price, brokers are able to sell homes to veterans who otherwise could not afford to purchase them. In such cases the veteran pays only the closing costs. Normally a veteran is entitled to only one VA loan; however, in some cases the loan can be transferred to another eligible veteran, and the original borrower's right to a loan is then restored.

Conventional mortgage.   In recent years the percentage of FHA and VA mortgages has been decreasing. The majority of mortgages made today by most lenders are conventional. Conventional loans are preferred by lenders for two basic reasons. First, lenders have the flexibility to create loans that reflect their own requirements. This permits individualized programs that are in the best interest of both parties.

Second, more paperwork and red tape are required for loans that are guaranteed or insured, and the administrative costs of such loans are higher.

Generally, a conventional mortgage requires a larger down payment than do either FHA or VA mortgages. In both the FHA and VA programs, the borrower is not allowed to pay points. (Points are a discount from the face amount of the loan which increases the yield to the lender. They are discussed in greater detail in Chapter 17.) In conventional mortgages, however, borrowers are allowed, and in many cases do, pay loan fees or discount points.

Mortgages by method of payment

Straight (or straight-term) mortgage.   A loan in which only interest payments are made periodically with the entire amount due at maturity is called a straight (or straight-term) loan. Although such loans are not used frequently to finance the purchase of single-family houses, they are used quite often in land transactions. If this is done, developers are able to pay for the land after development and sale. In the interim, they pay interest only.

Amortized mortgage.   A fully amortized loan is one that is completely paid off by equal, periodic payments. This is the standard type of loan used to finance single-family homes today. It is also the most frequently used type of loan for income-producing properties, although partially amortized loans are sometimes used to finance these types of properties. Payments on fully amortized mortgages are usually required monthly. At maturity of the loan, the loan balance is zero.

Partially amortized mortgage.   If a loan is not completely paid off by equal, periodic payments, but periodic payments are required, it is a partially amortized loan. In other words, the loan is partially paid off by periodic payments, but at maturity a balance will remain, which must be paid off. This remaining balance on a partially amortized loan is called a *balloon* or a *balloon payment.*

Mortgages by purpose

Mortgage forms vary in their payback provisions, in their terms of agreement, and in the types of property they use as security. Some mortgage forms are created to achieve specific purposes or to fit the needs of the individual borrower. The types of mortgages, classified according to purpose, are as follows.

Purchase-money mortgage. A purchase-money mortgage is a mortgage on property purchased, given by the buyer to the seller as partial payment for the property. Purchase-money mortgages are common in all types of real estate purchases. In the purchase of raw land in large quantities by a developer, the landowner may accept a partial cash payment and take a mortgage for the remainder of the selling price. As the developer sells lots from the completed subdivision, the mortgage is paid off. In effect, the landowner becomes a partner with the developer through the use of a purchase-money mortgage.

Purchase-money mortgages are also common in transactions involving residential properties. The need arises when the buyer does not have a sufficient down payment. The remainder may be obtained by assuming an existing mortgage or by giving the seller a new mortgage. Either way, the seller is willing to take a mortgage as part of the payment.

Example

Consider the following example to illustrate the use of a purchase-money mortgage in residential properties. Seller A is asking $80,000 for a single-family residence. The lending institution will loan only $64,000 on the house. Buyer B likes the house but has only $10,000 for a down payment. To be able to sell the house, seller A agrees to take a purchase-money mortgage for $6,000 from buyer B. In addition to taking this purchase-money mortgage, seller A is willing to accept a lower priority of claim if buyer B should default. In this case, the lending institution has the first claim because it has a first mortgage. The purchase-money mortgage is a second mortgage.

Participation mortgage. A participation mortgage is a loan agreement under which a lender receives part of the income from an investment in addition to the interest payments. Participation mortgages become popular during periods of high interest rates as a device by which lenders can increase their yields. The participation feature enables them to share in the expected success of income-producing properties but also protects the borrower from abnormally high payments, if income projections are not realized. The participation is usually a specified percentage of gross or net income.

The use of a closely related term, *mortgage participation*, occurs when two or more lending institutions combine their funds to finance a real estate project. Possibly one lender does not want the risk of a project as large as the one for which an investor is seeking a loan. In this case the "primary" lender may call upon another lender to "participate" in the loan, thereby creating a participation. For example, an investor may need $100 million to purchase a very large hotel complex. The lending institution to which the investor applies for a loan may not be able to lend that much money. By obtaining one or more "participants," the original lender is able to obtain the money needed by the investor. In return, all lenders receive evidence of debt from the borrower, as well as an instrument pledging the property as security for each lender's note.

Blanket mortgage. A blanket mortgage covers more than one parcel of land. Developers of subdivisions employ this type of mortgage, which permits small portions of the land (residential lots) to be paid off and released from the mortgage. The percentage of the original mortgage that is released is usually smaller than the pro rata dollar amount. For example, the developer may have a note for $100,000 on a subdivision with 20 lots. The lender will usually require the payment of more than $1/20$ of the mortgage dollar amount before one lot is released.

Package mortgage. A package mortgage allows homebuyers to pledge items of home-related personal property, in addition to the real estate, as security for a loan. Lending institutions may allow items such as a range, refrigerator, dishwasher, or air conditioner to serve as security, thereby allowing the homebuyer to finance major appliances over the term of the loan at relatively low mortgage interest rates. This practice allows lenders to increase the amount of a loan with no added administrative costs and little additional risk. It allows buyers to purchase home appliances and other major items of equipment they might not be able to afford otherwise.

Mortgages by priority of lien

First mortgage. A first mortgage is the mortgage instrument that creates the first lien on a property. As explained in the example on the purchase-money mortgage, the claims of the holder of the note secured by the first mortgage will be satisfied before those of any subsequent mortgages.

Junior mortgage. Any mortgage that is not a first mortgage is "junior" to the first mortgage. This means that in case of default the claims of the holder of a note secured by a second mortgage or a mortgage of even lower priority will not be satisfied until the claims of the first mortgage has been satisfied. Because of the subordinated nature of junior mortgages, they carry a higher level of risk than first mortgages. With more risk, lenders generally charge a higher interest rate.

TRANSFERRING MORTGAGED PROPERTY

In the transfer of mortgaged property two cases normally arise: (1) the mortgagor sells the property; or (2) the mortgagee sells the mortgage. When the mortgagor sells the property, the buyer may take the property "subject to" the mortgage or the buyer may "assume" the mortgage. When the mortgagee sells its mortgage interest, the sale must be by "assignment."

Transfer of property subject to mortgage

When a buyer takes property subject to a mortgage, the buyer only recognizes the existence of the mortgage. So long as the buyer makes the mortgage payments, no problems arise. Suppose, however, that the buyer defaults. The seller is still liable for the debt and may elect to make the payments. If the seller does not make the payments, however, the lender will foreclose and the property will be sold. If the sale price is not adequate to pay off the debt, the seller, not the buyer, is held responsible for the deficiency.

Mortgage assumption

When a buyer assumes a mortgage, the buyer covenants and promises to pay any deficit that might occur from a subsequent default. Therefore, if the buyer goes into default and money is still owed on the debt after the foreclosure sale, then both the buyer and the seller may be held responsible for the deficit.

Mortgage assignment

A mortgage assignment occurs when a mortgagee sells a mortgage. The assignment is a brief form stating that the mortgagee, the assignor, transfers and assigns the mortgage and mortgage note to the purchaser, the assignee. Prior to the assignment, the assignee should give the mortgagor written notice of the assignment and should also obtain a certificate of estoppel from the mortgagor. The certificate of estoppel is a written document stating the balance due on the debt and all defenses or claims against the mortgagee.

Default and foreclosure

Default.   Default is defined as the nonperformance of a duty or an obligation, whether arising under a contract or otherwise, such as the failure to make payment called for by a note. Default can also occur if the mortgagor fails to pay taxes or insurance premiums, or otherwise breaches any of the covenants contained in the mortgage instrument.

Default does not necessarily lead to foreclosure. After default occurs, lenders usually try to avoid foreclosing. Foreclosure action usually arises only after default has occurred and the mortgagee decides that the amount owed cannot be collected through normal negotiation with the borrower.

Foreclosure.   If a borrower defaults on a secured loan, the mortgagee must bring foreclosure action to eliminate the mortgagor's interest in the property. In most states the usual method of foreclosure is by *public sale.* The proceeds of the sale are then applied to the indebtedness. When the property sells for more than the debt, the mortgagor receives the remaining balance, saving at least some of the investment.

When a foreclosed property sells for less than the debt, the mortgagee must look to the note for the remainder of the debt. To do this, the mortgagee first obtains a *deficiency judgment* against the signotaries to the note and attempts collection against their personal assets.

When foreclosure begins, all junior lienholders should join in the suit. If the property sells for less than the debt, the junior lienholders can then sue the mortgagor on the note. If the property sells for more than the debt, the junior lienholders are paid off in order of their priority, with the mortgagor receiving the remaining balance. The purchaser of the property then receives the property free and clear of the first lien (which was foreclosed) and all liens junior to it. All real estate tax liens must be paid from the foreclosure sale, or the property passes to the purchaser subject to all unpaid taxes. The purchaser must then pay these taxes or lose the property.

OTHER TECHNIQUES USED IN FINANCING REAL ESTATE

In recent years techniques other than typical mortgage loans have been employed in financing real estate. The techniques most widely used are condominium, contract for deed, sale and leaseback, sale and contract-back, and wraparound mortgages.

Condominium

Condominium ownership has become an extremely important arrangement for financing real estate. Approximately 20 percent of all new housing units are of the condominium type. Condominium ownership can be regarded as a method of financing real estate because it divides multi-unit properties into more affordable single-units. It is ownership in fee simple of a single unit in a multi-unit structure, coupled with ownership of an undivided interest in the land and other elements of the structure that are held in common with other unit owners.

Expenses for maintenance, improvements, and services are paid by each owner in the form of monthly assessments, which are determined by an owners' association. Condominium owners are legally bound by the declaration and bylaws of the owners' association. These documents determine owners' voting rights, management policies, and the amount of assessments.

Four main documents define the rights and obligations of condominium owners. The *declaration* creates the condominium, identifies the physical elements of ownership, and contains provisions relating to such matters as the name of the association, membership and voting rights, the bylaws, easements, covenants, and restrictions. The *bylaws* govern the administration of the association, including its powers, duties, manner of selection, removal, and compensation; meetings; rules and regulations; removal of officers; and bylaws amendment. A *map* is necessary to describe a condominium unit in terms of its legal description. In many condominiums vertical as well as horizontal dimensions must be specified. The *conveyance* is a general warranty deed that contains provisions relating to the special aspects of a condominium. These special provisions concern the airspace, common elements, private areas, rights in additional construction or improvements, and the right of the grantor to convey similar interests in other units.

Financing the purchase of a condominium unit is similar to the financing of a detached unit. Financial institutions grant mortgage loans on condominiums, and FHA insurance is available under Section 234 of the National Housing Act.

Contract for deed

A contract for deed, or a land contract, is an instrument by which a prospective buyer will obtain title to some property in the future. The primary characteristic of the contract for deed is that at the time of closing the buyer does *not* receive title to the property being purchased. Instead, the buyer receives a commitment that title will be transferred if certain conditions are met. The buyer usually receives title when all payments have been made.

The contract for deed may also be used as an "interim" financing instrument. In this case the buyer and seller sign a contract for deed, and as soon as a sufficient amount is paid, the buyer assumes the mortgage obtained by the original seller. For example, builders may build homes in the $80,000 price range; however, mortgages in the area are available for only $60,000. The builders may find that many buyers want this type of home, but cannot afford $20,000 as a down payment. In this situation, builders may use their credit to obtain the mortgage, and when payments have been made that reduce the remaining balance to $25,000, the mortgage is assumed by the buyer and the title is transferred.

In some states the contract for deed is considered to have passed equitable title to the buyer, and in case of default the typical foreclosure proceedings must be carried out. Admittedly, this instrument increases the marketability of many properties. However, buyers should be advised to use the instrument with caution, and to rely upon the advice of their own legal counsel.

Sale and leaseback

Sale and leaseback is a financing arrangement in the sense that it allows payment for the use of property to be extended through the entire period of use. It requires two simultaneous steps. First, an investor such as a life insurance company, pension fund, or charitable institution purchases real estate owned and used by a business firm. Second, the property is leased back to the firm by the purchaser-investor. From these two simultaneously executed steps, the name "sale and leaseback" is derived. The property does not have to be in existence at the time such an arrangement is made. For example, a large retailer may purchase a site for a new department store. The site may be sold to a large investor, such as an insurance company. The insurance company builds the store, usually according to the tenant's specifications, and leases it to the merchandising chain. Many of the large retail chains have chosen not to invest heavily in real estate and have therefore used sale and leaseback quite extensively.

Lease terms. Sale and leaseback is employed when an investor considers the future tenant to be a well-established firm or one with success potential. Customarily, the term of the lease ranges from 20 to 40 years. The rental is quoted as net to lessor (owner), and the lease agreement is known as a *net lease.* The lessee pays all taxes, insurance, maintenance, utilities, and other expenses. This net rental income is fixed so that the lessor can at least recover the purchase price of the building and receive a return on the land and building equal to that of government AAA corporate bonds.

Leases may have other provisions calling for various types of payment patterns. When a lease calls for the same payments over its entire term, it is called a *level payment* or *flat lease.* Most leases today, however, call for payments that increase over the term of the lease. Leases requiring payments that increase at regular intervals are termed *step-up leases,* while leases that increase a specified amount, each year or in relation to some index (such as the consumer price index), are termed *escalator leases.*

Sometimes a lessee will sublease the leasehold estate. For example, if tenant Brown who has a 20-year lease for some reason finds that he must give up his business, he may be able to lease his 20-year leasehold to someone else. If Brown can lease his estate for a higher rental rate, such an arrangement becomes especially attractive. Brown's lease may call for payments of $1,000 per month for 20 years, and he may be able to sublease the property for $1,200 per month with a step-up provision. Brown would then have a *sandwich lease,* as his position is between the fee simple owner and the sublessee.

Reason for use.   Only in recent years has the sale and leaseback technique become popular. One of the major reasons is scarcity of equity capital from outside sources. Resorting to borrowed capital, which is normally limited to 60–75 percent of the appraised value, may not be appropriate for business firms that do not wish to invest large amounts of equity in real estate. In situations where more capital is needed, the opportunity to secure 100 percent of value through sale and leaseback is an attractive financing arrangement. This plan also provides more funds for expansion and for additional working capital at a lower cost and for a longer period of time than are possible by other methods. The funds that are released from the sale may be invested to produce a higher return in the firm's business operation. The plan is a flexible form of financing the business, resulting in a minimum investment in fixed assets. While this type of financing may be advantageous from a tax viewpoint, each project must be considered individually.

A major drawback of this plan for both the lessee and the lessor arises when there is no repurchase option and the value of the property appreciates in value. Without a repurchase agreement, the lessee will not share in any value increases. However, if there is a repurchase provision or a sharing in any value increases, the IRS will usually disallow any depreciation or other benefits of ownership to the lessor.

Tax counsel should *always* be obtained when structuring sale-leaseback transactions.

Sale and contract-back

This technique is similar to sale and leaseback. However, instead of leasing back the property, the seller agrees to buy back the property in a land contract. Only the interest portion of the monthly (or other periodic) payments is deductible for tax purposes. However, the seller-buyer builds up equity in the land contract and is able to obtain the benefits of any property appreciation.

Wraparound mortgage

Wraparound mortgages have become desirable financing tools in certain situations during periods of high interest rates. When an owner requires additional financing and obtains a new mortgage in a larger amount than the remaining balance on the original loan, the new loan is known as a wraparound mortgage. The old loan is taken over by the new lender, who makes the periodic payments out of the payments received on the new loan. The old loan is not paid off because it carries a low interest rate or a high repayment penalty. The borrower receives the difference between the new amount borrowed and the balance on the old loan.

For example, Brown owes $300,000 on a motel secured by a first mortgage that has an annual debt service of $30,000 at 7 percent interest. In order to expand the facility, Brown, the owner, arranges with a pension fund for a wraparound mortgage of $700,000 at an interest rate of 8 percent. The annual debt service is $64,750 (0.0925 constant). At closing, Brown receives $400,000. The pension fund continues to pay off the original mortgage at a rate of $30,000 per year out of the $64,750. By servicing this debt, the pension fund is able to earn a return well above the 8 percent nominal return on its mortgage note.

The wraparound mortgage is a second mortgage. That is, it is a junior lien, and many financial institutions are not allowed to make such loans. In some states, however, wraparound mortgages are regarded as first mortgages because of the manner in which the transactions are made. In other states, regulated institutions have made wraparound mortgages under leeway provisions which permit them to make a limited number of investments based on business judgment, without regard to lien priority. As mentioned earlier, the return earned by the lender far exceeds the nominal rate of the mortgage. There have been indications in some states that courts may find this in violation of usury laws.

PRIVATELY INSURED MORTGAGES

Private mortgage insurance has been an attractive alternative for buyers who have been reluctant to seek FHA/VA government assistance. Since 1971, private insurers have covered more new one–four-family mortgage loans each year than have the FHA/VA programs.

Prior to the 1930s, when the federal government initiated various insurance/guarantee programs, private companies were the exclusive insurers of mortgages. However, they concentrated their efforts on large commercial and high-rise apartment buildings. Regional in nature and inadequately regulated, these firms ceased to exist in the late 1930s.

Finally, in 1957, after some 20 years of absence, private mortgage insurers again appeared. Licensed by the Wisconsin insurance commissioner in 1957, the Mortgage Guaranty Insurance Corporation (MGIC) was organized nationwide. While today there are a number of private mortgage insurance companies, such as Foremost Guaranty Corporation, PMI, Inc., and AMI, Inc., MGIC is by far the largest, accounting for over 60 percent of the mortgages insured by private companies.

Private mortgage insurance companies offer insurance to approved lenders against financial loss where mortgagors fail to make their payments. Ordinarily, this insurance is not utilized unless the loan exceeds 80 percent of the appraised value. For example, most companies insure the top 20 percent of the loan, regardless of the balance, up to a maximum of 95 percent of the appraised value. Thus, if a borrower defaults on a loan, the private insurer would reimburse the lender up to 20 percent of the amount of the loan. The lender can usually recoup the remainder of the loss from foreclosure proceeds. With this protection, lenders are able to increase their volume of conventional loans by lending at loan to value ratios normally excluded under typical lending policies.

Mortgage insurance companies approve only loans that meet their underwriting standards. When a loan is approved by a mortgage insurer, one of two types of loan policies is normally issued. One type, typically called the "annual plan," requires a premium of 1 percent of the loan for the first year and one fourth of 1 percent of the declining balance of the loan for each succeeding year. The second type has a single premium in the amount of 2½ percent of the initial loan. Regardless of which type is used, the premium is paid by the borrower.

SECONDARY FINANCING

Second mortgages are often considered to be speculative investments because their lien position is inferior to that of first mortgages. If default of the first mortgagee occurs and foreclosure takes place, the first-mortgage holder will be paid in full before the second-mortgage holder receives anything. Therefore, second mortgages are usually written for shorter terms and higher interest rates than first mortgages. On many occasions, however, owners, buyers, and developers cannot obtain sufficient funds to carry out a project from equity and first-mortgage sources, and additional funds are needed. Such occasions produce a strong demand for secondary financing in real estate.

Sources of secondary financing

Savings and loan associations and commercial banks.   Until 1980, savings and loan associations and commercial banks were prohibited by law from making loans secured by second mortgages. They could only take second mortgages as additional security for other loans having primary security. Now, however, these institutions are permitted to make second mortgages, and their activity in this type of lending is expected to expand greatly.

Life insurance companies and mutual savings banks.   In most states the *basket clause* (or *leeway provisions*) of the regulations that pertain to insurance companies and mutual savings banks allow these institutions to make investments that would otherwise be prohibited up to a small percentage of their assets (usually 3–5 percent). Life insurance companies are therefore particularly good sources of large second-lien loans.

Mortgage investment trusts.   As discussed previously, these trusts experienced severe difficulties during the 1973–75 recession. Nevertheless, some of them continue to operate in the second-mortgage market.

Real estate finance companies.   Established to make risky loans, these firms have a reputation for shady operations. Borrowers should be wary in seeking loans from this source.

State and local development authorities.   These quasi-governmental agencies will sometimes make second-mortgage loans in order to attract industries to a state or community.

Individuals, material suppliers, and foreigners.   Situations sometimes occur when small businesses or individuals can obtain needed funds from domestic or foreign investors. Material suppliers are occasionally willing to finance a small business's inventory by providing the material and taking back a second mortgage.

Secondary financing situations

Home financing.   Builders will sometimes lend buyers part of the purchase price on a second mortgage in order to make more sales. The total debt in such situations often approaches 100 percent of the sale price. Interest rates on such mortgages are usually 1 or 2 percent higher than those for conventional first mortgages, and the mortgages have five- to ten-year maturities (often with balloon payments).

Interim financing. A typical developer often finances the purchase of land by giving the landowner a mortgage as part or all of the purchase price. However, the developer must then borrow funds to develop the land and construct buildings. Development and construction loans usually require a first lien, which cannot be obtained when there is already a first mortgage on the land. In such situations the owner may be willing to subordinate the first mortgage to a development and/or construction loan. During the period of subordination of land, the seller's lien is second in priority and the interest rate paid to the seller usually increased. For this period the financing is termed interim financing.

Gap financing. The builder of a large apartment project may only be able to obtain permanent financing that is conditional upon the achievement of a certain occupancy rate by the time the loan is closed. If the specified rate has not been achieved, the loan amount will be lower. Nevertheless, the builder must usually obtain a construction loan for a larger amount, which would normally be paid off with the proceeds of the permanent loan. The construction lender recognizes the possibility that the occupancy rate required to obtain the larger amount will not be achieved, in which case the construction loan could not be paid off. Therefore, the construction lender will typically require the borrower to obtain a second-mortgage commitment to cover the potential gap. Because of the risk involved if the second mortgage is needed, both the commitment fees and the interest rates on such loans are high.

Improvement financing. Often both homeowners and commercial property owners desire to improve their property but do not have the funds to do so and may not have an open-end mortgage. Since there is usually a first mortgage on the property, such owners must find junior or unsecured financing. FHA Title I loans for home modernization are unsecured loans, although lenders may require a second mortgage as additional security.

Equity capital for large investment properties. Owners having a sizable equity in a property may borrow against the equity with a second mortgage in order to finance the remaining equity. Since institutional investors are limited to loans of 90 percent or less of the property's value, a large owner equity may exist which can be used for this purpose. Even if the borrower defaults in this case, the holder of the second mortgage can foreclose subject to the first mortgage, and the property can be sold easily.

Leasehold financing.   Buyers or owners of leaseholds usually resort to junior financing because the fee simple owners typically have first mortgages against such properties. The leaseholds must have a substantial remaining term, and the properties must be desirable. In case of default the mortgagee must, of course, take over the lease. The borrower must be able to meet both the lease payments and the mortgage payments to avoid default. Such loans are made only to the most creditworthy borrowers.

Typically the fee simple mortgagee is asked to subordinate the first mortgage to the lease so that the leasehold owner (tenant) can obtain financing. The fee mortgage remains a first lien on the fee, subject to the lease. If the lessee (leasehold owner) does not make timely rent payments to the fee simple owner, the owner may default on the fee mortgage. Thus, the fee mortgagee will require a highly creditworthy lessee and a favorable lease in order to subordinate. There will also be legal provisions protecting the amount of the rental payments, and the mortgage will carry a higher interest rate. From the standpoint of the leasehold lender, the value of the mortgage security is equal to the value of the fee simple interest. The leasehold mortgage in effect has a first lien against the property.

Wraparound mortgage.   As discussed previously, the wraparound mortgage involves a second or junior mortgage. However, it is not a situation requiring secondary financing, but a financing technique; therefore, it is not discussed further in this section.

SUMMARY

Chapter 16 deals with alternative methods of financing real estate transactions. This process involves seeking debt capital and obtaining mortgage terms which satisfy the requirements of both the lender and the borrower. In seeking debt capital, the real estate investor attempts to tap into the flow of funds available for such financing. The principal institutional sources of debt capital are savings and loan associations, commercial banks, life insurance companies, and mutual savings banks. Mortgage bankers play a facilitating role by granting loans for real estate use and then selling the loans to institutional lenders.

Some of the basic legal documents used in real estate finance—the note, the mortgage, and the deed of trust—are discussed in terms of their significance to the investor. By knowing the possible relationships that these documents can establish, one can be creative in designing financing arrangements that meet the needs of both equity capital providers and debt capital providers.

The mortgage and its various forms and types are emphasized. Each specific mortgage type is designed to aid the borrower or lender in overcoming particular obstacles to completion of the loan transaction. Mortgages are classified according to purpose, lien priority, payment method, and loan underwriters.

The transfer of mortgaged property or a mortgage occurs when the mortgagor sells the property or the mortgagee sells the mortgage. Property rights are also transferred during foreclosure, usually through a public sale of the property. Buyers of mortgaged or foreclosed properties should be careful to find out exactly what liabilities will be passed on to them. Sellers of mortgaged properties need to realize that they may be held liable for future unpaid debts on the property.

During periods of national or regional economic duress, inventive financing is a necessity if real property exchanges are to occur. Some of the techniques used in place of typical mortgage lending include the condominium, the contract for deed, sale and leaseback, and the wraparound mortgage. This list serves only as a basis for further innovations.

Finally, private mortgage insurance and secondary financing are discussed. Private mortgage insurance is usually required by the lender as protection for a larger loan than would normally be provided. Secondary financing is obtained by the borrower for amounts needed in addition to the primary loan.

QUESTIONS FOR REVIEW

1. Why are mortgage bankers not shown as an important source of mortgage funds in the U.S. flow of funds accounting system?

2. Why do savings and loan associations and mutual savings banks lend a much higher percentage of their savings on mortgages than do commercial banks?

3. Why were mortgage trusts so popular in the early 1970s? What type of investors would find these trusts attractive? What events led to the downfall of REITs?

4. Explain the difference between a note and a mortgage. Why do lending institutions require borrowers to sign both instruments?

5. Discuss lien theory, title theory, and deed of trust.

6. Why did the Federal Home Loan Bank Board recently approve the use of renegotiable rate mortgages and variable rate mortgages? Do you think these instruments will be widely used? Why or why not?

7. What is the difference between an FHA-insured mortgage and a VA-guaranteed mortgage?

8. Describe the process that is followed during foreclosure.

9. What are the advantages of a wraparound mortgage over a second mortgage? What are the institutional sources of secondary financing?

10. What are the advantages and dangers of purchasing and selling by contract for deed? How would you protect yourself against the dangers?

11. What is the purpose of private mortgage insurance?

REFERENCES

Bagby, Joseph R. *Real Estate Financing Desk Book.* Englewood Cliffs, N. J.: Institute for Business Planning, 1975.

Britton, James A., and Kerwood, Lewis O. *Financing Income-Producing Real Estate.* New York: McGraw-Hill, for the Mortgage Bankers Association of America, 1977.

Crean, Michael J. *Principles of Real Estate Analysis.* New York: D. Van Nostrand, 1979, chaps. 10–14.

Hines, Mary Alice. *Real Estate Finance.* Englewood Cliffs, N.J.: Prentice-Hall, 1978.

Hoagland, Henry E.; Stone, Leo D.; and Brueggeman, William B. *Real Estate Finance.* 6th ed. Homewood, Ill.: Richard D. Irwin, 1977.

Smith, Halbert C. "Institutional Aspects of Interregional Mortgage Investment." *Journal of Finance* 23, no. 2 (May 1968): 349–58.

————. *Interregional Mortgage Placement: Lenders' Policies, Practices, and Characteristics.* Storrs: Center for Real Estate and Urban Economic Studies, University of Connecticut, 1969.

————. "Regional Placement of Mortgage Funds by Life Insurance Companies and Mutual Savings Banks." *Journal of Risk and Insurance* 31, no. 3 (September 1964): 429–36.

chapter 17

Real estate financing 2:

The borrowing and

lending decisions

Potential purchasers of real estate may apply for a loan from one or more of the various lenders that typically provide funds for real estate. Usually it is wise for such would-be borrowers to shop for funds. Lenders will usually quote interest rates and terms on standard or "prime" single-family home loans. Applicants for such loans usually either qualify or they do not. An institutional lender does not vary terms and interest rates for different applicants. However, there may well be differences among lenders in the interest rates and terms on mortgage loans being made available to borrowers.

For larger, income-producing properties, lending institutions often tailor the interest rate and loan terms to the borrower and the loan security. In financing these types of properties, the borrowing and lending decisions may be quite complex. The lender may demand special security provisions and possibly a share in the property's earnings. The borrower may find such security provisions onerous or riskier than anticipated. The interest rate, repayment provisions, a discount (or points), and loan maturity are all additional considerations that may affect the desirability of a loan—from the standpoints of both the borrower and the lender.

The position of lenders is usually relatively inflexible. A lender will typically analyze a loan request and decide whether to make a loan or not, and if so, on what terms. A prospective borrower must then decide whether to "take it or leave it." Occasionally, a borrower may be able to convince a lender that a different security requirement, loan term, or even interest rate will increase the probability of the borrower's successful operation of the property, and thus enhance the lender's security in the loan. Modification of a prospective loan agreement, however, would usually require a trade-off. For example, a lender might be willing to accept a lower interest rate but might then require a larger front-end discount. Or a lender might be willing to forgo personal liability for a loan if the borrower would agree to provide additional real estate as mortgage security. Both the borrower and the lender must analyze carefully all terms of a proposed loan to make certain that the risk to each is minimized and the probability of creating a successful investment is maximized.

SINGLE-FAMILY RESIDENTIAL PROPERTY

The borrowing decision

Potential home purchasers should consider the financial risk and burden they will assume in borrowing funds to purchase a home. They should expect to be able to meet the monthly payment schedule and still have enough monthly income remaining to pay other living expenses; meet other debt obligations; pay for property maintenance, repairs, and taxes; provide for some level of entertainment and recreation; and provide for a cash reserve and savings program. Family misfortunes such as sickness, accidents, divorce, and employment setbacks may cause loss of the property. Lower down payments mean larger monthly payments and greater risk. Ownership of a home and related financial obligations can become great burdens on a family, and these burdens should be carefully weighed in terms of the family's needs and long-term objectives.

The lending decision

In evaluating loan applications, or even in providing information or advice to potential loan applicants, lenders must be extremely careful not to discriminate against loan applicants on the basis of race, national origin, religion, sex, marital status, or age. Furthermore, lenders may not discount various types of income received from public assistance programs. Borrowers' rights are protected by the Equal Credit Opportunity Act and the Federal Reserve Board of Governors' Regulation B, which implements the act.

The act does not preclude an analysis of the *quality* of an applicant's income sources. The criterion for quality, however, must be the *probability of continuance* of any income, whether from salary, wages, social security, alimony, food stamps, and so on. Furthermore, a lender may not discriminate against anyone who exercises or attempts to exercise his or her rights under the law.

In analyzing a loan application, a lender must attempt to measure both the quantity and the quality of the applicant's income. The income must be great enough to cover the applicant's living expenses, debt obligations, and property expenses and the loan's debt service. Generally, a lender must include all sources of income in determining the applicant's creditworthiness. For example, a spouse's income and income from alimony, public assistance, or a retirement fund must be included. Arbitrary rules of thumb or ratios may not be used to disqualify applicants.

A lender may evaluate the quality of each source of an applicant's income. Quality is judged by the source's creditworthiness and record of reliability and by the length of time income has been received from the source. Arbitrary discounts may not be applied to any source, but the probability of the income's continuing from that source may be evaluated. If there is a significant likelihood that income from a given source will not continue or will be sporadic, the lender may decide to omit that source from the quantity of funds available to the applicant.

Generally, lenders today attempt not to refuse loan applications for home ownership and occupancy. Clear financial insufficiency is usually required for a lender to turn down a loan request. Lenders may, however, adopt nondiscriminatory policies against granting loans for certain purposes. For example, during periods of tight credit, lenders may cut off all lending for second homes or commercial properties. Lenders may also refuse to make loans to college students for home ownership during their college tenure. Such loans may be considered short term and speculative. Furthermore, occupancy by students of single-family homes may be regarded as detrimental to real estate values in the area.

INCOME-PRODUCING PROPERTY

The borrowing decision

Buyers of income-producing properties are usually motivated by a desire to enhance their financial position. They may seek periodic income and/or cash flows from the properties, appreciation in the properties' values, or shelter from federal income taxes. While nonfinancial considerations, such as a desire for status and prestige, may play a motivating role for some purchasers, usually the financial aspects are the primary, if not the only, factors in determining whether to invest in real properties.

Most buyers of income-producing properties seek to borrow a large portion of the purchase price. The vast majority of buyers do not have enough cash to pay 100 percent with their own funds. And even those buyers who could pay cash for a property usually prefer to finance the purchase. The reason for this preference by those who could avoid financing is twofold. First, borrowing conserves their own equity funds for investment in other assets. An investor, for example, could purchase several properties, rather than only one, by borrowing to pay for all of them. Business firms can use the funds so conserved to invest in other assets needed by the businesses—machines, inventory, advertising campaigns, and so on.

In addition to conserving and stretching equity funds, borrowing may enable investors to earn a higher rate of return on their investments than could be obtained without borrowing. The use of borrowed funds to finance the purchase of an asset is termed *leverage* (and sometimes *trading on the equity*), and borrowers seek to obtain the positive effect of leverage. The positive effect is a higher rate of return than would otherwise be realized. Leverage may also produce a negative effect in which the rate of return is lower than the rate that would have been obtained without borrowing.

In order to analyze the effect of leverage and other indicators of investment desirability, a property that is expected to produce the following financial characteristics will be evaluated:

Purchase price	$250,000
Potential gross income	45,500
Vacancy and collection losses	2,000
Effective gross income	$ 43,500
Operating expenses (including replacement reserves of $2,000)	13,500
Net operating income	$ 30,000

Additionally, the potential buyers believe they can obtain a monthly amortized loan of $187,500 for 20 years at 10 percent interest. The total annual debt service would be $21,713, leaving a cash throw-off of $8,287.

Net operating income	$30,000
Annual debt service	21,713
Cash throw-off	$ 8,287

If the property were purchased with all cash by the equity investors, the annual equity return would be equal to the overall return on the property:

$$OAR = \text{Equity return} = \frac{\$30,000}{\$250,000} = 0.12, \text{ or } 12\%$$

However, by using borrowed funds requiring interest expense of 10 percent, the investors increase their rate of return. To show the effect of leverage, the repayment of principal on the mortgage for the year must be calculated and subtracted from the annual debt service to find the amount of interest paid for the year.

$$\begin{aligned} \frac{\text{Principal}}{\text{repayment}} &= (12 \times \text{SFF*}_{10,20}) \quad \times \quad \frac{\text{Mortgage}}{\text{amount}} \\ &= (12 \times 0.001317) \quad \times \$187,500 \\ &= \$2,963 \end{aligned}$$

* Monthly sinking fund factor at 10 percent for 20 years.

By subtracting the amount of annual principal repayment from total annual debt service, the amount of annual interest remains:

$$\begin{aligned} \text{Annual interest} &= \text{Total debt service} - \text{Principal repayment} \\ &= \$21,713 - \$2,963 \\ &= \$18,750 \end{aligned}$$

The return to the equity investors is then calculated as the relationship between NOI minus interest expense and the amount of equity:

$$\begin{aligned} \text{Equity return} &= \frac{\text{NOI} - \text{Annual interest}}{\text{Equity}} \\ &= \frac{\$30,000 - \$18,750}{\$62,500} \\ &= 0.18, \text{ or } 18\% \end{aligned}$$

Therefore, the effect of leverage would be positive. The equity investors' return would be increased from 12 percent to 18 percent because the interest rate on the borrowed funds is less than the overall return on the entire property. Furthermore, the amount of interest would decrease each year on an amortizing loan, causing the return on equity to increase each year.

The effect of leverage can also be negative. If the interest rate on the borrowed funds in the above example had been higher than 12 percent, the equity investor's return would have been reduced to a rate below 12 percent. Obviously, most real estate investors hope and expect to obtain positive leverage when using borrowed funds. However, if NOI decreases below expectations, the effect of leverage can be disastrous because mortgage payments must continue to be made regardless of the level of NOI.

The loan constant. While purchasers of income-producing properties usually attempt to take advantage of the positive effect of leverage, such investors may look to a number of other criteria to judge the soundness and desirability of a particular financial arrangement. Several of these criteria (as well as the effect of leverage) involve the calculation of the total annual debt service required by different lending arrangements. Such calculations require the use of a loan constant.

By definition, a loan constant is the percentage of the original loan that is paid periodically for principal and interest. Recall that column 6 of the compound interest tables contains level annuity factors for income streams providing either monthly or annual payments. Since amortized loans produce the same pattern of income, the factors from column 6 are loan constants.

To illustrate the calculation of debt service, let us return to the example being followed in this chapter. A 20-year mortgage loan is obtainable for a property which can be purchased for $250,000. The annual debt service on this monthly amortized loan was estimated to be $21,713. This amount was calculated in the following manner. A monthly loan constant of 0.009650 was obtained from column 6 of the monthly 10 percent table for 20 years (240 months). This monthly constant was then multiplied by 12 to obtain an annual constant for this monthly amortized loan. The annual constant was then multiplied by the amount of the loan to obtain the total annual debt service.

Monthly constant	Number of months	Annual constant
0.009650 ×	12 =	0.1158

Annual constant	Amount of loan	Annual debt service
0.1158 ×	$187,500 =	$21,713

If the loan were amortized annually, the annual constant for the annually amortized loan would be obtained directly from column 6 of the annual 10 percent table. This constant is 0.117460, giving an annual debt service of $22,024. Note that the annual debt service for the monthly payment loan is lower than for the annual payment loan. This difference occurs because the monthly payment loan produces principal amortization through the year, while the principal balance is not reduced through the year with an annually amortized loan.

To understand the nature of a loan constant, recall that a column 6 rate comprises two components—the interest rate and a sinking fund factor. For example, the annual constant for the 10 percent, 20-year, annually amortized loan of 0.117460 is composed of the interest rate of 10 percent plus the sinking fund factor of 0.017460 from column 3 of the 10 percent table for 20 years.

Interest rate	Sinking fund factor	Annual constant
0.10 +	0.017460 =	0.117460

Similarly, the monthly constant for the monthly amortized loan is composed of the effective monthly interest rate of 0.00833 plus the monthly sinking fund factor of 0.001317.

Annual interest rate		Number of months		Effective monthly rate
0.10	÷	12	=	0.008333

Effective monthly rate		Monthly sinking fund factor		Monthly constant
0.008333	+	0.001317	=	0.009650

Therefore, the loan payments to the lender will provide both a return on the lender's outstanding funds plus recapture of a portion of the loan. For our monthly amortized loan, the sinking fund is $0.1158 - 0.10$, or 0.0158. The amounts of return on investments and capital recapture for the first year of the loan will be as follows:

$$\$187,500 \times 0.10 = \$18,750 \quad \text{Interest}$$
$$\$187,500 \times 0.0158 = \begin{array}{l} \$\ 2,963 \quad \text{Principal} \\ \overline{\$21,713} \quad \text{Total payment} \end{array}$$

For succeeding years the principal repayments will reduce the outstanding balance of the loan. Thus, the amounts allocated to interest will decline, and the amounts allocated to principal repayment will increase.

Cash throw-off and the equity dividend rate.   In analyzing the desirability of various borrowing plans, investors often consider the magnitude of cash throw-off and the equity dividend rate. The cash throw-off is the amount of periodic cash generated by a property after subtracting periodic debt service. It is sometimes termed "gross spendable income" or "before-tax cash flow."

The equity dividend rate (sometimes called the "cash on cash return") is the ratio of cash throw-off to the amount of equity funds invested in the property. It is an important and widely used ratio in real estate investment and financial analysis because it is an indication of the return to investors on their cash contribution to a project. The formula is:

$$\text{Equity dividend rate} = \frac{\text{Cash throw-off}}{\text{Equity}}$$

In our example, in which a $187,500 loan is obtained for a $250,000 property, the equity dividend rate would be:

$$EDR = \frac{\$8,287}{\$62,500} = 0.1326, \text{ or } 13.3\%$$

Value of mortgage and equity income. Astute readers may have realized that in a financing situation both the lender and the equity investor want a return on and of their portion of the investment. Stated another way, each wants an annual income and the original investment returned in a certain period of time. Net operating income must provide both the investor and the lender with sufficient dollars to provide these amounts. When the dollars to the investor and the dollars to the lender are capitalized, the sum of the two values is the total property value.

In our continuing example, the value of the mortgage loan is $187,500. This amount could be obtained by capitalizing the annual debt service by the loan constant:

$$\$21,713 \div 0.1158 = \$187,500$$

Similarly, the value of the equity can be obtained by capitalizing the cash throw-off by the equity dividend rate of 13.26 percent:

$$\$8,287 \div 0.1326 = \$62,500$$

Proof that the value of the property is equal to the value of the mortgage plus the value of the equity can be provided by a "band of investment" analysis. This analytical technique is used to derive an overall capitalization rate based on the weight that each interest contributes to the total value. The appropriate capitalization rate in each case—the mortgage constant and the equity dividend rate—is multiplied by its respective weight.

$$
\begin{aligned}
\text{Mortgage:} \quad & 0.75 \times 0.1158 = 0.0868 \\
\text{Equity:} \quad & 0.25 \times 0.1326 = \underline{0.0332} \\
\text{Overall rate:} \quad & 0.1200
\end{aligned}
$$

This rate can then be used to capitalize the total NOI:

$$\$30,000 \div 0.12 = \$250,000$$

Thus, the value of the property is shown to be the value of the NOI capitalized by an overall rate weighted by the proportion that each interest represents in the property. It should be noted that both components of the overall rate—the loan constant and the equity dividend rate—provide for return on and of the investment. The lender's investment will be recaptured over the life of the loan (20 years), while the equity investment will be recaptured over the equity investment period.

The practical significance of this technique is that investors can quickly determine whether the purchase price of a property will allow an adequate return to both the financing and the equity positions. Or the rates relevant to both positions can be combined into an overall rate that can be used to capitalize the expected NOI. The resulting value represents a price which should provide both interests with adequate returns.

Discounts or points.   Lenders often charge discounts, or points, on loans to raise their effective yields. The amount of money represented by the points is simply deducted from the payout of the loan at the time the loan is closed. For example, if a borrower obtains a loan for $100,000 at a 12 percent interest rate and 2 points, the borrower would actually receive $98,000 at closing (98% × $100,000). The borrower then makes loan payments on the full amount of the loan, $100,000.

In our example, if the lender charges 2 points, the borrower would receive $138,750 (0.98 × $187,500). The lender's effective yield would be:

$$\text{Loan yield} = \frac{\text{Annual interest}}{\text{Outstanding balance of loan}}$$
$$= \frac{\$18,750}{\$183,750}$$
$$= 0.102, \text{ or } 10.2\%$$

The interest rate and effective yield are extremely important considerations to a lender—often more important than the down payment or term of the loan. Thus, borrowers can sometimes obtain better noninterest rate terms if they are willing to pay a slightly higher interest rate or more points. The effect on the borrower of changes in interest rate and other terms can be calculated as demonstrated below.

Sensitivity analysis.   Many times, borrowers are interested in knowing what effect different loan terms and interest rates will have on monthly mortgage payments. In addition to the interest rate, borrowers can analyze the effect of changes in the down payment and the loan term. The effect on the monthly payments resulting from changes in each of these variables is presented below. Then the effects on cash throw-off and the equity dividend rate are shown for three financing plans. We follow our continuing example of a property having a purchase price of $250,000 which is expected to produce NOI of $30,000. One loan plan requiring a 25 percent down payment, a 10 percent interest rate, and a 20-year term has already been analyzed. It would result in monthly payments of $1,809.38 and annual payments of $21,712.50. Cash throw-off from this plan would amount to $8,287.50, and the equity dividend rate would be 13.26 percent.

a. Changing the down payment.   If the borrower had the option of obtaining either an 80 percent or a 70 percent loan, how would the monthly payments, annual debt service, and cash throw-off be affected? An 80 percent loan would be for $200,000 and would require monthly payments of $1,930 and annual debt service of $23,160. A 70 percent loan would be for $175,000 and would require monthly payments of $1,688.75 and annual debt service of $20,265.00. Cash throw-off would be $6,840 and $9,735, respectively.

b. *Changing the term of the loan.*   If the borrower could obtain a loan having a maturity of 25 years or one having a maturity of 15 years, what results would occur, other terms remaining unchanged? A 25-year loan would require monthly payments of $1,703.81 and annual debt service of $20,445.75. A 15-year loan would require monthly payments of $2,014.88 and annual debt service of $24,178.50. Cash throw-off would be $9,554.25 and $5,821.50, respectively.

c. *Changing the interest rate.*   Other loan terms remaining unchanged, a lower interest rate will lower monthly payments and annual debt service and will raise cash throw-off. A higher interest rate will have the opposite effect. In our example, a 9 percent interest rate would require monthly payments of $1,686.94 and annual debt service of $20,243.25. An 11 percent interest rate would require monthly payments of $1,917.77 and annual debt service of $23,013.28. Cash throw-off would be $9,756.75 and $6,986.72, respectively.

Comparing loan packages.   Borrowers may face the availability of several alternative loan packages. That is, they probably cannot adjust some terms without having the lender require adjustments in other terms. And different institutional lenders may offer different loan arrangements on a "take it or leave it" basis. The borrowers must then analyze which loan package is best for them in terms of down payment, annual debt service, cash throw-off, equity dividend rate, and risk. Table 17–1 presents data concerning three potential loan packages for our continuing example.

TABLE 17–1
Loan package comparison

Loan	Down payment	Annual constant	Annual debt service	Cash throw-off	Equity dividend rate
1. 75%, 20-year, 10%	$62,500	0.115800	$21,712.50	$8,287.50	13.26%
2. 80%, 25-year, 12%	50,000	0.126384	25,276.80	4,723.20	9.45
3. 70%, 15-year, 9%	75,000	0.121716	21,300.30	8,699.70	11.60

From this presentation, it can be seen that loan 2 will require the lowest down payment and loan 3 will require the highest down payment. However, loan 2 will produce the smallest cash throw-off and equity dividend rate, while loan 3 will produce the largest cash throw-off and the second highest equity dividend rate. Loans 1 and 3 are fairly close in the annual debt service they require, while loan 2 is significantly higher in this requirement.

A major consideration for most borrowers is the size of down payment required. Borrowers often have minimal amounts of equity funds and therefore accept whatever loan package has the smallest down payment requirement. As illustrated here, however, such a loan may require the borrower to sacrifice cash throw-off and equity return. Furthermore, lower down payments increase financial risk. Nevertheless, during inflationary periods, or in areas experiencing rapid growth, a strategy of minimizing down payments at the cost of higher interest rates may pay off handsomely. The debt service is a fixed amount (unless the lender requires participation in the property income), which allows the borrower-owner to realize any increases in NOI and property value. Clearly, this strategy has been the key to success for many real estate investors in recent years.

The lending decision

Nonresidential lending decisions usually are based on a single factor—income. Prospective borrowers for nonresidential properties typically see an opportunity to increase their net worth by purchasing an income-producing property. Even speculative vacant land purchases are made for this purpose. The lender is faced with the task of determining the validity of the borrower's estimate of items such as income, expenses, and taxes. If these are regarded as realistic and valid, the lender must then evaluate the probability that the income produced by the property will be sufficient to meet the mortgage payments. This consideration is judged primarily by four ratios—the debt service coverage ratio, the operating expense ratio, the cash break-even ratio, and the margin of safety ratio. The lender also wants to be assured that in the event of default and foreclosure, the value of the property will be sufficient to pay off the outstanding balance of the loan. The loan to value ratio is the principal indicator of this consideration.

Just as with residential property loan applications, lenders may not discriminate against applicants for income property loans on the basis of race, national origin, religion, sex, marital status, age, and so forth. Nevertheless, lenders must judge the quality of the property that will serve as security for a loan and the amount of risk entailed in making the loan. The property and the income to be derived from it are much more important in income property lending than in residential lending. For our property and loan request being evaluated in this section, the ratios would be calculated as follows:[1]

---

[1] These ratios are also discussed in Chapter 5.

Loan to value ratio.   The loan to value ratio is a measure of financial risk associated with borrowing money. A lender realizes that the higher the loan to value ratio, the lower the cushion of value should the borrower default. This ratio typically ranges between 60 percent and 90 percent, depending on the nature of the property. It is calculated as follows:

$$\text{Loan to value ratio} = \frac{\text{Loan amount}}{\text{Price or value}}$$

For our property having a loan of $187,500 and price of $250,000 the loan to value ratio is:

$$L/V = \frac{\$187,500}{\$250,000} = 0.750 \text{ or } 75.0\%$$

Debt service coverage.   When prospective borrowers apply for loans on income-producing properties, they normally will already have estimated the effective gross income for the property. From this income figure, all operating expenses are subtracted to yield net operating income. A lender is concerned about the amount of cash throw-off remaining after the mortgage payment has been made. One may ask the question, "Why are lenders concerned about this amount? They have their payment." To answer this question, consider another question a lender might ask. "How much can NOI decrease and still be adequate to cover the mortgage payment?"

$$\text{Debt service coverage} = \frac{\text{Net operating income}}{\text{Mortgage payment}}$$

Therefore, with $30,000 NOI and a mortgage payment of $21,713, debt service coverage is:

$$DSC = \frac{\$30,000}{\$21,713} = 1.38$$

This means that NOI could decrease by 27.6 percent and the lender would still be assured of receiving the mortgage payment. Generally, lenders require a minimum debt service coverage ratio of around 1.3.

Operating expense ratio.   The operating expense ratio is used to show the percentage of effective gross income consumed by operating expenses. Since the investor obtains income only after these expenses are subtracted, the lower the operating ratio, the better. It is calculated as follows:

$$\begin{aligned}
\text{Operating expense ratio} &= \frac{\text{Operating expenses}}{\text{Effective gross income}} \\
&= \frac{\$13,500}{\$43,500} \\
&= 31.0\%
\end{aligned}$$

Typical operating expenses include management, janitorial services, maintenance, repairs, and supplies. *Remember:* Mortgage payments and depreciation are not operating expenses.

Cash break-even ratio.   The cash break-even ratio provides investors with a measure of all cash charges against effective gross income. Reserves are subtracted from the operating expenses since they are not a cash expense. Also, recall that depreciation is not an operating expense and thus is not included in the ratio. This ratio usually varies between 60 percent and 80 percent.

$$\text{Cash break-even ratio} = \frac{\substack{\text{Operating} \\ \text{expenses}} + \substack{\text{Annual debt} \\ \text{service}} - \substack{\text{Replacement} \\ \text{reserves}}}{\text{Effective gross income}}$$

$$= \frac{\$13,500 + \$21,713 - \$2,000}{\$43,500}$$

$$= 0.7635, \text{ or about } 76.4\%$$

In other words, the project must realize 76.4 percent of its projected revenue to break even.

Margin of safety.   The margin of safety between cash receipts and cash disbursements is the difference between 1.00 and the cash break-even ratio. For our example, the relative margin of safety would be:

$$MS = 1.00 - CBE$$
$$= 1.00 - 0.764$$
$$= 0.236, \text{ or } 23.6\%$$

This could be considered as the maximum vacancy rate allowable before expenses exceed revenues.

Based upon these ratios, the loan appears to be safe and prudent from the lender's point of view. The loan to value ratio indicates there would be a sizable cushion of value should the borrower default and the lender foreclose. The debt service coverage ratio indicates that the borrowers should be able to meet the periodic payments from NOI with no difficulty. And, finally, the operating expense ratio, the cash break-even ratio, and the margin of safety ratio all indicate that the property could lose a significant amount of revenue before it would no longer be sufficient to cover expenses and mortgage payments.

Role of financial analysis

In applying for a loan from an institutional lender, the borrower-developer will be required to submit an estimate of expected costs and a projection of future income and expenses. Examples of such schedules are shown in Tables 17–2 and 17–3. The lender will analyze the financial plan to determine whether it is accurate and realistic. An

TABLE 17–2
Presidential Manor apartment project estimated costs

Land:	
15.013 acres, or 655,263 sq. ft., at $0.46/sq. ft.	$ 301,420
Improvements:	
29 apartment buildings, 252,000 sq. ft. at $14.50/sq. ft.	3,654,000
Blacktop, 191,000 sq. ft. at $0.40/sq. ft.	76,400
Laundry and maintenance building, 1,350 sq. ft. at $11/sq. ft.	14,850
Estimated total cost	$4,046,670

appraisal will be made by either the lender's appraisal staff or an independent appraiser. The lender may accept the plans and projections, suggest modifications, or reject them. Of course, a lender may believe that a proposed development has merit, yet not grant a loan because of a current lack of loanable funds or because of the availability of other desirable projects.

One large apartment project, Presidential Manor, recently proposed to a life insurance company, contained estimates of cost as shown in Table 17–2.

The builder should have the building costs itemized for all materials, assemblies, parts, and labor. The costs should include the costs of plans and blueprints, permits, city fees, construction financing, legal fees, marketing, and overhead and profit, as well as the direct materials and labor costs. If lenders are convinced that the buildings as planned, the land, and other improvements can be obtained for the estimated costs, they will proceed with an analysis of income and expense projections. The Presidential Manor proposal contained the income and expense projections shown in Table 17–3.

If lenders agree with these projections of income and expense, they can capitalize the net income stream to estimate the property's value. If a capitalization rate of 10 percent is appropriate and an economic life of the improvements of 40 years is used, the level annuity factor of 9.8 produces an estimated value of $4,220,624, or approximately $4,220,600. To this is added the present value of the land reversion ($301,420 × 0.022) of $6,631, for a total value of $4,227,200. On the basis of this value, a life insurance company in this state can legally lend 80 percent, or $3,381,760. The borrower has requested this amount from the insurance company in the form of a 20-year, annually amortized mortgage loan, bearing a 9 percent interest rate.

Assuming that the insurance company is satisfied that the income and expense projections are as realistic and accurate as can be determined, the lender will still want to examine other factors and may propose an alternate financing arrangement to the developer. Important additional considerations are (a) the relation of the cash flow to be generated from the property to the financing payments and (b) the effect of the federal income tax on the stream of earnings.

The income projection of Table 17–3 can be extended as follows:

Net operating income		
(first year)		$430,676
Less annual depreciation (40 years straight-line on		
building only)...	$ 91,350	
Less interest (first year)	304,358	395,708
Net taxable income		$ 34,968
Income tax (50%)		17,484
Net income (after depreciation, interest expense,		
and income tax)		17,484
Add: Depreciation	$ 91,350	
Deduct: Mortgage principal payment (first year)*	66,100	25,250
Net cash flow (first year)		$ 42,734

* Calculation of principal payment:

Total mortgage payment (9%)		$370,458
Interest (first year)		304,358
Principal payment (first year)		$ 66,100

It is evident that by dipping into the funds earmarked for depreciation, the borrowers would be able to meet their mortgage payments and have some cash ($42,734) left over. The margin is not great, however, and both borrowers and lender should consider the possibility that the rental estimates may be optimistic. If rents should turn out to be less than anticipated, the borrowers might not be able to meet their mortgage commitment. The lender, therefore, proposed a different financing arrangement.

The new arrangement proposed that the lender grant a loan of $3 million for 25 years at 10 percent interest (amortized annually) and purchase the land for $300,000. The borrowers would lease back the land for $30,000 per year (10 percent), this amount being deductible by the borrowers for income tax purposes. Additionally, to protect itself against the risk of inflation, the lender wanted a "kicker." The kicker took the form of additional rent on the ground, tied to net operating income. The lender would be entitled to 25 percent of any additional operating income above that obtained in the current rental schedule. The kicker would continue for the length of the lease on the ground, although the mortgage would in all probability be paid off much sooner. Additionally, the lender stipulated that the property could not be sold or refinanced without its permission for 12 years.

The cash flow generated by the new financing arrangement was estimated as shown in Figure 17–1.

TABLE 17–3
Presidential Manor projected income and expenses

Unit type	Num-ber of units	Monthly rental	Sq. ft./ unit	Mo. rent/ sq. ft.	Num-ber of rooms	Rent/ room/ month	Total
1-bedroom flat	80	$160	620	25.8¢	3	$53.33	$153,600
2-bedroom flat	152	185	812	22.8	4	46.25	337,440
2-bedroom townhome	76	200	928	21.6	4	50.00	182,400

Total projected annual rental income	$673,440
Other income: Laundry at $25/unit	7,700
Gross annual income	$681,140
Less: Vacancy and collection allowance at 5%	34,072
Effective gross income	$647,068
Less expenses:	
Operating:	
Management at 4½%	$ 29,118
Custodial	17,000
Heating and air conditioning at $25/room	28,900
Electric (common areas only)	6,000
Maintenance at $12/room	13,872
Painting and redecorating at $12/room	13,872
Miscellaneous	5,000
Total operating expenses...................................	$113,762
Fixed:	
Real estate taxes at $200/unit	$ 60,160
Insurance at $40/unit	12,320
Reserve for replacements	30,150
Total fixed expenses	$102,630
Total operating and fixed expenses	216,392
Net operating income	$430,676

FIGURE 17–1
Estimated cash flow produced by bank-proposed financing arrangement (first year)*

Net operating income		$430,676
Less:		
Rent	$ 30,000	
Interest	300,000	
Depreciation	93,665	423,665
Taxable income		$ 7,011
Income tax (50%)...		3,505
Net income after tax		$ 3,506
Add depreciation		93,665
		$ 97,171
Deduct mortgage principal payment (1st year).............		30,504
Cash flow (first year)		$ 66,667

* Loan terms: Amount—$3,000,000; term—25 years; amortization—annual; annual payment—$330,504; constant—0.110168; interest rate—10%.

Although the interest rate for the lender's proposed loan is higher than for the loan requested by the developer, the cash flow is greater. The better cash position results because of two factors: (*a*) the term of the loan is longer, reducing the annual mortgage payment; and (*b*) the ground rent is tax deductible, producing a lower income tax liability for the developer.

If rental income did not increase or if expenses increased as much as income, of course the lender would obtain no increased yield from the kicker. In its projections, however, the lender assumed that net operating income (gross income less vacancy and operating expenses) would increase 3 percent per year. The property's cash flow would increase each year under the assumption, and both the lender's and the developer's yields would increase, as shown in Tables 17–4 and 17–5. Thus, for the second year $12,920 additional operating income would be generated, the lender receiving $3,230 and the developer receiving the remainder. The rates of return for each year are calculated by adding the total inflows to each party—the lender and the developer—and dividing by the total investment of each. Income to the lender consists of mortgage interest, ground rent, and kicker income.

The developer's before-tax cash return to invested equity is calculated by deducting from net operating income ground rent and total debt service (mortgage interest plus principal payments) and adding the expected increases in net operating income, after subtracting the

TABLE 17–4
Lender's rate of return for 12-year locked-in period*

Year	Net operating income	Additional income over previous year	Kicker (25 percent of additional income)	Interest + Ground rent + Kicker	Lender's investment (mortgage balance + land)	Lender's rate of ROI†
1	$430,676	–0–	–0–	$330,000	$3,300,000	10.00%
2	443,596	$12,920	$3,230	330,180	3,269,496	10.09
3	456,896	13,308	3,327	326,921	3,235,942	10.10
4	470,204	13,705	3,426	323,329	3,199,032	10.10
5	484,310	14,106	3,527	319,370	3,158,431	10.11
6	498,839	14,529	3,632	315,009	3,113,770	10.11
7	513,804	14,965	3,741	310,205	3,064,643	10.12
8	529,218	15,414	3,854	304,914	3,010,603	10.12
9	545,095	15,877	3,969	299,085	2,951,159	10.13
10	561,448	16,353	4,088	292,665	2,885,771	10.14
11	578,291	16,843	4,211	285,585	2,813,744	10.14
12	595,640	17,349	4,337	227,798	2,734,614	10.15

* Amount of loan—$3,000,000; term—25 years; interest rate—10 percent; amortization—annual; mortgage constant—0.110168; annual payment—$330,504.

† Return on investment = $\dfrac{\text{Total income}}{\text{Outstanding investment}}$

TABLE 17–5
Developer's before-tax rate of return for 12-year locked-in period

Year	Developer's additional NOI	Total income to developer	Developer's ROI*
1.	–0–	$ 70,172†	9.41%
2.	$ 9,690	79,862	10.71
3.	9,981	89,843	12.05
4.	10,279	100,122	13.43
5.	10,579	110,701	14.85
6.	10,897	121,598	16.31
7.	11,224	132,822	17.82
8.	11,560	144,382	19.37
9.	11,908	155,290	20.83
10	12,265	167,555	22.48
11	12,632	180,187	24.17
12	13,012	193,199	25.92

* Return on investment = $\dfrac{\text{Total income}}{\text{Outstanding investment}}$

Developer's investment calculated as follows:

Cost of improvements	$3,745,250
Less mortgage	3,000,000
	$ 745,250

† Income to developer = 1st year's NOI – Ground rent and debt service
= $430,676 – ($30,000 + $330,504)
= $70,172

kicker paid to the lender. Although the mortgage principal payments serve to build up equity in the property, it can be assumed that depreciation equals the annual principal payments. The resulting rate of return is equal to increasing the developer's investment each year by the amounts of the principal payment and increasing the developer's cash by the same amount of depreciation.

From the example it is clear that the developers of the apartment complex are able to obtain the financing necessary to produce the project and to realize an extremely attractive rate of return. The rate of return, however, is dependent upon the assumption of an annual, compounded 3 percent growth rate of net income. The requirement that the developers pay a higher interest rate (10 percent versus 9 percent) and extend the maturity five years has worked to their advantage. Their annual mortgage payments are lower, thus giving them a greater cash flow. If the apartment project is successful, the higher interest rate and longer maturity will not be burdensome and they will have gained a more secure financial position. On the other hand, the insurance company will have gained a higher rate of return, which is very important to it.

Obviously, any number of different financing schemes could be worked out. Interest rates, maturities, amortization schedules, and kickers could be changed to reflect the best combination for one or both parties. In recent years the field of income property financing has experienced almost every conceivable financing arrangement. There is no such thing as a "standard" or even "preferred" type of loan package.

The clear implication for real estate developers is that they need to understand the various instruments and techniques of real estate finance. They need to realize that they can and should shop around for a lender who will put together a financing package suitable for their requirements. Even better, they need to be able to suggest financing arrangements to lenders that will meet the lender's requirements for legality and safety, yet will provide the required amount of funds at the proper place and time. The key to most successful real estate developments is financing.

SUMMARY

Obtaining financing on favorable terms and at a reasonable cost is an important aspect of creating successful real estate projects. Although some amount of equity funds will normally be required in the production or purchase of real estate, the bulk of funds constitute the debt capital committed to a project.

This chapter begins with a discussion on the borrowing and lending decisions for single-family residential properties. Lending institutions are generally less flexible with mortgage terms for these type of loans than with mortgage terms for income-producing properties. Both the borrowing and the lending decision are made primarily on the basis of an applicant's income flow. Enough income must be earned so that the borrower can pay all debts and living expenses.

Income-producing-property loans are more complex. Borrowers for such loans attempt to enhance their financial position through cash flows, tax shelters, or capital gains. Investors must be certain that the effects of these incomes are positive and that their wealth does not diminish because of them. In analyzing a proposed real estate project, the developers should compute their expected rate of return by relating forecasted net income to the required capital investment. Expenses, as well as rental income, should be evaluated carefully and projected as realistically as possible for the expected life of the investment. Vacancy rates, management expense, and replacement reserves must be included in the expense forecast.

Income-producing-property borrowers generally attempt to finance their investments through the use of debt, even if they can provide 100 percent equity themselves. The rationale behind this is that a higher rate of return on equity may be achieved by using borrowed funds. On the other hand, if the mortgage interest rate is greater than the actual overall returns on the property, leverage will have a negative effect on equity returns.

One criterion used by investors to make decisions concerning mortgage loan acceptability is the amount of debt service that must be paid each year. This can be calculated using the loan constant, which is found by multiplying the column 6 factor in the compound interest table by 12. The loan constant represents the percentage of the total amount borrowed which must be repaid annually. This constant provides for both return on investment and capital recapture to the lender.

The lender is not the only party interested in recapturing invested capital and receiving a return on the investment. The borrower views the equity investment as comparable in nature to the lender's mortgage investment. Both the lender's and the borrower's requirements in this respect must be satisfied before a lending/borrowing agreement is put into effect. The sum of the mortgage and the equity value is the total property value.

Other factors affecting loan desirability include the loan to value ratio, the debt service coverage ratio, the cash break-even ratio, and the margin of safety. Although the equity dividend rate is a widely used indication of return, it is rather simplistic and does not account for the time value of money. More sophisticated methods of measuring return are presented in Chapter 5.

When shopping for loans, real estate investors need to understand the legal framework, characteristics, and practices of institutional lenders, described in Chapter 16. In addition, investors need to investigate alternative financing plans and various mortgage term arrangements. These provide a basis on which borrowers can bargain with lenders. Borrowers may often be prepared to concede a point of relatively small importance to them (such as a somewhat higher interest rate) in order to obtain a feature of great importance to them but of less importance to the lender (such as a higher loan-to-value ratio). The terms on which a borrower can receive a loan are very important, as they can make or break a project.

QUESTIONS FOR REVIEW

1. What guidelines do lenders follow when evaluating loan applications for single-family residential properties? What are the differences and similarities of the borrower's viewpoint and the lender's viewpoint with regard to the acceptability of a mortgage agreement?

2. How does financing influence a developer's expected return on invest-

ment? How is cash flow influenced by financing? What role is played by principal repayment?

3. Why is the sinking fund factor added to the effective interest rate when a loan constant is developed?

4. What is the "band of investment" technique? What role do the equity dividend rate and the loan constant play in the overall rate computation? Why is the band of investment technique particularly useful when evaluating a potential real estate project?

5. What is a *kicker*? Do you believe kickers will continue to exist during periods of lower interest rates?

PROBLEMS

1. Calculate the cash throw-off and taxable income associated with the following facts:

Gross income.......................	$500,000
Vacancy allowance	5 percent of gross
Variable expenses..................	27 percent of gross
Fixed expenses	$50,000
Mortgage (new)	$1,800,000
Debt service constant	0.0967
Interest rate on mortgage	8.5 percent
Depreciation—1st year	$100,000

2. Prepare a numerical example that shows an after–income tax advantage of owning a condominium apartment over renting the same apartment. Incorporate the following data into your example:

Rental level if rented	$300 per month
Purchase price	$35,000
Mortgage..........................	90 percent of price
Marginal income tax rate	40 percent
Utilities and maintenance...........	$800 per year
Real estate taxes	$700 per year

REFERENCES

Beaton, William R. *Real Estate Finance.* Englewood Cliffs, N.J.: Prentice-Hall, 1975.

Britton, James A., and Kerwood, Lewis O. *Financing Income-Producing Real Estate.* New York: McGraw-Hill, for the Mortgage Bankers Association of America, 1977.

Epley, Donald R., and Millar, James A. *Basic Real Estate Finance and Investments.* New York: John Wiley and Sons, 1980.

Hines, Mary Alice. *Real Estate Finance.* Englewood Cliffs, N.J.: Prentice-Hall, 1978.

Hoagland, Henry E.; Stone, Leo D.; and Brueggeman, William B. *Real Estate Finance.* 6th ed. Homewood, Ill.: Richard D. Irwin, 1977.

Smith, Halbert C., and Tschappat, Carl J. "Monetary Policy and Real Estate Values." *Appraisal Journal* 34, no. 1 (January 1966): 18–26.

Wiedemer, John P. *Real Estate Finance.* Reston, Va.: Reston, 1974.

Real estate planning

Planning is one of the principal functions of management in the execution stage of microadministration (along with organizing, directing, and controlling). Planning is especially important to real estate development and urban growth because of the long-term commitment to which most land uses subject a community. Once the characteristics of real estate development are determined, they establish a community's economic and social pattern. This pattern, in turn, helps determine the nature of further development and growth. Thus, careful planning is necessary to achieve the desired type of land-use pattern through the guidance of future growth.

Although there are many areas of overlap, real estate planning can generally be divided between public planning and private planning. Public planning is often termed *city* (or *urban*) *planning*, while private planning is usually termed *land planning*. Generally, either type of planning involves an attempt to guide development so as to achieve maximum efficiency, utility, and attractiveness for a community or a neighborhood. In this sense, planning is a problem-solving process, and a step-by-step approach is required in order to formulate a good plan.

PUBLIC PLANNING

Comprehensive planning

The formulation of a plan for a city, county, or region requires a planning agency to take an overall approach to the planning problem. Planning involves much more than merely the physical aspects; social, economic, and governmental-political-legal matters must all be considered. Kent has emphasized that the proper role of the public planner is usually that of land-use adviser to an elected public body—typically a city council or a county commission.[1] The planner must forecast the jurisdiction's future needs for utilities, streets, roads, public service buildings, parks and recreational facilities, police and fire protection, and public welfare. And, in the most general view, the public planner must forecast tax and other revenues for the jurisdiction and recommend ways to balance revenues against needed expenditures. Although the extent of the planner's role in these matters is a continual issue of debate, any general, or broad, approach to public planning is termed *comprehensive planning*. There are five basic steps in the continuing process of urban planning.

Define fundamental land-use goals for the constituency to be served. Fundamental land-use goals are determined in a public forum, through the making of key decisions by elected public officials. Clearly defined community goals are often obscured by a plethora of conflicting interests and individual concerns. Examples of such conflicts have occurred in a number of cities which have established the goal of a maximum future population. These cities have planned for a fixed number of citizens, and they consider the impact of every requested rezoning or new building permit in light of this overriding goal. Some local citizens, developers, and builders, however, have not been in agreement with this type of goal. They represent conflicting interests which have often resulted in heated political and legal battles.

The cities of Atlanta, Washington, D.C., and San Francisco have established a goal of promoting rapid transit systems by limiting the development of new parking structures in congested downtown areas. New office buildings are not designed to accommodate employees' and customers' total parking needs. One important implication of this goal for the private sector is that decisions must be based upon judgments regarding the success of yet uncompleted rapid transit facilities. While New York, Chicago, and Montreal have had rapid transit facilities for many years, the experience of newer systems, such

---

[1] T. J. Kent, Jr., *The Urban General Plan* (San Francisco: Chandler, 1964).

as BART in San Francisco and Metro in Washington, D.C., is insufficient to allow an unequivocal forecast of success for this goal.

Formulate alternative plans to accomplish the goals. In formulating a comprehensive plan, many needs and desires must be considered. Priorities must be determined and political implications weighed. Any proposed plan must reflect a balancing of diverse concerns and interests in the community. For example, the need for an adequate road system must be balanced by the desire of residents of existing neighborhoods not to have streets widened to accommodate additional traffic. Moreover, the planner's research must establish the need for funding and create the understanding of its importance. Ruth Mack has commented upon the frustration felt by planners as they encounter this bartering process.[2] However, it is a political fact of life which planners cannot avoid.

In formulating a comprehensive plan, the following steps are usually necessary.

Inventory existing conditions. The planner must evaluate the location of utilities (sewerage, gas, water, telephone, and power) and who provides these services; the status of street, highway, and expressway improvements; the provision of such services as medical care, police and fire protection, transit, sanitation, and welfare; the age and condition of structures; the availability of unimproved or underdeveloped land; property ownership patterns; and community facilities for business and recreation. Inventory maps must be developed which reflect what the jurisdiction contains and the condition of private and public improvements. Both air and water pollution must be considered in this process. Goals for improvement can then be established, followed by formal policy statements and priorities for use of scarce monetary resources.

Prepare an assessment of trends in population, employment, and business growth. Identify clearly the direction and magnitude of growth.

Prepare independent plans for municipal utilities (sewer and water), community facilities, streets and roads, and public housing. Estimate costs for each plan.

Analyze potential funding sources. The capacity of the property tax and other local sources of revenue must be analyzed to determine their potential for financing the plan. Additional support may be available from state and federal agencies. Funding programs have a major impact upon the ability of a local planner to forecast future revenues.

---

[2] Ruth Prince Mack, *Planning on Uncertainty* (New York: Wiley-Interscience, 1971).

The planner must catalog the requirements of federal- and state-aid programs and prepare drafts of application for such aid. The potential use of special taxing districts, new bond issues, general tax increases, and new taxes must be assessed.

Assemble data from earlier steps and overlay them on a single set of base maps for use in developing alternate comprehensive plans. Given that costs have been estimated for subelements, overall cost estimates can be made for each alternative plan. Such costs should be aligned with potential funding sources and strategies devised regarding sources of specific revenues and the timing of expenditures. The plan should be kept reasonably general; urban design alternatives should be considered within the plan.

Select the plan that best meets the goals, within political and funding constraints. Selection of the plan that best meets goals and constraints is made by the political governing body, for example, the city council or the county commission. However, the plan selected can be influenced by the advantages and disadvantages identified by the planners. Additionally, public reactions to alternative plans can influence (and often determine) which plan is chosen.

When a new plan is formulated or an existing plan is substantially revised, public hearings are usually required. At such hearings citizen opinions and inputs to the plan are obtained. Based upon these reactions and suggestions, the plan may be selected, rejected, or modified to include components of alternative plans. Needless to say, public approval of a plan usually requires citizen input during its formulation, "selling" of the plan to elected officials, and commitment to and selling of the plan by these officials to their constituents.

Implement the plan. Implementation of the comprehensive plan is accomplished through zoning. Zoning may be defined as the regulation of land use, population density, and building size by district. The overall zoning pattern and rezoning decisions should be made in conformance with the comprehensive plan.

Monitor the operation of the plan, and modify it as required. Plans must be modified as conditions change or as the plans are found to be deficient. One of the key tests of a plan's success is the extent to which it is accepted by the area's residents. A substantial outpouring of criticism or court challenges to the plan will likely cause the plan to be modified. A successful plan normally contains both a strong element of rigidity and provisions for flexibility. Once the plan has been adopted, capricious changes should be precluded. At the same time, however, changes of a more general nature should be allowed, if they are based upon well-founded reasoning and research. The comprehensive plan should be regarded as a document subject to continual review, analysis, and modification.

Zoning

Zoning may be regarded as a phase of comprehensive planning. As noted previously, zoning is the process by which a plan is implemented. This process involves the delineation of zones or districts, within which certain land uses are permitted and others are prohibited. The broadest categorization of zones is residential, commercial, and industrial. The category of residential would be indicated by R; commercial, by C; and industrial, by I. These categories are further divided into many subcategories. For example, R1a may designate that only detached single-family residences may be built on lots of a specified minimum size and shape; R1b may allow smaller lots; R2 may allow duplexes; and R3 may allow high-density apartments. The zoning code for a moderate-sized city may contain several hundred pages of small print to identify and explain the various zones.

Objective.   The objective of the zoning process is to bring order to the otherwise uncontrolled market of private competition for land. Without zoning, many diverse opinions as to the most profitable use of land would undoubtedly result in widely differing uses of adjacent parcels. Offices, apartments, and even factories could be constructed in a neighborhood of single-family homes. Or homes could be constructed in an area subject to pollution, poor drainage, or industrial usage. The ultimate result of these types of practices is a reduction of all land values (compared with land values under zoning control). Thus, the main advantage claimed for zoning is that land values are preserved and enhanced.

Legal basis.   The legal basis for zoning is the police power of the government. The police power is the inherent right of government to protect the general welfare by the regulation of public health, morals, and safety. Legislative enabling acts confer the specific zoning authority upon local governments.

As mentioned previously, a number of cities, including Petaluma, California; Boca Raton, Florida; Mount Laurel, New Jersey; and Ramapo, New York, have attempted to control and limit growth by enacting zoning ordinances that restrict the number of new housing units that could be constructed. The restrictions have been based upon the need for planned provision of services for residential development and the necessity for growth to conform to a comprehensive plan. The ordinances have been challenged in court by developers and builders who contend that the ordinances constitute exclusionary zoning, denial of due process, denial of the right to travel, and inverse condemnation.

The courts generally have held that zoning ordinances which are reasonable, provide for all types of housing, and are based upon a long-range comprehensive plan are constitutional. For example, although the federal district court ruled against the Petaluma plan, the Ninth Circuit U.S. Court of Appeals reversed the district court. It found that the Petaluma plan is not arbitrary and unreasonable. Neither was it considered exclusionary, since the plan contains provisions for multiunit dwellings and for low- and moderate-income housing. The U.S. Supreme Court later refused to review the circuit court's ruling.[3]

In the Ramapo case, the highest court in New York State approved the city's ordinance. The court noted that the restrictions on development were of limited duration and concluded:

> In sum, where it is clear that the existing physical and financial resources of the community are inadequate to furnish the essential services and facilities which a substantial increase in population requires, there is a rational basis for "planned growth" and hence, the challenged ordinance is not violative of the Federal and State Constitutions.[4]

The court also determined that the ordinance was not exclusionary, partially because the plan provided for low- and moderate-income housing and partially because it attempted to provide a balanced, cohesive community.

While the courts have approved some controversial zoning ordinances that attempt to control growth, others have been turned down. For example, Mount Laurel, New Jersey, attempted to limit housing to single-family dwellings and prescribed large lot and structure sizes. Furthermore, the town zoned almost 30 percent of its land for industrial and related uses, far exceeding reasonable expectations of industrial development. The New Jersey Supreme Court concluded that this ordinance was exclusionary and overturned it.[5] Similarly, a Boca Raton ordinance that attempted to limit the number of dwelling units that could be constructed within the city was overturned by state courts for being arbitrary and exclusionary. Thus, zoning ordinances that are reasonable in attempting to control growth, while not excluding any racial groups or income classes, will probably be upheld. Zoning ordinances that do not meet these criteria will probably be defeated.

Since zoning limits the right of property owners to develop and use property as they may desire, zoning has been attacked in the courts as a method of taking property *without* compensation. Many such attacks

---

[3] 522 F.2d 897, 8 ERC 1001 (9th Cir. 1975), *cert. denied*, 96 S. Ct. 1148 (February 23, 1976).

[4] 285 N.E. 2d at 304–305.

[5] 336 A. 2d at 731–732.

have been unsuccessful; the courts have upheld the concept of zoning as a legitimate exercise of police power. However, a California U.S. district court case, *Arastra Limited Partnership* v. *City of Palo Alto*, suggests that there are definite limits to zoning powers. The court ruled that Palo Alto's open-space zoning regulations precluded private development of land that the city had intended to buy and thus constituted "inverse condemnation"—illegal taking of land. The implications of the case will likely be quite significant. Local governments or agencies which downzone property that they had intended to buy may find that they have gone beyond the limits of zoning authority.[6]

Additionally, zoning must be applied fairly, impartially, and in conformance with a community's comprehensive plan. Many specific applications of zoning have been overturned when these criteria were not met. For example, the Georgia Supreme Court ruled in 1975 that the commissioners of Cobb County were arbitrary and capricious in failing to rezone a developer's property.[7] Further, the court warned that the state courts would be looking over the shoulders of all zoning bodies to see that all future decisions are made in consideration of the public health, safety, morals, and general welfare. Within six months after this decision, more than 100 zoning cases in several states were placed on court dockets.

In recent years, the emphasis of courts in zoning has been upon the constitutionality of zoning. Basically, the issues are: (1) Is a denial of use change equivalent to a confiscatory taking of an individual's property? (2) Can the zoning authority prove to the court's satisfaction that the public's benefit in denying a rezoning equals or exceeds the applicant's detriment? The major result of judicial involvement in zoning is that local governments are forced to consider the interests of individual property owners as well as community-wide land-use objectives. The court's purpose is to achieve a balance between the interests of individual property owners and the perceived public benefit.

The increasing use of private planners who present expert testimony in various public forums has led to a new category of planners—the *advocacy planners*. Altshuler, Bolan, and others have developed the viewpoint that the public hearing mechanism for making land-use decisions requires greater involvement by professional planners.[8] Although such professionals are advocates, it is believed

---

[6] "The Limits on Zoning," *Business Week*, May 3, 1976, p. 74.

[7] Earnest W. Barrett et al., *Commissioners* v. *Doyle Hamby*, Ext. 30 Ga. 015, decided September 16, 1975.

[8] Alan A. Altshuler, *The City Planning Process: A Political Analysis* (Ithaca, N.Y.: Cornell University Press, 1965); and Richard S. Bolan, "Emerging Views of Planning," *Journal of the American Institute of Planners*, July 1967, pp. 233–45.

that they can present pertinent facts and develop solutions that will meet the required criteria.

Requests for rezoning are typically made to the chief staff planner, or zoning administrator. The property owner must submit an application for rezoning, accompanied by a plan for the property which reflects the proposed use. Larger rezoning requests must also be reviewed by state and federal agencies, school officials, and utility companies that will be affected by the proposed plan.

Administration. Appendix B describes the administrative structure for planning and zoning in Gainesville, Florida, a city of approximately 100,000 population. The structure is typical, in that a planning commission of appointed, nonprofessional planners is the planning agency for the city. The planning commission hires a staff of professional planners who carry out the day-to-day planning and zoning activities. The planning commission approves, rejects, or modifies its staff's recommendations. In planning and zoning matters, the commission's decisions then become recommendations to the city commission, which has the final decision-making authority. The planning commission holds final authority for the approval of site plans, subdivision plats, and commercial signs and billboards.

Following these reviews, a notice of the rezoning request is posted on the property and surrounding property owners are notified of the proposed rezoning. The request is then scheduled for public hearing, where the pteitioner presents the proposal, affected property owners are asked to testify, and the zoning administrator is asked to recommend for or against the proposal. The commission then makes a recommendation to the elected governing body, which in turn holds a hearing and renders a final approval or denial.

The political power of the zoning administrator should be analyzed by anyone seeking a rezoning. In some jurisdictions the governing body rarely votes in opposition to the administrator, while in others the recommendations have little or no effect on the final decision. The hearings in this process are tending to become more formal in most jurisdictions, and the administrator's ideas are typically given more attention than in the past. Thus, the administrator's political power over land-use decisions appears to be increasing.

Social and economic issues

Because of the pervasive impact of planning and zoning decisions, they have been subject to many controversies. The legal issue regarding whether zoning results in confiscation without compensation has been noted. Although the general authority to zone is well established, legal battles will continue to be waged over the question of whether specific planning and zoning decisions meet the criteria of reasonable-ness, fairness, and necessity to the general welfare. It has been shown that the courts will not hesitate to intervene in zoning decisions to uphold the fundamental tests.

In addition to the legal issues, economic and social concerns have been expressed regarding the effects of zoning on the private enter-prise system and upon groups of citizens. These issues are discussed in the following paragraphs.

Zoning interferes with the efficient operation of the private mar-ket. Zoning seeks to guide and direct market decisions in ways that enhance all land values. To accomplish this goal, however, zoning must anticipate market needs. In effect, land must be zoned so as to reflect decisions that the private market might well have made without the zoning. Land zoned for single-family residences should be gener-ally recognized as appropriate for that use, and land zoned for com-mercial uses should be amenable to that type of use.

Planning and zoning decisions may not, however, accurately fore-cast market activity. Too much land may be zoned for one purpose and not enough for another. Or, land zoned for one use may not fit in with the trends of development and other uses. These inaccurate market interpretations lead to imbalances in supply and demand relation-ships. Market inefficiency is the result, with the price of some land being too high and that of other land too low.

Siegan has attacked the basic premise of zoning by contending that zoning does not improve upon the private market's ability to produce a desirable structure of land uses.[9] In his study of Houston, the only major U.S. city without zoning, he concluded that the private market produced a structure of land uses as desirable as the structure pro-duced under zoning in other cities. Although Siegan's research and value judgments can be (and have been) questioned, the basic issue of the relationship between planning, zoning, and the private market will continue to be debated. Perhaps the most satisfactory resolution of the issue is to assure sufficient flexibility in the comprehensive plan and in the planning and zoning processes so that changes can be made to reflect market realities.

The administration of planning and zoning is inherently subject to favoritism and political manipulation. Given the administrative structure of planning and zoning, perhaps favoritism and political in-fluence are unavoidable and should be recognized as a definitional aspect of these activities. Nevertheless, when these types of consid-erations affect zoning or rezoning decisions, they defeat the fundamen-

---

[9] Bernard H. Siegan, *Land Use without Zoning* (Lexington, Mass.: D. C. Heath, 1972).

tal criteria which form zoning's legal justification. The economic effect of manipulative influences is, as with any antimarket force, to subvert the operation of the market and to produce prices that are too high or too low. Some land may be developed too soon, while other land development may be delayed. And, of course, some property owners or developers profit at the expense of the general public. As Audrey Moore, a member of the Board of Supervisors of Fairfax County, Virginia, has expressed it: "Every time they meet, the local zoning boards create wealth for some to the detriment of others."[10]

The increasing use of professional planners in the planning and zoning process is perhaps the most important way of preventing or limiting favoritism and political influence. The lay members of the planning and zoning commission can serve to insulate the professional staff. After the staff's recommendations have been made, the commission may endorse or reject them, but the commission's decisions are subject to careful public scrutiny. Rejection of professional advice focuses attention upon the personalities, the process, and the influencing factors.

The appointment of well-qualified, highly regarded, ethical, and moral members of planning and zoning commissions is always a desirable form of protection from favoritism and political influence. Given the economic and social importance and the pervasiveness of planning and zoning decisions, appointees to the commission should be of the highest caliber. However, political cronies and underqualified candidates cannot always be identified and their appointments prevented. Probably the only answer to this issue is to be aware of the problem and to obtain the greatest possible scrutiny of planning and zoning activities.

Zoning is used to discriminate against low-income and minority groups. With the attainment of open-housing laws and court decisions,[11] minority groups undoubtedly expected housing in middle- and upper-class suburbs to be more easily attainable. Very few inroads have been made, however. Minority and low-income families have found their attempts to obtain such housing thwarted by high prices and costs. Provision of lower priced housing in such areas has been made impossible by zoning ordinances which impose strict limits upon density. Minimum lot sizes (in some cases of one to three acres), building sizes, height and setback restrictions, utilities, and street requirements have limited access to the more desirable living areas.

The issue of exclusionary zoning practices has been taken to several

---

[10] Audrey Moore, "The Case against Zoning," *Central Atlantic Environment News* 3, no. 1 (January 1973): 2.

[11] See Appendix A.

courts. To date the court decisions have not settled the question of exclusionary zoning; however, the net effect seems to have been the upholding of community authority to impose such zoning.

Another important factor in the issue of exclusionary zoning is the role of the federal government. When the federal government supplies vast sums of money for the construction of public housing or the subsidization of other housing, it may have the obligation to assure that this housing does not perpetuate racial segregation. Indeed, the U.S. Supreme Court ruled unanimously in 1976 that federal courts could order low-cost public housing for minorities in suburban areas as an effort to relieve racial segregation in inner-city housing. The U.S. Department of Housing and Urban Development was found guilty of fostering segregation in public housing programs it had supported. However, the Court indicated that the decision did not mean that public housing projects could be forced automatically on suburban communities which did not request them.

PRIVATE PLANNING

The private planning process parallels the public planning process. Private planners inventory a site's physical features and the utilities and roads available to the site. They study the markets for all of the site's proposed uses and study the legal, social, and economic constraints to the site's use. Several alternative use plans are prepared, and one is selected that appears to balance costs and revenues over a reasonable planning period. Within design and pollution control parameters, the use mix is devised. The plan is then promoted to the developer and lenders, with implementation leading to continuous monitoring.

An example of a land plan for Kimball Knoll prepared by a prominent planner in Atlanta, Dr. Terrence L. Love,[12] is presented in Figure 18–1. This plan reflects the development of a new access road connecting Kimball Bridge Road and Haynes Bridge Road (see inset map), offering ready access to Georgia Highway 400. Georgia Highway 400 is a four-lane, limited-access highway which connects north Atlanta to Lake Lanier. It carries 5,000 to 7,000 automobiles per day past the site, and its volume of traffic is expected to grow steadily. The highway has been a popular road for apartment and office park development. The subject site is sewered and has water, gas, and electric utilities available at its border. It has a moderately steep slope that varies in altitude from a low of 1,005 feet above mean sea level in the southwest corner

---

[12] Dr. Love is a member of the American Institute of Architects (AIA) and the American Institute of Certified Planners (AICP).

FIGURE 18–1
Site plan for Kimball Knoll

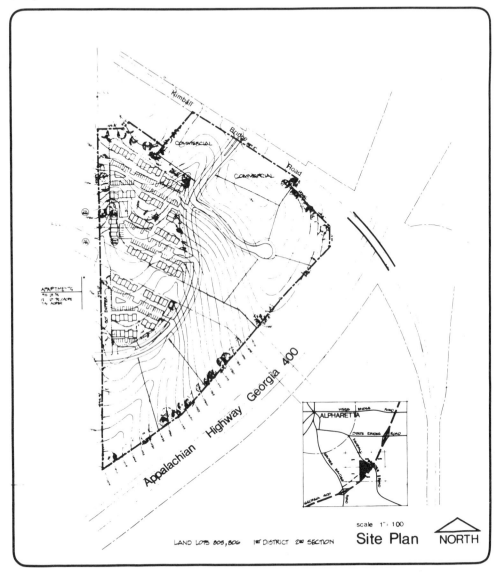

Source: Land Development Analysts, Atlanta, Georgia.

of the tract to a high of 1,140 feet at the crown near the northeast corner, and is thus highly visible from Georgia 400. The property lies less than 15 minutes' driving time from more than 50 office parks and three regional shopping centers. It is a prestige location.

The plan is overlaid on a topographic base map having five-foot intervals of elevation. The development plan calls for 90 apartment units on 7.5 acres, 7 office building sites on 8 acres, and 2 commercial tracts totaling 4 acres. The site is 19.5 acres in size.

The commercial usage lies on Kimball Bridge Road, anchoring the subject tract's end to the new access road. All of the office sites lie above Highway 400, providing excellent commercial visibility, coupled with ease of access via Haynes Bridge Road. The apartments terrace a gentle hillside, providing excellent separation of tiers of units to render a feeling of spaciousness even though a density of 12 units per acre is maintained.

The wide band which bisects the property from east to west is a power company easement. The power lines lie in a swail, or depressed area, so they are not visually prominent. The easement area is grassed, and it provides substantial open space within the apartment area. It is not felt to be a development hindrance by the planner.

The use program shown for Kimball Knoll is felt to bring the 19.5-acre property to its highest and best use. The land plan is schematic only—it is not precise enough to permit specific building siting. An engineer will next overlay the plan on a two-foot-interval topographic map and prepare plans for specific building siting, water runoff, and utility line placements.

Most land planners work first at the concept level, relying on market analyses of the amount and types of space that will be demanded. Then they prepare a rough schematic plan like the one shown here. This is followed by a final engineered plan suitable for courthouse recording as a final use program. The last step involves a sewer plan, a water plan, an underground electric/telephone line plan, and a gas line plan, coupled with a new topographic survey. This final step is quite expensive compared with the preliminary efforts, and it is normally completed immediately prior to the start of development.

This example identifies the process involved in land planning for a relatively simple project. High-density projects with several subterranean levels and interconnecting buildings, joint parking garages, and sophisticated fire-fighting systems require extremely complex development plans. These plans must then be integrated into architectural efforts. For low-density work, the planner is typically trained as a pure planner or as a landscape architect. As density increases, so must the planner's knowledge of architecture.

TRENDS AND THE FUTURE

The planning process is characterized by conflict and compromise. It has been implemented poorly in many past efforts, and it has developed a poor public image because of seemingly arbitrary decisions on the part of political decision makers. However, the authors are finding that developers have begun to prepare better justifications for their proposed projects. Prior to rezoning they are now often required to prepare "A–95" review documents in which every impacted state, federal, and local agency must identify problems that the proposed development might cause if implemented according to plan. These problems must be worked out prior to rezoning. Many development lenders, sensitive to criticism of poorly planned projects, are requiring that residential projects be approved by the FHA and/or the VA prior to development. Many local jurisdictions have retained trained planners to aid developers in eliminating future problems at the planning stage.

This is not to say that cities will be able to plan themselves out of blight and into vitality. Funds are limited, and many causes of blight are related to people who will not, or cannot, improve their properties to meet code standards. Planners have developed few tools with which to solve social problems, and there seems to be no economically practical vehicle to provide quality housing for low-income families. Environmental analysis techniques are crude, and few programs exist to aid in keeping our air and water pure while cities go through the inevitable process of change.

Planning has come a long way in the past 50 years, but only recently has it reached the point at which private and public planners work together to prevent the "fast buck" developer from stripping a site and building substandard structures for quick resale. The American Planning Association, an organization designed to serve as a forum for discussing the planning process, is focusing attention on solving the public/private equation. Developers should be aware of these efforts and seek to incorporate the long-range planning perspective into the profit equation.

SUMMARY

Real estate planning occurs in two spheres—the public sector and the private sector. Public planning agencies plan for the logical and orderly development of a community, while private planning involves the formulation of a plan that will maximize the utility and efficiency of a site or tract of land. Whether public or private, the planning process requires a definition of land-use goals, preparation of possible alternative plans, selection of one plan, promotion and implementation of the plan, and monitoring and modification of the plan as necessary. The planning process must consider the physical characteristics of the site or community, its social aspects, its economic aspects, and urban design principles.

Public planning is usually carried on by a planning commission that is assisted by a professional staff. The commission is normally in charge of implementing the approved comprehensive plan by the process of zoning. Zoning involves the delineation of districts that allow and prohibit specified uses. Nevertheless, in most matters the commission is advisory to the governing council of the jurisdiction.

Private planning is undertaken to design for an owner or developer a property's use to serve a specific market. The plan seeks to attract workers, residents, or customers having specified socioeconomic characteristics. The plan is formulated in recognition of existing public facilities, such as sewers, water, schools, churches, and libraries. The plan may call for additional public facilities to be provided in the project, or it may contemplate public construction of additional facilities. The private planner must cooperate closely with public planners and service agencies in seeking rezoning, utility services, building permits, public transportation, and other required approvals.

The zoning process is based upon the police power. It must be administered fairly, impartially, and in conformance with the comprehensive plan. Even more fundamentally, zoning should not go so far as to confiscate property without compensation. The goal of zoning is to guide the market in its ultimate determination of land uses and values.

Several socioeconomic issues regarding planning and zoning are discussed in the chapter. Whether zoning interferes with efficient operation of the private market, is inherently subject to favoritism and political manipulation, and is used as a tool for racial and class discrimination are overriding questions of continuing concern. While there are undoubtedly significant elements of truth in a positive response to all of these questions, the solution to date has been to try to improve the existing system and to limit its abuses. Abandonment of the system seems very unlikely.

QUESTIONS FOR REVIEW

1. What is *land planning?* Distinguish between "private" land planning and "public" city or county planning.
2. What are the basic goals of a private land planner? How do they differ from the basic goals of a public planner?

3. Can a planner assume the role of an advocate in public proceedings? Why is the planner's role different from that of a real estate appraiser?

4. Is it prop_r for the planner to be a key person in implementing a goal adopted by a county commission?

5. Identify several potential conflicts among public agencies that tend to arise as the planner establishes priorities in preparing a comprehensive plan.

6. How often should a comprehensive plan be redone? What steps can be taken to extend the life of such a plan?

7. Do you feel that the planner is the proper person to serve as zoning administrator? Who else could logically do the job?

8. Is the political power of the public planner increasing or decreasing? Comment upon the positive and negative considerations involved in your answer.

REFERENCES

Altshuler, Alan A. *The City Planning Process: A Political Analysis.* Ithaca, N.Y.: Cornell University Press, 1965.

Black, Alan. *The Comprehensive Plan: Principles and Practice of Urban Planning.* Washington, D.C.: International City Managers Association, 1968, pp. 349–78.

Bolan, Richard S. "Emerging Views of Planning." *Journal of the American Institute of Planners,* July 1967, pp. 233–45.

Cartwright, Timothy J. "Problems, Solutions, and Strategies: A Contribution to the Theory and Practice of Planning." *Journal of the American Institute of Planners,* May 1973, pp. 179–87.

Friedmann, John. "Notes on Societal Action." *Journal of the American Institute of Planners,* September 1969, pp. 311–18.

Kent, T. J., Jr. *The Urban General Plan.* San Francisco: Chandler, 1964.

Mandelker, Daniel R., and Cunningham, Roger A. *Planning and Control of Land Development.* New York: Bobbs-Merrill, 1979.

Natural Resources Defense Council. *Land Use Controls in the United States.* Elaine Moss, editor. New York: Dial Press/James Wade, 1977.

Williams, Charles W., Jr. "Inventing a Future Civilization." *The Futurist* (Bethesda, Md.: World Future Society), August 1972, pp. 137–41.

part four

Real estate administration

in the public sector

chapter 19

The role of government

in real estate decisions

Real estate decision making and decision implementation have been analyzed in previous chapters as processes within the private sector of the economy. The thesis of the book is that the decision maker as an individual, household, or firm collects relevant information, engages in rational problem-solving behavior, and reaches decisions based upon objectives and priorities. The term *administration* is used to describe this individual decision-making process and its implementation. As discussed in the immediately preceding section (Part Three), the activities of real estate marketing, production, financing, and private planning are the principal business functions involved in the creation and exchange of real estate resources.

This chapter provides an overview of the process of decision making in the public sector. It is concerned with identification of decision makers, their decision-making processes, and the manner in which alternatives are generated.

Subsequent chapters focus on decision making and decision implementation by the public sector in the areas of housing and community development, and environmental preservation. Attention is deliberately focused on the expenditure decision in the public sector. It must be recognized that all actions taken by the public sector (including regulatory activities, such as the formulation of a master plan and its implementation through zoning) require expenditures. The funds for these expenditures must, of course, be obtained by taxation, profit-making ventures (such as utility operations), or debt financing.

Decisions made by the federal government can affect cities and communities throughout the nation or within an entire region, such as the Tennessee Valley or Appalachia. Federal programs and policies in areas such as housing, community development, and environmental preservation have a pervasive impact on all urban development. It should also be recognized that decisions made at the local government level may have a macroeffect within the community. For example, a decision to improve an urban arterial route sets in motion repercussions throughout the community. Travel patterns may be affected, the demand for transit altered, and the linkages among land uses changed drastically. The final result often is a restructuring of values among individual parcels of real estate in the community.

Administration of urban real estate resources may also produce a widespread impact because of the relatively large-scale investment undertaken. Investors in the private sector continually demolish existing structures and construct new improvements, but rarely, if ever, is reconstruction undertaken in the magnitude of an urban renewal project. Public investment, such as an urban renewal project or subsidized housing, often produces a macroeffect in the community and becomes an input to the microadministration of private real estate projects. For example, the construction of a Section 8 or Section 235 housing project may make construction of additional unsubsidized housing for moderate-income families impracticable.

THE ROLE OF GOVERNMENT

When economists debate the relative magnitudes of expenditures and investments to be made by the public sector of our economy, their opinions are based upon the value judgments that influence any individual in the selection of goals and the means for meeting them. Economists differ in their goals and selection of means, as do other citizens. As a nation we have been committed by tradition and philosophy to the tenets of capitalism, individual freedom, and equality of opportunity. We advocate a competitive market, free enterprise, and the sovereign consumer. Different individuals define these goals differently, or they may repudiate one or more of them entirely. Indeed, our collective goal of individual freedom sanctions this right to disagree.

Regardless of the personal philosophy of the citizen, economic principles in their most abstract form are universal and apply in any culture. Two economic principles are relevant for any nation. *First, a country's resources and production should be distributed between the public sector and the private sector in such a manner that the margi-*

*nal satisfaction from the last dollar spent (invested by) the public
sector just equals the marginal satisfaction from the last dollar spent
(invested by) the private sector. Second, total welfare is maximized
when the resources controlled by each sector of the economy are
utilized in the most efficient manner.* Application of these principles
could produce government budgets of different magnitude in nations
equal in total resources and technology. Our nation might obtain a
lesser quantum of satisfaction from a dollar spent by the public sector
than would a country which embraces goals of government ownership
of the means of production and a high degree of income equality
among its citizens.

Additionally, as Hendon points out, we must be concerned with
who gains in the attempt to maximize the present value of benefits
over the present value of costs. He suggests that the decision maker
can see these results by developing a table that shows who receives the
benefits of government activities, classified by age, race, and income.
"The maximizing statement relates to efficiency, but the distribution of
benefits relates to equity."[1]

Our society accepts public expenditures for the purchase of goods
and services, investment in social overhead capital, and transfer payments. The provision of public services requires that persons be paid
as administrators, legislators, civil servants, and judges and that materials and consumer goods be purchased (primarily from the private
sector) for programs of national defense, space exploration, housing,
and other government activities. Bridges, schools, public buildings,
housing projects, highways, and parks are constructed and become
public investments in social capital. Social Security payments, unemployment compensation, and partial payments of rent or mortgage
payments are examples of transfer payments that redistribute income
in the attempt to achieve equity. In considering the role and size that
are best for the federal government, the three major types of involvement by the government can be identified, and the amount of government activity in each area can then be debated.

Transfer payments. Some government expenditures result from
perceived needs, with the perceptions being determined by our values
and attitudes. Transfer programs such as old-age assistance, veterans'
cash bonuses, housing subsidies, unemployment compensation, and
farm subsidies belong in this category. These programs transfer income among groups in our society, but they do not necessarily cause
resources to bypass the market. Rather, the income provided by these
programs is likely spent upon a different array of products and services
than it would have been otherwise.

---

[1] William S. Hendon, *Economics for Urban Social Planning* (Salt Lake City: University of Utah Press, 1975), p. 84.

A different approach has been taken in the attempt to provide safe and sanitary housing for some low-income families. The approach has provided standard housing, rather than cash income, to qualifying households. The value judgment was made by our elected representatives that the national welfare would be maximized by providing safe, sanitary, and adequate housing to needy families. Nevertheless, these families might have obtained a higher level of total satisfaction if they had been given money income and allowed to vote dollars in the marketplace for housing, automobiles, food, and other goods and services.

Technical monopolies. Other public expenditures for social overhead capital and for purchase of goods and services from the private sector may be justified because of the existence of a "technical monopoly."[2] A technical-monopoly results when only one firm or entity can economically afford to serve a particular function in a given market. Efficient operation of power-generating or public transit facilities, for example, may result in losses, requiring a subsidy for such operations to stay in business. If the public, through its elected representatives, decides that the power-generating facility or the public transportation system is worth retaining, a subsidy is required. In these situations, government may intervene as a regulator of a private monopoly or as the provider of a public-owned enterprise. For example, many private power companies are regulated by state regulatory commissions; airlines have been subsidized and are regulated by the federal government; and many cities own public transit systems. Note that in some cases a private industry may be both regulated and subsidized.

Public goods. A public good is the extreme case in which the marginal cost of additional use of the good or service is zero. Once produced, the good or service can be divided among innumerable users, and the benefits received by each user do not detract from the benefits received by others. The national defense is close to being a pure public good. All citizens benefit equally, and the benefit obtained by one of us does not reduce the benefits available to all. Many goods and services qualify to a greater or lesser extent as public goods. Schools, parks, highways, street lighting, police protection, sanitation facilities, public health programs, and urban renewal are examples. When such goods or services are provided, their benefits are available to everyone, and it is not feasible to charge any users for benefits that differ among citizens.

---

[2] A technical monopoly occurs in a strongly decreasing cost industry having a high original fixed cost and very low variable unit cost. Electric power and public transit companies are among these industries.

Public goods have "neighborhood" or spillover effects. It is usually not possible to identify the magnitude of such effects on users and nonusers in order to assign a differential charge. Friedman points out that neighborhood effects can either penalize or benefit an individual in the market.[3] The penalty side occurs when property owners believe they cannot economically maintain or improve their properties. Net income after improvement is not sufficient to generate the additional value necessary to cover the costs of the improvement. A neighborhood effect results when individual inaction on the part of separate owners produces a blighted condition for the entire area. Individuals have then become prisoners of the inaction of their neighbors. Residents elsewhere in the community may also suffer because of higher costs of police protection, fire protection, schooling, and other public services provided residents in the blighted area.

The beneficial type of neighborhood effect may be obtained when urban renewal is undertaken to remove the blight. Renewal may have a positive neighborhood effect because it benefits many groups that do not necessarily bear the cost of the public action in proportion to their respective net benefits. The renewal action itself produces a pattern of benefits and costs among groups in the community that makes it very difficult to identify the beneficiaries of the action and to charge them according to the benefits received. Thus, urban renewal exhibits the elements of a public good.

Friedman points out that in such a case the social costs of the neighborhood effects prior to and following public intervention must be carefully weighed. Although the blighted area exhibits many social costs, such as unsanitary and unhealthful housing, higher crime rates, lower educational levels of inhabitants, and higher requirements for police and fire protection, the costs of urban renewal are also huge. These costs must be borne by all taxpayers, whose aftertax incomes are thereby reduced. And after the costs are incurred and urban renewal is carried out, it may be that the blighted area is relocated in another section of the community. This would be the anticipated result, if increases were not achieved in residents' incomes, educational levels, and social adaptability.

Once again, our values and goals influence our decisions concerning the propriety of public action and the magnitude of action needed. If one felt, like Friedman, that any government intervention in the free operation of the market reduces the sphere of individual freedom, then

---

[3] Milton Friedman, "The Role of Government in a Free Society," in *Private Wants and Public Needs,* edited by Edmund S. Phelps (New York: W. W. Norton, 1965), pp. 104–17. Also see Milton Friedman, *Capitalism and Freedom* (Chicago: University of Chicago Press, 1962).

a large increment might be added to social costs for the government's intrusion into the private market.

How much government?

The question of "how much government" will undoubtedly be debated as long as our republic continues to exist. Some citizens believe, as does J. K. Galbraith, that our national affluence permits more government activity than is presently undertaken in our society. This viewpoint would support more and larger programs in education, housing, job training, health insurance, and so on. In contrast, Professor Friedman would restrict government activity when the persons benefited can be identified and charged. He would classify a city park and a city street as public goods that justify government expenditures. The national park and the limited-access freeway, however, would not be public goods, because their users could be identified and charged directly for construction and maintenance of the facilities.

Public sector decision makers

The atomistic decision maker in the public sector is the public servant—perhaps a government executive, an elected or appointed administrator, a judge, or a legislator. These elected or appointed officials can be classified into four branches in both the federal and state governments: the legislative, executive, and judiciary branches and the bureaucracy. The legislative, executive, and judicial branches are commonly recognized as the primary sources of power and decision making in our government. The bureaucracy, comprising regulatory and administrative agencies such as the Federal Trade Commission, the Federal Communications Commission, the Federal Aviation Administration, and the Federal Home Loan Bank Board, is sometimes regarded as politically neutral and subordinate to the other three branches, each of which exercises some control over agency policy and operations. The bureaucracy, however, is better viewed as an active participant in decision making in the public sector.[4] For example, the rules promulgated by the Federal Home Loan Bank Board, under authority of a basic law, may largely determine whether a builder or developer is able to obtain a loan to finance a proposed project.

At times, an administrative agency acts in an advisory capacity to other decision-making units. Congressional committees and govern-

---

[4] The concept of the administrative agency as an active participant in government decision making, rather than simply an extension of the executive branch, has been developed by Millett. See John D. Millett, *Organization for the Public Service* (New York: D. Van Nostrand, 1966), p. 159.

ment executives call upon the professional expertise of administrators when proposing legislation pertaining to the area of policy adminis-tered by, say, the Department of Housing and Urban Development, the Environmental Protection Agency, or the Department of Energy. The administrative agency also formulates and implements policy at the operational level, where it functions in its own right, within limits, as a decision-making unit.

THE DECISION-MAKING PROCESS IN THE PUBLIC SECTOR

Behavioral aspects.   Administration of real estate in the private sector assumes that the decision-making unit behaves in ways that are believed to maximize personal profit, satisfaction, or utility. Utility maximization by individuals can also explain how decisions are reached in the public sector.[5] Public servants array the benefits and costs associated with each decision as they perceive them, assess the subjective probabilities of their realization, and make the trade-offs necessary to reach their preferred positions, that is, the decision and course of action that maximize their net satisfaction. The concept of benefit can be defined broadly enough to include all alternatives that produce satisfaction for the individual. A decision made "for the public good" (as the individual legislator perceives it) may result in enough personal satisfaction to overcome a result which may be considered distasteful or damaging in some way (a cost to that legislator). For instance, legislators who own developable real estate may vote in favor of environmental legislation because they believe it is for the public good.

Another explanation of the decision-making process in government has been termed by Downs as the "economic theory of democracy." The central premise in this theory is that each political party designs its budget, both revenues and expenditures, to maximize its candi-dates' chances of winning the next election.[6] The budget is a mix of expenditure programs and taxation or borrowing proposals to finance these programs. Voters act to maximize their own positions by deciding which budget produces the greatest net benefit for the candidates who, in their estimation, will maximize their personal satisfaction. The vic-torious candidates have until next election to demonstrate their ability to perform as expected.

---

[5] Roland N. McKean, *Public Spending* (New York: McGraw-Hill, 1968), p. 13; and McKean, "The Unseen Hand in Government," *American Economic Review* 40, no. 3 (June 1965): 496–506.

[6] Anthony Downs, *An Economic Theory of Democracy* (New York: Harper & Row, 1957).

The ultimate decision or policy made in the public sector represents the end result of a complex bargaining process. Compromises and trade-offs are arranged among individuals and various interest groups. For example, within a regulatory agency, a senior staff member may propose a rule change to alleviate an undesirable restriction upon the regulated industry. Other staff members will voice their opinions, and the commission or board will decide according to majority vote whether to issue a proposed rule. If a rule is proposed, it is published, but it cannot go into effect until public comments are obtained and considered. Comments will likely be received from industry members, public interest groups, and other interested parties. For example, environmental groups would undoubtedly protest a rule that would allow the industry more lenient pollution standards. Industry groups would likely support such a rule change. There would also likely be some disagreement among staff members.

In any regulatory, administrative, legislative, or judicial action, a decision is reached, and the regulatory or administrative agency speaks with a single voice. In the case of a legislative or judicial action, however, a disparate opinion may be expressed openly by a minority of legislators or justices. The bargaining process preceding a decision in the public sector performs the function of the marketplace in the private sector. As McKean explains: "Both mechanisms tend to substitute voluntary exchange for direct coercion and induce decision makers to take into account many of the indirect or external impacts of their decisions."[7]

Power and influence.   Decisions made at the community level reflect basic characteristics of the community and its leadership and decision-making structure.[8] Sociologists attempt to relate these decisions to the demographic, economic, legal-political, and cultural characteristics of the community. The integrating functions performed by local political and voluntary organizations (such as the Democratic and Republican parties, the League of Women Voters, and Common Cause) are also important in arriving at the final decision. The activities of these organizations permit groups of individuals in the community to have a voice in the decision process.

Power and influence are involved in the analysis of leadership and the structure of decision making. Power is defined as the "potential ability of an actor or actors to select, to change, and to attain the goals of a social system." Influence is defined as the "exercise of power that brings about change in a social system."[9] Power can be regarded as a

---

[7] McKean, *Public Spending*, p. 19.

[8] Terry N. Clark, ed., *Community Structure and Decision-Making: Comparative Analyses* (San Francisco: Chandler, 1968), pp. 15–24 and 57–58.

[9] Ibid., pp. 46–47.

static distribution of resources at a point in time. Clark identifies the resources providing power as money and credit, control over jobs, control of mass media, high social status, knowledge and specialized technical skills, popularity and esteemed personal qualities, legality, subsystem solidarity, the right to vote, social access to community leaders, commitments of followers, manpower and control of organization, and control over the interpretation of values. The exercise of influence is a dynamic process which relates the existing distribution of power to the final decision.

Nutall, Scheuch, and Gordon report an example of power and influence culminating in the final decision on an urban renewal project in Cambridge, Massachusetts.[10] The authors identify four separate decision processes occurring over time. The first decision process was the planning stage, begun in 1957, involving the Cambridge Redevelopment Authority, the Housing and Home Finance Agency (HHFA),[11] the mayor and the city manager, major local business people and bankers, and the CIO union, which was to be the eventual owner and operator of the new buildings. Following the lengthy administrative planning process, the first public .hearing was held in 1961. At this point, new actors, including families and small business people in the renewal area, a church in the area, and low-income groups residing outside the area, were able to exercise their influence. The person speaking for the church emphasized that persons in the renewal area would pay more for the new low-income housing than they were then paying for rent. Blacks and low-income families elsewhere in the community were fearful of future displacement if renewal was begun in Cambridge.

The second decision process occurred in the political arena when the city council had to ratify the proposed project. The dissident groups possessed power and the ability to exercise influence in this arena. On the other hand, the HHFA, the local redevelopment authority, the CIO union, and the large business people and bankers found their influence limited in the political debate. The second decision process resulted in defeat of the proposed renewal plan.

The third decision process involved reformulation of the plan. This time, the administrative process included a citizen's advisory committee representing residents, small business people in the renewal area, and the church. The reformulated plan received the greatest opposition in public hearings from large business people who held property in the area, two city council representatives whose constituents were

---

[10] Ronald L. Nuttall, Erwin K. Scheuch, and Chad Gordon, "In the Structure of Influence," in Clark, *Community Structure and Decision-Making*, pp. 349–80.

[11] This agency was later superseded by HUD.

black, and low-income persons from other parts of the city. As a result of a threat of legal action by the large business people, the mayor effected a compromise in their behalf before the city council finally approved the plan. This approval was the fourth decision process.

The case study of the Cambridge urban renewal project demonstrates the bargaining and compromise which occur in all public decision making that is not routine and institutionalized. The influence of certain individuals and groups was brought to bear on the issue over time. Although some groups were not appeased by the final decision (the black and low-income elements outside the renewal area), they were able to exercise whatever influence their power base permitted.

Institutional aspects. Decisions made in the public sector and their implementation depend in large part upon the institutional structure of government. Power, influence, and political factors are channeled through these institutions in the bargaining process that culminates in final decisions. As discussed earlier in this chapter, the primary institutions in government are the executive, legislative, and judicial branches. The regulatory and administrative agencies comprising the bureaucracy are an extension of both the executive and legislative branches. While they have extensive regulatory responsibilities, their ultimate authority is derived from the legislature. Our system of government incorporates this separation of power among institutions, but it also involves a sharing of power among the federal, state, and local governments. The U.S. Constitution enumerates the powers of our federal government, while the states retain all other powers, including the police power.

Today, state and local governments can best be described as exercising concurrent power with the federal government.[12] The exercise of concurrent powers necessitates a system of shared administrative responsibilities. Federal, state, and local administrative agencies are concerned with a particular activity but are not formally subordinate to each other. For example, the U.S. Department of Housing and Urban Development administers housing subsidy programs, but a state may also have a housing agency to oversee the activities of communities participating in the federal programs. Additionally, each community or county may have a local housing authority that owns and operates the public housing and administers other housing programs. The interagency problems are to define respective spheres of influence and to resolve conflicts of authority.

It is through administrative agencies (such as HUD, a state department of housing, or a city planning commission) that public policy is translated into highways and streets, subsidized housing, the city plan,

---

[12] Millett, *Organization for the Public Service,* pp. 19–20.

zoning enforcement, and other public sector activities. The operating policies and regulations established by the agencies in carrying out the legal mandate of Congress or the legislature have the force of law and control the character of the public good or service provided. Control over operations of the agency to insure that it continues to fulfill its policy objectives is exercised by congressional oversight committees, budgetary review, and, in extreme instances, congressional or legislative investigation. At the federal level, the department, agency, commission, or board head must submit requests for operating funds to the president, who reviews the requests in context will all other needs and sources of funds for operation of the government. Broad national goals must be considered, including the need for economic growth, full employment, and price stability. The budget is then sent to Congress, where it is reviewed once again. The administrator may be called upon to inform congressional committees of programs and policies. The authorization of funds and their ultimate appropriation for administrative activity will depend at least partly upon the ability of the administrator and other expert witnesses to convince Congress or the legislature that a public need will be met. The size of the government budget determines the extent to which the government participates in the total economy. The administrative agencies play an important role in determining both the size of the total budget and the proportion devoted to each area of concern, such as housing, national defense, education, and other public needs.

ECONOMIC ANALYSIS IN THE DECISION-MAKING PROCESS

The broadest goal our government could attain would be to maximize the welfare of all citizens collectively by assuming control only over functions delegated by the citizens and by organizing to carry out its assigned roles efficiently. McKean points out that several levels of decision making are involved in this process.[13] First, there is the problem of how much control over national resources should be given to the government. Second, the resources available to the government must be allocated among perceived needs. Third, after it has been decided to support various public needs in varying proportions, the policymaker is faced with almost infinite alternatives for carrying out each program. A choice must be made among these alternative courses of action. Fourth, given a course of action for each program, the most efficient organization for producing the desired results must be developed.

---

[13] Roland N. McKean, *Efficiency in Government through Systems Analysis* (New York: John Wiley, 1958). The following problems in the economic analysis of public expenditures are among those discussed by McKean.

These decisions are not independent of one another. For example, the case for giving more control over our resources to government may rest upon the argument that a centralized entity will be more efficient in producing desired results. The demonstrated or expected ability of one government agency to get more utility than other agencies from its appropriations can influence the division of the total budget. The ability of administrators to select the most appropriate program for translating policy into action and the organizational efficiency of their agencies can enhance their image with the chief executive and can influence the share of the budget devoted to their agencies' programs.

Political factors, judgment, and personal bias influence decision making at all levels. These factors are particularly important in determining the extent of government control over resources and the allocation of these resources among perceived needs. Analytical tools are useful at the third and fourth levels of decision making, where the problems involve selection of an alternative course of action for carrying out the policy decision and the most efficient form of organization to achieve the goal.

Economic analysis at the third level of decision making, where alternative programs are considered, may demonstrate efficiency in the form of benefits minus costs, the ratio of benefits to costs, cost minimization given a specified goal, or benefit maximization given a specified cost. A continual difficulty in the economic analysis of government programs is the inability to quantify all costs and benefits. Not only are spillover effects too numerous to identify completely, but social costs and benefits often defy measurement in dollars and cents. What is the dollar value of the human lives saved by improvement of a city street or control of pollution?

Another inescapable problem arises from the fact that a public program can affect different groups in our society. Higher-income groups may experience a net disbenefit to provide subsidized housing for a lower-income group, which experiences a net benefit. Before the program is undertaken, a value judgment must be made that society will experience a net benefit from it. Still another problem in the economic analysis of public programs is that alternative programs available to meet a perceived need are too numerous for each of them to be considered separately. Consequently, the analysis of an expenditure decision usually involves suboptimal or partial analysis.

Analysis should also be made of the impact of the financing required to make the expenditure possible. This analysis should include the incidence of the tax, the effect of borrowing to finance the expenditure, and the economic effect of expanding the money supply. In many instances, the financing side of government decisions is not explicitly considered in the analysis of program alternatives. Often the budget for a program is considered as given, with the problem being how to spend the money most efficiently. Viewed in this manner, the problem of scale is not adequately considered. Significant cost savings or net benefits could perhaps be achieved by either increasing or decreasing the scale of expenditures in a given program. Furthermore, government programs are interrelated, and expenditures for one program may affect the costs and benefits of another. Spending for public housing or other subsidized housing, for instance, may enhance worker productivity and affect the costs and benefits of the welfare program. Tracing and quantifying these side effects is usually beyond the capability of the analysts.

Economic analysis, whether it is cost-benefit analysis, systems analysis, or simulation, admittedly will not replace the public decision maker. The analysis of alternative programs, however, does provide the decision maker with better knowledge and understanding, and it permits more consistent and logical choices to be made. Subsequent chapters deal with various areas for public decisions and the types of economic considerations involved in determining taxation levels, public expenditures, and types of programs.

SUMMARY

Decisions in the private sector are not made in a vacuum. Factors considered in the administration of our real estate resources include the results of public sector decision making on such matters as the nature of our financial system, transportation policy, urban renewal, subsidized housing, tax policy, and planning and zoning. If such factors are taken as given, administration in the private sector is based upon partial analysis, where the problem is typically to maximize profit and satisfaction within the constraints imposed by government regulation and government programs. The private decision maker must also usually work with the existing social overhead capital in the form of streets, schools, sewers, and utilities. The role of government in our economy is to provide the optimal level of regulation and social overhead capital, while preserving the greatest possible degree of individual freedom and responsibility.

A general analysis of the production and use of our urban real estate resources would consider decisions, actions, and results in both the private and public sectors, and their interrelationships. To borrow two current buzzwords, the interfaces between systems would be examined. A circular system would be conceptualized in which the decisions, actions, and results of the private sector are recognized as inputs to the public sector. It would also be recognized that the public sector, in turn, generates outputs affecting administration in the private sector.

This chapter examines some of the characteristics of administration in the public sector. The extent of government involvement in the economy is constrained by our values. Any government regulation or expenditure reflects this value system, as well as our framework of government, in which behavioral aspects, power and influence, and institutional aspects play important roles. Our values and perceptions of need influence the selection of programs involving transfer payments that redistribute income among segments of our society. Government actions in dealing with technical monopolies and in providing public goods are influenced importantly by these factors. Economic analyses of government programs and expenditure decisions are useful in generating alternative courses of action for implementation of policy and in quantifying at least some of the costs and benefits. Economic analysis may contribute to the formulation of consistent and logical choices by public sector decision makers, but it is usually, by necessity, partial and suboptimal analysis.

QUESTIONS FOR REVIEW

1. How does administration in the public sector differ from administration in the private sector?
2. How can you justify government spending for transfer payments?
3. What are the roles of power and influence in the decision-making process of government?
4. What is the role of economic analysis in the government decision-making process?
5. What is meant by *cost-benefit analysis*? Is it comparable to the investment analysis discussed in preceding chapters?
6. What is the *bureaucracy*? What types of decisions are made in a federal regulatory agency?
7. What is the economic theory of democracy?
8. What types of considerations influence a public decision maker, such as a member of the Securities and Exchange Commission or the secretary of HUD?

REFERENCES

Clark, Terry N., ed. *Community Structure and Decision-Making: Comparative Analyses.* San Francisco: Chandler, 1968.

Due, John F., and Friedlaender, Ann F. *Government Finance: Economics of the Public Sector.* 5th ed. Homewood, Ill.: Richard D. Irwin, 1973.

Hendon, William S. *Economics for Urban Social Planning*. Salt Lake City: University of Utah Press, 1975.

McKean, Roland N. *Efficiency in Government through Systems Analysis*. New York: John Wiley, 1958.

_____. *Public Spending*. New York: McGraw-Hill, 1968.

Margolis, Julius, ed. *The Analysis of Public Output*. New York: National Bureau of Economic Research, 1970.

Millett, John D. *Organization for the Public Service*. New York: D. Van Nostrand, 1966.

Phelps, Edmund S., ed. *Private Wants and Public Needs*. New York: W. W. Norton, 1965.

chapter 20

Government involvement

in real estate

The federal government influences real estate in many ways. It subsidizes housing for certain segments of the population, provides mortgage insurance programs for other segments, regulates the supply of funds and interest rates, sponsors secondary markets for mortgages, provides block grants to communities for community development, and insures savings accounts in real estate financing institutions. As can be noted, most of these activities involve the financing of real estate. Thus, governmental influence on real estate is largely indirect—through the financing mechanism. This influence, although indirect, is pervasive.

The role of government has been to improve the population's housing condition and to stimulate home ownership. In this way the government has created business for real estate brokerage firms, although this was not the primary motivation. The principal reasons for government involvement have been that a large segment of the housing stock is substandard, stimulation of the construction industry is beneficial to the economy, and poor housing is regarded as an important element of social problems.

In 1980 approximately 14 percent of all housing units were classified as substandard in one or more aspects. This condition continued to exist more than 30 years after the U.S. Congress declared in 1949 its intent to pursue the goal of "a decent home and suitable living environment for every American family." In 1969 the President's Committee on Urban Housing estimated the need for new and rehabilitated housing units over the following ten years at 26 million units. Six million of this total would need to be subsidized.[1]

Construction is our nation's largest industry. As has been vividly demonstrated in several recessions during the last 25 years, declines in construction activity can have disastrous effects upon the nation's economy. The building industry is an extremely important component of the gross national product; a healthy construction industry is needed for a growing economy.

While substandard housing is often viewed as an effect of inadequate income, poor health, and underemployment, poor housing may also be a cause of underemployment, poor health, and lower levels of education and income. It may be impossible to provide needy elements of the population with social services and the like, and have their overall social condition improve permanently, if their housing is inadequate. The motivation for additional and sustained improvement may be thwarted by a depressing physical environment for everyday living.

Regulation of the supply of funds and interest rates

The supply of funds and the level of interest rates in the economy are influenced by several factors, including Federal Reserve policy, the debt management policies of the U.S. Treasury, the financing of new plant and equipment purchases by large corporations, and the financing needs of individual investors and consumers. The Federal Reserve System is perhaps the most important of these determinants. Its function is to establish, maintain, and supervise the monetary system for the country. It has direct control of the supply of money in the economy and of certain interest rates, which in turn influence all interest rates. This control is exercised through the instruments of monetary regulation—the discount rate, reserve requirements, and open market operations. Through the operation of these instruments, the board of governors of the Federal Reserve System can effectively increase or decrease the rate of growth of the money supply and can drive interest rates upward or downward. The organization structure of the Federal Reserve System is shown in Figure 20–1.

The important point to bear in mind in considering the Federal Reserve System is that the policies adopted by its board of governors influence real estate to a greater extent than any other economic good.

---

[1] Report of the President's Committee on Urban Housing (Kaiser Report), *A Decent Home* (Washington, D.C.: U.S. Government Printing Office, 1969), p. 39.

FIGURE 20–1

Federal Reserve System organization structure

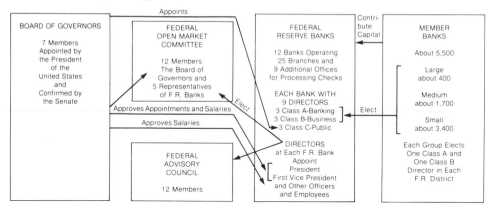

If the board of governors decides to slow the rate of growth of the money supply and to drive interest rates upward, the effect is to make real estate financing more difficult and costly for many would-be purchasers. With the decreased availability of funds and higher interest rates, many persons will stay out of the market. On the other hand, during periods of monetary ease, when the money supply is growing at an ample rate and interest rates are relatively low, financing is more readily available to a greater number of people. Marginal buyers will be able to obtain financing, and real estate activity will tend to increase.

Obviously, this analysis is oversimplified. Other factors may at times be equal in importance or perhaps even more important to real estate financing than Federal Reserve policy. For example, if there is general pessimism about the future of the economy, an increased rate of growth of the money supply and lower interest rates will not by themselves overcome this factor. Also, if there is a great increase in the government's or private industry's demand for funds for non–real estate purposes, an increase in the total availability of funds might not benefit real estate interests. Nevertheless, the influence of Federal Reserve policies must be considered both in terms of their own effects on real estate finance and in relation to the other considerations that we have just discussed. The importance of financing to almost every real estate transaction means that Federal Reserve policy will often mean the difference between whether a buyer can or cannot afford to complete a transaction.

The Federal Home Loan Bank System influences real estate credit and interest rates through regulation of federal savings and loan associations. The governing body of the system, the Federal Home Loan Bank Board, can set reserve and liquidity requirements for member associations within specified ranges. Borrowing by the twelve Federal Home Loan Banks to provide funds for member associations also can exert a significant impact upon the capital markets. The organization structure of the Federal Home Loan Bank System is shown in Figure 20–2.

FIGURE 20–2
Federal Home Loan Bank System organization structure

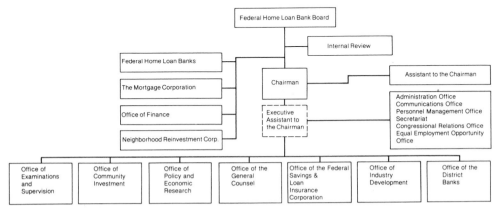

The financing of the national debt of the United States also has important bearing on the financing of real estate. The amount which the U.S. government owes holders of short-term and long-term debt is well over $870 billion. Since the debt continues to grow and there is no thought that it will be paid off to any significant extent, the Treasury must continually refinance it. As this refinancing takes place, the amounts of funds drained from the capital market and the interest rates paid on the securities that are issued have a significant impact upon the amount of funds available and the interest rate levels in the economy. In general, as interest rates rise and government bonds become relatively more attractive, funds are siphoned off from potential real estate use. When funds become more readily available and interest rates on government securities are relatively low, mortgage investment is more attractive, and funds flow into real estate finance.

Secondary markets for mortgages

A secondary market is a market in which existing assets are bought and sold; a primary market is one in which the original issuance or sale of assets takes place. The New York Stock Exchange is perhaps the best-known example of a secondary market. In it, existing stocks and bonds are traded among sellers and buyers. Secondary markets make primary markets more efficient and viable. The NYSE creates a wider market for securities, thus making more feasible the sale of new issues of corporate stocks and bonds. The primary mortgage market derives the same benefits from the secondary mortgage market. If a financial institution can sell its existing mortgages, it can then make more new loans to homebuyers.

Three organizations—two quasi-governmental and one totally governmental—comprise the organized secondary mortgage market. These organizations are the Federal National Mortgage Association (FNMA), the Federal Home Loan Mortgage Corporation (FHLMC), and the Government National Mortgage Association (GNMA).[2] Until FNMA was created, there was only a small amount of trading of mortgages among a few financial institutions. FNMA was created in 1938 as a government agency under the Reconstruction Finance Corporation for the purpose of providing a secondary market for FHA-insured mortgages.

Federal National Mortgage Association.   In addition to its original purpose of buying (and occasionally selling) FHA-insured mortgages, FNMA's authority was expanded in 1948 to include the purchase of VA-guaranteed mortgages. In 1954 FNMA was rechartered to include the following functions:

1.   To support the secondary mortgage market through private financing (selling bonds in the private market) instead of borrowing from the U.S. Treasury.
2.   To provide special assistance to various housing subsidy programs.
3.   To manage and liquidate its existing portfolio of mortgages.

In 1970 FNMA became a partially private organization by the sale of one third of its outstanding capital stock to private owners. However, one third of its board of directors are appointed by the president of the United States, and it may continue to borrow from the U.S. Treasury. It is also obligated to help attain the national housing goal of safe and decent housing for low- and moderate-income families. In 1970 FNMA was also authorized to purchase conventional loans.

The National Housing Act of 1968, which gave FNMA the authority to obtain private ownership, also created another government organization, the Government National Mortgage Association (GNMA), under the Department of Housing and Urban Development. As dis-

---

[2] The organizations are sometimes called by their nicknames, respectively, Fannie Mae, Freddie Mac, and Ginnie Mae.

cussed below, GNMA took over some of FNMA's previous responsibilities, leaving FNMA to concentrate in the business operation of the secondary market.

FNMA's primary function today is to buy and sell both conventional and government-underwritten mortgages. It obtains funds to do this by selling stocks and bonds in the private capital markets, by selling mortgages from its portfolio, by obtaining commitment fees for loan purchases, and by obtaining interest income from its mortgage portfolio and other investments.

Government National Mortgage Association. When GNMA was created in 1968, two main areas of responsibility were transferred to it from FNMA—the special assistance function and the function of managing and liquidating the mortgage portfolio that FNMA had acquired since its creation.

1. *Special assistance function.* GNMA's special assistance function involves a number of programs which are established from time to time by Congress or the president of the United States. These programs involve making purchase commitments on certain types and categories of home mortgages which otherwise would not be readily salable due either to the unconventional nature of the risk or to uncompetitive low yields. For example, GNMA has the authority to make mortgage loan purchases for housing programs in emergency areas, for the armed services for construction advances, and for mortgages at below-market interest rates.

A particularly useful arrangement by which GNMA carries out its special assistance function is the Tandem Plan. The Tandem Plan is a two-part process in which GNMA makes a commitment to purchase mortgages, usually to FNMA, at the current discount rate. Thus, under the Tandem Plan GNMA provides a subsidy for a portion of the discount. For example, if GNMA buys a $50 million package of special assistance mortgages, it can turn around and resell the package to FNMA at current discount rates for, say, $48 million. In this way it subsidizes $2 million of the discount but still has $48 million to reinvest in other special assistance projects. So the Tandem Plan in effect multiplies GNMA's funds. GNMA may tandem a special assistance mortgage project with any investor, especially when the sale can be made at discount rates more favorable than those quoted by FNMA.

2. *Management and liquidation function.* When GNMA was created in 1968, it received the responsibility of managing and liquidating all mortgage loans acquired by FNMA since 1938. These old mortgages were to be transferred into private financing channels as quickly as possible and at a minimum cost to the federal government, with all funds returned to the U.S. Treasury. To aid GNMA in the process of managing and liquidating FNMA's mortgage portfolio, it

was given the authority to guarantee all securities issued by itself or any other approved insurer. It developed the mortgage-backed security program whereby it sells securities backed by pools of insured or guaranteed mortgages by the FHA, VA, or Farmers Home Administration. Ginnie Mae's securities are also guaranteed by the full faith and credit of the federal government; therefore, these securities are virtually risk free.

Federal Home Loan Mortgage Corporation.   FHLMC was created in 1970 by the Emergency Home Finance Act. The primary purpose of this act was to tap sources of funds that were previously unavailable for housing, such as pension and trust funds. It did this by creating FHLMC and authorizing FNMA to purchase conventional as well as government-underwritten loans. Investment by pension and trust funds in the securities of FNMA and FHLMC thus allows these organizations to purchase vast amounts of mortgages from primary institutions.

FHLMC's purpose, like that of FNMA, is to develop the secondary market for mortgages. Unlike FNMA, however, which deals mostly with mortgage bankers and insurance companies, FHLMC deals primarily with savings and loan associations. In fact, its original capital of $100 million was obtained from the 12 Federal Home Loan banks, and its board of directors consists of the three members of the Federal Home Loan Bank Board. Also, while FNMA has been a large net purchaser of government-underwritten mortgages, FHLMC has attempted to even out its purchases with sales and to buy conventional as well as government-underwritten loans.

A major obstacle to the development of a viable secondary market for conventional mortgages has long been the lack of uniform documents. FHLMC has taken the lead in developing such documents, and all loans submitted to it must involve such documents as the standardized FHLMC-approved note, mortgage, and appraisal. These documents have been developed in consultation with FNMA and GNMA and are acceptable to those organizations as well.

FHLMC buys FHA–VA loans, conventional whole loans, and mortgage participations. In the participation program, FHLMC purchases a percentage of all the conventional loans in a specified pool of mortgages. The pool may consist of all one–four-family home mortgages, all multifamily mortgages, or a combination of the two.

Like FNMA, FHLMC raises capital by selling loans in its portfolio to other purchasers (such as financial institutions), by selling mortgage-backed bonds or GNMA-guaranteed mortgage-backed securities, by selling participation certificates in a pool of mortgages, and by its interest earnings above acquisition costs.

Insurance of accounts and supervision

The Federal Deposit Insurance Corporation (FDIC) and the Federal Savings and Loan Insurance Corporation (FSLIC) insure deposits up to $100,000 per account in commercial banks and savings and loan associations, respectively. In their insuring function, these agencies of the federal government provide relief in the rare instances when a financial institution goes bankrupt, and they engender public confidence as to the safety of funds deposited in insured institutions.

The FDIC and FSLIC regulate and supervise institutions under their jurisdiction to make certain that their insurance function will not often be needed. Additionally, the Federal Reserve Board and the comptroller of the currency regulate and supervise certain aspects of commercial bank operations. The Federal Home Loan Bank Board performs these functions for savings and loans. (The members of the Federal Home Loan Bank Board also constitute the board of directors of the FSLIC.) State regulatory agencies supervise the operations of banks and savings and loan associations that are chartered by the states and are not members of the Federal Reserve System or the Federal Home Loan Bank System. All of these institutions are required to abide by specific regulations and standards in regard to the loans they make. The supervisory function is for the purpose of assuring that the standards and regulations are observed by the various institutions.

The system of federal regulation, supervision, and insurance of financial depository institutions has been instrumental in providing adequate funds for mortgage finance. Without this system public confidence would not be adequate to induce savers to hold their funds in institutions that make mortgage loans. Such funds would then undoubtedly flow to other investment media, such as government bonds, corporate securities, and life insurance. The FDIC and FSLIC were established in 1934 because public confidence had been badly shaken during the Great Depression of the late 1920s and 1930s.

Mortgage insurance and guaranty

Perhaps the government programs having the greatest direct impact upon real estate activity are the FHA insurance and VA (Veterans Administration) guaranty programs. These programs underwrite mortgage loans to the general public and veterans, respectively, for the purchase of housing units meeting specified minimum standards. Millions of purchasers have been able to participate in home ownership through these programs.

Federal Housing Administration. The Federal Housing Administration was created by the National Housing Act of 1934 to promote the construction of new homes and home ownership by encouraging lenders to release greater amounts of funds for home financing. It performs this function by insuring mortgage loans that meet its requirements. This enables qualified buyers to obtain higher loan-to-value ratios and longer mortgage terms, thus giving millions of Americans the opportunity to own their own home. The FHA does not lend money; it insures mortgage loans. For this insurance the borrower pays a premium of one half of 1 percent per annum on the average debt balance outstanding during the year. The FHA comes under the authority of the Assistant Secretary for Housing—Federal Housing Commissioner—Department of Housing and Urban Development, as shown in Figure 20–3. The FHA has the same basic purposes today as it had when it was created. These are:

1. Promoting home ownership.
2. Upgrading and improving housing standards.
3. Providing and creating sound patterns for mortgage loan financing.

The lending standards of the FHA are generally high. It will not insure loans on obsolete homes or on properties poorly located with respect to transportation and vital community services. Buildings must

FIGURE 20–3
Department of Housing and Urban Development organization structure

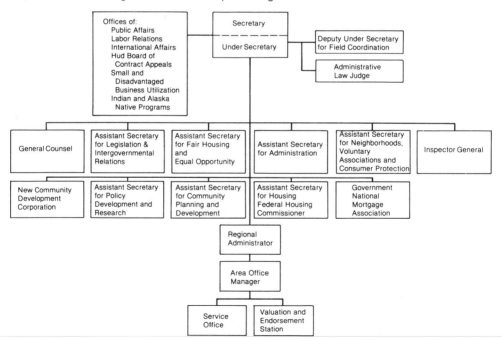

meet FHA construction standards, and all essential utilities must be included. The lender must rate whether the following six factors pertaining to the borrower's creditworthiness are acceptable:

1. Credit characteristics.
2. Adequacy of available assets.
3. Motivating interest in ownership.
4. Stability of effective income.
5. Importance of monetary interest.
6. Adequacy of effective income.

The principal FHA programs are concentrated in Sections 203 and 207 of the National Housing Act. Section 203 provides for the insurance of privately granted, long-term, fully amortized loans to borrowers for the purchase of one–four-family properties. The properties must meet minimum standards for size and construction. Section 207 authorizes the FHA to insure loans for the construction of rental apartments (five units or more). Title I of the act also authorizes insurance for loans to repair or improve existing housing.

Altogether, the FHA today has over 50 programs of housing finance assistance. It has special help programs for servicemen and disaster victims, as well as programs in experimental housing, urban renewal, and housing for the elderly and handicapped. Some of the major provisions of the more widely used programs are described below.

On one–four-family loan insurance, the limit on the insurable amount is currently $67,500 for one-family dwellings, $76,000 for two-family dwellings, $92,000 for three-family dwellings, and $107,000 for four-family dwellings. Maximum terms of loan cannot exceed 30 years. A borrower must pay down 3 percent of the first $25,000 of value and closing costs, plus 5 percent of value and closing costs in excess of $25,000.

Loans on residential condominium units are insurable at the same rates as loans on single-family properties. Home improvement loans insured by FHA (Title I) may be made for a maximum amount of $15,000 for 15 years.

A relatively new graduated payments program is simply a variant on the regular insurance program for single-family residences (Section 203b). It is not available for two–four-family residences. Whereas the "regular program" calls for level payments or a fully amortized loan, this program (Section 245) allows payments for up to ten years that begin lower but increase to an amount which then remains level for the remainder of the loan term. Because the interest charges in the early years are greater than the periodic payments, the outstanding balance increases for several years. For example, on a five-year graduated payment loan, the monthly payments increase by about $20 per month each of the first five years. The factors for computing the monthly payment per $1,000 of original loan amount on a 10 percent, 30-year loan are as follows:

Year	Factor
1	6.6704
2	7.1706
3	7.7084
4	8.2866
5	8.9081
Remaining	9.5762

The highest outstanding balance occurs in year 6 and is $1055.2642 per $1,000 of loan amount. The mortgage amount is computed from the following formula:

$$\text{Mortgage amount} = \frac{\text{Sale price} \times 0.97}{\text{Highest outstanding balance per dollar}}$$

Therefore, on a $35,000 home the mortgage amount would be ($35,000 × 0.97) ÷ 1.0552642 = $32,172. This amount can be compared with the amount obtainable on a level payment loan, which would be $33,750. The payments for the first year with the graduated payment loan are $32,172 × 6.6704 = $214.60, while the payments on the level payment loan are $296.19. For the sixth year to maturity, however, payments are higher for the graduated payment loan than for the level payment loan, at $308.09.

Multifamily rental housing can be insured at loan to value ratios of up to 90 percent, with the insurable amount per unit varying as to type of construction and size of unit.

Property improvement loans for multifamily structures can be insured up to a maximum amount of $25,000. Special assistance multifamily rental housing for low- and moderate-income families can be insured up to 100 percent of estimated replacement cost, if owned by a nonprofit organization.

For mobile homes the FHA will insure single-wides up to $16,000 and double-wides up to $24,000. The maximum maturity on these loans is 15 years and 32 days. To be eligible for these loans the mobile home must be serviced by electrical, water, and sewer hookups.

Land development loans are insurable up to 80 percent of land value before development plus 90 percent of the estimated costs of development. However, such loans may not exceed 85 percent of the estimated value upon completion.

Veterans Administration. Toward the end of World War II it became apparent to Congress that legislation would be needed to help returning war veterans adjust to civilian life. Thus, in 1944 the Servicemen's Readjustment Act was passed by Congress. It contained a section empowering the Veterans Administration to grant veterans a partial guaranty on first-mortgage real estate loans or to grant loans directly to veterans, if they cannot otherwise obtain credit. Thus, the VA has two areas of authority with regard to mortgage loans:

1. The power to guarantee partially mortgage loans made to veterans by qualified lenders.
2. The power to make direct loans to veterans in areas where mortgage credit is not available.

Lenders of VA-guaranteed loans are divided into two categories—"supervised lenders" and "nonsupervised lenders." Supervised lenders are subject to periodic examination and are supervised by federal or state agencies. They do not have to obtain prior approval from the VA in order to make a VA-guaranteed loan, but they usually obtain a prior commitment from the VA in order to safeguard themselves against unforeseen technicalities. Nonsupervised lenders are required to obtain prior VA loan approval before closing a VA-underwritten loan.

Maximum interest rates on VA-guaranteed loans are set by the administrator of the Veterans Administration. The rate is usually set to conform with the FHA rate. Any discount on a VA-guaranteed loan must be paid by the seller; it is against the law for a veteran to pay any premium for a VA loan.

The VA will guarantee loans made for the construction or purchase of a home (including a mobile home) by a veteran. The property may be one–four units, and it must be used by the veteran borrower as his or her place of residence. On home loans the VA may guarantee up to 60 percent of any one loan or a maximum of $27,500, whichever is less, for terms up to 30 years 32 days. This guaranty need not be used immediately or in any single transaction. For example, if a veteran has used a $20,000 guaranty to purchase a home, he or she can sell that home and still have $7,500 of guaranty left to purchase another home.

Besides making guaranteed loans, the VA has the power to make direct loans to veterans in areas where credit is not generally available. In recent times, however, this power has not been used often.

Private mortgage insurers. In recent years, a number of private mortgage insurance companies have been formed. These companies insure the top 15–20 percent of a mortgage for a fee of approximately 1 percent of the amount insured plus an annual premium of 0.25 percent. An example is a 95 percent loan with a 15 percent insurance coverage. If the insured lender forecloses the loan and sells the property for 85 percent of the loan amount, the insurer pays the 10 percent loss (or buys the property for the full loan amount). This permits the primary lender or secondary lender to gain protection similar to that provided by the FHA and the VA, but with less difficult administrative procedures. The large private insurers such as Mortgage Guaranty Insurance Corporation (MGIC), Foremost Guaranty, and PMI, Inc., now underwrite a large portion of mortgages written in excess of 90 percent of appraised value.

TABLE 20–1
Functions and government agencies associated with real estate finance

Function	Government agency
Regulation of the supply of funds and interest rates	1. Federal Reserve System. 2. U.S. Treasury (debt management).
Secondary market activities	1. Federal National Mortgage Association. 2. Federal Home Loan Mortgage Corporation. 3. Government National Mortgage Association—Department of Housing and Urban Development.
Supervision and insurance	1. Federal Reserve System. 2. Federal Deposit Insurance Corporation. 3. Comptroller of the Currency. 4. Federal Home Loan Bank Board. 5. Federal Savings and Loan Insurance Corporation. 6. State Regulatory Agencies.
Special aid for low-income housing and community development	1. Offices for Housing Production and Mortgage Credit, Housing Management, and Community Development—Department of Housing and Urban Development. 2. Government National Mortgage Association.
Mortgage loan insurance and guaranty	1. Federal Housing Administration—Department of Housing and Urban Development. 2. Veterans Administration.
Taxation	1. U.S. Internal Revenue Service. 2. Local taxing authorities (real estate tax).

Subsidized housing programs

Through the years Congress has sought to encourage the construction of housing for specific purposes by providing subsidies in FHA programs. Also, many of the urban renewal and community development subsidy programs are administered by the FHA. For example, Section 101 provides rent supplement payments to owners of private housing projects that serve eligible low-income tenants. Section 202 provides below-market interest rate (BMIR) loans for construction of multifamily rental projects for the elderly or handicapped. Section 221 (d)(3) provides insurance for below-market rate or market rate loans for low- and moderate-income multifamily projects. And Sections 235 and 236 provide insurance for single-family and multifamily projects serving low- and moderate-income families, which also obtain interest and rent subsidies. As shown in Table 20–2, many of the programs have been replaced or are dormant.

Special aid for low-income housing and urban renewal

The Department of Housing and Urban Development functional offices for Community Development, Housing Management, and Housing Production and Mortgage Credit—FHA are primarily responsible for the government effort in the fields of low-income housing and community development.

Taxation

It should be recognized here that income, estate, and gift taxes exert a great influence on real estate decisions. Tax rates applied to various types and amounts of income, and the rules promulgated to calculate the tax burden, must be considered when analyzing an investment decision. The rules regarding allowable economic lives and rates of depreciation are particularly important in this regard. When the rules governing these matters are changed, the relative attractiveness of real estate investments may be altered drastically. For example, the Tax Reform Act of 1976 greatly altered such matters as construction period interest and taxes, long-term capital gain periods, depreciation recapture, and deductions for offices in homes and vacation homes. Investment in some types of real estate projects thus became considerably less desirable.

The primary subsidized housing program currently in effect is contained in Section 8 of Title II of the Housing and Community Development Act of 1974. As described in Table 20–2 this program authorizes the leasing of new and rehabilitated private housing units, not in ghetto areas, to low-income families. Families must contribute at least 15 percent, but no more than 25 percent, of family income to rent. The government subsidizes the difference between a family's contribution to rent and the fair market rental of the unit, as determined by the FHA.

Also operative at the present time is a modified Section 235 program. This program provides insurance on loans whose interest rates are subsidized down to 5 percent. The loans are made to purchase single-family houses. The developer, in the case of new construction, obtains FHA approval for inclusion of the homes in the Section 235 program. Builders obtain their profits from an overhead and profit allowance of 12–13 percent of total replacement cost. The FHA-determined value for mortgage lending purposes considers lot value,

TABLE 20–2
Historical summary of federal housing programs

Year	Type of program	Principal provisions	Current status
1934 *a.* Mortgage insurance	Established FHA and insurance programs	Operative
b. Insurance of accounts in thrift institutions	Established FSLIC	Operative
1937 Public housing	Capital grants and loans plus annual contribution to local housing authorities to provide low-rent housing for low-income families.	Dormant
1949 *a.* Subsidized housing	Established principle of governmental assistance to privately constructed housing.	Principle and goal are still being pursued
b. National housing goal	Established national housing goal of a "decent home and suitable living environment for every American family."	Principle and goal are still being pursued
c. Slum clearance and urban redevelopment	Initiated slum clearance and urban redevelopment.	Replaced
1954 Conservation and rehabilitation	Broadened scope of Housing Act of 1949 by adding conservation and rehabilitation programs for housing in renewal areas. Also required a "workable program" for funds to be provided for renewal or subsidized housing.	Replaced
1961 Section 221(d)(3) BMIR	Subsidized the interest rate on subsidized housing for moderate-income families sponsored by limited dividend and nonprofit organizations.	Dormant
1965 *a.* Rent supplements	Paid subsidies to landlords for difference between 25 percent of tenants' income and fair market rent.	Dormant
b. Leased public housing	Permitted public housing units to be leased from private owners.	Dormant
1966 *a.* Blighted area FHA loans	Allowed standard FHA-insured loans (Section 203) to be made in blighted areas.	Replaced
b. Model cities	Provided grants and technical assistance to cities which had an acceptable comprehensive plan for dealing with the social, economic, and physical problems of selected neighborhoods.	Replaced
1967 Home counseling service	Provided prospective homeowners with information about opportunities under various FHA programs and explanations of FHA procedures.	Operative

TABLE 20–2 (continued)

Year	Type of program	Principal provisions	Current status
1968 a.	Subsidized housing (Sections 235 and 236)	Subsidized homebuyers (235) and multi-family rental housing (236).	Section 235 revived, but modified, Section 236 dormant
b.	Special credit risk mortgage insurance (Section 237)	Provided mortgage insurance for families which could not meet credit requirements under other sections of the act.	Dormant
c.	National housing partnership	Profit-making organization was to produce subsidized housing.	Dormant
d.	Rehabilitation	Permitted nonprofit organizations to rehabilitate housing for resale to low-income families.	Dormant
e.	Mortgage insurance for displaced families	Provided mortgage insurance for families displaced by government actions.	Dormant
f.	Multifamily FHA financing	Provided favorable financing for new or rehabilitated units for low- and moderate-income families.	Dormant
g.	Subsidies for nonprofit sponsors of subsidized housing	Provided subsidies for nonprofit sponsors of subsidized housing.	Replaced
1974	Housing and Community Development Act		Operative
a.	Title I: community development	Consolidated several existing programs into a single program providing block grants.	
b.	Title II: assisted housing	Authorized the leasing of new and rehabilitated private housing, not in ghetto areas, to low-income families. Families had to contribute not less than 15 percent but no more than 25 percent of family income to rent.	
c.	Title III: mortgage credit assistance	Raised FHA single-family home mortgage limits.	Basic applicable housing law
d.	Title IV: comprehensive planning	Provided funds for comprehensive planning by communities to determine housing needs.	
e.	Title V: rural housing	Liberalized existing rural housing law.	
f.	Title VI: mobile home construction	Established construction safeguards and enforcement of safety standards for mobile home manufacturers.	
g.	Title VII: consumer home mortgage assistance	Raised loan limits for federal savings and loans and revised the real estate lending authority of national banks.	

TABLE 20–2 (concluded)

Year	Type of program	Principal provisions	Current status
h.	Title VIII: miscellaneous	Authorized urban homesteading; authorized a demonstration program for solar heating and cooling; authorized an experimental housing allowance program; raised FNMA and GNMA mortgage purchase limits; made communities eligible for national flood insurance at subsidized rates; outlawed discrimination on the basis of sex; encouraged the formation of state housing and development agencies.	

Source: Authors' summary, 1980.

closing costs, sale expense (broker's commission), structure cost, and on-site improvements. The builder's profit and overhead allowance is included in the value, which can be adjusted up or down within limits to reflect the quality of construction. The final value estimated by FHA is usually very close to sale price.

COMMUNITY DEVELOPMENT

The owners of property in a blighted or slum area are subject to the external diseconomies imposed by the surrounding neighborhood.[3] They cannot afford to rehabilitate their properties because the values of these properties will be constrained by those of adjacent properties. Each property owner is faced with a "prisoner's dilemma."[4] Also, property values in a community may be negatively affected by inadequate public facilities and services. Unpaved streets, an absence of sanitary and storm sewers, inadequate police and fire protection, poor garbage pickup, and other substandard municipal services inhibit the desire and feasibility of property owners to improve existing properties or construct new ones. Therefore, the federal government has provided programs for communities to upgrade or construct new community facilities, to renew blighted sections of cities, and to encourage property owners to conserve and rehabilitate deteriorating properties. From the beginning of various types of community development programs, the concepts of subsidization have changed dramatically. In 25 years the major type of financial assistance to communities has evolved

---

[3] This is discussed in depth in Chapters 19 and 20.

[4] Otto A. Davis and Andrew B. Whinston, "Economics of Urban Renewal," *Law and Contemporary Problems* 26, no. 1 (Winter 1961): 105–17.

from slum clearance administered under federal aegis to community block grants for uses that are locally determined.

URBAN RENEWAL

As shown in Table 20–2, the National Housing Act of 1949 initiated slum clearance and urban redevelopment that evolved into large urban renewal projects. Urban renewal was accomplished in cities by a local renewal agency. The agency purchased or condemned (if necessary) properties in the blighted area, demolishing existing improvements and providing or improving streets, utilities, schools, and municipal buildings as planned in the reuse of the area. Sites in the renewal area were sold to private developers who agreed to build improvements suggested by the renewal plan. The sites were sold at prices low enough to induce the desired development.

The subsidy in urban renewal was the difference between (*a*) the proceeds realized from the resale of sites and (*b*) the costs of purchasing the blighted properties, razing them, and supplying the required municipal improvements. The federal government supplied two thirds of this subsidy, and the local government provided one third, which could be in the form of labor and municipal improvements.

Rationale.   The rationale for urban renewal includes the contention that removal of neighborhood externalities permits improvement of an area that could not occur in normal operation of the market. Only removing the blighted condition of the neighborhood can attract families which are willing and able to pay the necessary rents. Other reasons given for urban renewal include attracting middle-class families back to the central city; increasing the city's property tax base and tax revenues; removing aesthetically unattractive structures; and reducing the cost of police and fire protection, health services, and education by eliminating the slum conditions that make provision of these services necessary and costly.

Problems.   Urban renewal was beset by problems. Blighted areas had to be identified, and concerned citizens protested having neighborhoods classified as "blighted" and therefore eligible for renewal. At what point does an area contain sufficient substandard properties to be blighted? The relocation of families displaced from the renewal areas presented continual complications. Before an urban renewal program was authorized, the local agency had to demonstrate that sufficient standard housing was available in the community within the financial means of families to be displaced and reasonably close to their places of work. At times, public housing had to be provided before renewal was begun. The local public agency was required to provide counseling and relocation assistance to displaced families. However, families forced to move did not have to take advantage of this service. Urban renewal was accused of shifting slum conditions from the renewal area to other low-income neighborhoods. The broad generalization that renewal merely shifts slum conditions to other neighborhoods in all instances is not supported by empirical evidence, although in some communities displaced families did concentrate in other neighborhoods.[5] Each local public agency was required to trace the displaced families and assess their new housing condition and housing expense. A summary of several of these relocation studies concludes that relocated families generally were better housed, but they were paying more in housing expenses.[6]

The reuse of urban renewal sites for offices, commercial, and other nonhousing purposes has been severely criticized. Similarly, replacement of low-rent housing with units priced for higher-income families has been questioned. A decrease in the supply of units within the financial means of low-income families is a disbenefit for all such families in the community.

If the "benefits" view of filtering is accepted, reuse of a renewal area for higher-priced residential units can be viewed as less of a problem than reuse for nonresidential purposes. The higher-rent units could result in vacancies elsewhere in the market as families move to the new housing, precipitating the filtering process. Ultimately, better quality units than they are occupying may be available to low-income families at the same or lower housing expense.

It is our contention, however, that filtering is a slow and uncertain process, which can be impeded by net in-migration, undoubling of households, and new household formations that absorb vacancies.[7] The cost of moving, unwillingness to move because of neighborhood ties, lack of knowledge about the availability of better housing, and prejudice that restricts freedom of choice in the housing market further hamper the process. Rents and prices in the market can be slow to fall as landlords tolerate marginal increases in vacancy rate and property owners accept longer waiting periods for sale of their properties. If blight exists because people are poor, the filtering down of better-quality housing will not prevent blight from recurring.[8] Properties which filter down may have maintenance and repair forgone over time because rental income is insufficient to induce normal upkeep. Eventually, the properties will become physically substandard.

---

[5] Chester Hartman, "The Housing of Relocated Families," *Journal of the American Institute of Planners* 30, no. 4 (November 1964): 266–86.

[6] Ibid.

[7] See Chapter 9 for additional discussion of the filtering concept.

[8] Hugh O. Nourse, "The Economics of Urban Renewal," *Land Economics* 42, no. 1 (February 1966): 67.

Urban renewal has the potential of increasing land values in the renewal area and increasing the property tax base of the central city. Land values in the vicinity of the renewal area may also appreciate. When the metropolitan area is considered as a whole, however, the net long-term effect on land values may be minimal.[9] If aggregate land value is some multiple of aggregate rent, the total value of land following urban renewal increases to the extent that households pay more in total rent after renewal. This increase in aggregate rent may be very small. Land values increase in the renewal area because new residents can afford to pay more rent than the displaced families. However, the increased rental income realized in the renewal area may be lost by owners of competitive properties in the market who are experiencing a higher vacancy loss. Displaced families moving elsewhere in the market may be faced with higher rents and may choose to buy less housing. Certainly, they are limited in the amount of additional housing expense they can tolerate. The renewal project may alter the pattern of land values in the metropolitan area without appreciably affecting the aggregate value.

Increases in land value resulting from the location of commercial and other establishments in the renewal area can be counted as a net increase in aggregate land value only if these establishments would not have located elsewhere in the community. Renewal may increase the community's aggregate income and the demand for goods and services, since the federal subsidy dollars can be, in part, a net gain to the community. These dollars are acted upon by the local income multiplier to produce a greater regional or community income. This amount would be small, and the additional derived demand for commercial and other nonresidential improvements generated by this increased local purchasing power should not be expected to call forth construction of any magnitude.

Empirical studies of the costs and benefits of urban renewal have been attempted by Messner and Mao.[10] Rothenberg, however, notes that the most important benefits of urban renewal may be the reduced social costs of slum living.[11] Fire hazards and crime may be lessened; health hazards are reduced; and the conditions fostering personality problems are removed. These items are difficult to quantify in rigorous cost-benefit analysis.

---

[9] Ibid., pp. 68–69.

[10] J. C. T. Mao, *Efficiency in Public Urban Renewal Expenditures through Capital Budgeting*, Research Report no. 27 (Berkeley: University of California, Center for Real Estate and Urban Economics, 1965); and Stephen D. Messner, "Urban Redevelopment in Indianapolis: A Benefit-Cost Analysis." *Journal of Regional Science* 8, no. 2 (Winter 1968): 149–58.

[11] Jerome Rothenberg, *Economic Evaluation of Urban Renewal* (Washington, D.C.: Brookings Institution, 1967), p. 175.

Rehabilitation and conservation

Disenchantment with urban renewal resulted in programs designed to rehabilitate deteriorating properties and to conserve "gray" areas that might deteriorate further. The model cities program initiated in 1966 provided grants and technical assistance to municipalities or other government bodies which proposed an acceptable comprehensive plan for dealing with the social, economic, and physical problems of selected neighborhoods. Proposals for grants to assist in carrying out a model cities program were required to show that several social and economic criteria would be met.

Rehabilitation of deteriorating properties in urban renewal areas and in neighborhoods designated for conservation had to be facilitated by strict code enforcement. However, landlords decide to make necessary improvements only if the cost is no greater than the loss of value experienced by abandoning their property. And some landlords seem capable of inordinately extending the period of compliance. Furthermore, declaring units unfit for human habitation and boarding the windows does not solve the housing problem of the occupants, who must seek housing elsewhere. Nor does an increase in rent following improvement of the property aid low-income families to achieve adequate housing within their financial means. If strict code enforcement is effectively to encourage rehabilitation, the availability of credit and other incentives must make rehabilitation the viable alternative to abandonment without unduly increasing the rent of the units.

The federal government has helped provide credit for rehabilitation, both directly as grants and loans and indirectly in the form of mortgage insurance or rehabilitation loans. Further incentive to provide rehabilitated units for low- and moderate-income families was incorporated into the 1969 Tax Reform Act and extended by the 1976 and 1978 Tax Reform Acts. The 1978 act permits a maximum of $20,000 of rehabilitation expenditures per unit to be written off using straight-line depreciation over five years.

Direct block grants

Title I of the Housing and Community Development Act of 1974 consolidated several programs (such as urban renewal, public facility loans, model cities supplemental grants, and rehabilitation loans) into a single program of direct block grants. Eighty percent of the funds ($2.5 billion to $2.95 billion per year) are allocated to urban cities and counties; 20 percent are allocated to nonurban areas. The formula which determines the amount each community obtains is complex; it considers such factors as (*a*) the population of the community, (*b*) the extent of poverty in the community, and (*c*) the extent of overcrowded housing.[12] The grants are to be used by the community in terms of its priorities for eliminating slums and blight, increasing public services, improving land use, and preserving property values.

IMPACT OF FEDERAL HOUSING PROGRAMS

Federal housing programs are available to familes that vary not only in size, income, and assets, but also in tastes and preferences, stage in the family cycle, and other characteristics. Some families have more than one wage earner; others have none. Moreover, the places of employment of these wage earners can be widely distributed over the urban area. These characteristics determine the location and type of unit occupied in the private housing market by families eligible for subsidized housing. Since the subsidized programs admit families having different income distributions (and different distributions of other characteristics), it can be expected that each program would admit families from units in the housing market that vary in type (single-family residence or apartment), size, physical condition, location, rent, and value. One study showed that in Columbus, Ohio, families moving into federal housing generally came from the inner city, from apartments, from deteriorating and dilapidated units, and from low-rent units. Various programs affected differing proportions of occupants coming from the inner city or from various types of housing units.[13]

New housing developed under the federal programs has been recognized as a factor contributing to the filtering process when it provides a net increase in the number of units available in the market. The vacancy rate in the nonsubsidized portion of the local housing market would rise in this instance, contributing to the potential for a decline in the level of rents in the submarkets affected and permitting low-income families to better their housing condition at the same or less expense. In reality, it would be very difficult indeed to separate the net impact of units provided by the federal programs from other forces operating in the market to influence the demand for and supply of housing. The net increase in total housing units represented by these programs and the rise in the level of vacancies in the housing submarkets affected can only be viewed as a marginal change that may

---

[12] Wallace B. Agnew, "The Housing and Community Development Act of 1974: An Interpretation," *Real Estate Appraiser* 41, no. 1 (January–February 1975): 9–11.

[13] Ronald L. Racster, Halbert C. Smith, and William B. Brueggeman, "Federal Housing Programs in the Local Housing Market," *Appraisal Journal* 39, no. 3 (July 1971): 402–6.

be swamped by in-migration of households, undoubling of existing households, new household formations, and loss of units from demolition and conversion, all of which simultaneously affect this part of the local housing market. Further, as we have seen, supply-oriented housing programs, over the longer run, probably result in little or no overall improvement in the housing condition of families in the market.[14]

Rehabilitated units supplied by the federal programs improve the quality of the housing stock, but they do not increase the number of units available in the market. Large-scale rehabilitation could increase the prices of properties in lower quality submarkets as investors and public agencies bid for units suitable for placement in the federal programs. This increase in market prices could give incentive to owners of better quality units to allow their properties to filter down into the lower quality housing stock by forgoing maintenance and repair.[15] Better quality submarkets thus lose units to the lower quality submarkets that are experiencing relatively higher prices. Prices, in turn, rise in these better quality submarkets, attracting units from submarkets of still higher quality. The process repeats itself until it reaches those submarkets which are competitive with new properties and calls forth new construction.

Policy for the provision of adequate housing

The decision to improve the housing condition of the ill-housed is reached at a high level of government, where the problem is to allocate the national budget among broad categories of perceived needs. At a lower level of decision making, methods of meeting the need must be determined. Our present federal housing programs are the result of past decisions at this level. However, there are unresolved problems that deserve consideration and further analysis. For example, should income supplements be provided to low-income families rather than subsidizing the development and operation of their housing? Our national housing policy, to date, has provided housing developed specifically for disadvantaged families. An alternative solution would be to give income to these families which they could spend for housing if they choose, or for other goods and services. The negative income tax is one proposal for this purpose. Another variation on income supplements is the housing allowance program, which has been tried experimentally in selected cities. The housing allowance is tied to expenditure for housing, but it may be spent on any standard unit in the

---

[14] See Chapter 9.

[15] Edgar O. Olsen, "A Competitive Theory of the Housing Market," *American Economic Review* 59, no. 4 (September 1969): 612–22.

private market. The housing allowance program seems to have the capability of replacing present federal housing programs that provide new and rehabilitated housing for low- and moderate-income families.

If the decision is to subsidize low-income families by providing housing directly, what form of subsidized program should be used? Should only the housing of low-income families be subsidized, or should subsidization be extended to the housing of moderate-income families? What mix of subsidized housing should be provided? Public housing directly admits low-income families, improving their housing condition and at the same time reducing their housing expense. However, the subsidy cost per public housing unit is relatively large. Units available to moderate-income families in Section 235, Section 8, and other programs can be supplied at a lower subsidy cost per unit. Federal appropriations for housing subsidies are limited. Therefore, should a greater number of moderate-income program units be supplied from a given appropriation, or should fewer low-income program units be supplied?

Income redistribution effects

The economic analysis of subsidized housing can involve the examination of broader income redistribution effects. In one analysis of income redistribution. Nourse uses the example of the development and operation of conventional public housing.[16] A schematic presentation of the potential shifts in income from this housing program is depicted in Figure 20–4. Nourse notes a potential increase in national income if construction workers would have been unemployed otherwise, or a shift from the development of other types of real estate to public housing (with no change in national income) if these workers would have been employed elsewhere. If the public housing program places additional demands upon the construction industry during full employment, wage and construction cost increases are to be expected, with income shifting to favor persons in the building industry. Raising funds by issuing bonds to finance public housing shifts income from other investments. A local government may get more or less tax revenue from the housing project (which pays 10 percent of rent collected in lieu of the property tax) than from the properties condemned for project construction, depending upon the relative intensity of site use before and after project development. Whether or not slum landlords whose property is taken for the project experience a net benefit or disbenefit will depend upon their condemnation award. If they are

---

[16] Hugh O. Nourse, "Redistribution of Income from Public Housing," *National Tax Journal* 19, no. 1 (March 1966): 27–37.

FIGURE 20–4

Channels of potential income redistribution in the development and operation of public housing

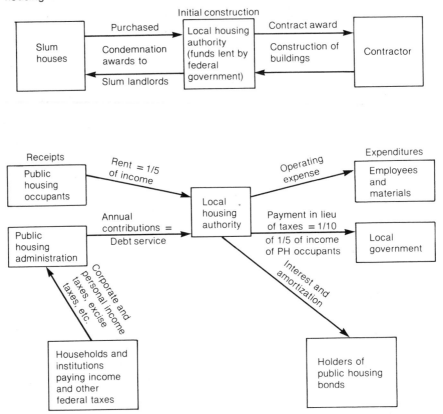

Source: Hugh O. Nourse, "Redistribution of Income from Public Housing," *National Tax Journal* 19, no. 1 (March 1966): 37.

paid more than the fair market value of their property, they benefit at the expense of the taxpayer. The most important shift of income is from the taxpayer to the public housing tenants. The following point made by Nourse should be kept in mind: the economist can trace potential income redistribution effects, but it is not possible to state objectively that the total national welfare has been increased following redistribution. The decision to provide public housing or any form of subsidized housing remains a value judgment.[17]

Currently, the emphasis in the federal subsidization of housing is on the direct subsidization of rents in apartment units and the subsidiza-

---

[17] Ibid.

tion of the interest rate in single-family homes. The latter type is a "shallow" subsidy, permitting marginal purchasers to afford standard housing. The same number of subsidy dollars is thus spread among more beneficiaries. Large-scale community development programs, such as urban renewal and model cities, have been disbanded in favor of block grants to communities. This approach seems to be part of the trend to shift more decisions from the federal level back to the states and communities. Whether it will be more effective and efficient in solving urban problems than more direct federal involvement can only be determined with the passage of time.

Employment, education, and equality of opportunity will, in the longer run, alleviate the socioeconomic problems besetting our minority groups and low-income families. In the interim, the direct provision of decent housing for some disadvantaged families can only be a partial solution.

SUMMARY

This chapter deals with the pervasive influence of government on real estate finance. While government agencies do not become directly involved in private financing transactions and arrangements, their influence plays a prominent role in determining the quantity and types of financing available. The Federal Reserve System, the Federal Home Loan Bank System, the U.S. Treasury, the comptroller of the currency, the Federal Home Loan Mortgage Corporation, the Federal National Mortgage Association, the U.S. Department of Housing and Urban Development, and the Veterans Administration establish and operate a framework of interest rate determination, institutional supervision and regulation, secondary mortgage market activity, loan insurance, and special-purpose assistance within which real estate finance must function.

Our national housing policy is to provide "a decent home and suitable living environment for every American family." In pursuit of this goal, several federal housing programs have been initiated. Public housing was a depression-born program designed to provide adequate housing for low-income families. Over time, public housing has evolved from high-rise projects to less intensive developments and to lease or purchase programs and the public housing home ownership program. The rent supplement program enables low-income families to occupy adequate housing without paying a disproportionate share of their income for rent. Housing for moderate-income families has been made available through the Section 221(d)(3) BMIR, Section 236, Section 235, and Section 8 programs. Both new and rehabilitated housing are included in these programs. Other federal programs have provided grants and loans for renovation and rehabilitation of housing in renewal and conservation districts.

The emerging intent of these programs has been to encourage private enterprise to construct, own, and operate the needed housing. Federal subsidy is provided when necessary to encourage development. The subsidy permits below-market rents and housing expense to be charged, and at the same time it gives the developer and investor satisfactory profits. With the exception of the rent supplements, federal programs have focused upon the provision of housing units for the underhoused. Other alternatives are possible, such as the housing allowance program, which can supplement the income of poor families, although the subsidy would still be earmarked for housing expense. Proposals for unrestricted income supplements have not been well received.

QUESTIONS FOR REVIEW

1. Look up an annual report of the U.S. Department of Housing and Urban Development. What are the principal kinds of programs carried on by this agency?

2. Why are the effects of monetary policies of the board of governors of the Federal Reserve System so keenly felt in the field of real estate finance?

3. How does the developer-investor profit from a Section 235 project?

4. Discuss the effects on the local housing market of the simultaneous provision of housing units in two or more subsidy programs.

5. Not every low- or moderate-income family can be provided with a subsidized housing unit. Given a total allocation for subsidy, what factors are involved in an analysis of the alternatives of providing fewer units with a higher subsidy cost per unit directly to low-income families versus providing a larger number of units to moderate-income families?

6. What prevents the economist from stating that federal housing programs increase the total national welfare?

7. Explain the rationale for urban renewal.

8. Do you agree with the statement: "Blight exists because people are poor"? Is this contention a complete analysis of the problem?

9. What potential advantages and disadvantages do you see in the housing allowance program?

10. Do you prefer to have the government make block grants to communities or to have specific programs for community development, such as urban renewal? Why?

REFERENCES

Agnew, Wallace B. "The Housing and Community Development Act of 1974: An Interpretation." *Real Estate Appraiser* 41, no. 1 (January–February 1975): 9–11.

Brueggeman, William B.; Racster, Ronald L.; and Smith, Halbert C. "Research Report: Multiple Housing Programs and Urban Housing Policy." *Journal of the American Institute of Planners* 38, no. 3 (1972): 161–67.

Grigsby, William G. *Housing Markets and Public Policy.* Philadelphia: University of Pennsylvania Press, 1963.

Lansing, J. B.; Clifton, C. W.; and Morgan, J. N. *New Homes and Poor People: A Study of Chains of Moves.* Ann Arbor: University of Michigan, Institute for Social Research, 1969.

O'Block, Robert P., and Kuehn, Robert H., Jr. *An Economic Analysis of the Housing and Urban Development Act of 1968.* Boston: Harvard University, Graduate School of Business Administration, Division of Research, 1970.

Racster, Ronald L.; Smith, Halbert C.; and Brueggeman, William B. "Federal Housing Programs in the Local Housing Market." *Appraisal Journal* 39, no. 3 (July 1971): 402–6.

Report of the President's Committee on Urban Housing. *A Decent Home.* Washington, D.C.: U.S. Government Printing Office, 1969.

Rothenberg, Jerome. *Economic Evaluation of Urban Renewal.* Washington, D.C.: Brookings Institution, 1967.

Smith, Halbert C., and Tschappat, Carl J. "Monetary Policy and Real Estate Values." *Appraisal Journal* 34, no. 1 (January 1966): 18–26.

Smith, Wallace F. *Housing: The Social and Economic Elements.* Berkeley: University of California Press, 1970.

U.S. Department of Housing and Urban Development. *Digest of Insurable Loans and Summaries of Other Federal Housing Administration Programs.* Washington, D.C.: U.S. Government Printing Office, 1978.

chapter 21

Environmental issues and

real estate development

Two alternatives available to our society—the preservation of the environment and the development of real estate—often appear to be mutually exclusive. Real estate developers are sometimes regarded as rapists of the countryside, while defenders of the environment are viewed as naive do-gooders who would sabotage economic growth in order to preserve some wildlife and vegetation. Laws have been passed at all levels of government to help preserve the environment. Many of these laws have imposed restrictions and additional costs upon both the developers and the users of real estate. The purpose of this chapter is to examine the nature and background of environmental issues, the responses to the issues, and the impact of these responses upon real estate investors.

RISE OF ENVIRONMENTAL CONCERN

Deterioration of the environment is a relatively recent issue in national affairs. Agitation for legal means of environmental protection began to occur in the mid-1960s and early 1970s. During this period significant and far-reaching legislation was imposed at the federal level. Additionally, a number of states enacted restrictive laws which more directly affected real estate development and investment.

This period also saw efforts at the local level to increase standards in land-use controls, to impose more comprehensive planning, and to limit population growth. Candidates for political office at all levels became known as proponents or opponents of environmental preservation or of further growth and development. The traditional form of land-use control—zoning—was both attacked and defended in regard to its impact upon environmental issues. Urban environmentalists saw zoning as the principal tool by which suburban and high-income groups kept inner-city (usually black) low-income people from escaping the congested, polluted, deteriorated central portions of cities. Middle- and high-income groups saw zoning as a device to prevent congestion, maintain property values, exclude low-income residents, and discourage development of all but single-family housing.

Underlying factors of environmental concern

Attempting to assign sources to the rise in environmental concern is, as always in attempting to analyze motivations, hypothetical and hazardous. Nevertheless, we can note other social trends and their close relationship to environmental issues. Some substnatial degree of cause and effect can reasonably be assigned to factors such as population trends, industrialization and urbanization, economic prosperity, the extension of civil rights, and the energy crisis.

Population trends.   An increase in the U.S. population from approximately 140 million in 1940 to approximately 223 million in 1980 has required a substantially large drain upon our natural resources. More food and fiber have been required for food and clothing. The increased need for housing, transportation, education, employment, and other goods and services has added to the complexity of society. Public and private institutions have multiplied and changed to accommodate this growth perhaps more than during any comparable period in our country's history. The growth has contributed to congestion in our urban areas and to urbanization in formerly rural and isolated regions.

Coupled with net natural increases in population, migratory growth patterns have contributed to fast growth rates in some areas. Population growth rates have been above average in states having climatic and scenic advantages, such as Florida, California, Arizona, Texas, Colorado, and Oregon. For these states and regions, the impact upon natural resources, social complexity, public and private institutions, and the need for all goods and services has been even greater.

With population increases emanating from net natural increase and net migration, many urban centers have experienced more concentrated living patterns. High-rise apartments and condominiums have added to the demands for urban services and resources in cities such as

New York, Chicago, Washington, D.C., Atlanta, St. Louis, Seattle, and Toronto. Additionally, other areas such as the lower southeast and southwest coasts of Florida, southern California, and the mid-Atlantic coast have been developed with hotels and resort accommodations, as well as high-rise residential buildings. These concentrations of population have inevitably contributed to pressures and frictions in everyday living and have placed heavy demands upon resources and environmental systems.

Industrialization and urbanization. The industrial resolution of the late 19th and early 20th centuries led to the development of industrial centers and the consequent urbanization of society. Early manufacturing centers, such as New York, Chicago, Detroit, Pittsburgh, and Cleveland, attracted large numbers of rural residents with the promise of relatively high-paying jobs and the hope of prosperity. Further advances in transportation and communication, particularly jet airplanes, television, and the interstate highway system, extended the ideas and values of urban America to rural areas. Leisure time, planned obsolescence, throwaway containers, conspicuous consumption, and "buy now—pay later" credit plans became distinguishing characteristics of American society. Until the mid-1960s, little concern was shown that continued adherence to these tenets would place intolerable strains upon the land resources of the nation.

Economic prosperity. The continued industrialization and urbanization of the United States, particularly after World War II, produced an economic prosperity greater than any country had previously known. Along with population growth, technology, and mass markets, a high degree of purchasing power became characteristic of large segments of the urbanized society. Increasing numbers of people, the pent-up demand from World War II, and the large amounts of savings from the war period initiated a cycle of production and consumption that was to last over 25 years. Furthermore, the cycle was self-sustaining through the economic processes of employment, investment, and consumption. If the economy incurred an occasional downturn, the government primed the pump with stimulative monetary and fiscal policies. America prospered through two large-scale wars, and it was drawn to a standstill only by the shortage of fossil fuels in the late 1970s. The desire to sustain past lifestyles is currently causing reduced savings, and reliance on foreign fuel sources has created a severe drain on the nation's balance of trade. The need for environmental control is emphasized as we seek to regain the prosperity that has been taken for granted but is now uncertain.

Civil rights. Also during the 1960s, the major push by minority groups to attain their full civil rights and to increase their proportionate share of the American economic pie brought into question some of the traditional values and theories of American capitalism. Could the system operate without exploiting people? If the system had relied to any extent upon the exploitation of people, had it also relied upon the exploitation of resources and the environment? Do firms that discriminate in hiring and advancement policies also exploit the majority by dumping wastes into lakes and streams? Do firms that manufacture throwaway containers transfer part of their costs of cleanup and disposal to the taxpayers? And are firms that discriminate against certain groups in hiring and promotion capable or trustworthy enough to make decisions affecting the general welfare through the environment? Certainly it seems plausible that an increased awareness of discrimination and exploitation carried over to increased concern for the environment.

Additionally, minority groups became vocal and even violent about the quality of the central city environments into which many of their members were drawn and contained by overt and economic discrimination. The dissatisfaction and frustration of central city residents led to skyrocketing crime rates and to the suburban migration of white residents. The downtown areas of major cities became no-man's-land at night. Urban decay, crime, pollution, and fear began to spread like cancer from the inner city to outlying areas of the city, and even to suburban enclaves of the privileged classes. The urban environment had become truly repressive and disheartening to many Americans who lived in cities.

The energy crisis. The Arab oil embargo of 1973, followed by dramatic cost increases for all forms of energy, painfully accentuated our dependence upon the world's limited supply of raw materials and natural resources. The American public realized for the first time that the United States did not have unlimited access to basic resources. Furthermore, U.S. technology was incapable of replacing oil with a substitute energy source, except at huge cost, long delays, and great risk. The need to conserve energy suggested the desirability of conserving other resources, including the environment.

As the 1980s began, the high cost of energy consumption was revealed. Automobile makers emphasized mileage, and utility companies encouraged customers to reduce energy consumption. The effect on the U.S. economy was not positive; the history of growth in the American economy appeared to have been based upon energy exploitation.

RESPONSES TO ENVIRONMENTAL CONCERN

Legislation to preserve the environment has been enacted at all governmental levels. Generally, legislation enacted at the state and local levels has more directly affected land use and control than have federal laws. Federal laws have generally dealt with pollution standards and control and with the organization of administrative agencies to enforce pollution legislation. In 1974, when the U.S. Congress considered land planning and control legislation, strong elements of opposition were successful in preventing its passage. This legislation would have established standards and criteria for land planning and control for areas as small as counties and municipalities. If planning and control did not meet the federal standards, federal funds could be withheld from the jurisdiction. It seems doubtful that the country has seen the end of efforts to enact such legislation.

Federal response

The federal response to environmental concern consists of several significant laws and an administrative structure to carry out many aspects of environmental preservation. While the legislative effort in this field is not new—examples of pioneering legislation are the Public Health Service Act of 1912, the Oil Pollution Act of 1924, and the Water Pollution Control Act of 1948—our attention will be focused upon legislation and executive activity from the mid-1960s to the present time. Several of the laws enacted during this period were amendments to existing laws that had been passed earlier. For example, the Water Pollution Control Act Amendments of 1972 were only the latest in a series of amendments to the 1948 act.

Federal Water Pollution Control Act Amendments of 1972.   This act was a complete rewrite of all existing water pollution control laws on the federal statute books. It sets as a national goal the elimination of all pollution from America's waters by 1985. It requires secondary treatment for all municipal wastes by mid-1977, and the application of more advanced disposal methods by mid-1983. For industry, it establishes a two-phase cleanup program, with increasingly tight restrictions on industrial pollution, backed up by penalties of fines and imprisonment for violators.

President's Reorganization Plan No. 3 of 1970.   This executive order by President Nixon established the Environmental Protection Agency and transferred numerous functions and personnel from other departments and agencies to the new EPA. For example, the functions formerly vested in the Federal Water Quality Administration of the Department of the Interior and functions of the National Air Pollution Control Administration, the Environmental Control Administration, the Bureau of Solid Waste Management, the Bureau of Water Hygiene, and the Bureau of Radiological Health of the Department of Health, Education, and Welfare were mandated to the EPA.

The purpose of the EPA is to protect the health and welfare of

Americans by controlling environmental pollution hazards. The agency establishes and enforces air and water pollution standards, establishes drinking water standards, regulates the sale and use of pesticides, sets standards for noise and ambient radiation, develops techniques and procedures for solid waste management, studies toxic substances, conducts research, and demonstrates new pollution control methods and technology. Major federal laws administered by the agency include the Clean Air Act; the Federal Water Pollution Control Act; the Safe Drinking Water Act; the Solid Waste Disposal Act; the Federal Insecticide, Fungicide, and Rodenticide Act; and the Noise Control Act.

Clean Air Act of 1963. This act and its amendments[1] established comprehensive and specific requirements for the maintenance and improvement of air quality. Some of the act's more significant aspects were the following:

1. Establishment of various types of research programs relating to air pollution and pollutants.
2. Establishment of air quality control regions.
3. Requirement for the EPA administrator to establish ambient air quality standards.
4. Implementation plans and schedules.
5. Establishment of standards of performance of new stationary sources emitting air pollutants.
6. Establishment of emission standards for moving sources (such as automobiles and airplanes) of air pollutants.
7. Establishment of national emission standards for hazardous air pollutants.
8. Establishment of the president's Air Quality Advisory Board.

Noise Control Act of 1972. This legislation requires the EPA administrator to identify major sources of noise, noise criteria, and noise control technology. The administrator is charged with developing noise emission standards for products distributed in commerce, railroads, and motor carriers, and with assessing the adequacy of noise emission standards for new and existing aircraft and airports. Included in this charge is provision for the control of aircraft noise and sonic boom.

Solid Waste Disposal Act of 1965. This act seeks to promote the demonstration, construction, and application of solid waste management and resource recovery systems which preserve and enhance the

---

[1] Amendments to this act were made in the Motor Vehicle Air Pollution Control Act of 1965, the Clean Air Act Amendments of 1966, the Air Quality Act of 1967, and the Clean Air Amendments of 1970, 1971, 1973, and 1977.

quality of air, water, and land resources; to provide technical and financial assistance to states and local governments and interstate agencies in the planning and development of resource recovery and solid waste disposal programs; and to promote research and development in solid waste disposal and recycling.

National Materials Policy Act of 1970. This act established the National Commission on Materials Policy. It was the commission's task to develop a comprehensive policy with regard to the priorities, use, disposition, recycling, and environmental impact of various materials. The commission terminated after submission of its report to the president.

National Environmental Policy Act of 1969. This act established the Council on Environmental Quality within the executive office of the president and directed the president to submit an annual report to Congress on environmental quality. It also stated:

> It is the continuing policy of the federal government, in cooperation with state and local governments, and other concerned public and private organizations, to use all practicable means and measures, including financial and technical assistance, in a manner calculated to foster and promote the general welfare, to create and maintain conditions under which man and nature can exist in productive harmony, and fulfill the social, economic, and other requirements of present and future generations of Americans.

Among other provisions to implement this policy, the act requires all agencies of the federal government, in every recommendation or report on proposals for legislation and other major federal actions significantly affecting the quality of the human environment, to include a detailed statement on its environment impact, unavoidable adverse environmental effects, short-run versus long-run considerations, commitments of resources involved, and alternatives to the proposed action.

Coastal Zone Management Act of 1972. This law provides grants for any coastal state to develop a coastal zone management plan and program for the land and water resources of its coastal zones. The plans must identify permissible land and water uses and indicate how the state will enforce compatibility among land uses. The plans must also identify areas of particular concern and describe the planning and regulatory provisions for effectively managing the coastal zone. This act is administered by the National Oceanic and Atmospheric Administration of the U.S. Department of Commerce. Its goal is to avoid adverse impacts upon the coastal waters, which include the Great Lakes; the Atlantic, Pacific, and Arctic oceans; the Gulf of Mexico; and Long Island Sound.

Safe Drinking Water Act of 1974.   This act empowered the EPA to develop standards to safeguard public drinking water supplies from contaminants such as bacteria, inorganic chemicals, and organic pesticides. The standards have applied to more than 240,000 public water supplies since June 1977.

Energy Supply and Environmental Coordination Act of 1974 (ESECA).   This act requires the EPA to perform comprehensive planning activities which relate the utilization of energy and all aspects of the environment that are affected by such utilization. Energy programs such as nuclear power plants are particularly affected; evidence must be presented that air pollutants and contamination will not affect surrounding populations.

Speed limit law and gasoline rationing.   A limitation of highway speeds to 55 miles per hour and President Carter's 1980 Emergency Gasoline Rationing Act are designed to reduce fuel consumption and provide a logical plan for distributing fuel during an emergency. If an emergency occurs, the Rationing Act could lead to a dramatic change in where people live and work.

Historical register.   The federal government has provided for the registration of buildings and other landmarks which have historic significance. Once registered, the property is to be preserved if at all possible. If it is destroyed without meeting Register requirements, the property owner is disallowed federal income tax deductions that could normally be taken on demolition costs.

U.S. Army Corps of Engineers

In addition to the EPA, the U.S. Army Corps of Engineers has important regulatory authority over the nation's waterways. The corps' authority in this area derives from the Constitution through several laws and court decisions. The Constitution empowers Congress to "regulate commerce with foreign nations and among the several states," and it has been held that the power to regulate commerce includes the power to regulate navigation. The following laws and court decisions provide the authority for the regulatory activities of the U.S. Army Corps of Engineers.

River and Harbor Act of 1899.   Sections 9 through 20 of this act form the original basis for the corps' authority. Most important are Sections 9 and 10, which prohibit unauthorized construction in navigable waters of the United States.

Fish and Wildlife Act of 1958.   This act requires that consideration be given to fish and wildlife resources, and that federal and state fish and wildlife agencies coordinate their activities.

Zabel v. *Tabb* (1968).   This court decision established the precedent that all "public interest factors" must be considered in permit applications for dredge and fill operations.

National Environmental Policy Act of 1969.   As described previously, this act states the national policy of encouraging productive and enjoyable harmony between people and their environment.

Federal Water Pollution Control Act of 1972.   As described previously, this law governs the disposal of dredged or fill material in waterways.

Marine Protection Research and Sanctuaries Act of 1972.   This law regulates the transportation of dredged material for the purpose of dumping in ocean waters.

Coastal Zone Management Act of 1972.   As described previously, this act requires coordination with a state's coastal zone management plan.

In 1975 the corps was directed by a U.S. district court ruling to expand its regulatory authority to include *all waters* of the United States. This decision is estimated to extend the corps' jurisdiction over navigable waters from 50,000 miles to 5.5 million miles. Additionally, tributaries of navigable waters, marshlands, wetlands adjacent to navigable waters, interstate waters, and intrastate waters used for interstate purposes are included.

Revised regulations expanded the corps' responsibilities in three phases, as shown in Figure 21–1. These regulations require permits for activities such as construction of dams or dikes; obstruction or alteration of navigable water; construction of piers, wharves, bulkheads, pilings, marinas, or docks; dredging; and filling of waters or wetlands. No permit is granted unless its issuance is found to be in the public interest.

State response

A number of states have enacted legislation that affects many types of real estate developments more directly than do federal laws. Additionally, regional and local planning councils have become more concerned with environmental effects of proposed developments. Consequently, the planning councils and local governing bodies they advise have become more demanding in specifying the characteristics and features of developments to preserve the environment. Such requirements often add substantially to the costs of new developments or encourage developers to plan smaller and perhaps less efficient projects. In many cases, the concern of regional and local planning agencies results from state laws mandating their supervision. State legislation can generally be classified as to requirements for environmental

FIGURE 21–1
Regulatory authority of U.S. Army Corps of Engineers

PRIOR TO 25 JULY 1975

Regulatory authority under River and Harbor Act of 1899. (Includes all "navigable waters" and coastal areas)

Typical River Basin

Coastal Area

PHASE I

* Effective 25 July 1975
* Extends existing permit procedures to include adjacent wetlands
* Wetlands – – Endangered and valuable resource

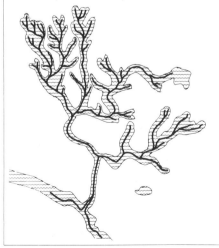

PHASE II

* Effective 1 July 1976
* Initiate regulation of discharges of dredged or fill material into:

  Primary tributaries of navigable waters
  Lakes greater than five acres
  Adjacent wetlands

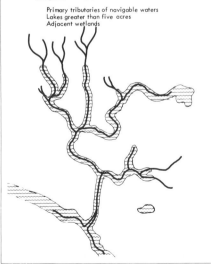

PHASE III

* Effective 1 July 1977
* Regulate discharges of dredged or fill material into other waters up to their headwaters of 5 cubic feet per second or less (Includes all tributaries)

impact statements, preservation of environmentally endangered zones, and planning and zoning.

Environmental impact statements.   A number of states require that developers of projects of certain size or having certain characteristics prepare a detailed analysis of the impact of these projects upon the environment or upon such subsystems as water, sewers, and transportation. In California, for example, the Environmental Quality Act of 1970 is modeled after the National Environmental Policy Act of 1969 and requires the preparation of environmental impact reports (EIR) on all state and local projects which are permitted or funded by state or local agencies. Any EIR must contain the following information:

1. Environmental impact of the proposed action.
2. Adverse environmental effects which cannot be avoided if the proposal is implemented.
3. Measures proposed to minimize the impact.
4. Alternatives to the proposed action.
5. Relationship between short-term and long-term considerations.
6. Irreversible environmental changes which the proposed action might cause.
7. Growth-inducing impact of the proposed action.

The Florida Environmental Land and Water Management Act of 1972 requires approval for any proposed development which, because of its character, magnitude, or location, would have a substantial effect on the health, safety, or welfare of citizens of more than one county. The application must contain a detailed analysis of these items:

1. Environment and natural resources.
2. Regional economy.
3. Public facilities.
4. Public transportation.
5. Housing.
6. Other relevant areas.

Such projects are termed "developments of regional impact" (DRIs), and are defined for various types of uses. For example, a *residential* development is deemed to be a DRI if it is planned to contain more than the following numbers of units:

1. 250 units—in counties of less than 25,000 population.
2. 500 units—in counties with a population between 25,000 and 50,000.
3. 750 units—in counties with a population between 50,000 and 100,000.

4. 1,000 units—in counties with a population between 100,000 and
    250,000.
5. 2,000 units—in counties with a population between 250,000 and
    500,000.
6. 3,000 units—in counties of more than 500,000 population.

Estimates of cost for the preparation of an environmental impact
statement or a DRI application range from $20,000 to $40,000 for a
straightforward residential project to $150,000 for a large, fairly com-
plex residential project. The cost of environmental impact statements
for commercial projects ranges from $50,000 for a small shopping
center to $250,000 for a regional shopping center. And, of course, these
costs do not include additional charges or requirements which may be
imposed for approval of the project. Frequently, developers must add
or upgrade sewer treatment plants, water systems, water drainage retention ponds, and transportation systems. Needless to say, environmentally motivated requirements have greatly increased the "front-
end costs" of developments. If the demand for these developments is
inelastic, the costs can be transferred to consumers through increased
rents and prices, while an elastic demand structure will result in the
project's inability to cover costs. Investment decisions resulting from a
consideration of total costs should thus reflect more accurately the
environmentally related costs and social priorities.

Preservation of environmentally endangered lands. Some states
have passed laws that stringently regulate environmentally endangered zones or provide for outright purchase by the state of such
areas. Again, Florida and California have been leaders in this type of
legislation. Some states, such as Oregon, Maryland, and Nevada, require state government review of local zoning decisions that would
have broader, regional impact. California's Coastal Zone Conservation
Act of 1972 gives a state commission and six regional commissions the
task of developing a comprehensive, enforceable plan for the conservation and management of the entire California coastal zone. The zone is
defined as an area extending from three miles offshore to the highest
elevation of the mountain range closest to shore, or five miles from the
mean high tide line. Additionally, the commissions are empowered to
regulate all construction up to 1,000 yards inland from the mean high
tide line by denial of permits for development within their territorial
jurisdictions. These permits are required in addition to other, customary required approvals such as zoning, subdivision, and building permits.

The Florida legislation allows the governor and cabinet to designate
areas of critical state concern. Once an area has been so designated, the
local governments within the area must adopt land development regu-

lations that are satisfactory to the state land planning agency, the governor, and the cabinet. If such regulations are not adopted and implemented, the state may impose its own regulations. The threat of such a state imposition of development regulations created a great deal of controversy when it was applied to the Florida Keys. As reported by *Business Week*, some local business people were afraid that the regulations would discourage development and disrupt the local tax base. Robert Matthews of the Council of State Governments stated, "It is the first time a state government has stepped in to take over the local planning function."[2]

Planning and zoning. As noted above, several states encourage or require adequate planning to preserve and protect the environment. States review local planning and zoning regulations and decisions that affect larger areas or environmentally endangered areas. And states have established regional planning agencies and commissions, as well as state agencies, to review and approve large-scale developments or developments in environmentally threatened areas. Hawaii, Vermont, Florida, Maine, Minnesota, and Oregon currently have the greatest influence in statewide land-use planning and control. However, many predominantly rural counties and communities in almost all states still have weak local land-use controls. Additional state intervention in local areas where minimal planning and zoning exist seems inevitable.

ECONOMIC ASPECTS OF ENVIRONMENTAL ISSUES

A major shift in public attitudes toward the environment suggests a national reordering of priorities, costs, and economic advantage. The need for such reordering reflects an inappropriate structure of charges applied to the production and delivery of many goods and services. This structure has not recognized the full costs of both private and public products. It has encouraged greater, not lesser, consumption and destruction, rather than conservation, of the environment. In attempting to steer a changed course of direction through the murky waters of environmental concern, policymakers at all levels need to be cognizant of the economic effects of externalities, marginal cost pricing, efficiencies of scale, and cost-benefit analysis.

Externalities

External economies or diseconomies result from goods that have a positive or negative effect upon people other than those who produce

---

[2] "A State Crackdown Scares the Developers," *Business Week*, August 11, 1975, pp. 22–24.

or own the good. For example, an external economy occurs when one class of ticket purchasers for a concert pay a price higher than the cost of their seats so that others may attend at a subsidized price. External economies also occur when property owners landscape the front of their properties so that others may enjoy the beauty. When external economies are applicable on a wide scale, the product or service is a good candidate for governmental provision. Bridges, highways, police and fire protection, and other commonly provided services are provided more cheaply per customer through common purchase by the government than through separate purchase by each individual. Perhaps national defense is the most conspicuous example of external economies achieved by governmental activity. It would be prohibitively expensive for citizens to provide their own systems of national defense.

External diseconomies occur when costs or inconveniences are imposed by an individual or a firm upon other people. For example, the person who litters imposes the costs of cleanup upon other people. The business firm that erects an unattractive sign imposes the cost of offensive visual sensations upon all who must pass the sign. Similarly, the factory that spews forth smoke, soot, and fumes imposes serious costs upon all who happen to be in the path of the pollutants. The costs imposed by radioactive fallout from the testing of thermonuclear weapons constitute perhaps the most dramatic example of external diseconomies of wide geographic scope.

Exploitation of the environment typically produces external diseconomies. When an individual or a business firm pollutes water or air, despoils the countryside, or allows property to deteriorate, the resulting costs, inconveniences, and offenses must be borne by many people. When a manufacturer does not include such costs in the price of the products, purchasers of the products pay a price that is too low. If the prices had to be set to cover all costs (including those required to prevent or clean up pollution), fewer items would be sold. Thus, a redistribution of costs would produce a shift in the priorities among various products and services that would more accurately reflect economic preferences. Conversely, subsidized costs tend to establish inappropriate preference patterns that fail to reflect the true priorities of social needs. Some goods cost too much; others cost too little. Inefficiency is the result.

Federal and state laws that require standards to be met in such areas as air pollution, water pollution, or oil spills raise the cost of certain products. For example, equipping automobiles with antipollution devices raises their cost. Such costs are then usually transmitted to the products' purchasers in the form of increased prices. Depending upon the price elasticity for the products, manufacturers may be able to cover the additional cost fully, or they may have to absorb part of the increased cost. Some manufacturers may be forced out of business; others may have to drop or modify some product lines.

In the real estate field, state and local regulations often require developers and builders to design and construct projects in a more costly manner than would be done otherwise. Zoning ordinances and building codes have long imposed certain kinds of additional costs upon builders that they might choose not to incur otherwise. More recently, however, additional laws and regulations that require developers of large projects to consider the impact of these projects upon regional systems and environmental concerns have greatly added to development costs. Such considerations often require developers to widen public roads, construct pedestrian walkways and overpasses, provide for the handicapped, preserve natural features of the terrain, construct sewage treatment systems, install traffic lights, and take any other steps needed to conform to the recommendations of local, regional, or state planning agencies.

As mentioned previously, the result of laws and regulations that impose additional costs upon real estate developers, as well as manufacturers and other business firms, is to shift the burden of many external diseconomies to the consumers of the products. Such shifts represent an attempt to internalize previously external costs or diseconomies.

Marginal cost pricing

The U.S. economy has tended to reward larger numbers and size over smaller numbers and size. For example, manufacturers of automobiles tend to produce additional cars as long as marginal revenue exceeds marginal costs. Profit margins are greater for standard-size automobiles than for compacts, for luxury cars than for more modest models. Utility companies have been classic examples of a decreasing cost industry in which unit costs are lowered by higher levels of output. Thus the tendency has been to encourage greater use of utility services by pricing marginal amounts lower than the average costs. Such pricing breaks have typically given large customers lower per unit prices and have encouraged greater, rather than lesser, use of utility services. Rapidly increasing energy costs have shifted the relationship between fixed and variable costs. With variable fuel costs taking a much larger share of total costs, the old decreasing rate pricing policies may no longer reflect the marginal costs incurred.

On the other side of marginal price influences has been the tendency of some city services, such as water and garbage removal, to be priced at average cost when marginal costs are actually increasing. In other words, new outlying areas of communities are sometimes provided with such services at prices lower than the costs incurred to provide the services. The effect of such pricing, of course, is to subsidize and encourage new development at the periphery of cities. In its extreme form, such subsidization helps produce urban sprawl. And urban sprawl produces added social costs of its own, in terms of transportation costs, increased burdens on community services, and various forms of pollution.

As demonstrated by Guntermann, the economically correct and efficient solution to the problem of pricing products and services whose production contributes to environmental degradation is to internalize all environmental costs, as well as other production costs, and to charge prices reflecting total marginal costs.[3] This solution, however, is extremely difficult and costly to impose. After all, how do we know when all costs are truly internalized? The costs of air pollution or urban sprawl, for example, are virtually impossible to measure.

Additionally, there are costs associated with identifying, measuring, and enforcing antipollution requirements. One recently reported example illustrates a situation in which the control of pollution from one source may generate even more pollution from another source:

> Coming clean, or maybe not. Armco Steel Corp. says special pollution-control equipment it had to install at one plant cleans up 21.2 pounds of visible iron oxide dust every hour. But the equipment is run by a 1,020-horsepower electric motor, Armco notes. "Producing that power at the electric utility's plant spews out 23 pounds an hour of sulphur and nitrogen oxides and other gaseous pollution," the company claims.[4]

Thus, another economic principle should be recognized with respect to pollution control: the marginal cost associated with identifying, measuring, and enforcing environmental protection efforts should not exceed the value of the marginal benefit to be derived from doing so.

The goal of marginal cost pricing is to reflect accurately in consumer prices the full cost of producing the unit to be consumed. If the costs of environmental preservation are included in these costs, the total stock of wealth in the economy is not diminished. As Boulding has expressed this view:

> The essential measure of the success of the economy is not production and consumption at all, but the nature, extent, quality and complexity of the total capital stock. . . . And any technological change which results

---

[3] Karl L. Guntermann, "Cost-Benefit Analysis and the Economics of Air Pollution" in *Real Estate and Urban Land Analysis*, edited by James R. Cooper and Karl L. Guntermann (Lexington, Mass.: D. C. Heath, 1974), pp. 151–63.

[4] *The Wall Street Journal*, March 25, 1976, p. 1.

in the maintenance of a given total stock with a lessened throughput (that is, less production and consumption) is clearly a gain.[5]

Economies of scale

The basic economic principle of increasing returns to scale is indirectly responsible for a large part of our environmental difficulties. It explains why many of our goods and products are produced by large companies in large factories. The principle states that when all input factors are increased at the same time in the same proportion, output may be increased by an even greater proportionate amount. The key is, as those readers who have been students of economics may remember, that *all* inputs are increased. Decreasing returns may occur when some inputs are increased, while others are held constant or are increased by a smaller proportionate amount.

Since many production processes go through a stage of increasing returns to scale, there is a natural tendency for firms to expand the size of their manufacturing facilities to take advantage of the increased output. And, of course, the number of managers and other support personnel and facilities must also be expanded. Along with the greater output of goods and products, however, is also produced a proportionately greater quantity of pollutants. In other words, the undesirable outputs obtain the scalar effects, just as do the desirable outputs. Thus, the smoke, soot, and chemical pollutants *may* be increased more than two times with a doubling of factory size (if technological improvements to control pollution are not incorporated into the new factory).

On the other side, it should be noted that the higher productivity and profit levels emanating from larger scale operations may enable firms to expend larger amounts to curtail or limit environmental pollutants. Whether firms voluntarily incur such costs often determines what net effect the increased size of operations has on the environment.

The steel industry in Pittsburgh provides a good example of the stages of physical growth, environmental pollution, and subsequent cleanup. The industry's plants expanded through the 1940s, emitting ever-increasing amounts of pollutants. During the 1950s, however, a concerted, largely voluntary, community-industry program resulted in substantial cleanup efforts by the industry, removal of dilapidated business structures from downtown, and construction of many new, mod-

---

[5] Kenneth E. Boulding, "The Economics of the Coming Spaceship Earth," in *Environmental Quality in a Growing Economy,* edited by Henry Jarrett (Baltimore: Johns Hopkins Press, for Resources for the Future, 1966), pp. 9–10.

ern buildings in Pittsburgh's "golden triangle." Industry leaders saw curtailment of pollution as an absolute necessity for the continued viability, and even survival, of the city. And many external costs were internalized through the expenditure of retained profits, obtained from operations based upon efficiencies of scale.

Other types of developments and projects may also have potential environmental advantages, as well as disadvantages, resulting from scalar size. Although large shopping centers create environmental problems (such as traffic, water and waste disposal, and inharmonious relationships with neighboring residential areas), one large shopping center may be less environmentally damaging than several smaller ones. And one large, well-planned residential area may contain more adequate environmental safeguards than several smaller developments. For example, the larger development can utilize one water system, one sewage disposal system, and one system of other municipal services. Smaller, less-well-planned areas may place proportionately larger burdens upon the community and the environment. Thus, some current environmental legislation may have the effect of defeating the potential benefits from economies of scale.

Cost-benefit analysis

We have already noted the principle that the marginal costs of identifying, measuring, and enforcing environmental protection measures should not exceed the value of the marginal benefit to be derived from doing so. While the principle is a valid proposition of economic theory, it is often a hazardous and tenuous basis upon which to make many types of decisions.

Hazards stem from the difficulties of quantifying both sides of the equation. First, the costs associated with environmental preservation or cleanup may be extremely high. The direct costs of installing special equipment, water and sewage treatment systems, water runoff retaining ponds, special landscaping, traffic facilitation and control devices, and so on, may easily double the cost of a project. Additionally, however, indirect costs may be even higher and virtually impossible to measure. The costs of preserving or restoring the environment may involve extending or enlarging the area's transportation system (for example, the Disney World development in central Florida, which required an expansion of the highway system for many miles in all directions), the provision of additional water and sewage facilities and other municipal services, or the curtailment of some private rights and privileges (perhaps limiting the use of private automobiles in smog-susceptible areas such as Los Angeles, Phoenix, or Washington, D.C.).

The benefits obtained by incurring such costs are usually even more difficult to measure. What is the value of the prevention of disease and early death from smoke and chemical pollution for an undeterminable number of an area's residents? What is the value of preventing consumers from being poisoned by the mercury found in fish products from Lake Erie? And what is the value of wildlife preservation, clear streams, and the aesthetic appeal of residential, commercial, or even industrial developments?

Cost-benefit analysis is used to attempt the measurement of such costs and benefits. Costs are conceptually easier to measure because they involve capital outlays, capitalized expenditures, or outflows. Benefits, however, often involve nonfinancial matters. The cost of preventing the mercury contamination of Lake Erie may be quantifiable; the benefits are more subjective.

To utilize cost-benefit analysis, some measurement of the benefits, as well as the costs, must be undertaken. The income to the Lake Erie fishing industry would be one of the benefits in the example. The average earning power of the people who would otherwise die from mercury poisoning, for the average length of life curtailed, might be the measure of another major benefit. This average benefit would be applied to the estimated number of people so benefited, and the total earning power saved would be discounted at the appropriate rate for human life. Other, less-major benefits, such as the preservation of safe swimming and plant life in the lake, would also be included in the analysis.

Although the task may be difficult, values can be estimated for the various benefits. As can be seen, the benefits are usually measured by the value of damages avoided. Such values will often require large amounts of judgment and informed guesses. As Guntermann concludes, however: "Even rough estimates of damages are better than none at all and may allow those in a policy position to make more rational control decisions."[6] Nevertheless, the nature of the estimates and the types of judgments entering into them should be clearly understood by policymakers in deciding the types and amounts of environmental preservation efforts to be undertaken.

TRENDS AND THE FUTURE

Hopefully, the previous sections provide some idea of the outpouring of legislation that has been designed to counteract specific aspects of environmental degradation. Although the various federal laws do not directly address the problems and issues of land-use control, sev-

---

[6] Guntermann, "Cost-Benefit Analysis," p. 162.

eral of them contain general references or inferences regarding land-use regulation. For example, the Water Pollution Control Act of 1972 refers to land-use control as one means of achieving the goals of reduced pollution of rivers and lakes. And the Clean Air Act of 1970 specifies that land-use controls and state review of new sources of air pollution be utilized to achieve and maintain national air quality standards.

The State A–95 Review process requires that developers submit plats of their proposed developments to agencies for determination that these will not pose pollution problems. The agencies go even further, requiring that archaeologists inspect the property to prevent developments which might cause a loss of any artifacts or elements which are of significance to our national heritage.

Even more directly, however, the additional front-end costs imposed both by federal and state environmental legislation forebode a restructuring of costs and priorities. Whether the marginal benefits will prove to equal the marginal costs required to alleviate the perceived difficulties can only be ascertained over the long-term future. Perhaps an even more realistic question is whether the laws and regulations can come close to accomplishing their stated objectives, no matter what level of cost is incurred. Given the numerous federal and state programs that have failed totally or partially, the question seems fair.

It is also apparent that the state and federal legislative response to environmental concerns has resulted in a hodgepodge of requirements and regulations to cover concerns of the moment. Pamela C. Mack terms this the "ad hoc approach" and demonstrates that such an approach to other types of concerns has often produced unintended results which turned out to be worse than the original problems.[7] Her principal concern, however, is that although the various environmental laws contain important land-use implications, they are not coordinated in any comprehensive land-use policy. Such laws may even be counterproductive. "For example, implementation of the water act could mean sewer moratoriums in prime suburban areas. The developer would then seek land further out where sewer permits are available. Thus, leapfrog development occurs and results in more urban sprawl."[8]

Finally, it seems clear that environmental concerns and legislation have been spawned by growth—demographic and economic. People generate pollution, and more people generate more pollution. And

---

[7] Pamela C. Mack, "Piecemeal Approach Dilutes Federal Environmental Laws," *Mortgage Banker* 34, no. 12 (September 1974): 6–10.

[8] Ibid., p. 7.

when combined with continually increasing levels of production of every conceivable type of consumer good, pollution has reached unacceptable magnitudes. As Ralph R. Widner has stated: "Most of our concerns with the problems of growth now center upon the undesired consequences that flow from the development of a metropolitanized, land-hungry, high-energy, high-consumption society."[9] These consequences have taxed the capacity of the air, the lakes, the oceans, and natural resources—all of which seemed to have infinite capacity only a few years ago. Thus, growth control policies and laws will inevitably be intertwined with environmental policies and laws. The combined impact upon land use and development can only involve more government involvement and control. Such control must attempt to balance the often conflicting demands of private property rights, environmental preservation, and economic advancement.

It seems likely that the future role of land-use determination and real estate development will be regarded as a matter for public concern. Private property rights will be increasingly constrained by laws and regulations expressing the public's concern for the environment, growth control, and efficiency in land utilization. Land seems destined to be increasingly regarded as a public resource; developers will find their alternatives limited and buffeted by often costly, sometimes capricious, but almost always serious and searching public review.

SUMMARY

Increasing concern about preservation of the environment has produced additional factors that must be considered in real estate development and investment. These factors often result in increased costs of development for projects to meet various requirements imposed by federal, state, and local governments. Criteria for the maintenance of water and air quality, disposal of solid waste, control of noise, protection of drinking water supplies, and preservation of coastal zones have been mandated by federal legislation. Requirements for environmental impact reports, the purchase or control of environmentally endangered lands, and regulation of local planning and zoning procedures have been instituted in some states.

The dramatic rise of environmental concern during the last 15 years undoubtedly stems from such phenomena as the increasing population and population shifts, industrialization and urbanization of society, unprecedented economic prosperity, the struggle for full civil

---

[9] Ralph R. Widner, "State Growth and Federal Policies: A Reassessment of Responsibilities," in *Management and Control of Growth* (Washington, D.C.: Urban Land Institute, 1975), vol. 3, p. 404.

rights by minority groups, and the realization that energy supplies and other natural resources are not unlimited. Although the resulting legislation and administrative structures have expressed the country's desire to preserve the environment, severe burdens have sometimes been placed upon real estate development. In addition to the added direct costs, developers may also incur indirect costs through changed traffic patterns, shifts in migratory patterns, encouragement of less efficient developments, and imposition of requirements that do not accomplish their stated objectives. The justification for the added costs must be the internalization of a development's total costs, including environmental charges.

In determining whether environmental costs should be imposed, the economic principle that the additional benefits should at least equal the added costs should prevail. In attempting to implement the principle, policymakers should consider such economic concepts as externalities, marginal cost pricing, efficiencies of scale, and cost-benefit ratios. Their proper use and measurement would produce costing and pricing policies that reflect the value placed by society upon a clean, healthful environment.

QUESTIONS FOR REVIEW

1. What environmental legislation has been enacted by your state's legislature within the past ten years? In what ways does it affect real estate development?

2. How could air pollution affect real estate values? Do you believe it is in the best interest of real estate developers to allow pollution to increase? Why or why not?

3. What is the role of the Environmental Protection Agency? Identify some of the laws administered by the agency.

4. Explain the economic principle that should determine the level of costs that is imposed upon developers and consumers for environmental preservation.

5. What is cost-benefit analysis, and how does it relate to the analysis of environmental legislation and programs?

6. How may some types of environmental requirements encourage less efficient developments?

7. How does marginal cost pricing relate to internalization of the costs of environmental preservation?

REFERENCES

Beaton, William R., and Bond, Robert J. *Real Estate.* Pacific Palisades, Calif.: Goodyear, 1976, chap. 25.

Boulding, Kenneth E. "The Economics of the Coming Spaceship Earth." In *Environmental Quality in a Growing Economy,* edited by Henry Jarrett. Baltimore: Johns Hopkins Press, for Resources for the Future, 1966, pp. 9–10.

Guntermann, Karl L. "Cost-Benefit Analysis and the Economics of Air Pollution." In *Real Estate and Urban Land Analysis,* edited by James R. Cooper and Karl L. Guntermann. Lexington, Mass.: D. C. Heath, 1974, pp. 151–63.

Hodges, Allan A. "California Environmental Laws Challenge Real Estate and Finance Industries." *Mortgage Banker* 36, no. 1 (October 1975): 42–48.

Mortgage Banker 34, no. 12 (September 1974). Entire issue is devoted to articles on environmental matters.

Natural Resources Defense Council. *Land Use Controls in the United States.* Elaine Moss, editor. New York: Dial Press/James Wade, 1977.

Urban Land Institute. *Management and Control of Growth.* Vols. 1, 2, and 3. Washington, D.C.: Urban Land Institute, 1975.

chapter 22

Overview

Readers who have perused this volume from the beginning may have become very impatient with the authors. "When," they may ask, "are they going to discuss the important aspects of real estate?" Most of our readers, we suspect, became acquainted with our book because of curiosity about the real estate business or because they heard that real estate might be a profitable investment. The successful ventures of real estate investors and operators are reported daily in the popular press. *Syndication, joint ventures, tax-free income,* and other terms have become part of our vocabulary. Books such as Nickerson's *How I Turned $1,000 into a Million in Real Estate in My Spare Time*[1] are not uncommon. Readers whose eagerness has been whetted by such material may wonder when the authors will explain the secrets of how to make a killing in real estate.

The authors believe that they have discussed the attributes which cause real estate to be a profitable and satisfying investment for many persons and a successful occupation for others. There would be not real estate success stories without the basic want-satisfying power of the economic good. Consequently, a portion of this treatise has been devoted to the characteristics of real estate that yield productivity and value.

---

[1] William Nickerson, *How I Turned $1,000 into a Million in Real Estate in My Spare Time* (New York: Simon and Schuster, 1959).

Analytical approach.   An analytical approach to real estate investment has been proposed, in which market value and investment value are central concepts. Appraisal methodologies provide techniques for estimating market value, which can be adapted to computations of investment value or justified investment price. Other return on investment calculations have been examined as additional criteria for ranking investment alternatives.

These measurements of the relative value or worth of a real estate investment in Chapters 4, 5, 6 and 7 show the mathematical end product of the many determinants affecting the future productivity and risk of the investment. These physical, locational, economic, and social determinants are too numerous to recount in detail in this brief overview. However, among the major factors affecting real estate value are the physical characteristics of the land and improvements; the character of the neighborhood or district in which the property is located; the market conditions in which the property is competing; the economic strength and stability of the local, regional, and national economies; property rights transferred and other legal aspects; form of ownership; financing; tax factors; and the public actions, controls, and regulations affecting the property and its future productivity.

Real estate business.   Several sections of this book concern various types of real estate businesses. In the minds of most people, the real estate business is most closely associated with real estate brokerage. Brokers and their sales staffs are the most visible participants in the real estate business. Most of us have utilized or will utilize their services in buying or selling our homes and other properties. The real estate business, however, encompasses a variety of occupations in the private and public sectors related to land development and construction, financing, management, law, appraisal, consulting, and brokerage. Each of these occupations has its specialties. Real estate brokerage, for instance, includes persons who specialize in one type of real estate (such as single-family residences or industrial properties), in negotiating leases, in arranging exchanges, and in effecting transactions.

The real estate business utilizes the economic and institutional aspects of real estate in organizing for the planning, production, financing, and marketing of the product. When persons in the business are creative in combining the various determinants of value, a profit should materialize. The real estate business has always offered great potential for creativity and resultant imitation as others attempt to duplicate successful ventures. We can all recount the history of several recent "innovations," such as 95 percent conventional loans, condominiums and quadraminiums, planned unit developments, new towns, resort communities and ranchettes for $10 down and $10 a

month, wraparound mortgages, variable rate and renegotiated rate
mortgages, equity participations, joint ventures and syndications, and
prefabricated and modular units; the list continually lengthens. These
newsworthy developments in the real estate business obtain the most
publicity. Many of the developments have been mentioned in this text,
although the authors believe that detailed treatment should be reserved for advanced courses.

Administrative processes.   Another major emphasis of this text has
been on the decision-making process. In this regard, the authors have
chosen to place the process in the context of an administrative framework. The close relationship between administration in the private
sector and administration in the public sector has been stressed. Individuals and firms in the private sector combine land and improvements to create useful properties and valuable assets that are attractive
to investors. The functions of production, financing, marketing, and
management in the real estate business are manifestations of administration in the private sector. Administration in the public sector by the
executive, legislative, and judicial branches and the bureaucracy results in laws, regulations, and programs which may have nationwide
effects. Zoning regulations, building codes, federal housing, community development, the property tax, and transportation policies and
subsidies are examples of publicly enacted rules and programs which
become inputs to the administration of our real estate resources. They
comprise part of the list of determinants of real estate productivity and
value.

PROGNOSIS

The excitement of real estate as an academic field of study comes
from two principal sources. First, there is the challenge of adapting the
theory, concepts, and analytical methods from several disciplines in
the process of analyzing the production of real estate and its investment qualities. Then, there is the need to impose ever-changing institutional factors upon the analytical framework.

Theory and concepts.   Real estate "principles," divested of their
institutional wrappings, are economic principles. Economic models
are used to analyze urban economies and local housing markets. Recent developments in regional and urban economics blend with materials often included in real estate courses, particularly in the analyses
of urban economies and the location of firms and households. The
analysis of real estate investments claims kinship with the financial
analysis of the firm, capital budgeting, and security analysis. General
marketing and management theories and concepts are applicable to
the real estate business. City planning, sociology, psychology, and

geography make their contributions. Advancements in the state of the art in real estate investment analysis and appraisal; in housing market research; in understanding the motivations of investors, homebuyers, and renters; in organizing for efficient production and marketing of the product; and in other aspects of the field of real estate undoubtedly will come from continued adaptation of work in fields related to real estate problems.

Institutional factors.   The study of real estate is differentiated from other academic fields by the institutional characteristics of the subject. Legal aspects, for instance, are a large part of these institutional characteristics. The law mirrors the attitudes and mores of our society. In recent years, statutory law and court interpretations have combined in a manner that affects real estate investment and the actions of persons involved in the real estate business. Civil rights legislation, open-housing requirements, and court decisions in antitrust cases have been in the forefront of the evolution of the law.

The provision of new housing in our cities is primarily dependent upon the economic and demographic factors underlying the demand for shelter. However, enabling legislation permitting ownership of condominium units has created a new housing submarket. Legislation permitting the formation of real estate investment trusts has enabled the small investor to obtain the benefits and risks of real estate investments. Each new federal tax law has had repercussions on the profitability of real estate investment. The so-called tax shelters available to real estate investors were created initially to stimulate investment in needed social capital. In several recent "tax reform" acts, however, Congress pared away some of the shelters it previously created.

The real estate cycle is wasteful of our precious human and natural resources and has been ruinous to many individuals and firms in the real estate business. To a large extent, the fluctuations in real estate construction have been attributable to monetary conditions. New channels for the flow of funds into the mortgage market have been opened by the deregulation of financial institutions and through innovations introduced under the auspices of the Federal Home Loan Bank Board, the Federal Home Loan Mortgage Corporation, the Federal National Mortgage Association, and the Government National Mortgage Association. Federal housing (Section 235, Section 8, and so on) has continued in quantity even in periods of tight monetary policy. The combined impact of these actions has the potential of containing fluctuations in housing starts within tolerable limits. Further efforts to stabilize the availability of credit and construction are to be expected.

The physical character of the housing unit is progressing to modular components and modular units, and further innovations in construction techniques and materials are being encouraged by government programs. Concomitant with new construction techniques has been the industrialization of housing, applying the concept of mass production to the housing industry. Large-scale developments worthy of being called "new towns" have been fairly common. The profitability of real estate developments has attracted insurance companies into joint ventures with developers who obtain the needed long-term commitments of equity capital for developments on a very large scale. American industry has also experimented with large-scale real estate development as a potentially profitable activity and, in some instances, as a market for their products. The scale of developments in general has become larger. Real estate development firms are often merged or controlled by industrial corporations, providing them with the capital necessary to undertake larger projects. The scale of development is reflected in the diversification of the firms in the real estate business. A single firm and its subsidiaries may include a mortgage company, a brokerage company, a construction company, an investment company to buy and hold land and other properties, and a property management company.

Government involvement with real estate has been increasing. Our nation is experiencing changes in social attitudes as we become more wealthy and urbanized. Acquisition of the means to obtain a better quality of life and increased interdependence in an urban environment reduce our tolerance for nuisances, for inequities in the distribution of opportunities, and for self-seeking actions considered to be detrimental to the social welfare. At the same time, our falling level of tolerance has been met by the rising intensity of certain nuisances, such as congestion and pollution. Government regulation, subsidies, and other actions are often prompted by these conditions. Hopefully, our democratic form of government will continue to permit the will of the majority of our citizens to be reflected in these actions. The authors of this basic text find that, over time, a larger part of their courses in real estate principles has been devoted to what we have called "administration" of our real estate resources. This trend is expected to continue.

Appendixes

appendix A

Laws prohibiting

discrimination in housing

Title VIII of the Civil Rights Act of 1968, which is better known as the Federal Fair Housing Law, bans discrimination in the sale, rental, and leasing of housing in the United States because of race, color, religion, or national origin.

Under this law the following are typical discriminatory acts which are declared illegal:

1. Refusing to sell, rent, or deal with any person.
2. Making different terms and conditions for buying or renting housing.
3. Advertising housing as available to only certain buyers.
4. Denying that housing is available for inspection for sale or rental when it is actually available.
5. Persuading someone to sell housing by telling him minority groups are moving in—commonly called *blockbusting*.
6. Denying home loans or making different home loan terms by lender.
7. Denying or limiting the use of real estate services to anyone.
8. Coercing, intimidating, or interfering with any person in the exercise or enjoyment of these federal rights.

Enforcement procedures and penalties are as follows:

1. An aggrieved person may file a complaint with HUD, which can attempt to conciliate after investigation.
2. A civil suit may be filed by an individual in a federal or state court.
3. The U.S. Department of Justice can investigate and bring suit if the attorney general has reasonable cause to believe there is a pattern or practice of resistance to the act, or if the attorney general believes that the case is one of general public importance.
4. The court may issue an injunction requiring or preventing the home or apartment sale or rental.
5. *Damages may be assessed against the defendant.*

Properties and people covered by this law include housing in the United States except the rental of apartments up to four families if the owner occupies one, religious organizations and private clubs, and homeowners who do not use the services of a real estate broker or advertise discriminatorily in the sale of a single-family home.

These exemptions have been negated by many state fair housing laws, such as the Ohio Fair Housing Act of 1969 and a provision of the Federal Civil Rights Act of 1866, as interpreted by the U.S. Supreme Court in a case known as *Jones* v. *Mayer Co.*, decided in 1968.

U.S. SUPREME COURT DECISION

Jones v. Mayer Co. (June 17, 1968)

In *Jones* v. *Mayer Co.*, a case emanating from St. Louis and charging racial discrimination in the sale of housing, the U.S. Supreme Court ruled that a law, enacted at the close of the Civil War in 1866 and reenacted in 1870 to protect the freed slaves and assure them equal citizenship, was applicable today in housing.

The law "bars all racial discrimination, private as well as public, in the sale or rental of property."

This law and its present-day application make it clear that racial discrimination by anyone in the sale or rental of property is illegal.

Under this mandate, no exemptions such as are permitted under the 1968 Federal Fair Housing Act can exist. No discrimination on a racial basis in housing can exist.

This ruling is enforceable by the federal district court or an appropriate state court.

STATE OF OHIO FAIR HOUSING LAW (HOUSE BILL 432)

As of November 12, 1969, when sections 4112.01 and 4112.99 of the Ohio Revised Code became effective, discrimination in the sale, rental, or leasing of housing on the basis of race, color, religion, national origin, or ancestry became illegal.

This law prohibits the following actions or activities in housing in Ohio by property owners or their agents:

1. Falsely denying availability.
2. Refusing to show.
3. Refusing to sell, rent, and so on, because of the race, religion, or ethnic background of any actual or prospective owner, occupant, or user of the property.
4. Inquiring into the keeping of records relating to property sales or rentals concerning race, religion, or ethnic origin.
5. Advertising or circulating any statement indicating a preference or limitation based on race, religion, or ethnic origin in connection with sales or rentals.
6. Aiding or abetting the commitment of any unlawfully discriminatory act or obstructing another person from complying with the law.
7. Inducing or soliciting real estate activity by representing that the presence or anticipated presence of persons of any race, religion, and so forth, will have any of the following effects:
    a. lowering of property value.
    b. change in the racial, religious, or ethnic composition of the area.
    c. an increase in criminal or antisocial behavior.

Real estate agents following the mandates of this law are protected from harassment and intimidation. Threats by neighbors of retaliation against real estate brokers in the event a home is sold to unwanted neighbors are not allowed and are violations of the law.

All real property in the state of Ohio is covered by this law. There are no exceptions! From single-family homes to vacant lots—from hotel rooms to graveyards.

These courses of action are open to aggrieved persons:

1. The court may order affirmative action.
2. The court may issue an injunction if it finds a discriminatory practice has occurred or is about to occur.
3. Temporary or permanent injunctions may be granted by the court.
4. Actual damages and court costs may be assessed against the guilty party.
5. A penalty fine of not less than $100 nor more than $500 may be assessed.

Other provisions of the Ohio law are:

1. The accused may not be compelled to testify against himself.
2. Attorneys will be provided for plaintiffs if they don't have the money to hire one.
3. A bond must be posted by the plaintiff before temporary relief or a restraining order will be issued.

appendix B

Administrative structure for

planning and zoning in

Gainesville, Florida

The top level in the administrative decision-making structure of Gainesville is the City Commission. The commission is composed of five members elected by the citizens of the city at large. It is the legislative body of the city, and thus must approve any changes in the zoning ordinance.

Directly below the City Commission is the City Planning Commission, or Plan Board, which is the main advisory body to the City Commission. Its function is to provide advice to the City Commission in the areas of current and future planning. The Plan Board is composed of seven lay members appointed by the City Commission. The appointive system presumably minimizes the political pressure to which elected officials might be subject from constituent groups, thus allowing them to act more independently in reviewing controversial issues. In appointing these members, the legislative body is required to select a cross section of citizens in order to prevent minority interests from being suppressed.

To assist it in carrying out its functions, the Plan Board hires a full-time, paid staff. At present the staff is composed of nine professionally trained urban planners, most of whom hold master's degrees in urban planning. The staff performs the research and analysis required in the formulation of planning concepts and developments. Its two main functions are: (1) to plan for current needs and (2) to develop and continually update the city's Comprehensive Development Plan.

Current planning involves primarily zoning and ordinance changes. This phase is subdivided into three functions: (*a*) small area land-use plans, (*b*) zoning, and (*c*) site plan approval.

Small area land-use plans

These are land-use plans for small areas which the Comprehensive Plan does not include. When adopted by the City Commission, the plans are used for determining land uses in the area in the immediate future. Small area land-use plans were used extensively before the city adopted a Comprehensive Plan several years ago. Since that time, these plans have generally not been needed.

Zoning

In this function, a request is filed by a property owner or his representative to change a zoning classification. The filing fee is $112. The professional staff analyzes requests in light of the city's Comprehensive Plan and its small area land-use plans. The Plan Board then establishes a time and place for a public hearing on the zoning request. The public must be notified at least 16 days prior to the hearing. Notification is given by three methods. The first method involves publishing in a newspaper an agenda of items to be covered at the hearing and stating the change in zoning (e.g., "RI-A to Mobile Home Park"). The second method is to place a sign on the subject property stating the agenda and zoning change request. Third, all property owners within 300 feet of the site to be rezoned must be notified by mail. If more than 20 percent of these owners object to the rezoning, the vote of the City Commission must be 4 out of 5 to accomplish the zoning change.

Then comes the public hearing. The Plan Board listens to the advice of the staff, arguments of the property owner and to anyone who is against the zoning change. The request is then voted upon by the board. If the decision confirms the zoning change, it is passed on to the City Commission for final consideration.

Site plan approval

The approval of site planning and development by the Plan Board is required for multiunit residential developments of four or more units and for shopping centers. The board's decision about a site plan is final; if there is any appeal, it must be made directly to the courts. Site planning includes all the physical aspects of the development. It involves such matters as architectural style, layout of the land, location of buildings on the site, access to parking areas, and landscaping.

PLANNING FOR THE FUTURE

The second major function of the planning staff is to develop a future planning guide. This guide is better known as the Comprehensive Plan. It is a land-use plan for the growth of an area, usually figured ten years ahead of the present. It includes present and proposed land uses, such as the type and number of recreational areas to be located in the city, proposed highways, police and fire stations, schools, and areas designated for residential, commercial, and industrial use.

Six background studies support the Comprehensive Plan. First and most important is the population study, designed to provide present population data and future growth statistics. Second is the economic base study, which analyzes the city's economy. These two studies attempt to predict the size and economic needs of the city ten years hence. Third is the land-use study, which provides a physical inventory of all land in the area at the present time. Fourth is a recreation study, which provides an inventory of the recreational areas and attempts to relate the city's recreational needs to its future size and geographic distribution. Fifth is a physiographic study showing all soil conditions and qualities. Last is the land-use and transportation study.

Another important agency in the zoning process is the Board of Adjustment. It is a semijudicial body appointed by the City Commission for the purpose of providing flexibility in the zoning ordinances. Its decisions are final; the only appeal is to the courts. It provides flexibility in two ways. First, it has the power to vary the strict letter of the zoning ordinance, that is, to grant a variance. Although a variance does not involve changing the zoning law, it does involve changing the use requirements. To obtain a variance, owners must show that they have a hardship (not caused by themselves) which prevents them from following the normal zoning requirements. The Board of Adjustment will consider the request for a variance in accordance with criteria that it has established.

Second, the board makes special exceptions to the zoning law. Under this method, the board has the power to allow a use that is not a matter of right in a given area. By applying criteria established by the Plan Board, the Board of Adjustment can change the zoning limitations to allow a prohibited type of use for a given parcel.

appendix C

Queens Gate Apartments

Mr. Queensworth recently purchased an obsolete, deteriorating factory building on 14.5 acres of land near the central business district. He hoped to use the building, a 160,000 square foot, three-story structure, as a boutique-oriented shopping center.

A market analysis showed a lack of demand for the shopping center, but it suggested that the salvage market would accept the building's materials at high prices. The land was shown to be ideal for apartment usage in a strong apartment market.

Mr. Queensworth paid $175,000 for the property. Within two months, he sold two small commercial frontage sites for $60,000 and netted $120,000 from the sale of scrap metal, hard pine, a water tank, an air conditioner, and so on. Thus, he more than recaptured his initial cash investment, and he owned an excellent apartment site of 9.5 acres (net of internal streets) plus commercial frontage sites of approximately 2.5 acres.

The financial analysis indicated as projection 1 shows the return that would result for apartment investors under market-based financing, rental, and expense projections. A net aftertax return of approximately 11 to 12 percent per year is shown for year 1, a return that is low for apartment investors.

Not shown in the projection are the following case facts:

1. The land is sold to the partnership at a substantial profit to Mr. Queensworth.
2. Mr. Queensworth absorbs all risks of construction cost overrun and slow rent-up. His $180,000 land sales income funds this risk.
3. Mr. Queensworth retains 80 percent of any funds remaining in the construction loan accounts at the time the permanent loan is closed. He draws no developer's fee.
4. Mr. Queensworth sells 80 percent of the equity for cash and retains 20 percent of the equity for his services.
5. The project is structured as a limited partnership.
6. All profits, losses, refinancing expenses, and sales proceeds are distributed on a pro rata basis to investors and Mr. Queensworth based upon ownership share.

Mr. Queensworth did not think that his partnership shares would sell well based upon 11 to 12 percent aftertax total earnings and a cash flow of less than 8 percent. Thus, he worked out projection 2 to improve the earnings picture.

Projection 2 utilizes the same market-based revenue and expense data, but it is premised upon a gross construction cost per square foot of $20, as compared with $22 in projection 1. It also assumes an 80 percent mortgage rather than a 75 percent mortgage. This situation leads to aftertax earnings of approximately 20 to 22 percent, but it requires a higher-than-market mortgage amount, and it reduces the project cost to a level that offers little or no protection from cost overruns.

Realizing the difficulties associated with projection 2, Mr. Queensworth reduced the loan amount to 75 percent and increased the cost of construction to $22 per square foot. In reviewing the market conditions, he also increased the loan interest rate from 11 percent to 11.5 percent and reduced the capitalization rate from 10.5 percent to 10 percent. This led to projection 3, which he decided was a sound structure for his project. He then prepared his pro forma financial statements upon this basis.

Throughout the three sets of calculations, Mr. Queensworth consistently retained a price of $175,000 for his land input. This was a profit to him, and it provided the financial assets needed to underwrite the risk of cost overruns.

The amount of equity money needed in the project varied from a high of $550,000 in projection 1 to a low of $263,000 in projection 2. In either event, the amount of equity was sufficient to pay the full land price in year 1.

Proposed Queens Gate Apartments, analysis of apartment offering, projection 1 (October 1981)

Gross annual rental income:	
25, 1-BR @ 700 sq. ft. @ $245/mo.	$ 73,500
75, 2-BR @ 950 sq. ft. @ $335/mo.	301,500
Total	$ 375,000
Less: Vacancy and collection loss allowance—5%	18,750
Effective gross income	$ 356,250
Less: Operating expenses @ 37% (tenants electricity, gas)	131,813
Net operating income	$ 224,437
Value (net income capitalized at 10.5%)	$2,137,495
say	$2,140,000
Loan—75%	$1,605,000
Loan constant, 11% interest, 30 years	0.1143
Cash throw-off analysis:	
Net operating income	$ 224,437
Debt service (0.1143 × $1,605,000)	183,452
Cash throw-off	$ 40,985
Cash equity required:	
Improvement cost (90,000 sq. ft. @ $22)	$1,980,000
Land at cost	175,000
Total cost	$2,155,000
Deduct loan proceeds	1,605,000
Cash equity required	$ 550,000
Taxable income:	
Interest at 11%	$ 176,550
Depreciation—double-declining balance, 33 years	120,000
Total	$ 296,550
Net operating income	224,437
First-year taxable income	$ (72,113)
Investment position: Total equity	
Sell 80% of total project for cash—20 shares at $27,500 each	$ 550,000
Distribute first-year cash throw-off pro rata 80% of $40,985	$ 32,788
Distribute first-year tax loss pro rata 80% of $72,113 = $57,690	$ 57,690
Benefit for 40% taxpayer	$ 23,076
Benefit for 50% taxpayer	$ 28,845
Distribute first-year mortgage equity payments pro rata 80% of $6,902 × $5,522	$ 5,522

Return on investment:
40% bracket taxpayers:

$$\frac{\$32,788 + \$23,076 + \$5,522}{\$550,000} = 11.2\% \text{ aftertax}$$

50% bracket taxpayers:

$$\frac{\$32,788 + \$28,845 + \$5,522}{\$550,000} = 12.2\% \text{ aftertax}$$

Proposed Queens Gate Apartments, analysis of apartment offering, projection 2 (October 1981)

Gross annual rental income:	
25, 1-BR @ 700 sq. ft. @ $245/mo.	$ 73,500
75, 2-BR @ 950 sq. ft. @ $335/mo.	301,500
Total	$ 375,000
Less: Vacancy and collection loss allowance—5%	18,750
Effective gross income	$ 356,250
Less: Operating expenses @ 37% (tenants pay electricity, gas)	131,813
Net operating income	$ 224,437
Value (net income capitalized at 10.5%)	$2,137,495
say	$2,140,000
Loan—80%	$1,712,000
Loan constant, 11% interest, 30 years	0.1143
Cash throw-off analysis:	
Net operating income	$ 224,437
Debt service (0.1143 × $1,712,000)	195,682
Cash throw-off	$ 28,755
Cash equity required:	
Improvement cost (90,000 sq. ft. @ $20)	$1,800,000
Land at cost	175,000
Total cost	$1,975,000
Deduct loan proceeds	1,712,000
Cash equity required	$ 263,000
Taxable income:	
Interest at 11%	$ 188,320
Depreciation—double-declining balance, 33 years	109,091
Total	$ 297,411
Net operating income	224,437
First-year taxable income	$ (72,974)
Investment position: Total equity	
Sell 80% of total project for cash—20 shares at $13,150 each	$ 263,000
Distribute first-year cash throw-off pro rata 80% of $28,755	$ 23,004
Distribute first-year tax loss pro rata 80% of $72,974 = $58,379	$ 58,379
Benefit for 40% taxpayer	$ 23,352
Benefit for 50% taxpayer	$ 29,190
Distribute first-year mortgage equity payments pro rata 80% of $7,362 = $5,890	$ 5,890

Return on investment:
40% bracket taxpayers:

$$\frac{\$23,004 + \$23,352 + \$5,890}{\$263,000} = 19.9\% \text{ aftertax}$$

50% bracket taxpayers:

$$\frac{\$23,004 + \$29,190 + \$5,890}{\$263,000} = 22.1\% \text{ aftertax}$$

Proposed Queens Gate Apartments, analysis of apartment offering, projection 3 (October 1981)

Gross annual rental income:

25, 1-BR @ 700 sq. ft. @ $245/mo.	$ 73,500
75, 2-BR @ 950 sq. ft. @ $335/mo.	301,500
Total	$ 375,000
Less: Vacancy and collection loss allowance—5%	19,150
Effective gross income	$ 363,850
Less: Operating expenses @ 37% (tenants pay electricity, gas)	134,625
Net operating income	$ 229,225
Value (net income capitalized at 10.5%)	$2,292,250
Loan—75%	$1,719,188
Loan constant, 11.5% interest, 30 years	0.1188

Cash throw-off analysis:

Net operating income	$ 229,225
Debt service ($1,719,188 × 0.1188)	204,240
Cash throw-off	$ 24,985

Cash equity required:

Improvement cost (90,000 sq. ft. @ $21)	$1,890,000
Land at cost	175,000
Total cost	$2,165,000
Deduct loan proceeds	1,719,188
Cash equity required	$ 345,812

Taxable income:

Interest at 11.5%	$ 197,707
Depreciation—double-declining balance, 33 years	114,545
Total	$ 312,252
Net operating income	229,225
First-year taxable income	$ (83,027)

Investment position: Total equity

Sell 80% of total project for cash—20 shares at $17,291 each	$ 345,812
Distribute first-year cash throw-off pro rata 80% of $24,985	$ 19,988
Distribute first-year tax loss pro rata 80% of $83,027 = $66,422	$ 66,422
Benefit for 40% taxpayer	$ 26,569
Benefit for 50% taxpayer	$ 33,211
Distribute first-year mortgage equity payments pro rata 80% of $6,533 = $5,226	$ 5,226

Return on investment:
40% bracket taxpayers

$$\frac{\$19,988 + \$26,569 + \$5,226}{\$345,812} = 15\% \text{ aftertax}$$

50% bracket taxpayers:

$$\frac{\$19,988 + \$33,211 + \$5,226}{\$345,812} = 16.9\% \text{ aftertax}$$

Proposed Queens Gate Apartments, pro forma statement of revenue and expenses

	Year 1	Year 2	Year 3	Year 4	Year 5	Year 6	Year 7	Year 8	Year 9	Year 10
Gross annual rental income:										
25, 1-Br @ 700 sq. ft......	$ 73,500	$ 73,500	$ 73,500	$ 75,705	$ 75,705	$ 75,705	$ 79,975	$ 79,975	$ 79,975	$ 79,975
75, 2-BR @ 950 sq. ft......	301,500	301,500	301,500	310,545	310,545	310,545	319,860	319,860	319,860	319,860
Laundry, telephone, miscellaneous	8,000	8,000	8,000	8,0000	8,000	8,000	8,000	8,000	8,000	8,000
Total	$383,000	$383,000	$383,000	$394,250	$394,250	$394,250	$407,835	$407,835	$407,835	$407,835
Less: Vacancy and collection loss allowance— 5%...........	19,150	19,150	19,150	19,713	19,713	19,713	20,392	20,392	20,392	20,392
Effective gross income	$363,850	$363,850	$363,850	$374,537	$374,537	$374,537	$387,443	$387,443	$387,443	$387,443
Less: Operating expenses:										
Common area electricity, water and sewer	$ 7,000	$ 7,000	$ 7,000	$ 7,210	$ 7,210	$ 7,210	$ 7,426	$ 7,426	$ 7,426	$ 7,426
Trash, service	2,400	2,400	2,400	2,472	2,472	2,472	2,546	2,546	2,546	2,546
Janitor/yardman	8,320	8,320	8,320	8,570	8,570	8,570	8,827	8,827	8,827	8,827
Painting and decorating	4,250	4,250	4,250	4,250	4,378	4,378	4,509	4,509	4,509	4,509
General repairs	10,000	10,000	10,000	10,300	10,300	10,300	10,609	10,609	10,609	10,609
Reserve for replacements	24,050	24,050	24,050	24,772	24,772	24,772	25,515	25,515	25,515	25,515
Supplies	5,000	5,000	5,000	5,150	5,150	5,150	5,305	5,305	5,305	5,305
Resident manager	12,540	12,540	12,540	12,916	12,916	12,916	13,303	13,303	13,303	13,303
Cable TV	2,400	2,400	2,400	2,472	2,472	2,472	2,546	2,546	2,546	2,546
Insurance	3,500	3,500	3,500	3,605	3,605	3,605	3,713	3,713	3,713	3,713
Property taxes	29,110	29,110	29,110	29,983	29,983	29,983	30,882	30,882	30,882	30,882
Management fee	18,190	18,190	18,190	18,727	18,727	18,727	19,372	19,372	19,372	19,372
Advertising	1,200	1,200	1,200	1,236	1,236	1,236	1,273	1,273	1,273	1,273
Landscaping	6,000	6,000	6,000	6,180	6,180	6,180	6,365	6,365	6,365	6,365
Telephone	480	480	480	494	494	494	509	509	509	509
Total expenses........	$134,440	$134,440	$134,440	$138,465	$138,465	$138,465	$142,700	$142,700	$142,700	$142,700
Net operating income	$229,410	$229,410	$229,410	$236,072	$236,072	$236,072	$244,743	$244,743	$244,743	$244,743

Proposed Queens Gate Apartments, ten-year return on investment

	Year 1	Year 2	Year 3	Year 4	Year 5	Year 6	Year 7	Year 8	Year 9	Year 10
Total return on investment:										
Gross revenue	$383,000	$383,000	$383,000	$394,250	$394,250	$394,250	$407,835	$407,835	$407,835	$407,835
Less: Vacancy and collection loss allowance—5%	19,150	19,150	19,150	19,713	19,713	19,713	20,392	20,392	20,392	20,392
Effective gross income	$363,850	$363,850	$363,850	$374,537	$374,537	$374,537	$387,443	$387,443	$387,443	$387,443
Less: Operating expenses	134,440	134,440	134,440	138,465	138,465	138,465	142,700	142,700	142,700	142,700
Net operating income	$229,410	$229,410	$229,410	$236,072	$236,072	$236,072	$244,743	$244,743	$244,743	$244,743
a. Deduct:										
Interest	$197,707	$196,955	$196,118	$195,184	$194,142	$192,981	$191,686	$190,242	$188,633	$186,838
Depreciation	114,545	107,603	101,082	94,956	89,201	83,795	78,716	73,946	69,464	65,193
Net taxable income	($ 82,842)	($ 75,148)	($ 67,790)	($ 54,068)	($ 47,271)	($ 40,704)	($ 25,659)	($ 19,445)	($ 13,354)	($ 7,288)
b. Deduct:										
Debt service	$204,240	$204,240	$204,240	$204,240	$204,240	$204,240	$204,240	$204,240	$204,240	$204,240
Cash throw-off	$ 25,170	$ 25,170	$ 25,170	$ 31,832	$ 31,832	$ 31,832	$ 40,503	$ 40,503	$ 40,503	$ 40,503
Principal payments on mortgage	$ 6,533	$ 7,285	$ 8,122	$ 9,056	$ 10,098	$ 11,259	$ 12,554	$ 13,998	$ 15,607	$ 17,402
Return on 80% investors' shares										
Cash throw-off return on investment	5.8%	5.8%	5.8%	7.4%	7.4%	7.4%	9.4%	9.4%	9.4%	9.4%
Adjust for tax benefit (detriment) for 40% bracket taxpayer	7.7	7.0	6.3	5.0	4.4	3.8	2.4	1.8	1.2	0.7
Add mortgage payment value (assumes constant property value)	1.5	1.7	1.9	2.1	2.3	2.6	2.9	3.2	3.6	4.0
Total aftertax effective return on investment (property value does not change)	15.0%	14.5%	14.0%	14.5%	14.1%	13.8%	14.7%	14.4%	14.2%	14.1%

Note: A single 4 percent share costing $17,291 would receive $1,007 cash plus a tax refund of $1,325 plus a mortgage equity value of $261 in year 1 if the above projections are correct. These are only projections, even though they are based upon current market information.

FHA housing market

analysis outline

The following outline is indicative of the scope and sequence of subject matter to be considered in an overall market analysis. It does not reflect geographic submarket considerations; these can be incorporated by the analyst at appropriate points wherever feasible and to the extent required by each analysis. An abbreviated form of analytical treatment is adaptable from these components.

Preface

If a brief statement of the purpose of the analysis, that is, the specific problem which occasioned the need for the market study, is desired, it could be included as a preface. Alternatively, the statement of purpose may be omitted or it may be incorporated into a letter or memorandum of transmittal.

Summary and conclusions

Generally, a summary is desired to provide a quick, overall perspective on the principal findings and conclusions of the analysis, preferably at the beginning rather than at the end of the report. The summary is not intended to be a résumé of the entire analysis. To achieve its purpose most effectively it should be limited to the salient statistical findings and major conclusions and presented concisely in a series of brief paragraphs in the same sequence of subject matter that is followed in the text. Specific page references to parallel subject matter in the text may be utilized to facilitate ready access to pertinent details.

Housing market area

1. Definition (delineation), including identification of entire area encompassed and principal cities; geographic submarkets discussed and defined
2. Description, including:
    a. Size (total population)
    b. Major topographical features
    c. Principal transportation arteries (highway, rail, water) and distance to other urban areas
    d. General urban structure and direction of growth
    e. Special features, characteristics, or considerations
    f. Major community developments in process or planned which are germane to the present analysis
    g. Net (in or out) commutation; significance
3. Map of area

Economy of the housing market area

1. Economic character and history
    a. General description
    b. Principal economic activities and developments—past and present
2. Employment—total, wage and salary, other
    a. Current estimate
    b. Past trend (last eight–ten years)
    c. Distribution by major industry
        (1) Current
        (2) Comparison with previous years
    d. Female employment participation rate
    e. Trend of employment participation rate
3. Discussion of principal employers
    a. Manufacturing
    b. Nonmanufacturing
    c. Military, if any (history and mission)
    d. Other
4. Unemployment
    a. Current level and composition
    b. Past trend

5. Estimated future employment
   a. Total and annual increments
   b. Analytical exposition
6. Income
   a. Average weekly wages of manufacturing workers
      (1) Current level
      (2) Trend since last census
   b. Other data from state estimated for counties, if available
   c. Estimates of current family income distribution (after tax) for all families, for renter households, and for other segmental groups, if necessary

Demographic analysis

1. Population
   a. Current estimate
   b. Past trend
   c. Estimated future population—total and annual increments
   d. Net natural increase and imputed migration
   e. Distribution by age
   f. Trend of military and military-connected civilian strength, if applicable
   g. Trend of college enrollment, if applicable
2. Households
   a. Current estimate
   b. Past trend
   c. Estimated future households—total and annual increments
   d. Household size trends
   e. Military and military-connected civilian households, if applicable
      (1) Present—on-base and off-base, with distribution by minor civil divisions
      (2) Projected
   f. College-oriented households, faculty and student, present and projected

Housing stock and market conditions

1. Housing supply
   a. Current estimate
   b. Past trends, including last census date
   c. Principal characteristics: last census and current estimates
      (1) Type of structure
      (2) Year built

      (3) Condition

      (4) Plumbing facilities

2. Residential building activity, by type

    a. Annually, last ten years

    b. Monthly, January to latest month for current and previous year

    c. Units under construction

    d. Demolition and conversion trends and projections

3. Tenure of occupancy

    a. Current estimate

    b. Past trends

4. Vacancy

    a. Last census—net available

      (1) Overall, homeowner, and rental

      (2) Number of units lacking one or more plumbing facilities

    b. Postal vacancy surveys—current and previous, if any, and conversion and adjustment to census concepts of owner and renter unit vacancy

    c. Other occupancy-vacancy indicators and surveys, including surveys of FHA-insured projects

    d. Current estimates—net available (qualified for units lacking one or more plumbing facilities)

      (1) Owner

      (2) Renter

      (3) Quality differentials

      (4) Evaluation

5. Mortgage market

    a. Sources and availability of funds

    b. FHA participation

    c. Interest rates and terms of mortgages

    d. Mortgage and deed recordings

6. Sales market

    a. General market conditions—strong and weak points

    b. Major subdivision activity

    c. Speculative versus contract building

    d. Marketing experience—new and existing

    e. Price trends—new and existing

    f. Unsold inventory of new houses

      (1) Price

      (2) Months unsold

      (3) Comparison with previous period, if available

    g. Houses under construction—volume and quality

    h. Foreclosures

      (1) Overall trend

          (2)   FHA and other

          (3)   Sales versus acquisitions

    i.   Outlook

7.   Rental market

    a.   General market conditions—strong and weak points

    b.   New rental housing, FHA and other, by years, type, and rents

          (1)   General marketing experience

          (2)   Competitive status with existing rental housing

    c.   Rental housing under construction

          (1)   Volume, type, and quality

          (2)   Probable, marketing schedule

    d.   Rental housing committed but not started—volume, type, and quality

    e.   Foreclosures—FHA and other

8.   Urban renewal activity, if applicable (federal, state, and local)

    a.   Summation: Overall renewal plan and progress

    b.   Urban renewal areas

          (1)   Identification and location (street boundaries)

          (2)   Description and renewal plans of areas

          (3)   Environment (surrounding area)

          (4)   Housing unit demolitions and replacements

          (5)   Present status and time schedule

9.   Military housing, if applicable

    a.   Housing available to military (including military-connected civilians, i.e., civil service and contractor employees)

          (1)   Number of units by type and construction status, on-base and off-base

          (2)   Physical adequacy

          (3)   Occupancy status

    b.   Current and projected housing requirements and deficits

          (1)   Eligible military personnel

          (2)   Ineligible military personnel

          (3)   Civilians, including contractor employees

10.   Subsidized housing, Section 221(d)(3); rent supplement, Section 235, Section 236; quantity, (existing, under construction, and planned), rents, income limits, vacancy

Demand for housing

1.   Quantitative demand (annual basis)

    a.   Projected increase in households

    b.   Adjustments

    c.   Net quantitative demand (privately financed), by tenure

    d.   Net quantitative demand by geographic submarkets

    e. Occupancy potentials for subsidized types, with submarket proportions

2. Qualitative demand
    a. Demand for single-family housing (nonsubsidized)
    b. Demand for multifamily housing (nonsubsidized)
    c. General locations favorable to market absorption
    d. Qualitative occupancy potential for subsidized housing, Section 221(d)(3); rent supplement, Section 235, Section 236; public housing.
    e. Geographic demand distribution for nonsubsidized housing and subsidized potential

3. Submarkets of demand: At times, the purpose of the housing market analysis may require an estimate of demand for one or more of the submarkets identified in Chapter 9. Subject matter pertinent to a particular submarket may be integrated with the discussion of the broader scope of the respective subject matter in the comprehensive analysis; or it may be consolidated and presented as a supplement following the overall estimates of qualitative demand for housing.

Statistical appendix

The statistical appendix is intended to contain the detailed tables of only the key data used in the analysis. It should not be used as a catchall for extensive statistical material of less than primary importance in the analysis.

Much of the data used in the analysis can be included in text tables or the narrative in the body of the report. Text tables, maps, and charts are helpful when used effectively. They provide sharp focus on important facts, relationships, and trends which require special emphasis otherwise achievable only by lengthy narration. Text tables, however, must be carefully selected and strategically integrated with the discussion; they must be simple and highly condensed; and their use must be minimized rather than maximized. The accompanying text must be analytical and interpretative, revealing the significance of the data shown in the tables rather than serving as a mere repetition of these data in narrative form. Caution must be exercised, of course, to avoid overloading the text with statistics—thus rendering the report difficult to read and distracting from the salient facts and findings.

appendix E

The Columbus Area economy:

Structure and growth, 1950 to 1985*

By James C. Yocum

This article presents some highlights of an intensive, three-volume economic base study of the Columbus Area, with detailed projections to 1985. The study was undertaken by the Bureau of Business Research for the Comprehensive Regional Plan of Columbus and Franklin County, Ohio, and required the assembly of a special research staff,[1] including members of the Bureau Staff and other faculty from the College of Commerce and Administration.

The long-term economic and demographic projections developed by this study are primarily for use in the preparation of a comprehensive, long-range Master Plan for Franklin County. The projections, and the historical and structural analysis of the economy of the Area, are useful as well in gaining a better understanding of the workings of the

* Reprinted from *Bulletin of Business Research*, College of Commerce and Administration, Ohio State University, vol. 41, no. 11 (November 1966): 1, 6–9.

[1] Members of the staff were: James C. Yocum, Professor of Business Reearch and Director, Bureau of Business Research; Richard A. Tybout, Professor of Economics; Henry L. Hunker, Professor of Geography; Gilbert Nestel, Assistant Professor of Business Research and Economics; and Wilford L'Esperance, Associate Professor of Economics and Business Research. Kent P. Schwirian, Associate Professor of Sociology, was also a member of the staff as Principal Investigator for the population segment of the study.

Area's economy as it has been in the recent past and as it is likely to be in the future, and provide a basis for assessing the viability of the Area's industrial location factors in the light of changing technology and U.S. regional trends in the location of population and industry.

Volume 1, *Employment, and Value Added by Manufacture*, analyzes the economic structure of the Columbus Area, its historic and recent growth, and its interrelationships both internally and with the rest of the world, and makes projections to 1985 of number employed, by 33 major industry classifications, and of dollar value added by manufacture, by 17 SIC two-digit manufacturing industry classifications and for manufacturing industry classifications not now in the Columbus Area.

Volume 2, *Income, Trade, Housing*, provides projections to 1985 of other economic parameters for the Columbus Area, including personal income, income distribution, retail sales, household automobile population, number of households by household type, and housing demand by housing unit tenure.

Volume 3, *Population and Labor Force*, develops projections to 1985 of population and labor force of the Columbus Area and of some principal population characteristics.

Volume 1 is the basic work (comprising 466 pages) since it deals with the recent growth and industry distribution of employment and output, and their projection to 1985 in the light of changes in technology and productivity likely for the Columbus Area economy. The employment projections underlie and are the principal determinants of the projected levels of population, labor force, households, income, and other economic variables developed in the other volumes.

For this reason, and because of space limitations, the highlights presented here, and the summary of the projection methodologies employed, are chiefly from Volume 1, and relate to number employed.

The Columbus Area—location and growth

Although Ohio for decades has been one of the nation's leading manufacturing states, Columbus, despite its location, for many years was principally a capital city, education, transportation, and finance-and-trading center.

By 1940, when the population of Ohio was 6,908,000, the Franklin County population was 388,700; Franklin County had 138,662 employed, of which only 23.6 percent were employed in Manufacturing. World War II, however, brought new industrial activity to the Area and was the catalyst to an industrial expansion that continues to the present and that has changed the character of the Area's economy. With war's end, the Columbus Area had the labor, space, facilities, and the recognized location to attract new manufacturing firms. The dynamic growth of the Columbus Area's economy in the 1940s continued in the 1950s. By 1960, the population of Franklin County had risen to 683,000 and resident employment to 256,684.

The Area's growth in these two decades was the result of two main forces: the surging industrial expansion, especially in durables manufacture, that stemmed from a somewhat belated recognition of the locational advantages of the Area for many kinds of manufacturing; and the continuing growth of elements related to the strong and long-established orientation of the Columbus Area as a political, educational, and financial-and-trading center.

Present economic structure

By 1960 the industrial growth of the Columbus Area had proceeded to the point where Manufacturing accounted for 27.2 percent of total resident employment (adjusted), compared to 25.6 percent in 1950 and approximately 23.6 percent in 1940. The general pattern of industry composition of the Columbus Area in 1960 more closely resembled that of the United States than that of Ohio—e.g., Manufacturing accounted for 28.3 percent of total employment in the United States, 38.3 percent in Ohio. The principal departures of the Columbus Area from the U.S. pattern are the substantially lower proportions of Agricultural employment, and higher percentages of employment in Professional Services (including Education), in Services generally, in Government, and in Insurance.

The makeup of Columbus Area Manufacturing, however, is less diversified than the United States or than Ohio but more nearly resembles Ohio than the United States.

The growth of Manufacturing in the Columbus Area since 1940 was primarily in durable goods, with five durable goods industry classifications accounting for almost 90 percent of the total increase in Manufacturing employment. Increasingly, therefore, Franklin County has become oriented to durable goods production, so that in 1960 durable goods manufacturing represented 67 percent of its total Manufacturing employment.

By 1965, although Manufacturing employment had increased 7.2 percent from 1960, larger increases in other industry classifications resulted in a decline to 26.0 percent in the Area's ratio of Manufacturing to all employment. In economic base terms, in which "Basic Industries" and "Local Industries" are defined on the basis of an external (exogeneous)–internal (endogeneous) dichotomy with respect to the source of their demands (with Basic Industries selling primarily to buyers outside the Area and generating activity whose multiplicative and cumulative effects are conceived as determining the demands [internal] of the Local Industries), the Columbus Area economy, despite the industrial expansion of the previous 25 years, still retains the advantage of a relatively large reliance on Local Supporting Industries, as the following table shows:

Classification	Percent of total employment, 1965
Basic Industries—Total	46.0
Products (Manufacturing, Construction, Quarrying, Agriculture)	(31.8)
Services (Exogenous)	(14.2)
Local Supporting and Services Industries	54.0
Total	100.0

Employment in the Local Industries and Basic Services is notably more stable, much less cyclically sensitive, than in Manufacturing and Construction.

Projections

The central concern of the study was with the rate of growth at which the Area's economy can be expected to proceed in the future, the probable nature and dimensions of the changes among the principal divisions of the economy, and the structure of the economic base, at five-year intervals, 1970 through 1985.

The projections of number employed by industry classifications were critical to the projections of all the other variables, and special pains were taken, therefore, in their preparation. Rather than relying on a *single* methodology and accompanying assumptions, a pluralistic research design was employed. As a safeguard, to minimize the deviations of the projected values from true future values, it might be said that redundancy was deliberately incorporated in the research design.

Thus, projections of employment for each industry classification were made by several methods. For the (existing) Manufacturing industry classifications these methods were:

a.   Franklin County Share of U.S. Total

For each industry classification, ratios of Franklin County/U.S. value added by manufacture and of Franklin County/U.S. value added per employee were developed from historical data; subjective determinations of the possible range ("High," "Intermediate," and "Low") of these two ratios in the projection period were made; and projected High, Intermediate, and Low Franklin County industry employment was derived from the projected ratios using the National Planning Association's projections of U.S. value added and number employed, by industry.

b. Manufacturers' Markets

Empirical data were obtained by questionnaire from Franklin County manufacturers showing distribution of their 1963 sales by industry (industrial goods) and/or by U.S. region (consumer goods). Sales were then projected to 1985, using NPA's projections of U.S. gross output by manufacturing industry classifications, and of personal income by U.S. regions; projected employment of each industry classification was then obtained by dividing the projected sales by the respective projected sales/employee ratios.

c. Input-Output

A table of Franklin County 1958 interindustry transactions and external sales was specially constructed, which, for each industry expresses its total output (sales) as the sum of the purchases of its output by every other category of local business, plus its output exported outside Franklin County. A matrix of technical coefficients, representing for each industry, for each dollar of its output, the value of its inputs from each other Franklin County industry, was computed. The matrix was inverted, and projected total sales of each Franklin County industry were computed by multiplying the inverse matrix by the matrix of projected exports. Projected sales were then converted to projected employment as in *b* above.

The projections from these separate methods were then compared (as illustrated in Chart 1, reproduced from chart C.4, volume 1 of the study) and used to develop a "Judgment Intermediate" (or implicitly a "most likely") level, and upper and lower bounds, which may be taken as "possible high" and "possible low." Where the projections by the various methods were closely confirming, the range between the upper and lower bounds is relatively small (as in the case of the Fabricated Metals industry in Chart 1). In a few industries in which the projections showed substantial dispersion (as in the case of the Primary Metals industry in Chart 1) the assumptions underlying the projection methods and subjective evaluations of the future prospects of the industry were restudied, and if a firm basis for decision among the alternatives was available, judgmental determinations were made; or if not, the range between the upper and lower bounds was left commensurately larger.

Historical and projected employment for all major industry classifications is shown in Chart 2 (reproduced from chart 9.1, volume 1).

In summary it may be noted that on the basis of these projections no major structural changes in the employment of the Columbus Area are anticipated. Continuing large gains in manufacturing per-employee productivity, however, will limit the employment growth in this prin-

CHART 1

Manufacturing industries (SIC 33 and 34) establishment employment: Projections by three methods, and final projections (high, judgment intermediate, and low), Franklin County, 1963, and projected, 1965–1985

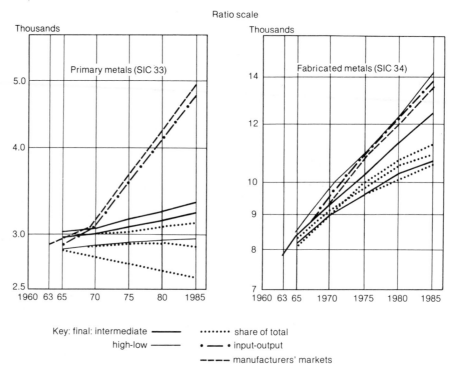

Ratio scale

Key: final: intermediate ——— ········ share of total
high-low ——— • —— • input-output
–––– manufacturers' markets

CHART 2

Major industry classifications: Franklin County resident employment, 1950, 1960, and 1965, and projected (judgment intermediate), 1970–1985

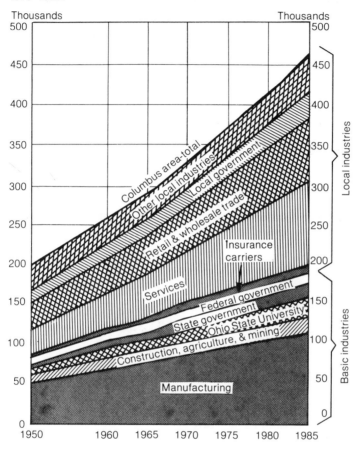

cipal segment of the Basic Industries, so that by 1985 it will account for 23.6 percent of the total Area employment compared to 26.1 percent in 1965.

The rate of growth of employment projected for the Columbus Area, 1965–85, compared with its recent historic rate, and with the United States as projected by NPA, is summarized in the following table:

Area	*Average annual percent increase*	
	1950–1965	*1965–1985*
Columbus Area total civilian resident employment		
High	—	2.7
Judgment Intermediate	2.5	2.3
Low	—	1.7
U.S. civilian employment	1.2	1.8

Projections of other selected economic variables are summarized in the accompanying table.

appendix F

Use of compound

interest tables

Tables in Appendix G are provided for selected rates of return from 3 percent to 25 percent (shown at the top of each table). These rates of return represent what is sometimes called the "effective rate," the "risk rate of interest," the "discount rate," the "speculative rate," or the "return needed *on*" the amount invested. This rate of return shown at the top of each table is an interest rate, not a capitalization rate. A capitalization rate or factor includes both the return *on* investment and the return *of* investment.

Two sets of tables are provided in Appendix G for each rate of return. The Annual Compound Interest Tables assume that interest is compounded annually and that the successive increments of income will come at annual intervals; the Monthly Compound Interest Tables assume monthly compounding of income and that the successive increments of income will come at monthly intervals. Tables are also available for quarterly, semiannual, and other periodic payments. Compound interest factors in the annual tables extend to the 50th year and in the monthly tables to the 40th year. Tables are available for factors for 100 years, and factors in the 50- and 40-year tables can be extended in the absence of a more complete table.

The following discussion of the six columns in the compound interest tables uses the 8 percent annual table for illustration.

Column 1

Column 1 is headed "Amount of $1 at Compound Interest." The factors in column 1 indicate the magnitude reached after a given number of years by a *single sum* (a one-time event) deposited *at the beginning* of year 1, if interest is compounded at the rate of 8 percent annually. The deposit today of $100 (a single sum) at 8 percent compound interest will accumulate to $125.97 (rounded) by the end of three years.

Example

To find the future value of any single sum given that interest is to be compounded at 8 percent for three years, the procedure is:

Factor × Single sum = Future value of the single sum
1.259712 × $100 = $125.97

Demonstration of what is assumed to occur during the three years:

Year	Outlay	Interest during year	Balance at end of year
1	$100	$8.00	$108.00
2	—	8.64	116.64
3	—	9.33	125.97 (answer)

Interest each year is calculated on the outstanding balance at the end of the preceding year. The original balance and accumulated interest total $125.97 by the end of the third year.

Note

The compound interest formula for calculating the factors in column 1 is:

$$(1 + r)^n$$

Substituting

$$(1 + 0.08)^3 = 1.259712.$$

Column 2

Column 2 in the table is headed "Accumulation of $1 per Period." The factors in column 2 indicate the magnitude reached after a given number of years by *a series of equal annual amounts* deposited *at the end* of each successive year, if interest is compounded at the rate of 8 percent annually. The deposit of $100 each year at 8 percent compound interest will accumulate to $324.64 at the end of three years.

Example

To find the future value of any series of equal annual outlays for three years, given that interest is to be compounded at 8 percent, the procedure is:

Factor × Annual amount deposited = Future value of the annual deposits
$$3.246400 \times \$100 = \$324.64$$

Demonstration of what is assumed to occur during the three years:

Year	End-of-year outlay	Interest during year	Balance at end-of-year
1	$100	$ 0.00	$100.00
2	100	8.00	208.00
3	100	16.64	324.64
			(answer)

Interest each year is calculated on the outstanding balance at the end of the preceding year. The series of three equal annual payments plus accumulated interest total $324.64 by the end of the third year.

Note

The compound interest formula for calculating the factors in Column 2 is:

$$\frac{(1 + r)^n - 1}{r}$$

Substituting:

$$\frac{(1 + 0.08)^3 - 1}{0.08} = 3.2464$$

Column 3

Column 3 is headed "Sinking Fund Factor." In other books, the percentages in this column may be found in a table headed "Amortization Rates" or "Deposits Needed to Accumulate $1." The percentages in column 3 indicate the equal annual amounts necessary to set aside at the end of each year at 8 percent compound interest in order to accumulate to a certain sum at the end of a given number of years. The equal annual amount necessary to set aside in an 8 percent sinking fund to accumulate to $100 at the end of three years is $30.80 (rounded); that is, $30.80 each year will amortize the investment, assuming that the annual amortization payment is put at compound interest of 8 percent.

Example

To find the annual payment into the sinking fund, given that the fund earns 8 percent and that the $100 investment is amortized over three years, the procedure is:

$$\text{Percentage} \times \text{Sum to be amortized} = \text{Sinking fund payment}$$

or

$$0.308034 \times \$100 = \$30.80$$

Demonstration of what is assumed to occur during the three years:

Year	End-of-year deposit in fund	Interest on fund during year	Balance at the end of year
1	$30.80	$0.00	$30.80
2	30.80	2.46	64.06
3	30.80	5.12	99.98*

* Discrepancy from $100 caused by rounding.

Interest each year is calculated on the outstanding balance at the end of the preceding year. The series of three equal annual payments into the fund plus accumulated interest total $100 by the end of the third year.

Note

The compound interest formula for calculating the percentages in column 3 is:

$$\frac{r}{(1 + r)^n - 1}$$

Substituting:

$$\frac{0.08}{(1 + 0.08)^3 - 1} = 0.308034$$

Column 4

Column 4 is headed "Present Value of Reversion of $1." The factors in column 4 indicate the value today of a *single sum* (a one-time event) to be received at the end of a given number of years, discounted at 8 percent annual compound interest. The discounting phenomenon (or the process of capitalization) arises because of the fact that a dollar today is more valuable to us than a dollar that we expect to receive at some future time. If we had the dollar in hand today, we could invest it and earn a return; we would be liquid; and we would avoid risk of loss of capital. In this case, we need 8 percent to induce us to wait three years for the receipt of $100. The $100 (a single sum) to be received at the end of three years from today, discounted at 8 percent compound interest, is worth $79.38 (rounded) today.

Example

To find the present value of a single payment to be received at the end of three years, given that the rate of discount is 8 percent, the procedure is:

Factor × Amount to be received = Present value of the single sum

or

$$0.793832 \times \$100 = \$79.38 \text{ (rounded)}$$

Demonstration of what is assumed to occur during the three years:

Year	Original outlay	Interest during year	Balance at end of year
1	$79.38	$6.35	$ 85.73
2	—	6.86	92.59
3	—	7.41	100.00
			(single sum to be received at end of year three)

The receipt of $100 at the end of year three has permitted earning 8 percent interest compounded annually.on the original investment of $79.38.

Note

The compound interest formula for calculating the factors in column 4 is:

$$\frac{1}{(1 + r)^n}$$

Substituting:

$$\frac{1}{(1 + 0.08)^3} = 0.793832$$

Column 5

Column 5 is headed "Present Value of Ordinary Annuity of $1 per Period." The factors in column 5 indicate the value today of a series of equal annual payments (an income stream) to be received *at the end* of each successive year for a given number of years, discounted at 8 percent annual compound interest. Income of $100 to be received at the end of each of three years, discounted at 8 percent compound interest, is worth $257.71 (rounded) today.

Example

To find the present value of a series of equal annual payments to be received at the end of each year for three years, given that the rate of discount is 8 percent, the procedure is:

Factor × Equal annual payment

= Present value of series of equal annual payments

or

2.577097 × $100 = $257.71 (rounded)

Demonstration of what is assumed to occur during the three years:

Year	Payment to be received at end of year	Interest on outstanding balance of investment	Recapture of principal	End-of-year outstanding balance of investment
1	$100	$20.62*	$ 79.38	$178.33†
2	100	14.27	85.73	92.60
3	100	7.41	92.59	—
Totals	$300	$42.30	$257.70	

* 8% × original investment of $257.71 made at beginning of year.
† $257.71 less $79.38.

The original investment of $257.71 is fully recaptured out of the annual receipts of $100 over the three years and the investor has earned 8 percent on the outstanding balance of the original investment each year. (Note that the portion of each annual receipt of $100 designated as recapture of principal increases each year as the interest earned on the reducing balance decreases.)

Note

The compound interest formula for calculating factors in column 5 is:

$$\frac{1 - (1 + r)^{-n}}{r}$$

Substituting:

$$\frac{1 - (1 + 0.08)^{-3}}{0.08} = 2.577097$$

Column 6

Column 6 is headed "Installment to Amortize $1." In other books, the percentages in this column may be found in a table headed "Partial Payment of $1 of Loan." This table is often called a mortgage amortization table. The percentages in column 6 indicate the equal annual payment necessary to amortize fully the principal balance of a mortgage over its term and to provide the lender a given rate of return on the outstanding balance of unamortized principal each year. Payments are assumed to be made at the end of each successive year. The percentages in column 6 are often called mortgage constants and are sometimes referred to as whole numbers. Thus a constant of 38.80 is

38.80 *percent,* or 0.3880. A loan of $100 with a term of three years and bearing a face rate of interest of 8 percent (compound interest) requires an equal annual payment of $38.80.

Example

To find the equal annual installment necessary to amortize the 8 percent, three-year loan, the procedure is:

Percentage × Original amount of the loan = Annual payment

or

$$0.388034 \times \$100 = \$38.80 \text{ (rounded)}$$

Demonstration of what is assumed to occur during the three years:

Year	Payment to be made at end of year	Interest on outstanding balance of loan	Repayment of principal	End-of-year outstanding balance of loan
1	$ 38.80	$ 8.00*	$30.80	$69.20
2	38.80	5.54	33.26	35.94
3	38.80	2.88	35.92	—
Totals ...	$116.40	$16.42	$99.98†	

* 0.08 × original balance of $100.
† Discrepancy from $100 total caused by rounding.

The original loan of $100 is repaid from the three equal installments of $38.80, and the lender receives 8 percent interest calculated annually on the outstanding balance of the loan.

Note

The compound interest formula for calculating the percentages in column 6 is:

$$\left[\frac{1}{1 - (1 - r)^{-n}} \right] \div r$$

Substituting:

$$\left[\frac{1}{1 - (1 - 0.08)^{-3}} \right] \div 0.08 = 0.388034$$

Interrelation of columns 1–6

The factors and percentages in columns 1 through 6 are all based upon the compound interest premise and therefore are all related as discussed below.

1. Factors in column 4 (present value of reversion of $1) are the reciprocals of factors in column 1 (amount of $1 at compound interest), and vice versa.

Example

$$\frac{1}{1.259712} \text{ (column 1, 8\%, 3 years)} = 0.793832 \text{ (column 4, 8\%, 3 years)}$$

2. If the column 2 factors (accumulation of $1 per period) were calculated as though the equal annual increment of income were deposited at the beginning of each year, as is the case with the column 1 factors, then a column 2 factor for any given year can be shown to be the sum of successive column 1 factors. Column 2 factors in the annual table can be converted to beginning-of-year payments by subtracting 1.0 from the next year's factor.

Example

$100 deposited at the beginning of each year for three years at 8 percent compound interest has a future worth of $350.61.

$$\$100 \times (4.506112 \text{ [column 2, 4 years, 8\%]} - 1.0) = \$100 \times 3.506112$$
$$= \$350.611$$

The column 2 factor for beginning-of-year payments (3.506112) equals the sum of each column 1 factor for years 1–3.

1.080000	Column 1, 8%, 1 year
1.166400	Column 1, 8%, 2 years
1.259712	Column 1, 8%, 3 years
3.506112	Total

3. In similar fashion, a column 5 factor is the sum of successive column 4 factors.

Example

0.925926	Column 4, 8%, 1 year
0.857339	Column 4, 8%, 2 years
0.793832	Column 4, 8%, 3 years
2.577097	Column 5, 8%, 3 years

4. Column 6 factors are reciprocals of column 5 factors.

Example

$$\frac{1}{2.577097}(\text{column 5, 8\%, 3 years}) = 0.388034 \ (\text{column 6, 8\%, 3 years})$$

5. Column 5 factors are the reciprocals of column 3 factors plus the rate of discount.

Example

$$\frac{1}{0.08 \ (\text{rate of discount}) + 0.308034 \ (\text{column 3, 8\%, 3 years})}$$
$$= 2.577097 \ (\text{column 5, 8\%, 3 years})$$

Note

The column 3 factor is a sinking fund factor that tells us what percentage of the total investment must be deposited each year in a sinking fund assumed to draw 8 percent compound interest over three years in order to accumulate to the total investment at the end of those three years. Appraisers often call this assumption the "Inwood Premise" for amortization of the investment. It might be pointed out that the column 4 factors also are based upon the Inwood Premise regarding recapture of investment.

Additional capitalization assumptions

Capitalization to perpetuity. An assumed perpetual level income stream (land income) is capitalized into present value by dividing the annual income by the rate of return *on* investment.

Example

Given that the rate of discount is 8 percent and the annual payments are $100 each, the procedure is:

$$\frac{\text{Annual income}}{\text{Rate of interest}} = \text{Present value of perpetuity}$$

or

$$\frac{\$100}{0.08} = \$1,250$$

You would pay $1,250 today for the right to receive $100 a year to perpetuity if you need 8 percent to induce you to wait to receive the income over time.

Demonstration of what is assumed to occur:

Year	Payment to be received at end of year	Interest on outstanding balance of investment	Recapture of investment	Outstanding balance at end of year
1	$100	$100*	0	$1,250
2	100	100	0	1,250
99 to infinity	100	100	0	1,250

* (0.08 × outstanding balance at beginning of year, or $1,250).

The original investment of $1,250 is never recaptured from future income, the total of which represents interest at the rate of 8 percent on the full investment year after year. The original investment is recaptured only by selling the asset.

The 8 percent return on investment in the above example is treated as a capitalization rate and when used to discount land income to present value, it is sometimes called the "land capitalization rate." Rather than view this land capitalization rate as an exception to the rule that every capitalization rate has two components, the return *on* investment (8 percent in this instance) and the return *of* investment, it is contended that the return of investment component is present but that it has fallen to zero.

Straight-line capitalization. Other columns could be provided in addition to the six which have been discussed. A column of capitalization rates or capitalization factors (reciprocals of the rates) could be included for capitalization of future income projected to decline in a straight line.

A "straight-line capitalization rate" is composed of (*a*) the speculative rate of discount (8 percent) and (*b*) a rate of amortization that permits recapture of the investment over the duration of the income stream (25-year income stream = 4 percent rate of recapture; 50-year stream = 2 percent rate of recapture; 3-year stream = 33.3 percent rate of recapture; the rate of recapture can be found by dividing the number of years in the income stream into 1.0). A straight-line capitalization factor is the reciprocal of the straight-line capitalization rate.

Example

A three-year income stream beginning at $100 in the first-year discounted at 8 percent using a straight-line capitalization rate has a present value of $241.94 (rounded). To find the present value of a three-year income stream beginning at $100 given that the rate of discount is 8 percent, the procedure is:

$$\frac{\text{Income in first year}}{\text{Rate}} = \text{Present value}$$

$$\frac{\$100}{0.08 \text{ rate of discount} + 0.333 \text{ rate of recapture}} = \$241.94$$

Alternatively:

$$\text{Factor} \times \text{Income in first year} = \text{Present value}$$

$$\left[\frac{1}{0.08 + 0.333} \right] \times \$100 = \$241.94$$

Appraisal literature has assumed that straight-line capitalization determined the present value of an income stream which declines in a straight line over time, with the rate of decline given by the formula:

$$\frac{R \times d}{R + d}$$

where

R = Capitalization rate
d = Rate of recapture (reciprocal of the years of remaining economic life)

Thus, with a rate of discount of 0.08 and a recapture rate of 0.3333 (one-third each year), the annual rate of decline would be:

$$\frac{0.08 \times 0.3333}{0.08 + 0.3333} = \frac{0.02666}{0.4133} = 0.0645$$

An income stream beginning at $100 in year 1 would be projected to fall to $93.54 in year 2 and to $87.09 in year 3. Graphed, this income stream would appear as a straight line:

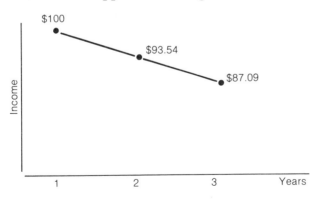

The assumption has been that the annual recapture of investment under the straight-line capitalization method is not reinvested. The following example demonstrates this assumption:

Year	Income to be received at end of year	Interest on outstanding balance of investment	Recapture of principal	End-of-year outstanding balance of investment
1	$100.00	$19.36*	$ 80.64	$161.30
2	93.54	12.90	80.64	80.66
3	87.09	6.45	80.64	—
	$280.63	$38.71	$241.92	

* 0.08 × $241.94.

The assumption in much of appraisal literature regarding straight-line capitalization is that the recapture of the original amount of the investment is in equal annual amounts (in this case, $80.64 each year). Since interest each year is calculated on the remaining outstanding balance of the investment at the beginning of that year, the portion of each annual increment of income designated as interest declines year by year (from $19.36 in year 1 to $6.45 in year 3). Income received each year from the investment is the sum of the annual recapture plus interest in that year, resulting in an income stream beginning at $100 in year 1 and declining to $87.09 in year 3.

Recent articles have pointed out that the so-called straight-line capitalization process is but one special case of the more general present value formulation which assumes that the annual recapture of investment is reinvested at the speculative rate.[1] That is, straight-line capitalization has the same reinvestment rate assumption (the Inwood Premise) as the present value factors in columns 4 and 5.

Thus, the present value of a three-year stream discounted at 8 percent and assumed to decline by 6.45 percent each year can be found by using the column 4 factors:

Year	Income to be received at end of year		Column 4: Present value of reversion of $1		
1	$100.00	×	0.925926	=	$ 92.59
2	93.54	×	0.857339	=	80.20
3	87.09	×	0.793832	=	69.13
	$280.63				$241.92 (answer)

---

[1] Joseph Strung, "The Internal Rate of Return and the Reinvestment Presumptions," *Appraisal Journal*, January 1976, pp. 23–33; Schall and Kerr, "The Validity of Existing Capitalization Methods," *Engineering Economist*, 24, (1979): 29–35; and John Glascock and Donald Cunningham, "The Straight-Line Income Capitalization Model: A Special Case of Present Value and IRR Analysis" (Ohio State University, unpublished paper, 1980). The interested reader is referred to these papers for the proof of this formulation.

The contention that the reinvestment rate for annual recapture is zero is not correct. The reinvestment rate in so-called straight-line capitalization is the speculative rate of discount (0.08 in the above example).

Other assumptions. Capitalization rates and factors can be calculated for discounting level income streams to present value assuming that the annual recapture of investment is reinvested at an interest rate less than the speculative rate of discount. Appraisers have called this recapture assumption the "Hoskold Premise." A Hoskold capitalization rate for a three-year level income stream of $100 each year, discounted at 8 percent and assuming that the annual recapture will be reinvested at 6 percent, is obtained by adding the 8 percent return *on* investment to the column 3 sinking fund factor for three years at 6 percent. This rate is converted to a factor by taking its reciprocal (1/rate).

Example

0.08 return on investment + 0.314110 return of investment*

$$= 0.394110 \text{ Hoskold capitalization rate}$$

$$\frac{\text{Income}}{\text{Rate}} = \text{Value}$$

$$\frac{\$100}{0.394110} = \$253.74$$

* Column 3, 6 percent, three years.

The Hoskold Premise is a special case of more general assumptions concerning reinvestment rates in the sinking fund concept of recapture of investment. Sinking fund factors at any assumed reinvestment rate can be added to the discount rate to obtain a capitalization rate.

Still other capitalization rates and factors have been calculated for income streams assumed to take different flow patterns. For instance, Frederick Babcock developed tables for income streams assumed to decline in a curvilinear fashion over their duration.[2]

---

[2] Frederick Babcock, *Valuation of Real Estate* (New York: McGraw-Hill, 1932), pp. 543–99.

appendix G

Interest tables*

* Tables in this appendix are taken from Paul Wendt and Alan R. Cerf, *Tables for Investment Analysis* (Berkeley: Center for Real Estate and Urban Economics, Institute of Urban and Regional Development, University of California), © 1966. The Regents of the University of California, pages 22, 25, 54, 57, 70, 73, 78, 81, 86, 89, 94, 97, 102, 105–6, 109–10, 113–14, 117–18, 121, 126, 129, 138, 141, 158, 161, 178, and 181.

3.00%   MONTHLY COMPOUND INTEREST TABLES   3.00%
                                   EFFECTIVE RATE 0.250

	1	2	3	4	5	6	
	AMOUNT OF $1 AT COMPOUND INTEREST	ACCUMULATION OF $1 PER PERIOD	SINKING FUND FACTOR	PRESENT VALUE REVERSION OF $1	PRESENT VALUE ORD. ANNUITY $1 PER PERIOD	INSTALMENT TO AMORTIZE $1	
MONTHS							
1	1.002500	1.000000	1.000000	0.997506	0.997506	1.002500	
2	1.005006	2.002500	0.499376	0.995019	1.992525	0.501876	
3	1.007519	3.007506	0.332501	0.992537	2.985062	0.335001	
4	1.010038	4.015025	0.249064	0.990062	3.975124	0.251564	
5	1.012563	5.025063	0.199002	0.987593	4.962718	0.201502	
6	1.015094	6.037625	0.165628	0.985130	5.947848	0.168128	
7	1.017632	7.052719	0.141789	0.982674	6.930522	0.144289	
8	1.020176	8.070351	0.123910	0.980223	7.910745	0.126410	
9	1.022726	9.090527	0.110005	0.977779	8.888524	0.112505	
10	1.025283	10.113253	0.098880	0.975340	9.863864	0.101380	
11	1.027846	11.138536	0.089778	0.972908	10.836772	0.092278	
12	1.030416	12.166383	0.082194	0.970482	11.807254	0.084694	
YEARS							**MONTHS**
1	1.030416	12.166383	0.082194	0.970482	11.807254	0.084694	12
2	1.061757	24.702818	0.040481	0.941835	23.265980	0.042981	24
3	1.094051	37.620560	0.026581	0.914034	34.386465	0.029081	36
4	1.127328	50.931208	0.019634	0.887053	45.178695	0.022134	48
5	1.161617	64.646713	0.015469	0.860869	55.652358	0.017969	60
6	1.196946	78.779387	0.012694	0.835458	65.816858	0.015194	72
7	1.233355	93.341920	0.010713	0.810797	75.681321	0.013213	84
8	1.270868	108.347387	0.009230	0.786863	85.254603	0.011730	96
9	1.309523	123.809259	0.008077	0.763637	94.545300	0.010577	108
10	1.349354	139.741419	0.007156	0.741096	103.561753	0.009656	120
11	1.390395	156.158171	0.006404	0.719220	112.312057	0.008904	132
12	1.432686	173.074254	0.005778	0.697990	120.804069	0.008278	144
13	1.476262	190.504855	0.005249	0.677386	129.045412	0.007749	156
14	1.521164	208.465626	0.004797	0.657391	137.043486	0.007297	168
15	1.567432	226.972690	0.004406	0.637986	144.805471	0.006906	180
16	1.615107	246.042664	0.004064	0.619154	152.338338	0.006564	192
17	1.664232	265.692670	0.003764	0.600878	159.648848	0.006264	204
18	1.714851	285.940350	0.003497	0.583141	166.743566	0.005997	216
19	1.767010	306.803882	0.003259	0.565928	173.628861	0.005759	228
20	1.820755	328.301998	0.003046	0.549223	180.310914	0.005546	240
21	1.876135	350.454000	0.002853	0.533011	186.795726	0.005353	252
22	1.933199	373.279777	0.002679	0.517277	193.089119	0.005179	264
23	1.992000	396.799821	0.002520	0.502008	199.196742	0.005020	276
24	2.052588	421.035250	0.002375	0.487190	205.124080	0.004875	288
25	2.115020	446.007823	0.002242	0.472809	210.876453	0.004742	300
26	2.179350	471.739961	0.002120	0.458852	216.459028	0.004620	312
27	2.245637	498.254766	0.002007	0.445308	221.876815	0.004507	324
28	2.313940	525.576044	0.001903	0.432163	227.134679	0.004403	336
29	2.384321	553.728325	0.001806	0.419407	232.237341	0.004306	348
30	2.456842	582.736885	0.001716	0.407027	237.189382	0.004216	360
31	2.531569	612.627767	0.001632	0.395012	241.995247	0.004132	372
32	2.608570	643.427810	0.001554	0.383352	246.659253	0.004054	384
33	2.687912	675.164665	0.001481	0.372036	251.185586	0.003981	396
34	2.769667	707.866827	0.001413	0.361054	255.578310	0.003913	408
35	2.853909	741.563657	0.001349	0.350397	259.841368	0.003849	420
36	2.940714	776.285408	0.001288	0.340054	263.978590	0.003788	432
37	3.030158	812.063254	0.001231	0.330016	267.993688	0.003731	444
38	3.122323	848.929318	0.001178	0.320274	271.890268	0.003678	456
39	3.217292	886.916698	0.001128	0.310820	275.671828	0.003628	468
40	3.315149	926.059501	0.001080	0.301646	279.341764	0.003580	480

3.00% ANNUAL COMPOUND INTEREST TABLES 3.00%
EFFECTIVE RATE 3.00

	1	2	3	4	5	6
	AMOUNT OF $1 AT COMPOUND INTEREST	ACCUMULATION OF $1 PER PERIOD	SINKING FUND FACTOR	PRESENT VALUE REVERSION OF $1	PRESENT VALUE ORD. ANNUITY $1 PER PERIOD	INSTALMENT TO AMORTIZE $1
YEARS						
1	1.030000	1.000000	1.000000	0.970874	0.970874	1.030000
2	1.060900	2.030000	0.492611	0.942596	1.913470	0.522611
3	1.092727	3.090900	0.323530	0.915142	2.828611	0.353530
4	1.125509	4.183627	0.239027	0.888487	3.717098	0.269027
5	1.159274	5.309136	0.188355	0.862609	4.579707	0.218355
6	1.194052	6.468410	0.154598	0.837484	5.417191	0.184598
7	1.229874	7.662462	0.130506	0.813092	6.230283	0.160506
8	1.266770	8.892336	0.112456	0.789409	7.019692	0.142456
9	1.304773	10.159106	0.098434	0.766417	7.786109	0.128434
10	1.343916	11.463879	0.087231	0.744094	8.530203	0.117231
11	1.384234	12.807796	0.078077	0.722421	9.252624	0.108077
12	1.425761	14.192030	0.070462	0.701380	9.954004	0.100462
13	1.468534	15.617790	0.064030	0.680951	10.634955	0.094030
14	1.512590	17.086324	0.058526	0.661118	11.296073	0.088526
15	1.557967	18.598914	0.053767	0.641862	11.937935	0.083767
16	1.604706	20.156881	0.049611	0.623167	12.561102	0.079611
17	1.652848	21.761588	0.045953	0.605016	13.166118	0.075953
18	1.702433	23.414435	0.042709	0.587395	13.753513	0.072709
19	1.753506	25.116868	0.039814	0.570286	14.323799	0.069814
20	1.806111	26.870374	0.037216	0.553676	14.877475	0.067216
21	1.860295	28.676486	0.034872	0.537549	15.415024	0.064872
22	1.916103	30.536780	0.032747	0.521893	15.936917	0.062747
23	1.973587	32.452884	0.030814	0.506692	16.443608	0.060814
24	2.032794	34.426470	0.029047	0.491934	16.935542	0.059047
25	2.093778	36.459264	0.027428	0.477606	17.413148	0.057428
26	2.156591	38.553042	0.025938	0.463695	17.876842	0.055938
27	2.221289	40.709634	0.024564	0.450189	18.327031	0.054564
28	2.287928	42.930923	0.023293	0.437077	18.764108	0.053293
29	2.356566	45.218850	0.022115	0.424346	19.188455	0.052115
30	2.427262	47.575416	0.021019	0.411987	19.600441	0.051019
31	2.500080	50.002678	0.019999	0.399987	20.000428	0.049999
32	2.575083	52.502759	0.019047	0.388337	20.388766	0.049047
33	2.652335	55.077841	0.018156	0.377026	20.765792	0.048156
34	2.731905	57.730177	0.017322	0.366045	21.131837	0.047322
35	2.813862	60.462082	0.016539	0.355383	21.487220	0.046539
36	2.898278	63.275944	0.015804	0.345032	21.832252	0.045804
37	2.985227	66.174223	0.015112	0.334983	22.167235	0.045112
38	3.074783	69.159449	0.014459	0.325226	22.492462	0.044459
39	3.167027	72.234233	0.013844	0.315754	22.808215	0.043844
40	3.262038	75.401260	0.013262	0.306557	23.114772	0.043262
41	3.359899	78.663298	0.012712	0.297628	23.412400	0.042712
42	3.460696	82.023196	0.012192	0.288959	23.701359	0.042192
43	3.564517	85.483892	0.011698	0.280543	23.981902	0.041698
44	3.671452	89.048409	0.011230	0.272372	24.254274	0.041230
45	3.781596	92.719861	0.010785	0.264439	24.518713	0.040785
46	3.895044	96.501457	0.010363	0.256737	24.775449	0.040363
47	4.011895	100.396501	0.009961	0.249259	25.024708	0.039961
48	4.132252	104.408396	0.009578	0.241999	25.266707	0.039578
49	4.256219	108.540648	0.009213	0.234950	25.501657	0.039213
50	4.383906	112.796867	0.008865	0.228107	25.729764	0.038865

5.00%   MONTHLY COMPOUND INTEREST TABLES   5.00%
                         EFFECTIVE RATE 0.417

	1 AMOUNT OF $1 AT COMPOUND INTEREST	2 ACCUMULATION OF $1 PER PERIOD	3 SINKING FUND FACTOR	4 PRESENT VALUE REVERSION OF $1	5 PRESENT VALUE ORD. ANNUITY $1 PER PERIOD	6 INSTALMENT TO AMORTIZE $1	
MONTHS							
1	1.004167	1.000000	1.000000	0.995851	0.995851	1.004167	
2	1.008351	2.004167	0.498960	0.991718	1.987569	0.503127	
3	1.012552	3.012517	0.331948	0.987603	2.975173	0.336115	
4	1.016771	4.025070	0.248443	0.983506	3.958678	0.252610	
5	1.021008	5.041841	0.198340	0.979425	4.938103	0.202507	
6	1.025262	6.062848	0.164939	0.975361	5.913463	0.169106	
7	1.029534	7.088110	0.141081	0.971313	6.884777	0.145248	
8	1.033824	8.117644	0.123188	0.967283	7.852060	0.127355	
9	1.038131	9.151467	0.109272	0.963269	8.815329	0.113439	
10	1.042457	10.189599	0.098139	0.959272	9.774602	0.102306	
11	1.046800	11.232055	0.089031	0.955292	10.729894	0.093198	
12	1.051162	12.278855	0.081441	0.951328	11.681222	0.085607	
YEARS							MONTHS
1	1.051162	12.278855	0.081441	0.951328	11.681222	0.085607	12
2	1.104941	25.185921	0.039705	0.905025	22.793898	0.043871	24
3	1.161472	38.753336	0.025804	0.860976	33.365701	0.029971	36
4	1.220895	53.014885	0.018863	0.819071	43.422956	0.023029	48
5	1.283359	68.006083	0.014705	0.779205	52.990706	0.018871	60
6	1.349018	83.764259	0.011938	0.741280	62.092777	0.016105	72
7	1.418036	100.328653	0.009967	0.705201	70.751835	0.014134	84
8	1.490585	117.740512	0.008493	0.670877	78.989441	0.012660	96
9	1.566847	136.043196	0.007351	0.638225	86.826108	0.011517	108
10	1.647009	155.282279	0.006440	0.607161	94.281350	0.010607	120
11	1.731274	175.505671	0.005698	0.577609	101.373733	0.009864	132
12	1.819849	196.763730	0.005082	0.549496	108.120917	0.009249	144
13	1.912956	219.109391	0.004564	0.522751	114.539704	0.008731	156
14	2.010826	242.598290	0.004122	0.497308	120.646077	0.008289	168
15	2.113704	267.288944	0.003741	0.473103	126.455243	0.007908	180
16	2.221845	293.242809	0.003410	0.450076	131.981666	0.007577	192
17	2.335519	320.524523	0.003120	0.428170	137.239108	0.007287	204
18	2.455008	349.202022	0.002864	0.407331	142.240661	0.007030	216
19	2.580611	379.346715	0.002636	0.387505	146.998780	0.006803	228
20	2.712640	411.033669	0.002433	0.368645	151.525313	0.006600	240
21	2.851424	444.341787	0.002251	0.350702	155.831532	0.006417	252
22	2.997308	479.354011	0.002086	0.333633	159.928159	0.006253	264
23	3.150656	516.157528	0.001937	0.317394	163.825396	0.006104	276
24	3.311850	554.843982	0.001802	0.301946	167.532948	0.005969	288
25	3.481290	595.509709	0.001679	0.287250	171.060047	0.005846	300
26	3.659400	638.255971	0.001567	0.273269	174.415476	0.005733	312
27	3.846622	683.189213	0.001464	0.259968	177.607590	0.005630	324
28	4.043422	730.421325	0.001369	0.247315	180.644338	0.005536	336
29	4.250291	780.069922	0.001282	0.235278	183.533283	0.005449	348
30	4.467744	832.258635	0.001202	0.223827	186.281617	0.005368	360
31	4.696323	887.117422	0.001127	0.212933	188.896185	0.005294	372
32	4.936595	944.782889	0.001058	0.202569	191.383498	0.005225	384
33	5.189161	1005.398630	0.000995	0.192709	193.749748	0.005161	396
34	5.454648	1069.115587	0.000935	0.183330	196.000829	0.005102	408
35	5.733718	1136.092425	0.000880	0.174407	198.142346	0.005047	420
36	6.027066	1206.495925	0.000829	0.165918	200.179632	0.004996	432
37	6.335423	1280.501402	0.000781	0.157843	202.117759	0.004948	444
38	6.659555	1358.293140	0.000736	0.150160	203.961555	0.004903	456
39	7.000270	1440.064850	0.000694	0.142852	205.715609	0.004861	468
40	7.358417	1526.020157	0.000655	0.135899	207.384291	0.004822	480

ANNUAL COMPOUND INTEREST TABLES
EFFECTIVE RATE 5.00

	1 AMOUNT OF $1 AT COMPOUND INTEREST	2 ACCUMULATION OF $1 PER PERIOD	3 SINKING FUND FACTOR	4 PRESENT VALUE REVERSION OF $1	5 PRESENT VALUE ORD. ANNUITY $1 PER PERIOD	6 INSTALMENT TO AMORTIZE $1
YEARS						
1	1.050000	1.000000	1.000000	0.952381	0.952381	1.050000
2	1.102500	2.050000	0.487805	0.907029	1.859410	0.537805
3	1.157625	3.152500	0.317209	0.863838	2.723248	0.367209
4	1.215506	4.310125	0.232012	0.822702	3.545951	0.282012
5	1.276282	5.525631	0.180975	0.783526	4.329477	0.230975
6	1.340096	6.801913	0.147017	0.746215	5.075692	0.197017
7	1.407100	8.142008	0.122820	0.710681	5.786373	0.172820
8	1.477455	9.549109	0.104722	0.676839	6.463213	0.154722
9	1.551328	11.026564	0.090690	0.644609	7.107822	0.140690
10	1.628895	12.577893	0.079505	0.613913	7.721735	0.129505
11	1.710339	14.206787	0.070389	0.584679	8.306414	0.120389
12	1.795856	15.917127	0.062825	0.556837	8.863252	0.112825
13	1.885649	17.712983	0.056456	0.530321	9.393573	0.106456
14	1.979932	19.598632	0.051024	0.505068	9.898641	0.101024
15	2.078928	21.578564	0.046342	0.481017	10.379658	0.096342
16	2.182875	23.657492	0.042270	0.458112	10.837770	0.092270
17	2.292018	25.840366	0.038699	0.436297	11.274066	0.088699
18	2.406619	28.132385	0.035546	0.415521	11.689587	0.085546
19	2.526950	30.539004	0.032745	0.395734	12.085321	0.082745
20	2.653298	33.065954	0.030243	0.376889	12.462210	0.080243
21	2.785963	35.719252	0.027996	0.358942	12.821153	0.077996
22	2.925261	38.505214	0.025971	0.341850	13.163003	0.075971
23	3.071524	41.430475	0.024137	0.325571	13.488574	0.074137
24	3.225100	44.501999	0.022471	0.310068	13.798642	0.072471
25	3.386355	47.727099	0.020952	0.295303	14.093945	0.070952
26	3.555673	51.113454	0.019564	0.281241	14.375185	0.069564
27	3.733456	54.669126	0.018292	0.267848	14.643034	0.068292
28	3.920129	58.402583	0.017123	0.255094	14.898127	0.067123
29	4.116136	62.322712	0.016046	0.242946	15.141074	0.066046
30	4.321942	66.438848	0.015051	0.231377	15.372451	0.065051
31	4.538039	70.760790	0.014132	0.220359	15.592811	0.064132
32	4.764941	75.298829	0.013280	0.209866	15.802677	0.063280
33	5.003189	80.063771	0.012490	0.199873	16.002549	0.062490
34	5.253348	85.066959	0.011755	0.190355	16.192904	0.061755
35	5.516015	90.320307	0.011072	0.181290	16.374194	0.061072
36	5.791816	95.836323	0.010434	0.172657	16.546852	0.060434
37	6.081407	101.628139	0.009840	0.164436	16.711287	0.059840
38	6.385477	107.709546	0.009284	0.156605	16.867893	0.059284
39	6.704751	114.095023	0.008765	0.149148	17.017041	0.058765
40	7.039989	120.799774	0.008278	0.142046	17.159086	0.058278
41	7.391988	127.839763	0.007822	0.135282	17.294368	0.057822
42	7.761588	135.231751	0.007395	0.128840	17.423208	0.057395
43	8.149667	142.993339	0.006993	0.122704	17.545912	0.056993
44	8.557150	151.143006	0.006616	0.116861	17.662773	0.056616
45	8.985008	159.700156	0.006262	0.111297	17.774070	0.056262
46	9.434258	168.685164	0.005928	0.105997	17.880066	0.055928
47	9.905971	178.119422	0.005614	0.100949	17.981016	0.055614
48	10.401270	188.025393	0.005318	0.096142	18.077158	0.055318
49	10.921333	198.426663	0.005040	0.091564	18.168722	0.055040
50	11.467400	209.347996	0.004777	0.087204	18.255925	0.054777

INTEREST TABLES

6.00%   MONTHLY COMPOUND INTEREST TABLES   6.00%
                           EFFECTIVE RATE 0.500

	1 AMOUNT OF $1 AT COMPOUND INTEREST	2 ACCUMULATION OF $1 PER PERIOD	3 SINKING FUND FACTOR	4 PRESENT VALUE REVERSION OF $1	5 PRESENT VALUE ORD. ANNUITY $1 PER PERIOD	6 INSTALMENT TO AMORTIZE $1	
MONTHS							
1	1.005000	1.000000	1.000000	0.995025	0.995025	1.005000	
2	1.010025	2.005000	0.498753	0.990075	1.985099	0.503753	
3	1.015075	3.015025	0.331672	0.985149	2.970248	0.336672	
4	1.020151	4.030100	0.248133	0.980248	3.950496	0.253133	
5	1.025251	5.050251	0.198010	0.975371	4.925866	0.203010	
6	1.030378	6.075502	0.164595	0.970518	5.896384	0.169595	
7	1.035529	7.105879	0.140729	0.965690	6.862074	0.145729	
8	1.040707	8.141409	0.122829	0.960885	7.822959	0.127829	
9	1.045911	9.182116	0.108907	0.956105	8.779064	0.113907	
10	1.051140	10.228026	0.097771	0.951348	9.730412	0.102771	
11	1.056396	11.279167	0.088659	0.946615	10.677027	0.093659	
12	1.061678	12.335562	0.081066	0.941905	11.618932	0.086066	

YEARS							MONTHS
1	1.061678	12.335562	0.081066	0.941905	11.618932	0.086066	12
2	1.127160	25.431955	0.039321	0.887186	22.562866	0.044321	24
3	1.196681	39.336105	0.025422	0.835645	32.871016	0.030422	36
4	1.270489	54.097832	0.018485	0.787098	42.580318	0.023485	48
5	1.348850	69.770031	0.014333	0.741372	51.725561	0.019333	60
6	1.432044	86.408856	0.011573	0.698302	60.339514	0.016573	72
7	1.520370	104.073927	0.009609	0.657735	68.453042	0.014609	84
8	1.614143	122.828542	0.008141	0.619524	76.095218	0.013141	96
9	1.713699	142.739900	0.007006	0.583533	83.293424	0.012006	108
10	1.819397	163.879347	0.006102	0.549633	90.073453	0.011102	120
11	1.931613	186.322629	0.005367	0.517702	96.459599	0.010367	132
12	2.050751	210.150163	0.004759	0.487626	102.474743	0.009759	144
13	2.177237	235.447328	0.004247	0.459298	108.140440	0.009247	156
14	2.311524	262.304766	0.003812	0.432615	113.476990	0.008812	168
15	2.454094	290.818712	0.003439	0.407482	118.503515	0.008439	180
16	2.605457	321.091337	0.003114	0.383810	123.238025	0.008114	192
17	2.766156	353.231110	0.002831	0.361513	127.697486	0.007831	204
18	2.936766	387.353194	0.002582	0.340511	131.897876	0.007582	216
19	3.117899	423.579854	0.002361	0.320729	135.854246	0.007361	228
20	3.310204	462.040895	0.002164	0.302096	139.580772	0.007164	240
21	3.514371	502.874129	0.001989	0.284546	143.090806	0.006989	252
22	3.731129	546.225867	0.001831	0.268015	146.396927	0.006831	264
23	3.961257	592.251446	0.001688	0.252445	149.510979	0.006688	276
24	4.205569	641.115782	0.001560	0.237779	152.444121	0.006560	288
25	4.464970	692.993962	0.001443	0.223966	155.206864	0.006443	300
26	4.740359	748.071876	0.001337	0.210954	157.809106	0.006337	312
27	5.032734	806.546875	0.001240	0.198699	160.260172	0.006240	324
28	5.343142	868.628484	0.001151	0.187156	162.568844	0.006151	336
29	5.672696	934.539150	0.001070	0.176283	164.743394	0.006070	348
30	6.022575	1004.515043	0.000996	0.166042	166.791614	0.005996	360
31	6.394034	1078.806895	0.000927	0.156396	168.720844	0.005927	372
32	6.788405	1157.680906	0.000864	0.147310	170.537996	0.005864	384
33	7.207098	1241.419693	0.000806	0.138752	172.249581	0.005806	396
34	7.651617	1330.323306	0.000752	0.130691	173.861732	0.005752	408
35	8.123551	1424.710299	0.000702	0.123099	175.380226	0.005702	420
36	8.624594	1524.918875	0.000656	0.115947	176.810504	0.005656	432
37	9.156540	1631.308097	0.000613	0.109212	178.157690	0.005613	444
38	9.721296	1744.259173	0.000573	0.102867	179.426611	0.005573	456
39	10.320884	1864.176825	0.000536	0.096891	180.621815	0.005536	468
40	10.957454	1991.490734	0.000502	0.091262	181.747594	0.005502	480

6.00%   ANNUAL COMPOUND INTEREST TABLES   6.00%
                              EFFECTIVE RATE   6.00

	1 AMOUNT OF $1 AT COMPOUND INTEREST	2 ACCUMULATION OF $1 PER PERIOD	3 SINKING FUND FACTOR	4 PRESENT VALUE REVERSION OF $1	5 PRESENT VALUE ORD. ANNUITY $1 PER PERIOD	6 INSTALMENT TO AMORTIZE $1
YEARS			*NEEDS SAVED*			
1	1.060000	1.000000	1.000000	0.943396	0.943396	1.060000
2	1.123600	2.060000	0.485437	0.889996	1.833393	0.545437
3	1.191016	3.183600	0.314110	0.839619	2.673012	0.374110
4	1.262477	4.374616	0.228591	0.792094	3.465106	0.288591
5	1.338226	5.637093	0.177396	0.747258	4.212364	0.237396
6	1.418519	6.975319	0.143363	0.704961	4.917324	0.203363
7	1.503630	8.393838	0.119135	0.665057	5.582381	0.179135
8	1.593848	9.897468	0.101036	0.627412	6.209794	0.161036
9	1.689479	11.491316	0.087022	0.591898	6.801692	0.147022
10	1.790848	13.180795	0.075868	0.558395	7.360087	0.135868
11	1.898299	14.971643	0.066793	0.526788	7.886875	0.126793
12	2.012196	16.869941	0.059277	0.496969	8.383844	0.119277
13	2.132928	18.882138	0.052960	0.468839	8.852683	0.112960
14	2.260904	21.015066	0.047585	0.442301	9.294984	0.107585
15	2.396558	23.275970	0.042963	0.417265	9.712249	0.102963
16	2.540352	25.672528	0.038952	0.393646	10.105895	0.098952
17	2.692773	28.212880	0.035445	0.371364	10.477260	0.095445
18	2.854339	30.905653	0.032357	0.350344	10.827603	0.092357
19	3.025600	33.759992	0.029621	0.330513	11.158116	0.089621
20	3.207135	36.785591	0.027185	0.311805	11.469921	0.087185
21	3.399564	39.992727	0.025005	0.294155	11.764077	0.085005
22	3.603537	43.392290	0.023046	0.277505	12.041582	0.083046
23	3.819750	46.995828	0.021278	0.261797	12.303379	0.081278
24	4.048935	50.815577	0.019679	0.246979	12.550358	0.079679
25	4.291871	54.864512	0.018227	0.232999	12.783356	0.078227
26	4.549383	59.156383	0.016904	0.219810	13.003166	0.076904
27	4.822346	63.705766	0.015697	0.207368	13.210534	0.075697
28	5.111687	68.528112	0.014593	0.195630	13.406164	0.074593
29	5.418388	73.639798	0.013580	0.184557	13.590721	0.073580
30	5.743491	79.058186	0.012649	0.174110	13.764831	0.072649
31	6.088101	84.801677	0.011792	0.164255	13.929086	0.071792
32	6.453387	90.889778	0.011002	0.154957	14.084043	0.071002
33	6.840590	97.343165	0.010273	0.146186	14.230230	0.070273
34	7.251025	104.183755	0.009598	0.137912	14.368141	0.069598
35	7.686087	111.434780	0.008974	0.130105	14.498246	0.068974
36	8.147252	119.120867	0.008395	0.122741	14.620987	0.068395
37	8.636087	127.268119	0.007857	0.115793	14.736780	0.067857
38	9.154252	135.904206	0.007358	0.109239	14.846019	0.067358
39	9.703507	145.058458	0.006894	0.103056	14.949075	0.066894
40	10.285718	154.761966	0.006462	0.097222	15.046297	0.066462
41	10.902861	165.047684	0.006059	0.091719	15.138016	0.066059
42	11.557033	175.950545	0.005683	0.086527	15.224543	0.065683
43	12.250455	187.507577	0.005333	0.081630	15.306173	0.065333
44	12.985482	199.758032	0.005006	0.077009	15.383182	0.065006
45	13.764611	212.743514	0.004700	0.072650	15.455832	0.064700
46	14.590487	226.508125	0.004415	0.068538	15.524370	0.064415
47	15.465917	241.098612	0.004148	0.064658	15.589028	0.064148
48	16.393872	256.564529	0.003898	0.060998	15.650027	0.063898
49	17.377504	272.958401	0.003664	0.057546	15.707572	0.063664
50	18.420154	290.335905	0.003444	0.054288	15.761861	0.063444

6.50%   MONTHLY COMPOUND INTEREST TABLES   6.50%
EFFECTIVE RATE 0.542

	1 AMOUNT OF $1 AT COMPOUND INTEREST	2 ACCUMULATION OF $1 PER PERIOD	3 SINKING FUND FACTOR	4 PRESENT VALUE REVERSION OF $1	5 PRESENT VALUE ORD. ANNUITY $1 PER PERIOD	6 INSTALMENT TO AMORTIZE $1	
MONTHS							
1	1.005417	1.000000	1.000000	0.994613	0.994613	1.005417	
2	1.010863	2.005417	0.498649	0.989254	1.983867	0.504066	
3	1.016338	3.016279	0.331534	0.983924	2.967791	0.336951	
4	1.021843	4.032618	0.247978	0.978624	3.946415	0.253395	
5	1.027378	5.054461	0.197845	0.973351	4.919766	0.203262	
6	1.032943	6.081839	0.164424	0.968107	5.887873	0.169841	
7	1.038538	7.114782	0.140552	0.962892	6.850765	0.145969	
8	1.044164	8.153321	0.122649	0.957704	7.808469	0.128066	
9	1.049820	9.197485	0.108725	0.952545	8.761014	0.114142	
10	1.055506	10.247304	0.097587	0.947413	9.708426	0.103003	
11	1.061224	11.302811	0.088474	0.942309	10.650735	0.093890	
12	1.066972	12.364034	0.080880	0.937232	11.587967	0.086296	
YEARS							MONTHS
1	1.066972	12.364034	0.080880	0.937232	11.587967	0.086296	12
2	1.138429	25.556111	0.039130	0.878404	22.448578	0.044546	24
3	1.214672	39.631685	0.025232	0.823268	32.627489	0.030649	36
4	1.296020	54.649927	0.018298	0.771593	42.167488	0.023715	48
5	1.382817	70.673968	0.014149	0.723161	51.108680	0.019566	60
6	1.475427	87.771168	0.011393	0.677770	59.488649	0.016810	72
7	1.574239	106.013400	0.009433	0.635227	67.342623	0.014849	84
8	1.679669	125.477348	0.007970	0.595355	74.703617	0.013386	96
9	1.792160	146.244833	0.006838	0.557986	81.602576	0.012255	108
10	1.912184	168.403154	0.005938	0.522962	88.068500	0.011355	120
11	2.040246	192.045460	0.005207	0.490137	94.128569	0.010624	132
12	2.176885	217.271134	0.004603	0.459372	99.808260	0.010019	144
13	2.322675	244.186218	0.004095	0.430538	105.131446	0.009512	156
14	2.478229	272.903856	0.003664	0.403514	110.120506	0.009081	168
15	2.644201	303.544767	0.003294	0.378186	114.796412	0.008711	180
16	2.821288	336.237756	0.002974	0.354448	119.178820	0.008391	192
17	3.010235	371.120256	0.002695	0.332200	123.286152	0.008111	204
18	3.211836	408.338901	0.002449	0.311348	127.135675	0.007866	216
19	3.426938	448.050147	0.002232	0.291806	130.743570	0.007649	228
20	3.656447	490.420930	0.002039	0.273490	134.125004	0.007456	240
21	3.901326	535.629362	0.001867	0.256323	137.294192	0.007284	252
22	4.162605	583.865486	0.001713	0.240234	140.266456	0.007129	264
23	4.441382	635.332073	0.001574	0.225155	143.048282	0.006991	276
24	4.738830	690.245473	0.001449	0.211023	145.657372	0.006865	288
25	5.056198	748.836525	0.001335	0.197777	148.102695	0.006752	300
26	5.394821	811.351528	0.001233	0.185363	150.394529	0.006649	312
27	5.756122	878.053277	0.001139	0.173728	152.542509	0.006556	324
28	6.141620	949.222165	0.001053	0.162823	154.555664	0.006470	336
29	6.552936	1025.157366	0.000975	0.152603	156.442457	0.006392	348
30	6.991798	1106.178087	0.000904	0.143025	158.210820	0.006321	360
31	7.460052	1192.624917	0.000838	0.134047	159.868185	0.006255	372
32	7.959665	1284.861250	0.000778	0.125633	161.421521	0.006195	384
33	8.492739	1383.274822	0.000723	0.117748	162.877357	0.006140	396
34	9.061513	1488.279333	0.000672	0.110357	164.241813	0.006089	408
35	9.668379	1600.316190	0.000625	0.103430	165.520625	0.006042	420
36	10.315889	1719.856364	0.000581	0.096938	166.719167	0.005998	432
37	11.006763	1847.402364	0.000541	0.090853	167.842480	0.005958	444
38	11.743906	1983.490356	0.000504	0.085151	168.895284	0.005921	456
39	12.530417	2128.692413	0.000470	0.079806	169.882006	0.005886	468
40	13.369602	2283.618920	0.000438	0.074797	170.806793	0.005855	480

6.50%   ANNUAL COMPOUND INTEREST TABLES   6.50%
                              EFFECTIVE RATE 6.50

	1 AMOUNT OF $1 AT COMPOUND INTEREST	2 ACCUMULATION OF $1 PER PERIOD	3 SINKING FUND FACTOR	4 PRESENT VALUE REVERSION OF $1	5 PRESENT VALUE ORD. ANNUITY $1 PER PERIOD	6 INSTALMENT TO AMORTIZE $1
YEARS						
1	1.065000	1.000000	1.000000	0.938967	0.938967	1.065000
2	1.134225	2.065000	0.484262	0.881659	1.820626	0.549262
3	1.207950	3.199225	0.312576	0.827849	2.648476	0.377576
4	1.286466	4.407175	0.226903	0.777323	3.425799	0.291903
5	1.370087	5.693641	0.175635	0.729881	4.155679	0.240635
6	1.459142	7.063728	0.141568	0.685334	4.841014	0.206568
7	1.553987	8.522870	0.117331	0.643506	5.484520	0.182331
8	1.654996	10.076856	0.099237	0.604231	6.088751	0.164237
9	1.762570	11.731852	0.085238	0.567353	6.656104	0.150238
10	1.877137	13.494423	0.074105	0.532726	7.188830	0.139105
11	1.999151	15.371560	0.065055	0.500212	7.689042	0.130055
12	2.129096	17.370711	0.057568	0.469683	8.158725	0.122568
13	2.267487	19.499808	0.051283	0.441017	8.599742	0.116283
14	2.414874	21.767295	0.045940	0.414100	9.013842	0.110940
15	2.571841	24.182169	0.041353	0.388827	9.402669	0.106353
16	2.739011	26.754010	0.037378	0.365095	9.767764	0.102378
17	2.917046	29.493021	0.033906	0.342813	10.110577	0.098906
18	3.106654	32.410067	0.030855	0.321890	10.432466	0.095855
19	3.308587	35.516722	0.028156	0.302244	10.734710	0.093156
20	3.523645	38.825309	0.025756	0.283797	11.018507	0.090756
21	3.752682	42.348954	0.023613	0.266476	11.284983	0.088613
22	3.996606	46.101636	0.021691	0.250212	11.535196	0.086691
23	4.256386	50.098242	0.019961	0.234941	11.770137	0.084961
24	4.533051	54.354628	0.018398	0.220602	11.990739	0.083398
25	4.827699	58.887679	0.016981	0.207138	12.197877	0.081981
26	5.141500	63.715378	0.015695	0.194496	12.392373	0.080695
27	5.475697	68.856877	0.014523	0.182625	12.574998	0.079523
28	5.831617	74.332574	0.013453	0.171479	12.746477	0.078453
29	6.210672	80.164192	0.012474	0.161013	12.907490	0.077474
30	6.614366	86.374864	0.011577	0.151186	13.058676	0.076577
31	7.044300	92.989230	0.010754	0.141959	13.200635	0.075754
32	7.502179	100.033530	0.009997	0.133295	13.333929	0.074997
33	7.989821	107.535710	0.009299	0.125159	13.459088	0.074299
34	8.509159	115.525531	0.008656	0.117520	13.576609	0.073656
35	9.062255	124.034690	0.008062	0.110348	13.686957	0.073062
36	9.651301	133.096945	0.007513	0.103613	13.790570	0.072513
37	10.278636	142.748247	0.007005	0.097289	13.887859	0.072005
38	10.946747	153.026883	0.006535	0.091351	13.979210	0.071535
39	11.658286	163.973630	0.006099	0.085776	14.064986	0.071099
40	12.416075	175.631916	0.005694	0.080541	14.145527	0.070694
41	13.223119	188.047990	0.005318	0.075625	14.221152	0.070318
42	14.082622	201.271110	0.004968	0.071010	14.292161	0.069968
43	14.997993	215.353732	0.004644	0.066676	14.358837	0.069644
44	15.972862	230.351725	0.004341	0.062606	14.421443	0.069341
45	17.011098	246.324587	0.004060	0.058785	14.480228	0.069060
46	18.116820	263.335685	0.003797	0.055197	14.535426	0.068797
47	19.294413	281.452504	0.003553	0.051828	14.587254	0.068553
48	20.548550	300.746917	0.003325	0.048665	14.635919	0.068325
49	21.884205	321.295467	0.003112	0.045695	14.681615	0.068112
50	23.306679	343.179672	0.002914	0.042906	14.724521	0.067914

7.00%

MONTHLY COMPOUND INTEREST TABLES
EFFECTIVE RATE 0.583

7.00%

	1 AMOUNT OF $1 AT COMPOUND INTEREST	2 ACCUMULATION OF $1 PER PERIOD	3 SINKING FUND FACTOR	4 PRESENT VALUE REVERSION OF $1	5 PRESENT VALUE ORD. ANNUITY $1 PER PERIOD	6 INSTALMENT TO AMORTIZE $1	
MONTHS							
1	1.005833	1.000000	1.000000	0.994200	0.994200	1.005833	
2	1.011701	2.005833	0.498546	0.988435	1.982635	0.504379	
3	1.017602	3.017534	0.331396	0.982702	2.965337	0.337230	
4	1.023538	4.035136	0.247823	0.977003	3.942340	0.253656	
5	1.029509	5.058675	0.197680	0.971337	4.913677	0.203514	
6	1.035514	6.088184	0.164253	0.965704	5.879381	0.170086	
7	1.041555	7.123698	0.140377	0.960103	6.839484	0.146210	
8	1.047631	8.165253	0.122470	0.954535	7.794019	0.128304	
9	1.053742	9.212883	0.108544	0.948999	8.743018	0.114377	
10	1.059889	10.266625	0.097403	0.943495	9.686513	0.103236	
11	1.066071	11.326514	0.088288	0.938024	10.624537	0.094122	
12	1.072290	12.392585	0.080693	0.932583	11.557120	0.086527	
YEARS							MONTHS
1	1.072290	12.392585	0.080693	0.932583	11.557120	0.086527	12
2	1.149806	25.681032	0.038939	0.869712	22.335099	0.044773	24
3	1.232926	39.930101	0.025044	0.811079	32.386464	0.030877	36
4	1.322054	55.209236	0.018113	0.756399	41.760201	0.023946	48
5	1.417625	71.592902	0.013968	0.705405	50.501993	0.019801	60
6	1.520106	89.160944	0.011216	0.657849	58.654444	0.017049	72
7	1.629994	107.998981	0.009259	0.613499	66.257285	0.015093	84
8	1.747826	128.198821	0.007800	0.572139	73.347569	0.013634	96
9	1.874177	149.858909	0.006673	0.533568	79.959850	0.012506	108
10	2.009661	173.084807	0.005778	0.497596	86.126354	0.011611	120
11	2.154940	197.989707	0.005051	0.464050	91.877134	0.010884	132
12	2.310721	224.694985	0.004450	0.432765	97.240216	0.010284	144
13	2.477763	253.330789	0.003947	0.403590	102.241738	0.009781	156
14	2.656881	284.036677	0.003521	0.376381	106.906074	0.009354	168
15	2.848947	316.962297	0.003155	0.351007	111.255958	0.008988	180
16	3.054897	352.268112	0.002839	0.327343	115.312587	0.008672	192
17	3.275736	390.126188	0.002563	0.305275	119.095732	0.008397	204
18	3.512539	430.721027	0.002322	0.284694	122.623831	0.008155	216
19	3.766461	474.250470	0.002109	0.265501	125.914077	0.007942	228
20	4.038739	520.926660	0.001920	0.247602	128.982506	0.007753	240
21	4.330700	570.977075	0.001751	0.230910	131.844073	0.007585	252
22	4.643766	624.645640	0.001601	0.215342	134.512723	0.007434	264
23	4.979464	682.193909	0.001466	0.200825	137.001461	0.007299	276
24	5.339430	743.902347	0.001344	0.187286	139.322418	0.007178	288
25	5.725418	810.071693	0.001234	0.174660	141.486903	0.007068	300
26	6.139309	881.024426	0.001135	0.162885	143.505467	0.006968	312
27	6.583120	957.106339	0.001045	0.151904	145.387946	0.006878	324
28	7.059015	1038.688219	0.000963	0.141663	147.143515	0.006796	336
29	7.569311	1126.167659	0.000888	0.132112	148.780729	0.006721	348
30	8.116497	1219.970996	0.000820	0.123206	150.307568	0.006653	360
31	8.703240	1320.555383	0.000757	0.114900	151.731473	0.006591	372
32	9.332398	1428.411024	0.000700	0.107154	153.059383	0.006533	384
33	10.007037	1544.063557	0.000648	0.099930	154.297770	0.006481	396
34	10.730447	1668.076622	0.000599	0.093193	155.452669	0.006433	408
35	11.500152	1801.054601	0.000555	0.086910	156.529709	0.006389	420
36	12.337932	1943.645569	0.000514	0.081051	157.534139	0.006348	432
37	13.229843	2096.544450	0.000477	0.075587	158.470853	0.006310	444
38	14.186229	2260.496403	0.000442	0.070491	159.344418	0.006276	456
39	15.211753	2436.300456	0.000410	0.065739	160.159090	0.006244	468
40	16.311411	2624.813398	0.000381	0.061307	160.918839	0.006214	480

7.00%   ANNUAL COMPOUND INTEREST TABLES   7.00%
                              EFFECTIVE RATE 7.00

	1	2	3	4	5	6
	AMOUNT OF $1 AT COMPOUND INTEREST	ACCUMULATION OF $1 PER PERIOD	SINKING FUND FACTOR	PRESENT VALUE REVERSION OF $1	PRESENT VALUE ORD. ANNUITY $1 PER PERIOD	INSTALMENT TO AMORTIZE $1
YEARS						
1	1.070000	1.000000	1.000000	0.934579	0.934579	1.070000
2	1.144900	2.070000	0.483092	0.873439	1.808018	0.553092
3	1.225043	3.214900	0.311052	0.816298	2.624316	0.381052
4	1.310796	4.439943	0.225228	0.762895	3.387211	0.295228
5	1.402552	5.750739	0.173891	0.712986	4.100197	0.243891
6	1.500730	7.153291	0.139796	0.666342	4.766540	0.209796
7	1.605781	8.654021	0.115553	0.622750	5.389289	0.185553
8	1.718186	10.259803	0.097468	0.582009	5.971299	0.167468
9	1.838459	11.977989	0.083486	0.543934	6.515232	0.153486
10	1.967151	13.816448	0.072378	0.508349	7.023582	0.142378
11	2.104852	15.783599	0.063357	0.475093	7.498674	0.133357
12	2.252192	17.888451	0.055902	0.444012	7.942686	0.125902
13	2.409845	20.140643	0.049651	0.414964	8.357651	0.119651
14	2.578534	22.550488	0.044345	0.387817	8.745468	0.114345
15	2.759032	25.129022	0.039795	0.362446	9.107914	0.109795
16	2.952164	27.888054	0.035858	0.338735	9.446649	0.105858
17	3.158815	30.840217	0.032425	0.316574	9.763223	0.102425
18	3.379932	33.999033	0.029413	0.295864	10.059087	0.099413
19	3.616528	37.378965	0.026753	0.276508	10.335595	0.096753
20	3.869684	40.995492	0.024393	0.258419	10.594014	0.094393
21	4.140562	44.865177	0.022289	0.241513	10.835527	0.092289
22	4.430402	49.005739	0.020406	0.225713	11.061240	0.090406
23	4.740530	53.436141	0.018714	0.210947	11.272187	0.088714
24	5.072367	58.176671	0.017189	0.197147	11.469334	0.087189
25	5.427433	63.249038	0.015811	0.184249	11.653583	0.085811
26	5.807353	68.676470	0.014561	0.172195	11.825779	0.084561
27	6.213868	74.483823	0.013426	0.160930	11.986709	0.083426
28	6.648838	80.697691	0.012392	0.150402	12.137111	0.082392
29	7.114257	87.346529	0.011449	0.140563	12.277674	0.081449
30	7.612255	94.460786	0.010586	0.131367	12.409041	0.080586
31	8.145113	102.073041	0.009797	0.122773	12.531814	0.079797
32	8.715271	110.218154	0.009073	0.114741	12.646555	0.079073
33	9.325340	118.933425	0.008408	0.107235	12.753790	0.078408
34	9.978114	128.258765	0.007797	0.100219	12.854009	0.077797
35	10.676581	138.236878	0.007234	0.093663	12.947672	0.077234
36	11.423942	148.913460	0.006715	0.087535	13.035208	0.076715
37	12.223618	160.337402	0.006237	0.081809	13.117017	0.076237
38	13.079271	172.561020	0.005795	0.076457	13.193473	0.075795
39	13.994820	185.640292	0.005387	0.071455	13.264928	0.075387
40	14.974458	199.635112	0.005009	0.066780	13.331709	0.075009
41	16.022670	214.609570	0.004660	0.062412	13.394120	0.074660
42	17.144257	230.632240	0.004336	0.058329	13.452449	0.074336
43	18.344355	247.776496	0.004036	0.054513	13.506962	0.074036
44	19.628460	266.120851	0.003758	0.050946	13.557908	0.073758
45	21.002452	285.749311	0.003500	0.047613	13.605522	0.073500
46	22.472623	306.751763	0.003260	0.044499	13.650020	0.073260
47	24.045707	329.224386	0.003037	0.041587	13.691608	0.073037
48	25.728907	353.270093	0.002831	0.038867	13.730474	0.072831
49	27.529930	378.999000	0.002639	0.036324	13.766799	0.072639
50	29.457025	406.528929	0.002460	0.033948	13.800746	0.072460

7.50%   MONTHLY COMPOUND INTEREST TABLES   7.50%
                                EFFECTIVE RATE 0.625

	1 AMOUNT OF $1 AT COMPOUND INTEREST	2 ACCUMULATION OF $1 PER PERIOD	3 SINKING FUND FACTOR	4 PRESENT VALUE REVERSION OF $1	5 PRESENT VALUE ORD. ANNUITY $1 PER PERIOD	6 INSTALMENT TO AMORTIZE $1	
MONTHS							
1	1.006250	1.000000	1.000000	0.993789	0.993789	1.006250	
2	1.012539	2.006250	0.498442	0.987616	1.981405	0.504692	
3	1.018867	3.018789	0.331259	0.981482	2.962887	0.337509	
4	1.025235	4.037656	0.247668	0.975386	3.938273	0.253918	
5	1.031643	5.062892	0.197516	0.969327	4.907600	0.203766	
6	1.038091	6.094535	0.164081	0.963307	5.870907	0.170331	
7	1.044579	7.132626	0.140201	0.957324	6.828231	0.146451	
8	1.051108	8.177205	0.122291	0.951377	7.779608	0.128541	
9	1.057677	9.228312	0.108362	0.945468	8.725076	0.114612	
10	1.064287	10.285989	0.097220	0.939596	9.664672	0.103470	
11	1.070939	11.350277	0.088104	0.933760	10.598432	0.094354	
12	1.077633	12.421216	0.080507	0.927960	11.526392	0.086757	

YEARS							MONTHS
1	1.077633	12.421216	0.080507	0.927960	11.526392	0.086757	12
2	1.161292	25.806723	0.038750	0.861110	22.222423	0.045000	24
3	1.251446	40.231382	0.024856	0.799076	32.147913	0.031106	36
4	1.348599	55.775864	0.017929	0.741510	41.358371	0.024179	48
5	1.453294	72.527105	0.013788	0.688092	49.905308	0.020038	60
6	1.566117	90.578789	0.011040	0.638522	57.836524	0.017290	72
7	1.687699	110.031871	0.009088	0.592523	65.196376	0.015338	84
8	1.818720	130.995147	0.007634	0.549837	72.026024	0.013884	96
9	1.959912	153.585857	0.006511	0.510227	78.363665	0.012761	108
10	2.112065	177.930342	0.005620	0.473470	84.244743	0.011870	120
11	2.276030	204.164753	0.004898	0.439362	89.702148	0.011148	132
12	2.452724	232.435809	0.004302	0.407710	94.766401	0.010552	144
13	2.643135	262.901620	0.003804	0.378339	99.465827	0.010054	156
14	2.848329	295.732572	0.003381	0.351083	103.826705	0.009631	168
15	3.069452	331.112276	0.003020	0.325791	107.873427	0.009270	180
16	3.307741	369.238599	0.002708	0.302321	111.628623	0.008958	192
17	3.564530	410.324766	0.002437	0.280542	115.113294	0.008687	204
18	3.841254	454.600560	0.002200	0.260332	118.346930	0.008450	216
19	4.139460	502.313599	0.001991	0.241577	121.347615	0.008241	228
20	4.460817	553.730725	0.001806	0.224174	124.132131	0.008056	240
21	4.807122	609.139496	0.001642	0.208025	126.716051	0.007892	252
22	5.180311	668.849794	0.001495	0.193039	129.113825	0.007745	264
23	5.582472	733.195558	0.001364	0.179132	131.338863	0.007614	276
24	6.015854	802.536650	0.001246	0.166227	133.403610	0.007496	288
25	6.482880	877.260872	0.001140	0.154252	135.319613	0.007390	300
26	6.986163	957.786129	0.001044	0.143140	137.097587	0.007294	312
27	7.528517	1044.562771	0.000957	0.132828	138.747475	0.007207	324
28	8.112976	1138.076109	0.000879	0.123259	140.278506	0.007129	336
29	8.742807	1238.849131	0.000807	0.114380	141.699242	0.007057	348
30	9.421534	1347.445425	0.000742	0.106140	143.017627	0.006992	360
31	10.152952	1464.472331	0.000683	0.098494	144.241037	0.006933	372
32	10.941152	1590.584339	0.000629	0.091398	145.376312	0.006879	384
33	11.790542	1726.486751	0.000579	0.084814	146.429801	0.006829	396
34	12.705873	1872.939621	0.000534	0.078704	147.407398	0.006784	408
35	13.692263	2030.762007	0.000492	0.073034	148.314568	0.006742	420
36	14.755228	2200.836555	0.000454	0.067773	149.156386	0.006704	432
37	15.900715	2384.114432	0.000419	0.062890	149.937560	0.006669	444
38	17.135129	2581.620647	0.000387	0.058360	150.662457	0.006637	456
39	18.465374	2794.459783	0.000358	0.054155	151.335133	0.006608	468
40	19.898889	3023.822174	0.000331	0.050254	151.959350	0.006581	480

ANNUAL COMPOUND INTEREST TABLES
EFFECTIVE RATE 7.50

	1	2	3	4	5	6
	AMOUNT OF $1 AT COMPOUND INTEREST	ACCUMULATION OF $1 PER PERIOD	SINKING FUND FACTOR	PRESENT VALUE REVERSION OF $1	PRESENT VALUE ORD. ANNUITY $1 PER PERIOD	INSTALMENT TO AMORTIZE $1
YEARS						
1	1.075000	1.000000	1.000000	0.930233	0.930233	1.075000
2	1.155625	2.075000	0.481928	0.865333	1.795565	0.556928
3	1.242297	3.230625	0.309538	0.804961	2.600526	0.384538
4	1.335469	4.472922	0.223568	0.748801	3.349326	0.298568
5	1.435629	5.808391	0.172165	0.696559	4.045885	0.247165
6	1.543302	7.244020	0.138045	0.647962	4.693846	0.213045
7	1.659049	8.787322	0.113800	0.602755	5.296601	0.188800
8	1.783478	10.446371	0.095727	0.560702	5.857304	0.170727
9	1.917239	12.229849	0.081767	0.521583	6.378887	0.156767
10	2.061032	14.147087	0.070686	0.485194	6.864081	0.145686
11	2.215609	16.208119	0.061697	0.451343	7.315424	0.136697
12	2.381780	18.423728	0.054278	0.419854	7.735278	0.129278
13	2.560413	20.805508	0.048064	0.390562	8.125840	0.123064
14	2.752444	23.365921	0.042797	0.363313	8.489154	0.117797
15	2.958877	26.118365	0.038287	0.337966	8.827120	0.113287
16	3.180793	29.077242	0.034391	0.314387	9.141507	0.109391
17	3.419353	32.258035	0.031000	0.292453	9.433960	0.106000
18	3.675804	35.677388	0.028029	0.272049	9.706009	0.103029
19	3.951489	39.353192	0.025411	0.253069	9.959078	0.100411
20	4.247851	43.304681	0.023092	0.235413	10.194491	0.098092
21	4.566440	47.552532	0.021029	0.218989	10.413480	0.096029
22	4.908923	52.118972	0.019187	0.203711	10.617191	0.094187
23	5.277092	57.027895	0.017535	0.189498	10.806689	0.092535
24	5.672874	62.304987	0.016050	0.176227	10.982967	0.091050
25	6.098340	67.977862	0.014711	0.163979	11.146946	0.089711
26	6.555715	74.076201	0.013500	0.152539	11.299485	0.088500
27	7.047394	80.631916	0.012402	0.141896	11.441381	0.087402
28	7.575948	87.679310	0.011405	0.131997	11.573378	0.086405
29	8.144144	95.255258	0.010498	0.122788	11.696165	0.085498
30	8.754955	103.399403	0.009671	0.114221	11.810386	0.084671
31	9.411577	112.154358	0.008916	0.106252	11.916638	0.083916
32	10.117445	121.565935	0.008226	0.098839	12.015478	0.083226
33	10.876253	131.683380	0.007594	0.091943	12.107421	0.082594
34	11.691972	142.559633	0.007015	0.085529	12.192950	0.082015
35	12.568870	154.251606	0.006483	0.079562	12.272511	0.081483
36	13.511536	166.820476	0.005994	0.074011	12.346522	0.080994
37	14.524901	180.332012	0.005545	0.068847	12.415370	0.080545
38	15.614268	194.856913	0.005132	0.064044	12.479414	0.080132
39	16.785339	210.471181	0.004751	0.059576	12.538989	0.079751
40	18.044239	227.256520	0.004400	0.055419	12.594409	0.079400
41	19.397557	245.300759	0.004077	0.051553	12.645962	0.079077
42	20.852374	264.698315	0.003778	0.047956	12.693918	0.078778
43	22.416302	285.550689	0.003502	0.044610	12.738528	0.078502
44	24.097524	307.966991	0.003247	0.041498	12.780026	0.078247
45	25.904839	332.064515	0.003011	0.038603	12.818629	0.078011
46	27.847702	357.969354	0.002794	0.035910	12.854539	0.077794
47	29.936279	385.817055	0.002592	0.033404	12.887943	0.077592
48	32.181500	415.753334	0.002405	0.031074	12.919017	0.077405
49	34.595113	447.934835	0.002232	0.028906	12.947922	0.077232
50	37.189746	482.529947	0.002072	0.026889	12.974812	0.077072

8.00%   MONTHLY COMPOUND INTEREST TABLES   8.00%
                                 EFFECTIVE RATE 0.667

	1 AMOUNT OF $1 AT COMPOUND INTEREST	2 ACCUMULATION OF $1 PER PERIOD	3 SINKING FUND FACTOR	4 PRESENT VALUE REVERSION OF $1	5 PRESENT VALUE ORD. ANNUITY $1 PER PERIOD	6 INSTALMENT TO AMORTIZE $1	
MONTHS							
1	1.006667	1.000000	1.000000	0.993377	0.993377	1.006667	
2	1.013378	2.006667	0.498339	0.986799	1.980176	0.505006	
3	1.020134	3.020044	0.331121	0.980264	2.960440	0.337788	
4	1.026935	4.040178	0.247514	0.973772	3.934212	0.254181	
5	1.033781	5.067113	0.197351	0.967323	4.901535	0.204018	
6	1.040673	6.100893	0.163910	0.960917	5.862452	0.170577	
7	1.047610	7.141566	0.140025	0.954553	6.817005	0.146692	
8	1.054595	8.189176	0.122112	0.948232	7.765237	0.128779	
9	1.061625	9.243771	0.108181	0.941952	8.707189	0.114848	
10	1.068703	10.305396	0.097037	0.935714	9.642903	0.103703	
11	1.075827	11.374099	0.087919	0.929517	10.572420	0.094586	
12	1.083000	12.449926	0.080322	0.923361	11.495782	0.086988	

YEARS							MONTHS
1	1.083000	12.449926	0.080322	0.923361	11.495782	0.086988	12
2	1.172888	25.933190	0.038561	0.852596	22.110544	0.045227	24
3	1.270237	40.535558	0.024670	0.787255	31.911806	0.031336	36
4	1.375666	56.349915	0.017746	0.726921	40.961913	0.024413	48
5	1.489846	73.476856	0.013610	0.671210	49.318433	0.020276	60
6	1.613502	92.025325	0.010867	0.619770	57.034522	0.017533	72
7	1.747422	112.113308	0.008920	0.572272	64.159261	0.015586	84
8	1.892457	133.868583	0.007470	0.528414	70.737970	0.014137	96
9	2.049530	157.429535	0.006352	0.487917	76.812497	0.013019	108
10	2.219640	182.946035	0.005466	0.450523	82.421481	0.012133	120
11	2.403869	210.580392	0.004749	0.415996	87.600600	0.011415	132
12	2.603389	240.508387	0.004158	0.384115	92.382800	0.010825	144
13	2.819469	272.920390	0.003664	0.354677	96.798498	0.010331	156
14	3.053484	308.022574	0.003247	0.327495	100.875784	0.009913	168
15	3.306921	346.038222	0.002890	0.302396	104.640592	0.009557	180
16	3.581394	387.209149	0.002583	0.279221	108.116871	0.009249	192
17	3.878648	431.797244	0.002316	0.257822	111.326733	0.008983	204
18	4.200574	480.086128	0.002083	0.238063	114.290596	0.008750	216
19	4.549220	532.382966	0.001878	0.219818	117.027313	0.008545	228
20	4.926803	589.020416	0.001698	0.202971	119.554292	0.008364	240
21	5.335725	650.358746	0.001538	0.187416	121.887606	0.008204	252
22	5.778588	716.788127	0.001395	0.173053	124.042099	0.008062	264
23	6.258207	788.731114	0.001268	0.159790	126.031475	0.007935	276
24	6.777636	866.645333	0.001154	0.147544	127.868388	0.007821	288
25	7.340176	951.026395	0.001051	0.136237	129.564523	0.007718	300
26	7.949407	1042.411042	0.000959	0.125796	131.130668	0.007626	312
27	8.609204	1141.380571	0.000876	0.116155	132.576786	0.007543	324
28	9.323763	1248.564521	0.000801	0.107253	133.912076	0.007468	336
29	10.097631	1364.644687	0.000733	0.099033	135.145031	0.007399	348
30	10.935730	1490.359449	0.000671	0.091443	136.283494	0.007338	360
31	11.843390	1626.508474	0.000615	0.084435	137.334707	0.007281	372
32	12.826385	1773.957801	0.000564	0.077964	138.305357	0.007230	384
33	13.890969	1933.645350	0.000517	0.071989	139.201617	0.007184	396
34	15.043913	2106.586886	0.000475	0.066472	140.029190	0.007141	408
35	16.292550	2293.882485	0.000436	0.061378	140.793338	0.007103	420
36	17.644824	2496.723526	0.000401	0.056674	141.498923	0.007067	432
37	19.109335	2716.400273	0.000368	0.052330	142.150433	0.007035	444
38	20.695401	2954.310082	0.000338	0.048320	142.752013	0.007005	456
39	22.413109	3211.966288	0.000311	0.044617	143.307488	0.006978	468
40	24.273386	3491.007831	0.000286	0.041197	143.820392	0.006953	480

ANNUAL COMPOUND INTEREST TABLES
EFFECTIVE RATE 8.00

	1	2	3	4	5	6
	AMOUNT OF $1 AT COMPOUND INTEREST	ACCUMULATION OF $1 PER PERIOD	SINKING FUND FACTOR	PRESENT VALUE REVERSION OF $1	PRESENT VALUE ORD. ANNUITY $1 PER PERIOD	INSTALMENT TO AMORTIZE $1
YEARS						
1	1.080000	1.000000	1.000000	0.925926	0.925926	1.080000
2	1.166400	2.080000	0.480769	0.857339	1.783265	0.560769
3	1.259712	3.246400	0.308034	0.793832	2.577097	0.388034
4	1.360489	4.506112	0.221921	0.735030	3.312127	0.301921
5	1.469328	5.866601	0.170456	0.680583	3.992710	0.250456
6	1.586874	7.335929	0.136315	0.630170	4.622880	0.216315
7	1.713824	8.922803	0.112072	0.583490	5.206370	0.192072
8	1.850930	10.636628	0.094015	0.540269	5.746639	0.174015
9	1.999005	12.487558	0.080080	0.500249	6.246888	0.160080
10	2.158925	14.486562	0.069029	0.463193	6.710081	0.149029
11	2.331639	16.645487	0.060076	0.428883	7.138964	0.140076
12	2.518170	18.977126	0.052695	0.397114	7.536078	0.132695
13	2.719624	21.495297	0.046522	0.367698	7.903776	0.126522
14	2.937194	24.214920	0.041297	0.340461	8.244237	0.121297
15	3.172169	27.152114	0.036830	0.315242	8.559479	0.116830
16	3.425943	30.324283	0.032977	0.291890	8.851369	0.112977
17	3.700018	33.750226	0.029629	0.270269	9.121638	0.109629
18	3.996019	37.450244	0.026702	0.250249	9.371887	0.106702
19	4.315701	41.446263	0.024128	0.231712	9.603599	0.104128
20	4.660957	45.761964	0.021852	0.214548	9.818147	0.101852
21	5.033834	50.422921	0.019832	0.198656	10.016803	0.099832
22	5.436540	55.456755	0.018032	0.183941	10.200744	0.098032
23	5.871464	60.893296	0.016422	0.170315	10.371059	0.096422
24	6.341181	66.764759	0.014978	0.157699	10.528758	0.094978
25	6.848475	73.105940	0.013679	0.146018	10.674776	0.093679
26	7.396353	79.954415	0.012507	0.135202	10.809978	0.092507
27	7.988061	87.350768	0.011448	0.125187	10.935165	0.091448
28	8.627106	95.338830	0.010489	0.115914	11.051078	0.090489
29	9.317275	103.965936	0.009619	0.107328	11.158406	0.089619
30	10.062657	113.283211	0.008827	0.099377	11.257783	0.088827
31	10.867669	123.345868	0.008107	0.092016	11.349799	0.088107
32	11.737083	134.213537	0.007451	0.085200	11.434999	0.087451
33	12.676050	145.950620	0.006852	0.078889	11.513888	0.086852
34	13.690134	158.626670	0.006304	0.073045	11.586934	0.086304
35	14.785344	172.316804	0.005803	0.067635	11.654568	0.085803
36	15.968172	187.102148	0.005345	0.062625	11.717193	0.085345
37	17.245626	203.070320	0.004924	0.057986	11.775179	0.084924
38	18.625276	220.315945	0.004539	0.053690	11.828869	0.084539
39	20.115298	238.941221	0.004185	0.049713	11.878582	0.084185
40	21.724521	259.056519	0.003860	0.046031	11.924613	0.083860
41	23.462483	280.781040	0.003561	0.042621	11.967235	0.083561
42	25.339482	304.243523	0.003287	0.039464	12.006699	0.083287
43	27.366640	329.583005	0.003034	0.036541	12.043240	0.083034
44	29.555972	356.949646	0.002802	0.033834	12.077074	0.082802
45	31.920449	386.505617	0.002587	0.031328	12.108402	0.082587
46	34.474085	418.426067	0.002390	0.029007	12.137409	0.082390
47	37.232012	452.900152	0.002208	0.026859	12.164267	0.082208
48	40.210573	490.132164	0.002040	0.024869	12.189136	0.082040
49	43.427419	530.342737	0.001886	0.023027	12.212163	0.081886
50	46.901613	573.770156	0.001743	0.021321	12.233485	0.081743

8.50%   MONTHLY COMPOUND INTEREST TABLES   8.50%
                                      EFFECTIVE RATE 0.708

	1	2	3	4	5	6	
	AMOUNT OF $1 AT COMPOUND INTEREST	ACCUMULATION OF $1 PER PERIOD	SINKING FUND FACTOR	PRESENT VALUE REVERSION OF $1	PRESENT VALUE ORD. ANNUITY $1 PER PERIOD	INSTALMENT TO AMORTIZE $1	
MONTHS							
1	1.007083	1.000000	1.000000	0.992966	0.992966	1.007083	
2	1.014217	2.007083	0.498235	0.985982	1.978949	0.505319	
3	1.021401	3.021300	0.330983	0.979048	2.957996	0.338067	
4	1.028636	4.042701	0.247359	0.972161	3.930158	0.254443	
5	1.035922	5.071337	0.197187	0.965324	4.895482	0.204270	
6	1.043260	6.107259	0.163740	0.958534	5.854016	0.170823	
7	1.050650	7.150519	0.139850	0.951792	6.805808	0.146933	
8	1.058092	8.201168	0.121934	0.945098	7.750906	0.129017	
9	1.065586	9.259260	0.108000	0.938450	8.689356	0.115083	
10	1.073134	10.324846	0.096854	0.931850	9.621206	0.103937	
11	1.080736	11.397980	0.087735	0.925296	10.546501	0.094818	
12	1.088391	12.478716	0.080136	0.918788	11.465289	0.087220	
YEARS							MONTHS
1	1.088391	12.478716	0.080136	0.918788	11.465289	0.087220	12
2	1.184595	26.060437	0.038372	0.844171	21.999453	0.045456	24
3	1.289302	40.842659	0.024484	0.775613	31.678112	0.031568	36
4	1.403265	56.931495	0.017565	0.712624	40.570744	0.024648	48
5	1.527301	74.442437	0.013433	0.654750	48.741183	0.020517	60
6	1.662300	93.501188	0.010695	0.601576	56.248080	0.017778	72
7	1.809232	114.244559	0.008753	0.552721	63.145324	0.015836	84
8	1.969152	136.821455	0.007309	0.507833	69.482425	0.014392	96
9	2.143207	161.393943	0.006196	0.466590	75.304875	0.013279	108
10	2.332647	188.138416	0.005315	0.428698	80.654470	0.012399	120
11	2.538832	217.246858	0.004603	0.393882	85.569611	0.011686	132
12	2.763242	248.928220	0.004017	0.361894	90.085581	0.011101	144
13	3.007487	283.409927	0.003528	0.332504	94.234798	0.010612	156
14	3.273321	320.939504	0.003116	0.305500	98.047046	0.010199	168
15	3.562653	361.786353	0.002764	0.280690	101.549693	0.009847	180
16	3.877559	406.243693	0.002462	0.257894	104.767881	0.009545	192
17	4.220300	454.630657	0.002200	0.236950	107.724713	0.009283	204
18	4.593337	507.294589	0.001971	0.217707	110.441412	0.009055	216
19	4.999346	564.613533	0.001771	0.200026	112.937482	0.008854	228
20	5.441243	626.998951	0.001595	0.183782	115.230840	0.008678	240
21	5.922199	694.898672	0.001439	0.168856	117.337948	0.008522	252
22	6.445667	768.800112	0.001301	0.155143	119.273933	0.008384	264
23	7.015406	849.233766	0.001178	0.142543	121.052692	0.008261	276
24	7.635504	936.777024	0.001067	0.130967	122.686994	0.008151	288
25	8.310413	1032.058310	0.000969	0.120331	124.188570	0.008052	300
26	9.044978	1135.761595	0.000880	0.110559	125.568199	0.007964	312
27	9.844472	1248.631307	0.000801	0.101580	126.835785	0.007884	324
28	10.714634	1371.477676	0.000729	0.093330	128.000428	0.007812	336
29	11.661710	1505.182546	0.000664	0.085751	129.070487	0.007748	348
30	12.692499	1650.705711	0.000606	0.078787	130.053643	0.007689	360
31	13.814400	1809.091800	0.000553	0.072388	130.956956	0.007636	372
32	15.035468	1981.477780	0.000505	0.066509	131.786908	0.007588	384
33	16.364466	2169.101112	0.000461	0.061108	132.549457	0.007544	396
34	17.810936	2373.308640	0.000421	0.056145	133.250078	0.007505	408
35	19.385261	2595.566257	0.000385	0.051586	133.893800	0.007469	420
36	21.098742	2837.469426	0.000352	0.047396	134.485244	0.007436	432
37	22.963679	3100.754635	0.000323	0.043547	135.028655	0.007406	444
38	24.993459	3387.311862	0.000295	0.040010	135.527934	0.007379	456
39	27.202654	3699.198142	0.000270	0.036761	135.986665	0.007354	468
40	29.607121	4038.652333	0.000248	0.033776	136.408142	0.007331	480

8.50%   ANNUAL COMPOUND INTEREST TABLES   8.50%
                        EFFECTIVE RATE 8.50

	1 AMOUNT OF $1 AT COMPOUND INTEREST	2 ACCUMULATION OF $1 PER PERIOD	3 SINKING FUND FACTOR	4 PRESENT VALUE REVERSION OF $1	5 PRESENT VALUE ORD. ANNUITY $1 PER PERIOD	6 INSTALMENT TO AMORTIZE $1
YEARS						
1	1.085000	1.000000	1.000000	0.921659	0.921659	1.085000
2	1.177225	2.085000	0.479616	0.849455	1.771114	0.564616
3	1.277289	3.262225	0.306539	0.782908	2.554022	0.391539
4	1.385859	4.539514	0.220288	0.721574	3.275597	0.305288
5	1.503657	5.925373	0.168766	0.665045	3.940642	0.253766
6	1.631468	7.429030	0.134607	0.612945	4.553587	0.219607
7	1.770142	9.060497	0.110369	0.564926	5.118514	0.195369
8	1.920604	10.830639	0.092331	0.520669	5.639183	0.177331
9	2.083856	12.751244	0.078424	0.479880	6.119063	0.163424
10	2.260983	14.835099	0.067408	0.442285	6.561348	0.152408
11	2.453167	17.096083	0.058493	C.407636	6.968984	0.143493
12	2.661686	19.549250	0.051153	0.375702	7.344686	0.136153
13	2.887930	22.210936	0.045023	0.346269	7.690955	0.130023
14	3.133404	25.098866	0.039842	0.319142	8.010097	0.124842
15	3.399743	28.232269	0.035420	0.294140	8.304237	0.120420
16	3.688721	31.632012	0.031614	0.271097	8.575333	0.116614
17	4.002262	35.320733	0.028312	0.249859	8.825192	0.113312
18	4.342455	39.322995	0.025430	0.230285	9.055476	0.110430
19	4.711563	43.665450	0.022901	0.212244	9.267720	0.107901
20	5.112046	48.377013	0.020671	0.195616	9.463337	0.105671
21	5.546570	53.489059	0.018695	0.180292	9.643628	0.103695
22	6.018028	59.035629	0.016939	0.166167	9.809796	0.101939
23	6.529561	65.053658	0.015372	0.153150	9.962945	0.100372
24	7.084574	71.583219	0.013970	0.141152	10.104097	0.098970
25	7.686762	78.667792	0.012712	0.130094	10.234191	0.097712
26	8.340137	86.354555	0.011580	0.119902	10.354093	0.096580
27	9.049049	94.694902	0.010560	0.110509	10.464602	0.095560
28	9.818218	103.743741	0.009639	0.101851	10.566453	0.094639
29	10.652766	113.561959	0.008806	0.093872	10.660326	0.093806
30	11.558252	124.214725	0.008051	0.086518	10.746844	0.093051
31	12.540703	135.772977	0.007365	0.079740	10.826584	0.092365
32	13.606663	148.313680	0.006742	0.073493	10.900078	0.091742
33	14.763229	161.920343	0.006176	0.067736	10.967813	0.091176
34	16.018104	176.683572	0.005660	0.062429	11.030243	0.090660
35	17.379642	192.701675	0.005189	0.057539	11.087781	0.090189
36	18.856912	210.081318	0.004760	0.053031	11.140812	0.089760
37	20.459750	228.938230	0.004368	0.048876	11.189689	0.089368
38	22.198828	249.397979	0.004010	0.045047	11.234736	0.089010
39	24.085729	271.596808	0.003682	0.041518	11.276255	0.088682
40	26.133016	295.682536	0.003382	0.038266	11.314520	0.088382
41	28.354322	321.815552	0.003107	0.035268	11.349788	0.088107
42	30.764439	350.169874	0.002856	0.032505	11.382293	0.087856
43	33.379417	380.934313	0.002625	0.029959	11.412252	0.087625
44	36.216667	414.313730	0.002414	0.027612	11.439864	0.087414
45	39.295084	450.530397	0.002220	0.025448	11.465312	0.087220
46	42.635166	489.825480	0.002042	0.023455	11.488767	0.087042
47	46.259155	532.460646	0.001878	0.021617	11.510384	0.086878
48	50.191183	578.719801	0.001728	0.019924	11.530308	0.086728
49	54.457434	628.910984	0.001590	0.018363	11.548671	0.086590
50	59.086316	683.368418	0.001463	0.016924	11.565595	0.086463

9.00%   MONTHLY COMPOUND INTEREST TABLES   9.00%
                                 EFFECTIVE RATE 0.750

	1	2	3	4	5	6	
	AMOUNT OF $1 AT COMPOUND INTEREST	ACCUMULATION OF $1 PER PERIOD	SINKING FUND FACTOR	PRESENT VALUE REVERSION OF $1	PRESENT VALUE ORD. ANNUITY $1 PER PERIOD	INSTALMENT TO AMORTIZE $1	
MONTHS							
1	1.007500	1.000000	1.000000	0.992556	0.992556	1.007500	
2	1.015056	2.007500	0.498132	0.985167	1.977723	0.505632	
3	1.022669	3.022556	0.330846	0.977833	2.955556	0.338346	
4	1.030339	4.045225	0.247205	0.970554	3.926110	0.254705	
5	1.038067	5.075565	0.197022	0.963329	4.889440	0.204522	
6	1.045852	6.113631	0.163569	0.956158	5.845598	0.171069	
7	1.053696	7.159484	0.139675	0.949040	6.794638	0.147175	
8	1.061599	8.213180	0.121756	0.941975	7.736613	0.129256	
9	1.069561	9.274779	0.107819	0.934963	8.671576	0.115319	
10	1.077583	10.344339	0.096671	0.928003	9.599580	0.104171	
11	1.085664	11.421922	0.087551	0.921095	10.520675	0.095051	
12	1.093807	12.507586	0.079951	0.914238	11.434913	0.087451	
YEARS							MONTHS
1	1.093807	12.507586	0.079951	0.914238	11.434913	0.087451	12
2	1.196414	26.188471	0.038185	0.835831	21.889146	0.045685	24
3	1.308645	41.152716	0.024300	0.764149	31.446805	0.031800	36
4	1.431405	57.520711	0.017385	0.698614	40.184782	0.024885	48
5	1.565681	75.424137	0.013258	0.638700	48.173374	0.020758	60
6	1.712553	95.007028	0.010526	0.583924	55.476849	0.018026	72
7	1.873202	116.426928	0.008589	0.533845	62.153965	0.016089	84
8	2.048921	139.856164	0.007150	0.488062	68.258439	0.014650	96
9	2.241124	165.483223	0.006043	0.446205	73.839382	0.013543	108
10	2.451357	193.514277	0.005168	0.407937	78.941693	0.012668	120
11	2.681311	224.174837	0.004461	0.372952	83.606420	0.011961	132
12	2.932837	257.711570	0.003880	0.340967	87.871092	0.011380	144
13	3.207957	294.394279	0.003397	0.311725	91.770018	0.010897	156
14	3.508886	334.518079	0.002989	0.284991	95.334564	0.010489	168
15	3.838043	378.405769	0.002643	0.260549	98.593409	0.010143	180
16	4.198078	426.410427	0.002345	0.238204	101.572769	0.009845	192
17	4.591887	478.918252	0.002088	0.217775	104.296613	0.009588	204
18	5.022638	536.351674	0.001864	0.199099	106.786856	0.009364	216
19	5.493796	599.172747	0.001669	0.182024	109.063531	0.009169	228
20	6.009152	667.886870	0.001497	0.166413	111.144954	0.008997	240
21	6.572851	743.046852	0.001346	0.152141	113.047870	0.008846	252
22	7.189430	825.257358	0.001212	0.139093	114.787589	0.008712	264
23	7.863848	915.179777	0.001093	0.127164	116.378106	0.008593	276
24	8.601532	1013.537539	0.000987	0.116258	117.832218	0.008487	288
25	9.408415	1121.121937	0.000892	0.106288	119.161622	0.008392	300
26	10.290989	1238.798494	0.000807	0.097172	120.377014	0.008307	312
27	11.256354	1367.513924	0.000731	0.088839	121.488172	0.008231	324
28	12.312278	1508.303750	0.000663	0.081220	122.504035	0.008163	336
29	13.467255	1662.300631	0.000602	0.074254	123.432776	0.008102	348
30	14.730576	1830.743483	0.000546	0.067886	124.281866	0.008046	360
31	16.112406	2014.987436	0.000496	0.062064	125.058136	0.007996	372
32	17.623861	2216.514743	0.000451	0.056741	125.767832	0.007951	384
33	19.277100	2436.946701	0.000410	0.051875	126.416664	0.007910	396
34	21.085425	2678.056697	0.000373	0.047426	127.009850	0.007873	408
35	23.063384	2941.784473	0.000340	0.043359	127.552164	0.007840	420
36	25.226888	3230.251735	0.000310	0.039640	128.047967	0.007810	432
37	27.593344	3545.779215	0.000282	0.036241	128.501250	0.007782	444
38	30.181790	3890.905350	0.000257	0.033133	128.915659	0.007757	456
39	33.013050	4268.406696	0.000234	0.030291	129.294526	0.007734	468
40	36.109902	4681.320272	0.000214	0.027693	129.640902	0.007714	480

9.00% ANNUAL COMPOUND INTEREST TABLES 9.00%
EFFECTIVE RATE 9.00

	1 AMOUNT OF $1 AT COMPOUND INTEREST	2 ACCUMULATION OF $1 PER PERIOD	3 SINKING FUND FACTOR	4 PRESENT VALUE REVERSION OF $1	5 PRESENT VALUE ORD. ANNUITY $1 PER PERIOD	6 INSTALMENT TO AMORTIZE $1
YEARS						
1	1.090000	1.000000	1.000000	0.917431	0.917431	1.090000
2	1.188100	2.090000	0.478469	0.841680	1.759111	0.568469
3	1.295029	3.278100	0.305055	0.772183	2.531295	0.395055
4	1.411582	4.573129	0.218669	0.708425	3.239720	0.308669
5	1.538624	5.984711	0.167092	0.649931	3.889651	0.257092
6	1.677100	7.523335	0.132920	0.596267	4.485919	0.222920
7	1.828039	9.200435	0.108691	0.547034	5.032953	0.198691
8	1.992563	11.028474	0.090674	0.501866	5.534819	0.180674
9	2.171893	13.021036	0.076799	0.460428	5.995247	0.166799
10	2.367364	15.192930	0.065820	0.422411	6.417658	0.155820
11	2.580426	17.560293	0.056947	0.387533	6.805191	0.146947
12	2.812665	20.140720	0.049651	0.355535	7.160725	0.139651
13	3.065805	22.953385	0.043567	0.326179	7.486904	0.133567
14	3.341727	26.019189	0.038433	0.299246	7.786150	0.128433
15	3.642482	29.360916	0.034059	0.274538	8.060688	0.124059
16	3.970306	33.003399	0.030300	0.251870	8.312558	0.120300
17	4.327633	36.973705	0.027046	0.231073	8.543631	0.117046
18	4.717120	41.301338	0.024212	0.211994	8.755625	0.114212
19	5.141661	46.018458	0.021730	0.194490	8.950115	0.111730
20	5.604411	51.160120	0.019546	0.178431	9.128546	0.109546
21	6.108808	56.764530	0.017617	0.163698	9.292244	0.107617
22	6.658600	62.873338	0.015905	0.150182	9.442425	0.105905
23	7.257874	69.531939	0.014382	0.137781	9.580207	0.104382
24	7.911083	76.789813	0.013023	0.126405	9.706612	0.103023
25	8.623081	84.700896	0.011806	0.115968	9.822580	0.101806
26	9.399158	93.323977	0.010715	0.106393	9.928972	0.100715
27	10.245082	102.723135	0.009735	0.097608	10.026580	0.099735
28	11.167140	112.968217	0.008852	0.089548	10.116128	0.098852
29	12.172182	124.135356	0.008056	0.082155	10.198283	0.098056
30	13.267678	136.307539	0.007336	0.075371	10.273654	0.097336
31	14.461770	149.575217	0.006686	0.069148	10.342802	0.096686
32	15.763329	164.036987	0.006096	0.063438	10.406240	0.096096
33	17.182028	179.800315	0.005562	0.058200	10.464441	0.095562
34	18.728411	196.982344	0.005077	0.053395	10.517835	0.095077
35	20.413968	215.710755	0.004636	0.048986	10.566821	0.094636
36	22.251225	236.124723	0.004235	0.044941	10.611763	0.094235
37	24.253835	258.375948	0.003870	0.041231	10.652993	0.093870
38	26.436680	282.629783	0.003538	0.037826	10.690820	0.093538
39	28.815982	309.066463	0.003236	0.034703	10.725523	0.093236
40	31.409420	337.882445	0.002960	0.031838	10.757360	0.092960
41	34.236268	369.291865	0.002708	0.029209	10.786569	0.092708
42	37.317532	403.528133	0.002478	0.026797	10.813366	0.092478
43	40.676110	440.845665	0.002268	0.024584	10.837950	0.092268
44	44.336960	481.521775	0.002077	0.022555	10.860505	0.092077
45	48.327286	525.858734	0.001902	0.020692	10.881197	0.091902
46	52.676742	574.186021	0.001742	0.018984	10.900181	0.091742
47	57.417649	626.862762	0.001595	0.017416	10.917597	0.091595
48	62.585237	684.280411	0.001461	0.015978	10.933575	0.091461
49	68.217908	746.865648	0.001339	0.014659	10.948234	0.091339
50	74.357520	815.083556	0.001227	0.013449	10.961683	0.091227

MONTHLY COMPOUND INTEREST TABLES
EFFECTIVE RATE 0.792

	1 AMOUNT OF $1 AT COMPOUND INTEREST	2 ACCUMULATION OF $1 PER PERIOD	3 SINKING FUND FACTOR	4 PRESENT VALUE REVERSION OF $1	5 PRESENT VALUE ORD. ANNUITY $1 PER PERIOD	6 INSTALMENT TO AMORTIZE $1	
MONTHS							
1	1.007917	1.000000	1.000000	0.992146	0.992146	1.007917	
2	1.015896	2.007917	0.498029	0.984353	1.976498	0.505945	
3	1.023939	3.023813	0.330708	0.976621	2.953119	0.338625	
4	1.032045	4.047751	0.247051	0.968950	3.922070	0.254967	
5	1.040215	5.079796	0.196858	0.961340	4.883409	0.204775	
6	1.048450	6.120011	0.163398	0.953789	5.837198	0.171315	
7	1.056750	7.168461	0.139500	0.946297	6.783496	0.147417	
8	1.065116	8.225211	0.121577	0.938865	7.722360	0.129494	
9	1.073548	9.290328	0.107639	0.931490	8.653851	0.115555	
10	1.082047	10.363876	0.096489	0.924174	9.578024	0.104406	
11	1.090614	11.445923	0.087367	0.916915	10.494940	0.095284	
12	1.099248	12.536537	0.079767	0.909713	11.404653	0.087684	

YEARS							**MONTHS**
1	1.099248	12.536537	0.079767	0.909713	11.404653	0.087684	12
2	1.208345	26.317295	0.037998	0.827578	21.779615	0.045914	24
3	1.328271	41.465760	0.024116	0.752859	31.217856	0.032033	36
4	1.460098	58.117673	0.017206	0.684885	39.803947	0.025123	48
5	1.605009	76.422249	0.013085	0.623049	47.614827	0.021002	60
6	1.764303	96.543509	0.010358	0.566796	54.720488	0.018275	72
7	1.939406	118.661756	0.008427	0.515622	61.184601	0.016344	84
8	2.131887	142.975186	0.006994	0.469068	67.065090	0.014911	96
9	2.343472	169.701665	0.005893	0.426717	72.414648	0.013809	108
10	2.576055	199.080682	0.005023	0.388190	77.281211	0.012940	120
11	2.831723	231.375495	0.004322	0.353142	81.708388	0.012239	132
12	3.112764	266.875491	0.003747	0.321258	85.735849	0.011664	144
13	3.421699	305.898776	0.003269	0.292253	89.399684	0.011186	156
14	3.761294	348.795027	0.002867	0.265866	92.732722	0.010784	168
15	4.134593	395.948628	0.002526	0.241862	95.764831	0.010442	180
16	4.544942	447.782110	0.002233	0.220025	98.523180	0.010150	192
17	4.996016	504.759939	0.001981	0.200159	101.032487	0.009898	204
18	5.491859	567.392681	0.001762	0.182088	103.315236	0.009679	216
19	6.036912	636.241570	0.001572	0.165648	105.391883	0.009488	228
20	6.636061	711.923546	0.001405	0.150692	107.281037	0.009321	240
21	7.294674	795.116775	0.001258	0.137086	108.999624	0.009174	252
22	8.018653	886.566731	0.001128	0.124709	110.563046	0.009045	264
23	8.814485	987.092874	0.001013	0.113450	111.985311	0.008930	276
24	9.689302	1097.595994	0.000911	0.103207	113.279165	0.008828	288
25	10.650941	1219.066282	0.000820	0.093888	114.456200	0.008737	300
26	11.708022	1352.592202	0.000739	0.085412	115.526965	0.008656	312
27	12.870014	1499.370247	0.000667	0.077700	116.501054	0.008584	324
28	14.147332	1660.715658	0.000602	0.070685	117.387195	0.008519	336
29	15.551421	1838.074212	0.000544	0.064303	118.193330	0.008461	348
30	17.094862	2033.035174	0.000492	0.058497	118.926681	0.008409	360
31	18.791486	2247.345541	0.000445	0.053216	119.593820	0.008362	372
32	20.656495	2482.925693	0.000403	0.048411	120.200725	0.008319	384
33	22.706602	2741.886606	0.000365	0.044040	120.752835	0.008281	396
34	24.960178	3026.548765	0.000330	0.040064	121.255097	0.008247	408
35	27.437415	3339.462955	0.000299	0.036447	121.712011	0.008216	420
36	30.160512	3683.433122	0.000271	0.033156	122.127671	0.008188	432
37	33.153870	4061.541498	0.000246	0.030162	122.505803	0.008163	444
38	36.444312	4477.176216	0.000223	0.027439	122.849795	0.008140	456
39	40.061322	4934.061676	0.000203	0.024962	123.162729	0.008119	468
40	44.037311	5436.291914	0.000184	0.022708	123.447408	0.008101	480

9.50%   ANNUAL COMPOUND INTEREST TABLES   9.50%
                              EFFECTIVE RATE   9.50

	1	2	3	4	5	6
	AMOUNT OF $1 AT COMPOUND INTEREST	ACCUMULATION OF $1 PER PERIOD	SINKING FUND FACTOR	PRESENT VALUE REVERSION OF $1	PRESENT VALUE ORD. ANNUITY $1 PER PERIOD	INSTALMENT TO AMORTIZE $1
YEARS						
1	1.095000	1.000000	1.000000	0.913242	0.913242	1.095000
2	1.199025	2.095000	0.477327	0.834011	1.747253	0.572327
3	1.312932	3.294025	0.303580	0.761654	2.508907	0.398580
4	1.437661	4.606957	0.217063	0.695574	3.204481	0.312063
5	1.574239	6.044618	0.165436	0.635228	3.839709	0.260436
6	1.723791	7.618857	0.131253	0.580117	4.419825	0.226253
7	1.887552	9.342648	0.107036	0.529787	4.949612	0.202036
8	2.066869	11.230200	0.089046	0.483824	5.433436	0.184046
9	2.263222	13.297069	0.075205	0.441848	5.875284	0.170205
10	2.478228	15.560291	0.064266	0.403514	6.278798	0.159266
11	2.713659	18.038518	0.055437	0.368506	6.647304	0.150437
12	2.971457	20.752178	0.048188	0.336535	6.983839	0.143188
13	3.253745	23.723634	0.042152	0.307338	7.291178	0.137152
14	3.562851	26.977380	0.037068	0.280674	7.571852	0.132068
15	3.901322	30.540231	0.032744	0.256323	7.828175	0.127744
16	4.271948	34.441553	0.029035	0.234085	8.062260	0.124035
17	4.677783	38.713500	0.025831	0.213777	8.276037	0.120831
18	5.122172	43.391283	0.023046	0.195230	8.471266	0.118046
19	5.608778	48.513454	0.020613	0.178292	8.649558	0.115613
20	6.141612	54.122233	0.018477	0.162824	8.812382	0.113477
21	6.725065	60.263845	0.016594	0.148697	8.961080	0.111594
22	7.363946	66.988910	0.014928	0.135797	9.096876	0.109928
23	8.063521	74.352856	0.013449	0.124015	9.220892	0.108449
24	8.829556	82.416378	0.012134	0.113256	9.334148	0.107134
25	9.668364	91.245934	0.010959	0.103430	9.437578	0.105959
26	10.586858	100.914297	0.009909	0.094457	9.532034	0.104909
27	11.592610	111.501156	0.008969	0.086262	9.618296	0.103969
28	12.693908	123.093766	0.008124	0.078778	9.697074	0.103124
29	13.899829	135.787673	0.007364	0.071943	9.769018	0.102364
30	15.220313	149.687502	0.006681	0.065702	9.834719	0.101681
31	16.666242	164.907815	0.006064	0.060002	9.894721	0.101064
32	18.249535	181.574057	0.005507	0.054796	9.949517	0.100507
33	19.983241	199.823593	0.005004	0.050042	9.999559	0.100004
34	21.881649	219.806834	0.004549	0.045700	10.045259	0.099549
35	23.960406	241.688483	0.004138	0.041736	10.086995	0.099138
36	26.236644	265.648889	0.003764	0.038115	10.125109	0.098764
37	28.729126	291.885534	0.003426	0.034808	10.159917	0.098426
38	31.458393	320.614659	0.003119	0.031788	10.191705	0.098119
39	34.446940	352.073052	0.002840	0.029030	10.220735	0.097840
40	37.719399	386.519992	0.002587	0.026512	10.247247	0.097587
41	41.302742	424.239391	0.002357	0.024211	10.271458	0.097357
42	45.226503	465.542133	0.002148	0.022111	10.293569	0.097148
43	49.523020	510.768636	0.001958	0.020193	10.313762	0.096958
44	54.227707	560.291656	0.001785	0.018441	10.332203	0.096785
45	59.379340	614.519364	0.001627	0.016841	10.349043	0.096627
46	65.020377	673.898703	0.001484	0.015380	10.364423	0.096484
47	71.197313	738.919080	0.001353	0.014045	10.378469	0.096353
48	77.961057	810.116393	0.001234	0.012827	10.391296	0.096234
49	85.367358	888.077450	0.001126	0.011714	10.403010	0.096126
50	93.477257	973.444808	0.001027	0.010698	10.413707	0.096027

10.00%   MONTHLY COMPOUND INTEREST TABLES   10.00%
                                  EFFECTIVE RATE 0.833

	1 AMOUNT OF $1 AT COMPOUND INTEREST	2 ACCUMULATION OF $1 PER PERIOD	3 SINKING FUND FACTOR	4 PRESENT VALUE REVERSION OF $1	5 PRESENT VALUE ORD. ANNUITY $1 PER PERIOD	6 INSTALMENT TO AMORTIZE $1	
MONTHS							
1	1.008333	1.000000	1.000000	0.991736	0.991736	1.008333	
2	1.016736	2.008333	0.497925	0.983539	1.975275	0.506259	
3	1.025209	3.025069	0.330571	0.975411	2.950686	0.338904	
4	1.033752	4.050278	0.246897	0.967350	3.918036	0.255230	
5	1.042367	5.084031	0.196694	0.959355	4.877391	0.205028	
6	1.051053	6.126398	0.163228	0.951427	5.828817	0.171561	
7	1.059812	7.177451	0.139325	0.943563	6.772381	0.147659	
8	1.068644	8.237263	0.121400	0.935765	7.708146	0.129733	
9	1.077549	9.305907	0.107459	0.928032	8.636178	0.115792	
10	1.086529	10.383456	0.096307	0.920362	9.556540	0.104640	
11	1.095583	11.469985	0.087184	0.912756	10.469296	0.095517	
12	1.104713	12.565568	0.079583	0.905212	11.374508	0.087916	
YEARS							MONTHS
1	1.104713	12.565568	0.079583	0.905212	11.374508	0.087916	12
2	1.220391	26.446915	0.037812	0.819410	21.670855	0.046145	24
3	1.348182	41.781821	0.023934	0.741740	30.991236	0.032267	36
4	1.489354	58.722492	0.017029	0.671432	39.428160	0.025363	48
5	1.645309	77.437072	0.012914	0.607789	47.065369	0.021247	60
6	1.817594	98.111314	0.010193	0.550178	53.978665	0.018526	72
7	2.007920	120.950418	0.008268	0.498028	60.236667	0.016601	84
8	2.218176	146.181076	0.006841	0.450821	65.901488	0.015174	96
9	2.450448	174.053713	0.005745	0.408089	71.029355	0.014079	108
10	2.707041	204.844979	0.004882	0.369407	75.671163	0.013215	120
11	2.990504	238.860493	0.004187	0.334392	79.872986	0.012520	132
12	3.303649	276.437876	0.003617	0.302696	83.676528	0.011951	144
13	3.649584	317.950102	0.003145	0.274004	87.119542	0.011478	156
14	4.031743	363.809201	0.002749	0.248032	90.236201	0.011082	168
15	4.453920	414.470346	0.002413	0.224521	93.057439	0.010746	180
16	4.920303	470.436376	0.002126	0.203240	95.611259	0.010459	192
17	5.435523	532.262780	0.001879	0.183975	97.923008	0.010212	204
18	6.004693	600.563216	0.001665	0.166536	100.015633	0.009998	216
19	6.633463	676.015601	0.001479	0.150751	101.909902	0.009813	228
20	7.328074	759.368836	0.001317	0.136462	103.624619	0.009650	240
21	8.095419	851.450244	0.001174	0.123527	105.176801	0.009508	252
22	8.943115	953.173779	0.001049	0.111818	106.581856	0.009382	264
23	9.879576	1065.549097	0.000938	0.101219	107.853730	0.009272	276
24	10.914097	1189.691580	0.000841	0.091625	109.005045	0.009174	288
25	12.056945	1326.833403	0.000754	0.082940	110.047230	0.009087	300
26	13.319465	1478.335767	0.000676	0.075078	110.990629	0.009010	312
27	14.714187	1645.702407	0.000608	0.067962	111.844605	0.008941	324
28	16.254954	1830.594523	0.000546	0.061520	112.617635	0.008880	336
29	17.957060	2034.847259	0.000491	0.055688	113.317392	0.008825	348
30	19.837399	2260.487925	0.000442	0.050410	113.950820	0.008776	360
31	21.914634	2509.756117	0.000398	0.045632	114.524207	0.008732	372
32	24.209383	2785.125947	0.000359	0.041306	115.043244	0.008692	384
33	26.744422	3089.330596	0.000324	0.037391	115.513083	0.008657	396
34	29.544912	3425.389448	0.000292	0.033847	115.938387	0.008625	408
35	32.638650	3796.638052	0.000263	0.030639	116.323377	0.008597	420
36	36.056344	4206.761236	0.000238	0.027734	116.671876	0.008571	432
37	39.831914	4659.829677	0.000215	0.025105	116.987340	0.008548	444
38	44.002836	5160.340305	0.000194	0.022726	117.272903	0.008527	456
39	48.610508	5713.260935	0.000175	0.020572	117.531398	0.008508	468
40	53.700663	6324.079581	0.000158	0.018622	117.765391	0.008491	480

10.00%
ANNUAL COMPOUND INTEREST TABLES
EFFECTIVE RATE 10.00
10.00%

	1 AMOUNT OF $1 AT COMPOUND INTEREST	2 ACCUMULATION OF $1 PER PERIOD	3 SINKING FUND FACTOR	4 PRESENT VALUE REVERSION OF $1	5 PRESENT VALUE ORD. ANNUITY $1 PER PERIOD	6 INSTALMENT TO AMORTIZE $1
YEARS						
1	1.100000	1.000000	1.000000	0.909091	0.909091	1.100000
2	1.210000	2.100000	0.476190	0.826446	1.735537	0.576190
3	1.331000	3.310000	0.302115	0.751315	2.486852	0.402115
4	1.464100	4.641000	0.215471	0.683013	3.169865	0.315471
5	1.610510	6.105100	0.163797	0.620921	3.790787	0.263797
6	1.771561	7.715610	0.129607	0.564474	4.355261	0.229607
7	1.948717	9.487171	0.105405	0.513158	4.868419	0.205405
8	2.143589	11.435888	0.087444	0.466507	5.334926	0.187444
9	2.357948	13.579477	0.073641	0.424098	5.759024	0.173641
10	2.593742	15.937425	0.062745	0.385543	6.144567	0.162745
11	2.853117	18.531167	0.053963	0.350494	6.495061	0.153963
12	3.138428	21.384284	0.046763	0.318631	6.813692	0.146763
13	3.452271	24.522712	0.040779	0.289664	7.103356	0.140779
14	3.797498	27.974983	0.035746	0.263331	7.366687	0.135746
15	4.177248	31.772482	0.031474	0.239392	7.606080	0.131474
16	4.594973	35.949730	0.027817	0.217629	7.823709	0.127817
17	5.054470	40.544703	0.024664	0.197845	8.021553	0.124664
18	5.559917	45.599173	0.021930	0.179859	8.201412	0.121930
19	6.115909	51.159090	0.019547	0.163508	8.364920	0.119547
20	6.727500	57.274999	0.017460	0.148644	8.513564	0.117460
21	7.400250	64.002499	0.015624	0.135131	8.648694	0.115624
22	8.140275	71.402749	0.014005	0.122846	8.771540	0.114005
23	8.954302	79.543024	0.012572	0.111678	8.883218	0.112572
24	9.849733	88.497327	0.011300	0.101526	8.984744	0.111300
25	10.834706	98.347059	0.010168	0.092296	9.077040	0.110168
26	11.918177	109.181765	0.009159	0.083905	9.160945	0.109159
27	13.109994	121.099942	0.008258	0.076278	9.237223	0.108258
28	14.420994	134.209936	0.007451	0.069343	9.306567	0.107451
29	15.863093	148.630930	0.006728	0.063039	9.369606	0.106728
30	17.449402	164.494023	0.006079	0.057309	9.426914	0.106079
31	19.194342	181.943425	0.005496	0.052099	9.479013	0.105496
32	21.113777	201.137767	0.004972	0.047362	9.526376	0.104972
33	23.225154	222.251544	0.004499	0.043057	9.569432	0.104499
34	25.547670	245.476699	0.004074	0.039143	9.608575	0.104074
35	28.102437	271.024368	0.003690	0.035584	9.644159	0.103690
36	30.912681	299.126805	0.003343	0.032349	9.676508	0.103343
37	34.003949	330.039486	0.003030	0.029408	9.705917	0.103030
38	37.404343	364.043434	0.002747	0.026735	9.732651	0.102747
39	41.144778	401.447778	0.002491	0.024304	9.756956	0.102491
40	45.259256	442.592556	0.002259	0.022095	9.779051	0.102259
41	49.785181	487.851811	0.002050	0.020086	9.799137	0.102050
42	54.763699	537.636992	0.001860	0.018260	9.817397	0.101860
43	60.240069	592.400692	0.001688	0.016600	9.833998	0.101688
44	66.264076	652.640761	0.001532	0.015091	9.849089	0.101532
45	72.890484	718.904837	0.001391	0.013719	9.862808	0.101391
46	80.179532	791.795321	0.001263	0.012472	9.875280	0.101263
47	88.197485	871.974853	0.001147	0.011338	9.886618	0.101147
48	97.017234	960.172338	0.001041	0.010307	9.896926	0.101041
49	106.718957	1057.189572	0.000946	0.009370	9.906296	0.100946
50	117.390853	1163.908529	0.000859	0.008519	9.914814	0.100859

12.00%   MONTHLY COMPOUND INTEREST TABLES   12.00%
                                  EFFECTIVE RATE 1.000

	1 AMOUNT OF $1 AT COMPOUND INTEREST	2 ACCUMULATION OF $1 PER PERIOD	3 SINKING FUND FACTOR	4 PRESENT VALUE REVERSION OF $1	5 PRESENT VALUE ORD. ANNUITY $1 PER PERIOD	6 INSTALMENT TO AMORTIZE $1	
MONTHS							
1	1.010000	1.000000	1.000000	0.990099	0.990099	1.010000	
2	1.020100	2.010000	0.497512	0.980296	1.970395	0.507512	
3	1.030301	3.030100	0.330022	0.970590	2.940985	0.340022	
4	1.040604	4.060401	0.246281	0.960980	3.901966	0.256281	
5	1.051010	5.101005	0.196040	0.951466	4.853431	0.206040	
6	1.061520	6.152015	0.162548	0.942045	5.795476	0.172548	
7	1.072135	7.213535	0.138628	0.932718	6.728195	0.148628	
8	1.082857	8.285671	0.120690	0.923483	7.651678	0.130690	
9	1.093685	9.368527	0.106740	0.914340	8.566018	0.116740	
10	1.104622	10.462213	0.095582	0.905287	9.471305	0.105582	
11	1.115668	11.566835	0.086454	0.896324	10.367628	0.096454	
12	1.126825	12.682503	0.078849	0.887449	11.255077	0.088849	
YEARS							**MONTHS**
1	1.126825	12.682503	0.078849	0.887449	11.255077	0.088849	12
2	1.269735	26.973465	0.037073	0.787566	21.243387	0.047073	24
3	1.430769	43.076878	0.023214	0.698925	30.107505	0.033214	36
4	1.612226	61.222608	0.016334	0.620260	37.973959	0.026334	48
5	1.816697	81.669670	0.012244	0.550450	44.955038	0.022244	60
6	2.047099	104.709931	0.009550	0.488496	51.150391	0.019550	72
7	2.306723	130.672274	0.007653	0.433515	56.648453	0.017653	84
8	2.599273	159.927293	0.006253	0.384723	61.527703	0.016253	96
9	2.928926	192.892579	0.005184	0.341422	65.857790	0.015184	108
10	3.300387	230.038689	0.004347	0.302995	69.700522	0.014347	120
11	3.718959	271.895856	0.003678	0.268892	73.110752	0.013678	132
12	4.190616	319.061559	0.003134	0.238628	76.137157	0.013134	144
13	4.722091	372.209054	0.002687	0.211771	78.822939	0.012687	156
14	5.320970	432.096982	0.002314	0.187936	81.206434	0.012314	168
15	5.995802	499.580198	0.002002	0.166783	83.321664	0.012002	180
16	6.756220	575.621974	0.001737	0.148012	85.198824	0.011737	192
17	7.613078	661.307751	0.001512	0.131353	86.864707	0.011512	204
18	8.578606	757.860630	0.001320	0.116569	88.343095	0.011320	216
19	9.666588	866.658830	0.001154	0.103449	89.655089	0.011154	228
20	10.892554	989.255365	0.001011	0.091806	90.819416	0.011011	240
21	12.274002	1127.400210	0.000887	0.081473	91.852698	0.010887	252
22	13.830653	1283.065278	0.000779	0.072303	92.769683	0.010779	264
23	15.584726	1458.472574	0.000686	0.064165	93.583461	0.010686	276
24	17.561259	1656.125905	0.000604	0.056944	94.305647	0.010604	288
25	19.788466	1878.846626	0.000532	0.050534	94.946551	0.010532	300
26	22.298139	2129.813909	0.000470	0.044847	95.515321	0.010470	312
27	25.126101	2412.610125	0.000414	0.039799	96.020075	0.010414	324
28	28.312720	2731.271980	0.000366	0.035320	96.468019	0.010366	336
29	31.903481	3090.348134	0.000324	0.031345	96.865546	0.010324	348
30	35.949641	3494.964133	0.000286	0.027817	97.218331	0.010286	360
31	40.508956	3950.895567	0.000253	0.024686	97.531410	0.010253	372
32	45.646505	4464.650519	0.000224	0.021907	97.809252	0.010224	384
33	51.435625	5043.562459	0.000198	0.019442	98.055822	0.010198	396
34	57.958949	5695.894923	0.000176	0.017254	98.274641	0.010176	408
35	65.309595	6430.959471	0.000155	0.015312	98.468831	0.010155	420
36	73.592486	7259.248603	0.000138	0.013588	98.641166	0.010138	432
37	82.925855	8192.585529	0.000122	0.012059	98.794103	0.010122	444
38	93.442929	9244.292938	0.000108	0.010702	98.929828	0.010108	456
39	105.293832	10429.383172	0.000096	0.009497	99.050277	0.010096	468
40	118.647725	11764.772510	0.000085	0.008428	99.157169	0.010085	480

12.00%   ANNUAL COMPOUND INTEREST TABLES   12.00%
                                      EFFECTIVE RATE 12.00

	1 AMOUNT OF $1 AT COMPOUND INTEREST	2 ACCUMULATION OF $1 PER PERIOD	3 SINKING FUND FACTOR	4 PRESENT VALUE REVERSION OF $1	5 PRESENT VALUE ORD. ANNUITY $1 PER PERIOD	6 INSTALMENT TO AMORTIZE $1
YEARS						
1	1.120000	1.000000	1.000000	0.892857	0.892857	1.120000
2	1.254400	2.120000	0.471698	0.797194	1.690051	0.591698
3	1.404928	3.374400	0.296349	0.711780	2.401831	0.416349
4	1.573519	4.779328	0.209234	0.635518	3.037349	0.329234
5	1.762342	6.352847	0.157410	0.567427	3.604776	0.277410
6	1.973823	8.115189	0.123226	0.506631	4.111407	0.243226
7	2.210681	10.089012	0.099118	0.452349	4.563757	0.219118
8	2.475963	12.299693	0.081303	0.403883	4.967640	0.201303
9	2.773079	14.775656	0.067679	0.360610	5.328250	0.187679
10	3.105848	17.548735	0.056984	0.321973	5.650223	0.176984
11	3.478550	20.654583	0.048415	0.287476	5.937699	0.168415
12	3.895976	24.133133	0.041437	0.256675	6.194374	0.161437
13	4.363493	28.029109	0.035677	0.229174	6.423548	0.155677
14	4.887112	32.392602	0.030871	0.204620	6.628168	0.150871
15	5.473566	37.279715	0.026824	0.182696	6.810864	0.146824
16	6.130394	42.753280	0.023390	0.163122	6.973986	0.143390
17	6.866041	48.883674	0.020457	0.145644	7.119630	0.140457
18	7.689966	55.749715	0.017937	0.130040	7.249670	0.137937
19	8.612762	63.439681	0.015763	0.116107	7.365777	0.135763
20	9.646293	72.052442	0.013879	0.103667	7.469444	0.133879
21	10.803848	81.698736	0.012240	0.092560	7.562003	0.132240
22	12.100310	92.502584	0.010811	0.082643	7.644646	0.130811
23	13.552347	104.602894	0.009560	0.073788	7.718434	0.129560
24	15.178629	118.155241	0.008463	0.065882	7.784316	0.128463
25	17.000064	133.333870	0.007500	0.058823	7.843139	0.127500
26	19.040072	150.333934	0.006652	0.052521	7.895660	0.126652
27	21.324881	169.374007	0.005904	0.046894	7.942554	0.125904
28	23.883866	190.698887	0.005244	0.041869	7.984423	0.125244
29	26.749930	214.582754	0.004660	0.037383	8.021806	0.124660
30	29.959922	241.332684	0.004144	0.033378	8.055184	0.124144
31	33.555113	271.292606	0.003686	0.029802	8.084986	0.123686
32	37.581726	304.847719	0.003280	0.026609	8.111594	0.123280
33	42.091533	342.429446	0.002920	0.023758	8.135352	0.122920
34	47.142517	384.520979	0.002601	0.021212	8.156564	0.122601
35	52.799620	431.663496	0.002317	0.018940	8.175504	0.122317
36	59.135574	484.463116	0.002064	0.016910	8.192414	0.122064
37	66.231843	543.598690	0.001840	0.015098	8.207513	0.121840
38	74.179664	609.830533	0.001640	0.013481	8.220993	0.121640
39	83.081224	684.010197	0.001462	0.012036	8.233030	0.121462
40	93.050970	767.091420	0.001304	0.010747	8.243777	0.121304
41	104.217087	860.142391	0.001163	0.009595	8.253372	0.121163
42	116.723137	964.359478	0.001037	0.008567	8.261939	0.121037
43	130.729914	1081.082615	0.000925	0.007649	8.269589	0.120925
44	146.417503	1211.812529	0.000825	0.006830	8.276418	0.120825
45	163.987604	1358.230032	0.000736	0.006098	8.282516	0.120736
46	183.666116	1522.217636	0.000657	0.005445	8.287961	0.120657
47	205.706050	1705.883752	0.000586	0.004861	8.292822	0.120586
48	230.390776	1911.589803	0.000523	0.004340	8.297163	0.120523
49	258.037669	2141.980579	0.000467	0.003875	8.301038	0.120467
50	289.002190	2400.018249	0.000417	0.003460	8.304498	0.120417

15.00%   MONTHLY COMPOUND INTEREST TABLES   15.00%
                                    EFFECTIVE RATE 1.250

	1	2	3	4	5	6
	AMOUNT OF $1 AT COMPOUND INTEREST	ACCUMULATION OF $1 PER PERIOD	SINKING FUND FACTOR	PRESENT VALUE REVERSION OF $1	PRESENT VALUE ORD. ANNUITY $1 PER PERIOD	INSTALMENT TO AMORTIZE $1

MONTHS

1	1.012500	1.000000	1.000000	0.987654	0.987654	1.012500
2	1.025156	2.012500	0.496894	0.975461	1.963115	0.509394
3	1.037971	3.037656	0.329201	0.963418	2.926534	0.341701
4	1.050945	4.075627	0.245361	0.951524	3.878058	0.257861
5	1.064082	5.126572	0.195062	0.939777	4.817835	0.207562
6	1.077383	6.190654	0.161534	0.928175	5.746010	0.174034
7	1.090850	7.268038	0.137589	0.916716	6.662726	0.150089
8	1.104486	8.358888	0.119633	0.905398	7.568124	0.132133
9	1.118292	9.463374	0.105671	0.894221	8.462345	0.118171
10	1.132271	10.581666	0.094503	0.883181	9.345526	0.107003
11	1.146424	11.713937	0.085368	0.872277	10.217803	0.097868
12	1.160755	12.860361	0.077758	0.861509	11.079312	0.090258

YEARS   MONTHS

1	1.160755	12.860361	0.077758	0.861509	11.079312	0.090258	12
2	1.347351	27.788084	0.035987	0.742197	20.624235	0.048487	24
3	1.563944	45.115506	0.022155	0.639409	28.847267	0.034665	36
4	1.815355	65.228388	0.015331	0.550856	35.931481	0.027831	48
5	2.107181	88.574508	0.011290	0.474568	42.034592	0.023790	60
6	2.445920	115.673621	0.008645	0.408844	47.292474	0.021145	72
7	2.839113	147.129040	0.006797	0.352223	51.822185	0.019297	84
8	3.295513	183.641059	0.005445	0.303443	55.724570	0.017945	96
9	3.825282	226.022551	0.004424	0.261419	59.086509	0.016924	108
10	4.440213	275.217058	0.003633	0.225214	61.982847	0.016133	120
11	5.153998	332.319805	0.003009	0.194024	64.478068	0.015509	132
12	5.982526	398.602077	0.002509	0.167153	66.627722	0.015009	144
13	6.944244	475.539523	0.002103	0.144004	68.479668	0.014603	156
14	8.060563	564.845011	0.001770	0.124061	70.075134	0.014270	168
15	9.356334	668.506759	0.001496	0.106879	71.449643	0.013996	180
16	10.860408	788.832603	0.001268	0.092078	72.633794	0.013768	192
17	12.606267	928.501369	0.001077	0.079326	73.653950	0.013577	204
18	14.632781	1090.622520	0.000917	0.068340	74.532823	0.013417	216
19	16.985067	1278.805378	0.000782	0.058875	75.289980	0.013282	228
20	19.715494	1497.239481	0.000668	0.050722	75.942278	0.013168	240
21	22.884848	1750.787854	0.000571	0.043697	76.504237	0.013071	252
22	26.563691	2045.095272	0.000489	0.037645	76.988370	0.012989	264
23	30.833924	2386.713938	0.000419	0.032432	77.405455	0.012919	276
24	35.790617	2783.249347	0.000359	0.027940	77.764777	0.012859	288
25	41.544120	3243.529615	0.000308	0.024071	78.074336	0.012808	300
26	48.222525	3777.802015	0.000265	0.020737	78.341024	0.012765	312
27	55.974514	4397.961118	0.000227	0.017865	78.570778	0.012727	324
28	64.972670	5117.813598	0.000195	0.015391	78.768713	0.012695	336
29	75.417320	5953.385616	0.000168	0.013260	78.939236	0.012668	348
30	87.540995	6923.279611	0.000144	0.011423	79.086142	0.012644	360
31	101.613606	8049.088447	0.000124	0.009841	79.212704	0.012624	372
32	117.948452	9355.876140	0.000107	0.008478	79.321738	0.012607	384
33	136.909198	10872.735858	0.000092	0.007304	79.415671	0.012592	396
34	158.917970	12633.437629	0.000079	0.006293	79.496596	0.012579	408
35	184.464752	14677.180163	0.000068	0.005421	79.566313	0.012568	420
36	214.118294	17049.463544	0.000059	0.004670	79.626375	0.012559	432
37	248.538777	19803.102194	0.000050	0.004024	79.678119	0.012550	444
38	288.492509	22999.400698	0.000043	0.003466	79.722696	0.012543	456
39	334.868983	26709.518627	0.000037	0.002986	79.761101	0.012537	468
40	388.700685	31016.054774	0.000032	0.002573	79.794186	0.012532	480

15.00%   ANNUAL COMPOUND INTEREST TABLES   15.00%
                              EFFECTIVE RATE 15.00

	1	2	3	4	5	6
	AMOUNT OF $1 AT COMPOUND INTEREST	ACCUMULATION OF $1 PER PERIOD	SINKING FUND FACTOR	PRESENT VALUE REVERSION OF $1	PRESENT VALUE ORD. ANNUITY $1 PER PERIOD	INSTALMENT TO AMORTIZE $1
YEARS						
1	1.150000	1.000000	1.000000	0.869565	0.869565	1.150000
2	1.322500	2.150000	0.465116	0.756144	1.625709	0.615116
3	1.520875	3.472500	0.287977	0.657516	2.283225	0.437977
4	1.749006	4.993375	0.200265	0.571753	2.854978	0.350265
5	2.011357	6.742381	0.148316	0.497177	3.352155	0.298316
6	2.313061	8.753738	0.114237	0.432328	3.784483	0.264237
7	2.660020	11.066799	0.090360	0.375937	4.160420	0.240360
8	3.059023	13.726819	0.072850	0.326902	4.487322	0.222850
9	3.517876	16.785842	0.059574	0.284262	4.771584	0.209574
10	4.045558	20.303718	0.049252	0.247185	5.018769	0.199252
11	4.652391	24.349276	0.041069	0.214943	5.233712	0.191069
12	5.350250	29.001667	0.034481	0.186907	5.420619	0.184481
13	6.152788	34.351917	0.029110	0.162528	5.583147	0.179110
14	7.075706	40.504705	0.024688	0.141329	5.724476	0.174688
15	8.137062	47.580411	0.021017	0.122894	5.847370	0.171017
16	9.357621	55.717472	0.017948	0.106865	5.954235	0.167948
17	10.761264	65.075093	0.015367	0.092926	6.047161	0.165367
18	12.375454	75.836357	0.013186	0.080805	6.127966	0.163186
19	14.231772	88.211811	0.011336	0.070265	6.198231	0.161336
20	16.366537	102.443583	0.009761	0.061100	6.259331	0.159761
21	18.821518	118.810120	0.008417	0.053131	6.312462	0.158417
22	21.644746	137.631638	0.007266	0.046201	6.358663	0.157266
23	24.891458	159.276384	0.006278	0.040174	6.398837	0.156278
24	28.625176	184.167841	0.005430	0.034934	6.433771	0.155430
25	32.918953	212.793017	0.004699	0.030378	6.464149	0.154699
26	37.856796	245.711970	0.004070	0.026415	6.490564	0.154070
27	43.535315	283.568766	0.003526	0.022970	6.513534	0.153526
28	50.065612	327.104080	0.003057	0.019974	6.533508	0.153057
29	57.575454	377.169693	0.002651	0.017369	6.550877	0.152651
30	66.211772	434.745146	0.002300	0.015103	6.565980	0.152300
31	76.143538	500.956918	0.001996	0.013133	6.579113	0.151996
32	87.565068	577.100456	0.001733	0.011420	6.590533	0.151733
33	100.699829	664.665525	0.001505	0.009931	6.600463	0.151505
34	115.804803	765.365353	0.001307	0.008635	6.609099	0.151307
35	133.175523	881.170156	0.001135	0.007509	6.616607	0.151135
36	153.151852	1014.345680	0.000986	0.006529	6.623137	0.150986
37	176.124630	1167.497532	0.000857	0.005678	6.628815	0.150857
38	202.543324	1343.622161	0.000744	0.004937	6.633752	0.150744
39	232.924823	1546.165485	0.000647	0.004293	6.638045	0.150647
40	267.863546	1779.090308	0.000562	0.003733	6.641778	0.150562
41	308.043078	2046.953854	0.000489	0.003246	6.645025	0.150489
42	354.249540	2354.996933	0.000425	0.002823	6.647848	0.150425
43	407.386971	2709.246473	0.000369	0.002455	6.650302	0.150369
44	468.495017	3116.633443	0.000321	0.002134	6.652437	0.150321
45	538.769269	3585.128460	0.000279	0.001856	6.654293	0.150279
46	619.584659	4123.897729	0.000242	0.001614	6.655907	0.150242
47	712.522358	4743.482388	0.000211	0.001403	6.657310	0.150211
48	819.400712	5456.004746	0.000183	0.001220	6.658531	0.150183
49	942.310819	6275.405458	0.000159	0.001061	6.659592	0.150159
50	1083.657442	7217.716277	0.000139	0.000923	6.660515	0.150139

20.00%   MONTHLY COMPOUND INTEREST TABLES   20.00%
                              EFFECTIVE RATE 1.667

	1	2	3	4	5	6	
	AMOUNT OF $1 AT COMPOUND INTEREST	ACCUMULATION OF $1 PER PERIOD	SINKING FUND FACTOR	PRESENT VALUE REVERSION OF $1	PRESENT VALUE ORD. ANNUITY $1 PER PERIOD	INSTALMENT TO AMORTIZE $1	

MONTHS							
1	1.016667	1.000000	1.000000	0.983607	0.983607	1.016667	
2	1.033611	2.016667	0.495868	0.967482	1.951088	0.512534	
3	1.050838	3.050278	0.327839	0.951622	2.902710	0.344506	
4	1.068352	4.101116	0.243836	0.936021	3.838731	0.260503	
5	1.086158	5.169468	0.193444	0.920677	4.759408	0.210110	
6	1.104260	6.255625	0.159856	0.905583	5.664991	0.176523	
7	1.122665	7.359886	0.135872	0.890738	6.555729	0.152538	
8	1.141376	8.482551	0.117889	0.876136	7.431865	0.134556	
9	1.160399	9.623926	0.103908	0.861773	8.293637	0.120574	
10	1.179739	10.784325	0.092727	0.847645	9.141283	0.109394	
11	1.199401	11.964064	0.083584	0.833749	9.975032	0.100250	
12	1.219391	13.163465	0.075968	0.820081	10.795113	0.092635	

YEARS							MONTHS
1	1.219391	13.163465	0.075968	0.820081	10.795113	0.092635	12
2	1.486915	29.214877	0.034229	0.672534	19.647986	0.050896	24
3	1.813130	48.787826	0.020497	0.551532	26.908062	0.037164	36
4	2.210915	72.654905	0.013764	0.452301	32.861916	0.030430	48
5	2.695970	101.758208	0.009827	0.370924	37.744561	0.026494	60
6	3.287442	137.246517	0.007286	0.304188	41.748727	0.023953	72
7	4.008677	180.520645	0.005540	0.249459	45.032470	0.022206	84
8	4.888145	233.288730	0.004287	0.204577	47.725406	0.020953	96
9	5.960561	297.633662	0.003360	0.167769	49.933833	0.020027	108
10	7.268255	376.095300	0.002659	0.137585	51.744924	0.019326	120
11	8.862845	471.770720	0.002120	0.112831	53.230165	0.018786	132
12	10.807275	588.436476	0.001699	0.092530	54.448184	0.018366	144
13	13.178294	730.697658	0.001369	0.075882	55.447059	0.018035	156
14	16.069495	904.169675	0.001106	0.062230	56.266217	0.017773	168
15	19.594998	1115.699905	0.000896	0.051033	56.937994	0.017563	180
16	23.893966	1373.637983	0.000728	0.041852	57.488906	0.017395	192
17	29.136090	1688.165376	0.000592	0.034322	57.940698	0.017259	204
18	35.528288	2071.697274	0.000483	0.028147	58.311205	0.017149	216
19	43.322878	2539.372652	0.000394	0.023082	58.615050	0.017060	228
20	52.827531	3109.651838	0.000322	0.018930	58.864229	0.016988	240
21	64.417420	3805.045193	0.000263	0.015524	59.068575	0.016929	252
22	78.550028	4653.001652	0.000215	0.012731	59.236156	0.016882	264
23	95.783203	5686.992197	0.000176	0.010440	59.373585	0.016843	276
24	116.797184	6947.831050	0.000144	0.008562	59.486289	0.016811	288
25	142.421445	8485.286707	0.000118	0.007021	59.578715	0.016785	300
26	173.667440	10360.046428	0.000097	0.005758	59.654512	0.016763	312
27	211.768529	12646.111719	0.000079	0.004722	59.716672	0.016746	324
28	258.228656	15433.719354	0.000065	0.003873	59.767648	0.016731	336
29	314.881721	18832.903252	0.000053	0.003176	59.809452	0.016720	348
30	383.963963	22977.837794	0.000044	0.002604	59.843735	0.016710	360
31	468.202234	28032.134021	0.000036	0.002136	59.871850	0.016702	372
32	570.921630	34195.297781	0.000029	0.001752	59.894907	0.016696	384
33	696.176745	41710.604725	0.000024	0.001436	59.913815	0.016691	396
34	848.911717	50874.703013	0.000020	0.001178	59.929321	0.016686	408
35	1035.155379	62049.322767	0.000016	0.000966	59.942038	0.016683	420
36	1262.259241	75675.554472	0.000013	0.000792	59.952466	0.016680	432
37	1539.187666	92291.259934	0.000011	0.000650	59.961018	0.016678	444
38	1876.871717	112552.303044	0.000009	0.000533	59.968032	0.016676	456
39	2288.640640	137258.438382	0.000007	0.000437	59.973784	0.016674	468
40	2790.747993	167384.879554	0.000006	0.000358	59.978500	0.016673	480

20.00%   ANNUAL COMPOUND INTEREST TABLES   20.00%
                             EFFECTIVE RATE 20.00

	1 AMOUNT OF $1 AT COMPOUND INTEREST	2 ACCUMULATION OF $1 PER PERIOD	3 SINKING FUND FACTOR	4 PRESENT VALUE REVERSION OF $1	5 PRESENT VALUE ORD. ANNUITY $1 PER PERIOD	6 INSTALMENT TO AMORTIZE $1
YEARS						
1	1.200000	1.000000	1.000000	0.833333	0.833333	1.200000
2	1.440000	2.200000	0.454545	0.694444	1.527778	0.654545
3	1.728000	3.640000	0.274725	0.578704	2.106481	0.474725
4	2.073600	5.368000	0.186289	0.482253	2.588735	0.386289
5	2.488320	7.441600	0.134380	0.401878	2.990612	0.334380
6	2.985984	9.929920	0.100706	0.334898	3.325510	0.300706
7	3.583181	12.915904	0.077424	0.279082	3.604592	0.277424
8	4.299817	16.499085	0.060609	0.232568	3.837160	0.260609
9	5.159780	20.798902	0.048079	0.193807	4.030967	0.248079
10	6.191736	25.958682	0.038523	0.161506	4.192472	0.238523
11	7.430084	32.150419	0.031104	0.134588	4.327060	0.231104
12	8.916100	39.580502	0.025265	0.112157	4.439217	0.225265
13	10.699321	48.496603	0.020620	0.093464	4.532681	0.220620
14	12.839185	59.195923	0.016893	0.077887	4.610567	0.216893
15	15.407022	72.035108	0.013882	0.064905	4.675473	0.213882
16	18.488426	87.442129	0.011436	0.054088	4.729561	0.211436
17	22.186111	105.930555	0.009440	0.045073	4.774634	0.209440
18	26.623333	128.116666	0.007805	0.037561	4.812195	0.207805
19	31.948000	154.740000	0.006462	0.031301	4.843496	0.206462
20	38.337600	186.688000	0.005357	0.026084	4.869580	0.205357
21	46.005120	225.025600	0.004444	0.021737	4.891316	0.204444
22	55.206144	271.030719	0.003690	0.018114	4.909430	0.203690
23	66.247373	326.236863	0.003065	0.015095	4.924525	0.203065
24	79.496847	392.484236	0.002548	0.012579	4.937104	0.202548
25	95.396217	471.981083	0.002119	0.010483	4.947587	0.202119
26	114.475460	567.377300	0.001762	0.008735	4.956323	0.201762
27	137.370552	681.852760	0.001467	0.007280	4.963602	0.201467
28	164.844662	819.223312	0.001221	0.006066	4.969668	0.201221
29	197.813595	984.067974	0.001016	0.005055	4.974724	0.201016
30	237.376314	1181.881569	0.000846	0.004213	4.978936	0.200846
31	284.851577	1419.257883	0.000705	0.003511	4.982447	0.200705
32	341.821892	1704.109459	0.000587	0.002926	4.985372	0.200587
33	410.186270	2045.931351	0.000489	0.002438	4.987810	0.200489
34	492.223524	2456.117621	0.000407	0.002032	4.989842	0.200407
35	590.668229	2948.341146	0.000339	0.001693	4.991535	0.200339
36	708.801875	3539.009375	0.000283	0.001411	4.992946	0.200283
37	850.562250	4247.811250	0.000235	0.001176	4.994122	0.200235
38	1020.674700	5098.373500	0.000196	0.000980	4.995101	0.200196
39	1224.809640	6119.048200	0.000163	0.000816	4.995918	0.200163
40	1469.771568	7343.857840	0.000136	0.000680	4.996598	0.200136
41	1763.725882	8813.629408	0.000113	0.000567	4.997165	0.200113
42	2116.471058	10577.355290	0.000095	0.000472	4.997638	0.200095
43	2539.765269	12693.826348	0.000079	0.000394	4.998031	0.200079
44	3047.718323	15233.591617	0.000066	0.000328	4.998359	0.200066
45	3657.261988	18281.309940	0.000055	0.000273	4.998633	0.200055
46	4388.714386	21938.571928	0.000046	0.000228	4.998861	0.200046
47	5266.457263	26327.286314	0.000038	0.000190	4.999051	0.200038
48	6319.748715	31593.743577	0.000032	0.000158	4.999209	0.200032
49	7583.698458	37913.492292	0.000026	0.000132	4.999341	0.200026
50	9100.438150	45497.190751	0.000022	0.000110	4.999451	0.200022

25.00%   MONTHLY COMPOUND INTEREST TABLES   25.00%
                                      EFFECTIVE RATE 2.083

	1 AMOUNT OF $1 AT COMPOUND INTEREST	2 ACCUMULATION OF $1 PER PERIOD	3 SINKING FUND FACTOR	4 PRESENT VALUE REVERSION OF $1	5 PRESENT VALUE ORD. ANNUITY $1 PER PERIOD	6 INSTALMENT TO AMORTIZE $1	
MONTHS							
1	1.020833	1.000000	1.000000	0.979592	0.979592	1.020833	
2	1.042101	2.020833	0.494845	0.959600	1.939192	0.515679	
3	1.063811	3.062934	0.326484	0.940016	2.879208	0.347318	
4	1.085974	4.126745	0.242322	0.920832	3.800041	0.263155	
5	1.108598	5.212719	0.191838	0.902040	4.702081	0.212672	
6	1.131694	6.321317	0.158195	0.883631	5.585712	0.179028	
7	1.155271	7.453011	0.134174	0.865598	6.451310	0.155007	
8	1.179339	8.608283	0.116167	0.847932	7.299242	0.137001	
9	1.203909	9.787622	0.102170	0.830628	8.129870	0.123003	
10	1.228990	10.991531	0.090979	0.813676	8.943546	0.111812	
11	1.254594	12.220521	0.081830	0.797070	9.740616	0.102663	
12	1.280732	13.475115	0.074211	0.780804	10.521420	0.095044	

	1	2	3	4	5	6	MONTHS
YEARS							
1	1.280732	13.475115	0.074211	0.780804	10.521420	0.095044	12
2	1.640273	30.733120	0.032538	0.609654	18.736585	0.053372	24
3	2.100750	52.835991	0.018926	0.476021	25.151016	0.039760	36
4	2.690497	81.143837	0.012324	0.371679	30.159427	0.033157	48
5	3.445804	117.398588	0.008518	0.290208	34.070014	0.029351	60
6	4.413150	163.831191	0.006104	0.226596	37.123415	0.026937	72
7	5.652060	223.298892	0.004478	0.176927	39.507522	0.025312	84
8	7.238772	299.461053	0.003339	0.138145	41.369041	0.024173	96
9	9.270924	397.004337	0.002519	0.107864	42.822522	0.023352	108
10	11.873565	521.931099	0.001916	0.084221	43.957406	0.022749	120
11	15.206849	681.928746	0.001466	0.065760	44.843528	0.022300	132
12	19.475891	886.842782	0.001128	0.051346	45.535414	0.021961	144
13	24.943389	1149.282656	0.000870	0.040091	46.075642	0.021703	156
14	31.945785	1485.397684	0.000673	0.031303	46.497454	0.021507	168
15	40.913975	1915.870809	0.000522	0.024442	46.826807	0.021355	180
16	52.399819	2467.191326	0.000405	0.019084	47.083966	0.021239	192
17	67.110102	3173.284913	0.000315	0.014901	47.284757	0.021148	204
18	85.950026	4077.601254	0.000245	0.011635	47.441536	0.021079	216
19	110.078911	5235.787733	0.000191	0.009084	47.563949	0.021024	228
20	140.981536	6719.113709	0.000149	0.007093	47.659530	0.020982	240
21	180.559502	8618.856102	0.000116	0.005538	47.734160	0.020949	252
22	231.248253	11051.916141	0.000090	0.004324	47.792431	0.020924	264
23	296.166936	14168.012922	0.000071	0.003376	47.837929	0.020904	276
24	379.310342	18158.896417	0.000055	0.002636	47.873455	0.020888	288
25	485.794726	23270.146862	0.000043	0.002058	47.901193	0.020876	300
26	622.172638	29816.286623	0.000034	0.001607	47.922851	0.020867	312
27	796.836134	38200.134414	0.000026	0.001255	47.939762	0.020860	324
28	1020.533185	48937.592880	0.000020	0.000980	47.952966	0.020854	336
29	1307.029059	62689.394819	0.000016	0.000765	47.963275	0.020849	348
30	1673.953366	80301.761578	0.000012	0.000597	47.971325	0.020846	360
31	2143.884907	102858.475544	0.000010	0.000466	47.977611	0.020843	372
32	2745.741063	131747.571026	0.000008	0.000364	47.982518	0.020841	384
33	3516.557237	168746.747367	0.000006	0.000284	47.986350	0.020839	396
34	4503.765838	216132.760226	0.000005	0.000222	47.989342	0.020838	408
35	5768.115051	276821.522428	0.000004	0.000173	47.991678	0.020837	420
36	7387.406991	354547.535558	0.000003	0.000135	47.993502	0.020836	432
37	9461.285285	454093.693657	0.000002	0.000106	47.994927	0.020836	444
38	12117.366668	581585.600079	0.000002	0.000083	47.996039	0.020835	456
39	15519.093924	744868.508353	0.000001	0.000064	47.996907	0.020835	468
40	19875.793381	953990.082294	0.000001	0.000050	47.997585	0.020834	480

25.00%   ANNUAL COMPOUND INTEREST TABLES   25.00%
                                 EFFECTIVE RATE 25.00

	1	2	3	4	5	6
	AMOUNT OF $1 AT COMPOUND INTEREST	ACCUMULATION OF $1 PER PERIOD	SINKING FUND FACTOR	PRESENT VALUE REVERSION OF $1	PRESENT VALUE ORD. ANNUITY $1 PER PERIOD	INSTALMENT TO AMORTIZE $1
YEARS						
1	1.250000	1.000000	1.000000	0.800000	0.800000	1.250000
2	1.562500	2.250000	0.444444	0.640000	1.440000	0.694444
3	1.953125	3.812500	0.262295	0.512000	1.952000	0.512295
4	2.441406	5.765625	0.173442	0.409600	2.361600	0.423442
5	3.051758	8.207031	0.121847	0.327680	2.689280	0.371847
6	3.814697	11.258789	0.088819	0.262144	2.951424	0.338819
7	4.768372	15.073486	0.066342	0.209715	3.161139	0.316342
8	5.960464	19.841858	0.050399	0.167772	3.328911	0.300399
9	7.450581	25.802322	0.038756	0.134218	3.463129	0.288756
10	9.313226	33.252903	0.030073	0.107374	3.570503	0.280073
11	11.641532	42.566129	0.023493	0.085899	3.656403	0.273493
12	14.551915	54.207661	0.018448	0.068719	3.725122	0.268448
13	18.189894	68.759576	0.014543	0.054976	3.780098	0.264543
14	22.737368	86.949470	0.011501	0.043980	3.824078	0.261501
15	28.421709	109.686838	0.009117	0.035184	3.859263	0.259117
16	35.527137	138.108547	0.007241	0.028147	3.887410	0.257241
17	44.408921	173.635684	0.005759	0.022518	3.909928	0.255759
18	55.511151	218.044605	0.004586	0.018014	3.927942	0.254586
19	69.388939	273.555756	0.003656	0.014412	3.942354	0.253656
20	86.736174	342.944695	0.002916	0.011529	3.953883	0.252916
21	108.420217	429.680869	0.002327	0.009223	3.963107	0.252327
22	135.525272	538.101086	0.001858	0.007379	3.970485	0.251858
23	169.406589	673.626358	0.001485	0.005903	3.976388	0.251485
24	211.758237	843.032947	0.001186	0.004722	3.981111	0.251186
25	264.697796	1054.791184	0.000948	0.003778	3.984888	0.250948
26	330.872245	1319.488980	0.000758	0.003022	3.987911	0.250758
27	413.590306	1650.361225	0.000606	0.002418	3.990329	0.250606
28	516.987883	2063.951531	0.000485	0.001934	3.992263	0.250485
29	646.234854	2580.939414	0.000387	0.001547	3.993810	0.250387
30	807.793567	3227.174268	0.000310	0.001238	3.995048	0.250310
31	1009.741959	4034.967835	0.000248	0.000990	3.996039	0.250248
32	1262.177448	5044.709793	0.000198	0.000792	3.996831	0.250198
33	1577.721810	6306.887242	0.000159	0.000634	3.997465	0.250159
34	1972.152263	7884.609052	0.000127	0.000507	3.997972	0.250127
35	2465.190329	9856.761315	0.000101	0.000406	3.998377	0.250101
36	3081.487911	12321.951644	0.000081	0.000325	3.998702	0.250081
37	3851.859889	15403.439555	0.000065	0.000260	3.998962	0.250065
38	4814.824861	19255.299444	0.000052	0.000208	3.999169	0.250052
39	6018.531076	24070.124305	0.000042	0.000166	3.999335	0.250042
40	7523.163845	30088.655381	0.000033	0.000133	3.999468	0.250033

Glossary of terms

A-95 review Comprehensive analysis of a proposed project by all affected governmental, environmental, citizens', or other groups.

Abstract of title History of documents affecting title to real property.

Acceleration clause Mortgage contract clause that makes all payments due immediately if a scheduled payment is missed.

Accretion Growth in size, especially by addition or accumulation; the addition of soil to land by gradual, natural deposits.

Accrued depreciation Loss of value from any cause.

Ad valorem Latin for "according to value."

Adaptive reuse Changing the property to a different use, usually refers to a historically significant structure.

Adjusted tax basis Original tax basis plus any capital improvements, less depreciation taken.

Adverse possession Acquisition of title to real property by action of law through fulfilling certain statutory requirements.

Advocacy planner One who defends the role of a client, usually in a public hearing.

Agency Law governing the relationship between employers and their agents.

Amenities The pleasant satisfactions, other than money, which are obtained in using real property.

Amortization Systematic apportionment of costs, loan principal, or other input to discrete periods of time such as months, years, and so on.

Apportionment of basis Division of income tax basis (or investment in asset) between depreciable improvements and nondepreciable land. This division must be acceptable to the Internal Revenue Service.

Assessed value The dollar amount assigned to taxable property for tax purposes by the assessor or county property appraiser. It is usually a statutory percentage of market value.

Avulsion The sudden transference of a piece of land from one person's property to another's without change of ownership, as by a change in the course of a stream.

Balloon payment Amount of principal of loan remaining unamortized and outstanding at the end of the mortgage term.

Bargain and sale deed A deed which conveys the land itself rather than the ownership interest.

Base line An east/west line in the rectangular survey system from which land lying north or south is described in rows of townships.

Beta coefficient This is a measure of systematic risk in the capital asset pricing model.

Blanket mortgage Mortgage lien secured by several land parcels.

BMIR (below-market interest rate) Subsidy by FHA to private lending institutions which lowers the amount of interest paid by low-income families on mortgage loans while giving lenders their market interest rate via the subsidy.

Boot Cash or other nonreal estate assets exchanged for real property.

Break-even cash throw-off Operating expenses plus mortgage payment divided by gross income.

Broker In real estate, a person licensed to buy, sell, lease, rent, exchange, auction, or appraise real property as an agent for another, for compensation.

Building residual technique An income capitalization methodology in which site value is known and net operating income is divided into site income and building income. Building income is discounted to present value and added to site value (given) to estimate the market value of the property.

Business risk Possibility of losses caused by internal operating inefficiencies and external factors.

Capital gain Net sale price less the adjusted base.

Capital improvement A modification which adds to value of real estate, extends its useful life, or adapts the property to a different use.

Capital recapture Expression of the manner in which the dollars of investment in a property are to be returned to investors. Stated as a rate or dollar amount per unit of time.

Capital structure The ratio of debt financing to equity value.

Capitalization Process of converting a net operating income into value. Usually shown by the formula $V = I \div R$ where R is a predetermined return rate.

Capitalization rate Percentage of return required from an investment which provides for investor income, principal and interest on debts, and loss in value from depreciation.

CARS (computer aided routing system) Personalized door-to-door public transportation service.

Cash flow aftertax Cash throw-off minus income taxes paid or plus income tax deduction benefits.

Cash throw-off Net operating income minus annual debt service on a mortgage loan.

Central place theory An attempt to explain city size through examination of market areas.

Certificates of beneficial interest Ownership shares of a trust or mutual fund.

Closing Event at which title to real estate is transferred.

Closing costs Expenses resulting from the purchase of real property.

Cognovit clause Borrower confesses judgment or authorizes lender to secure a judgment that can be attached to borrower's property as a lien.

Collateral Assets that are pledged to secure or guarantee the discharge of an obligation.

Comprehensive planning   The formulation of a land-use program for a city, county, or other region in terms of social, economic, governmental, political, and legal criteria.

Condemnation   A declaration that property is legally appropriated for public use; also, a declaration that something is unfit for use or service (example: the condemnation of a slum tenement).

Condominium   An arrangement under which tenants in an apartment building or in a complex of multi-unit dwellings hold full title to their own units and joint ownership in the common grounds.

Conduit   A channel for conveying income from one entity to another wherein only the final recipient incurs the income tax consequences of the income.

Confiscation   Private property which is seized for the public treasury, usually as a penalty.

Conspicuous consumption   Purchasing and displaying a good primarily for its prestige value. An example is parking a Cadillac in front while keeping a Volkswagen in the garage.

Contract for deed   An agreement under which buyer does not receive title to property until certain conditions are met.

Contract for sale   Legal document between buyer and seller which states the manner in which ownership rights are to be transferred and the purchase price.

Contract rent   Rental fixed by agreement among parties which may or may not be comparable to rentals of similar properties.

Conventional mortgage   Mortgage not insured by a public or private agency.

Conversion   Changing the use of the property, usually by remodeling.

Conveyancing   Passage of title or ownership to real estate.

Cooperative   Ownership form in which a single property is divided into several use portions, with each user owning stock in a corporation that owns the property.

Corporate risk   Business risk plus financial risk.

Corporeal   Ownership estates in real property that give the right to use and to occupy.

Cost of capital   Charge that must be paid to attract money into an investment project.

CPM   Certified Property Manager.

Cross-elasticity of demand   The effect of a change in the price of a good on the quantity supplied of another good.

Curable deterioration or obsolescence   The cost to correct the item of physical deterioration or functional obsolescence is matched by the value added to the property.

Dealer   Person or entity who cannot depreciate real estate held or take capital gains on real estate sold because the properties are his or her stock in trade.

Debt capital   Borrowed long-term money.

Debt service   Annual mortgage payment.

Debt service coverage   Requirement imposed by lender that earnings be a percentage or dollar sum higher than debt service.

Declaration   A document which creates a condominium, identifies the physical elements of ownership, and contains provisions relating to such matters as the name of the association, membership and voting rights, bylaws, easements, covenants, and restrictions.

Deed   Document transferring title to real property.

Deed convenants   Warranties made by a seller of property to protect the buyer against items such as liens, encumbrances, or title defects.

Deed of trust   Transfer of ownership interest to a trustee acting on behalf of a money lender. The trustee is usually instructed to supervise collection of the debt and return the trust deed to the borrower upon retirement of the debt.

Deed restrictions Land-use constraints imposed in the deed passed from seller to buyer. These constraints then pass with the property in future transfers.

Defeasance clause Prevents the mortgagee from foreclosing so long as the debtor fulfills the conditions of the mortgage.

Demographic Characteristics of population, size, age, density, and economic distribution.

Depreciable basis Portion of original tax basis representing value or cost of improvements.

Depreciation (1) Loss in value from all causes; (2) apportionment of improvement cost to time periods.

Descent Transfer of ownership upon death by action of law as stated in the state's Statute of Descent.

Development of regional impact (DRI) In Florida, any proposed development which is large enough to have a measurable effect upon the economy, environment, or public services of more than one county.

Devise Transfer of ownership by means of a will.

Direct capitalization Processing net operating income into value by dividing by an overall capitalization rate.

Direct sales comparison A value estimation methodology utilizing the sales prices of comparable properties to which adjustments are made to reflect value-creating differences between the property under appraisal and the comparables.

Discount Additional interest taken by a lender by lending less actual cash than the mortgage loan principal.

Discount rate Relationship between dollars transmitted from a lender to a borrower and dollars that must be repaid by the borrower. If a lender advances $960 and the borrower must repay $1,000, the discount rate is $40/$1,000 = 4 percent.

Discounting Process of converting any cash flow into present value at a selected rate of return. Based on the idea that one would pay less than $1 today for the right to receive $1 at a future date.

Dower That part of man's property which his widow inherits for life.

Earnest money Money paid to evidence good faith when a contract of purchase is submitted to a property owner by a prospective purchaser.

Easement A right or privilege that a person may have in another's land, as the right-of-way.

Economic base analysis Study of a community's employment and income to forecast population changes and to plan for future expansion of basic and service employment.

Economic good Any material or immaterial thing which satisfies human desire and which is relatively scarce, such that it commands a price in market exchange.

Economic life The length of time improvements (usually buildings) will produce a competitive return; land may have an infinite economic life.

Economies of scale The situation in which costs of production per unit are less for large firms than for smaller firms.

EDUCARE Educational Foundation for Computer Applications in Real Estate.

Efficient market A market in which competitive investments earn the same risk-adjusted rate of return in the equilibrium condition.

Egress A way out; exit.

Elastic demand The phenomenon of a large response in quantity demanded to a small change in price.

Elasticity Ability of supply of real estate to respond to price increases over a short period of time.

Ellwood technique   A mortgage-equity income capitalization methodology for estimating market value or determining investment value.

Embargo   An action by one government prohibiting trade with another country.

Eminent domain   The right of a government or agency thereof to take private property for a public purpose. Just compensation must be paid to the owner whose property is taken.

Encumbrance   A claim against title, such as a mortgage, tax lien, or mechanic's lien.

Environmental impact report (EIR)   A detailed analysis of a project's potential effect upon environmental subsystems, such as air, water, sewer, and transportation of the area.

Environmental Protection Agency (EPA)   Federal agency set up to protect the health and welfare of Americans by controlling environmental pollution hazards.

Equity   Share of property possessed by residual owners after allowing for borrowed funds.

Equity-dividend rate   Cash throw-off divided by the initial equity investment. May be before or after taxes.

Escalator clause   Permits a lender to vary the mortgage interest rate unilaterally, usually upward. Variance is not tied to an index.

Escheat   Revision of real property to the government when the owner dies without a will or heirs.

Escrow   Real estate transactions are accomplished in escrow when the deed is delivered to a third party (escrow agent) for delivery to the buyer upon performance of a condition. The condition may be that title shows clear in the buyer. Escrow also refers to earmarked bank accounts in which are kept earnest money or other funds designated for a particular use.

Escrow agreement   Establishment of a fiduciary who holds documents, cash, or both until all elements of a transaction can be completed.

Estate   The quantity, duration, or extent of interest in real property.

Excess depreciation   Accelerated depreciation taken less depreciation that would have been taken using straight-line.

Exchange   Ownership of like-kind properties are transferred between two or more owners; can result in postponement of part or all of the capital gain tax for one or more of the parties to the exchange.

Exclusive listing   Agreement between seller of property and broker in which broker is assured a commission if the seller's property is sold by anyone other than the seller.

Exclusive right to sell listing   Agreement between seller of property and broker in which broker is assured a commission if the property is sold, no matter how or by whom it is sold.

Exculpatory clause   A clause in the mortgage which relieves the borrower of personal liability to repay the loan.

Expected value   A weighted average of values of an experiment's outcome. This is a measure of central tendency.

FDIC   Federal Deposit Insurance Corporation.

Feasibility analysis   Study of the cash flow, profitability potential, and overall desirability of a project.

Fee simple absolute   The entire bundle of rights to use and control of real property.

FHA (Federal Housing Administration)   Agency of the Department of Housing and Urban Development (HUD) which insures private lending institutions against loss on loans under various housing programs established by Congress.

FHLMC   Federal Home Loan Mortgage Association.

Filtering Movement of people of one income group into homes that have recently dropped in price and that were previously occupied by persons in the next higher income group.

Financial risk Possibility of losses caused by the amount of and legal provisions concerning borrowed funds.

Firm advertising Advertising intended to call attention to the firm and its specific offerings.

First user First owner of the real estate to take tax depreciation on improvement value.

Fixture Fittings or furniture of a property attached to a building and ordinarily, and legally, considered to be a part of the real estate.

Flat lease Equal rental payments are made over the term of the lease.

Flow of funds accounts Governmental system of accounting for movement of money throughout the economy.

FNMA (Fanny Mae) Federal National Mortgage Association.

Foreclosure The act of depriving a borrower of the right to redeem a mortgage when regular payments have not been kept up.

Forfeiture Anything lost or given up because of some crime, fault, or neglect of duty; specifically, a fine or penalty.

Freehold estate An estate in land held for life or with the right to pass it on through inheritance.

Friction of space The effort required to move persons and goods between geographically separate sites and to communicate between establishments; results in transfer costs.

FSLIC Federal Savings and Loan Insurance Corporation.

Functional capability The capacity of the structure to perform its intended use.

Functional obsolescence Decline in value of property caused by changes in technology or by defects in design, layout, or size of building. Loss of a building's ability to perform its function.

Funds Cash or any resource having value which is capable of being sold in order to buy some other asset.

Generative establishments The retail establishments which customers intend to visit; these are major traffic generators.

GNMA (Ginny Mae) Government National Mortgage Association, a buyer in the secondary mortgage market for some programs of federally-sponsored loans.

Government (rectangular) survey A method of providing a legal description for land involving the use of principal meridians, base lines, ranges, and townships.

Graduated (graded, step-up) lease Rental payments are changed over term of lease as stipulated by contract.

Grantee Purchaser of rights to real property.

Grantor Person selling rights to real property.

Gross equity yield Aftertax cash flow plus mortgage principal repayment divided by equity investment.

Gross income Total dollars of revenue generated by an investment property.

Gross income multiplier (GIM) Expression of value based upon a multiple of project gross income.

Gross national product (GNP) Governmental system of accounting for annual output or production of the economy.

Ground lease A long-term lease of the site.

Guaranteed mortgage The Veterans Administration idemnifies the lender for a portion of the mortgage debt in the event sale at foreclosure does not satisfy the entire obligation.

HHFA   Housing and Home Finance Agency.

Highest and best use   Vacant site—that use of the site which results in maximum productivity and return on investment. Improved property—existing improvements remain the highest and best use until a new use of the site generates sufficient value for the site to permit acquisition and demolition of the existing improvements.

Historic preservation   Restoration of a property to its original form.

Homestead   Primary domicile, as declared by the head of a family and filed with county clerk of courts. Purpose is to exempt homestead from claims of creditors.

Homestead exemption   A deduction from assessed value for purposes of real estate tax calculation, granted by state laws to the head of a family on property designated as his or her homestead.

IAAO   International Association of Assessing Officials.

Imputed interest   In an installment sale, the Internal Revenue Service establishes an interest payment schedule even when the principals to a transaction mention no interest. This causes part of the seller's capital gain to be treated as ordinary interest income.

Incorporeal   The right to use the land of another or to remove minerals (profit) without having title and ownership.

Incurable deterioration or obsolescence   The cost to correct the item of physical deterioration or functional obsolescence exceeds the value added to the property.

Inelastic demand   The situation in which a change in price produces a proportionately smaller change in quantity demanded.

Ingress   A place or means of entering; entrance.

Input-output accounts   Measurement of products exported from a community and goods and services imported into the same community.

Installment sale   Disposition of a property that permits deferral of capital gain over time provided certain rules are observed.

Institutional advertising   Advertising intended to popularize an industry such as real estate.

Insured loan   A loan for which an insurance premium is part of the monthly payments. If the loan is defaulted by the borrower, FHA (or the private insuror) will reimburse the lender from these premiums.

Insured mortgage   Mortgage insured by the Federal Housing Administration or a private insurance agency such as Mortgage Guaranty Insurance Corporation, or Foremost Guaranty Corporation.

Interest rate risk   The risk of an investment's price change in reaction to interest rate changes.

Intermediate title theory   With respect to the rights conferred to the mortgagee, an intermediate title theory state lies between a title theory and lien theory state.

Internal rate of return   The interest rate which discounts future cash flows and cash reversion from a project equal to the initial investment.

Investment holding period   Length of time that the investor is assumed to hold the property before sale or exchange.

Investment property   An asset owned for the purpose of earning an investment return as opposed to one held as stock in trade or one held for operation in the ordinary course of business.

Investment value   Value to investors based upon their particular requirements.

Investor   One who holds real estate for the production of income; may take depreciation and capital gains.

Joint tenancy   Special ownership situation in which two or more owners hold equal shares, acquire shares concurrently, and have equal rights of possession. The rights of one owner pass to the other owner upon the one's death.

Kicker Surcharge payment on a loan; any loan payment in excess of ordinary principal and interest.

Land contract A method of conveying title to real property in which legal title does not pass to the buyer until the contract for deed is fulfilled. The contract for deed usually requires the purchase price to be paid in installments.

Lease Contract providing for the transfer of a right to use real estate.

Leaseholds Less than freehold estates that are usually considered to be personal property.

Level annuity Equal amounts of income over time; discounting a level annuity assumes the annual recapture of investment in improvements is reinvested at the rate of discount.

Leverage Use of money borrowed at a fixed rate of interest in an investment project, with the expectation of obtaining a higher rate of return on the equity investment as a result.

License A formal permission to do some specified thing, especially some activity authorized by law; also, a document, permit, and so on, indicating such permission has been granted.

Lien A claim against property whereby the property is security for a debt. The holder of the lien is entitled to sell the property to satisy the debt.

Lien theory State law permitting lenders to secure a lien against property as collateral for a loan.

Limited partnership Ownership form in which a general partner performs all management functions and assumes all operating liabilities on behalf of passive investors known as limited partners.

Linkage Time and distance relationship between a subject site and an important location such as a school, a shopping area, or a place of employment.

Liquidity Relationship between a speedy sale price and the total number of dollars invested in a property.

Liquidity risk The risk that an asset cannot be sold quickly for an amount equal to or above the amount invested.

Location coefficient The ratio of national employment figures in an industry to total national employment subtracted from the ratio of local employment figures in the same industry to total local employment. identifies basic industries.

Location quotient The ratio of local percentage employment in an industry to national percentage employment. Identifies whether activities are basic or nonbasic.

Locational characteristics A property's geographic relationship to other parcels of real estate. These characteristics involve the cost of transferring people, information, goods, and services from one site to another.

Locational obsolescence Decline in value of property caused by deterioration in the quality of its neighborhood; also known as economic obsolescence.

Locked-in period Time period in which a mortgage loan borrower is not permitted by contract to prepay any of the loan principal.

Marginal Increment of change.

Marginal cost Increment of cost resulting from a given business decision.

Marginal rate of return The return on investment received by holding the property one more year.

Marginal revenue Increment of revenue resulting from a given business decision.

Market analysis Study of the market in which a developer might supply new real estate resources; study of the reasons why current prices are being paid.

Market rent Rental level ascertained by seeking out similar properties in a selected market area.

Market risk   The result of downward market trends causing a loss in market value. Also known as systematic or nondiversifiable risk.

Market segmentation   Identification and delineation of the submarket to be served.

Market value   The price which a property will bring in a competitive market when there has been a normal offering time, no coercion, an arms-length transaction, typical financing, and informed buyers and sellers; exchange value.

Marketability   Relationship between a speedy sale price and the current market value of a property.

Marketability risk   The risk that an asset cannot be sold quickly for an amount equal to or above the amount invested.

Marketer   Person engaged in marketing of a product or service; deals with the satisfaction of human needs on a broad scale.

Marketing myopia   Failure to focus upon needs and people who have needs.

Metes and bounds   A mete is a unit of measure (foot, mile); a bound is a boundary marker. A method of legally describing real estate.

Millage rate   Expressed as tax dollars payable per $1,000 assessed value of property; for example, 15 mills implies $15 tax on each $1,000 of assessed property value.

Model city   A comprehensive plan dealing with the social, economic, and physical problems of selected neighborhoods.

Monopolistic competition   Control of a market by a number of parties who differentiate their services effectively.

Monopoly   Control of a market by one party.

Monument   A permanent marker indicating a corner of a parcel of land. A method of legally describing real estate.

Mortgage   Written evidence of the right of a creditor to have property of a debtor sold upon default of the debt.

Mortgage bank correspondents   Mortgage bankers in local communities who serve as agents of lenders in placing and servicing loans.

Mortgage constant   Percentage of original loan balance represented by constant periodic mortgage payment. A payment of $100,000 per year on $1 million mortgage converts to a 10 percent constant.

Multiple listing   Sharing of property sales listings by several real estate brokers.

Mutual ownership   Used in Chapter 16 to mean a financial institution that is owned by its depositors.

NAR (National Association of Realtors®)   An organization of real estate brokers which sponsors educational and research activities in all areas of the real estate industry.

Net income multiplier   Expression of value based upon a multiple of project net income.

Net lease   Lease agreement under which lessee pays all taxes, insurance, maintenance, utilities, and other expenses.

Net listing   The seller specifies the amount which he or she will accept from the sale of his or her property, with the broker keeping all proceeds in excess of that amount.

Net operating income (NOI)   Gross possible revenue minus an allowance for vacancies and for operating expenses.

Net present value   The difference between the aftertax cash flow and the aftertax cash reversion discounted at the investor's required rate of return and the initial equity investment.

Nominal rate of return   The rate of return on investment unadjusted for inflation or other risk.

Nonmarketable securities   Usually notes taken in an installment or deferred payment sale that contain restrictive clauses that hinder their marketability. This hindrance may be designed to reduce the seller's income tax liability.

Note (promissory)   Document evidencing a debt and describing the terms by which the debt is to be paid.

Occupancy   The period during which a house or other real estate is kept in possession; in law, the taking possession of a previously unowned object, thus establishing ownership.

Officer's deeds   Record transfers of property from a public official to an auction purchaser, with the ownership rights of the foreclosed owner being cut off after a stated redemption period. No warranties are made.

Oligopoly   Control of a market by a small number of participants.

100 percent site   Location past which the largest number of customers or space users pass (within a given market area).

Open-end mortgage   Permits additional sums to be borrowed on a single mortgage.

Open listing   Agreement between seller of property and broker which permits broker to receive a commission if he or she sells the seller's property. No exclusive protection is provided the broker.

Operating expense ratio   Relationship between operating expenses and project gross income.

Option   Contract given by a landowner to another person, giving the latter the right to buy (lease) the property at a certain price within a specified time.

Original tax basis   Cost of acquisition of the real estate or cost of construction of improvements new plus the acquisition cost of the site.

OSHA   Occupational Safety and Health Act of 1973.

Package mortgage   A debt secured by pledge of both real property and personalty (range, refrigerator, and so on).

Participation mortgage   Lender participates in profits or ownership as well as receiving contract interest.

Patent   A special type of deed which conveys title to land owned by the federal government to a private party.

Payback period   Length of time required for cash throw-off from project to equal amount of money invested.

Personal property (personalty)   A chattel; an item of property that is neither the land nor is permanently attached to the land.

Physical characteristics   The nonlocational attributes of a property and its immediate surroundings.

Physical deterioration   Loss of utility resulting from impairment in physical condition.

Planned obsolescence   Attempting to increase sales by purposefully manufacturing goods or products to wear out or lose utility more quickly than would be necessary.

Plat   Drawing that shows boundaries, shape, and size of a parcel of land.

Plottage value   Value added to land by assembling small parcels into large tracts.

Points   Additional interest charged by the lender; one point equals 1 percent of the mortgage loan principal.

Police power   The constitutional authority of government to limit the exercise of private property rights as necessary to protect the health, safety, and welfare of all citizens. It constitutes the legal basis for zoning.

Population density gradient   The ratio of population per unit of land to the distance from the central business district.

Portfolio   A collection of investments.

Predeveloped land   Land which has been zoned, planned, and made ready for immediate development.

Prepaid interest   Payment in advance of a portion of the total interest due over term of the loan.

Prepayment privilege   Mortgage contract clause permitting borrower to pay loan payments in advance of their due dates.

Prescription   One who uses the land of another for a period of time stated by law obtains the right of easement to the subject land.

Present value   Today's value derived by measuring all future benefits of an investment and converting those benefits into terms of today's dollars.

Prisoner's dilemma   The situation in which an individual owner's desire for action is restrained by surrounding owners' inaction, as in the case of neighborhood deterioration.

Private planning   Employed by landowner, developer, builder, or other nongovernment entity to prepare comprehensive plan for a parcel of land. Private planning frequently relies upon governmental agencies for provision of utilities, schools, garbage collection, highways, and other urban services.

Productivity   The relationship between output in the production process and the total of all inputs.

Profitability index   The present value of the aftertax cash flows divided by the initial equity investment.

Property residual technique   An income capitalization methodology which discounts net operating income and the site reversion value to present value without separating NOI into income attributable to the building and to the site.

Proration   Allocation of costs or revenues between buyer and seller of real property.

Public planning   Process followed by a public agency to prepare communitywide comprehensive plans.

Purchase money mortgage   Mortgage taken by the seller of property as part of the purchase price.

Purchasing power risk   The devaluation of assets due to inflation and the decreasing purchasing power of a dollar.

Qualified fee   An estate in real property which terminates with the occurrence of a specified event.

Quantity survey   Method of estimating building replacement cost in which all elements of labor, materials, and overhead are priced and totaled to obtain building cost.

Quitclaim deed   A deed which passes ownership rights without guarantees.

Range   A north/south line from which land lying east or west is described in columns of ranges.

Rapid write-off (accelerated) depreciation   All tax depreciation methods that permit taking depreciation expense greater than that which would have been taken using straight-line depreciation.

Real estate   Land, including the buildings or improvements, and its natural assets, as minerals, water, and so forth.

Real estate investment trust (REIT)   A passive investment vehicle whose distributed earnings are taxed only to investors who receive them. Similar to a corporation in every way except for the permitted avoidance of double taxation of dividends.

Real property   The legal rights to possession, use, and disposition of real estate.

Realtor®   Registered trademark reserved for members of the National Association of Realtors; Realtors subscribe to an idealistic code of ethics which sets standards for conduct and integrity in all business dealings.

Reappraisal lease   Lease having a clause calling for periodic reevaluation of rental levels.

Recapture (depreciation)   The disallowance of a portion of rapid depreciation income tax deductions caused by disposing of the depreciable asset at a time when accumulative rapid depreciation exceeds the amount of depreciation that would have been taken during the holding period if straight-line depreciation had been used. Only the amount by which accumulative depreciation exceeds straight-line depreciation is disallowed.

Reconcilliation   Process of evaluating data, conclusions, or value indications to reach a single answer.

Redemption clause   A clause in the mortgage giving a defaulting borrower the right to pay principal and interest owed on a property prior to foreclosure.

Redlining   Delineation of geographical areas in which a lender does not make real property loans or in which loans are made on terms less favorable than those found in preferred areas.

Regressive tax   A tax which requires a proportionately higher percentage of lower income taxpayers' incomes than higher income taxpayers' incomes.

Rehabilitation   Restoration of a property to satisfactory condition without changing the plan, form, or style of a structure.

Reinvestment rate of return   The aftertax internal rate of return over the holding period which results when the annual recapture of investment is assumed to be reinvested at a specified rate of return different from the speculative rate of return.

Reliction   A receding water boundary which leaves dry land to be added to the title holders' property.

Remainder   The right held by someone other than the grantor to receive title to the property after an intervening estate, such as a life estate.

Remodeling   Renovation of a property which changes the plan, form, or style of a structure to remove functional or economic obsolescence.

Reproduction cost   The cost at current prices of constructing a duplicate of the improvements.

Reserve for replacements   An operating expense account by which the prorated cost of replacing short-lived items is deducted from effective gross income.

Residual techniques   Assignment of a portion of income to part of an asset, with the remainder (or residual) flowing automatically to the rest of the asset. Also, the assignment of part of the income to cover debt payments with the balance accruing to the equity.

RESPA   Real Estate Settlement Procedures Act of 1973.

Return on investment (ROI)   A percentage relationship between the price paid by an investor and the stream of income dollars obtained from the investment.

Reversion   The return of an estate to the grantor and his or her heirs by operation of law after the period of grant is over.

Reversion value   Worth of the site at a time when improvements value is zero (end of their economic life); worth of the property (improvements and site) at the end of an investment holding period.

Right-of-way   Right to passage, as over another's property; also, land over which a public road, an electric power line, and so forth, passes.

Riparian rights   Property rights transferred through the movement of a body of water.

Risk   The variation potential in estimates of a project's net present value.

Risk-adjusted rate of return   A return on investment from which the premium for business risk has been removed.

Salvage value   Estimated market value of improvements or other depreciable assets at the end of their useful life.

Sandwich lease The lease with which a lessee sublets a leasehold estate.

Secondary financing market A market composed of purchasers of mortgages from institutions that originate mortgage loans to individual users. The principal entities in the secondary home loan market are the Federal National Mortgage Association (FNMA), the Federal Home Loan Mortgage Corporation (FHLMC), and the Government National Mortgage Association (GNMA).

Section 8 subsidized occupancy program A program of rent supplements established in 1975 by HUD and allocated to local governments.

Section 1231 property Includes property used in one's trade or business and many income properties held by investors; property must be held more than six months.

Security market line The linear relationship between risk and return.

Sensitivity analysis The changes in selected dependent variables (aftertax internal rate of return, etc.) resulting from a given change in one or more independent variables (rents, vacancy levels, mortgage terms, etc.).

Settlement Final accounting in a real estate transaction which shows amounts owed by seller and buyer and to whom payable; closing.

Simulation Computer-assisted investment analysis which assigns probabilities of occurrence to variables such as rents, vacancy rates, and operating expenses in order to observe the resulting distributions of dependent variables (rates of return, property values).

Site residual technique An income capitalization methodology in which building cost is assumed to equal building value. Net operating income is divided into building income and site income, which is capitalized into site value and added to building value (cost) to obtain market value of the property.

Social class Group of people delineated by selected social characteristics.

Special assessment A charge made by government against properties to defray costs of public improvements which especially benefit the properties assessed.

Special warranty deed A deed in which grantors covenant only against claims arising from the time during which they owned the property.

Specifications Restrictions imposed on the quantity and quality of materials and labor to be used in a construction project.

Standard deviation A measure of dispersion about a central value. Mathematically, it is the square root of the variance.

Statement of consideration Statement in a deed that affirms the fact that the purchaser actually paid something for the property.

Statute of frauds Legal requirement that all matters affecting title to real estate must be in writing if they are to be enforced by a court of law.

Statutory redemption period Time permitted delinquent borrowers to cure their deficiencies before their property is taken permanently from them.

Straight-line capitalization Process of discounting future income into present value given the assumption that the investment in improvements is recaptured in equal annual amounts that are not reinvested.

Straight-term loan No repayment of the principal of the loan until the due date.

Subdividing Separation of a parcel of land into smaller parcels. Selling more than five parcels in a single year can cause investors to become dealers in real property.

Submarket (housing) A collection of housing units considered to be close substitutes by a relatively homogeneous group of households; similar housing units that provide equal utility or satisfaction.

Surcharge An additional amount added to the usual charge.

Suscipient establishments Convenience establishments which rely on passersby for business.

Syndicate Group of individuals, corporations, or trusts who pool money to undertake economic ventures. The syndicate can take the form of a corporation, a trust, a partnership, a tenancy in common, or any other legal ownership form.

Syndication   The formation of an association of individuals or corporations to carry out a financial venture.

Systematic risk   Undiversifiable risk in a portfolio. This is the same as market risk.

Tax abatement   Forgiveness of all or a portion of the real property tax that would otherwise be owed.

Tax credit   Allowable reduction in the amount of income tax owed.

Tax deferral (postponement)   The payment of the tax bill is deferred to a later date (but not avoided).

Tax preference items   Include excess depreciation and the deductible one-half of any net long-term capital gain; under federal income tax rules, tax preference items greater than a certain amount are liable for a surtax.

Tax shelter   Net loss that can be deducted from other income for income tax purposes.

Tax shelters   Legally permissible methods of reducing or postponing the burden of the federal income tax, including accelerated depreciation, capital gains, exchanges, and so on.

Taxable income   Gross possible revenue minus an allowance for vacancies, operating expenses, depreciation, and interest paid on borrowed funds.

Threshold size   The market area necessary for a firm's survival in a central place of the nth order.

Title   Right of ownership, especially of real estate.

Title insurance   Insurance paying monetary damages for loss of property from superior legal claims not expected in the policy.

Title theory   State law permitting lenders to secure title to property as collateral for a loan.

Torren's certificate   Method of providing evidence of ownership to real property.

Trading on the equity   Synonymous with leverage.

Transfer characteristics   The movement of goods, persons, and messages among geographically separated sites and establishments that result in transfer costs.

Transfer costs   Costs of overcoming the friction of space.

Transfer payments   A redistribution of private sector income via the government to citizens or groups, in an attempt to achieve equity.

Trust deed   Conveyance of contingent title to a trustee who holds it as security for the lender; used in some states in lieu of a mortgage.

Trustee   One who administers property held in trust for another.

Unit-in-place costs   Method of estimating building replacement cost in which quantities of materials are costed on an in-place basis and summarized to obtain building cost.

Unsystematic risk   Diversifiable risk in a portfolio of investments.

Urban decay   Falling of urban centers to a condition of disrepair.

Urban renewal   Process of renovation or rehabilitation of deteriorated areas within a city.

Useful life   Period of time permitted by the Internal Revenue Service for computing annual depreciation expense.

VA   Veterans Administration.

Value   A ratio at which goods exchange; the relative worth of an object, usually measured in money terms.

Value in exchange   Price an investment asset is expected to bring based upon comparable market transactions.

Value in use   Price an investor would pay based upon his or her personal assessment of the investment asset's merit.

Variance   A statistical measure of dispersion about a central value. The mathematical formula is

$$\sigma^2 = \sum_{i=1}^{n} (k_i - k)^2 P_i.$$

Warehousing (loans)   Provision of funds to a mortgage banker so that he or she may increase the inventory of mortgage loans. Typically a commercial bank does the warehousing of loans.

Warrenty deed   The most desirable type of deed from a buyer's viewpoint. Guarantees include the covenant of seisin, covenant against encumbrances, and covenant for quiet enjoyment.

Wraparound mortgage   A junior lien on a property which enables the borrower to add financing to the original loan without paying off the original loan or encumbering the higher interest rates of most other types of secondary financing.

Yield   Relationship between income or cash received from an investment and the value of the capital producing the income or cash.

Zoning   The regulation of land use, population density, and building size by district. May be viewed as a phase of comprehensive planning in which the plan's implementation is enforced through police power.

Index

*This book has been set VIP, in 10 and 9 point
Caledonia, leaded 2 points. Part numbers are
14 point Helvetica bold and chapter numbers
are 14 and 24 point Helvetica Light. Part titles are 16 point Helvetica Light and chapter
titles are 16 point Helvetica bold. The size of
the type page is 30 by 46 picas.*